COLONIAL
VOICES

UQP AUSTRALIAN AUTHORS

General Editor: L.T. Hergenhan
Reader in Australian Literature
University of Queensland

Also in this series:

Marcus Clarke edited by Michael Wilding
Henry Lawson edited by Brian Kiernan
Five Plays for Stage, Radio and Television edited by Alrene Sykes
The 1890s: Stories, Verse and Essays edited by Leon Cantrell
Rolf Boldrewood edited by Alan Brissenden
The Jindyworobaks edited by Brian Elliott
Hal Porter edited by Mary Lord
Barbara Baynton edited by Sally Krimmer and Alan Lawson
Henry Kingsley edited by J.S.D. Mellick
Joseph Furphy edited by John Barnes
New Guinea Images in Australian Literature edited by Nigel Krauth
Australian Science Fiction edited by Van Ikin
The Australian Short Story: An Anthology from the 1890s to the 1980s edited by Laurie Hergenhan
R.D. FitzGerald edited by Julian Croft
Catherine Helen Spence edited by Helen Thomson
James McAuley edited by Leonie Kramer
Nettie Palmer edited by Vivian Smith

In preparation:

Randolph Stow edited by A.J. Hassall
John Shaw Neilson edited by Clifford Hanna

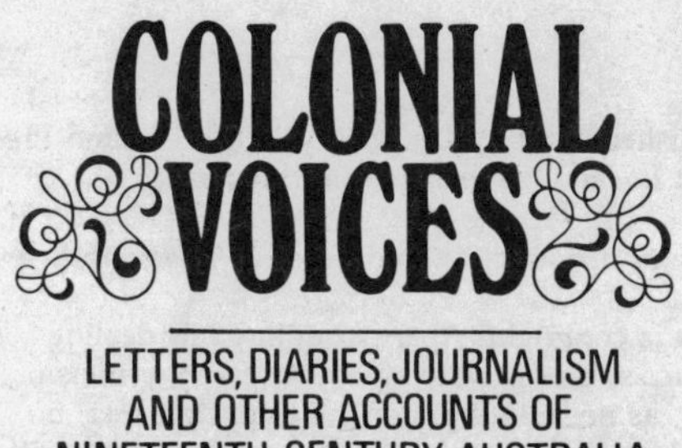

COLONIAL VOICES

LETTERS, DIARIES, JOURNALISM AND OTHER ACCOUNTS OF NINETEENTH-CENTURY AUSTRALIA

Edited by Elizabeth Webby

University of Queensland Press

First published 1989 by University of Queensland Press
Box 42, St Lucia, Queensland 4067 Australia

Typeset by University of Queensland Press
Printed in Australia by The Book Printer, Melbourne

Distributed in the USA and Canada by
International Specialized Book Services, Inc.,
5602 N.E. Hassalo Street, Portland, Oregon 97213-3640

Cataloguing in Publication Data
National Library of Australia

Colonial voices : letters, diaries, journalism, non-fiction from nineteenth century Australia.

Bibliography.

1. Australian prose literature. 2. Australian prose literature – 19th century. I. Webby, Elizabeth. (Series : UQP Australian authors).

A828'.08

ISBN 0 7022 2171 6

Contents

3 Settling Down

4 Travelling

5 Floods, Flies, Fauna

6 Town and Bush

7 Friends, Lovers, Sexual Commerce

8 Rituals and Celebrations

9 Protest and Revolution

Acknowledgments

During the preparation of this anthology, many people have offered advice and suggestions, not all of which, unfortunately, could be included. I should particularly like to thank Debra Adelaide, Jim Davidson, Robert Dixon, Richard Fotheringham, Mary Gaudron, Teresa Pagliano, Lucy Sussex and G.A. Wilkes. Harold Love deserves special thanks for kindly supplying copies of J.E. Neild material. I am grateful to Laurie Hergenhan for his helpful editorial suggestions.

Acknowledgment is made to Angus and Robertson for permission to include extracts from *The Letters of Henry Lawson* (ed. Colin Roderick, 1970) and from Max Brown, *Ned Kelly* (1948); to Fremantle Arts Centre Press for extracts from *A Faithful Picture* (ed. Peter Cowan, 1977); to Heinemann for extracts from *The New Australia* (trans. and ed. Russel Ward, 1973); to Oxford University Press for extracts from *The Diaries and Letters of G.T.W.B. Boyes* (vol. I, ed. P. Chapman, 1985); to the William Dixson Foundation for extracts from *Journal of a First Fleet Surgeon*; to *Meanjin* for extracts from James Smith's diary; to Bruce Bennett for extracts from *Cross Currents* (1981); and to the National Library of Australia for extracts from *Audrey Tennyson's Vice-Regal Days* (ed. A. Hasluck, 1978) and for the manuscript letters of David Blair, printed here with the permission also of Miss F. Baverstock.

Introduction

As the end of the twentieth century approaches, it becomes more apparent that the nineteenth was the great age of the written and printed word. The industrial revolution required a large, concentrated workforce which was also skilled and sober. Books were among the cheapest and most effective tools for self-improvement. The technology which demanded a mass reading public conveniently also provided the means for ensuring one. By 1900, books, magazines and newspapers were no longer expensive luxuries but part of everyday life.

The European settlement of Australia gave a considerable boost to manufacturers of ink, paper and books. A whole new continent was revealed, with unknown people, landscapes, flora and fauna to be described. Until mid-century, when the camera and lithography made the creating and reproducing of visual images much cheaper and easier, these descriptions were mainly verbal. Letters were the initial means of communication between Australia and Europe and, as can be seen from those included here, Australian letter writers were well aware of their roles as harbingers and interpreters of the new and strange. Many apologise for the length of their descriptions but most are also aware that they are writing for a larger audience than the person to whom their letter is addressed. George Worgan, surgeon on the *Sirius*, having already filled seventeen sheets of paper, advises his reader "rally your Patience Brother Dick", and proceeds to transcribe his journal entries from January to July 1788:

> a string of little Transactions, Occasions, Excursions and Adventures which I could not introduce in the preceding Narrative without thrusting them in Head and Shoulders to the utter Confusion of the whole: and as

> these Incidents have happened in almost an unknown Part of the World, I am unwilling to omit them, because I think they may, possibly, afford You and Your Friends half an hours Amusement, and a new Topic to Reflect and Comment upon in your Social Meetings.[1]

After many further pages, Worgan concludes by noting that he has "no less than 31 Letters (& 5 of them almost as long as y^r)" ready to despatch to England the next day (12 July 1788) on two returning transport ships. He adds, furthermore, the postscript "I have sent you 2 Letters beside this in different ships." While such marathon letter writing seems amazing today, it was commonplace in the early settler's life. Since ships returned infrequently, every opportunity of sending mail was seized. Some of them might not reach their destinations, so it was best to send more than one letter, and information was repeated from letter to letter. So the convict Thomas Watling, writing to his aunt in Dumfries from Sydney Cove on 12 May 1793, took the precaution of enclosing a copy of an earlier letter, sent from the Cape of Good Hope in December 1791, in case it had never reached her.

Watling also advised his aunt to publish his letters if, "after the revisal by an abler hand", they could be "in the least conducive" to her interest.[2] Accordingly, they were published in Penrith, Scotland in 1794 prefaced

> THE PUBLISHER OF THE ENSUING PRODUCTION, SENDS IT INTO THE WORLD FOR THE TWO FOLLOWING REASONS.
>
> First; he hopes it may contribute a little to the relief of an old, infirm, and friendless woman, to whom it is addressed
>
> And Secondly; he imagines the account here given of a country so little known, may be interesting to some, and amusing to *all*. With the original, which is now in his hands, he declines taking any liberty, but leaves the unfortunate exile to tell his story exactly in his own words, and how he acquits himself, the public must determine. (p. 15)

Most other accounts of the beginning of white settlement in Australia were also based on letters or published in the form of letters or journals. *The Voyage of Governor Phillip to Botany Bay* (1789) was edited from Phillip's despatches by its publisher, John Stockdale. George Worgan's letter mentions the narratives being prepared by Watkin Tench and David Collins, which also take the form of letters or journals. These remained popular models for later writers about Australia. Most explorers' accounts, for example, were written in the form of journals. Peter Cunningham's *Two Years in New South Wales* (1827) is subtitled "A series of letters"; the letter is also the structural model of William Howitt's *Land, Labour and Gold* (1855).

Cunningham's lengthy subtitle also refers to "Sketches of the Actual State of Society". The term "sketch" crops up in many other nineteenth-century titles including Louisa Anne Meredith's *Notes and*

Sketches of New South Wales (1842) and James Martin's *The Australian Sketch Book* (1838). Martin's title points to his major source of inspiration, Washington Irving's very popular *The Sketch Book* (1819–20). Irving, the first American writer to achieve an international reputation, popularised the sketch as a type of descriptive writing based on observations of people and places. The best known Australian examples are probably Henry Lawson's "Hungerford", "In a Dry Season" and "In a Wet Season". The latter two are included here to show the way in which Lawson, usually seen as a pioneer of Australian literature, actually inherited a very long literary, particularly journalistic, tradition of writing. In this collection, the reader can trace the progressive modification of the sketch in the hands of Richard Rowe, Marcus Clarke and J.S. James ("The Vagabond"). Though later collected and published as volumes, these sketches were originally published in newspapers and magazines.

If the letter and the journal were the primary forms of writing in the early days of white settlement (though no doubt some poems were also penned) and remained significant forms throughout the nineteenth century, newspapers and magazines were the primary outlets for writers wishing to publish in Australia. There was a great demand – as George Worgan recognised early – for information about Australia in England and Europe. The books produced to meet this demand, all of course published in Britain, came in progressive waves throughout the century: the First Fleet accounts, the journals of exploration, descriptions of the goldfields and finally the works of the "touring experts" in the 1880s and 1890s. During most of the century demand in Australia worked in a reverse direction. Here the thirst was for information from Britain: there were many accounts of the eagerness with which new arrivals were greeted with requests for news and newspapers. English novels and English magazines were to be found on all the library tables, both public and private. Though there was some local publishing, it was usually of poetry, plays and other works for which there was no market in Britain and it was done at the author's expense, which normally meant the author's loss. Local magazines were also a losing proposition until after the gold rushes when two Melbourne weeklies, *Melbourne Punch* (1855–1929) and the *Australian Journal* (1865–1958), settled down for long runs. *Melbourne Punch* had the advantage of topical, local material which, with advertisements, had sustained local newspapers since their beginning in 1803. The success of the *Australian Journal* was more surprising, since it specialised in fiction, roughly half local and half imported, offered in a very cheap format. This suggests an awakening of interest in the local literary product, particularly if it was available at competitive prices. The *Australian Journal* was able to maintain its competitiveness by not paying for contributions sent by freelance writers.

The earliest Australian newspapers, the *Sydney Gazette* (1803–42) and the *Hobart Town Gazette* (1816–27), were established as vehicles for government notices. In any spare columns, they carried local advertisements and summaries of overseas news, for which, as already noted, there was a great hunger. There were occasional reports of important local happenings, such as the 1811 Sydney murder trial included here, original poems and essays, and reprints of selections from British and American authors. By the 1820s the government monopoly over print had ceased. The *Australian* (1824–48) and the *Sydney Monitor* (1826–41) were commenced in Sydney as rivals to the *Gazette*. Both often carried editorials, articles and letters critical of official policies and practices. When Andrew Bent began to do the same in Hobart, Governor Arthur set up a rival *Hobart Town Gazette*, forcing Bent to change his paper's title to the *Colonial Times* (1825–57). The establishment of these independent and more critical papers gave greater scope, as well as more outlets, to local writers, allowing for the development of genres like the satirical essay, as seen in Henry Savery's sketches, collected in *The Hermit in Van Diemen's Land* (1829) but originally published in the *Colonial Times*. With more papers and pages to fill there was also room for more descriptive writing, of the type seen in William Dumaresq's letters on "A Ride to Bathurst", originally written for the *Australian* in 1827.

The first magazine to be printed in Australia, named, appropriately enough, the *Australian Magazine* (1821–22), was published in Sydney by a group of Wesleyan missionaries but carried mainly reprinted material. One of the next, though also called the *Australian Magazine* (1838), took the opposite line, boldly announcing that "the most arduous part of it was written by the *Sons of Australia*".[3] There was considerable debate – akin to later arguments about the content of Australian theatre, film and television – as to whether the primary purpose of local magazines should be to encourage the development of Australian writing by printing original contributions or whether it was first necessary to establish correct standards of literary taste in Australia by printing only the best material from overseas. One or two excellent early monthlies, such as the *Hobart Town Magazine* (1833–34) and the *South Australian Magazine* (1841–43) printed a high proportion of original material. But, as their dates of publication demonstrate, there was insufficient demand to allow them to survive for long in the face of competition from many better known, and cheaper, British magazines.

By the 1860s, as noted earlier, the gold discoveries of the previous decade had increased Australia's population sufficiently to allow some weekly and monthly magazines to gain continuing support. Melbourne was now the centre of Australian journalism, a position it was to hold until the 1890s and the growing success of the Sydney

Bulletin (1880-). As well as the *Melbourne Punch* and the *Australian Journal*, Melbourne was home to the *Australasian* (1864–1946) and the *Leader* (1856–1957), two weekly journals associated with the *Argus* (1846–1957) and the *Age* (1854-) newspapers respectively. Such weekly newspapers attached to major metropolitan dailies were the mainstay of Australian literary journalism, and of many writers, during the second half of the nineteenth century. They provided a summary of the week's news, intended primarily for country readers who had little use for daily papers that arrived days late, and substantial literary and other supplements.

The Melbourne *Leader*, the earliest to appear, published work by Marcus Clarke, among many others, and James Smith, its first editor. Clarke also published in the rival *Australasian*, which Smith edited at one time. The *Australasian* emphasised literature and literary matters and published many leading local writers, including Rolf Boldrewood, Catherine Spence, Mary Gaunt, Ada Cambridge, Louisa Meredith and J.E. Neild, to name only those included in this anthology. A third Melbourne weekly, the *Weekly Times* (1869-), initially associated with the *Daily Telegraph* (1869–92), and later with the *Herald* (1840-), also carried contributions from Marcus Clarke, including his sketch "Nasturtium Villas", reproduced here.

After the *Australasian*, the best known weekly was the *Sydney Mail* (1860–1938), published in association with the *Sydney Morning Herald* (1831–). Though its literary material was not of the same quality or quantity as that of the *Australasian*, the *Mail* can claim the honour of serialising Rolf Boldrewood's *Robbery Under Arms* after it had been rejected by both the *Australasian* and the *Australian Town and Country Journal* (1870–1919). The *Sydney Mail* published fiction and articles by Louisa Atkinson, the first Australian-born woman novelist. Its local rival was the *Town and Country Journal*, associated with the Sydney *Evening News* (1867–1931). Louisa Atkinson, Boldrewood and many other notable writers also published there. Long-lasting weeklies of this type also appeared in Brisbane and Adelaide during this period. Leading writers and journalists connected with the *Queenslander* (1886–1939), the weekly companion of the *Brisbane Courier* (1846–1933), included Marcus Clarke and Francis Adams, as well as many not represented in this anthology, such as Mary Hannay Foott and Ernest Favenc.

Several novels by Catherine Helen Spence were originally serialised in the *Adelaide Observer* (1843–1931), which began as an independent journal but later became the weekly associated with the *South Australian Register* (1839–1900). A later rival was the Adelaide *Advertiser's* (1858–) *South Australian Chronicle* (1858–1975). Readers in Tasmania and Western Australia also supported successful weeklies: the *Tasmanian Mail* (1877–1935) and the *Western Mail* (1885–1955) respectively.

As the century wore on, and the population of Australia continued to increase, newspapers and magazines became more specialised and diversified, a process which, combined with the coming of television in the 1950s, would eventually kill off even the most popular of the newspaper weeklies. The one major nineteenth-century Australian magazine to have survived to the present, the *Bulletin*, has done so by undergoing successive changes of format and direction, to cope with a changing readership. Its early numbers, with their emphasis on sport, sex and scandal, had little to distinguish them from earlier magazines aimed at a male readership. But, thanks to the journalistic and literary skills of J.F. Archibald and, later, A.G. Stephens, the *Bulletin* developed into Australia's most famous magazine.[4] While Louisa Lawson was not Australia's first woman editor – that distinction belongs to Cora Ann Weekes, also represented in this anthology – her monthly, the *Dawn: A Journal for Australian Women* (1888–1905), was the first journal for women to be edited by a woman.[5] It also had the distinction of employing women to print the magazine as well as write and edit it, and it lasted much longer than earlier attempts run and edited by men such as the *Australian Women's Magazine* (1882–84) and *Women's World* (1886–87).

Newspapers and magazines aimed at working class readers had been around since the 1840s but towards the end of the century they took on a much more radical tone. Two of the more famous were produced in Brisbane – the *Boomerang* (1887–92) and the *Worker* (1890–1974). William Lane was associated with both of them, while A.G. Stephens, Francis Adams and Henry Lawson also contributed to the *Boomerang*.

Much literary journalism, particularly of the sketch type, highlights the difficulty of making rigid distinctions between fiction and non-fiction. Indeed, it has been claimed that the only real difference is that the fiction writer has to work harder to seduce the reader.[6] Readers feel less guilty about reading non-fiction, since they assume that they are doing something useful or practical, not just being escapist. Distrust of fiction was particularly strong early in the nineteenth century, when novels were thought of rather as television is today – a useful form of relaxation but likely to be abused (especially by women and children). Travel books, histories and biographies were more highly favoured and clearly satisfied many readers' desires for exciting narratives set in exotic places. Indeed, who needed fiction when there were new worlds like Australia to be explored and described?

The distinction between writing for publication and writing for oneself or one's friends is just as difficult to maintain with any degree of certainty as that between fiction and non-fiction.[7] Dr Worgan wrote to his brother in the expectation that his letters and journal would reach a much wider audience; Thomas Watling wrote to his aunt with the firm expectation of publication. In the case of Eliza Brown, an early settler in Western Australia, the writer made a triple switch from a private to a public audience and then back to a private one. During a trip upcountry, Eliza kept a journal which was thought sufficiently interesting to be published in a Perth newspaper; she sent the published journal to her father as a supplement to her usual long letters. Annie Baxter copied letters to her English friends into her private journal, which was later used as the basis for her *Memories of the Past* (1873). David Blair wrote letters to his family in the guise of a travel book entitled "Dottings from the Diary of a Travelling Technological Commissioner". As often as possible, examples have been included of authors writing both for publication and in letters and journals. Readers can, for example, compare Henry Lawson's description of his trip to Bourke in "In a Dry Season" with that given in his 21 September 1892 letter to his aunt. Writing directed at an audience was, of course, in the nineteenth century more circumspect than that done for oneself alone. While some journals, especially early ones like Worgan's or G.T.W.B. Boyes's, were clearly composed with an eye to a wider audience, there was a considerable difference between the subjects and tone of James Smith's diary entries and those of his journalism and reviews. A.G. Stephens's public writings showed more evidence of his strong interest in sexual matters, but even the *Bulletin* could never have printed the scurrilous Henry Parkes stories he recorded in his diary.

These dirty stories recorded by Smith and Stephens also indicate the strong oral literary culture which continued in the nineteenth century. Though this century may, as noted earlier, have been the great age of print, earlier ways of transmitting information did not completely die out, any more than today's increasingly visual culture has killed off writing. As well as the perennial human love of swapping stories around the lunch and dinner table, there was a flourishing public oral culture. To the Sunday sermon and the after-dinner, celebratory or political speech were added the public lecture and the penny reading. Lectures and readings were particularly associated with movements for mass education, such as that of the Mechanics' Institutes. Originally set up to teach science to working men, these institutes, also known as Schools of Arts, soon widened both their curricula and their audiences, to include the humanities, the middle classes and women.[8] Cora Ann Weekes's lecture on "Female Heroism in the Nineteenth Century", given at the Sydney School of Arts in December 1859, may well have been the first given there by a woman. Though her magazine, the *Spectator* (1858–59) had a particular interest in printing an extensive report of Mrs Weekes's lecture, lengthy reports of lectures were a regular feature of Australian newspapers of the period.[9] One interesting, and often amusing, feature is the attempt to represent audience response to the lecture, seen also in the report of J.D. Lang's lecture on "The Coming Event". Lang's lecture was published as a pamphlet, so reports of "prolonged cheers" were an essential part of the propaganda effort. Other political speeches included here – by Daniel Deniehy and Henry Parkes – were printed in a more sober manner appropriate to their context of memorial or celebratory collections of speeches.

Some reformers, of course, chose to use the pen rather than the voice. Ned Kelly had no choice – he was captured before his audience could be – and his famous Jerilderie letter was not printed in his lifetime. To ensure publication of radical material, it was necessary to own a newspaper or at least to edit one; Louisa Lawson did both with the *Dawn*.

Newspaper editorials, with their strong exhortations to readers, often adopted the rhetorical tricks of the pulpit, stage and lecture hall. There was again something of a breakdown of customary binary oppositions – that between oral and written. Many writers before Lawson used the direct address and colloquial style appropriate to the yarn, as in A.J. Boyd's "The Shepherd". Raffaello Carboni's *The Eureka Stockade* (1855), a marvellous polyglot work, jumbled together fiction and non-fiction, public and private, oral and written with a blithe disregard for the conventions. Sometimes oral forms were deliberately parodied by writers. There has been no space in this volume for *Sydney Punch's* spoof "Lecture on Australian Literature" [10] but I have included the *Bulletin*'s "Centennial Oration", a speech definitely not delivered anywhere in 1888.

Sydney Punch's spoof lecture was omitted partly because of a desire to prevent this anthology becoming too "literary" in the narrow sense, but also because of lack of space. Lectures on literary topics, literary criticism and most reviews have been left out. Where reviews have been included, as with J.E. Neild's of a 1889 performance of Ibsen's *The Doll's House* – they have been chosen for the nineteenth-century Australian attitudes to women and sexuality they reveal rather than for their comments about the work being reviewed. They have also been included as forceful and exciting pieces of writing. Style as much as content was my initial criterion in selecting material. I was looking for pieces or passages which stood out from the mass, which could be read more than once. When one is reading hundreds of pages of (often) small print, this is a fair criterion.

While the selection process was begun with no idea other than that of including writing which was particularly vivid and interesting, a number of themes emerged as my reading went on. These have formed the basis for the arrangement of the anthology. Inevitably, some themes and subjects overlap the boundaries. The book follows a roughly chronological order, beginning with some first impressions of Australia, or, more specifically, of New South Wales, Tasmania and Victoria. These, particularly the earlier ones, naturally included some references to Aborigines. "Aboriginal Encounters" deals specifically with relations between the original inhabitants of Australia and the white invaders. It begins with Watkin Tench's description of Governor Phillip's attempts to capture and civilise some Aborigines and ends with another vice-regal encounter as Audrey Tennyson, wife of the governor of Western Australia, describes a corroboree arranged for their benefit. By that stage, the Aborigines had been well and truly "conciliated". The extract from John West's *History of Tasmania* (1852) gives a graphic account of the conciliation process in that island, while the explorers Sturt and Mitchell provide other perspectives. John Morgan's ghosted autobiography of William Buckley, "the wild white man" who lived with Aborigines in Victoria for many years, shows how perceptions of Aborigines could be influenced by fiction as well as fact. His reference to *Robinson Crusoe* is hardly necessary, to guess the literary model being drawn upon here. Note, too, Mitchell's comparison of the "savages" he encounters to the witches in *Macbeth*.

A contrast to these highly sophisticated literary narratives is provided by the simple jottings of a thirteen-year-old, Gordon McCrae, in the next part of the book, "Settling Down". McCrae's encounters with Ben-Benjie are part of everyday life on his father's station, and his description of a corroboree forms a useful contrast to the one given by Audrey Tennyson. These early experiences clearly influenced McCrae's later writing; he was one of the first whites to take Aborigines and their culture as the basis for serious poetry. "Settling Down" concentrates on the first generations of white settlement, again seen from various perspectives. McCrae and Boyes recorded events as they happened (though Boyes was much more self-conscious), W.C. Wentworth and Peter Cunningham provided contemporary interpretations for British readers, and the extracts from writings of Annie Baxter and Rolf Boldrewood look back; both directed their gaze at the Baxters' Victorian property, Yambuck.

Parts 4 and 5, "Travelling" and "Floods, Flies, Fauna", focus mainly on the Australian landscape and some of its pleasant and unpleasant features. "Travelling" also, incidentally, gives a potted history of how people got around Australia during the nineteenth century. Beginning with Oxley, Dumaresq and Louisa Atkinson traversing New South Wales on foot and horseback, readers move on to Richard Rowe going to Maitland on the steamer, Giles crossing the desert by camel, and David Blair and Henry Lawson taking the iron rail in and out of Sydney. Lawson, however, also describes his tramp from Bourke to Hungerford, so readers return to the beginning. "Town and Bush" is more concerned with the human inhabitants of both areas than with landscape and locale. Both William Howitt and A.J. Boyd describe bush types who clearly were forerunners of Lawson's much better known ones.

Like "Town and Bush", parts 7, 8 and 9 are largely made up of material written in the second half of the century. Though still written within a specifically Australian context, they deal with such universal issues as relations between men and women, politics, reform and religion. There is a description of the growth and breakdown of a friendship in a series of letters written by Charles Harpur to Henry Parkes over a twenty-year period; David Blair's love letter heralds the beginning of a marriage, which may be compared with his reminiscences of his courtship, written nearly forty years later, and included in the earlier part, "Travelling". Readers will discover how many practices were transported from Europe and readily adapted to Australian conditions: prostitution, the theatre, murder trials, the celebration of Christmas. Some, of course, were vigorously resisted. James Smith opposes the new art movement of impressionism; Robert Lowe the continuation of the transportation of convicts; Daniel Deniehy successfully ridicules Wentworth's "bunyip aristocracy".

As in the earlier parts of the book, an attempt has been made here to mix the unknown with the well-known, with respect to the writers, the extracts chosen, and the events described. Most of the major historical events of Australia in the second half of the century have been included: the Eureka Stockade, Ned Kelly, federation, the centenary, the fight for universal and women's suffrage, together with descriptions of many of the leading figures, though sometimes seen from unfamiliar perspectives. This is particularly true of Henry Parkes who, though certainly not by design, has ended up rather as the hero, or antihero, of this volume.

He can be seen in his official role as "father of Federation", speaking on "The Federal and Separate Interests of the Colonies" in 1867, and in all his glory as premier twenty years later, through the eyes of a long-time admirer, David Blair, editor of his *Speeches*. However, readers will also discover the disillusionment of another friend, Charles Harpur, and notice the contemporary gossip and scandal concerning Parkes as recorded in A.G. Stephens's diary for 1896. The *Bulletin* for 1888 savagely attacks Parkes in its spoof "Centennial Oration"; for this writer the real Australian heroes are J.D. Lang and Peter Lalor, and 3 December 1854, the date of Eureka Stockade, deserves celebration far more than 26 January 1788. Briefer alternative glimpses are also given of Annie Baxter (through the eyes of Rolf Boldrewood), Daniel Deniehy (in James Smith's Diary) and Louisa Lawson.

Though Louisa Lawson is at last getting some of the recognition she deserves, few have heard of that earlier pioneer woman journalist and lecturer, Cora Ann Weekes. She is included here, with other unsung heroines like Eliza Brown and Jane Watts, pioneers of Western and South Australia respectively. Every effort has been made to represent marginalised figures and regions in this anthology. But, though there are many accounts of Aborigines, there are no Aboriginal writers and few from working class or non-English backgrounds. This is, after all, not a revisionist social history, though informed by some that have been written recently, but a literary anthology. While "literature" has been defined here more widely than usual, one cannot escape the fact that most memorable nineteenth-century Australian writers were from a middle or upper class English background.

Many who read this anthology will bring other perspectives to bear on the material. As a guide to those with a particular interest in studying some of the different forms and styles used by letter writers, diarists, journalists and public speakers throughout the century, such a categorisation is offered in the notes at the end of the book. The letters included here, for example, range stylistically from Thomas Watling's very rhetorical and mannered ones written to his aunt in Dumfries to Henry Lawson's blunt, down-to-earth letters sent to his aunt in Sydney. There are many other letters written to friends and relatives in England and Australia, David Blair's previously unpublished love letter to his future wife and John Oxley's official summary for Governor Macquarie of the results of his explorations. Perhaps the most curious of all is Ned Kelly's "Jerilderie" letter, a work of protest and self-justification intended for publication but never published. Maybe this is just as well, for any copy-editor would surely have cleaned up the erratic spelling and syntax to be found in the manuscript version reprinted here.

However *Colonial Voices* is read, and in whatever order, I hope it will give some indication of the wealth of entertaining and outstanding writing produced in nineteenth-century Australia. Many equally fascinating writers and passages were left out – a book of similar size and quality could easily have been put together for each of the individual sections. Much research remains to be carried out on nineteenth-century Australian magazines and newspapers and on collections of manuscripts, often uncatalogued, in libraries and private ownership. Perhaps some readers may be inspired to read, and research, further. I hope this book will give those reading it some of the delight of discovery that was mine during its preparation.

Notes

1. *Journal of a First Fleet Surgeon* (Sydney, 1978), p. 26.
2. *Letters from an Exile at Botany-Bay, to His Aunt in Dumfries, 1794* (Sydney, 1945), p. 37.
3. See Elizabeth Webby, "Before the *Bulletin*: Nineteenth Century Literary

Journalism" in Bruce Bennett (ed.), *Cross Currents. Magazines and Newspapers in Australian Literature* (Melbourne, 1981), pp. 3–34.
4. See further Sylvia Lawson, *The Archibald Paradox* (Melbourne, 1983).
5. See further Brian Matthews, *Louisa* (Melbourne, 1987).
6. See Ross Chambers, "Narrative Point", *Southern Review* 16 (1983), p. 71.
7. See Robert Dixon, "Public and Private Voices: Non-Fictional Prose", in Laurie Hergenhan (ed.), *The Penguin New Literary History of Australia* (Ringwood, 1988), pp. 123–35.
8. See Elizabeth Webby, "Dr Crowther Lectures at the Hobart Town Mechanics' Institute", in A. Atkinson and M. Aveling (eds.), *Australians 1838* (Sydney, 1987), pp. 254–600.
9. See Elizabeth Webby, "Literary Lectures in Early Australia", *Southerly* 40 (1980), pp. 268–83.
10. 8 and 15 October 1864, pp. 160, 163.

Note on the Text

As far as possible, the texts given here are those of an item's first publication, whether in a newspaper, a magazine or a book, as indicated in the notes for each section. Some obvious misprints have been corrected and, for ease of reading, there has been some standardisation of punctuation and spelling in accordance with UQP house style. Consistent methods of dating and addressing letters and diary entries have also been adopted. Where the editor has omitted material from within an extract, this has been indicated by three centred asterisks. Material omitted from within a paragraph has been shown by three dots. Titles enclosed in square brackets have been supplied by the editor. Sources for the extracts in this book are given on pages 459 to 469, and notes on the authors can be found by interested readers on pages 470 to 481.

1

First Impressions

EDITOR'S NOTE

This part collects some of the impressions of Australia recorded by people arriving here for the first time, mainly between 1788 and the middle of the nineteenth century. Only one of the six writers, George Worgan, had any official standing, being a surgeon on the First Fleet ship *Sirius*. Of the others, three were males, and convicts, and two were women. All, however, were well educated and consciously writing for an audience.

Going to Australia in 1788 must have been not unlike going to the moon today. Many stories and legends were circulated, but there was little precise knowledge about the voyagers' destination. Worgan, like all early writers who discussed Australia, pays particular attention to the Aborigines, but also strives to convey an accurate picture of the country and its products and of the events since the Fleet's arrival in January. His descriptions, of course, obey the aesthetic conventions of the period. So Sydney Harbour "exhibits a Variety of Romantic Views, all thrown together in sweet Confusion by the careless hand of Nature".

The artist, and convicted forger, Thomas Watling, writing of the same scenes five years later, refers even more elaborately to the "elysian scenery of a Telemachus; – the sweet recesses for a Thomson's musidora". Like Worgan, however, he also notes the deceptive nature of the landscape, which promises much but delivers little. So one of the dominant notes of Australian literature, the uneasy relationship between the white man and the land, was present right from the beginning. Watling's involuntary exile adds a tinge of bitterness to his impressions. While Worgan plays with the notion of the Antipodes, the upside-down country, for Watling Australia is the land where the wicked prosper and good men (such as himself) suffer.

By 1829, when Henry Savery's "Hermit" arrived in Hobart, wonderful strides had been made along the road to "civilisation". But appearances were still highly deceptive. "Simon Stukeley" is amazed by the sights of Hobart – "Oh! thought I, this must be the effect of a virtuous and industrious population". When he discovers that he has lost his pocket watch he pictures to himself "what delight would be the portion of him who had found it, when he should know to whom it was to be returned". He soon learns better. A similar irony informs all of Savery's sketches. His account of a trial in Hobart's civil court may be compared with the newspaper report of a Sydney murder trial included in a later section of this book, "Rituals and Celebrations".

While Savery was chiefly interested in Hobart and its inhabitants, the Irish political prisoner John Mitchel wrote more generally about the Tasmanian landscape. Like many earlier, and later, exiles he found Australia almost totally alienating: "The birds have a foreign tongue: the very trees whispering to the wind, whisper in accents unknown to me". Like many others, too, he found that the land and its creatures punctured romantic dreams or at least offered an ironic counterpoint. While Mitchel is reminiscing on European naiads, "plump into the water, just under the bank, tumbles a *Platypus*, uncouth, amphibious quadruped". It is hardly surprising that Mitchel left Tasmania as soon as he could.

Though Ellen Clacy was to spend only a short time in Australia, in contrast to Ada Cambridge, who spent the rest of her life here, both women's first impressions are marked more by excitement and enthusiasm for new sights and scenes than by irony or romantic visions. Clacy provides a very succinct and graphic description of Bendigo at the height of gold fever; her account of a goldfield store, for example, vividly conveys sounds and smells as well as visual images. Australian tastes are also prominent in Ada Cambridge's recollections of her arrival in Melbourne, reminding us that monotonous food was an inescapable, if often unremarked, part of the long voyage from Europe. She gives a delightful picture of herself and her husband retiring surreptitiously to each eat a whole pineapple. She was later to show she could cope equally well with the bush and its hazards.

George Worgan

LETTER TO HIS BROTHER

Sirius, Sydney Cove, Port Jackson
June 12th 1788

Dear Richard,

I think I hear You saying, "Where the D–ce is Sydney Cove Port Jackson?" and see You whirling the Letter about to find out the Name of the Scribe: Perhaps You have taken up Salmons Gazetteer, if so, pray spare your Labour, and attend to Me for half an Hour – We sailed from the *Cape of Good Hope* on the 12th of November 1787 – As that was the last civilised Country We should touch at, in our Passage to *Botany Bay* We provided ourselves with every Article, necessary for the forming a civilised Colony, Live Stock, consisting of Bulls, Cows, Horses, Mares, Colts, Hogs, Goats, Fowls and other living Creatures by Pairs. We likewise, procured a vast Number of Plants, Seeds & other Garden articles, such as Orange, Lime, Lemon, Quince Apple, Pear Trees, in a Word, every Vegetable Production that the Cape afforded. Thus Equipped, each Ship like another Noah's Ark, away we steered for *Botany Bay*, and after a tolerably pleasant Voyage of 10 Weeks & 2 Days *Governour Phillip*, had the Satisfaction to see the whole of his little Fleet safe at Anchor in the said *Bay*.

As we were sailing in We saw 8 or 10 of the Natives, sitting on the Rocks on the South Shore, and as the Ships bordered pretty near thereto, we could hear them hollow, and observe them talking to one another very earnestly, at the same time pointing towards the Ships; they were of a black reddish sooty Colour, entirely naked, walked very upright, and each of them had long Spears and a short Stick in their hands; soon after the Ships had anchored, the Indians went up into the Wood, lit a Fire, and sat Around about it, as unconcerned (apparently) as tho' nothing had occurred to them. Two Boats from the *Sirius*, were now Manned and armed, and the *Governor*, accompanied by Captn. Hunter, and several other Officers, went towards the Shore, where they had seen the Natives, who perceiving the Boats making towards the Beach, came out of the Wood, and walked along, some distance from the Water-side, but immediately on the Boats landing, they scampered up into the Woods again, with great Precipitation. On this, the Governor, advised, that we should seem quite indifferent about them, and this apparent Indifference had a good Effect, for they very soon appeared in sight of Us, When, the Governor held up some Beads, Red Cloth & other Bawbles and made signs for them to advance, but they still were exceedingly shy & timid, and would not be enticed by our allurements; which the Governor perceiving, He shewed them his Musket, then laid it on the Ground, advancing singly towards them, they now seeing that He had nothing in his Hands like a Weapon, one of ye oldest of the Natives gave his Spears to a younger, and approached to meet the Governor, but not without discovering manifest tokens of Fear, and distrust, making signs for the things to be laid on the Ground which, the *Governor* complying with, He advanced, tooke them up, and went back to his Companions; Another, came forth and wanted some of the same kind of Presents, which, were given to Him by the same Method, at length, after various Methods to impress them with the Belief that We meant them no harm, they suffered Us to come up to them, and after making them all presents, which they received with much the same kind of Pleasure, which Children shew at such Bawbles, just looking at them, then holding out their Hands for more, some laughing heartily, and jumping extravagantly; they began to shew a Confidence, and became very familiar, and curious about our Cloaths, feeling the Coat, Waistcoat, and even the Shirt and on seeing one of the Gentlemen pull off his Hat, they all set up a loud Hoop, one was curious enough to take hold of a Gentlemans Hair that was cued, and called to his Companions to look at it, this was the occasion of another loud Hoop, accompanied with other Emotions of Astonishment. In a Word, they seemed pretty well divested of their Fears, and became very funny Fellows.

They suffered the Sailors to dress them with different coloured Papers, and Fools-Caps, which pleased them mightily, the strange contrast these Decorations made with their black Complexion brought strongly to my Mind, the Chimney-Sweepers in London on a May-Day. – They were all Men & Boys in this Tribe.

I should have told You, that the Governor, left the *Sirius* soon after we sailed from the *Cape of Good Hope*; and Embarked on Board the *Supply Brig* & Gave up the Command of ye Convoy to Captn. Hunter, in order that he might proceed on before the main Body of the Fleet, but he arrived in Botany Bay, only two Days before Us. In this Time, He had obtained an Intercourse or two, with some Natives on the *North Shore*, but, as the Means which he took to gain their Confidence, and effect a Parley, were much the same as those, I have given you an account of, I shall only mention a few singular Circumstances that occurred in these Intercourses. The *Supply Brig*, arrived in ye *Bay* about 2 ºClk in the Afternoon of ye 18th January and at 4 ºClock, The Governor, attended by several Officers, went in two armed Boats towards a part of the Shore where, 6 of the Natives, were, and had been sitting the whole time the *Supply* was entering the Bay, looking and pointing at Her with great Earnestness; When the Boats had approached pretty near this Spot, two of the Natives got up, and came close to the Waters-Edge, making Motions, pointing to another part of the Shore and talking very fast & loud, seemingly, as if the Part to which they pointed, was better landing for the Boats, they could not however, discern any thing unfriendly, or threatening in the Signs and Motions which the Natives made. – Accordingly the Boats coasted along the Shore in a Direction for the Place, to which, they had been directed, the Natives following on the Beach. In the mean Time, the Governor, or somebody in his Boat, made Signs that they wanted Water, this they signified by putting a Hat over the Side of the Boat and seeming to take up some of the salt Water put it to his Mouth, the Natives, immediately, understood this Sign and with great Willingness to Oblige, pointed to the Westward, and walked that Way, apparently with an Intention to show their Visitors the very Spot. The Boats steered towards the Place, and soon discovered the Run of fresh Water, opposite to which, they landed, and tasting it found it to be very good. The Natives had stopped about 30 Yards from ye Place where the Boat landed, to whom, the Gentlemen made signs of thanks for their friendly Information, at the same time offering Presents, and doing everything they could think of, to make them lay aside their Fears and advance towards them, but this point was gained only, by the Methods that I have mentioned: and when they did venture to come and take the things out of the Governor's & the other Gentlemen's Hands, it was with evident Signs of Fear, the Gentlemen now having distributed all their Presents among them, returned on Board.

Thus, was our first Intercourse obtained, with these *Children of Nature*. – About 12 of the Natives appeared the next Morning, on the Shore opposite to the *Supply*, they had a Dog with them, (something of the Fox Species); The Governor and the same Gentlemen that were of his Party Yesterday went on Shore, and very soon came to a Parley with them, there were some of their Acquaintances among the Number, and these advanced first (leaving their Spears with their Companions who remained behind at a little Distance) as they had done Yesterday; They all of them in a short time became Confident, Familiar & *vastly funny* took anything that was offered them, holding out their Hands and making Signs for many things that they saw, laughed when we laughed, jumped extravagantly, and grunted by way of Music, & Repeated many Words & Phrases after Us. The Gentlemen having passed about an hour with them, returned on Board, but could not induce any of the Natives to accompany them there. A Party of Us made an Excursion up an Arm in the North part of the *Bay*, where we had not been long landed before we discovered among the Bushes a Tribe of the Natives, who at first did not discover such an inoffensive & friendly Disposition, as those I have spoke of, above; for these rude, unsociable Fellows, immediately threw a Lance, which fell very near one of the Sailors, and stuck several Inches in the Ground, we returned the Compliment by firing a Musket over their Heads, on which I thought they would have broken their Necks with running away from Us. About an hour after, we, in our Ramble, fell in with them again, they stood still, but seemed ready for another Start. One of Us, now laid down the Musket and advanced towards them singly, holding out some Bawbles, and making Signs of Peace; In a little time they began to gain Confidence, and two of them approached to meet the Gentlemen who held out the Presents, the Introduction being amicably settled, they all joined Us, and took the Trinkets we offered them; The same Emotions of Pleasure, Astonishment, Curiosity & Timidity, appeared in these poor Creatures, as had been observed in our first Acquaintances – There were some Old and young Women in this Tribe, whom the Men seemed very jealous & careful of, keeping them at Distance behind some young Men, who were armed with Spears, Clubs & Shields, apparently as a Guard to them. We could see these curious *Evites* peeping through the Bushes at Us, and we made signs to the Men, who were still with Us, that We wished to give some Trinkets to the Women, on which, One of their Husbands, or Relations (as we supposed) hollowed to them in an authoritative Tone, and one of these Wood-Nymphs (as naked as Eve before she knew Shame) obeyed and came up to Us; when; we presented her with a Bracelet of blue Beads for her obliging Acquiescence; She was extremely shy & timid, suffering Us, very reluctantly, even to touch Her; Indeed, it must be merely from the Curiosity, to see how they would behave, on an Attempt to be familiar with them, that one would be induced to touch one of Them, for they are Ugly to Disgust, in their Countenances and stink of Fish-Oil & Smoke, *most sweetly*. – I must not omit mentioning a very singular Curiosity among the Men here, arising from a Doubt of what Sex we are, for from our not having, like themselves, long Beards, and not seeing when they open our Shirt-Bosoms (which they do very roughly and without any Ceremony) the usual distinguishing Characteristics of Women, they start Back with Amazement, and give a Hum! with a significant look, implying. What kind of Creatures are these?! – As it was not possible for Us to satisfy their Inquisitiveness in this Particular, by the simple Words. *Yes* or *No*, We had Recourse to the Evidence of *Ocular Demonstration*, which made them laugh, jump & Skip in an extravagant Manner. – In a Tribe of these funny, curious Fellows, One of them, after having had His Curiosity gratified by this mode of Conviction, went into the Wood, and presently came forth again, jumping & laughing with a Bunch of broad Leaves tied before Him, by Way of a Fig-leaf Veil. – Before we took our leave of the Tribe that threw the Lance; they endeavoured to convince Us, that it was not thrown by general Consent, and one of them severely reprimanded the Man who threw it, and several of them struck him, but more to shew Us their Disapprobation of what he had done, than as a Punishment for it.

During our stay at *Botany Bay*, the *Governor* had made himself well acquainted with the Situation of the Land Nature of the Soil etc. etc. which he not finding so Eligible, as he could Wish, for the Purpose of forming a Settlement, He determined, before he fixed on it, to visit an Inlet on the Coast, about 12 Miles to the Northward of this *Bay* which, our great Circumnavigator, *Captn. Cook*, discovered, and named, (in honour of one of the then Commissioners of the Navy) *Port Jackson* accordingly, the Governor, attended by a Number of Officers went in 3 Boats, on this Expedition, and the third day, they returned, gave it as their Opinion, that *Port Jackson* was one of the most spacious and safe Harbours in the known World, and said they had already fixed on a Spot, on which the Settlement was to be formed. In Consequence of this Success, the Idea was entirely given up, of establishing a Colony at *Botany Bay*, and three days after, the Wind favouring our Designs, the Fleet sailed for *Port Jackson* and in the Evening of the Day of our Departure, We arrived, and anchored in one of the many beautiful Coves which it Contains, which *Cove* Sir, the *Governor* has (in honour of *Lord Sydney*), named *Sydney Cove*.

Though the Description given by the Gentlemen who first, visited this *Port* was truly luxuriant, and wore the air of Exaggeration, Yet they had by no means done its Beauties and Conveniences Justice, for as an Harbour, None, that has hitherto been described, equals it in Spaciousness and Safety. the Land forms a Number of pleasant Coves in most of which 6 or 7 Ships may lie secured to the Trees on Shore. It contains likewise a Number of small Islands, which are covered with Trees and a variety of Herbage, all which appears to be Evergreens. The Whole, (in a Word) exhibits a Variety of Romantic

Views, all thrown together into sweet Confusion by the careless hand of Nature. Well, Dear Dick, now I have brought you all the way to *Sydney Cove*, I must tell you what we have done, since our arrival in these Seas, & in this Port – what we are doing, what has happened etc. etc.

On the Evening of our Arrival (26th January 1788) The Governor & a Number of the Officers assembled on Shore where, they Displayed the British Flag and each Officer with a Heart, glowing with Loyalty drank his Majesty's Health and Success to the Colony. The next Day, all the Artificers & an 100 of the Convicts were landed, carrying with them the necessary Utensils for clearing the Ground and felling the Trees. By the Evening, they were able to pitch a Number of Tents and some Officers and private Soldiers slept on shore that Evening. In the Interval of that time and the Date of this Letter, the principal Business has been the clearing of Land, cutting, Grubbing and burning down Trees, sawing up Timber & Plank for Building, making Bricks, hewing Stone, Erecting temporary Store-houses, a Building for an Hospital, another for an Observatory, Enclosing Farms & Gardens, making temporary Huts, and many other Conveniences towards the establishing of a Colony.

A small Settlement has been established on an Island, which is about a Fort-night's sail from this place, and named by Captn. Cook *Norfolk Island*, the Intention of this Settlement I believe, is on account of the fine Pine Trees, of wh. the Island is full, and to try what the Soil will produce.

We have discovered an Island in these Seas, never before seen by our Navigators, We have named it, *Lord Howe's Island*. It affords Turtle in the Summer Season, and the *Supply Brig*, brought away 18 very fine Ones, on which, we feasted most luxuriously, it also, abounds with Birds of the Dove Species, which are so stupid, as to suffer us to take them off the Bushes with our Hands. As this Island is not above 4 or 5 Days sail from Port Jackson, we hope, to have Turtle Feasts frequently: if this be the Case, I suppose We shall have a Ship-load of Aldermen coming out to New South Wales.

As I mean to annex to this Letter, a kind of Journal of each Day's Transaction and Occurrences, I shall pass over many things in this Narrative, and enter immediately on a rough Sketch of the Country of New South Wales, its Inhabitants etc. etc. as far, at least, as We have been able to learn. *Botany Bay, Port Jackson*, and another Inlet (8 Miles to the Northward of *Port Jackson*, which Captn. Cook calls *Broken Bay,)* lie between the Latitudes of 35° & 40° South. This Part of the Coast (which is as much as we have been near enough, to judge of) is moderately high and regular, forming small Ridges, Plains, easy ascents and descents. It is pretty generally clothed with Trees and Herbage Inland; The Shore is rocky and bold, forming many bluff Heads, and overhanging Precipices. On approaching the Land which forms *Botany Bay* (but I shall speak more particularly to that which forms *Port Jackson*) It suggests to the Imagination Ideas of luxuriant Vegetation and rural Scenery, consisting of gentle risings & Depressions, beautifully clothed with variety of Verdures of Evergreens, forming dense Thickets, & lofty Trees appearing above these again, and now & then a pleasant checquered Glade opens to your View. – Here, a romantic rocky, craggy Precipice over which, a little purling stream makes a Cascade – There, a soft vivid-green, shady Lawn attracts your Eye: Such are the prepossessing Appearances which the Country that forms *Port Jackson* presents successively to your View as You sail along it.

Happy were it for the Colony, if these Appearances did not prove so delusive as upon a nearer Examination they are found to do; For though We meet with, in many parts, a fine black Soil, luxuriantly covered with Grass, & the Trees at 30 or 40 Yards distant from each other, so as to resemble Meadow Land, yet these Spots are frequently interrup. in their Extent by either a rocky, or a sandy, or a Swampy Surface crowded with large Trees, and almost impenetrable from Brush-wood which, being the Case, it will necessarily require much Time and Labour to cultivate any considerable Space of Land together. To be sure in our Excursions Inland, which I believe have not exceeded 30 or 40 Miles in any Direction, we have met with a great Extent of Park-like Country, and the Trees of a moderate Size & at a moderate distance from each other, the Soil, apparently, fitted to produce any kind of Grain and clothed with extraordinarily luxuriant Grass, but from its Situation, and the Quantity of Wood, though in a moderate Quantity in Comparison with that in other Parts. It is the general Opinion here, that it would be a great Length of Time, and require a vast Number of Cultivators to render it fit to produce Grain enough to supply a small Colony. About 50 Miles to the West, and North West Inland, there appears to be some mountainous Country and from our having seen Smoke on it, now & then, We are led to suppose that it is Inhabited. The Governour intends to visit these Mountains shortly, and I have his permission to accompany Him in this Excursion, but I don't think, he will go, before he has discharged, and despatched all the Ships for England.

Thomas Watling

LETTERS FROM AN EXILE

Sydney Cove, Port Jackson, New South Wales
May 12th, 1793

My Ever Revered Aunt,

Embracing the opportunity of a returning vessel, I would waft you, from this place, a second testimonial of my insuperable attachment and remembance. My first letter per the Atlantic, I hope you have received before; but should it be otherwise, after speaking to the present state of my mind, I shall hastily recapitulate its principal contents.

In my saddest hours, and God knows there are many of them, I have observed you are then most busy with my memory. Melancholy's sombre shadow louring over my soul, endears the fleeting moment by impelling me to write to you. Indeed, it is solely owing to this despondent state of mind, that ought I have produced for those last four years proceeds. When this gloom frowns dreadful over the vista of my being, I but too much indulge the dreary prospect – exploring the wide domain of adversity terminated only by the impending darkness; – hence it is, that whatever flows from my pen, or is laboured by my pencil, affects, in some degree, the tone of mind that possess me at the period of its production.

Recurring now to my former letter :– it informed that I had wrote you from *Rio de Janeiro* ; that I had escaped at the *Cape of Good-Hope*, where I was betrayed by the mercenary *Dutch*, and remanded to captivity; whence, after seven months of imprisonment, the *Royal Admiral* E. Indiaman landed me here; where the pur-blind jurisprudence of a *Scottish* tribunal, doubtless, first intended me.

To lead you through the labyrinth of all my sufferings, from the 28th of December, 1791, down to the present period, is a thing utterly impossible ; neither is it my duty to harrow up your feelings by the attempt. – It better becomes me to soothe those sorrows that vague report in the public prints has most likely excited, than to give an additional stab to so valued a life – a life I have already, though innocently, almost extinguished.

* * *

Britain, I believe, still entertains, and very justly, an idea of the sterility and miserable state of *N. S. Wales*. It will be long before ever it can even support itself. – Still that country so famed for charity and liberality of sentiment I doubt not will persevere to continue it. – When I have seen so much wanton cruelty practised on board the *English* hulks, on poor wretches, without the least colour of justice, what may I not reasonably infer ?–*French* Bastile, nor *Spanish* Inquisition, could not centre more of horrors.

Our longest day coincides exactly with your shortest; and *vice versa*. The climate is an extremely sultry one, especially in summer; and yet paradoxical as it may appear, it is in no wise propitious for tropical vegetation. A few *European* culinary vegetables grow, but never arrive to their pristine maturity, and when retransplanted dwindle unto nothing.–The face of the country is deceitful ; having every appearance of fertility ; and yet productive of no one article in itself fit for the support of mankind.

The flattering appearance of nature may be offered as the best apology for those mistaken eulogisms lavished by a late eminent circumnavigator upon this place. Perhaps nothing can surpass the circumambient windings, and romantic banks of a narrow arm of the sea, that leads from this to *Parramatta*, another settlement about fourteen miles off. The Poet may there descry numberless beauties ; nor can there be fitter haunts for his imagination. The elysian scenery of a Telemachus ;– the secret recesses for a Thomson's musidora ;–arcadian shades, or classic bowers, present themselves at every winding to the ravished eye.–Overhead the most grotesque foliage yields a shade, where cooling zephyrs breathe every perfume. Mangrove avenues, and picturesque rocks, entwined with non-descript flowers:- In short, were the benefits in the least equal to the specious external, this country need hardly give place to any other on earth.

Often amid these coveted solitudes do I wander by the silent moon, along the margin of some nameless stream, and pray for the most loved of aunts, and for my dearest C____. The willing tear will often fall when I reflect upon your widowed and impotent condition. – "If in existence," I exclaim, "alas ! indigence and pallid hunger most likely guards her humble door, whilst her modest heart pines in silence, unknown to, and unacquainted with philantrophy. God of the widow & the orphan, shield her helpless head, and shed abroad comfort and pious resignation in her agonised and solitary heart."

My worthy friend, Mr H—, may reasonably conclude, that these romantic scenes will much amuse my pencil ; though therein he is mistaken. The landscape painter, may in vain seek here for that beauty which arises from happy-opposed off-scapes. Bold rising hills, of azure distances would be a kind of phaenomena. The principal traits of the country are extensive woods, spread over a little-varied plain. I however confess, that were I to select and combine, I might avoid that sameness, and find engaging employment. Trees wreathing their old fantastic roots on high ; dissimilar in tint and foliage ; cumbent, upright, fallen, or shattered by lightning, may be found at every step ; whilst sympathetic glooms of twilight glimmering groves, and wildest nature lulled in sound repose, might much inspire the soul – all this I confess ; but all this, if I possibly can, shall be considered of hereafter.

In the warmer season, the thunder very frequently rolls tremendous, accompanied by a scorching wind, so intolerable as almost to obstruct respiration ;–whilst the surrounding horizon looks one entire sheet of uninterrupted flame. The air, notwithstanding, is in general dry. Fifteen months have been known to elapse without a single shower ; but though thus dry, the transitions of hot and cold are often surprisingly quick and contrasted without any discernible injury to the human system. I have felt one hour as intensely warm as if immediately under the line, when the next has made me shiver with cold, yet have I not experienced any harm there from ; owing, without a doubt, to the dryness and salubrity of the atmosphere.

The vast number of green frogs, reptiles, and large insects, among the grass and on the trees, during the spring, summer, and fall, make an incessant noise and clamour. They cannot fail to surprise the stranger exceedingly, as he will hear their discordant croaking just by, and sometimes all around him, though he is unable to discover whence it proceeds :–nor can he perceive the animals from whence the sounds in the trees issue, they being most effectually hid among the leaves and branches.

Should the curious Ornithologist, or the prying Botanist, emigrate here, they could not fail of deriving ample gratification in their favourite pursuits in this luxuriant museum. Birds, flowers, shrubs, and plants ; of these, many are tinged with hues that must baffle the happiest efforts of the pencil – Quadrupeds are by no means various; but we have a variety of fishes, the greater part of which, are dropped and spangled with gold and silver, and stained with dyes transparent and brilliant as the arch of heaven.

One great error in many of our voyagers, is the giving prematurely a decided opinion of what falls within the circle of their observation. That the inhabitants of *N. S. Wales*, are centuries behind some other savage nations, in point of useful knowledge, may be fact ; but in this there is no criterion of judging mental ability. Their huts and canoes, it is true, are extremely rude and ill informed ; but when we consider their non-acquaintance with iron tools, and the hardness of their wood, it is more surprising that they can use it at all. – It being so ponderous as to sink immediately in water, renders it entirely useless that way : – consequently no succedaneum here can be so easily moulded, or so fit for the purposes of forming their little vessels as the bark – and this, both as builders and sailors they manage with singular dexterity.

The people are in general very straight and firm, but extremely ill featured ; and in my opinion the women more so than the men. Irascibility, ferocity, cunning, treachery, revenge, filth, and immodesty, are strikingly their dark characteristics – their virtues are so far from conspicious, that I have not, as yet, been able to discern them.

One thing I may adduce to their credit, that they are not cannibals. They burn and bury their dead, but from what motive it is hard to conceive ; immolation it cannot be ; as they have not apparently the smallest idea of a Deity, much less of religion.

In imitation they are extremely apt, particularly in mimicry ; and they seem also in many other respects to be capable of much improvement ; but they are so very unsteady and indolent, that it would be almost next to a miracle to bring them to any degree of assiduity or perseverance.

Here I cannot help making what may appear rather an ill-natured remark ; our governors, for they are all such, have carried philosophy, I do not say religion, to such a pitch of refinement as is surprising. Many of these savages are allowed, what is termed, a freeman's ratio of provision for their idleness. They are bedecked at times, with dress which they make away with the first opportunity, preferring the originality of naked nature ; and they are treated with the most singular tenderness. This you will suppose not more than laudable ; but is there one spark of charity exhibited to poor wretches, who are at least denominated christians ? No, they are frequently denied the common necessities of life ! wrought to death under the oppressive heat of a burning sun ; or barbarously afflicted with often little merited arbitrary punishment – this may be philosophy, according to the calculation of our rigid dictators ; but I think it is the falsest species of it I have ever known or heard of.

The men and women, at an early age, devote to their chieftain, the former, one of the upper fore-teeth ; and the latter, the first joint of the little finger of the left hand, as a token of their fidelity.–This is one of their public ceremonies, and is performed in the most bungling manner : but it is impossible to descend to particulars in the limits of a narrow letter.

A canoe, spear, wooden sword, and shield, short bludgeon, stone hatchet, fishing tackle, and a rude basket formed of bark, comprise the whole of their domestic or offensive implements. Their subsitute for knives is ever at hand ; the first shell that occurs fully answering that purpose.

They are very quick eyed, and dextrous in the striking of fish, or aiming of the spear ; but they are neither so athletic or nimble as might reasonably be expected in a savage race.

Bedaubing, or streaking themselves in various forms with red or white earth, they would prefer to the most tawdry birth-day suit whatever. The same want of taste keeps them honest this way – but victuals, knives, or hatchets, vanish with them in a twinkling.

It pays no small compliment to poesy and painting, that they are affected by the most unenlightened as well as the most refined countries. The natives are extremely fond of painting, and often sit hours by me when at work. Several rocks round us have outre figures engraven in them ; and some of their utensils and weapons are curiously carved, considering the materials they have to work with.

Their Poets neither having the advantage of writing or printing, are necessitated to travel as the hedge-preachers in *Britain*, to extend their reputation. It is but lately that an itinerant sable *Ossian* called this way, and held forth to some hundreds of his countrymen, who after kindly entreating, escorted him to some other bourne, to further promulgate his composition.

Whatever may be their merits in this department, I confess that I am not connoisseur enough to guess at them. Of their music, however, I may aver that nothing can be more disagreeable, unless it be their other favourite amusement, dancing ; for if harmony be the foundation of the one, and grace of the other, these aborigines have not, as yet, the smallest idea of either.

The hair smeared with gum, and forked as the porcupine ; a bone or straw stuck horizontally through the middle cartilage of the nose ; and the body streaked over with red or white earth, completes the *ton* of dress of the inhabitants of *N. S. Wales*, either for war, love, or festivity.

Many of them are tatowed over the arms, back, and breast, in a very irregular manner, which seems to have been done at an early period of life, for which they can assign no other reason than that of ornament.

It were presumption in me to speak of their language, with which I am but little acquainted. Glossaries have been attempted by some of our pretending and aspiring gentry, who, I am conscious, are as much ignorant of it as myself. I think it is by no means copious, but rather confined to a few simple sounds ; but whether this is, or is not a beauty, I leave to the learned to determine. To an *European* ear the articulation seems uncommonly wild and barbarous ; owing, very likely, to those national prejudices every man imbibes, and perhaps cannot entirely divest himself of. One thing they have in common with more refined communities, that marks a clannish propinquity of kindred ; which is a similarity in the termination of their sir-names : Terribi-long, Benna-long, Bye-gong, Wye-gong, Cole-bree, Nan-bree, etc. etc., are full as striking as Thomson, Johnson, and Robson.

As it is impossible for me to be so particular as I could with, the barbarian *New Hollander* must give place to a few other remarks, I would inform you of ere I finish my letter.

Returning then back to general observations ; and supposing you to have heard something of the swiftness, meekness, and singular formation of the Kangaroo, of the Opposum, Guanoe, Lizards, etc., I may say, that not only these, but the whole appearance of nature must be striking in the extreme to the adventurer, and at first this will seem to him to be a country of enchantments. The generality of the birds and the beasts sleeping by day, and singing or catering in the night, is such an inversion in nature as is hitherto unknown.

The air, the sky, the land, are objects entirely different from all that a *Briton* has been accustomed to see before. The sky clear and warm ; in the summer very seldom overcast, or any haze discernible in the azure ; the rains, when we have them, falling in torrents, & the clouds immediately dispersing. Thunder, as said, in loud contending peals, happening often daily, & always within every two or three days, at this season of the year. Eruscations and flashes of lightning, constantly succeeding each other in quick and rapid succession. The land, an immense forest, extended over a plain country, the maritime parts of which, are interspersed with rocks, yet covered with venerable majestic trees, hoary with age, or torn with tempests. – In a word, the easy, liberal mind, will be here filled with astonishment, and find much entertainment from the various novel objects that every where present themselves.

To sum up natural reflection for the present – though there are a variety of objects to exercise the imagination, yet such a sameness runs through the whole of the animal and vegetable creation of *New South Wales*, that I think it would be no hard matter for the discerning naturalist to at once distinguish them from those of every other country, by their peculiarity. The various Banksias do not more appear to belong to one common family, than the Kangaroo, Opposum, and Kangaroo-rat, to that of the Kangaroo. The fruit and seed of the trees, and most of the underwood, ligneous and scarce penetrable to the hardest instrument, have all of them something of resemblance to each other. In short, from the savage native in the animal, and the towering red gum in the vegetable, everything indigenous to this colony, approaches or recedes by a very striking and singular gradation of proximity.

Sydney-Cove, from whence I write this letter, is the principal settlement, and is about 1/3 part as large as *Dumfries*. *Parramatta,* or *Rose-Hill*, that I have spoke of, is somewhat less ; and the latest settlement, called *Toongabbe*, about four miles farther inland, is the least of all. Many houses of the two former settlements, are built with brick, and covered with tiles ; but none of them, the governor's excepted, exceed the height of one storey. His Excellency's, indeed, is composed of the common and attic orders, with a pediment in front, and commands the most exalted station, but as neither the wood, brick, nor stone (lime there is none) are good for much, it is simple and without any other embellishment whatever.

It is impossible for a well-wisher to his country, not to breathe a sigh, should he visit us, nay, the genuine *British* patriot could scarce refrain from dropping a tear upon a survey of such mistaken policy. To see what has been done in the space of five or six years, of clearing, building, and planting, is astonishing. To behold hundreds of hands laboriously mis-employed, that might be of service, and not burthensome to their country, assuredly deserves attention and reformation ; for whatsoever interested men may advance to the contrary, I humbly declare, that it is my opinion, that all that has been done is of little service to our support, and of none at all to government ; and that neither this, nor the ensuing century will see us able to subsist ourselves, much less to retaliate what has been lavished upon so very wild an adventure.

Norfolk, is a small rocky island in the sea, and is governed by a deputy, named King. It lies in latitude 29° . 3. south, longitude 168° . 10. east. Its length does not exceed seven, nor its breadth four miles ; and it is about eight or ten days sail from *Sydney*. Capital offences done in this island, are reserved to the decision of this tribunal ; where the culprits are brought to undergo a form of trial. I will not say but justice in a criminal court may be administered impartially ; but instances of oppression, and mean souled despotism, are so glaring and frequent, as to banish every hope of generosity and urbanity from such as I am: – for unless we can flatter and cajole the vices and follies of superiors, with the most abominable servility, nothing is to be expected – and even this conduct, very often after all, meets with its just reward : – neglect and contempt.

As a late journalist is much anxious to insinuate the assiduity and virtue of governor P[hillip], in urging matrimonial connections, and forbidding illict ones, I think I may here remark the efficacy of his endeavours. Had such a scheme taken place, possibly something good might have accrued, though little I think could reasonably have been expected from the coupling of *whore* and *rogue* together. Be this as it may, I think that it would have been equally praise-worthy in his Excellency, to have recommended to our betters, the settling us a continent example ; in lieu of which, there is scarce a man without his mistress. The high class first exhibit it ; and the low, to do them justice, faithfully copy it.

I have observed instances in the papers, of ladies of easy virtue, stoutly withstanding the royal mercy, and bravely preferring death to *Botany-Bay* ; but I would beg them to permit me, who am also a prisoner, to encourage and advise them to behave more pliant in future, and by so doing obtain their best wishes. Henceforth, be they most forward in embracing every opportunity that occurs for transportation. They may rest assured, that they will meet with every indulgence from the humane officers and sailors in the passage ; and after running the gauntlet there, will, notwithstanding, be certain of coming upon immediate keeping at their arrival. Nay more, if any girl of uncommon spirit, with a happy talent for dissention, and no doubt but such there are, should attract the affection of one in office, she may console herself with the comfortable prospect of rendering everyone unhappy around her ; for by her duplicity and simulation, she may so far agitate her cully, supposing him one of the springs of our government, as to make our infant colony quake to the very centre.

But be she ever so despicable in person or in manners, here she may depend that she will dress and live better and easier than ever she did in the prior part of her prostitution.

Now for a contrast. – If a man's abilities are good, they are his bane, and impede his emancipation. He must abide upon the colony and become the property of some haughty despot ; or be lent about as an household utensil to his neighours – there to exert these abilities, without any other emoluments than illiberal reflection ; for the least apparent murmuring would instantaneously be construed insolence, and could not fail, though he had faithfully served years, to immediately damn him for ever in this life – for it would be burthened by cruelty, hunger, and the most laborious of employment.

Be my merits what they may, I am sorry to say, that they have been pursued by a good deal of this malign fortune I now mention ; and for which I quote myself, as one instance, to ascertain the truth of. My employment is painting for J. W—, esq., the non-descript productions of the country ; and for which, I have the rewards hinted at in the preceding sentence. The performances are, in consequence, such as may be expected from genius in bondage, to a very mercenary sordid person. There are, thank God, no fetters for the soul : collected in herself, she scorns ungenerous treatment, or a prostitution of her perfections ; nor will she meanly pluck the laurel from her own brow, to deck that of her unworthy governor. Let it suffice to *Britain*, that my youthful hopes and reputation are levelled in the dust, and that my old age will be unhoused and indigent ; but never let her presume to barter to interested men, the efforts of the artist, or powers of the mind ; for those are placed infinitely above her reach.

I could, along with this, point out many practices equally obnoxious to honour or justice ; but coming from my pen, they might savour so much of virulence, and so little of candour, that I shall wave them. Though I have nothing to expect from, or thank my natal abode for, still, fallen as I am, it would pain me to have my veracity even doubted of by those I am unknown to.

Should all, or any of these observations, seem not quite original, they may still prove entertaining from their simplicity and truth. If, therefore, the publication of such a letter, after the revisal by an abler hand, can be in the least conducive to the interest of my dear aunt, I shall yet account myself not altogether cast away ; and shall take care to furnish her with materials by every opportunity. There however are reflections, which I need not point out, that I could wish either entirely suppressed, or moulded into such a form, that should they recoil here, they may not create me cruel and invincible enemies. And if any person can be found, whose influence is so powerful as to extend here, and soften my ill-fated condition, one or two years would return me back with as correct an history, and as faithful and finished a set of drawings of the picturesque, botanic, or animate curiosities of *N. S. Wales*, as has ever yet been received in *England*.

Henry Savery

[THE VOYAGE]

No. 1 Hobart Town, June 5, 1829

> "There is not in the world a greater error than that which fools are so apt to fall into, and knaves with good reason to encourage, the mistaking a satirist for a libeller; whereas to a true satirist nothing is so odious as a libeller; for the same reason as to a man truly virtuous, nothing is so hateful as a hypocrite." – POPE.

Notwithstanding all modest men naturally feel a certain degree of diffidence when speaking of themselves, a courtesy which is due to the world, requires that a person who makes his first appearance in a given character, should say something of the pretences whereon he claims attention. Know then, most courteous reader, that he who this day addresses you, is derived from the ancient stock of the Stukeleys, of the West Riding of Yorkshire, a race "whose men were always brave, and women ever fair". Early disappointments of a tender nature led to a seclusion from the noise and discord of a busy world, at the very morning of my existence, and induced a retirement, from whence I could learn much, but said nothing. The fame of this distant Island having, however, reached my abode of privacy, and rumour having represented it as a place which was well adapted to my acquired habits and inclinations, I determined to judge of it for myself; and, changing the disguise which I had long worn, for a fashionable suit by Stultze, boots by Hoby, and hat by Bicknell, I took my passage by one of the vessels which were advertised to sail positively on the tenth of the coming month, being the seventh *positively* already announced, and destined to be succeeded by three others ere we departed. At length setting sail, and patiently enduring the usual ills of a long voyage, I put my foot upon Terra Firma a few weeks ago, and immediately re-exchanging my west-end fashionables, for the Hermit's gown, slippers and cap, I set about making my observations – but how have I been altogether deceived!

It was not necessary for me to wait the approach to this hemisphere, before I found that a ship load of passengers was another term for quarrelling, contention, and strife – that those who would be peaceable, had scarcely an opportunity afforded them of following the bent of their inclinations – those who were viciously disposed, had abundant aiders, encouragers, and supporters – those who were virtuous, could scarcely escape calumny and detraction. Ah! thought I, as I witnessed scenes, to which I had long been unaccustomed, as I heard language, calculated to stir up anger, or to inflame the passions and corrupt the mind, when I shall reach my destined shore all this will be over; I shall see only, primitive habits and manners – I shall mix with a population, who either not having found Old England good enough for them, must themselves be the purest of the pure, or who having been purified of their sins by punishment, must now have repented, and upon the principle, that a reformed rake makes the best husband, have become the most virtuous of the virtuous! But let no man who may chance to peruse the record of my disappointment, ever more presume to indulge in fairy hopes and dreams. It is for the good of all, who, like myself, are of a sanguine and yet a charitable temperament, that I have determined to commit my thoughts and observations to paper; but as the routine of certain official forms has placed me already, though so recently arrived, in all stages of public business, from the audience room of His Excellency, to the Prisoners' Barracks, as either under my real character or in my disguise, I have mixed in all societies, from the drawing-room at Government-house to the tap-room of the Macquarie Hotel; and, as I have been present in the Courts of Law, and incog. have witnessed the alternate petulance, firmness, sparring, and cutting between the lawyers, who, scissars-like ne'er hurt themselves, but only what's between – have therein also greatly admired the sudden transition between grotesque gravity and *"inimitable humour"* – have noticed the mode of conducting commercial affairs, so unlike what is practised at home, and have in a word, been grievously disappointed in the Utopian picture I had formed, I think myself qualified to impart my thoughts to the world; and having said thus much for the present, may perhaps make my second appearance this day week. In the interim, I say to all those who have honoured me, by having perused what I have now written, that I am their most obedient servant,

Simon Stukeley.

[ARRIVING FROM ENGLAND]

No. 2 Hobart Town, June 12, 1829

It was a remarkably fine clear day when I landed from the ship on the Wharf. What was my surprise, to observe the large handsome stone buildings, into which, porters were busily engaged rolling casks and other packages, and at several civil looking well dressed young men, who were standing with pens behind their ears, and memorandum books in their hands, paying the most diligent attention to what was going on. A number of other persons formed little knots or circles; and the hallooing of ferrymen, the cracking of whips, and the vociferation of carters, struck me as creating altogether, a scene of bustle and activity, which indeed I had little expected. For the moment it occurred to me, that our Captain, in the hurry and confusion which the quarrels on board had occasioned, has missed his reckoning, and had made a wrong port; and accordingly seeing a fat, portly, sleek-looking, apparently good-humoured Gentleman approaching, I enquired of him, with an apology, in what place I was? – Judging from my manner and appearance that I must be a stranger, he very civilly replied, that I was in Hobart Town, the capital of Van Diemen's Land, adding, "Perhaps, Sir, you would like to walk into our Commercial Room, to which I can introduce you." I then accompanied my new acquaintance up a flight of stone steps into a rather elegantly fitted-up room, in which were three or four plainly dressed Gentlemen reading Newspapers. One of them, who appeared bordering upon sixty, wore spectacles, and had a considerable degree of eagerness in his manner, rose upon my entrance, and addressed me, "Just from England, eh, Sir? What news, Sir, when you left? The Colony is much talked of at home, Sir. Suppose you heard of our Association, but things are not now as they used to be." Before I could make a reply, he offered me a Newspaper, farther acquainting me, that the town maintained three such publications; one of which, said he, is so dull and prosy, that nobody reads it; another has lately been at death's door, owing to some Government regulations, but has now, Phoenix-like, risen with redoubled splendour; and the other is made up of short paragraphs and country letters written in town, but commands an extensive circulation. I expressed my thanks for the information, and for my courteous reception, and mentally wondering at a commodious Wharf, fine Stone-buildings, a Chamber of Commerce, and three Newspapers, felt that so many other things, to be in character, must still await my attention, that I made my bow to the company, and proceeded on my tour through the town. The fat portly Gentleman was my companion to the end of the Wharf, and then, with a true John Bull air and manner, left me, and turned into one of the stone warehouses.

How great was my astonishment, at the magnificent straight line of street, extending apparently for more than a mile, by which my sight was greeted upon leaving the Quay. I could scarcely credit my senses, that I was in a town, which is only as it were of yesterday. As I proceeded along, my surprise was increased by seeing other fine streets, meeting at right angles, the one by which I was walking towards a handsome brick church, with a steeple like the extinguisher upon a flat candlestick, my left being flanked by well laid out gardens and shrubberies, in the centre of which stood the Governor's residence; and every here and there, the right being ornamented by large two storey brick or stone houses. The church door happening to be open, I took the opportunity of judging of its interior, and I could almost have fancied myself in one of the modern churches of the metropolis of the world. Such regular well-arranged pews, so beautifully a finished pulpit and reading desk, made of wood, which I at first thought was Spanish mahogany, quite astonished me; upon a nearer examination, however, and upon enquiry of a man who was dusting the aisles, I learnt that it was the produce of a tree, indigenous to the Colony, known by name of Myrtle. While I was thus employing myself, a Gentleman wearing a Clerical hat, approached, and with much affability of manner, addressed me as a stranger, and gave me some general information respecting the religious institutions of the place. He had a lisp in his speech, which was by no means disagreeable, and his well cased ribs bore evident marks that, whatever other doctrines he might preach, that of fasting was not one upon which he laid much stress, at least in its practice. He acquainted me, that independent of the congregations belonging to this large Church, a Presbyterian Chapel, a Roman Catholic Chapel, and a Wesleyan Meeting House, were each well attended every Sunday, and it gave me great pleasure afterwards to be told of this Gentleman, as he himself had beautifully expressed of his brother labourers in the vineyard, that in their lives and conduct the religion they all professed received its brightest ornament – that they each made a well formed cornerstone of the superstructure they supported. Oh! thought I, this must be the effect of a virtuous and industrious population. Arts, architecture, literature, religion, and commerce must here thrive so well, because so many excellent people, for whom Old England was not good enough, have congregated, and because so many others have been cleansed of their sins, and are now restored to innocence. Happy people, and thrice happy Simon Stukeley, to have left your retirement to come among them! –

Everything seemed indeed greatly superior to my expectations. Well dressed and elegant Ladies were promenading one street, well mounted Equestrians were galloping along another, respectably attired Pedestrians helped to add to the scene, which was still more enlivened by the relief-guard of the Military as it approached the Main-guard House from the Barracks, and by the rapid passing and re-passing of gigs, carts and other wheel vehicles. I was completely in a reverie, scarcely knowing through which street I would perambulate, or which object best claimed my attention. The entire absence of all beggars, or indigent persons, added to my wonder, but after a little reflection, I accounted for it in my own mind, by considering that as all the inhabitants were either pure or purified, it was quite of a piece with their religion and virtue to be charitable, this being the brightest of the cardinal gems. I continued my walk for a long time, each moment more astonished than before at the progress which had been made in laying out and building the town – at the excellent shops in the different streets – at the wide well macadamised thoroughfares, and their convenient causeways, and at a hundred other matters which excited my admiration, until I found myself in a quarter of the town situated on an eminence at some distance from the Church, and where the houses and inhabitants seemed rather of an inferior description to those I had before seen. In their manners and style of conversation, upon the different subjects, respecting which I interrogated them, they exhibited however all the easy confidence of virtue. The calls of my appetite now warned me that the day was fast waning, and I applied my hand to my fob to ascertain the hour, when to my utter dismay I found that one of Hawley's best gold watches, with which I had provided myself previous to my departure from England, was missing. To have lost it in any other manner than by accident, did not cross my mind for an instant, and I pictured to myself what delight would be the portion of him who had found it, when he should know to whom it was to be restored, and therefore pursued my journey to the Macquarie Hotel, with the view of taking up my quarters there, and obtaining some refreshment.

Having knocked at the door, it was opened by a smart dapper waiter, who ushered me into a large and well-furnished room, which I had scarcely entered before the Landlord, an obliging well-behaved man, paid his respects and enquired what I pleased to order. Upon my telling him that I was exceedingly hungry, he said that if I should not object to dine in a public room, dinner was now serving up, and that the company who were there, were all very respectable. I used to like table d'hote dinners before my seclusion from the world, and the idea now pleased me. Accordingly, I followed my host into the opposite room, in which were the Landlady, whose appearance and manners were greatly in her favour, and four visitors. They were all men well informed, and of lively conversation, and as I am ever a good listener, I brought this quality into full play on the occasion, carefully noting all that passed. It would be tedious to repeat what I then learned; one thing, however, I discovered to my sorrow, that my ideas of purity and virtue were like snow before the sun – beautiful, but easily dispelled, and that most probably my chronometer and I had parted company for ever. I determined however to make my loss the subject of a visit next morning to the Police-office. Ruminating upon the events of the day, and full of reflections at what I had heard and seen, I retired to my pillow, and being weary both in body and mind, was soon in the arms of Morpheus.

Amongst my plans for the succeeding day, I had purposed paying my respects at Government-house. Perhaps the result of my visit, as well there as at the Police-office, and the manner in which I spent the remainder of the day, may be communicated to my readers, when they next hear from me, till when, I am their obedient servant.

Simon Stukeley.

[AT THE COURT HOUSE]

No. 6 Hobart Town, July 10, 1829

Passing down Macquarie-street a few mornings ago, my attention was attracted by seeing a number of persons entering a large unfinished stone building, opposite the Church, and which upon enquiry, I found was the Court House, where the Criminal Sessions are held, and Civil Causes tried. – Among those who were pressing towards the doorway, apparently in great haste, was a tall thin Gentleman dressed in black, tripping along on his toes in a pace somewhat between a walk and a run. He leant his body forward, the projection of his back, which was unusually long, forming a very considerable angle. In his hand, which I noticed as he passed, was larger than ordinary, he held a bundle of papers. Just as he entered the broken enclosure in front of the Court House, he stopped for a minute or two to converse with another Gentleman, who was travelling the same road, but who, so far from having any hurry in his look, seemed wonderfully quiet and composed. Ever and anon during their short conference, the tall Gentleman had recourse to a snuff box of extra ordinary dimensions; the box indeed appeared to have been made for the hand, and the capacious power of the nose for both. The Gentleman, who helped to form the tète a tète, was also dressed in black. He was much the shortest of the two – wore his hat a little on one side, inclining the head a little further still; – had rather a pleasant smile on his countenance, which was likewise full of meaning or expression, and I observed that his mode of talking was remarkably quiet. Upon my enquiring of a Gentleman, whom I had met at the Macquarie Hotel, what all this was about, he told me there were some civil causes for trial, and I determined therefore to make one of the lookers-on, and to see in what form justice was administered. Before I had time to cross the street for this purpose, my attention was attracted by the approach of a curricle, at a very rapid rate, drawn by two ponies, who were scampering at full speed, the one in a canter with the left leg foremost, and the other in a run, such as is known in England by the name of the butcher's shuffle. The vehicle turned the corner with such velocity, that I was nearly run over, and only saved myself by a hasty retreat. It stopped at the entrance of the building, and the person who had been driving, alighted and bustled towards the door, as if all the affairs of the universe were upon his back. He was short and fat, of a very merry countenance, somewhat resembling such as a painter would select for the original of the laughter loving God, and there was a certain something in his air and manner, as much as to say *"Ecce magnus sed parvus homo."* I followed these personages and several others into the building, and passing through a small sort of entrance hall, presently found myself in a capacious room or chamber, with a number of windows opposite each other, which producing cross light, and admitting the full force of the sun's rays from the north side, must not unfrequently annoy the persons most requiring a steady and not glaring light. Across the middle of the room, about halfway from the door, was a bar or railing, within which stood a large table, in size and arrangement not very convenient for the profession, two pews or seats, resembling those of a Church, being on the left, close to the wall, and one of the same sort on the right, and immediately in front was an elevated seat across the room, in the centre of which was a sort of desk, as if intended for a Chairman or other person holding pre-eminence, and over which was an unsightly sounding-board, so unsoundly fixed as to threaten a sudden descent, and the natural consequence of putting out the light occasionally below it. Upon a chair at the left-hand corner of this desk, sat one of the Gentlemen, whom I had seen enter from the street; exactly opposite to him, in another chair, was a young man, in the costume of a Barrister, and whose countenance seemed familiar to me. – Round the table, upon forms, were several other Gentlemen, amongst whom I recognised the tall snuff-taker, and the short curricle-driver, whom I had before seen, together with many others. Presently a door in one corner of the room opened, and a tall Gentleman, wearing the gown and wig of an English Barrister, entered and immediately proceeded to the desk in the centre of the long seat under the front wall. His countenance did not seem unknown to me, although I could not immediately recollect where I had been introduced to him, but afterwards a friend brought to my recollection that it was at the Governor's dinner party. Some little preliminary business having been disposed of, and two more Gentlemen in plain clothes having joined him who last entered, one of those who were sitting on the form rose and said, "If His Honor pleased, the cause, Fitwell v. Testy, was ready for trial". The Court having nodded assent, the pleading began. From the opening speech of the Lawyer, I found that Fitwell was a tailor, and had been employed by Testy to make sundry articles of clothes, which he had done, and had sent them, accompanied by a bill or account, amounting to £11 3s. 10d. – Among other articles was a blue coat, charged at £5 15s. with the additional demand of fourteen shillings and sixpence for a velvet collar, which was the sole ground of action, Mr Fitwell having stated in his bill

A blue coat and trimmings complete £5 15 0
Velvet collar to ditto .... 0 14 6.

Whereas Testy contended, that it could not be complete without a collar, that it only had one, whether velvet or cloth was no matter, and that he was not therefore liable to pay as if the coat had been furnished with two collars. His Honor enquired if it could not be settled out of Court, but neither party chusing to accede to this proposal, the case proceeded. After witness for the plaintiff had been examined, the Gentleman who occupied the chair on the floor, on the Judge's left, rose, and putting his left hand into his breeches pocket, and giving his head the exact proper inclination to the right, cross-examined one of them as follows: –

What are you? – What am I, Sir? a man.

I did not ask you whether you were a man or woman, I wish to know what is your trade.

Witness. – A tailor.

Lawyer. – Well now Mr Mantailor, do you know a coat when you see it?

Witness. – I should think so.

Lawyer. – I did not ask you what you thought – answer my question, Sir.

Witness. – What sort of a coat do you mean, Sir?

Lawyer. – I ask you once more if you know a coat when you see it?

Witness. – Yes, Sir.

Lawyer. – Pray how many collars are there to a coat?

Witness. – How many collars are there to a coat, Sir, why everybody knows that.

Lawyer. – Well then, if everybody knows, you can have no difficulty in telling me – how many collars are there to a coat, I again ask?

Witness. – Why, sure Sir, you know as well as I how many collars there are to a coat.

Lawyer. – Perhaps I do, but still I wish you to tell me; come, Sir, I'll ask you another question, and perhaps we shall come round at last. How many tailors do you reckon there are to a man?

Witness. – One tailor to a coat, Sir.

Lawyer.—One what?

Witness.—Collar to a coat.

Lawyer.—(repeating) one collar to a coat.

Witness.—Yes, Sir.

Lawyer.—I thought we should come to the point in time; now, if there is only one collar to a coat, do you consider that a coat is complete without a collar?

The cross-examination was pursued much in this way for some time, when the case for the plaintiff being ended, the Lawyer, who had cross-examined the witness, rose and addressed the Jury on behalf of the defendant, commenting very happily on the admission of the plaintiff's witness, that a coat had but one collar, and that it was not complete without it.—The Gentleman neither wore a gown or wig. After he had ended, the young Barrister immediately opposite to him, addressed the Court in support of the plaintiff's claim. He had a good clear voice and a wonderful degree of self-possession, and his consumptive and delicate appearance would scarcely have warranted the expectation that his physical powers were equal to the deep sonorous tones which proceeded from him, or to the exertion which he displayed. The points upon which he chiefly laid stress were, that, although a coat might not be complete without a collar, it did not require a velvet collar, that the velvet collar was an extra, for which, it having been for the defendant's own pleasure and fancy, he was as much bound to pay as in a case where a contract might be made to complete a house or other work, and if the party afterwards chose to make alterations or additions not included in the contract, they were at his own cost and expence – that is £5 15s. had been the price named by Fitwell for the coat, to which Testy had agreed, and that he afterwards said, "let me have a velvet collar". He went on farther to argue, that it was by no means incontrovertible that coats might not have more than one collar – that he had seen coats with seven or eight collars, and had found the comfort of them when travelling in cold weather. Here he was interrupted by the opposite Lawyer, who said "capes – not collars", – that even one collar was not necessary to complete a coat, for it was within the daily observation of everyone that there were some coats of that peculiar make as to shew no collar, unless the straight neck-piece might be called a collar, and which might with equal propriety be termed a cape, as the other pieces of cloth, the mention of which had drawn upon him the interruption of the learned Counsel. Under these circumstances he confidently trusted to receive a verdict for the plaintiff.

The Judge then recapitulated the evidence in a husky tone of voice, frequently altogether inaudible, making constant breaks, or hesitations, and taking large quantities of snuff as he proceeded. He doubted very much upon which side the evidence preponderated –

it was entirely a question of fact rather than law. He explained, however, what the law was with respect to contracts, and left the case wholly in the hands of the Assessors, who presently returned a verdict for the defendant. During my attention to the arguments and decision of this cause, I discovered how extremely difficult the construction of this building had rendered it to hear what passed – that in fact, at a very short distance from the elevated seat before mentioned, nothing could be distinctly made out, when the voice of the speaker was not raised, and when perfect silence was not maintained. As I left the Court, I fell into Conversation with a Gentleman with whom I was slightly acquainted, and who, like myself, had been a byestander, observing to him, that from what I had that morning witnessed, I presumed law was very cheap in this Colony. – "Cheap, Sir," he replied, with the utmost astonishment, "you were never more mistaken in your life – Law, Sir, is not only very scarce here, but it is very dear – there is a certain bastard commodity called law, which is very current, but even this is so much clogged by expenses, that it is perfectly ruinous, and yet the most surprising thing is, almost every person encourages it." "That's very strange, Sir," said I, "the Gentleman who cross-examined the witness seemed clever and ingenious, and I thought the Judge explained the law clearly." "Pretty well as to that," my friend replied, "the defendant's Counsel is about one of the best of them, but many of his geese are swans, and the Judge would do well enough, if he had not so much of the Ex-Chancellor's doubts about him, but you must come and dine with me, and I will then explain the subject more fully to you. You have only today heard or seen two or three of our Law-expounders. I will introduce you to the acquaintance of some more of them, and I will also let you into a knowledge of some of the sweets of the profession, and of the terrible consequences which attend such infatuation, as we have this morning witnessed, but which I am sorry to say is very common. The Law Establishment of this Colony is a grievous tax upon the Public, and a dreadful scourge to individuals, but we will talk more about it over a bottle of wine. Mind my dinner hour is five, and I shall expect you."

The information I acquired by my visit will be communicated some other time. In the interim, I subscribe myself, gentle readers, your faithful and obedient,

Simon Stukeley.

Ellen Clacy

[THE DIGGINGS]

Saturday, 18
Fine day; we now approached Bendigo. The timber here is very large. Here we first beheld the majestic iron bark, *Eucalypti*, the trunks of which are fluted with the exquisite regularity of a Doric column; they are in truth the noblest ornaments of these mighty forests. A few miles further, and the diggings themselves burst upon our view. Never shall I forget that scene, it well repaid a journey even of sixteen thousand miles. The trees had been all cut down; it looked like a sandy plain, or one vast unbroken succession of countless gravel pits–the earth was everywhere turned up – men's heads in every direction were popping up and down from their holes. Well might an Australian writer, in speaking of Bendigo, term it "The Carthage of the Tyre of Forest Creek". The rattle of the cradle, as it swayed to and fro, the sounds of the pick and shovel, the busy hum of so many thousands, the innumerable tents, the stores with large flags hoisted above them, flags of every shape, colour, and nation, from the lion and unicorn of England to the Russian eagle, the strange yet picturesque costume of the diggers themselves, all contributed to render the scene novel in the extreme.

We hurried through this exciting locality as quickly as possible; and, after five miles travelling, reached the Eagle Hawk Gully, where we pitched our tents, supped, and retired to rest – though, for myself at least, not to sleep. The excitement of the day was sufficient cure for drowsiness. Before proceeding with an account of our doings at the Eagle Hawk, I will give a slight sketch of the character and peculiarities of the diggings themselves, which are of course not confined to one spot, but are the characteristics that usually exist in any auriferous regions, where the diggers are at work. I will leave myself, therefore, safely ensconced beneath a tent at the Eagle Hawk, and take a slight and rapid survey of the principal diggings in the neighbourhood from Saw-pit Gully to Sydney Flat.

* * *

Let us take a stroll round Forest Creek – what a novel scene! – thousands of human beings engaged in digging, wheeling, carrying, and washing, intermingled with no little grumbling, scolding and swearing. We approach first the old Post-office Square; next our eye glances down Adelaide Gully, and over the Montgomery and White Hills, all pretty well dug up; now we pass the Private Escort Station, and Little Bendigo. At the junction of Forest, Barker, and Campbell Creeks we find the Commissioners' quarters – this is nearly five miles from our starting point. We must now return to Adelaide Gully, and keep alongside Adelaide Creek, till we come to a high range of rocks, which we cross, and then find ourselves near the head-waters of Fryer's Creek. Following that stream towards the Loddon, we pass the interesting neighbourhood of Golden Gully, Moonlight Flat, Windless and Red Hill; this latter which covers about two acres of ground is so called from the colour of the soil, it was the first found, and is still considered as the richest auriferous spot near Mount Alexander. In the wet season, it was reckoned that on Moonlight Flat one man was daily buried alive from the earth falling into his hole. Proceeding north-east in the direction of Campbell's Creek, we again reach the Commissioners' tent.

The principal gullies about Bendigo are Sailor's, Napoleon, Pennyweight, Peg Leg, Growler's, White Horse, Eagle Hawk, Californian, American, Derwent, Long, Piccaninny, Iron Bark, Black Man's, Poor Man's, Dusty, Jim Crow, Spring, and Golden – also Sydney Flat, and Specimen Hill – Haverton Gully, and the Sheep-wash. Most of these places are well-ransacked and tunnelled, but thorough good wages may always be procured by tin dish washing in deserted holes, or surface washing.

It is not only the diggers, however, who make money at the Gold Fields. Carters, carpenters, storemen, wheelwrights, butchers, shoemakers, etc. usually in the long run make a fortune quicker than the diggers themselves, and certainly with less hard work or risk of life. They can always get from £1 to £2 a day without rations, whereas they may dig for weeks and get nothing. Living is not more expensive than in Melbourne: meat is generally from 4d. to 6d. a pound, flour about 1s. 6d. a pound, (this is the most expensive article in housekeeping there) butter must be dispensed with, as that is seldom less than 4s. a pound, and only successful diggers can indulge in such articles as cheese, pickles, ham, sardines, pickled salmon, or spirits, as all these things, though easily procured if you have gold to throw away, are expensive, the last-named article (diluted with water or something less innoxious) is only to be obtained for 30s. a bottle.

The stores, which are distinguished by a flag, are numerous and well stocked. A new style of lodging and boarding house is in great vogue. It is a tent fitted up with stringy bark couches, ranged down each side of the tent, leaving a narrow passage up the middle. The lodgers are supplied with mutton, damper, and tea, three times a day, for the charge of 5s. a meal, and 5s. for the bed; this is by the week, a casual guest must pay double, and as 18 inches is on an average considered ample width to sleep in, a tent 24 feet long will bring in a good return to the owner.

The stores at the diggings are large tents generally square or oblong, and everything required by a digger can be obtained for money, from sugar-candy to potted anchovies; from East India pickles to Bass's pale ale; from ankle jack boots to a pair of stays; from a baby's cap to a cradle; and every apparatus for mining, from a pick to a needle. But the confusion – the din – the medley – what a scene for a shop walker! Here lies a pair of herrings dripping into a bag of sugar, or a box of raisins, there a gay-looking bundle of ribbons beneath two tumblers, and a half-finished bottle of ale. Cheese and butter, bread and yellow soap, pork and currants, saddles and frocks, wide-awakes and blue serge shirts, green veils and shovels, baby linen and tallow candles, are all heaped indiscriminately together; added to which, there are children bawling, men swearing, storekeeper sulky, and last, not *least*, women's tongues going nineteen to the dozen.

Most of the storekeepers are purchasers of gold either for cash or in exchange for goods, and many are the tricks from which unsuspecting diggers suffer. One great and outrageous trick is to weigh the parcels separately, or divide the whole, on the excuse that the weight would be too much for the scales; and then, on adding up the grains and pennyweights, the sellers often lose at least half an ounce. On one occasion, out of seven pounds weight, a party once lost an ounce and three quarters in this manner. There is also the old method of false beams – one in favour of the purchaser – and here, unless the seller weighs in both pans, he loses considerably. Another mode of cheating is to have glass pans resting on a piece of green baize; under this baize, and beneath the pan which holds the weights, is a wetted sponge; which causes that pan to adhere to the baize, and consequently it requires more gold to make it level; this, coupled with the false reckoning, is ruinous to the digger. In town, the Jews have a system of robbing a great deal from sellers before they purchase the gold-dust (for in these instances it must be *dust*): it is thrown into a zinc pan with slightly raised sides, which are well rubbed over with grease; and under the plea of a careful examination, the purchaser shakes and rubs the dust, and a considerable quantity adheres to the sides. A commoner practice still is for examiners of gold-dust to cultivate long finger-nails, and, in drawing the fingers about it, gather some up.

Sly grog selling is the bane of the diggings. Many – perhaps nine-tenths – of the diggers are honest industrious men, desirous of getting a little there as a stepping-stone to independence elsewhere; but the other tenth is composed of outcasts and transports – the refuse of Van Diemen's Land – men of the most depraved and abandoned characters, who have sought and gained the lowest abyss of crime, and who would a short time ago have expiated their crimes on a scaffold. They generally work or rob for a space, and when well stocked with gold, retire to Melbourne for a month or so, living in drunkenness and debauchery. If, however, their holiday is spent at the diggings, the sly grog-shop is the last scene of their boisterous career. Spirit selling is strictly prohibited; and although Government will license a respectable public-house on the *road*, it is resolutely refused *on* the diggings. The result has been the opposite of that which it was intended to produce. There is more drinking and rioting at the diggings than elsewhere, the privacy and risk give the obtaining it an excitement which the diggers enjoy as much as the spirit itself; and wherever grog is sold on the sly, it will sooner or later be the scene of a riot, or perhaps murder. Intemperance is succeeded by quarrelling and fighting, the neighbouring tents report to the police, and the offenders are lodged in the lock-up; whilst the grog-tent, spirits, wine, etc. are seized and taken to the Commissioners. Some of the stores, however, managed to evade the law rather cleverly – as spirits are not *sold*, "my friend" pays a shilling more for his fig of tobacco, and his wife an extra sixpence for her suet; and they smile at the store-man, who in return smiles knowingly at them, and then glasses are brought out, and a bottle produced, which sends forth *not* a fragrant perfume on the sultry air.

It is no joke to get ill at the diggings; doctors make you pay for it. Their fees are – for a consultation, at their own tent, ten shillings; for a visit out, from one to ten pounds, according to time and distance. Many are regular quacks, and these seem to flourish best. The principal illnesses are weakness of sight, from the hot winds and sandy soil, and dysentry, which is often caused by the badly-cooked food, bad water, and want of vegetables.

The interior of the canvas habitation of the digger is desolate enough; a box on a block of wood forms a table, and this is the only furniture; many dispense with that. The bedding, which is laid on the ground, serves to sit upon. Diogenes in his tub would not have looked more comfortless than anyone else. Tin plates and pannicans, the same as are used for camping up, compose the breakfast, dinner, and tea service, which meals usually consist of the same dishes – mutton, damper, and tea.

In some tents the soft influence of our sex is pleasingly apparent: the tins are as bright as silver, there are sheets as well as blankets on the beds, and perhaps a clean counterpane, with the addition of a dry sack or piece of carpet on the ground; whilst a pet cockatoo, chained to a perch, makes noise enough to keep the "missus" from feeling lonely when the good man is at work. Sometimes a wife is at first rather a nuisance; women get scared and frightened, then cross, and commence a "blow up" with their husbands; but all their railing generally ends in their quietly settling down to this rough and primitive style of living, if not without a murmur, at least to all appearance with the determination to laugh and bear it. And although rough in their manners, and not over select in their address, the digger seldom wilfully injures a woman; in fact, a regular Vandemonian will, in his way, play the gallant with as great a zest as a fashionable about town – at any rate, with more sincerity of heart.

Sunday is kept at the diggings in a very orderly manner: and among the actual diggers themselves, the day of rest is taken in *verbatim* sense. It is not unusual to have an established clergyman holding forth near the Commissioners' tent, and almost within hearing will be a tub orator expounding the origin of evil, whilst a "mill" (a fight with fisticuffs) or a dog fight fills up the background.

But night at the diggings is the characteristic time: murder here – murder there – revolvers cracking – blunderbusses bombing – rifles going off – balls whistling – one man groaning with a broken leg – another shouting because he couldn't find the way to his hole, and a third equally vociferous because he has tumbled into one – this man swearing – another praying – a party of bacchanals chanting various ditties to different time and tune, or rather minus both. Here is one man grumbling because he has brought his wife with him, another ditto because he has left his behind, or sold her for an ounce of gold or a bottle of rum. Donny-brook Fair is not to be compared to an evening at Bendigo.

John Mitchel

IN TASMANIA ON TICKET-OF-LEAVE

April, 1850–June, 1853

April 6th, 1850

The mountainous southern coast of Van Diemen's Land! It is a soft blue day; soft airs, laden with all the fragrances of those antarctic woods, weave an atmosphere of ambrosia around me. As we coast along over the placid waters, passing promontory after promontory, wooded to the waters' edge, and "glassing their ancient glories in the flood", both sea and land seem to bask and rejoice in the sunshine. Old Ocean smiles – that multitudinous rippling laugh seen in vision by the chained Prometheus. Even my own sick and weary soul (so kind and bounteous is our mother earth) feels lightened, refreshed, uplifted. Yet there, to port, loom the mountains, whereunto I am to be chained, for years, with a vulture gnawing my heart. Here is the very place: the Kaf, or Caucasus, where I must die a daily death.

It must have been on these mountains that strength and force bound the victim Demigod – for, did not *Kratos* say unto *Hephaistos*, "We have come now to the utmost verge of the earth"? Where was that but at the antipodes? – however, the limited geographical knowledge of the poet was unequal to his inspiration. Would that I had committed the godlike crime, and gathered fire from those empyrean urns whence the stars draw light – then might I hope to possess the godlike strength also of the Titan crucified! Oh! Divine

Æther! and ye swift-winged winds! ye gushing river-fountains! and thou boundless, endless, multitudinous chorus-laugh of ocean waves! Oh! Earth, mother of all things! and world-seeing circuit of the sun! – No answer; but, enter convict-servant with a mockery of dinner. Eating or sleeping is not for me these three days past; partly from severe illness, partly from the excited expectation of once more, at the end of two years, seeing the face of a friend. There, amongst or behind those shaggy mountains, wander Martin, O'Brien, Meagher, each alone in his forest-dungeon. Surely I shall contrive some means of meeting them *once*.

This evening we entered the inlet known as D'Entrecasteaux Channel, which runs up about twenty-five miles on the west side of Bruni Island, and divides it from the mainland of Tasmania. On the east side of Bruni spreads out Storm Bay, the ordinary approach to Hobart Town harbour; but this channel adjoins Storm Bay at the northern extremity of Bruni; from whence a wide estuary runs many miles farther inland. We are becalmed in the channel; but can see the huge mass of Mount Wellington, ending to the eastward in steep cliffs. In the valley at the foot of those cliffs, as they tell me, bosomed in soft green hills, bowered in shady gardens, with its feet kissed by blue the ripples of the Derwent – lies Hobart Town.

But as we lie here becalmed, between lonely wooded hills, the land seems virgin yet, as when La Perouse sailed up the same channel of old, startling the natives from their kangaroo flesh-pots on the shore. These woods are all of evergreen trees; and even from the deck I can see the long streamers of bark peeling off their trunks and festooned from branch to branch; for all this tribe, the *Eucalypti*, shed not their leaves but their bark. The trees seem almost all of great height; but on the whole the forest looks poor and ragged, because the boughs and branches are so conspicuous in their nakedness; and the foliage is thin compared with the bulk of the trunks. This is certainly the first impression made on an eye accustomed to the umbrageous masses of beech and sycamore that build up the cathedral arches and aisles of our European woodlands. But I can scarcely believe that I am verily to set my foot upon dry land again.

7th

We made our way this morning to the head of D'Entrecasteaux Channel, where it communicates by a narrow passage with the great Storm Bay – took a pilot on board at this passage, a little dark man, at whom I gazed as narrowly and curiously as ever did Abel Jans Tasman at the first Australasian savages he saw, or they at Abel. But, indeed, our little pilot was a mere Carthaginian in tweed pantaloons and round jacket; and he came down to his boat from a neat white cottage on a hill, with a greensward lawn sloping down from its door to the boat-pier, and some sweet-briar hedges protecting and adorning its garden.

Two o'clock afternoon

We are at anchor in the Derwent, a quarter of a mile from the quays and custom-house of Hobart Town. Why should I write down, here again, what I see, what everybody sees, at every sea-port? The town slopes from the river to the hills precisely like any other town. Several church steeples, of course; a small battery on a point; a windmill on a height; merchants' stores along the quays; wagons carrying merchandise hither and thither; and the wagons have wheels; and the horses are quadrupedal and solid-ungular. A good many ships lie in the harbour; and one Carthaginian frigate, the *Maeander*.

Our bold captain and surgeon-superintendent have dressed themselves (and the latter in sword and epaulettes looks grand enough), to await the official persons; the official persons ashore, with that deliberate dignity which becomes their high position, move slowly, and in their several convict bureaus, prepare their stationery and tape, that they may board us in due form. So I have time to dwell upon, to appropriate and assimilate, one of the loveliest scenes in all the world. The harbour is the broad estuary of the river Derwent. The town lies on the western side, backed by gardens and villas, rising on the slope of wooded hills and ravines, which all lose themselves in the vast gloomy mass of Mount Wellington. On the eastern side, which seems nearly uninhabited, there are low hills covered with wood; and directing the eye up the river valley, I see nothing but a succession of hill and forest, till blue mountains shut up the view. I long to walk the woods, and leave behind me the sight of the weariful sea.

8th

Some Hobart Town newspapers have come on board. O'Brien is still in very close confinement on an island off the east coast, called Maria Island, a rugged and desolate territory, about twelve miles in length, where the gaolers keep one of their main strongholds. He has refused to accept their "ticket-of-leave" on the terms of giving them his parole not to escape while he holds it; and the convict-authorities are much irritated by his determination.

Evening

An official person was brought to my cabin door half an hour ago, by the doctor, and introduced to me by the name of *Emmett*. – – A convict official by the name of Emmett! He handed me a communication from an individual styled "Comptroller-General", informing me that instructions had been received from the Secretary of State to allow me to reside at large in any one of the police-districts I might select (except those already used as the dungeons of my friends) – subject to no restriction, save the necessity of reporting myself to the district police-magistrate once a month. This condition of existence is, I find, called "Ticket-of-leave". I may accept it or not, as I think proper; or, having accepted, I may at any time resign it: but first of all, I must give my promise that so long as I hold the same "ticket", I shall not escape from the colony.

O'Brien, as I said, had refused to give this promise; but Martin, Meagher, O'Doherty, and the rest have done so. Some of them, as I hear, speak of surrendering their "comparative liberty", and, of course, withdrawing their promise, so soon as their health shall have been re-established by a few months' wandering in the bush. I decide to do as the majority of my friends have done, especially as Dr Gibson informs me that the close confinement of Maria Island would probably kill me at once. He seems, indeed, most anxious to get me ashore; and takes credit for bringing me so far alive, after my ten months' solitary confinement in Bermuda, and eleven months and seventeen days' cruising in the *Neptune*.

Wrote a note to the "Comptroller-General", and placed it in the hands of Emmett, informing him that I would promise not to escape so long as I should enjoy the "comparative liberty" of the ticket: and, on his suggestion and the doctor's, I wrote another note, telling the authorities I was very ill; had been ill for many months, and was utterly unfit to be sent off by myself to one of the remote districts, amongst entire strangers. The doctor is to back this with his professional authority; and he and Emmett say the governor will be sure to allow me to go up to a place called Bothwell, where John Martin vegetates. So Emmett left me.

Hobart Town has quite an imposing appearance from the water, standing out against its grand mountain background. Why should not I write a minute account of the town this evening, as I have leisure, and no prepossessions and no narrow personal observations to distract me? Sterne gave to the world a valuable directory of Calais upon that principle.

To my utter amazement, I had a letter today from Patrick O'Donoghue, who has been permitted to live in the city of Hobart Town, informing me that he has established a newspaper called the *Irish Exile*, enclosing me a copy of the last number, and proposing that *I should join him* in the concern. Herein is a marvellous thing. How happens it that the convict authorities permit him to conduct a paper at all? Or what would be the use of such a publication here, even if we were competent enough to manage it? The thing is a hideous absurdity altogether: but I am glad to learn that none of my friends have anything to do with it; though I suppose it assumes to be a sort of "organ" for them. The *Irish Exile* is bepuffing me now most outrageously: God preserve me from organs of opinion! Have I sailed round the terraqueous globe, and dropped in here in a cove of the far South Pacific, to find an "able editor" mounted stiltwise upon phrases tall, and blowing deliberate puffs in my face? Glady I would bare my brow to all the tornadoes and *ouragans* of the West Indies, to the black squalls of the tropics, to the heavy gales of the British channel, and the typhoons of the China seas, rather than to the flattering flatulence of these mephitic airs. I was tired, indeed, of the sea; but at sea there are, at any rate, no organs of opinion. Eurus and Boreas are often rude enough; but, at least, they blow where they list, and pipe not their notes under the censorship of a Comptroller-General.

To be sure, one may cite Virgil against me, with the Comptroller-General Æolus, and his *quos ego*.

But what of this? I retire to my cot tonight in a black humour, vilipending both sea and land.

12th

Sitting on the green grass by the bank of a clear, brawling stream of fresh water. Trees waving overhead; the sunshine streaming through their branches, and making a tremulous network of light and shade on the ground. It is Bothwell, forty-six miles from Hobart Town, from the *Neptune* and the sea, and high among the central mountains of Van Diemen's Land. Opposite sits John Martin, sometime of Loughorn, smoking placidly, and gazing curiously on me with his mild eyes.

* * *

July 22nd

Have had a serious consultation with John Martin, as to whether I should at length allow my wife and family to come out to Van Diemen's Land. None of our friends, except Mr O'Brien, seem to regard my speedy release as a thing at all probable. I may have to live the remaining twelve years of my sentence here, unless some chance arises of effecting an escape honourably. To escape *otherwise*, that is clandestinely, would indeed be easy to all of us at any time; but that is an idea not to be entertained.

It is grievous to think of bringing up children in this island; yet by fixing my residence in this remote, thinly-peopled, and pastoral district, engaging in some sort of farming and cattle-feeding, and mingling in the society of the good quiet colonists here, we might almost forget, at times, the daily and hourly outrage that our enemies put upon us in keeping us here at all, and enjoy the glorious health which this matchless climate would be almost sure to inoculate our veins withal. Several families (one especially, in which I have grown intimate) express a strong wish to see my family residing with me here. I could devote a good deal of time, also, to teaching the children; and, in short, I do so pine for something resembling a home – something that I could occasionally almost fancy a real home – that I have written this day to Newry, inviting all my household to the antipodes. Pray God, I have done right.

Visit from Terence MacManus; he has ridden up the valley of the Derwent and Clyde from New Norfolk, to see us by stealth. If discovered outside the bounds prescribed to him, he would be probably placed in custody and subjected to some punishment. He came to our door in the evening, and sent in his name (Dr Smith) by the little girl. We go up to the lakes again the day after tomorrow, and have induced him to prolong his trip so far along with us, though he will then be sixty-five miles from his dungeon; but the temptation of meeting Meagher and Kevin, and of seeing an actual congregation of five Irish rebels together again (more than enough, by law, to make a "riot") is too strong for him to resist. When we shall have drawn together such a power, we hope to be strong enough, if not to make a revolution, at least to shoot some ducks. The lakes swarm with a very fine kind of duck, the "black-duck", besides the "mountain-duck", a small kind with splendid plumage; teal, musk-duck, not to mention jet black swans, which swim either in pairs, or in fleets of five or six.

30th

MacManus made some days pass pleasantly for us, but he is gone home – that is, to his dungeon district. We have ridden about twelve miles north west from Bothwell, to see the Shannon. All the way, the country, the trees, the hills, have that sameness in figure and colour which makes the island so uniform – valley and bluff perpetually repeating its own features, and every wooded hill mirroring the wooded hill that stands opposite. On all the road, we passed but one house; a piece of Tudor barbarism in yellow stone, lately built by an eccentric settler in the dreariest spot he could find within many a league. At last we arrived at the brink of a deep valley, beyond which, on the western side, the hills rose more wild and mountainous. The valley spread just below us into a grassy plain, with a few fine "black-gums" dotting its green floor; and as we descended, we soon heard the murmurous dashing of a river hidden yet by the trees. It is the Shannon, a rushing, whirling, tumultuous stream that derives its water from the "Big Lake", a noble reservoir some thirty miles farther to the northwest, lying high on a desolate plateau of Tasmania. It is the greatest lake in the island, and is said to measure ninety miles round. Through the whole of its course this river runs very rapidly, having a fall of two thousand feet in those thirty miles; and like all the other Van Diemen's Land rivers, it is icy cold.

All my life long I have delighted in rivers, rivulets, rills, fierce torrents tearing their rocky beds, gliding dimpled brooks kissing a daisied marge. The tinkle, or murmur, or deep-resounding roll, or raving roar of running water is of all sounds my ears ever hear now, the most homely. Nothing else in this land looks or sounds like home. The birds have a foreign tongue: the very trees whispering to the wind, whisper in accents unknown to me; for the young gum-tree leaves are all hard, horny, polished as the laurel – besides, they have neither upper nor under side, but are set on with the plane of them vertical; wherefore they can never, never, let breeze pipe or zephyr breathe as it will, never can they whisper, quiver, sigh or sing, as do the beeches and the sycamores of old Rostrevor. Yes, all sights and sounds of nature are alien and outlandish – suggestive of the Tropic of Capricorn and the Antarctic Circle – save only the sparkle and the music of the streams. Well I know the voice of this eloquent river: it talks to me, and to the woods and rocks, in the same tongue and dialect wherein the Roe discoursed to me, a child; in its crystalline gush my heart and brain are bathed; and I hear, in its plaintive chime, all the blended voices of history, of prophecy, and poesy, from the beginning. Not cooler or fresher was the Thracian Hebrus; not purer were Abana and Pharpar; not more ancient and venerable is Father Nilus. Before the dynasty was yet bred that quaffed the sacred wave of Choaspes, "the drink of none but kings" – ere its lordly namesake river, in Erin of the streams, reflected yet upon its bosom a Pillar Tower, or heard the chimes from its seven churches, this river was rushing through its lonely glen to the southern sea, was singing its mystic song to these primeval woods.

Oh! Sun-loved River ! wherefore dost thou hum,
  Hum, hum, alway thy strange, deep, mystic song
Unto the rocks and strands ? – for they are dumb,
  And answer nothing as thou flowest along.
Why singest so, all hours of night and day ?
  Ah! river ! my best river ! thou, I know, art seeking
Some land where souls have still the gift of speaking
  With Nature in her own old wondrous way!

I delight in poets who delight in rivers; and for this do I love that sweet singer, through whose inner ear and brain the gush of his native Aufidus for ever streamed and flashed: – how some perennial brook of crystal glimmered for ever through all his day-dreams! how he yearned to marry his own immortality with the eternal murmuring hymn of that bright Bandusian fount ! Wisely, too, and learnedly did Clarence Mangan discourse with the rivers, and attune his notes to their wondrous music. How gloriously he interprets the German Moerike and his melodious theme! –

What on cold earth, is deep as thou? Is aught?

Love is as deep, Love only is as deep:
Love lavisheth all, yet loseth, lacketh naught ;
Like thee, too, Love can neither pause nor sleep.

Roll on, thou loving river, thou ! Lift up
Thy waves, those eyes bright with a riotous laughing !
Thou makest me immortal ! I am quaffing
The wine of rapture from no earthly cup !

So, too, with Mueller ; he delivers himself and you up to the entrancement of the Naiad: –

There danceth adown the mountain,
The child of a lofty race:
A streamlet, fresh from its fountain,
Hies through the valley apace.

Some fairy hath whispered, "Follow!"
And I have obeyed her well:
I thread the blossomy hollow,
With my pilgrim staff and shell.

On, on, behold me straying,
And ever beside the stream,
As I list its murmurous playing,
And mark how its wavelets gleam.

Can this be the path I intended?
Oh ! Sorceress, what shall I say ?
Thy dazzle and music blended,
Have wiled my reason away !

No mortal sounds are winging
Their wonted way along;
Oh, no ! some Naiad is singing
A flattering summer-song !

And loudlier doth she flatter
And loudlier, loudlier still –

But, behold ! plump into the water, just under the bank, tumbles a *Platypus*, uncouth, amphibious quadruped, with broad duck-bill; and shrill from a neighbouring gum-tree yells the "laughing-jackass" – a noisy bird so named by profane colonists.

Ada Cambridge

[ARRIVING IN MELBOURNE]

I suppose it was about nine o'clock when we dropped anchor. All we could see of the near city was a three-quarter ring of lights dividing dark water from dark sky – just what I see now every night when I come upstairs to bed, before I draw the blinds down. We watched them, fascinated, and – still more fascinating – the boats that presently found their way to us, bringing welcoming friends and relatives to those passengers who possessed them. We, strangers in a strange land, sat apart and watched these favoured ones – listened to their callings back and forth over the ship's side, beheld their embraces at the gangway, their excited interviews in the cuddy, their gay departures into the night and the unknown, which in nearly every case swallowed them for ever as far as we were concerned. Three only of the whole company have we set eyes on since – excepting the friend who became our brother – and one of these three renewed acquaintance with us but a year or two ago. Another I saw once across a hotel dinner-table. The third was the clergyman who had been so kindly foisted on us – or we on him – before we left England; and it was enough for us to see him afar off at such few diocesan functions as we afterwards attended together ; we dropped closer relations as soon as there was room to drop them. However, he was a useful and respected member of his profession, and much valued by his own parish, from which death removed him many a year ago. Quite a deputation of church members came off to welcome him on that night of his return from his English holiday, and to tell him of the things his *locum tenens* had been doing in his absence. He was furious at learning that this person – at the present moment the head of the Church of England in this state – had had the presumption to replace an old organ – *his* old organ – with a new one. In the deputation were ladies with votive bouquets for his wife; the perfume of spring violets in the saloon deepened the sense of exile and solitude that crept upon us when their boat and the rest had vanished from view, leaving but the few friendless ones to the hospitality of the ship for a last night's lodging.

However, in the morning, we had our turn. It was the loveliest morning, a sample of the really matchless climate (which we had been informed was exactly like that of the palm-houses at Kew), clear as crystal, full of sunshine and freshness; and when we awoke amid strange noises, and looked out of our porthole, we saw that not sea but wooden planks lay under it – Port Melbourne railway pier, exactly as it is now, only that its name was then Sandridge and its old piles thirty years stouter where salt water and barnacles gnawed them.

With what joy as well as confidence did we don our best clerical coat and our best purple petticoat and immaculate black gown (the skirt pulled up out of harm's way through a stout elastic waist-cord, over which it hung behind in a soft, unobtrusive bag, for street wear), and lay out our Peter Robinson jacket and bonnet, and gloves from the hermetically sealed bottle, upon the bare bunk! And the breakfast we then went to is a memory to gloat upon – the succulent steak, the fresh butter and cream, the shore-baked rolls, the piled fruits and salads; nothing ever surpassed it except the midday meal following, with its juicy sirloin and such spring vegetables as I had never seen. This also I battened on, with my splendidly prepared appetite, though G. did not. The bishop's representative – our first Australian friend, whose fine and kindly face is little changed in all these years, and which I never look upon without recalling that moment, my first and just impression of it and him – appeared in our cabin doorway early in the morning; and it was deemed expedient that G. should go with him to report himself at headquarters, and return for me when that business was done. So I spent some hours alone, watching the railway station at the head of the pier through my strong glasses. In the afternoon I too landed, and was driven to lodgings that had been secured for us in East Melbourne, where we at once dressed for dinner at the house of our newest friend, and for one of the most charming social evenings that I ever spent. The feature of it that I best remember was a vivid literary discussion based upon *Lothair*, which was the new book of the hour, and from which our host read excruciating extracts. How brightly every detail of those first hours in

Australia stands out in the mind's records of the past – the refined little dinner (I could name every dish on the dainty table), the beautiful and adored invalid hostess, who died not long afterwards, and whom those who knew her still speak of as "too good for this world"; the refreshment of intellectual talk after the banalities of the ship; the warm kindness of everybody, even our landlady, who was really a lady, and like a mother to me; the comfort of the sweet and clean shore life – I shall never cease to glow at the recollection of these things. The beautiful weather enhanced the charm of all, and – still more – the fact that, although at first I staggered with the weakness left by such long seasickness, I not only recovered as soon as my foot touched land, but enjoyed the best health of my life for a full year afterwards.

The second day was a Saturday, and we were taken out to see the sights. No description that we had read or heard of, even from our fellow-passengers whose homes were there, had prepared us for the wonder that Melbourne was to us. As I remember our metropolis then, and see it now, I am not conscious of any striking general change, although of course, the changes in detail are innumerable. It was a greater city for its age thirty years ago than it is today, great as it is today. I lately read in some English magazine the statement that tree-stumps – likewise, if I mistake not, kangaroos – were features of Collins Street "twenty-five years ago". I can answer for it that in 1870 it was excellently paved and macadamised, thronged with its wagonette-cabs, omnibuses, and private carriages – a perfectly good and proper street, except for its open drainage gutters. The nearest kangaroo hopped in the Zoological Gardens at Royal Park. In 1870, also – although the theatrical proceedings of the Kelly gang took place later – bushranging was virtually a thing of the past. So was the Bret Harte mining-camp. We are credited still, I believe, with those romantic institutions, and our local storywriters love to pander to the delusion of some folks that Australia is made up of them; I can only say – and I ought to know – that in Victoria, at any rate, they have not existed in my time. Had they existed in the other colonies, I must have heard of it. The last real bushranger came to his inevitable bad end shortly before we arrived. The cowardly Kellys, murderers, and brigands as they were, and costlier than all their predecessors to hunt down, always seemed to me but imitation bushrangers. Mining has been a sober pursuit, weighted with expensive machinery. Indeed, we have been quite steady and respectable, so far as I know. In the way of public rowdyism I can recall nothing worth mentioning – unless it be the great strike of 1890.

We went to see the Town Hall – the present one, lacking only its present portico; and the splendid Public Library, as it was until a few years ago, when a wing was added; and the Melbourne Hospital, as it stands today; and the University, housed as it is now, and beginning to gather its family of colleges about it. We were taken a-walking in the Fitzroy Gardens – saw the same fern gully, the same plaster statutes, that still adorn it; and to the Botanical Gardens, already furnished with their lakes and swans, and rustic bridges, and all the rest of it. And how beautiful we thought it all! As I have said, it was springtime, and the weather glorious. There had been excessive rains, and were soon to be more – rains which caused 1870 to be marked in history as "the year of the great floods" – but the loveliness of the weather as we first knew it I shall never forget.

We finished the week in the suburban parish that included Pentridge, the great prison of the State – an awesome pile of dressed granite then as now. The incumbent was not well, and G. was sent to help him with his Sunday duty. The first early function was at the gaol, from which they brought back an exquisitely-designed programme of the music and order of service, which I still keep amongst my mementoes of those days. It was done by a prisoner, who supplied one, and always a different one, to the chaplain each Sunday.

At his house – where again we were surprised to find all the refinements we had supposed ourselves to have left in England, for he and his wife were exceptionally cultivated persons – we slept on the ground floor for the first time in our lives, all mixed up with drawing-room and garden, which felt very strange and public, and almost improper. Now I prefer the bungalow arrangement to any other; I like to feel the house all round me, close and cosy, and to be able to slip from my bed into the open air when I like, and not to be cut off from folks when I am ill. For more than twenty years I was accustomed to it, sleeping with open windows and unlocked doors, like any Bedouin in his tent, unmolested in the loneliest localities by night-prowling man or beast. I miss this now, when I live in town and have to climb stairs and isolate myself – or sleep with shut windows (which I never will) in a ground-floor fortress, made burglar-proof at every point.

Bishop and Mrs Perry had a dinner-party for us on Monday. That day was otherwise given to our particular ship friend (of whom I shall say more presently); with him, a stranger in the land like ourselves, we had adventures and excursions "on our own", eluding the many kind folk who would have liked to play courier. We lunched plentifully at an excellent restaurant – I cannot identify it now, but it fixed our impression that we had indeed come to a land of milk and honey – and then rambled at large. The evening was very pleasant. Whether as host or guest, the first Bishop of Melbourne was always perfect, and we met some interesting people at his board. Others came in after dinner, amongst them two of the "sweetly pretty daughters", of whom we had heard in England, and who did not quite come up to our expectations. They are hoary-headed maiden ladies now – the youngest as white as the muslin of the frock she wore that night.

We did many things during the remainder of the week, which was full of business, pleasure, and hospitalities, very little of our time being spent in privacy. The shops were surprisingly well furnished and tempting, and we acted upon our supposition that we should find none to speak of in the Bush. We made careful little purchases from day to day. The very first of them, I think, was Professor Halford's snake-bite cure. We had an idea that, once out of the city, our lives would not be safe without it for a day. It was a hypodermic syringe and bottle of stuff, done up in a neat pocket-case. That case did cumber pockets for a time, but it was never opened, and eventually went astray and was no more seen – or missed. Yet snakes were quite common objects of the country then. I used to get weary of the monotony of sitting my horse and holding G.'s, while at every mile or so he stopped to kill one, during our Bush-rides in warm weather. English readers should know that in the bush it has ever been a point of honour, by no means to be evaded, to kill every snake you see, if possible, no matter how difficult the job, nor how great your impatience to be after other jobs. That probably is why they are so infrequent now that any chance appearance of the creature is chronicled in the papers as news.

Another early purchase was a couple of large pineapples, at threepence apiece. We each ate one (surreptitiously, in a retired spot), and realised one of the ambitions of our lives – to get enough of that delicacy for once.

On Saturday the 24th, the eighth day from our arrival, we turned our backs upon all this wild dissipation and our faces towards stern duty. We left Melbourne for the Bush.

2

Aboriginal Encounters

EDITOR'S NOTE

Descriptions of the Aboriginal inhabitants of Australia inevitably occupied a large part of early letters and journals, whether these were written by members of the First Fleet, by explorers or by settlers. The extracts from George Worgan's and Thomas Watling's letters, in "First Impressions" contain detailed accounts of the "natives" or "Indians", Watling's being coloured by his resentment that the Aborigines, in his opinion, received better treatment than did the convicts. In the next part, "Settling Down", Eliza Brown and George Gordon McCrae depict relatively harmonious relations between Aborigines and settlers in the pastoral districts of Western Australia and Victoria.

The extracts in this part are mainly concerned with specific encounters between Aboriginal people and the white invaders of their territories. Watkin Tench records initial "delicacy" on the part of the strangers and friendly curiosity on the part of the "Indians". Later, however, delicacy is put aside as Governor Phillip orders that some of the Aborigines be captured. Tench's description of Arabanoo – whom the whites initially call "Manly" – records the beginnings of the process of "civilising the natives". The point it had reached by the end of the nineteenth century can be seen in Audrey Tennyson's letters to her mother, describing a trip to Oodnadatta, part of a vice-regal progress made with her husband, then governor of South Australia.

In the intervening years, white explorers had encountered much Aboriginal hostility as they penetrated into the interior. Charles Sturt's journal describes how he prudently decides not to land in the midst of a war party; further disaster is averted by the arrival of four friendly Aborigines, though Sturt prefers to thank the "almost miraculous intervention of Providence in our favour". Thomas Mitchell also writes of encountering black resistance. Conscious that "we were rather unceremonious invaders of their country", he at first attempts conciliation. When the Aborigines refuse to be conciliated Mitchell is quick to picture them as "savages" and "fiends", comparing them with Milton's devils and Shakespeare's witches. For, as John West notes at the end of his account of the "long and disastrous conflict" between blacks and whites in Tasmania, "To judge of a people, during a season of extraordinary excitement, must tend to erroneous conclusions". It is instructive to compare the treatment of William Buckley by his Aboriginal "captors" with that given to Arabanoo. Buckley, a convict who escaped from the shortlived Port Phillip penal station in 1803, lived with the Aborigines in Victoria until 1835 and the re-establishment of white settlement. Arabanoo died of smallpox in May 1789, less than six months after his capture.

hearing him repeat his information, I flew upon deck, on which I had barely set my foot, when the cry of "another sail" struck on my astonished ear. Confounded by a thousand ideas which arose in my mind in an instant, I sprang upon the barricado, and plainly descried two ships of considerable size, standing in for the mouth of the Bay. By this time the alarm had become general, and everyone appeared lost in conjecture. Now they were Dutchmen sent to dispossess us, and the moment after storeships from England, with supplies for the settlement. The improbabilities which attended both these conclusions, were sunk in the agitation of the moment. It was by Governor Phillip, that this mystery was at length unravelled, and the cause of the alarm pronounced to be two French ships, which, it was now recollected, were on a voyage of discovery in the southern hemisphere. Thus were our doubts cleared up, and our apprehensions banished; it was, however, judged expedient to postpone our removal to Port Jackson, until a complete confirmation of our conjectures could be procured.

Had the sea breeze set in, the strange ships would have been at anchor in the Bay by eight o'clock in the morning, but the wind blowing out, they were driven by a strong lee current to the southward of the port. On the following day they reappeared in their former situation, and a boat was sent to them, with a lieutenant of the navy in her, to offer assistance, and point out the necessary marks for entering the harbour. In the course of the day the officer returned, and brought intelligence that the ships were the *Boussole* and *Astrolabe*, sent out by order of the King of France, and under the command of Monsieur De Perrouse. The astonishment of the French at seeing us, had not equalled that we had experienced, for it appeared, that in the course of their voyage they had touched at Kamschatka, and by that means learnt that our expedition was in contemplation. They dropped anchor the next morning, just as we had got under weigh to work out of the Bay, so that for the present nothing more than salutations could pass between us.

Before I quit Botany Bay, I shall relate the observations we were enabled to make during our short stay there; as well as those which our subsequent visits to it from Port Jackson enabled us to complete.

The Bay is very open, and greatly exposed to the fury of the S.E. winds, which, when they blow, cause a heavy and dangerous swell. It is of prodigious extent, the principal arm, which takes a S.W. direction, being not less, including its windings, than twenty-four miles from the capes which form the entrance, according to the report of the French officers, who took uncommon pains to survey it. At the distance of a league from the harbour's mouth is a bar, on which at low water, not more than fifteen feet are to be found. Within this bar, for many miles up the S.W. arm, is a haven, equal in every respect to any hitherto known, and in which any number of ships might anchor, secured from all winds. The country around far exceeds in richness of soil that about Cape Banks and Point Solander, though unfortunately they resemble each other in one respect, a scarcity of fresh water.

We found the natives tolerably numerous as we advanced up the river, and even at the harbour's mouth we had reason to conclude the country more populous than Mr Cook thought it. For on the *Supply*'s arrival in the Bay on the 18th of the month, they were assembled on the beach of the south shore, to the number of not less than forty persons, shouting and making many uncouth signs and gestures. This appearance whetted curiosity to its utmost, but as prudence forbade a few people to venture wantonly among so great a number, and a party of only six men was observed on the north shore, the Governor immediately proceeded to land on that side, in order to take possession of his new territory, and bring about an intercourse between its old and new masters. The boat in which his Excellency was, rowed up the harbour, close to the land, for some distance; the Indians keeping pace with her on the beach. At last an officer in the boat made signs of a want of water, which it was judged would indicate his wish of landing. The natives directly comprehended what he wanted, and pointed to a spot where water could be procured; on which the boat was immediately pushed in, and a landing took place. As on the event of this meeting might depend so much of our future tranquility, every delicacy on our side was requisite. The Indians, though timorous, shewed no signs of resentment at the Governor's going on shore; an interview commenced, in which the conduct of both parties pleased each other so much, that the strangers returned to their ships with a much better opinion of the natives than they had landed with; and the latter seemed highly entertained with their new acquaintance, from whom they condescended to accept of a looking glass, some beads, and other toys.

Owing to the lateness of our arrival, it was not my good fortune to go on shore until three days after this had happened, when I went with a party to the south side of the harbour, and had scarcely landed five minutes, when we were met by a dozen Indians, naked as at the moment of their birth, walking along the beach. Eager to come to a conference, and yet afraid of giving offence, we advanced with caution towards them, nor would they, at first, approach nearer to us than the distance of some paces. Both parties were armed; yet an attack seemed as unlikely on their part, as we knew it to be on our own. I had at this time, a little boy, of not more than seven years of age, in my hand. The child seemed to attract their attention very much, for they frequently pointed to him and spoke to each other; and as he was not frightened, I advanced with him towards them, at the same time baring his bosom and shewing the whiteness of the skin. On the cloaths being removed they gave a loud exclamation, and one of the party, an old man, with a long beard, hideously ugly, came close to us. I bade my little charge not to be afraid, and introduced him to the acquaintance of this uncouth personage. The Indian, with great gentleness, laid his hand on the child's hat, and afterwards felt his cloaths, muttering to himself all the while. I found it necessary, however, by this time to send away the child, as such a close connection rather alarmed him; and in this, as the conclusion verified, I gave no offence to the old gentleman. Indeed it was but putting ourselves on a par with them, as I had observed from the first, that some youths of their own, though considerably older than the one with us, were kept back by the grown people. Several more now came up, to whom we made various presents, but our toys seemed not to be regarded as very valuable; nor would they for a long time make any returns to them, though before we parted, a large club, with a head almost sufficient to fell an ox, was obtained in exchange for a looking-glass. These people seemed at a loss to know (probably from our want of beards) of what sex we were, which having understood, they burst into immoderate fits of laughter, talking to each other at the same time with such rapidity and vociferation as I had never before heard. After nearly an hour's conversation by signs and gestures, they repeated several times the word *whurra*, which signifies, begone, and walked away from us to the head of the Bay.

The natives being departed, we set out to observe the country, which, on inspection, rather disappointed our hopes, being invariably sandy and unpromising for the purposes of cultivation, though the trees and grass flourish in great luxuriancy. Close to us was the spring at which Mr Cook watered, but we did not think the water very excellent, nor did it run freely. In the evening we returned on board, not greatly pleased with the latter part of our discoveries, as it indicated an increase of those difficulties, which before seemed sufficiently numerous.

Between this and our departure we had several more interviews with the natives, which ended in so friendly a manner, that we began to entertain strong hopes of bringing about a connection with them. Our first object was to win their affections, and our next to convince them of the superiority we possessed: for without the latter, the former we knew would be of little importance. An officer one day prevailed on one of them to place a target, made of bark, against a tree, which he fired at with a pistol, at the distance of some paces. The Indians, though terrified at the report, did not run away, but their astonishment exceeded their alarm, on looking at the shield which the ball had perforated. As this produced a little shyness, the officer, to dissipate their fears and remove their jealousy, whistled the air of *Malbrooke*, which they appeared highly charmed with, and imitated him with equal pleasure and readiness. I cannot help remarking here, what I was afterwards told by Monsieur De Perrouse, that the natives of California, and throughout all the islands of the Pacific Ocean, and in short wherever he had been, seemed equally touched and delighted with this little plaintive air.

[ARABANOO]

Transactions of the Colony, from the Commencement of the Year 1789, until the End of March

Pursuant to his resolution, the governor on the 31st of December sent two boats, under the command of Lieutenant Ball of the *Supply*, and Lieutenant George Johnston of the marines, down the harbour, with directions to those officers to seize and carry off some of the natives. The boats proceeded to Manly Cove, where several Indians were seen standing on the beach, who were enticed by courteous behaviour and a few presents to enter into conversation. A proper opportunity being presented, our people rushed in among them, and seized two men: the rest fled; but the cries of the captives soon brought them back, with many others, to their rescue: and so desperate were their struggles, that, in spite of every effort on our side, only one of them was secured; the other effected his escape. The boats put off without delay; and an attack from the shore instantly commenced: they threw spears, stones, firebrands, and whatever else presented itself, at the boats; nor did they retreat, agreeable to their former custom, until many musquets were fired over them.

The prisoner was now fastened by ropes to the thwarts of the boat; and when he saw himself irretrievably disparted from his countrymen, set up the most piercing and lamentable cries of distress. His grief, however, soon diminished: he accepted and eat of some broiled fish which was given to him, and sullenly submitted to his destiny.

1789

When the news of his arrival at Sydney was announced, I went with every other person to see him: he appeared to be about thirty years old, not tall, but robustly made; and of a countenance which, under happier circumstances, I thought would display manliness and sensibility; his agitation was excessive, and the clamourous crowds who flocked around him did not contribute to lessen it. Curiosity and observation seemed, nevertheless, not to have wholly deserted him; he shewed the effect of novelty upon ignorance; he wondered at all he saw: though broken and interrupted with dismay, his voice was soft and musical, when its natural tone could be heard; and he readily pronounced with tolerable accuracy the names of things which were taught him. To our ladies he quickly became extraordinarily courteous, a sure sign that his terror was wearing off.

Every blandishment was used to soothe him, and it had its effect. As he was entering the governor's house, someone touched a small bell which hung over the door: he started with horror and astonishment; but in a moment after was reconciled to the noise, and laughed at the cause of his perturbation. When pictures were shewn to him, he knew directly those which resembled the human figure: among others, a very large handsome print of her royal highness the Dutchess of Cumberland being produced, he called out, woman, a name by which we had just before taught him to call the female convicts. Plates of birds and beasts were also laid before him; and many people were led to believe, that such as he spoke about and pointed to were known to him. But this must have been an erroneous conjecture, for the elephant, rhinoceros, and several others, which we must have discovered did they exist in the country, were of the number. Again, on the other hand, those he did not point out, were equally unknown to him.

1789

His curiosity here being satiated, we took him to a large brick house, which was building for the governor's residence: being about to enter, he cast up his eyes, and seeing some people leaning out of a window on the first storey, he exclaimed aloud, and testified the most extravagant surprise. Nothing here was observed to fix his attention so strongly as some tame fowls, who were feeding near him: our dogs also he particularly noticed; but seemed more fearful than fond of them.

He dined at a side-table at the governor's; and eat heartily of fish and ducks, which he first cooled. Bread and salt meat he smelled at, but would not taste: all our liquors he treated in the same manner, and could drink nothing but water. On being shewn that he was not to wipe his hands on the chair which he sat upon, he used a towel which was gave to him, with great cleanliness and decency.

In the afternoon his hair was closely cut, his head combed, and his beard shaved; but he would not submit to these operations until he had seen them performed on another person, when he readily acquiesced. His hair, as might be supposed, was filled with vermin, whose destruction seemed to afford him great triumph; nay, either revenge, or pleasure, prompted him to eat them! but on our expressing disgust and abhorrence he left it off.

To this succeeded his immersion in a tub of water and soap, where he was completely washed and scrubbed from head to foot; after which a shirt, a jacket, and a pair of trowsers, were put upon him. Some part of this ablution I had the honour to perform, in order that I might ascertain the real colour of the skin of these people. My observation then was (and it has since been confirmed in a thousand other instances) that they are as black as the lighter cast of the African negroes.

Many unsuccessful attempts were made to learn his name; the governor therefore called him Manly, from the cove in which he was captured: this cove had received its name from the manly undaunted behaviour of a party of natives seen there, on our taking possession of the country.

To prevent his escape, a handcuff with a rope attached to it, was fastened around his left wrist, which at first highly delighted him; he called it "*Ben-gàd-ee*" (or ornament), but his delight changed to rage and hatred when he discovered its use. His supper he cooked himself: some fish were given to him for this purpose, which, without any previous preparation whatever, he threw carelessly on the fire, and when they became warm took them up, and first rubbed off the scales, peeled the outside with his teeth, and eat it; afterwards he gutted them, and laying them again on the fire, completed the dressing, and ate them.

A convict was selected to sleep with him, and to attend him wherever he might go. When he went with his keeper into his apartment he appeared very restless and uneasy while a light was kept in; but on its extinction, he immediately lay down and composed himself.

Sullenness and dejection strongly marked his countenance on the following morning; to amuse him, he was taken around the camp, and to the observatory: casting his eyes to the opposite shore from the point where he stood, and seeing the smoke of fire lighted by his countrymen, he looked earnestly at it, and sighing deeply two or three times, uttered the word "*gweè-un*" (fire).

His loss of spirits had not, however, the effect of impairing his appetite; eight fish, each weighing about a pound, constituted his breakfast, which he dressed as before. When he had finished his repast, he turned his back to the fire in a musing posture, and crept so close to it, that his shirt was caught by the flame; luckily his keeper soon extinguished it; but he was so terrified at the accident, that he was with difficulty persuaded to put on a second.

1st January, 1789

Today being new-year's-day, most of the officers were invited to the governor's table: Manly dined heartily on fish and roast pork; he was seated on a chest near a window, out of which, when he had done eating, he would have thrown his plate, had he not been prevented: during dinner-time a band of music played in an adjoining apartment; and after the cloth was removed, one of the company sang in a very soft and superior style; but the powers of melody were lost on Manly, which disappointed our expectations, as he had before shown pleasure and readiness in imitating our tunes. Stretched out on his chest, and putting his hat under his head, he fell asleep.

To convince his countrymen that he had received no injury from us, the governor took him in a boat down the harbour, that they might see and converse with him: when the boat arrived, and lay at a little distance from the beach, several Indians who had retired at her approach, on seeing Manly, returned: he was greatly affected, and shed tears. At length they began to converse. Our ignorance of the language prevented us from knowing much of what passed; it was, however, easily understood that his friends asked him why he did not jump overboard, and rejoin them. He only sighed, and pointed to the fetter on his leg, by which he was bound.

In going down the harbour he had described the names by which they distinguish its numerous creeks and headlands: he was now often heard to repeat that of *Weè-rong* (Sydney), which was doubtless to inform his countrymen of the place of his captivity; and perhaps invite them to rescue him. By this time his gloom was chased away, and he parted from his friends without testifying reluctance. His vivacity and good humour continued all the evening, and produced so good an effect on his appetite, that he eat for supper two Kangaroo rats, each of the size of a moderate rabbit, and in addition not less than three pounds of fish.

Two days after he was taken on a similar excursion; but to our surprise the natives kept aloof, and would neither approach the shore, or discourse with their countryman: we could get no explanation of this difficulty, which seemed to affect us more than it did him. Uncourteous as they were, he performed to them an act of attentive benevolence; seeing a basket made of bark, used by them to carry water, he conveyed into it two hawks and another bird, which the people in the boat had shot, and carefully covering them over, left them as a present to his old friends. But indeed the gentleness and humanity of his disposition frequently displayed themselves: when our children, stimulated by wanton curiosity, used to flock around him, he never failed to fondle them, and, if he were eating at the time, constantly offered them the choicest part of his fare.

February, 1789

His reserve, from want of confidence in us, continued gradually to wear away: he told us his name, and Manly gave place to Ar-ab-a-noo. Bread he began to relish; and tea he drank with avidity: strong liquors he would never taste, turning from them with disgust and abhorrence. Our dogs and cats had ceased to be objects of fear, and were become his greatest pets, and constant companions at table. One of our chief amusements, after the cloth was removed, was to make him repeat the names of things in his language, which he never hesitated to do with the utmost alacrity, correcting our pronunciation when erroneous.

* * *

On the 17th of February the *Supply* again sailed for Norfolk Island. The governor went down the harbour in her, and carried Arabanoo with him, who was observed to go on board with distrust and reluctance; when he found she was under sail, every effort was tried without success to exhilarate him; at length, an opportunity being presented, he plunged overboard, and struck out for the nearest shore: believing that those who were left behind would fire at him, he attempted to dive, at which he was known to be very expert: but this was attended with a difficulty which he had not foreseen: his clothes proved so buoyant, that he was unable to get more than his head under water: a boat was immediately despatched after him, and picked him up, though not without struggles and resistance on his side. When brought on board, he appeared neither afraid or ashamed of what he had done, but sat apart, melancholy and dispirited, and continued so until he saw the governor and his other friends descend into a boat, and heard himself called upon to accompany them: he sprang forward, and his cheerfulness and alacrity of temper immediately returned, and lasted during the remainder of the day. The dread of being carried away, on an element of whose boundary he could form no conception, joined to the uncertainty of our intention towards him, unquestionably caused him to act as he did.

Charles Sturt

PROVIDENTIAL DELIVERANCE FROM DANGER

After breakfast, we proceeded onwards as usual. The river had increased so much in width that, the wind being fair, I hoisted sail for the first time, to save the strength of my men as much as possible. Our progress was consequently rapid. We passed through a country that, from the nature of its soil and other circumstances, appeared to be intersected by creeks and lagoons. Vast flights of wild fowl passed over us, but always at a considerable elevation, while, on the other hand, the paucity of ducks on the river excited our surprise. Latterly, the trees upon the river, and in its neighbourhood, had been a tortuous kind of box. The flooded-gum grew in groups on the spaces subject to inundation, but not on the levels above the influence of any ordinary rise of the stream. Still they were much smaller than they were observed to be in the higher branches of the river. We had proceeded about nine miles, when we were surprised by the appearance in view, at the termination of a reach, of a long line of magnificent trees of green and dense foliage. As we sailed down the reach, we observed a vast concourse of natives under them, and, on a nearer approach, we not only heard their war-song, if it might so be called, but remarked that they were painted and armed, as they generally are, prior to their engaging in deadly conflict. Notwithstanding these outward signs of hostility, fancying that our four friends were with them, I continued to steer directly in for the bank on which they were collected. I found, however, when it was almost too

Watkin Tench

[THE INDIANS]

January, 1788

We had scarcely bid each other welcome on our arrival, when an expedition up the Bay was undertaken by the Governor and Lieutenant-Governor, in order to explore the nature of the country, and fix on a spot to begin our operations upon. None, however, which could be deemed very eligible, being discovered, his Excellency proceeded in a boat to examine the opening, to which Mr Cook had given the name of Port Jackson, on an idea that a shelter for shipping within it might be found. The boat returned on the evening of the 23rd, with such an account of the harbour and advantages attending the place, that it was determined the evacuation of Botany Bay should commence the next morning.

In consequence of this decision, the few seamen and marines who had been landed from the squadron, were instantly reimbarked, and every preparation made to bid adieu to a port which had so long been the subject of our conversation; which but three days before we had entered with so many sentiments of satisfaction; and in which, as we had believed, so many of our future hours were to be passed. The thoughts of removal banished sleep, so that I rose at the first dawn of the morning. But judge of my surprise on hearing from a serjeant, who ran down almost breathless to the cabin where I was dressing, that a ship was seen off the harbour's mouth. At first I only laughed, but knowing the man who spoke to me to be of great veracity, and late to turn into the succeeding reach to our left, that an attempt to land would only be attended with loss of life. The natives seemed determined to resist it. We approached so near that they held their spears quivering in their grasp ready to hurl. They were painted in various ways. Some who had marked their ribs, and thighs, and faces with a white pigment, looked like skeletons, others were daubed over with red and yellow ochre, and their bodies shone with the grease with which they had besmeared themselves. A dead silence prevailed among the front ranks, but those in the background, as well as the women, who carried supplies of darts, and who appeared to have had a bucket of whitewash capsized over their heads, were extremely clamorous. As I did not wish a conflict with these people, I lowered my sail, and putting the helm to starboard, we passed quietly down the stream in mid channel. Disappointed in their anticipations, the natives ran along the bank of the river, endeavouring to secure an aim at us; but, unable to throw with certainty, in consequence of the onward motion of the boat, they flung themselves into the most extravagant attitudes, and worked themselves into a state of frenzy by loud and vehement shouting.

It was with considerable apprehension that I observed the river to be shoaling fast, more especially as a huge sand-bank, a little below us, and on the same side on which the natives had gathered, projected nearly a third-way across the channel. To this sand-bank they ran with tumultuous uproar, and covered it over in a dense mass. Some of the chiefs advanced to the water to be nearer their victims, and turned from time to time to direct their followers. With every pacific disposition, and an extreme reluctance to take away life, I foresaw that it would be impossible any longer to avoid an engagement, yet with such fearful numbers against us, I was doubtful of the result. The spectacle we had witnessed had been one of the most appalling kind, and sufficient to shake the firmness of most men; but at that trying moment my little band preserved their temper coolness, and if anything could be gleaned from their countenances, it was that they had determined on an obstinate resistance. I now explained to them that their only chance of escape depended, or would depend, on their firmness. I desired that after the first volley had been fired, M'Leay and three of the men would attend to the defence of the boat with bayonets only, while I, Hopkinson, and Harris, would keep up the fire as being more used to it. I ordered, however, that no shot was to be fired until after I had discharged both my barrels. I then delivered their arms to the men, which had as yet been kept in the place appropriated for them, and at the same time rounds of loose cartridge. The men assured me they would follow my instructions, and thus prepared, having already lowered the sail, we drifted onwards with the current. As we neared the sand-bank, I stood up and made signs to the natives to desist; but without success.

I took up my gun, therefore, and cocking it, had already brought it down to a level. A few seconds more would have closed the life of the nearest of the savages. The distance was too trifling for me to doubt the fatal effects of the discharge; for I was determined to take deadly aim, in hopes that the fall of one man might save the lives of many. But at the very moment, when my hand was on the trigger, and my eye was along the barrel, my purpose was checked by M'Leay, who called to me that another party of blacks had made their appearance upon the left bank of the river. Turning round, I observed four men at the top of their speed. The foremost of them as soon as he got ahead of the boat, threw himself from a considerable height into the water. He struggled across the channel to the sand-bank, and in an incredibly short space of time stood in front of the savage, against whom my aim had been directed. Seizing him by the throat, he pushed him backwards, and forcing all who were in the water upon the bank, he trod its margin with a vehemence and an agitation that were exceedingly striking. At one moment pointing to the boat, at another shaking his clenched hand in the faces of the most forward, and stamping with passion on the sand; his voice, that was at first distinct and clear, was lost in hoarse murmurs. Two of the four natives remained on the left bank of the river, but the third followed his leader, (who proved to be the remarkable savage I have previously noticed) to the scene of action. The reader will imagine our feelings on this occasion: it is impossible to describe them. We were so wholly lost in interest at the scene that was passing, that the boat was allowed to drift at pleasure. For my own part I was overwhelmed with astonishment, and in truth stunned and confused; so singular, so unexpected, and so strikingly providential, had been our escape.

We were again roused to action by the boat suddenly striking upon a shoal, which reached from one side of the river to the other. To jump out and push her into deeper water was but the work of a moment with the men, and it was just as she floated again that our attention was withdrawn to a new and beautiful stream, coming apparently from the north. The great body of the natives having posted themselves on the narrow tongue of land formed by the two rivers, the bold savage who had so unhesitatingly interfered on our account, was still in hot dispute with them, and I really feared his generous warmth would have brought down upon him the vengeance of the tribes. I hesitated, therefore, whether or not to go to his assistance. It appeared, however, both to M'Leay and myself, that the tone of the natives had moderated, and the old and young men having listened to the remonstrances of our friend, the middle-aged warriors were alone holding out against him. A part of about seventy blacks were upon the right bank of the newly discovered river, and I thought that by landing among them, we should make a diversion in favour of our late guest; and in this I succeeded. If even they had still meditated violence, they would have to swim a good broad junction, and that, probably, would cool them, or we at least should have the advantage of position. I therefore ran the boat ashore, and landed with M'Leay amidst the smaller party of natives, wholly unarmed, and having directed the men to keep at a little distance from the bank. Fortunately, what I anticipated was brought about by the stratagem to which I had had recourse. The blacks no sooner observed that we had landed, than curiosity took place of anger. All wrangling ceased, and they came swimming over to us like a parcel of seals. Thus, in less than a quarter of an hour from the moment when it appeared that all human intervention was at an end, and we were on the point of commencing a bloody fray, which, independently of its own disastrous consequences, would have blasted the success of the expedition, we were peacefully surrounded by the hundreds who had so lately threatened us with destruction; nor was it until after we had returned to the boat, and had surveyed the multitude upon the sloping bank above us, that we became fully aware of the extent of our danger, and of the almost miraculous intervention of Providence in our favour. There could not have been less than six hundred natives upon that blackened sward. But this was not the only occasion upon which the merciful superintendance of that Providence to which we had humbly committed ourselves, was strikingly manifested. If these pages fail to convey entertainment or information, sufficient may at least be gleaned from them to furnish matter for serious reflection; but to those who have been placed in situations of danger where human ingenuity availed them not, and where human foresight was baffled, I feel persuaded that these remarks are unnecessary.

It was my first care to call for our friend, and to express to him, as well as I could, how much we stood indebted to him, at the same time that I made him a suitable present; but to the chiefs of the tribes, I positively refused all gifts, notwithstanding their earnest solicitations. We next prepared to examine the new river, and turning the boat's head towards it, endeavoured to pull up the stream. Our larboard oars touched the right bank, and the current was too strong for us to conquer it with a pair only; we were, therefore, obliged to put a second upon her, a movement that excited the astonishment and admiration of the natives. One old woman seemed in absolute ecstasy, to whom M'Leay threw an old tin kettle, in recompense for the amusement she afforded us.

As soon as we got above the entrance of the new river, we found easier pulling, and proceeded up it for some miles, accompanied by the once more noisy multitude. The river preserved a breadth of one hundred yards, and a depth of rather more than twelve feet. Its banks were sloping and grassy, and were overhung by trees of magnificent size. Indeed, its appearance was so different from the water-worn banks of the sister stream, that the men exclaimed, on entering it, that we had got into an English river. Its appearance certainly almost justified the expression; for the greenness of its banks was as new to us as the size of its timber. Its waters, though sweet, were turbid, and had a taste of vegetable decay, as well as a slight tinge of green. Our progress was watched by the natives with evident anxiety. They kept abreast of us, and talked incessantly. At length, however, our course was checked by a net that stretched right across the stream. I say *checked*, because it would have been unfair to have passed over it with the chance of disappointing the numbers who apparently depended on it for subsistence that day. The moment was one of intense interest to me. As the men rested upon their oars, awaiting my further orders, a crowd of thoughts rushed upon me. The various conjectures I had formed of the course and importance of the Darling passed across my mind. Were they indeed realised? An irresistible conviction impressed me that we were now sailing on the bosom of that very stream from whose banks I had been twice forced to retire. I directed the Union Jack to be hoisted, and giving way to our satisfaction, we all stood up in the boat, and gave three distinct cheers. It was an English feeling, an ebullition, an overflow, which I am ready to admit that our circumstances and situation will alone excuse. The eye of every native had been fixed upon that noble flag, at all times a beautiful object, and to them a novel one, as it waved over us in the heart of a desert. They had, until that moment been particularly loquacious, but the sight of that flag and the sound of our voices hushed the tumult, and while they were still lost in astonishment, the boat's head was speedily turned, the sail was sheeted home, both wind and current were in our favour, and we vanished from them with a rapidity that surprised even ourselves, and which precluded every hope of the most adventurous among them to keep up with us.

Thomas Mitchell

[AT THE DARLING RIVER]

June 27

About nine o'clock this morning, Joseph Jones came in to report, that a native had pointed a spear at him when he was on the river-bank with the sheep; and that this native, accompanied by a boy, kept his ground in a position which placed the sheep entirely in his power, and prevented Jones from driving them back. He added, that on his holding out a green bough, the man had also taken a bough, spit upon it, and then thrust it into the fire. On hastening to the spot with three men, I found the native still there, no way daunted, and on my advancing towards him with a twig, he shook another twig at me, quite in a new style, waving it over his head, and at the same time intimating with it, that we must go back. He and the boy then threw up dust at us, in a clever way, with their toes.† These various expressions of hostility and defiance, were too intelligible to be mistaken. The expressive pantomime of the man plainly shewed the identity of

† Strange as this custom appears to us, it is quite consistent with some passages in the early history of mankind. King David and his host met with a similar reception at Bahurim. – "And as David and his men went by the way, Shimei went along on the hill's side over against him, and cursed as he went, and threw stones at him, *and cast dust*." 2 Sam. xvi. 13. So also we read in Acts xxii. 23, "They cried out, and cast off their clothes, *and threw dust into the air*." Frequent mention is made of this as the practice of the Arabians, in Ockley's

the human mind, however distinct the races, or different the language – but his loud words were, of course, lost upon us. Overseer Burnett very incautiously stole up, and sat unarmed and defenceless within five yards of him. All Burnett's endeavours to conciliate and inspire confidence, had but little effect upon the savage, who merely lowered his tone a little, and then advancing a few steps, addressed himself no longer to me, but to him. I felt some apprehension for the safety of Burnett, but it was too late to call him back. We were seated in the usual form, at the distance of at least one hundred yards from him, and the savage held a spear, raised in his hand. At length, however, he retired slowly along the river-bank, making it evident, by his gestures, that he was going for his tribe; and singing a war-song as he went. The boy in particular seemed to glory in throwing up the dust at us, and I had not the least doubt, but certainly not the slightest wish, that we should see this man again.

About half-past four in the afternoon, a party of the tribe made their appearance in the same quarter; holding out boughs, but according to a very different ceremonial from any hitherto observed towards us by the aborigines. They used the most violent and expressive gestures, apparently to induce us to go back, whence we had come; and as I felt, that we were rather unceremonious invaders of their country, it was certainly my duty to conciliate them by every possible means. Accordingly I again advanced, bearing a green branch on high, but the repulsive gestures then becoming much more violent than before, I stopped at some distance from the party. Honest Vulcan, our blacksmith (two or three men being near him), was at work with his bellows and anvil, near the river-bank. This man's labour seemed to excite very much their curiosity; and again the overseer and Bulger advanced quietly towards those natives, who had approached nearest to the blacksmith. Hearing at length much laughter, I concluded that a truce had been effected as usual, and I too walked forward with my branch. But on going to the spot, I found that all the laughter came from our party, the natives having refused to sit down, and continuing to wave the branches in our people's faces, having also repeatedly spit at them; the whole of which conduct was good-naturedly borne in hopes of establishing a more

---

History of the Sacracens, when they would express their contempt of a person speaking, and their abhorrence of what he publicly pronounces. We find also this directly stated in Light's Travels in Egypt, p. 64. "One more violent than the rest, *threw dust into the air*, the signal both of rage and defiance, ran for his shield, and came towards me dancing, howling, and striking the shield with the head of his javelin, to intimidate me."

amicable intercourse. As a peace-offering, I then presented the man who appeared to be the leader, with a tomahawk, the use of which he immediately guessed by turning round to a log and chopping at it. Two other stout fellows (our morning visitor being one of them), then rudely demanded my pistols from my belt; whereupon I drew one, and, curious to see the effect, I fired it at a tree. The scene which followed, I cannot satisfactorily describe, or represent, although I shall never forget it. As if they had previously suspected we were evil demons, and had at length a clear proof of it, they repeated their gesticulations of defiance with tenfold fury, and accompanied the action with demoniac looks, hideous shouts and a war-song – crouching, jumping, spitting, springing with the spear, and throwing dust at us, as they slowly retired. In short, their hideous crouching postures, measured gestures, and low jumps, all to the tune of a wild song, with the fiendish glare of their countenances, at times all black, but now all eyes and teeth, seemed a fitter spectacle for Pandemonium, than the light of the bounteous sun. Thus these savages slowly retired along the river-bank, all the while dancing in a circle like the witches in Macbeth, and leaving us in expectation of their return, and perhaps an attack in the morning. Any further attempt to appease them was out of the question. Whether they ceeded from some cause of disquiet or apprehension unimaginable by us; it was too probable, they might ere long force upon us the painful necessity of making them acquainted with the superiority of our arms. The manner and disposition of these people, were so unlike those of the aborigines in general, that I hoped they might be an exception to the general character of the natives we were to meet with: an evil disposed tribe perhaps, at war with all around them. The difference in disposition between tribes not very remote from each other was often striking. We had left, at only three days' journey behind us, natives as kind and civil as any I had met with; and I was rather at a loss now to understand, how they could exist so near fiends like these. I believe the peculiar character of different tribes, is not to be easily changed by circumstances. I could certainly mention more instances of well than evil disposed natives on the Darling; where indeed, until now, all had met us with the branch of peace. We had not yet accomplished one half of our journey to the Murray, from the junction of the Bogan and Darling; and it was no very pleasing prospect, to have to travel such a distance, through a country which might be occupied by inhabitants like these. In the present case I hoped, that our patient forbearance and the gift of the tomahawk, would deter our late visitors, if anything human were in their feelings, from annoying us more: and if not, that their great dread of the pistol, would at least keep them at a distance.

June 28

The natives did not appear in the morning, as we had expected, but at three in the afternoon, their voices were again heard in the woods. I ordered all the men to be on the lookout, and when the natives came near, I sent Burnett towards them, once more with a branch, but with orders to retire upon any indication of defiance. It turned out, as I had supposed, that their curiosity and desire to get something more, had brought them forward again. An old man was at length prevailed on to join Burnett, and to sit down by him. This was effected, however, but very slowly, the others standing at a great distance, and some who remained in the rear, still making signs of defiance. Others of the tribe at length joined the old man, but they prepared to return on my approach, recognising me perhaps as the owner of the pistol. On seeing this, I directed Burnett to give a clasp-knife to the old man, who seemed much pleased with the present. They next made a move towards the spot where the blacksmith was at work, commencing at the same time a kind of professional chaunt, and slowly waving their green boughs. The appearance of one of these men, in particular, was very odd. There was evidently some superstition in the ceremony, this personage being probably a *coradje* or priest. He was an old man with a large beard and bushy hair, and the lower part of his nose was wanting, so that the apex of that feature formed more than a right angle, giving him an extraordinary appearance. None, except himself and other ancients, wore any kind of dress; and this consisted of a small cloak of skins fastened over the left shoulder. While the man from the woods waved his bough aloft, and chaunted that monotonous hymn, an idea of the ancient druids arose in my mind. It was obvious the ceremony belonged to some strange superstition. He occasionally turned his back towards each of us, like "the grisly priest with murmuring prayer"; he touched his eyebrows, nose, and breast, as if crossing himself, then pointed his arm to the sky; afterwards laid his hand on his breast, chaunting with an air of remarkable solemnity, and abstracted looks, while at times his branch

he held on high,
With wasted hand and haggard eye,
And strange and mingled feelings woke,
While his anathema he spoke.† – *Scott.*

† Burder in his Oriental Customs says (no. 187), "An opinion prevailed both in those days and after ages, that some men had a power, by the help of their gods, to devote not only particular persons, but whole armies to destruction. This they are said to have done, sometimes by word of imprecation, of which there was a set form among some people, with Æschines calls *διοριζο-μενην αραν, the determinate curse.* Sometimes they also offered sacrifices, and used certain rites and ceremonies with solemn charms."

All this contrasted strangely with the useful occupation of honest Vulcan, whom I had positively enjoined not to laugh, or stop working. At length, I prevailed on an old man to sit down by me, and gave him a clasp-knife in order to check the search, he was disposed to make through my pockets. Meanwhile, the others came around the forge, and immediately began to pilfer, whatever they could lay either hand or foot upon. While one was detected making off with a file, another seized something else, until the poor blacksmith could no longer proceed with his work. One set his foot on an axe, and thus, all the while staring the overseer (who eyed him) in the face, he quickly receded several yards, jumping backwards, to another, who stood ready behind him to take the tool. Some jogged their neighbours at the moments most opportune for plundering; and an old man made amusing attempts to fish up a horseshoe into the hollow of a tree. The best of this part of the scene was, that they did not mind being observed by anyone, except the blacksmith, supposing that they were robbing him only. Vulcan was at last tempted to give one of them a push, when a scene of chaunting, spitting,†† and throwing dust, commenced on the part of the thief, who was a stout fellow and carried a spear, which he seemed inclined to use. Notwithstanding all the vigilance of several men appointed to watch the articles about the forge, an excellent rasp or file was carried off. The natives left our party, however, in a perfectly civil way, and we were right glad to feel at peace with them, on any terms.

June 29

At length we were ready to quit this spot, and gladly continued our journey, in hopes of leaving our troublesome neighbours also. After proceeding some way, however, Mr Larmer's horse pitched him over its head, and galloped back to the place, which we had so willingly quitted. Just then the natives emerged from their woods in greater numbers than ever, being painted white, many carrying spears, and shouting. This startled the horse and made him again gallop away, and we halted on the edge of a plain until Mr Larmer recovered the animal; which was the more easily accomplished, as the attention of the natives was fortunately fixed chiefly on us. They repeated all

†† "The malediction of the Turks, as of other oriental nations, is frequently expressed in no other way than by *spitting on the ground*." – *Clarke's Travels*, vol.iii.page 225. Mons. D'Arvieux tells us, "the Arabs are sometimes disposed to think, that when a person spits, it is done out of contempt; and that they never do it before their superiors. But Sir J. Chardin's MS. goes much further; he tells us, in a note on Numb. xii. 14, that spitting before anyone, or spitting upon the ground in speaking of any one's actions, is throughout the East, an expression of extreme detestation." – *Harmer*, vol.iv.page 429.

their menaces and expressions of defiance, and as we again proceeded, the whole of their woods appeared in flames. I never saw such unfavourable specimens of the aborigines as these children of the *smoke*, they were so barbarously and implacably hostile and shamelessly dishonest, and so little influenced by reason, that the more they saw of our superior weapons and means of defence, the more they shewed their hatred and tokens of defiance. The day's journey was over a firmer surface than usual, and we encamped on a bend of the river in latitude 31° 36′ 48″ S.

John Morgan

DISCOVERED BY NATIVES

He stood alone – beneath the deep dark shade
Of the *Australian* forest, where the trees,
A century old the youngest of them, made
Hollow and mournful music in the breeze.

One day when I was indulging in these meditations, and gazing round from my Robinson Crusoe hut upon the surface of the waters, I thought I heard the sound of human voices; and, on looking up, was somewhat startled at seeing three natives standing on the high land immediately above me. They were armed with spears, and had opossum skins thrown over their shoulders, partially covering their bodies. Standing as they did, on an elevated position, armed too, and being myself totally defenceless, I confess I felt alarmed; so that hoping I had not been seen, I crept into a crevice in a rock near at hand, where I endeavoured to conceal myself. They were however soon upon my track, and shouting what I considered to be a call for me to come out, I resolved to do so; indeed I could not have remained there long on account of the water. With but faint hopes of meeting with good treatment at their hands, I crawled out from my shelter, and surrendered at discretion. They gazed on me with wonder: my size probably attracting their attention. After seizing both my hands, they struck their breasts, and mine also, making at the same time a noise between singing and crying: a sort of whine, which to me sounded very like premeditated mischief. Pointing to my hut, they evinced a desire to examine it – so we entered. My new friends, if friends they were to be, made themselves very much at home, although uninvited. One made up a large fire, another threw off his rug and went into the sea for crayfish, which, on his return, he threw alive into the flame – at the same time looking at me with an expression as much as to intimate that they intended to grill me next, by way of a change of diet. I can afford to smile, and even laugh now at the recollection; but, at the time, I assure the reader, I was by no means satisfied with the prospect before me, or with my visitors. At length my suspense ended, by their taking the fish, fairly dividing them, and handing to me the first and best portion. Having finished our meal, they gave me to understand they wished me to follow them. To this I hesitated, not being satisfied as to their intentions, but after a time consented. On leaving the hut, two of them went before, and having thus only one to contend against, I thought of making my escape, but my armed guard was too vigilant; so that, defenceless as I was, no safe opportunity was afforded. We proceeded in this way until we came to their huts, two small turf cabins – in each of which there was just room enough for two persons to lay at length under their shelter. It was nearly dark, and finding that I was to have my sentry friend beside me, and that the other two were to occupy the second cabin, my hopes revived – that during the night an opportunity for my escape would offer. He however did not sleep a wink, but kept muttering to himself all the night, so that by the morning I was fairly worn out by anxiety and watching. At daylight they gave me to understand they were going farther, and that I must accompany them. I, on the contrary, thought it safer to come to an understanding at once, and with this view, mustering all my resolution, I intimated a refusal, that I would not do so. After a warm discussion by signs, and, to both parties, by sufficiently significant sounds, they apparently consented that I should remain; but, as they wished me not to leave until their return, my old and nearly worn-out stockings were required by them as an assurance offering. This I steadily declined complying with, so that after sundry striking of the breasts, and stamping with the feet, they were content to leave me unmolested. I watched them until I thought the coast was clear, and then began to consider in what direction I should steer, for I had not now the beach as a guide for my movements. Whilst thinking over the matter, one of them returned, bringing with him a rude kind of basket made of rushes. In it was some of the berries I have already mentioned, which he wished to barter for one of my much courted stockings. I however objected, being resolved on letting him know I was positive in that matter, hoping by so doing to give him a favourable opinion of my determination, on questions which might arise between us of greater consequence. Finding his negotiation useless, he left the fruit and followed his companions. When I thought them sufficiently far off, I took to my heels, in the direction, as I thought, for the sea coast, and fortunately I made it without much difficulty. Going musing along, I came to a high rock against which the waves were beating violently, the sea at the time being very tempestuous: it was a very grand but a dreary and melancholy scene. Whilst viewing it with a very aching and downcast heart and spirit, I observed a small rocky island a short distance from the beach, covered with the strangest looking animals I had ever seen. They appeared to be about four, or from four to six feet long, having a head similar to that of a pig, without feet, with tails like those of a fish, a large fin on each side, and a body covered with short glossy hair: I suppose them to be the fur seal, or sea elephant.

Finding night coming on, having no fire to warm me, and with so dreary a prospect of the future – without food of any kind – I began to repent having left the natives, and resolved on returning to their huts from whence I had made my escape. I accordingly traced my way back, but on my arrival found they had not returned. After remaining some hours, I decided on going in the direction I supposed them to have taken, but after a weary march, I found I had completely lost myself, and very much distressed, I laid myself down for the night, within the shelter of a large hollow tree, such as are to be found in the Australian forests. Having secured a fire-stick during the day, I made a good fire, it being very cold, and raining heavily.

I remember I had no sleep that night, for my fire attracted the notice of the wild dogs and opossums, whose horrid howls and noises were such as to render sleep impossible. The cries of the latter were like the shrieks of children, appearing to be at times over me, and at others close to my ear. Under these circumstances, I hailed the daylight very thankfully, and then proceeded on my solitary way, endeavouring to get upon the trail of the natives, who, as I supposed, had gone in that direction. In this I was not successful, and having entangled myself in the labyrinths of the forest, in a country entirely unknown to me, I became at length lost, and remained so for three days, without a morsel of food, or a drop of water, excepting small quantities which I occasionally met with in the clay holes. When I laid myself down to rest hoping to sleep, the same unearthly noises appeared to have followed me, and my mind for want of relaxation was failing, as the minds of the strongest men will fail, under such circumstances. I continued to wander about in this way, subsisting upon succulent shrubs and berries, until I came to a large lake, upon which I could see an abundance of ducks, and geese, and swans, and other wild fowl. From that lake I found a very considerable river flowing, as I concluded, toward the sea. I at once resolved to follow its course; and on reaching its entrance, saw the little rocky island already mentioned as having the seal, or sea elephants upon it; and it was a great comfort to me, to find myself once more not far from my old quarters where the three natives had left me. I soon after arrived at the turf cabins, having now acquired some acquaintance with the locality, and although suffering from much hunger, lay myself down and slept soundly. At daylight, I had the satisfaction to find some of the same kind of fruit the native had brought me in the rush basket. On these I made a great feast, and after remaining there that day, returned to my own hut on the beach. Here I must have remained many months – how long I cannot tell – subsisting as before; but at length it appeared likely that my supplies would fail, and I began again to reflect on my deplorable condition. My clothes were all in tatters, my shoes were worn out, my health was much impaired by want and exposure, and my spirits broken – so much so, that I determined on retracing my steps in order to regain the ship in the event of her remaining in the bay, and with the hopes of rejoining my companions, should they be still in existence. The winter was fast approaching, the weather had set in dreadfully cold and tempestuous, so that it was not without great difficulty I could go down amongst the rocks for shell fish, which, as I have already said, were now, from some cause or other, getting very scarce in that locality. I therefore bade goodbye to my lonely habitation and started on my return.

One night, whilst travelling along the beach, I was completely bewildered, having been stopped in my progress by a high perpendicular rock stretching out from the cliffs some distance into the sea. The tide running in fast, my only chance of escape was by climbing the rock. This I did with great difficulty, and just above high water mark I found a large cavern, into which I crept for shelter. Having had no fire for some time I was again living upon such raw shell fish as I could find in each day's journey, and with these was making my wretched meal, when I found I had intruded upon the lodgings of some of the tenants of the deep, who could only reach their rocky quarters when the tide was at the highest. I was completely horrified and knew not what to do, as it was nearly dark, and they were waddling in at the entrance. To rush out, appeared to be nothing less than certain death; but happening to make a noise, it struck terror into them, and tumbling one over the other into the sea, they left me once more master of the cavern. I remained during the rest of the night undisturbed, and the following morning again pursued my weary way.

John West

THE ABORIGINES

It would be useful to mankind, to trace the causes which led to that long and disastrous conflict, in which so many lives were sacrificed, and a people, all but a fading fragment, became extinct.

1st Among those mentioned by the government, was the admission into the colony of Sydney blacks, and the ascendancy which one of them acquired.

The emigrants of 1822 remember a number of natives, who roamed about the district, and were known as the "tame mob". They were absconders from different tribes, and separated from their chiefs. They often entered the town and obtained bread, tobacco, and even rum from the inhabitants. Their importunity was troublesome, and their appearance offensive: the eruptive disease which covered their skin, especially on the legs, most exposed to the heat of their fires, added to their squalor and wretchedness. They are thus described by the Rev. Mr Horton: he saw them at Pittwater, crouching round their fires, and entirely naked – a company of demoralised savages.

Musquito [Mosquito] became their head. He was transported from Sydney to this colony for the murder of a woman. For some time he acted as a stock-keeper; he was then employed as a guide, in tracking the bushrangers, having the keenness of vision, and almost canine instinct, by which in the slightest traces he discovered a certain clue. For this service, it is said, he was promised restoration to his country – a promise, unhappily, forgotten. He was odious to the prisoners, who taunted him as a *nose* for the hangman; his resentful nature could not brook the insult, and he struck down a convict who thus reviled him. He was then taken into custody; in alarm, he escaped to the bush. The muscular strength and superior skill of this man were supposed to have recommended him to the natives as their chief. He was seen, by Gilbert Robertson, to cut off the head of a pigeon with a stick, while flying. Musquito answered Mr Horton with intelligence, when that gentleman represented the misery of a vagrant life; he said that he should prefer to live like the white man, tilling the ground, but that none of his companions would join him. Before he united with the natives, he was accustomed to pursue them with all the virulence of a savage. In company with a convict servant he would face the darkness, and go out "to storm the huts" he had seen in the day. On one such occasion, in spite of prohibitions, he set out at night; but the natives had observed him, and decamped, leaving behind them large fires to deceive their enemy. Returning at midnight, he was mistaken for a Tasmanian black; and, but for discovery at the moment, would have suffered the fate he deserved.

It was said by Mr Robertson, that the first murders of Musquito were committed in self defence. He associated with the Oyster Bay tribe, and his power over them was great: he even prevailed on them to perform some rude agricultural labor. He had high notions of his own worth: he would stalk into the cottages of the settlers, seat himself with great dignity: his followers, to the number of one or two hundred, patiently awaiting his signal to approach.

As the influence of Musquito enlarged, it became more pernicious. He not only misled his immediate followers, but propagated his spirit. Deeds of great enormity were committed at his direction; several by his own hand. He drew a man from his house at Pittwater, by the *cooey*, and then speared him to death. A servant of Mr Cassidy, and another of Mr Evans, met a similar fate. In concert with Tom, a Tasmanian black, he became a terror to the colony. Their parties moved in large bodies, and acted under a common impulse. In carrying on their depredations, their tactics aimed at military unity and skill. A party of sixty appeared before the premises of Mr Hobbs, at the Eastern Marshes (1824): they watched the servants deliver their fire, and before they could reload their muskets, they rushed upon them, and by weight of numbers drove them off the ground. A few days after, the natives again appeared: a small party came forward first, and reconnoitred; then returning to a hill, they made signals to a body of a hundred and fifty, in an opposite direction. Both divisions bore down on the establishment. The English were now well armed, and maintained the post for five hours; but escaped when they saw the natives prepare to surround the dwelling with fire. Overcome with terror, for several days they refused to return, and the property was left to its fate. Mr Hobbs was specially unfortunate: his house lay in the track, both of the natives and bushrangers, and thrice in one season his premises were pillaged.

The arrest of Musquito became an object of importance, and Colonel Arthur, then Governor, offered a reward for his capture. Teague, an aboriginal boy, brought up by Dr Luttrell, was despatched with two constables. They overtook Musquito at Oyster Bay: he resisted, but was shot in the groin, and being unarmed was captured, with two women, and conveyed to Hobart Town.

It was resolved to bring him to justice. By the care of Dr Scott he was cured, and transferred from the hospital to gaol. Black Tom was subsequently taken, and both were tried for the murder of William Hollyoak and Patrick M'Arthur. Of the last of these offences, the Tasmanian was found guilty, but Musquito was convicted of both.

Mammoa, an Otaheitian, was killed with Hollyoak: Musquito had lingered in their neighbourhood, and watched their movements for days; he had visited their hut, and received provisions from their hands; but on the morning of the murder he purloined the guns and removed the dogs. Mammoa fell instantly; but the Englishman endured the misery of long pursuit and several wounds, and dropped at last, pierced through and through with spears.

Such were the men who, in February, 1825, suffered death with six European criminals. They were unassisted by counsel, and perhaps the evidence was not fully understood by them. It is useless, however, to extenuate their teachery: and their execution, whether politic or not, can scarcely be accounted unjust. But, unhappily, these deeds of barbarity were not left to the vengeance of the law. The colonists, of higher grades, preserved the distinction between the guilty and the innocent, which it is the object of public trials to establish; but the lower orders, and especially the dissolute and the worthless, justified hatred to the race, and finally, systematic massacre, by the individual acts of such men as Musquito.

It is instructive, if not amusing, to observe how nicely the theory of some philosophers and the sentiments of the lowest European robbers, meet together; how, what one predicts, the other executes. The supposed eternal laws of nature are accomplished by the wild licence of an English savage. It became the serious conviction of stockmen, that blacks are brutes, only of a more cunning and dangerous order – an impression which has long ceased in this colony, but which still flourishes in Australia Felix.

Bent, the proprietor of the only newspaper published at that time, referring to the outrages of the hostile blacks, seemed to dread these doctrines. With great consideration he detaches Musquito's guilt from the tribes in general: a distinction by no means trite or universally recognised. "Until corrupted by the Sydney natives they were", he asserts, "the most peaceable race in existence." These humane suggestions deserve more praise than the highest literary skill.

2nd The disposition to conciliate the blacks eventually contributed to the same disastrous consequences. A tribe of sixty, appeared in Hobart Town, November, 1824; they came in a peaceable manner, their visit was unexpected, and its cause unknown. On the first notice of their approach, the Governor went forth to meet them: he assigned three places for their fires, supplied them with food and blankets, and appointed constables to protect them. They departed suddenly, and on their journey attempted to spear a white man. Whether the abrupt retreat resulted from caprice or distrust, it did not prevent a similar visit to Launceston in the following December. There were 200 in this party. When crossing Paterson's Plains they were wantonly fired on by the whites, and in their return some of their women were treated with indescribable brutality; the ruffians who maltreated them were, indeed, punished with 25 lashes. When they reached the Lake River, two sawyers, who had never before suffered molestation, were wounded by their spears. The recent cruelty they had experienced fully accounted for their rage.

It was the anxious desire of the Governor to establish a native institution, deriving its funds partly from the public purse and partly from private benevolence. A code was prepared by the Rev. Messrs Bedford and Mansfield; and a public meeting held in the church of St David, the Governor presiding, approved the regulations; but at that time the colony was distracted by the ravages of robbers, and its financial resources were depressed: and the prevailing opinion that civilisation was impossible, still further embarrassed the project, and confined the hopes of the most sanguine to the rising generation. Mr Mansfield rested his expectation rather on the power of God than upon human probabilities.

The civilisation of a barbarous people is, perhaps, impossible, in the presence of organised communities of white men. The contrast is too great, and the points of contact too numerous and irritating. Never have colonists civilised aborigines; but the failure is easily explained, without recourse to egotistical superstition, that the white man's shadow is, to men of every other hue, by law of Heaven, the shadow of death.

The children of aborigines, adopted by the whites, when they grew to maturity, were drawn to the woods, and resumed the habits of their kindred. A black girl trained in Launceston, thus allured, laid aside her clothing, which she had worn nearly from infancy. It was thus with many: a sense of inferiority to the youth about them, united with the mysterious interest which every heart feels in kindred sympathies, is sufficient to account for these relapses. Examples will crowd upon the memory of the reader, in which the polish and caresses of the British capital did not disqualify the savage to re-enter with zest on the barbarous pursuits of his forefathers.

The desire for sugar, bread, and blankets, could only be regularly gratified by an abandonment of migratory habits. When remote from the government stores, the natives still coveted what they could not obtain, but as spoil. They had learned to prefer articles of steel to the crystal, and they acquired an imperfect mastery of fire-arms. Some were, however, exceedingly expert; a chief, conciliated by Mr G.A. Robinson, brought down an eagle hawk, with all the airs of a practised sportsman. Thus their untutored nature could not resist the temptation created by new wants: they watched the hut of the stock-keeper, which they stripped during his absence; till, growing more daring, they disregarded his presence; and even the populous districts, and establishments of considerable force, were not safe from their depredations.

At the time when they first became formidable, armed bushrangers scoured the colony; sometimes the allies of the natives, much oftener their oppressors. Outlaws themselves, they inculcated the arts of violence. The improved caution and cunning of the natives, so often noticed by the government were ascribed, in no small degree, to the treacherous lessons of degraded Europeans. But when the bushranger did not employ these people as the instrument of his designs, moved by fear or cruelty, often he destroyed them: thus Lemon and Brown set up the natives as marks to fire at. The irritated savage confounded the armed, though unoffending, stock-keeper, with his marauding countrymen, and missing the object of his premeditated vengeance, speared the first substitute he encountered. This conclusion is amply supported by facts. The common principles which affect the minds of nations towards each other; the reprisals, which are vindicated in civilised war, only differ in circumstances. A thousand injuries, never recorded, if stated in a connexion with these results, would enable us to see how often the harmless settler was sacrificed to passions, provoked by his robber countrymen.

In 1826, a remarkable instance of this was brought under the notice of government. Dunne, who at length met the punishment he deserved, seized a woman, and forced her to the hut of Mr Thompson, on the Shannon, where he detained her with violence; she, however, escaped to her people, and roused them to avenge her. Dunne, next morning, suddenly found himself in their midst: his musket protected him, and after hours of such torture as his conscience and fears might inflict, he managed to get off. On the following day, the woman led her tribe, vociferating threats, to the hut in which she had been maltreated, where they massacred James Scott, a man with whom they had lived in friendship for many years, and who, when warned a few days before to be on his guard, smiled at the notion of danger.

The treatment of some of these women was such as no one can be expected to credit, until prepared by extensive acquaintance with human depravation. A monster boasted that, having captured a native woman, whose husband he had killed, he strung the bleeding head to her neck, and drove her before him as his prize. Had not this fact been guaranted by formal enquiry, it could only have been admitted as a specimen of brutal gasconade, and in proof of how much a cruel fancy could exceed the actual guilt of mankind. It sometimes happened, that an unfortunate servant would receive the spear intended for his predecessor in the same employ, to whom it was justly due. Among the whites, there were men distinguished for the malicious vigour with which they tracked and murdered the native people. A lad, on his arrival from England, was sent into the interior, and warned never to wander from his dwelling; but he forgot the danger he did not see, and straying a short distance, he was murdered. He had never injured his destroyers; but then he lived on the lands just before in charge of a villian, and who, like a Roman warrior, took his name of "Abyssinian Tom", from the locality of his exploits.

3rd The infliction of judicial punishments, interrupted the friendly intercourse of the tribe that visited Hobart Town, and who were encouraged to resort to Kangaroo Point, where huts were erected for their use. The arrest of two of their number filled them with apprehension. The aborigines, Jack and Dick, were executed on the 13th September, 1826, an event which terminated all present hope of amicable relations. The murder of a shepherd at Oyster Bay, Great Swan Port, was proved against them by the evidence of convict stock-keepers; a topic of contemporary complaint: but the courts regularly relied on the same class of witnesses, and in this case there is no special reason for suspicion. The fact was not questioned: the culprits had been treated with kindness by the government, and efforts had been made by Colonel Arthur to acquaint them with the obligations of British subjects. He asserts that, by personal interviews, he was fully convinced that they understood the benevolent views of the Crown. One of these blacks was so far civilised, as to be admitted to the sacrament of the English church. His companion was a youth, and denied his guilt. The old black was carried to the scaffold, and resisted the execution: the younger, disentangled his arms, and struggled for his life. It was, indeed, a melancholy spectacle. Successive Governors had witnessed crimes against their race, atrocious and unpunished: hundreds had fallen unavenged by that public justice which treated them as murderers.

On the day of their execution, the Governor addressed the colony. He vindicated this act of severity, as requisite to intimidate the blacks; but he solemnly pledged his government to equal justice, and that the law should take its course on individuals of either race, who might violate "the common law of mankind".

The discussions which followed, proved the division of public opinion on the propriety of this measure. It was not clear, to many, that the natives were legally accountable, or that their punishment was just. Grotius and Vattel were quoted; writers, who have discoursed upon the relations of man, and distinguished the felon from the enemy. It was, however, simply a question between judicial and private vengeance: the interference of the court could alone prevent a general proscription. In the heat of anger, no provocation would be weighed – no palliative admitted; and the innocent would perish with the guilty. In sentencing Rodger, at Port Phillip, 1842, Judge Willis told him that he had been tried by an intelligent jury; that he could have challenged any of them; that to say he had never been in a court of justice before, was a common plea with white malefactors, and that he knew as much on the subject as many immigrants. When he was sentenced, the Rev. Mr Hurst explained to him, that he would be hanged! This was requisite, as the judge's address was utterly unintelligible.

4th The impression on the aborigines was unfavourable: they saw only the death of an unfortunate countryman, and, perhaps, the last act of the white man's warfare. Its moral influence was not great on either race: it neither softened the resentment of the British, nor intimidated the blacks: it was a mere variety in the forms of destruction. The brother of one of these men led the Oyster Bay tribe, and prompted the murders which, in 1830, filled the colony with wailing.

The rapid colonisation of the island from 1821 to 1824, and the diffusion of settlers and servants through districts hitherto unlocated, added to the irritation of the natives, and multiplied the agents of destruction. Land unfenced, and flocks and herds moving on hill and dale, left the motions of the native hunters free; but hedges and homesteads were signals which even the least rationality could not fail to understand, and on every reappearance the natives found some favourite spot surrounded by new enclosures, and no longer theirs.

The proclamations of the government assumed the fixed relations of the different tribes to particular districts. Oyster Bay and the Big River were deemed sufficiently precise definitions of those tribes, exposed to public jealousy and prosecution. It is true, they had no permanent villages, and accordingly no individual property in land; but the boundaries of each horde were known, and trespass was a declaration of war.

The English, of modern times, will not comprehend joint ownership, notwithstanding the once "common" property of the nation has been only lately distributed by law. The rights of the aborigines were never recognised by the Crown; yet it is not less certain that they saw with intelligence the progress of occupation, and felt that the gradual alienation of their hunting grounds implied their expulsion and extinction.

Native topography is, indeed, limited; but it is exact. Every mountain, valley, and river, is distinguished and named. The English have often been indebted to these primitive surveyors, for guidance through the forests which they came to divide. The tribes took up their periodical stations, and moved with intervals so regular, that their migrations were anticipated, as well as the season of their return. The person employed in their pursuit, by the aid of his native allies, was able to predict at what period and place he should find a tribe, the object of his mission; and though months intervened, he found them in the valley, and at the time he had foretold. Expectations of this sort could only be justified by the regularity of their movements, and the exact knowledge of the guides. Nor were they indifferent to the charms of a native land. A visitor enquired of a native woman at Flinders Island, whether she preferred that place to several others mentioned, where she had lived at times, and she answered with indifference; but when, to test her attachment to her early haunts, the querist said, "and not Ringarooma?" she exclaimed, with touching animation, "Oh yes! Ringarooma! Ringarooma!"

A chief accompanied the commandant to Launceston in 1847. At his own earnest request, he was taken to see the Cataract Basin of the South Esk, a river which foams and dashes through a narrow channel of precipitous rocks, until a wider space affords it tranquility. It was a station of his people; precisely the kind of spot which gypsies, on the "business of Egypt", would choose for their tents. As he drew nigh, his excitement became intense: he leaped from rock to rock, with the gestures and exclamations of delight. So powerful were his emotions, that the lad with him became alarmed, lest the associations of the scene should destroy the discipline of twelve years exile: but the woods were silent: he heard no voice save his own, and he returned pensively with his young companion. These examples shew, that the native was not an indifferent spectator of that rapid occupation, which must have appeared prodigious to scattered tribes.

A further cause of exasperation, consequent on the preceding, was the destruction of game. The extent to which it was carried was enormous. The skin of the kangaroo sold for a few pence, was the perquisite of the stock-keepers, and long the chief object of their daily enterprise. Their rugs, their clothing, were often composed of these spoils, and the pursuit did not slacken until the persecuted animal retired. Jeffreys, describing the field sports of his day, tells us that flocks of emu and kangaroo were found at short intervals, and that a cart might be loaded with their flesh by the sport of a morning; but he remained long enough, to observe a sensible diminution, and proposed limitations by law to the havoc of the whites; an idea, subsequently entertained by the *Aborigines' Committee*, which sat in 1830.

The dogs, trained to hunt the kangaroo, were at first serviceable to the natives, but they often increased the destruction by their spontaneous ravening. It is observed by a writer of 1827, that forty or fifty would be found within short distances, run down by the dogs, and left to rot.

Thus the food, on which the people depended for subsistence, was diminished, and the temptation to rob the settlers was regularly augmented at every return. Sir George Arthur, in his letter to the Secretary of State in 1828, notices this topic as a complaint of the natives against the intrusion of the whites, and seems to admit its truth; but three years after, he affirms that game was still abundant in the districts appointed for the tribes. It is, however, to be observed, that he wrote when the blacks, as a people, were dead; and when the high value of labour had withdrawn many from the chase; and that he implies a local, rather than a pervading abundance. "The extension of the settled districts upon their usual hunting grounds, has either driven them entirely from them, or removed the kangaroo. They are quite disappointed of their usual supplies. We have never known them to eat the flesh of either sheep or cattle."

The extent of their consumption, might be inferred from the increase after their exit. To preserve their crops, some settlers were obliged to employ hunters. In 1831, from Bothwell only, 100,000 skins were sent to Hobart Town, bearing a value of £2,000. As the natives passed through the settled districts to the sea shore, if numerous, their requirements would be great; but, by scattering themselves abroad, to obtain a sufficiency, their dangers would increase, and every evening they would muster fewer than in the morning.

5th Among the causes of enmity, referred to by writers of every period, the abduction of the women by sealers and others, is noticed the earliest, and continued to the last. The sealers were, chiefly, either convicts whose sentences had expired, or such as contrived to escape. In the islands of the Straits, they indulged the boundless licence of their passions, blending the professions of the petty pirate and the fisherman. A chain of rocks enabled them to rove to a considerable distance, picking up the refuse of the sea, and feeding on the aquatic birds which frequented the islets in great abundance. Many, however, perished, with the frail boats to which they committed their lives. Their first stage was known as "Clarke's Island"; from thence they made "Preservation Island": a succession of rocks formed landmarks in their course to New Holland, from which many found their way to Kangaroo Island, the Ultima Thule of their geography. In these places, they engaged in sealing; the produce of which they sold to the small craft trading among them, for guns, spirits, and tobacco. When the season was over, they retired to the interior, and passed their days in alternate slumber and intoxication.

So secure were some of these retreats, that they justified the apprehension, that formidable pirates would be trained up in their lawless and licentious communities. They were perpetually disturbed by violence. One old man spent thirteen years on an island, alone. He cultivated a plot of ground, and sold the produce to the boats which floated about. Several times robbed of his crops and clothing, by these contemptible spoilers, he, at last, was compelled to renounce his rude independence. In King's Island, families sat down; but Colonel Arthur, sensible of the great danger of these associations, sent the harbour master to the Straits, who arrested absconders, and released native women from slavery.

By these men, the black women and female children were captured in excursions to this island, and were liable to the ill-treatment, which might be expected from men who regarded them with passion and contempt. They were employed as slaves, on some islands, to strip the mutton bird, and in whatever irksome labour was within their capacity. It is said that one man (Harrison), had fourteen women in his service, whom he flogged with military severity, and some of whom he put to death.

Boatswain, an aged woman, stolen in her youth, related the manner of her abduction. She was induced to enter a boat, without suspicion of the design, when her captors rowed away, and confined her on an island in the Straits. She told her treatment, in broken English and expressive pantomime; first spreading forth her hands, as if fastened to the wall; then, with loud cries, gradually becoming fainter, she fell down into a pretended swoon: thus describing the mode and severity of her torture.

These men acquired an extraordinary dominion over the fears of the women, sufficient to induce them to dissemble in the presence of strangers. Backhouse relates, that two girls, Jumbo and Jackey, pretended, while in the company of their masters, either by silence, or feigned anger, to resent the proposal to take them away; but when they were assured that their liberty would be protected, they embraced it with joy.

Jeffreys, whose narrative is tinged with romance, depicts the fondness and contentment of the women in lively colours. Glad to escape the tyranny of their countrymen, they displayed to these amiable white men, warm, though jealous affection; – whose occasional absence they regretted, and for whose speedy return they invoked some imaginary deity in plaintive melodies! It is not improbable, that they were sensible of kindness, but it is very certain that this was not their ordinary lot. Unanimous testimony permits no doubt that they experienced the severity, which men of low intellect, and of fierce and capricious passions, inflict on women of an inferior race.

The sealers, when they came to the mainland, rarely brought their captives: they were in danger of losing them. Their fickleness or revenge, was sometimes fatal: in 1824, a party, engaged in an expedition to entice the girls of a tribe, took with them one who had a half-caste infant, and sent her on shore as a decoy. She returned, bringing promises from her country women to appear the following day; but at that time the blacks descended in great force, and all the adventurers, except one, were slain.

The sealers, by the names they gave the women, which were rarely feminine, and were sometimes ludicrously absurd, indicated the notions which prevailed. However slight their apparent importance, it has been justly observed, they betray the low civilisation of the persons who invented, and the degraded condition of those who bore them.

The intercourse of the stockmen was generally confined to the periods of migration: sometimes with the connivance, at others, the express consent of the men; but the detention was often compulsory. Dr Ross found a stock-keeper seated on a fallen tree, exhausted with hunger. He had chained a woman to a log, "to tame her", but she escaped, with his only shirt, which he had bestowed in his fondness. For five hours he had pursued her, catching glimpses of his shirt through the breaks of the forest: at last, this signal disappeared; and having lost his way for two days, he was in danger of starvation.

Such were the various causes, which combined first to alarm, and then to goad into madness, this unhappy people. They were troublesome, and were repelled. Wantonly wounded and shot down, they retaliated. Fresh wrongs produced their kind: at length, every white man was a *guerilla*, and every black an assassin. The original temper of both parties was changed. Dread detestation and treachery embittered every mind: even the humane yielded to the general sentiment. It became a question, which race should perish, and every man's verdict was in favour of his own.

From this, however, it is not to be inferred, that the natives were originally treacherous and cruel. It was stated by the Aborigines' Committee, in the middle of the conflict, that such dispositions were the substratum of their character, which, though disguised, only waited for time and opportunity. The colonists in general, at last, believed them to delight in blood, by an innate cruelty of temper – to find pleasure in the terrors they excited, and the convulsive agonies of the dying; but the records of mankind are full of such moral transformations. The Indians of America, we are informed by Dr Dwight, became corrupt, to a degree "enormous and dreadful: full of malice, cruelty, and murders". But he himself elsewhere remarks, that within his observation white men, commonly sober, moral, and orderly, on joining a mob, lost every one of these qualities; and, in a few hours of excitement, exhibited more vice than he had witnessed for years. The causes of degeneracy are not examined, when its mischief is suffered. Sir George Arthur, in his despatches, asserted that the natives were, and had been, "a most treacherous race", – a view, which the Committee adopted: these opinions were afterwards greatly modified; nor would it be just to admit their truth, without stronger evidence than history affords. Among the aborigines, some were distinguished for ferocity: such was a woman who led on the Big River tribe, and who was called by Mr Robinson, the "Amazon." A few were guilty of the crimes imputed to the race: and who were often their oppressors, rather than their avengers.

Though individuals, undoubtedly, displayed the vices imputed, who will condemn the natural disposition of a people for actions committed at long intervals, by solitary assassins and marauders? The English alone could preserve a record of the past, and after a careful examination no other conclusion is possible, than that whoever continued acts of ferocity and cruelty, the impulse and the example were European.

Dr Ross, arriving in 1822, passed into the interior, and settled on a farm. He was soon visited by the natives, whom he entertained with the consideration due to their ignorance and their rights. They had kindled their fires in perilous contiguity, and the flames threatened to destroy his crops. He pointed out his danger, and they instantly combined to extinguish the flame, and transfered their temporary resting place to a spot, from which no harm could be communicated. Dr Ross stood by, and watched their cookery, and they offered him a part of their food: he suffered himself to be amused with their loud merriment, and their evolutions in the water. They often renewed their visits, and rather contributed to his safety, by assisting in the pursuit of white robbers: and even when they inflicted dreadful outrages on many others, provoked by extraordinary maltreatment, they still preserved their kindness for this amiable man, until they were finally removed to Flinders' Island.

These incidents were not uncommon: – the cross lights, which seem to exhibit variously the character of a race, but in reality identify the family of man. To judge of a people, during a season of extraordinary excitement, must tend to erroneous conclusions: thus, when we turn to contemporary writings, we are amazed at the ferocity of expression – the sweeping and sanguinary appeals, by which they are disfigured; but this astonishment is corrected, when we examine the incidents they record, and recollect how little qualified men are to reason, when they are doomed to suffer. So with the native: the delirium of rage, and the taste for blood, had been produced by causes of long operation; and he appeared to be a fiend full of mischief and spite, marked out by his crimes for utter extinction.

Audrey Tennyson

LETTERS TO HER MOTHER

26 July 1899. Oodnadatta

Here we are right up in Central Australia as far as the railway goes & when we looked out of the train windows this morning it really looked as if we had come to the end of the world. Just close round us ½ a dozen white, low, one-storeyed houses of wood with iron roofs, an hotel rather larger than the rest, a railway station, a most primitive little school & besides that, nothing to be seen but dreary red soil, not a plant, a tree or shrub to be seen, but far away in the distance a slight rise in the ground of some hills. But I had better begin from when we left Adelaide on Monday in our special train at 3.10 . . . .

We dined the first night where we changed carriages at Terowie and had an excellent repast, I the only lady among all these men; then we went on in our new carriage & instead of our well-lit vice-regal carriage found it too dark to read. The man came in at 10 & made up the beds & I was very glad to go to bed for it was bitterly cold & to my great joy Clarke had brought my hot water bag and heated some water for it. I slept very well tho' of course waking every time the train stopped & to my great joy woke up with no headache . . . .

We were woken by children's voices singing God Save the Queen at a place called Beltana . . . . We next stopped at Leigh's Creek where we moved into the Railway Commissioner's carriage with whom we are travelling. Here at the station (a lovely morning but cold & crisp, about 8) we got out & bid goodbye to a Mr Gee. His wife and he were going to drive 600 miles to inspect the new gold mine at Worturpa which has just been found, or at least they hope so but it is doubtful yet whether it will turn out trumps or not . . . . Then on we went & next stopped at Farina about 10 & there we found about 50 schoolchildren with school mistress & master, the clergyman Mr Wilkinson, about a dozen blacks, men & women, two Afghans with turbans with their camels, & most of the leading inhabitants of the township. We got out after God Save the Queen was sung & I was given a bouquet or rather basket of flowers tied with red & yellow ribbons by one of the children, various little bunches of flowers by the other children & a basket of all the different minerals they find about there. It was quite pathetic the way they had all nearly got red & yellow rosettes . . . .

Everything, even every vegetable they have, is taken out fortnightly only by train so you may be sure they had to pay well for it. We shook hands & talked with all the adults including the blacks, all very warm & so delighted to see us, poor people, beaming. Then when the train had to go on the children sang the National Song of Australia; we got back into our carriage & were loudly cheered out of the little station.

These people are much better off than most of the townships. There are 200 inhabitants & church & school & clergyman, but many have none of these things, & have not even a store so they depend absolutely & entirely on the fortnightly train. And yet, somehow, perhaps with only two or three families, hundreds of miles from anybody they are all quite happy & contented & say they love the free bush life. All very well dressed – their parents if not they, having come from home, & are sometimes years without coming down to Adelaide. Their husbands mend the line or have the station, post & telegraph office all in one, or are store-keepers or little hotel-keepers – or own camels for carrying things from the train to the distant stations (farms). And at all these townships along the line the oxen & cattle are put into the trains having been driven 30, 40, 50 miles & more from the nearest stations & brought down to Adelaide either for export or for the town.

* * *

We arrived at Oodnadatta about midnight but had long before gone to bed & only got up the next morning in time for 9 o'clock breakfast. Hallam heard what he thought was a cow bellowing but it turned out to be a camel. It was a lovely bright morning, Wednesday, but with very cold wind & on looking out on this barren place we saw a touching little decoration of festoons of mixed coloured ribbons at the station & a large Union Jack & a large yellow flag with a red lion on it, floating at the Inn whence, after all greeting each other outside our carriages, we walked across to breakfast. The Hotel kept by a Scotchman, Mr Ferguson, & we were waited on by his two daughters, everything very good – porridge delicious, bacon & eggs etc. etc. After breakfast we walked back to the station to see Mr Winter the stationmaster who is "boss" of the whole place, postmaster, telegraph – marries & buries the people. He had married a Chinaman & a half-caste on the 1st June – when the Chinaman asked how much it would cost & was told £3, he said, "No, won't do, much too dear."

He & his friend another Chinaman keep a market garden about 5 miles off and we drove to see it in the afternoon – the most enormous cauliflowers & cabbage & heaps of vegetables coming on. They found this fertile strip near a creek and have worked at it splendidly – charge 4d. for a cauliflower. We were introduced with great pride to the bride, hideously ugly, and a small boy of three very like his father & a small *white* baby, as white as my own which was rather puzzling but I made no remarks & asked no questions. The bride was fetched out of a small tent just covered with thin unbleached calico – they must freeze at night – in which stood a bedstead covered with a striped rug on which she & the children were sitting, the one sole piece of furniture in this home & at a little distance the kitchen – no tent or covering, a hole dug in the sand for the fire, two or three pots & pans & a broken white case as larder in which was a basket of fresh eggs & some bits – rag & rubbish. The partner Chinaman had another little tent with just a few bedclothes on the ground. One of these men has £250 in the Bank.

After seeing Mr Winter, Mrs Winter was brought out to be presented to me & then asked me into her house, a very nice one, & I was invited to sit by the fire in the parlour. She has 8 children . . . & was much distressed at there being no sort of service or Sunday school on Sundays & the 18 little children at the school know nothing about religion. But what struck one at all these out-of-the-way places is the happiness & content of all these people. They say they love the free life. Mrs White told me a great deal about the natives. She has two – Mary Jane & Annie – as servants to help her & evidently likes the blacks & feels for them but she says they are very trying. She can teach them all the rough work – but at any moment they may come & say "I tired work – must go walkee-about one week or one moon etc." and off they go to the camp which is about 1½ miles from the township if any of their tribe happen to be there. There is always a camp of some tribe or other there, for at Oodnadatta stores & blankets are given away by Government every week to any blacks who come & ask for them. They are given out every Saturday now by the trooper (the Police Sergeant) who lives there with a black police "boy" under him. The present trooper, Mr Ireland, is the son of a

Gloucestershire well-to-do Rector, & a University man. His father wanted him to take Holy Orders & he did not care for it so he came out here 18 years ago to try his fortune & loves the life. He has a thoroughly nice cheery sensible colonial wife & one child, a boy 8 years old, Stanley de Courcy Ireland! who goes to the little school with all the other children . . . .

Mr Ireland told me that he has made a rule that the blacks before coming for their stores have to sweep & clean up the township, & all the refuse is then burnt. If they work, they get their stores, if lazy & won't, he says, "No, you not have flour today, you not work, you not have stores" & now they quite understand but it was very hard at first. (6 lbs flour a head, tea, sugar & tobacco.) He is devoted to his "black boy" (policeman) & when he drives away to his distant stations to inspect he puts the house & his wife & child under his care & he would die sooner than that anything should be touched.

They *never* steal except if food is put in their way too temptingly. If once they believe that a "white" means well to them they are devoted – but woe betide the man who treats them badly. Mr Ireland says he can go alone without any firearms anywhere among them, but many white men can't go a step without a pistol. They have been treated brutally by white men, but thank God, Government is taking up their cause very strictly this session & ill treatment will be most severely punished. They say those women I shook hands with at Farina will *never* forget it. Hallam wished one of them who could understand English to interpret to them how the Queen, he, & Government, were their friends. They are dying out fast however, & our making them wear clothes near white people & giving them blankets, alas helps to kill them for they throw off the clothes when they go off on their hunting grounds for lizards & kangaroos, emus & their eggs, rabbits & rats, & if fancy takes them, give away or leave behind their blankets.

* * *

4 August 1899. Government House, Adelaide

I sent off my huge budget yesterday and am beginning again at once to tell you about the Corroboree as I promised.

It seems a little doubtful as to whether they [the Aborigines] mix religion up in them or whether they are as a kind of acting, or as a festival of rejoicing. Anyhow they say they never throw the same spirit into it when it is done for the whites as when they just do it among themselves at their camp. At our corroboree there were three different tribes – the Arunta, Alberga & Macuna – who had congregated & had practised for it. In the afternoon when we went to visit the camp we found it almost deserted and the people all pointed towards the township saying, "Gone that way – over there – ready corroboree". They had been told to collect at sundown & we went out to them a little after 8, after dining first. There were quite a number of white people all collected, a great many bushmen who had probably come in to see it & were camping in the neighbourhood.

It was rather weird walking across this desert with lanterns accompanied by Trooper Ireland, his wife & little son, & the hotel people & our own party, with a few lanterns – a dark night but gorgeous stars – the Milky Way was marvellous in its beauty in that clear atmosphere – all wending towards a huge fire in the distance showing up occasionally figures moving about. As we approached, several of the natives snatched up big logs of burning wood & rushed to light up all the fires round they had prepared, & round the big fire already burning we found about 100 women and girls & two or three children all seated with their legs close to them like tailors, close to the fire & close to each other, grouped in a mass about 5 rows & 20 in a row, & in front of them two or three chiefs clothed with these dun-coloured felt government hats & long walking sticks, others sitting with wooden instruments in their hands. At the words of command these men began to hit them together & a low monotonous sort of chant was moaned out by them & then taken up by the women & then we saw about 50 or 60 naked natives (I was told after there was one woman among them but I did not make her out) all dressed with their war-paint & head-dresses, & the gypsum or white clay mixed with human blood in patterns all over their faces like masks & in patterns over their bodies & feathers – and all holding a bunch of emu's feathers in each hand. They all suddenly appeared in a sort of rush towards us from their wherleys where they had been hiding till our arrival, then they went thro' all sorts of weird gestures supposed to be representative of tracking an enemy or emu-hunting etc. Every few minutes the knocking of the sticks stopped & then the women stopped their dirge & off the dancers flew to the fires & almost touched the flames to get warm, & scratching their chests like monkeys or more often turning their backs close into the flames. H. & I say we shall always think of them when we see men standing with their backs to the fire with their coat tails removed, only that in this case there were no coat tails or unmentionables, & the outlines in the darkness against the firelight were extremely funny.

Then the moment the sticks beat & the singing began again, they rushed together for some new performance, tho', not understanding the ins & outs of the movements, they seemed to us a little monotonous. When we had had enough Hallam said so & thanked them in two or three simple words & then told them there were lots of lollies & apples & baccy & flour for them & pipes, all of which he gave them, & tea & sugar, and the government had also sent them up some shirts & blankets.

We then went back to our train to bed & after an early breakfast at the hotel again & a few last words to most of the inhabitants who congregated at the station to see us off with loud cheers, we started off about 9 Thursday morning on our homeward journey. We saw a most splendid mirage of a lake on our way up which we thought must be Lake Eyre but it was a great many miles off – & we passed quite close to the real thing later in the day. You see vast spaces of the desert quite white with salt & soda . . . . At Blanche Cup in driving to the Springs we came upon masses of bones & skeletons. These were of poor cattle that died in hundreds three years ago from the drought & simply fell down absolute skeletons to die .

3

Settling Down

EDITOR'S NOTE

Despite Aboriginal resistance, the white invaders gradually spread across the country and began to know and, in many cases, to love it. Children were born, towns and houses built; new customs and allegiances arose, though some people tried rigorously to cling to the old ones.

Elizabeth Macarthur writes to a friend in England of the beauty, peace and abundance of life in Australia. Though she notes that her children "speak of going home to England with rapture", she surmises (correctly) that some of them will return to live in Australia. For William Charles Wentworth, one of the first generation of Europeans to be born in Australia, Sydney is a place of infinite promise whose romantic vistas bear no trace of the deceitfulness observed by Worgan and Watling. Wentworth was, in Peter Cunningham's terms, a "Currency Lad" (born in Australia) and proud of it. Cunningham may have been the first to comment on the Australian abroad, who finds everything foreign inferior to the local. Cunningham also writes tellingly of the extreme class divisions in Sydney society. As the extracts from G.T.W.B. Boyes's diary show, such divisions were, if anything, even more of a feature of life in Hobart. A modern reader may have some difficulty coming to terms with a sensibility like Boyes's, which can enthuse over the natural sublime one minute and the next record in graphic detail the horrors of a penal station (and congratulate himself on being the first to do so).

The remaining four pieces describe the settler's life in Western Australia and Victoria from various perspectives: a wife and mother writing to her father in England; a young boy recording daily events of school and play in his journal; a woman and a man each looking back to an earlier period in their lives. With the last two examples there is the added interest that both Annie Baxter and Rolf Boldrewood write about the Baxters' Victorian station Yambuck (Boldrewood spells it without the "c" – I have assumed that its owner's memory was the more reliable). Boldrewood's reminiscences are more rose-coloured than Annie Baxter's, though hers have been considerably modified, as can be seen when her published account is compared with that given in her original diaries. Even Eliza Brown appears to spare her father many of the rawer details of pioneering life. One notices with wonder the way in which she keeps having babies apparently in between the paragraphs of her letters.

Elizabeth Macarthur

LETTER TO ELIZA KINGDON

Elizabeth Farm, Parramatta
1st Sept., 1795

Once again, my much loved friend, it is permitted me to sit down under a conviction that the letter I am about to write will be received by you with pleasure. By the capture of a ship off the coast of Brazil we were left without any direct intelligence from Europe for twelve months. We firmly believed that a Revolution or some national calamity had befallen Great Britain, and we should be left altogether to ourselves, until things at home had resumed some degree of order, and the tempest a little subsidised. These fears, however, have by a late arrival proved without foundation.

This country possesses numerous advantages to persons holding appointments under Government. It seems the only part of the Globe where quiet is to be expected. We enjoy here one of the finest climates in the World. The necessaries of life are abundant, and a fruitful soil affords us many luxuries. Nothing induces me to wish for a change but the difficulty of educating our children, and were it otherwise, it would be unjust towards them to confine them to so narrow a society. My desire is that they should see a little more of the world, and better learn to appreciate this retirement. Such as it is the little creatures all speak of going home to England with rapture. My dear Edward almost quitted me without a tear. They have early imbibed an idea that England is the seat of happiness and delight; that it contains all that can be gratifying to their senses, and that of course they are there to possess all they desire. It would be difficult to undeceive young people bred up in so secluded a situation, if they had not an opportunity given them of convincing themselves. But hereafter I shall much wonder if some of them make not this place the object of their choice. By the date of this letter you will see that we still reside on our farm at Parramatta, a native name signifying the head of a river, which it is. The town extends one mile in length from the landing-place, and is terminated by the Government House, which is built on an eminence, named Rose Hill. Our farm, which contains from 400 to 500 acres, is bounded on three sides by water. This is particularly convenient. We have at this time about 120 acres in wheat, all in a promising state. Our gardens, with fruit and vegetables, are extensive and produce abundantly.

It is now spring, and the eye is delighted with the most beautiful variegated landscape. Almonds, apricots, pear and apple trees are in full bloom. The native shrubs are also in flower and the whole country gives a grateful perfume. There is a very good carriage road now made from hence to Sydney, which by land is distant about 14 miles, and another from this to the river Hawkesbury, which is about 20 miles from hence in a direct line across the country. Parramatta is a central position between both. I have once visited the Hawkesbury, and made the journey on horseback. The road is through an uninterrupted wood, with the exception of the village of Toongabie, a farm of Government, and one or two others, which we distinguish by the name of Greenlands, on account of the fine grass, and there being few trees compared with the other parts of the country, which is occasionally brushy, and more or less covered with underwood.

The greater part of the country is like an English park, and the trees give it the appearance of a wilderness or shrubbery, commonly attached to the habitations of people of fortune, filled with a variety of native plants, placed in a wild irregular manner. I was at the Hawkesbury three days. It is a noble fresh water river, taking its rise in a precipitous range of mountains, that it has hitherto been impossible to pass; many attempts have been made, although in vain. I spent an entire day on this river, going in a boat to a beautiful spot, named by the late Governor, "Richmond Hill", high and overlooking a great extent of country. On one side are those stupendous barriers to which I have alluded, rising as it were immediately above your head; below, the river itself, still and unruffled; out of sight is heard a water fall whose distant murmurs add awfulness to the scene. I could have spent more time here, but we were not without apprehensions of being interrupted by the natives, as about that time they were very troublesome, and had killed many white people on the banks of the river. The soil in the valley of this river is most productive, and greatly superior to any that has been tilled in this country, which has induced numbers to settle there, but having no vessels there is at present much difficulty in transporting the produce to Sydney. Our stock of cattle is large; we have now fifty head, a dozen horses, and about a thousand sheep.

You may conclude from this that we kill mutton, but hitherto we have not been so extravagant. Next year, Mr Macarthur tells me, we may begin. I have now a very good dairy, and in general, make a sufficiency of butter to supply the family, but it is at present so great an object to rear the calves, that we are careful not to rob them of too much milk. We use our horses both for pleasure and profit; they alternately run in the chaise or cart.

Mr Macarthur has also set a Plough at work, the first which has been used in the country, and it is drawn sometimes by oxen and at others by horses. The ground was before tilled with the hoe. These details I am sensible have no other interest than as far as they serve to show the progressive state of this yet infant settlement.

Mr Macarthur once superintended the agricultural concerns of the Government, but since the arrival of Governor Hunter he has declined further interference. By the kindness of the commanding officer of the Regiment we are permitted to reside here, and there being a good road, as I have before observed, to Sydney, Mr M. is enabled to attend to all his duties at headquarters, although at times upon very short notice. Myself, or one or more of the children, occasionally accompany him. As the distance is convenient, our stay is prolonged as business or pleasure require, or we return the same day, but as our family is large we do not choose to be long absent from home together.

Mr Macarthur has frequently in his employment 30 or 40 people whom we pay weekly for their labour. Eight are employed as stockkeepers in the garden, stables and house; and five more, besides women servants; these we both feed and clothe, or, at least, we furnish them with the means of providing clothes for themselves. We have but two men fed at the expense of the Crown, altho' there are persons who contrive to get twenty or more, which the Governor does not or will not notice.

You will wonder how a return is made for the daily expense which it must appear to you we incur.

In the first place, some thousands of persons are fed from the public stores, perhaps between three or four thousand, all of whom were formerly supplied with flour from England to meet the demand for bread. But since so many individuals have cleared farms and have thereby been enabled to raise a great quantity of grain in the country, which at the present time is purchased by the Commissary at 10s. a bushel, and issued for what are termed rations, or the proportionate quantity due to each person instead of flour. In payment for which the Commissary issues a receipt, approved of by the Government; and these receipts pass current here as coin, and are taken by Masters of Ships and other adventurers who come to these parts with merchandise for sale. When any number of these have been accumulated in the hands of individuals they are returned to the Commissary, who gives a Bill on the Treasury in England for them. These bills amount to thirty or forty thousand pounds annually. How long Government may continue so expensive a plan it would be difficult to foresee. Pigs are bought upon the same system, as would also sheep and cattle, if their numbers would admit of their being killed. Beef might be sold at 4s., if not 5s. the lb. A good horse is worth £140 to £150. Be it ever so bad it never sells for less than £100. A cow is valued at about £80. An English cow that was the property of Colonel Grose sold for £100. From this statement you will perceive that those persons who took early precautions to raise livestock have at present singular advantages.

We have fattened and killed a great number of hogs in the year, which enables us to feed a large establishment of servants. These labourers are such as have been convicts, and whose time of transportation has expired. They then cease to be fed at the expense of Government, and employ themselves as they please. Some endeavour to procure a passage home to England; some become settlers, and others hire themselves out for labour. They demand an enormous price, seldom less than 4s. or 5s. a day. For such as have many in their employment it becomes necessary to keep on hand large supplies of such articles as are most needed by these people, for shops there are none. The officers in the Colony, with a few others possessed of money or credit in England, unite together and purchase the cargoes of such vessels as repair to this country from various quarters. Two or more are chosen from the number to bargain for the cargo offered for sale, which is then divided amongst them, in proportion to the amount of their subscriptions. This arrangement prevents monopoly, and the impositions that would be otherwise practised by masters of ships. These details which may seem prolix are necessary to show you the mode in which we are in our infant condition compelled to proceed.

I have had the misfortune to lose a sweet Boy of eleven months old, who died very suddenly by an illness occasioned by teething. The other three, Elizabeth, John, and Mary are well. I have lately been made very happy by learning the safe arrival of Edward in England. We often remember and talk over in the evening the hospitalities which we have both received in Bridgerule Vicarage, and happy shall I be if it is ever permitted me to mark my remembrance more strongly than is expressed in these lines.

If you are in the habit of visiting the Whitsline family I pray that you will kindly remember me to them. The benevolence of the Major's heart will dispose him to rejoice at the success which has attended us, and that the activity which was very early discernible in the mind of Mr Macarthur has had a field for advantageous exertion. How is it, my dearest friend, that you are still single? Are you difficult to please? or has the war left you so few bachelors from amongst whom to choose? But suffer me to offer you a piece of advice: abate a few of your scruples, and marry. I offer in myself an instance that it is not always, with all our wise foreseeings, those marriages which promise most or least happiness prove in their result such as our friends may predict. Few of mine, I am certain, when I married thought that either of us had taken a prudent step. I was considered indolent and inactive; Mr Macarthur too proud and haughty for our humble fortune or expectations, and yet you see how bountifully Providence has dealt with us. At this time I can truly say no two people on earth can be happier than we are. In Mr Macarthur's society I experience the tenderest affections of a husband, who is instructive and cheerful as a companion. He is an indulgent Father, beloved as a Master, and universally respected for the integrity of his character. Judge then my friend, if I ought not to consider myself a happy woman.

I have hither in all my letters to my friends forborn to mention Mr Macarthur's name, lest it might appear in me too ostentatious. Whenever you marry look out for good sense in a husband. You would never be happy with a person inferior to yourself in point of understanding. So much my early recollection of you and of your character bids me say.

E. M.

W.C. Wentworth

[SYDNEY AND PARRAMATTA]

The harbour of Port Jackson is perhaps exceeded by none in the world except the Derwent in point of size and safety; and in this latter particular, I rather think it has the advantage. It is navigable for vessels of any burden for about seven miles above the town, i.e. about fifteen from the entrance. It possesses the best anchorage the whole way, and is perfectly sheltered from every wind that can blow. It is said, and I believe with truth, to have a hundred coves, and is capable of containing all the shipping in the world. There can be no doubt, therefore, that in the course of a few years, the town of Sydney, from the excellence of its situation alone, must become a place of considerable importance.

The views from the heights of the town are bold, varied and beautiful. The strange irregular appearance of the town itself, the numerous coves and islets both above and below it, the towering forests and projecting rocks, combined with the infinite diversity of hill and dale on each side of the harbour, form altogether a coup d'oeil, of which it may be safely asserted that few towns can boast a parallel.

The neighbouring scenery is still more diversified and romantic, particularly the different prospects which open upon you from the hills on the South Head Road, immediately contiguous to the town. Looking towards the coast you behold at one glance the greater part of the numerous bays and islands which lie between the town and the heads, with the succession of barren, but bold and commanding hills, that bound the harbour, and are abruptly terminated by the water. Further north, the eye ranges over the long chain of lofty rugged cliffs that stretch away in the direction of the coal river, and distinctly mark the bearing of the coast, until they are lost in the dimness of vision. Wheeling round to the south you behold at the distance of seven or eight miles, that spacious though less eligible harbour, called "Botany Bay", from the prodigious variety of new plants which Sir Joseph Banks found in its vicinity, when it was first discovered and surveyed by Captain Cook. To the southward again of this magnificent sheet of water, where it will be recollected it was the original intention, though afterwards judiciously abandoned, to found the capital of this colony, you behold the high bluff range of hills that stretch away towards the five islands, and likewise indicate the trending of the coast in that direction.

If you afterwards suddenly face about to the westward, you see before you one vast forest, uninterrupted except by the cultivated openings which have been made by the axe on the summits of some of the loftiest hills, and which tend considerably to diminish those melancholy sensations its gloomy monotony would otherwise inspire. The innumerable undulations in this vast expanse of forest, forcibly remind you of the ocean when convulsed by tempests; save that the billows of the one slumber in a fixed and leaden stillness, and want that motion which constitutes the diversity, beauty, and sublimity of the other. Continuing the view, you arrive at that majestic and commanding chain of mountains called "the Blue Mountains", whose stately and o'ertopping grandeur forms a most imposing boundary to the prospective.

If you proceed on the South Head Road, until you arrive at the eminence called "Belle Vue", the scenery is still more picturesque and grand; since, in addition to the striking objects already described, you behold, as it were at your feet, although still more than a mile distant from you, the vast and foaming Pacific. In boisterous weather the surges that break in mountains on the shore beneath you, form a sublime contrast to the still, placid waters of the harbour, which in this spot is only separated from the sea by a low sandy neck of land not more than half a mile in breadth; yet is so completely sheltered, that no tempests can ruffle its tranquil surface.

The town of Parramatta is situated at the head of Port Jackson Harbour, at the distance of about eighteen miles by water, and fifteen by land, from Sydney. The river for the last seven or eight miles, is only navigable for boats of twelve or fifteen tons burden. This town is built along a small fresh water stream, which falls into the river. It consists principally of one street about a mile in length. It is surrounded on the south side by a chain of moderately high hills; and as you approach it by the Sydney road, it breaks suddenly on the view when you have reached the summit of them, and produces a very pleasing effect. The adjacent country has been a good deal cleared; and the gay mimosas, which have sprung up in the openings, form a very agreeable contrast to the dismal gloom of the forest that surrounds and o'ertops them.

The town itself is far behind Sydney in respect of its buildings; but it nevertheless contains many of a good and substantial construction. These, with the church, the government house, the new Orphan House, and some gentlemen's seats, which are situated on the surrounding eminences, give it, upon the whole, a very respectable appearance. There are two very good inns, where a traveller may meet with all the comfort and accommodation that are to be found in similar establishments in the country towns of this kingdom. The charges too are by no means unreasonable.

The population is principally composed of inferior traders, publicans, artificers, and labourers, and may be estimated, inclusive of a company which is always stationed there, on a rough calculation, at about twelve hundred souls.

There are two fairs held half yearly, one in March and the other in September; they were instituted about five years since by the present governor, and already begin to be very numerously and respectably attended. They are chiefly intended for the sale of stock, for which there are stalls, pens, and every other convenience, erected at the expense of the government; for the use of these pens, etc. and to keep them in repair, a moderate scale of duties is paid by the vender.

This town has for many years past made but a very inconsiderable progress compared with Sydney. The value of land has consequently not kept pace in the two places, and is at least 200 per cent less in the one than in the other. As the former, however, is in a central situation between the rapidly increasing settlements on the banks of the Hawkesbury and Nepean rivers, and the latter the great mart for colonial produce, landed property there and in the neighbourhood, will, without doubt, experience a gradual rise.

The public institutions are an Hospital, a Female Orphan House, into which it is intended to remove the orphans from Sydney, and a factory, in which such of the female convicts as misconduct themselves, and those also who upon their arrival in the colony are not immediately assigned as servants to families, are employed in manufacturing coarse cloth. There are upon an average about one hundred and sixty women employed in this institution, which is placed under the direction of a superintendent, who receives wool from the settlers, and gives them a certain portion of the manufactured article in exchange: what is reserved is only a fair equivalent for the expense of making it, and is used in clothing the gaol gang, the re-convicted culprits who are sent to the coal river, and I believe the inmates of the factory itself.

There is also another public institution in this town, well worthy of the notice of the philanthropist. It is a school for the education and civilisation of the aborigines of the country. It was founded by the present governor three years since, and by the last accounts from the colony, it contained eighteen native children, who had been voluntarily placed there by their parents, and were making equal progress in their studies with European children of the same age. The following extract from the *Sydney Gazette*, of January 4, 1817, may enable the reader to form some opinion of the beneficial consequences that are likely to result from this institution, and how far they may realise the benevolent intentions which actuated its philanthropic founder.

> On Saturday last, the 28th ult. the town of Parramatta exhibited a novel and very interesting spectacle, by the assembling of the native tribes there, pursuant to the governor's gracious invitation. At ten in the morning the market place was thrown open, and some gentlemen who were appointed on the occasion, took the management of the ceremonials. The natives having seated themselves on the ground in a large circle, the chiefs were placed on chairs a little advanced in front, and to the right of their respective tribes. In the centre of the circle thus formed, were placed large tables groaning under the weight of roast beef, potatoes, bread, &c. and a large cask of grog lent its exhilarating aid to promote the general festivity and good humour which so conspicuously shone through the sable visages of this delighted congress. The governor, attended by all the members of the native institution, and by several of the magistrates and gentlemen in the neighbourhood, proceeded at half past ten to the meeting, and having entered the circle, passed round the whole of them, enquiring after, and making himself acquainted with the several tribes, their respective leaders and residences. His Excellency then assembled the chiefs by themselves, and confirmed them in the ranks of chieftains, to which their own tribes had exalted them, and conferred upon them badges of distinction; whereon were engraved their names as chiefs, and those of their tribes. He afterwards conferred badges of merit on some individuals, in acknowledgment of their steady and loyal conduct in the assistance they rendered the military party, when lately sent out in pursuit of the refractory natives to the west and south of the Nepean river. By the time this ceremony was over, Mrs Macquarie arrived, and the children belonging to, and under the care of the native institution, fifteen in number, preceded by their teacher, entered the circle, and walked round it; the children appearing very clean, well clothed and happy. The chiefs were then again called together to observe the examination of the children as to their progress in learning and the civilised habits of life. Several of the little ones read; and it was grateful to the bosom of sensibility to trace the degrees of pleasure which the chiefs manifested on this occasion. Some clapped the children on the head; and one in particular turning round towards the governor with extraordinary emotion, exclaimed, "Governor, that will make a good settler, – that's my Pickaninny!" (meaning his child). And some of the females were observed

to shed tears of sympathetic affection, at seeing the infant and helpless offspring of their deceased friends, so happily sheltered and protected by British benevolence. The examinations being finished, the children returned to the institution, under the guidance of their venerable tutor; whose assiduity and attention to them, merit every commendation.

The feasting then commenced, and the governor retired amidst the long and reiterated acclamations and shouts of his sable and grateful congress. The number of the visitants (exclusive of the fifteen children), amounted to one hundred and seventy-nine, viz. one hundred and five men, fifty-three women, and twenty-one children. It is worthy of observation that three of the latter mentioned number of children (and the son of the memorable Bemni-long, was one of them) were placed in the native institution, immediately after the breaking up of the congress, on Saturday last, making the number of children now in that establishment, altogether eighteen; and we may reasonably trust that in a few years this benevolent institution will amply reward the hopes and expectations of its liberal patrons and supporters, and answer the grand object intended, by providing a seminary for the helpless offspring of the natives of this country, and opening the path to their future civilisation and improvement.

Peter Cunningham

[CURRENCY AND STERLING]

Letter XXI

Our colonial-born brethren are best known here by the name of *Currency*, in contradistinction to *Sterling*, or those born in the mother country.

The name was originally given by a facetious paymaster of the seventy-third regiment quartered here, the pound currency being at that time *inferior* to the pound sterling. Our Currency lads and lasses are a fine interesting race, and do honour to the country whence they originated. The name is a sufficient passport to esteem with all the well-informed and right-feeling portion of our population; but it is most laughable to see the capers some of our drunken old Sterling madonnas will occasionally cut over their Currency adversaries in a quarrel. It is then, "You saucy baggage, how dare you set up your *Currency* crest at me? I am *Sterling*, and that I'll let you know!"

To all acquainted with the open manly simplicity of character displayed by this part of our population, its members are the theme of universal praise; and, indeed, what more can be said in their favour, than that they are little tainted with the vices so prominent among their parents! Drunkenness is almost unknown with them, and honesty proverbial; the few of them that have been convicted having acted under the bad auspices of their parents or relatives. Nearly all the Currency criminals have, indeed, been furnished by three roguishly prolific families in the colony; and if the whole of the numbers of these have not hitherto been convicted, there are few who do not believe them deserving.

This fact forms, indeed, the best test of the utility of marriage in ministering to criminal reform; for the pliable disposition of youth can, in general, be so readily bent towards good or evil, that parents have almost always the power of forming the infant mind in whatever way their own ruling inclinations may tend; and as so few of our Currency youths have been trained up in the paths of Vice, we may naturally infer their parents have, at the least, made no attempts to mislead them. Hence the benefit of matrimony in a new colony does not less consist in peopling its dreary wilds with youthful and active native-born inhabitants, than in turning the inclinations of the old importations from thieving and immorality towards honesty and virtue.

The Currencies grow up tall and slender, like the Americans, and are generally remarkable for that Gothic peculiarity of fair hair and blue eyes which has been noticed by other writers. Their complexions, when young, are of a reddish sallow, and they are for the most part easily distinguishable – even in more advanced years – from those born in England. Cherry cheeks are not accompaniments of our climate, any more than that of America, where a blooming complexion will speedily draw upon you the observation, "You are from the old country, I see!"

The young females generally lose their teeth early, like the Americans and West Indians, this calamity always commencing about the period of puberty: it may possibly be ascribed to the climatising process, as we see nearly all plants and animals suffer considerable change in appearance on transplantation to a different latitude: we may therefore hope this defect will subside when a few generations have passed away. "The Currency lads" is now a popular standing toast, since it was given by Major Goulburn at the Agricultural dinner, while "The Currency lasses" gives name to one of our most favourite tunes.

The young men of low rank are fonder of binding themselves to trades, or going to sea, than passing into the employ of the settlers, as regular farm-servants. This no doubt arises partly from their unwillingness to mix with the convicts so universally employed on farms, partly from a sense of pride; for, owing to convicts being hitherto almost the sole agricultural labourers, they naturally look upon that vocation as degrading in the same manner as white men in slave colonies regard work of any kind, seeing that none *but* slaves *do* work. It is partly this same pride, as much as the hostile sentiments instilled into them by their parents, that makes them so utterly averse to fill the situation of petty constables, or to enlist as soldiers.

The young girls are of mild-tempered, modest disposition, possessing much simplicity of character; and, like all children of nature, credulous, and easily led into error. The lower classes are anxious to get into respectable service, from a laudable wish to be independent, and escape from the tutelage of their often profligate parents; and, like the "braw Scotch lasses", love to display their pretty curly locks, tucked up with tortoiseshell combs, and, slip-shod or bare-footed, trip it merrily along. They make generally very good servants, their wages varying from £10 to £15 per annum. They do not commonly appear to class chastity as the *very first* of virtues, which circumstance arises partly from their never being tutored by their parents so to consider it, but more especially from never perceiving its violation to retard marriage. They are all fond of frolicking in the water, and those living near the sea can usually swim and dive like water-hens.

The Currency youths are warmly attached to their country, which they deem unsurpassable, and few ever visit England without hailing the day of their *return* as the most delightful in their lives; while almost everything in the parent-land sinks in relative value with similar objects at home. Indeed, when comparing the exhilarating summer aspect of Sydney, with its cloudless sky, to the dingy gloom of a London street, no wonder a damp should be cast over the ethereal spirits of those habituated to the former; and who had possibly been led into extravagant anticipations regarding London, by the eulogiums of individuals reluctantly torn from its guilty joys.

A young Australian, on being once asked his opinion of a splendid shop on Ludgate Hill, replied, in a disappointed tone, "It is not equal to *Big Cooper's*" (a store-shop in Sydney), while Mrs Rickards' *Fashionable Repository* is believed to be unrivalled, even in Bond Street.

Some of them also contrive to find out that the English cows give *less* milk and butter than the Australian, and that the choicest Newmarket racers possess *less* beauty and swiftness than *Junius*, *Modus*, *Currency Lass*, and others of Australian turf pedigree; nay, even a young girl, when asked how she would like to go to England, replied with great *naivete*. "I should be afraid to go, from the *number of thieves* there," doubtless conceiving England to be a downright hive of such, that threw off its annual swarms to people the wilds of this colony.

Nay, the very miserable-looking trees that cast their annual coats of bark, and present to the eye of a raw European the appearance of being actually *dead*, I have heard praised as objects of incomparable beauty! – and I myself, so powerful is habit, begin to look upon them pleasurably. Our ideas of beauty are, in truth, less referable to a *natural* than an *artificial* standard, varying in every country according to what the eye has been habituated to, and fashion prescribes.

G.T.W.B. Boyes

[LIFE IN HOBART]

June 27th [1830]

At home all morning. Soaked my feet. Head aching from what cause I know not. I went to bed early, but did not go to sleep till 2 or 3, perhaps that was the cause.

Cold raw misty morning – but yesterday was the coldest morning I have observed this year.

The place is very quiet for the present. I heard of no parties and that at least is a relief, not that I care about them provided they overlook me in their invitations and that, I must do them the justice to say, they generally do.

I don't know any subject upon which people generally are so much mistaken as on party giving. Those who suppose that cards are issued with a view of making a panel of ladies and gentleman happy and merry – and that the said ladies and gentlemen don their finery and hie away with a determination to do the agreeable – cannot have many months emerged from the nursery confines – the odour of bread and butter must indeed be strong upon them.

No, no, the motives are well known to the initiated to be of a very different complexion. Speaking abstractedly it might be said that people come together of an evening to make themselves disagreeable and to exhibit to those in the secret how much tonish insolence they can throw off in the little half hour they thus devote to their friends.

Occasionally an individual has no other object than that of satisfying herself that Mrs A. looks as old as ever – a second to keep an eye on young George B. who has not been quite so sedulous as was expected of him – a third because there happened to be no other place open.

But there are some who are emulous of improving a naturally retentive memory by storing it with the various inventories of fripperie presented to the observation – others whose tastes are developed in the Department of the Confectioner seek opportunities for the exercise of their critical acumen at the turn out at the side tables. An epicure in tragedy horrors may find gratification for his passion in the doubtful colour of blanc mange which may become anything but a *white* meat in the hands of an unskilled artist – or in the opaque and fixed look of a jelly which in tenacity and impenetrability represents the contents of an artificer's glue pot. The goneby sweets of a cheesecake may also afford matter for moral reflection and the highly flavoured patty would naturally lead a mind cast in a Galway Martin mould to muse upon the cruelty that had been inflicted upon the unfortunate oyster by allowing it to spend its strength and die a lingering death and end its testacious solitude before its immersement for the evening's regale.

However you do sometimes see a few young Masters and Misses who have escaped from the nurserymaid – playing at hide and seek among the Draperised Madams and the Drapery Misses and with these Urchins only is any true enjoyment to be sought for.

* * *

February 13th [1831]

At home all morning. In the afternoon rode Bryant's horse beyond Roseway across the stream and into the woods on the other side. Magnificent scenery – Mount Wellington rearing his giant head above the tall trees at every turn – and the deep purple shadows of the Ravines formed fine contrasts with the bright parts rich with streams of yellow light from the declining sun.

Such scenes never fail to have a powerful effect over my mind and heart. The one appears to become sensible of its adaptation for the highest conceptions; seems to feel its connection with the great creator of all things; imbibes as it were conviction of its immortality. The other swells with gratitude to the being of whose fatherly protection and animating though awful presence, it feels itself the peculiar object. These sensations lose none of their freshness and strength by repetition; on the contrary, they seem to become more intense and perfect in their development by the frequency of their occurrence. This is not enthusiasm – there is no fanaticism in this. The heart and soul expand under the influence of such natural objects, wild and magnificent 'tis true, in the greatest degree – increase as it were in volume, become eminently susceptible of their enlarged capacity for enjoyment and all these as naturally as the lungs become inflated and invigorated with the pure and balmy breeze which seems to infuse new life and health and elasticity into the most secret recesses of our animal being.

If my sensations are participated by others generally – there requires little urging from our spiritual teachers to inspire us with a pure and a holy love of our creator.

Read in Joshua.

* * *

October 16th

Raining and blowing hard in Squalls. More snow upon the mountain than yesterday, and more yesterday than the day before. Cold wind. At home all day reading prayers and lessons and some chapters in the Bible. Flag up for a brig.

In my last visit to New Norfolk I was accompanied by a promising young man, the Assistant Surgeon of the 63rd Regiment – previously to our leaving on the Monday he had been requested to visit the Hospital at Bridgewater where there is about 100 men working in chains forming a bridge and causeway across the Derwent. A Mr Officer of New Norfolk whose duty it was to attend the sick at Bridgewater had, with the view of saving himself a twelve mile ride, made the request of my companion and apparently he could not have selected a substitute better calculated for summary proceedings:

The Chain gang is composed of Convict assigned servants and others, whose misconduct has brought them into a situation which to men not entirely callous to bodily suffering nor lost to a sense of human degradation, must be one of exquisite moral and physical misery.

The Convicts are there for a definite time varying from one to twelve months – and on expiration of their sentence they are either returned to their Masters or transferred to Public Works of less painful employment.

Wooden Barracks have been erected for their use and also for the military guard placed over them, the latter commanded by some subaltern officer – whose apparent tact has pointed him out to the Government as well adapted for such a duty. Here the convicts labour, and with short intervals of refreshment and repose it may be said incessantly. They quarry stone, break it, shape it – or not as required, wheel it to the Causeway and apply it either to form a foundation or in the erection of piers upon foundations already formed. The work is almost of an endless description – from the extent and depth of the mud in [?], which it is constructing, and the unhappy labourers are therefore not even cheered by viewing the progress of their daily toil.

Within the Court Yard appropriated for their use are seen some of the means by which discipline is preserved. Here stands constantly the triangle – and there ranged along one side of the small square are cells for close incarceration. These are of a peculiar construction and owe their origin to some modern Phalaris – who it is hoped brought the efficacy of the invention to the test in his own person.

Each cell is about 7 feet in length by 2 feet 6 in height and breadth; of course a stout man could not turn himself and when put in durance must be pushed in head foremost and when relieved drawn out by the heels – (However I need not indulge in speculation. There are few if any stout men amongst these poor wretches; a more speedy means of diminishing the bulk of human expansion could hardly have been devised than the treatment at this penal station.)

The cells when not occupied by the refractory are the depositories for the sick and when used on the latter occasion are dominated "The Hospital".

The entrance to each is secured by a strong wooden frame with a heavily barred gate swinging upon hinges which admits cold or heat in unmitigated intenseness.

There are other modes† of punishment besides the cells and Triangle – such as reducing the quantity of food, depriving one of soup and another of meat etc.

I have been thus particular in describing this penal station because it is very probably a specimen of the rest – and I believe they have never yet appeared on paper.

After a short consultation with the Officer commanding, the sick were ordered to be assembled and the Surgeon proceeded to inspect them. They consisted of 12 or 14 squalid famine stricken distressed wretches – drawn up in a line in front of the Barracks. Approaching the nearest the Surgeon enquired his complaint.

"I have got a bad eye Sir and can't bear the light."

"Let me look at them – how long have they been in this state?"

"They have been getting bad about ten days Sir."

The Surgeon, then speaking to the overseer in attendance:

"See that this man washes his eyes three or four times a day with warm water and let him work in the shade."

The second in the line was then asked what he had done to his arms?

†Modifications of punishment are also produced by varying the weight and length of the chains. The shortest are the most painful and embarrassing by affording the least possible space for the motion of the legs. I heard a man after receiving the cat o' nine tails once say that he would rather be hanged than forced to work in short chains.

"I haven't done anything Sir." replied the man, "but they are all come out in this way. I have no peace with them night or day."

"Oh!" exclaimed the Officer of the guard, "He has just got the itch, that's all!"

The surgeon then desired the overseer to give the man a dose of salts and let him go to work as usual.

"What is the matter with you?" said the Surgeon to a third.

"I don't know Sir – my knee is very much swelled and it has been getting worse and worse every day for the last month."

"Oh you have struck it, I perceive." rejoined the Surgeon, "You must bathe it several times a day in warm water, and, Overseer, let him rest today from work and tomorrow his knee will be well."

Another poor fellow's leg had been sore for three weeks and on the Surgeon's intimation took off a portion of a dirty cotton handkerchief under which was spread upon a broad unhealthy sore, about two square inches of an old chequed shirt much soiled with long use.

"I see how it is," said the Surgeon. "You don't keep it clean."

"Yes Sir," replied the man, "I do as well as I can."

"You do no such thing," reiterated the Surgeon, "Wash it frequently with warm water and, Overseer – take this man from the wheelbarrow for the present and let him break stones only."

"Why Martin," here interrupted the Officer on duty: "You were in hospital some time ago."

"Yes Sir," replied the poor wretch, "But I was very ill."

"Pooh," interjected the Officer, "I'll tell you what – a damned good flogging would be the best thing for him. However let him break stones as the Doctor directs."

"Thank you your honour," said the man, "I would rather go to work than stay in the Hospital." (I have already described the oven-like dens called the Hospital).

I was rather surprised at the extreme simplicity of the remedies prescribed by the young Surgeon which in every case consisted of either cold or warm water or a dose of salts, although the latter being a costly medicine was directed in only one instance.

I learnt afterwards that the prescription was regulated not by the necessity of the case but by the state of the medicine chest, which the Surgeon previously to the inspection had been informed contained neither more or less than a few ounces of Epsom salts. The Officer referred to in this mem. had been recently relieved from the station and was then in the temporary performance of duty during the illness of his successor. Upon finishing the Sick Inspection this Gentleman looked wise – shook his head and affected to complain of the number of Sick. While during the period of his commanding he said there were only two cases. One of these was ill when sent to the gang and the other had his leg crushed by a mass of rock falling upon it. He was of the opinion that a more liberal application of the Cat o' nine tails would render the attendance of a Medical Officer at the Station altogether superfluous, but it was no business of his and therefore he said nothing about it.

Eliza Brown

LETTERS FROM WESTERN AUSTRALIA

Grassdale
July 3, 1842
[In error. Should be 1841. W. Bussey]

My dear Papa,

We have now been four months in the Colony and not received a line from home, the only letter that has come to hand from a relative is one from Mr Brown's Brother Wm. which communicated the tidings of poor William's death, the circumstance was touched upon more in the way of a passing remark than with any idea that it would be the source from which we should first hear the melancholy intelligence. These were his words: "I have had a letter from Mr Bussey (relative to some business concerning the insurance of our mares, I believe) and was deeply grieved to hear from him of the death of his poor son". His letter is dated Janry. 27th, poor William did not survive many weeks then after we left England. I did not think poor fellow he would have been cut off so soon though I felt persuaded there was no hope of his final restoration. I am now more anxious than ever to hear from you being most solicitous to know how you support the trial. I feel assured your grief is deeply seated but trust to learn you have many consolations in the endearments of children still left to comfort you in whose peaceful and happy homes your sorrow will find alleviation, and I also trust that the God of consolation will send peace to your grieved spirit and be your support through this life, and to eternity.

I shall now be able to give you a more experienced account of what a settler's life is than when I wrote you three months since, and will candidly state that it has hitherto been one of great perplexity to us. Mr Brown has a most difficult task to perform in making it answer his purpose to have brought out so many labourers. The expense of providing for seven servants in addition to the wants of ourselves and little ones is a very serious matter, wheat being at present £1 per bushel and 2/6 for grinding and every other article of food in the same dear ration. The pork and other things we brought for domestic consumption are scarcely available to us from the great expense of bringing them up from the government store at Perth to this District and we are as yet almost without the common necessaries of life though it is only the distance of seventy miles that parts us from the household conveniences that we set out well provided with from England. We look forward to having them brought over the hills to our remote residence by degrees, but the first object is to get ploughing and sowing done to provide us all with bread next year. £25 per ton is the charge for conveying goods from Fremantle here, eight or nine times the cost of bringing them 13,000 miles over the sea from England, between Fremantle and Perth and from thence to Guildford the sand is so loose and deep that a horse of good strength cannot without difficulty draw an empty cart over it. The mode generally adopted for the transition of goods into the interior is to take them in boats up the Swan as far as Guildford, but in this way innumerable obstacles present themselves, the course of the river is very circuitous, several shoals come in the way over which the boats have to be dragged by the boatmen and there is no certainty of getting things conveyed in safety for it frequently happens that boats are swamped. The boatmen all bear a very bad character, there is said to be not one honest and sober man of that calling who plies on the river, we were run aground full twenty times in coming up to Mr Tanner's and coming up the Swan did really appear to me the most dangerous part of our voyage.

We have a team of four bullocks, two other bullocks, two strong horses (bought in the Colony) and one young horse (saved from the wreck of those we shipped from England) but all this force is not available for the purposes intended, namely the conveyance of goods from below and ploughing, the cattle being almost constantly lost in the Bush and the men's time taken up in looking for them, but when we become more accustomed to the wilds, understand the native language better by which we shall be able to make the Natives more useful to us than they are at present, we shall manage better I trust and get on with farming operations much more satisfactorily than it seems possible to do in the commencement of the undertaking in a primitive country, under a different clime from that to which we have been accustomed and the circumstances altogether so novel as to make it a matter of hesitation what to proceed with to the best advantage. Mr Brown toils incessantly, it is one unbroken period of manual labour with him from early dawn to bed time. The land has to be cleared previously to ploughing and our nights are generally illuminated with blazing fires. Tree after tree falls a sacrifice to the devouring element, first being felled either with the axe or sawn down then the men with Mr Brown to lead, encourage them and set an example pile several together and set fire to the heaps, we have sometimes eight or ten bonfires of this nature which continue burning for several days. With respect to cattle straying ours is by no means a solitary case, the old established settlers are equally subjected to the same inconvenience and quite smile when we express any anxiety lest they should not be found again. Instances have been known of horses, cows etc. being missed six and even twelve months yet returned to their original pasturage and rightful owners. We have a flock of about 600 ewe sheep that are attended with very little trouble, it is about a sufficient charge for one shepherd. The experience of all the Colonists goes to prove that great profits can be made from sheep, the climate being particularly suited to them, they increase rapidly and the wool becomes of good quality even should it not be so when a flock is first imported, ours are all long woolled sheep and considered very good ones.

Mr Brown has accepted the appointment (which came out in due form by the *Trusty*) of assistant surveyor to this Government, which will make matters pretty easy for us as regards sufficiency of income, but he will have a most difficult task to perform, not unattended with danger. Two soldiers will constantly attend him for protection and a civilian also to take care of baggage, instruments etc., and in case of any disturbances from the Natives a detachment of soldiers would be sent for from the nearest Barracks to quell it. The duties of the office will be entered upon in about three weeks from this time and it is arranged by the friendly concurrence of the Governor that the District where we reside shall be the first to be surveyed. This will give him an opportunity of overlooking concerns on the Farm, which locality I shall now proceed to describe to you.

Grass Dale is the name of the estate, it is about eleven square miles in extent and has a range of hills running through one part of it, the highest of which is called Mount Matilda. At the foot of this is our dwelling, a cottage consisting of two rooms, it is roughly built but of exceedingly picturesque appearance from the extreme beauty of the site where it is placed, rugged rocks are heaped in wild confusion around and a fertile valley stretches itself for full two miles and a half like a green lawn in front of the lowly habitation. There is an outhouse near which serves as a temporary sleeping place for the men, adjoining a stockyard where the bullocks, mares, etc. are penned at night. 5/- an acre was what Mr Brown gave for the land with the buildings upon it, since the purchase was made Government has raised the price of land to £1 per acre. We bought Grass Dale of Mr Bland the Government Resident at York. We are about four miles from York and attend service at church there, the Revd Wm. Mears is the name of the clergyman. We are on friendly terms with him, he preaches at Yanjedin, Mr Viveash's residence, every third Sunday in the afternoon. Yanjedin is about 9 miles from here and at a convenient part of the York District for a congregation to assemble who are not within reach of the place of worship at York. It adds to the pleasantness of our position that we are not cut off from social intercourse. The Viveashs are farther off than I would wish but they are within occasional visiting distance, and frequently the Doctor's profession and engagements bring him to York, on which occasions he is pretty sure to give us a call. I am sorry to say it will be a professional one very shortly, an increase to our family being looked forward to.

Mr and Mrs Hardey are our nearest neighbours, the Evans know them, their little boy Robt. comes daily on his pony to receive a lesson along with Kenneth. I take great delight in instructing them. Robt. Hardey is a nice companion for Kenneth, he is a vigorous boy but of gentle disposition and seven years old. My little Vernon has had such serious illnesses from time to time since we left England, Dr Viveash expected we should lose him once. We spent a month at Yanjedin after leaving Mr Tanner's and his worst illness was struggled with whilst there. His limbs were much swollen from debility when he was recovering from the last attack. He has gained strength since we came to Grass Dale and is now I hope likely to continue healthful. He is a child who attracts much interest and certainly is a pleasing little creature though unfortunately so delicate.

July 8th. Bedtime arrived before I had concluded my letter on the 3rd, I had therefore put the writing [away] intending to finish on the following morning. Then a little boy arrived during the night, resembling Kenneth for vigour and healthfulness but disabling me for resuming the pen again so early as intended and wholly frustrating my intention of writing dear Emma and Matilda at present. Mr Brown starts for Perth early tomorrow morning and will be the bearer of this to Miss Crocker one of our late fellow voyagers by the *Sterling* to this Colony. She is leaving by the *Trusty* and has offered to take charge of letters for us to England. I had many enquiries to make respecting Dorchester friends, regards to send etc. but must now only inform you that I am according to general phraseology on such occasions as well as can be expected, and remain

Dear Papa
Yr. Truly Affectionate Daughter
E. Brown
received June 3 1842

[no date]

My dearest Papa,

I am in the joyful possession of your letters to Mr Brown and myself of the dates Feby 26th from Cuddesdon and July 16th from the Isle of Wight. My husband was from home with his teams taking sandalwood down to Guildford, think what a delight it was to me to read your letters to him on his return which happened on the day I received them, Decr. 11th. I thought it so problematical whether you would find it convenient to help us or be willing to trust us further while we are still in your debt to so large an amount that the surprise was very great and you may judge that we are both of us very much elated and more thankful than we can express ourselves. Everything now looks up, sandalwood is increased in value since I last wrote, Mr Bland gives my husband twelve pounds per ton for it *delivered at Fremantle*. This was agreed upon and a large quantity contracted for on Mr Bland's part while reports were good with respect to its value in China. A trial cargo has been shipped which Luke Leake (son of Mrs Luke Leake our fellow passenger on the *Sterling*) went with in the *Bandicoot* to Hong Kong. He has very lately returned saying it was three weeks before he could dispose of his cargo and then only at sixteen pounds per ton. He was at first in high spirits as the merchants told him he would get forty but when they came to examine the wood they declared it to be of an inferior sort. Now Luke Leake has but a very young head on his shoulders, albeit a very steady trustworthy lad, and he may have been taken in. It looks well that he is going with another cargo and that the speculators have not ceased to buy. It is in the interest of these parties to keep prices in the Colony as low as possible and they would not be likely to sound a trumpet as to its great value in China. In general only seven or eight pounds per ton is given for it here now. I must drive Mr Brown to the pen to tell you of prices current, horses, cattle, sheep, and more particulars about Mr Bland and sandalwood, though under the rose let me tell you I have not lived within him these twelve years without becoming aware that he is a very awkward subject either to lead or drive, though if I do put the pen in his hand perhaps he will be telling you something just as pretty of me.

I have so much to tell you I hardly know what to begin with first, but as I know you are gallant enough to take a great interest in the fair sex I will introduce a young Lady to your notice, Matilda Brown, who opened her eyes upon this world on Thursday the 25th November. We call her a Kenneth child she is like him but has smaller features than he had when a baby. I write at the present moment with her in my arms, she is just a fortnight and four days old, at least will be before midnight. The Doctor was not here when I was taken poorly and when we sent for the Nurse she was prevented from coming by the obstinacy of her husband who declared she should not leave him and her children to wait on any lady. In the dilemma we applied to Mr Bland who very promptly sent his Housekeeper, a very experienced nurse who was with dear Mrs Bland in her fatal illness. I had such comfort from the kind attentions of this good creature, Mrs Heffron.

It is with a view of giving some insight into the social characteristics of this place that I mention the circumstance of having administered myself the necessary attentions to two women of the labouring class who were without Nurse, Doctor, or neighbour or any female but myself within several miles at the time of their illness. In both instances before their husbands returned who had been despatched for the Doctor the women were partaking of their gruel very snugly in bed with the Infant beside them in best bib and tucker.

And now my dear Papa I should make you tremble with what I have to relate did I not first tell you all is safe now, but Kenneth has been within a hair's breadth of having his life taken. He has been speared in the side, but not by a Native, the Natives when they saw he was wounded ran to his assistance intending to knock the barb off the spear but it was a blunt pointed spear without a barb, and Kenneth had pushed it out of his side before they reached it. It penetrated the flesh in his side the length of my forefinger, when I saw the wound which was four days from the time he received it, it was festering where the spear went in and where it came out. He concealed the injury from me all that time fearing it would make me ill to know of it. I had been but a few days confined and he saw that I was in delicate health. His Papa was on one of his weekly trips with the sandalwood. Our shepherd boy who did it was in agony of apprehension fearing for the child and wished it to be told but Kenneth made him be silent and went quietly over to Mr Hardey's to have it dressed. The evening before his Papa came home it all transpired for the servant girl told me, she had become alarmed because it was festering. My nerves are better than people think, I saw at once that the danger was over and was not agitated. I believe if there had been danger I should very calmly have endeavoured to mitigate it and sent in the meantime for a medical adviser. Kenneth is very fond of throwing the spear at a mark or at a bird and prides himself upon being able to jump a spear, that is jump out of the way of one after it is thrown. This he was attempting to do when he got wounded and I hope it will be a good lesson to him not to run such a risk again. Dr de Lille the military surgeon asked to see the wound (he happened to come up with Mr Brown) and he said that the spear very narrowly escaped fixing itself in the liver. How curious that we should receive a warning from you not to trust him in the way of the Natives just about the time that danger has threatened to happen to him from one of their missile weapons.

About the middle of October I went down to Perth, took little Aubrey this time. I had not visited the Capital for nearly two years, the old saying "out of sight out of mind" came into my head along with the wish to see and be seen. I met with no opposition from the quarter where I rather expected it, found my partner very complying, quite agreeable to my proposal, so he drove us down with great good humour.

We called at the Colonial Chaplain's (J.B. Wittenoom), he opened the door himself, his first exclamation was "A Star shot from its hemisphere". "Yes (I replied in a very dignified manner) to come jolting down in a spring cart." I had before been told there would be an eclipse of the sun upon my leaving York by the grave Mr Bland, which was literally true, but I gave him to understand that other spheres would not be brightened by that circumstance.

We met with great hospitality in Perth, dined out every day, first day luncheoned at the Governor's, engaged to dine there on the next. Perth dinner hour is seven o'clock, Aubrey soon found out that he dined at tea time. York dinner hour is twelve. The Colonial Secretary and his Lady spent the evening at the Governor's the day we were there. I must tell you their names, Mr and Mrs George Moore, the Lady was Miss Jackson daughter of Governor Clarke's wife by a former husband. Mrs Moore remembered our calling at Govt. House soon after she came to the Colony. Kenneth was with us then, she seemed particularly interested in him and told me a little story just gratifying the ambition of a fond mother, of her niece Sissy Moore having been brought to a confession of her before secret love by her, Mrs G. Moore, having found out that it was Kenneth Brown. On the second day we dined at Mr Wittenoom's, company in the evening, on the next Mr Lionel Samson's, on the next Mrs Luke Leake's, another day spent at Mrs Harris's, widow of the late Colonial Surgeon. Called, and called upon by Dr Ferguson (and his Lady) present Colonial Surgeon, the Honble the Advocate General and his Lady Mr and Mrs Burt, Mr and Mrs George Leake – spent a day with Mrs Viveash at Guildford, had many invitations on the Swan, Saml. Moore's, Rev. Mitchel's etc. which we declined and returned home very well satisfied with our trip. I am not much of a visitor but I feel it to be for the interest of my family to keep up a distant acquaintance with the higher circle that they may feel it to be their natural position when they grow up. I do not wish to know any person out of my own family very intimately for fear they should find out my many imperfections and like me less.

There is one more subject to discuss with you my dear Papa and that the most important of any that has yet been touched upon except your bounty in clearing us of our difficulties which will go far towards establishing my husband in worldly respect and honour. I cannot read your affectionate mention of my boys without emotion, your hint that one would be welcome were we to send him to England is not lost upon me. Were we at any time to act upon it it would be Kenneth I should send. I am in great hopes that your valuable life will be prolonged for many years and if when you write in reply to this the wish still continues to see my boy and you feel after all your acts of generosity that your income will bear the additional burden of getting him efficiently instructed I think I should be acting against his most important interests to keep him back from such a privilege. He has no idea of being a settler in this country, his thoughts revert to England from whence we brought him and where for the little time he dwelt he lived the life of an angel for happiness, health and advantages. The son of a settler becoming a settler in this Colony leads but a very obscure life, much more so than the parent who comes from England, I am aware of the fact but cannot now give the reasons. Before I am quite exhausted with writing I hope to give you my wishes of what he should be brought up to that his education may be conducted with a view to his after career. My hopes perhaps may be too ambitious. I wish him to jostle it with other boys at a public school for about four years, Eton, Westminster, Harrow, or the High School of Edinburgh, then if we are prosperous we might send him to College, then the Inner Temple and Lincolns Inn after which he would be eligible to go the circuit with the judges and make an excellent Sergeant Bother'em I fancy, he has a judicial turn and the boy seems to keep constant to the idea that he will be a Barrister.

Now my dearest Papa

Farewell
Yours gratefully and affectionately
Eliza Brown

(the midnight oil has fallen upon my paper)

Received May 2 1848

George Gordon McCrae

[CHRISTMAS IN THE BUSH]

December 19th, 1846. Saturday

This morning was rather rainy; Mr Barker called on his way to town. He told us that there were some blacks at the foot of the fence. We accordingly went down and recognised several of our old friends and amongst them Ben-Benjie who readily agreed to shoot ducks for us. We gave the gun to him after he had breakfasted and he set out. After breakfast we went to school and went over all the French history and we came out. Mr McLure went to dig potatoes for dinner with Willie. After dinner Ben-Benjie returned without the ducks and gave me the charge, and three bommerings as he was to go away tomorrow.

December 21st. Monday

Sandy and I arose early. We walked up along the beach and gathered some currants for a tart. After we returned we bathed and walked up to breakfast. Having breakfasted we went to school. We learned part of our French history, read a chapter in the Bible. I learned a part of the *Æneid*, Willie and Sandy began a new book in *Caesar's Commentaries* and Perry learned a part of the English history. We all wrote part of our lists of plants and went out. Sandy went to the lower garden to cut some lettuces for dinner while I ran up and called Ellen from the wash-house. We soon went to school. Mr McLure asked us a few questions on the map of Scotland, but the bell soon rang and we ran to dinner. Lucy brought into the house a salmon-coloured Mantis having a claret tinge and striped with white. Tom turned out "Duncan" this day. The school bell soon rang and we went to lessons. We read a part of Cornelius Nepos's life of Hannibal, a part of our *Latin Delectus*. We worked a few sums together tonight. Mr McLure and I went to Ellen's well and thinned the lettuces. Mamma gave me a book to sketch in but I have not as yet used it. Tom and the boys went to the beach and caught four small fishes resembling sprats and two or three flounders.

December 22nd, 1846. Tuesday

We rose rather late. Sandy and Perry and I walked to the beach where we stayed for some time. We walked up to breakfast. We had one hour of leisure after breakfast. We went to school: learned the reign of Charlemagne. I learned a part of Phaeton along with Willie and Sandy. We all wrote part of our lists of plants and after a time went out, it being very hot. After a time we came in again, were examined on the northern and middle countries, read a part of our *Latin Delectus* and came down to dinner. After dinner the wind suddenly changed to south having blown from north during the whole day. We went up to school. We all read a portion of Middleton's *Life of Cicero*, worked a few sums together, and went out. We went out in search of a kangaroo which Sancho had killed but could not find it. However we had a chase of three kangaroos. When we returned the wind was still blowing violently from the south. "Flora" was run down and terribly bitten by the other dogs. Paddy one of Mr Barker's men came here, he brought with him the two puppies that we had given to Mr Barker; they were so changed that I scarcely knew them. They were twice as large as our puppy.

December 23rd, 1846. Wednesday

We rose pretty early and walked down to the beach and bathed. I find swimming easier than it was at first. I walked in to the sea until the water touched my throat and threw myself forward, I then floated and striking out with my arms and legs I swam for a short space. After breakfast was over, we went to school, learned a part of the French history, read a part of a chapter in the Bible, and I, Willie, and Sandy, translated an account of the Battle of Phillipi from Velleius Paterculus, wrote a part of our lists of plants. We went out it being late and also near dinner-time. After dinner we had a long play but were interrupted by the lesson bell. So we went up. We took our slates and worked a few sums together in the rule of three. Willie called out that Papa was come and that somebody was with him. Mr McLure sent Perry to see who it was and to come back and tell. But Perry not returning he despatched Sandy and as he did not return he sent me. I went, came down, searched the house, but could not find him. I went into the kitchen and enquired where he was; while I was asking, who walked in but Jamie, the shoemaker (whose horse Willie had mistaken for "Don") and Dunn from the Survey instead of Papa! Jamie informed me that Mr Campbell of the Scotch school was coming here but could not on account of the flooded state of the Mordiallock Creek. Mr McLure and I walked along Mr Smith's road where we found many native raspberries and currants of which we brought home some to Mamma. The boys brought home a blossom of the native convolvulus.

December 24th, 1846. Thursday

After breakfast we went to lessons and as usual learned a part of the French history. We read a chapter in the Bible and a piece from Milton's *Paradise Lost*. I almost finished the third book of the *Æneid*. Willie and Sandy translated a part of *Caesar's Commentaries* and Perry read a part of his English history. We all wrote a part of our lists of plants with their botanical descriptions. We then went out. A black boy came here with a present of veal from Mr Smith shortly after we had come out. Papa returned riding on a mare which he had lately purchased. She had been lately imported from Van Diemen's Land and was very thin. We soon came into school again. We were again examined upon the map of Scotland, learned a part of the Latin Syntax and wrote more of our lists of plants. We then went to dinner. After dinner we went to lessons again. We worked a few sums in proportion and went out. I and the boys walked to the "Nose" and back before tea. I brought some wild clematis seed home as there is much of it ripe. Willie brought home a curious hollow stone from the "Nose". It might serve the purpose of an ink-bottle.

December 25th, 1846. Friday

Christmas! We all rose early and had a fine bathe.

After breakfast we had prayers and Papa read a sermon to us. We walked to the beach. I caught a fish which we supposed to be a young native salmon. Willie and Tom between them speared a dozen of toad fish. Papa and Mr McLure then came down and we walked to the Honeysuckles with them and collected some cockles. In the evening we managed to catch a sting ray (vulgarly termed stingaree) having speared two others without being able to hold them. That which we captured was young and like the rest armed with a barbed weapon on its tail.

December 26th, 1846. Saturday

We rose early and bathed. I stuck my spear into the back of a sting ray but he escaped. After breakfast Perry and I went to the beach in search of sting rays while Papa, Mr McLure, and Willie and Sandy went to the duck ponds to shoot ducks. We saw no rays but an enormous shark which was prowling about so close to the shore that I almost struck him with my spear. Papa, Mr McLure and the boys had better success, for they brought home two ducks, one white and one black magpie. The black magpie is of a different shape from the white. It has a curved bill and bright orange eyes inclining to scarlet and feet like those of a crow with this difference that it is pied black and white. We had the sting ray cooked for dinner today. It was very good, Tom brought back "Maggie" and her foal from the Survey having taken the new mare there in the morning. Tom saw Ben-Benjie and Eliza on this side of Dunn's they will be here tomorrow. While walking in quest of raspberries near the beach I saw a black lump on some rushes which lump proved to be a very small swarm of bees. I broke the rushes and carried the bees on them carefully to the house. I placed them in a small basket turned upside down previously smeared with honey and they are adhering to it.

December 28th, 1846. Monday

We rose and bathed. Ben-Benjie went out with the gun in search of ducks. We went to the scrub to look for seeds of the leafless creeper with blue pea blossoms but could not find any. After dinner Ben-Benjie returned with the hind quarters of a kangaroo, an opossum and a duck. A man came here today with a horse which he said he was bringing to Dr Hobson whom he said he expected here at night. Ben-Benjie amused us much tonight by throwing his bommerings. We gave him some flour, tea and sugar. The man came here to reap the barley. He is to begin tomorrow morning.

December 29th, 1846. Tuesday

We rose early as Papa and Mamma are to breakfast early. Ben-Benjie went out with the gun at break of day and returned with two ducks, one of the common kind and another of a new sort. It had a dark brown head, a blackish beak, with a broad blue band across it. It had eyes white with black pupils. Papa and Mamma started this morning for Mr Balcolmb's. Ben-Benjie, with Sandy Perry and me went to the "Nose" and speared four leather-jackets and four sting rays. We brought the fishes to Eliza and went out a second time. We saw no leather-jackets; but, as we returned Ben-Benjie struck a large Tem-Tem and brought it ashore.

After tea, late in the evening, Ben-Benjie, hearing the porpoises coming to the shore ran down to the beach and speared six large fishes each about 15 inches in length. He gave us all of these with the exception of one which he reserved for himself and Eliza.

* * *

January 15th, 1847. Friday

I helped Mamma to put some tea-box bottoms to some bottomless chairs and made a pretty good job of it. I made a kite this morning, that is to say, I pasted paper on a frame which I had made last night. After breakfast we went to school. We learned a part of the French history read a portion of Cornelius Nepos's life of Hannibal wrote our copies and went out. Shortly afterwards we came in again and I studied the geography of England. We were then examined on the construction of our Latin lesson of the former meeting etc. until dinner-time. After the dinner was finished I fastened a latch on to our bedroom door. We went to school and having worked some sums together came out . . . tried my kite (after having attached wings to it) but it would not go as there was not enough wind. Mr Merrick and Mr De Sailey called here in a gig on their way to town.

DESCRIPTION OF A CORROBOREE

When there is a Corrobera or Native War Dance the men assemble to prepare for the dance, the fire being lighted (for they dance round a fire), the dancers tie wisps of straw or grass round their legs; they take their weapons in their hands and feet and wait till the Corrobera sticks begin to beat and the native songs begin, they then begin to dance with the utmost fury, beating the clubs and spears together, cooeeing now and then. The clang of the weapons, the din of their songs and the trampling of their feet is enough to break the drums of one's ears. The men, women, and children each have a separate Corrobera. The Corrobera of the women is so like that of the men that it needs not be described. The Corrobera of the children . . . the children light a fire and dance round it, beating time with sticks till both their arms and legs get tired. As soon as they are tired they sit down and eat their repast. Each wraps himself in his opossum rug and retires to his miamia or native hut; they then huddle themselves up in their rugs and listen to the clamour of their seniors till they fall asleep. The dance ends, the men go to their huts to sing away till day-break for the dance is kept up nearly the whole night.

The men sleep one half of the day and send their wives or lubras to work while they sleep because they are too lazy to do it themselves.

Every black woman that is married is her husband's slave. The method of marrying is most brutal. The woman and her intended husband go to meet each other. The husband knocks her down with a stick and knocks his wife down on the spot. Sometimes the wife jumps up laughing. The blacks have two or three, even four wives. The wives are treated most cruelly by their husbands. While the men sleep the women go to or are rather sent to the nearest European Settlement to beg money. Sometimes they will take silver in preference to copper(!), and, if copper is offered and silver refused they will set up a great clamour.

Annie Baxter

AT YAMBUCK

At length we reached Yambuck, and here ended my journey overland, in exactly two months from the day we quitted Yesabba; and as we drove up to our tiny hut at our new home, I could not avoid wishing we had been returning to our old one. A young man made his appearance at the door of the domicile in his shirt sleeves, and they none of the cleanest. This was our superintendent. Out of a second hut ran five or six men and three small children. As we approached the dogs barked, men ran here, there, and everywhere, and the children screamed, and hid themselves behind a dray.

We dismounted, and walked into our small abode, comprising two rooms. It was thatched with the long native grass, and the inside was plastered and white-washed. A small deal table was in the middle of the sitting-room, covered with a dirty rug, pannikins, and crumbs of damper. A fire was in the fireplace, but as much smoke came into the room as went up the chimney, and this, added to the total look of discomfort, made me feel inclined to cry.

We were very hungry, and, as there was nothing for us to eat, a man went to the opposite sheep station and procured some mutton. When the meat came, and some chops were brought in, Mr Baxter, who was particular in what he ate, looked at them, and then asked the servant how they were cooked. The man answered –

"In the bottom of an iron pot."

This was Dutch to me then, but I've seen the operation since.

A rug was put up to the doorway, as there was no door between the two rooms, and I took possession of the inner room. I then found out where the gridiron of the establishment was; it composed my bed! How I did ache after lying on that split-wooden-gridiron. I could not rest for the first night at all; nor, indeed, until I made some alterations in it. The inner room had large cracks between the slabs of which the hut was composed, and these made it very airy. A pair of blankets was nailed round it, but they did not much prevent the draught. Opposite to my berth was a cask of corned beef, a chest of tea, and a bag of salt.

A little window place, having no glass in it, had a bag nailed up to keep out the rain or sun. On the mantelpiece in the sitting-room were sundry dirty clay pipes, knives, ink, and so on. The floors were earthern, and, from not having been swept and watered regularly, were in small heaps, and fleas abounded.

There was a vegetable garden in front of the hut, and cabbages did grow, certainly. Our superintendent was not a great florist, and the flowers consisted of stocks only; in fact, nothing is discussed but stock, from fat cattle to garden flowers. I hear of nothing but stock! First it is about the great weight of some bullocks; then as to what wool fetched at home, and strongly recommending sheep-farming; and when I turn to see the garden, alas! stock again is presented to my mind.

About two miles from Yambuck the sea dashes against rather an unsafe shore, so that we could distinctly hear its roar. I liked that, as I think turbulence in nature very grand, and I often used, after being settled, to go down and look at the waves which caused the roaring. Just before coming to the beach there was a salt water lake, and there were quantities of good fish in it; and on it black swans and wild ducks. We also had the wood-duck, which builds in a tree, and numbers of snipe, quail, and pigeons. Strange to say, the river that ran at the foot of the garden was beautiful fresh water, and about 500 yards from the hut there was a hill of sand, and on the side towards the sea the water was quite salt. We had another river, the Eumeralla, at the back of our run. The fish in the fresh water river were most plentiful and like smelt. I used to send a black boy down with a crooked pin fastened to some twine, and he used to collect his bait, i.e. worms, and catch a large dish of fish in a few minutes. The wild ducks used to be very plentiful there also, and I had a shot now and then at them with success; that was when I could sneak on them and shoot them from behind the trees.

In the afternoon of the day after our arrival, our horses came up to the river to water, and I went to pat them and say "How do you do" to them. They evidently thought they were to be harnessed as usual, but when they found this not to be the case one of them commenced kicking up his heels with joy, and, galloping off, was soon followed by the others.

We began building a new and larger hut immediately, and it was a very pleasant one when finished, as many a traveller can aver. It consisted of six rooms and a large veranda, and we made the old hut into a kitchen. We had then to build a store, as we were obliged to get flour, tea, sugar, and all other necessaries, in large quantities in the bush, as there are no shops to send to.

A gentleman was staying at Yambuck when we arrived, for whom I formed, on acquaintance, a sincere friendship. He was the son of a Major Smetham. If ever a kind heart dwelt in man, he had it. He was left in England at school, under the care of guardians, when his father, mother, and younger brother came to New South Wales. After being eight years at home, and hearing nothing from his parents, he determined on going to Sydney to see them, and before starting received a Government appointment from England. On his voyage he dreamed that he saw some letters in the post-office in Sydney, and one was addressed to his father, opposite to whose name was placed the word "dead", in large letters.

On his arrival in Sydney the first person whom he visited confirmed his dream; his father was dead. He was naturally much shocked, but immediately set out to see his remaining parent. When he got to her house she disowned him. Unnatural woman! What her reason was continued always a mystery to him; but he fancied, as she was an exceedingly vain, frivolous woman, that his age might have something to do with her not owning him as her child. She told him that he was Major Smetham's son by some foreigner, but not hers. It was supposed that his father had left him some property, but the supposition is all he ever knew of it. Poor fellow! he was of a most affectionate disposition, and has often told me that, if even then she would only own him as her child, he would give her all he either possessed then or was likely to possess. This so preyed on his mind that at night, in his sleep, he would repeat aloud what he had said to her on their meeting in Sydney –

"Cruel mother, to disown your son! You'll break my heart! I *am* your son!" He would remain silent for a time, and afterwards, in a subdued tone, would say, "My poor father! would you were alive."

His friends recommended him to write to England for the certificate of his baptism, and to go to law to recover any property that might be his by right; but he was unwilling to bring shame to his father's name by citing his worthless mother to appear before the public. Some time after we arrived at Yambuck Mr C. Smetham remained with us, and a few years later he studied for the church, and became a missionary to some of the South Sea Islands where he died.

I have often talked over my travels in Australia, and my friends have said, "You should publish them." But now that I am doing so I feel that my small journal is so poor and uninteresting that few will give themselves the trouble of buying or reading it.

My time in the bush passed sometimes very merrily, sometimes very sadly. Being of a happy temperament, I made friends, and every now and then some queer incident would occur to amuse me. I was very fond of riding and hunting, had some beautiful dogs, and plenty of kangaroos and dingoes to hunt.

A clerical friend of mine, who is now living in Portland, Victoria, and for whom I entertained the sincerest friendship, came to stay a day with us, and I was mischievous enough to plan a hunt for him. He said, in answer to my invitation to go for a ride, that he would be most happy, but that he never hunted, I must remember. Accordingly, we went; and when we got some distance from home I saw the dogs keeping a steady lookout, and presently they went after a forester kangaroo, or what we call "an old man". I cantered on, and heard my friend close behind me, but not a word did I say. The dogs, some of them, followed a second kangaroo, but Ada, my greyhound, kept to the old gentleman, and, seeing that he was too strong for her, and fearing lest she might be injured, I jumped off my horse and caught the animal by the tail to stop him from getting away. I put my arms around a sapling tree to prevent his moving, but he was too much for me, and away we went together, he taking me such hops as even Kent never saw. My friend could not move for laughing, and I don't know how the affair would have ended had not my shouts of "Hold him" brought the other dogs back to my assistance, and the forester's death.

Another time I remember we had to drive some cattle to a river about twenty miles from Yambuck, on their way to Portland, as they had been purchased by a butcher there. My clerical friend was going to the same place, and rode behind the cattle with Mr Baxter and the stockman. My place was in front of the bullocks, and as we got to a large swamp they broke in all directions. I found myself at one side of them, and tried to keep them together, but they were bent on going to their old haunts on some hummocks, so I followed and tried to head them. I had done this, for my horse was really a good one and could go the pace when he and I chose, and we had steadied the cattle a little, when the stockman rode up from behind me, thinking I should not be able to come up with the runaways.

"Why, what possesses the cattle, Will; I never knew any so tiresome before?" said I to the man.

"Ah! they knows they has a parson behind 'em, and that always do make 'em wild, ma'am," returned he.

I was told an admirable story in England of a clergyman who was very fond of following the hounds, but always did this to the letter, as he never could afford a horse which would keep up to them. The

Bishop of O— spoke to him about it, and said how sorry he was to hear of his attending balls and joining hunts. "You would think it strange to hear of my doing such things," said his lordship. "My lord, if I mistake not," humbly suggested the young minister, "I saw your name at the last ball at Buckingham Palace." "True, but the sovereign's invitation is an order, you know, and nobody ever saw me in the same room as the dancing," returned the bishop. "And I'll defy anyone, my lord, to say they ever saw me in the same field as the hounds," said the clergyman; to which, I believe, those around bore testimony and smiled.

We had been at Yambuck about three weeks; and it being then the commencement of winter, the small hut, with four regular inmates, was anything but comfortable; and as I could have no female servant, I had to act in that capacity myself. I can fancy in my mind's eye that I see poor Mr Smetham assisting me in my work by cleaning the knives and a pair of brass candlesticks. We were very merry over our work. The other gentlemen went out after the stock, when possible, but one day all were at home, owing to the downpour of rain, and one or other would go constantly to the door, give a look out, and then remark, "What a fine day for young ducks!" About two o'clock, to our astonishment, up drove a lady and gentleman in what is popularly called a "spring cart," but this in which they were seemed anything but that. Their horse, a very jaded one, appeared to relish the stop more than some of us did. The lady was wrapped up in a large plaid shawl, over that a silk cloak, lined with fur, and, to cover all, a policeman's cloak. Of course, they were invited into our mansion, and I took the lady into my room to take off her bonnet. She said she felt much ashamed to trespass on my kindness, that if it cleared up they would try and go on to Belfast, sixteen miles further, and a great deal more, which I listened to without answering. At last I said – "You'll have to sleep on my gridiron; but I promise not to heat it."

She appeared amazed, and told me after that she thought I was quizzing her.

We returned to the sitting-room, and passed a merry evening, and it would have been even merrier had we known that we were then entertaining a couple married that morning. Such a honeymoon!

The superintendent nearly found out the fact by saying to the bridegroom –

"Why Mr Allison, you have not been long making up your mind to marrying; I heard of your intention to get spliced, but thought the day named was not until tomorrow."

Mrs Allison said quickly, "You see we took Portland by surprise, and were married sooner, and are now going to pay some visits."

She told me the secret when we were alone, and I did not divulge it for some days after they left. They were weather-bound for three days with us, and Mrs Allison was distressed when she awoke each morning to see me lying on the floor between a mattress and a feather bed, quite in the German style, only the upper covering was not composed of eider down, and it nearly suffocated me; added to which, Ada, seeing me on the floor, thought it was camping in instead of out, and insisted on lying by my side, and on the bed.

The most laughable thing was to hear the people in the outer room groaning in their sleep with the hardness of their beds, for I had had the floor made very level and clean, and all these unfortunates had between them was a large tarpaulin, which would not soften their position much. I used to call these outcries "the groans of the wounded".

One night, before going to sleep, I heard someone of them say, "Oh! but it is hard! If Mrs Baxter would *only* let me scratch out a place for my hip to rest in I should be grateful." I answered, "Then indeed she won't!"

At the end of three days our young couple went on their way, I should think, rejoicing, to Belfast, and gave us a call on their return home, and very warm thanks they gave me for what they termed my hospitality.

Rolf Boldrewood

YAMBUK

Once upon a time, in a "kingdom by the sea", known to men as Port Fairy, Yambuk was a choice and precious exemplar of an old-fashioned cattle station. What a haven of peace – what a joyful, restful elysium, in these degenerate days of hurry and pressure and progress, and all that – could one but fall upon it. If one could only ride up now to that garden gate, receive the old cordial welcome, and turn his horse into the paddock, what a *fontaine de jouvence* it would be. Should one go and essay the deed? It could hardly be managed. We should not be able to find our way. There would be roads and cockatoo fences, with obtrusive shingled cottages, and wheat-fields, barns, and threshing machines – in short, all the hostile emblems of agricultural settlement, as it is called.

I like it not; I would the plain
Lay in its tall old groves again.

Touching the groves on the opposite side of the Shaw River, down to a bank of which the garden sloped, were broad limestone flats, upon which rose clumps of the beautiful lightwood or hickory trees, some of Australia's noblest growth, when old and umbrageous.

The cottage, low-roofed, veranda protected, was thatched at the early period I recall, the rafters being picked from the strongest of the slender ti-tree saplings in the brush which bordered the river side. The mansion was not imposing, but what of that? The rooms were of fair size, the hospitality refined, and pervading every look and tone;

and we, who in old days were wont to share it on our journeys to and from the metropolis of the district, would not have exchanged it for a palace.

People were not so ambitious then as of late years. Nor was the transcendent future of stock-holding visible to the mental eye, when companies and syndicates would compete for the possession of mammoth holdings, with more sheep and cattle depasturing thereon than we then believed the whole colony could carry.

No; a man with a thousand head of well-bred cattle, on a run capable of holding half as many more, so as to leave a reserve in case of bushfires and bad seasons, was thought fairly endowed with this world's goods. If prudent, he was able to afford himself a trip to Melbourne twice a year or so, and to save money in reason. He generally kept a few brood mares, and so was enabled to rear a superior hackney for himself or friend. As it was not the custom to keep more than a stockman, and one other man for general purposes, he had a reasonable share of daily work cut out for himself.

Yambuk was then an extremely picturesque station, combining within its limits unusual variety of soil and scenery, land and water. The larger grazing portion consisted of open undulating limestone ridges, which ran parallel with the sea beach. The River Shaw, deepening as it debouched into the ocean, was the south-eastern boundary of the run. The country for some miles up its course, past the village of Orford, then only known as The Crossing-place, and along the coast line towards Portland Bay, was originally within the bounds of the Yambuk run.

Beside the limestone ridges were sandy hillocks, thickly covered with the forest oak, which, growing almost to the beach, braved the stern sea blast. Very sound and well sheltered were these low hills, affording most advantageous quarters to the herd in the long, cold winters of the west.

When our dreamy summertime was o'er, a truly Arcadian season, with "blue and golden days", and purple-shadowed eves, wild wrathful gales hurtled over the ocean waste, rioting southward to the pole which lay beyond. Mustering then in bad weather was a special experience. Gathering on the sea-hills, the winter's day darkening fast, a drove of heavy bullocks perhaps lumbering over the sand ridges ahead of us, amid the flying sand and spume, their hoofs in the surf ever and anon, it was a season study, worth riding many a mile to see. No cove or bay restrained the angry waters. A misty cloud-rack formed the horizon, to which stretched the boundless ocean plain of the Pacific, while giant billows, rank on rank, foamed fiercely around, to meet in wrath and impotently rage on the lonely shore below us.

How often has that picture been recalled to me in later years! The sad-toned far-stretching shore – the angry storm-voices of the terrible deep – the little band of horsemen – the lowing, half-wild drove – the red-litten cloud prison, wherein the sun lay dying!

And how pleasant, again, in contrast, when the cattle were yarded and rails securely pegged, to unsaddle and walk into the house, where lights and glowing fires and well-appointed table awaited us, presided over by a Chatelaine, whose soft voice and ever-varied converse, mirthful or mournful, serious or satirical, practical or poetic, never failed to soothe and interest.

Stock riding in those days, half real business and half sport, as we youngsters held it to be, was certainly not one of those games into which, as Lindsay Gordon sings – "No harm could possibly find its way".

Part of the Yambuk run was distinctly dangerous riding. Where the wombats dug their treacherous shafts and galleries, how many a good steed and horseman have I seen overthrown. These peculiar night-feeding animals, akin to the badger of the old country, burrowed much among the coast hummocks. Their open shafts, though not particularly nice to ride among at speed, with your horse's head close behind the hard-pressed steer, were trifling drawbacks compared to the horizontal "drives" into which, when mined too near the surface, your horse's feet often broke. The solid turf would disappear, and, with your horse in a concealed pitfall up to the shoulder, gave a shock that often told tales in a strained joint or a broken collarbone. We fell lightly in those days, however, and, even when our nags rolled over us, rarely seemed to mind the trifling circumstance.

The limestone country, too, held cavities and fissures which caused the fiery steed to tremble and the ardent rider to pale temporarily, when suddenly confronted. At the south-eastern boundary of the run the forests were more dense, the marshes deeper, the country generally more difficult than on the coastline. The ruder portion of the herd "made out" that way, and many a hard gallop they cost us at muster-time. The run had been "taken up" for and on account of Lieutenant Baxter, formerly of Her Majesty's 50th Regiment, about a year before my time, that is in 1843, by Mr George Dumoulin, acting as overseer. This gentleman, a son of one of the early Imperial officials, and presumably of Huguenot descent, was a most amusing and energetic person. Inhering the *legèrté* of his Gallic ancestors, his disposition led him to be *toujours gai*, even under the most unpromising circumstances. A capital manager in the restricted sense then most appreciated, he spent no money, save on the barest necessaries, and did all the stock-keeping himself, with the occasional aid of a black boy. When I first set eyes on Yambuk head station, there were but two small thatched huts, no garden, no horse-paddock, and a very indifferent stockyard. The rations had rather run out lately – there was no salt, for one thing – and as the establishment had been living upon fresh veal for a fortnight, it was impressed upon me, forcibly, that no one there would look at fillets and cutlets of that "delicate meat that the soul loveth", under ordinary culinary conditions, for at least a year afterwards.

Mr Dumoulin, though wonderfully cheery as a general rule, was subject to occasional fits of despondency. They were dark, in proportion to his generally high standard of spirits. When this lowered tone set in, he generally alluded to his want of success hitherto in life, the improbability of his attaining to a station of his own, the easiest thing in those days if you had a very little money or stock. But capital being scarce and credit wanting for the use of enterprising speculators who had nothing but pluck and experience, it was hard, mostly impossible, to procure that necessary fulcrum. Regarding those things, and mourning over past disappointments, he generally wound up by affirming that "all the world would come right, but that poor Dumoulin would be left on his – beam ends – at the last". And yet what splendid opportunities lay in the womb of Time for him, for all of us. When Captain Baxter and his wife came from their New England home to take possession and live at Yambuk "for good", there was no necessity for Mr Dumoulin to abide there longer, the profits of a station of that size rarely permitting the proprietor and overseer to jointly administer. When the gold came we heard of him in a position of responsibility and high pay, but whether he rose to his proper status, or that malignant destiny refused promotion, we have no knowledge. He was a good specimen of the pioneers to whom Australia owes so much – brave to recklessness, patient of toil, hardy, and full of endurance – a good bushman and first-class stock-rider.

The captain, as he was generally called, and Mrs Baxter drove tandem overland the whole distance from New England to Yambuk, encamping regularly with a few favourite horses and dogs. Their journal, faithfully kept, of each day's journey and the road events was a most interesting one, and would show that even before the days of Miss Bird and Miss Gordon-Comyn there were lady travellers who dared the perils of the trackless wilderness, and its wilder denizens. A fine horse-woman, and passionately fond of her dumb favourites, Mrs Baxter was as happy in the company of her nice old roan Arab Kaffir, the beautiful greyhound Ada, and the collie Rogue, as many more *exigeantes*, though not more gently nurtured dames, would have been with all the materials of a society picnic.

One advantage of this sort of overland-route work is that when the goal is reached the humblest surroundings avail for a home, all luxury and privilege being comprehended in the idea that you have not to "move on" next day.

Once arrived, the abode *en permanence* is the great matter for thankfulness. The building may be unfinished and inadequate, not boasting even of a chimney, yet carpets and rugs are spread as by

Moslems in a caravansarai, and all thank Allah fervently in that we are permitted to stay and abide there for evermore.

With the arrival of the master and mistress speedy alterations for the better took place. The cottage was built – an Indian bungalow in architecture – with wooden walls, the roof and verandas thatched with the long tussock grass. A garden with fruit trees and flowers was organised, the fertile coffee-coloured loam responding eagerly. Furniture arrived, including a piano and other lady adjuncts. A detached kitchen was constructed. Mr Dumoulin's "improvements" were abandoned to the stockmen, and the new era of Yambuk was inaugurated, far pleasanter in every way, in my opinion, than any which have succeeded it in the land. The locale certainly had many advantages. It was only twelve miles from that fascinatingly pleasant little country town of Port Fairy – we didn't call it Belfast then, and didn't want to. The road was good, and admitted of riding in and out the same day. As it was a seaport town, stores were cheap, and everything could be procured from Melbourne or Sydney. There was then not an acre of land sold west of the Shaw before you reached Portland, and very little to the east, except immediately round the town. One cannot imagine a more perfect country residence, having regard to the period, and the necessities of the early squatting community. The climate was delightful, modified Tasmanian weather prevailed, nearly as cold in winter, quite sufficiently bracing but without frost, the proximity to the coast so providing. English fruits grew and bore splendidly. Finer apples and pears, gooseberries and cherries, no rejoicing schoolboy ever revelled in. The summers were surpassingly lovely, cooled with the breezes that swept over the long rollers of the Pacific, and lulling the sleeper to rest with the measured roll of the surge upon the broad beaches which stretched from the Moyne to Portland Bay. Talking of beaches, what a glorious sensation is that of riding over one at midnight!

> Ah, well do I remember
> That loved and lonely hour

when a party of us started one moonlight night to ride from Port Fairy to Portland, for the purpose of boarding an emigrant vessel, from which we hoped to be able to hire men-servants and maid-servants, then, as now, exceeding scarce commodities. My grand little horse Hope had carried me in from home thirty miles that day, but, fed and rested, he was not particular about a few miles further. We dined merrily, and at something before ten o'clock set forth. Lloyd Rutledge, who was my companion, rode his well-known black hackney and plater Molonglo Jack. As we started at a canter along the Portland road – the low moon nearly full, just rising, the night warm and cloudless – it was an Arabian night, one for romance and adventure. The other horses had been in their stalls all day, but as I touched my lower bridle rein my gallant little steed – one of the most awful pullers that ever funked a Christian [fail to take a jump] – rose on his hind legs and made as though about to jump on to the adjoining horses. This was only a trick I had taught him; at a sign he would rear and plunge "like all possessed", but it showed that he was ready for business, and I did not fear trying conclusions with the best horse then. Like Mr Sawyer's Jack-a-dandy, he would have won the Derby if it had not been more than half a mile. He did win the Port Fairy Steeplechase next year, over stiff timber, with Johnny Gorrie on his back, and in very good company, too.

Away we went. The sands lay some miles past Yambuk. When we rode down upon them, what wonders lay before us. The tide was out. For leagues upon leagues stretched the ocean shore – a milk-white beach, wide as a parade-ground and level as a tennis-court, and so hard under foot that our horses' hoofs rang sharp and clear; excited by the night, the moon, the novelty, they tore at their bits and raced one another in a succession of heats, which it took all our skill, aided by two effective double bridles of the Weymouth pattern, to moderate. As for our two companions they were left miles behind.

We were at the turn just ahead of Lady Julia Percy Island, which lay on the slumbering ocean's breast like some cloud fallen from the sky, or an enchanted isle, where the fairy princess might be imprisoned until the Viking's galley arrived, or the prince was conveniently cast away on the adjacent rocks.

Far as eye could see lay the illimitable ocean plain, star-brightened here and there. Southward a lengthening silver pathway rippled in the moon-gleam, shimmering and glowing far away towards the soft cloudland of the horizon. Tiny capes ran in from the fringe of forest, and barred the line of vision from time to time. Sweeping around these, our excited horses speeding as they had become winged, we entered upon a fresh bay, another stretch of beach fitted for fairy revels. While over all the broad and yellow moon shed such a flood of radiance that every twig and every leaf in the smallest tree was visible. So still was the night that even "the small ripple split upon the beach, most like unto the cream of your champagne", fell distinctly upon the ear.

As the pale dawn cloud rose in the east, the slumbering ocean began to stir and moan. A land breeze came sighing forth from the dense forest like a reproachful dryad as we charged the steep side of Lookout Hill, and saw the roofs of the town of Portland before us. It was a longish stage, but our horses still pressed as gaily forward as if the distance had been passed in a dream. We had no time to sentimentalise. Labour was scarce. We stabled our good horses, and transferred ourselves to a waterman's boat. When the employers of Portland came on board in leisurely fashion hours later, the flower of the farm labourers were under written agreement to proceed to Belfast. It rather opened the eyes of the Portlanders, whom, in the sauciness of our youth, we, of the rival township who called William Rutledge our mercantile chief, were wont to hold cheap. They needed servants for farm and station, as did we, but there was no help for it; they had to content themselves with what were left.

Personally, I had done well. The brothers Michael and Patrick Horan – two fine, upstanding Carlow men as one would wish to see – were indentured safely to me for a year. Many a day they served me well in the aftertime. Their brother-in-law, with his wife, as a married couple, and a smart "colleen" about sixteen, a younger sister, came with them. It was a "large order", but all our hands had cleared for Ballarat and Forest Creek; we had hardly a soul in the place but the overseer and myself. These immigrants were exactly of the class we wanted. I know a place where a few such shiploads would be of great and signal utility now. They were willing, well-behaved, and teachable. I broke in Pat Horan to the stock-riding business, and within a twelvemonth he could ride a buck-jumper, rope, brand, and draft with any old hand in the district. He repeatedly took large drafts of cattle to market in sole charge, and was always efficient and trustworthy. Mick showed a gift for ploughing and bullock-driving, and generally preferred farm work. They both remained with me for years – Pat, indeed, till the station was sold. They are thriving farmers, I believe, within a few miles of the spot, at the present day. I waited until nightfall, making arrangements to receive our *engagés* when they should arrive in Port Fairy, and then mounted Hope, in order to ride the thirty miles which lay between me and Squattlesea Mere. The old horse was as fresh as paint, and landed me there well on the hither side of midnight. One feels inclined to say there are no such horses nowadays, but there is a trifling difference in the rider's "form", I fancy, which accounts for much of this apparent equine degeneracy. Anyhow, Hope was a plum, and so was his mother before him. Didn't she give me a fall over a fence at Yambuk one day, laming me for a week and otherwise knocking me about – the only time I ever knew her make a mistake? But wasn't a lady looking on, and wouldn't I have broken my neck cheerfully, or any other important vertebra, for the sake of being pitied and petted after the event?

Soon after the gold discovery, and the consequent rise in prices, Captain Baxter was tempted to sell Yambuk with a good herd of cattle, and so departed for the metropolis. Then our society began to break up – its foundations to loosen. People got so rich that they voted station life a bore, and promoted their stockmen or put overseers in charge. Many of these were worthy people; but the charm of bush life had departed when the proprietor no longer greeted you on dismounting, and there was no question of books or music or cheery talk with which to while away the evening. And thinking over those pleasant homes in the dear old forest days, when one was always sure of sympathy and society, I know one wayworn pilgrim who will always recur to the *bon vieux temps* whereof a goodly proportion – sometimes for one reason, sometimes for another – was passed at Yambuk.

4

Travelling

EDITOR'S NOTE

Both Elizabeth Macarthur and Eliza Brown in part 3, "Settling Down", provide examples of one of the effects of distance on life in nineteenth-century Australia – the extended delays in communicating with the outside world. Australia was both a long way from Europe, and an immense land mass. The "tyranny of distance" was felt whenever people needed to travel. John Oxley, writing to Governor Macquarie from Bathurst, records the difficulties faced by early explorers, encountering rivers which unexpectedly dried up or flowed in the wrong direction. Ten years later, William Dumaresq wrote a series of letters for the *Australian* newspaper describing a ride to Bathurst – it was still far from being a pleasure trip. Such, ostensibly, is the reason why Richard Rowe, writing as "Peter Possum", journeys to the Hunter Valley. Actually, like Henry Lawson travelling to Bourke later in the century, he is on the lookout for literary "copy". "Possum" uses a whole series of conveyances, going by cab down to the harbour, then by steamer to Maitland. He intends to catch the mail coach to Singleton but falls in with a friend at the inn. Like several of Lawson's heroes, he leaves quietly the next day without paying his bill and hoofs it across country.

Rowe remarks that "Travelling in Australia is sadly monotonous". Such was certainly not the experience of Louisa Atkinson. "Cabbage-Tree Hollow" is one of many accounts of bush rambles and excursions she published in Sydney newspapers during the 1860s. All are full of the close observations of her environment, particularly its plant life, which are also found in her excellent sketches and drawings. "A Night Adventure in the Bush", more fictional in form though, she claims, equally true, gives a telling picture of the continuing difficulties of making any major expedition through the bush.

The contrasts between those who travelled for pleasure and those who did it to blaze a trail are also to be seen in the remaining little-known items in "Travelling". Edmund Marin La Meslée's account of touring Australia near the end of the century has been preferred to the better-known travel works of Anthony Trollope and Mark Twain. David Blair's travel diary – actually a series of letters sent to children back in Melbourne – describes the mixed blessings of travelling by rail from Melbourne to Sydney. Once in Sydney he makes many interesting comments on the changes since he first saw the city in the 1850s, and on his much admired friend Henry Parkes. Ernest Giles and Henry Lawson do their travelling in less comfort. A comparison between Lawson's letters to his aunt and the travel sketches based on the same trip provides insights into how life interacts with literature – how "real" experience undergoes progressive fictionalisation as it is written and rewritten.

John Oxley

LETTER TO GOVERNOR MACQUARIE

Bathurst
August 30, 1817

Sir,

I have the honour to acquaint your excellency with my arrival at this place last evening, together with the persons comprising the expedition to the westward, which your excellency was pleased to place under my direction.

Your excellency is already informed of my proceedings up to the 30th of April. The limits of a letter will not permit me to enter at large into the occurrences of nineteen weeks; and as I shall have the honour of waiting on your excellency in a few days, I trust you will in the meantime have the goodness to accept the summary account which I now offer.

I proceeded down the Lachlan in company with the boats until the 12th of May, the country rapidly descending, until the waters of the river rising to a level with it, and dividing themselves into numerous branches, inundated the land to the west and north-west, and prevented any farther progress in that direction, the river itself being lost among the marshes. Up to this point, it had received no accession of waters from either side; but on the contrary, was constantly dissipating itself in lagoons and swamps.

The impossibility of proceeding farther in conjunction with the boats being evident, I determined upon mature deliberation to haul them up; and divesting ourselves of everything that could possibly be spared, proceed with the horses loaded with the additional provisions from the boats, on such a course towards the coast as would intersect any stream that might arise from the divided waters of the Lachlan.

In pursuance of this plan, I quitted the river on the 17th of May, taking a south-west course towards Cape Northumberland, as the best adapted to answer my intended purpose. I will not here detail the difficulties and privations we experienced in passing through a barren and desolate country, without any water but such rain as was found remaining in holes and the crevices of rocks. I continued this course until the 9th of June, when having lost two horses through fatigue and want, and the others being in a deplorable condition, I changed our course to north, along a range of lofty hills running in that direction, as they afforded the only means of procuring water until we should fall in with some stream. On this course I continued until the 23rd of June, when we again fell in with a stream, which we had at first some difficulty to recognise as the Lachlan, it being little larger than one of the branches of it where we quitted it on the 17th of May.

I did not hesitate a moment to pursue the course of this stream, not that the nature of the country or its own appearance in any manner indicated that it would become navigable, or even permanent; but I was unwilling that the smallest doubt should remain whether any navigable waters fall westward into the sea, between the limits pointed out in my instructions.

I continued along the banks of the stream until the 8th of July, it having taken during this period a westerly direction, and passed through a perfectly level country, barren in the extreme, and being evidently at periods entirely under water. To this point the river had been gradually diminishing, and spreading its waters over stagnated lagoons and morasses, without receiving any tributary stream that we knew of, during the whole extent of its course. The banks were not more than three feet high, and the marks of flood on the shrubs and bushes showed that at times it rose between two and three feet higher, causing the whole country to become a marsh, and altogether uninhabitable.

Farther progress westward, had it been possible, was now useless, as there was neither hill nor rising ground of any kind within the compass of our view, which was bounded only by the horizon in every quarter, and entirely devoid of timber, unless a few dimunitive gum trees on the very edge of the stream might be so termed. The water in the bed of the lagoon, as it might now be properly denominated, was stagnant, its breadth about twenty feet, and the heads of grass growing in it showed it to be about three feet deep.

This unlooked for and truly singular termination of a river, which we had anxiously hoped, and reasonably expected, would have led to a far different conclusion, filled us with the most painful sensations.

We were full five hundred miles west of Sydney, and nearly in its latitude; and it had taken us ten weeks of unremitted exertion to proceed so far. The nearest part of the coast about Cape Bernoulli, had it been accessible, was distant above one hundred and eighty miles. We had demonstrated beyond a doubt, that no river could fall into the sea between Cape Otway and Spencer's Gulf, at least none deriving its waters from the eastern coast; and that the country south of the parallel of 34 degrees, and west of the meridian 147. 30. E. was uninhabitable, and useless for all the purposes of civilised men.

It now became my duty to make our remaining resources as extensively useful to the colony as our circumstances would allow; these were much diminished: an accident which happened to one of the boats in the outset of the expedition had deprived us of one-third of our dry provisions, of which we had originally a supply for only eighteen weeks, and we had been consequently for some time living on a reduced ration of two quarts of flour per man, per week. To return to the depot by the route we had come would have been as useless as impossible; and, seriously considering the spirit of your excellency's instructions, I determined, after the most mature deliberation, to take such a route, on our return, as would I hoped comport with your excellency's views, had our then situation ever been contemplated.

Returning up the Lachlan, I recommenced the survey of it from the point at which it was made on the 23rd of June, intending to continue up its banks until its connexion with the marshes where we quitted it on the 17th of May was satisfactorily established, as also to ascertain if any streams might have escaped our research. The connexion with all the points of the survey previously determined, was completed between the 19th of July and the 3rd of August. In the space passed over within that period, the river had divided itself into various branches, and formed three fine lakes, which, with one near the termination of our journey westward, were the only considerable pieces of water we had yet seen; and I now estimated that the river, from the place where it was first made by Mr Evans, had run a course, including all its windings, of upwards of one thousand two hundred miles; a length altogether unprecedented, when the single nature of the river is considered, and that its original source constitutes its only supply of water during that extent.

Crossing at this point, it was my intention to take a north-east course to intersect the country, and if possible to ascertain what had become of the Macquarie River, which it was clear had never joined the Lachlan. This course led us through a country to the full as bad as any we had yet seen, and equally devoid of water, the personal want of which again much distressed us. On the 7th of August the scene began to change, and the country to assume a very different aspect; we were now quitting the neighbourhood of the Lachlan, and had passed to the north-east of the high range of hills, which on this parallel bounds the low country to the north of that river. To the north-west and north the country was high and open, with good forest land; and on the 10th we had the satisfaction of falling in with the first stream running northerly. This renewed our hopes of soon falling in with the Macquarie, and we continued upon the same course, occasionally inclining to the eastward until the 19th, passing through a fine luxuriant country, well watered; crossing in that space of time nine streams, having a northerly course through rich valleys, the country in every direction being moderately high and open, and generally as fine as can be imagined.

No doubt remained upon our minds that those streams fell into the Macquarie, and to view it before it received such an accession, was our first wish. On the 19th, we were gratified by falling in with a river running through a most beautiful country, and which I should have been well contented to have believed to be the river we were in search of. Accident led us down this stream about a mile, when we were surprised by its junction with a river coming from the south, of such width and magnitude as to dispel all doubts as to this last being the river we had so long anxiously looked for. Limited as our resources were, we could not resist the temptation which this beautiful country offered us, to remain two days upon the junction of these rivers, for the purpose of examining its vicinity to as great an extent as possible.

Our examination increased the satisfaction we had previously felt; as far as the eye could reach, in every direction, a rich and picturesque country extended, abounding in limestone, slate, good timber, and every other requisite which could render an uncultivated country desirable.

The soil cannot be excelled; whilst a noble river of the first magnitude affords the means of conveying its productions from one part of the country to the other. Where we quitted, its course was northerly, and we were then north of the parallel of Port Stephens, being in latitude 32. 32. 45. S., and 148. 52. E. longitude.

It appeared to me that the Macquarie had taken a north-north-west course from Bathurst, and that it must have received immense accessions of water in its course from that place. We viewed it at a period best calculated to form an accurate judgment of its importance, when it was neither swelled by floods beyond its natural and usual height, nor contracted within its proper limits by summer droughts; of its magnitude when it should have received the streams we had crossed, independently of any which it may receive from the east (which, from the boldness and height of the country, I presume must be at least as many as from the south), some idea may be formed when I inform your excellency, that at this point it exceeded in breadth and apparent depth the Hawkesbury at Windsor, and that many of the reaches were of grander and more extended proportion than the admired one on the Nepean River, from the Warragamba to Emu Plains.

Resolving to keep as near the river as possible during the remainder of our course to Bathurst, and endeavour to ascertain at least on the west side what waters fall into it, on the 22nd we proceeded up the river, and, between the point quitted and Bathurst, crossed the sources of numberless streams all running into the Macquarie; two of them were nearly as large as that river itself is at Bathurst. The country whence all these streams derive their source was mountainous and irregular, and appeared equally so on the east side of the Macquarie.

This description of country extended to the immediate vicinity of Bathurst, but to the west of those lofty ranges the land was broken into low grassy hills and fine valleys, watered by rivulets rising on the western side of the mountains, which on their eastern side pour their waters directly into the Macquarie. These westerly streams appeared to me to join that which at first sight I had taken for the Macquarie, and, when united, to fall into it at the point on which it was first discovered on the 19th instant. We reached this place last evening, without a single accident having occurred to any one of the party during the whole progress of the expedition; which from this point has encircled within the parallels of 34. 30. S. and 32. S., and between the meridians of 149. 29. 30. E. and 143. 30. E. a space of nearly one thousand miles. I shall hasten to lay before your excellency the journals, charts, and drawings, explanatory of the various occurrences of our diversified route; amply gratified if our exertions should appear to your excellency commensurate with your expectations, and the ample means which your care and liberality placed at my disposal.

I feel the most particular pleasure in informing your excellency of the obligations I am under to Mr Evans, the deputy surveyor, for his able advice and cordial co-operation throughout the expedition; and, as far as his previous researches had extended, the accuracy and fidelity of his narrative was fully established.

It would perhaps appear presumptuous in me to hazard an opinion upon the merits of persons engaged in a pursuit in which I have little knowledge; the extensive and valuable collection of plants found by Mr A. Cunningham, the King's botanist, and Mr C. Frazer, the colonial botanist, will best evince to your excellency the unwearied industry and zeal bestowed in the discovery and preservation of them; in every other respect they also merit the highest praise.

From the nature of the greater part of the country passed over, our mineralogical collection is but small. Mr S. Parr did as much as could be done in that branch, and throughout endeavoured to render himself as useful as possible.

Of the men on whom the chief care of the horses and baggage devolved, it is impossible to speak in too high terms. Their conduct in periods of considerable privation, was such as must redound to their credit; and their orderly, regular, and obedient behaviour could not be exceeded. It may principally be attributed to their care and attention, that we lost only three horses; and that, with the exception of the loss of the dry provisions already mentioned, no other accident happened during the course of the expedition. I most respectfully beg leave to recommend them to your excellency's favourable notice and consideration.

I trust your excellency will have the goodness to correct any omissions or inaccuracies that may appear in this letter: the messenger setting out immediately will not allow me to revise or correct it.

I have the honour to remain, with the greatest respect,
Your excellency's most obedient and humble servant,
(Signed), J. Oxley, Surveyor General.

To His Excellency, Governor Macquarie, etc. etc. etc.

William Dumaresq

A RIDE TO BATHURST

Letter IV

I don't like the man who will travel from Dan to Beersheba, and tell us nothing. In a country like New South Wales, this disposition is particularly to be regretted, because everything is new, even to the high road; and what little knowledge we may acquire of our common country, should, in my opinion, be thrown into the general fund. That old gentlemanly vice, avarice, that last infirmity of man, is bad enough, when merely confined to cash, but an avarice of knowledge is hateful and injurious. But all our knowledge of this fine country is little, and might be put in a nut-shell; and when we come to think of the interior, we know no more of it than we do of the moon! "We are perfectly astonished", said the officers of the French squadron, when they lay in Port Jackson a year ago, "at your superb country." "What" replied a gentleman, "is it that most excites your surprise?" "That you have been so long in it, and know so little about it," was the severe answer. It was a just reproof, and ought to sink deep into the minds of those, who, by offering rewards of a few thousand acres of land, would set alive the spirit of discovery – draw the whole eyes of Europe to our shores – redeem the character of our country men from the reproach of the Frenchmen – and by thus fostering a laudable enterprise, secure to themselves an imperishable name! But it is no use talking – nothing will be done on a grand scale, the government hands are too full of business. Like the repentance of sailors in a storm,

They vow to amend their lives and yet they don't,
Because if drowned they *can't* – if saved they *won't*.

Collet's Inn is, I am sorry to say, only halfway to Bathurst, and bad as the preceding half was, the latter part of the journey is the worst. The vale of Clywdd reminds one of the valley of Bastan, in the pass of Ronscesvalles. But we must not forget mine host of the Golden Fleece and give him the *go by* in this way. I assure you there is only one better Inn in the whole Colony, for it is warm, comfortable, and commodious in the *inside*, as it is beautiful and picturesque *without*. The house is neat in the extreme, and the brightness, order and almost Dutch cleanliness of the kitchen pleased and surprised me. To arrive at Collet's, is like passengers going ashore from a weary voyage, everything appears *à couleur de rose*. There was just light enough the evening we got in, to see to shave and make ourselves comfortable after the filthy night at Springwood. Our horses were delivered over to the hostler, with perfect confidence that they would each get a belly full, for we were in a land of plenty; there was no necessity to stand by, *stroking their tails*, as somebody recommended in another place, while they devoured their thimble full of maize: – their chafed backs were well bathed in salt and water, and we adjourned to the house, and *discussed* a supper in the midst of the Blue Mountains, as good as we could have had, for aught I know, at the Blue Boar in Holborn. It was an American sort of supper, including excellent hyson tea, double refined sugar, plenty of cream and butter, as hard as cheese, and the water crystal itself. When I saw such a plenty of good furniture, glass and earthenware, I at first wondered how such fragile furniture could have been brought so safely across the mountains, but felt no surprise as soon as I heard that the *lime* itself of which the house was built was brought all the way from Parramatta, a distance of seventy miles; and of course when they can bring lime, they may as well bring loaf sugar. After supper and drinking the health of our Sydney friends, male and female, for it was Saturday night, we finished our cigars under the veranda, though rather chilly, and amused ourselves by listening to a man in the kitchen, who was busy reading aloud a ten day's old *Australian*, to a party round him. But though ten days old, it was new to them, for it had just arrived *in a dray*, such is the admirable state of our internal communications in New South Wales. After excellent beds, we resumed our journey in the morning. I would fain have stopped, but time would not permit – besides all this good accommodation is not had for nothing; some people thinking the charges high at this house under the hill, though for my part, I thought them extremely moderate, everything considered. I thought of the conceit once scribbled on a pane of glass at a similar place;

Our life is like a winter's day,
Some only breakfast, and away –

Others to dinner stay, and are well fed;
The oldest man but sups and goes to bed.
Hard is his fate, who lingers out the day;
Who *goes the soonest*, has the least to pay!

And away we cantered for Cox's River. Here was the first granite I had seen in the Colony, a granite sand and small particles of quartz forming the dust of the road. Wallurawang district lies to the right going from Collet's to Cox's River, and is said to be a fine valley for sheep and cattle, and a much shorter road to Bathurst than the one at present used over Mount Blaxland. There are some very respectable settlers in the valley of Wallurawang, whose ample scope of pasture is not likely to be curtailed for many years, unless the road proposed by Sir Thomas Brisbane, should be commenced along the valley. Five or six miles brought us to Cox's River, where we had two most dangerous fords to pass the horses over, owing to the deep holes of the first stream and the loose stones of the main river. The wreck of former bridges was lying on the spot, and apparently very old. The two fords are not a stone's throw from one another, and between them is the military station or barrack occupied by a non-commissioned officer, and ten or twelve men on the 57th under the command of a subaltern. Half a dozen men from the staff corps might repair these bridges, I should think, in a fortnight. I observed several soldiers belonging to the station enjoying themselves in perfect repose on benches, outside their neat whitewashed cottage, like so many pensioners at Chelsea, and while they sat looking at us almost breaking our horses' legs through the ford, I wished that the active officer in charge of roads and bridges had been with us, on a hundred guinea horse. This is the last stream that runs towards Sydney, and whose estuary is ascertained. Cox's River falling into the Warrugamba, into the Nepean, the Nepean into the Hawkesbury, and the Hawkesbury into the Pacific Ocean at Broken Bay. All the other rivers or streams beyond this, run the other way, into the interior of the country, refusing to have anything to do with the sea coast, and with the most unfilial, provoking obstinacy, deserting old father Ocean and his saline embraces, for the muddy repose of some mediterranean puddle! *Credat Judæus*. I wonder that some wag has not set on a foot a report that the Macquarie was met with in a certain meridian going up a hill, at the rate of seven knots an hour. This would remind one of a song that Theodore Hook sings, beginning,

Come, come, says Mrs Noah,
The ark is at the door, etc., etc., etc.

The road from Cox's River is good enough, but every quarter of an hour you must dismount, either to walk your horse *up* or *down* the hills, which are tremendous, and follow one another in rapid succession. Mount Blaxland is long and steep, and the road is taken over the very summit. The view does not repay you for the trouble of ascending, but ascend you must, or stop and starve, for it is a desolate and barren place. The high range of the Carmarthen Mountains bounds the horizon to the north, and exhibits three lofty peaks, the most remarkable of which is called Evans's Crown, after the deputy surveyor of Van Diemen's Land, who was despatched by Macquarie across the mountains on the return of Mr Lawson's party, to continue the discoveries of those enterprising gentlemen. The other two peaks are severally named Mount Lawson and Mount Wentworth. At this part of the road we met two government teams with wool, from his Majesty's farm at Bathurst. The steep road was swept clean like a sanded floor, by the tall trees tied with a chain behind the drays. I was now convinced that these hills required the resistance of very large trees, or the whole concern, bullocks and all, would go headlong to destruction. An occasional manna tree relieved the monotony of the journey over Mount Blaxland, and as I stopped to pick up the little pieces that had fallen underneath, I was agreeably surprised to find it real manna of commerce, of a very agreeable sweetness. It is as white as snow, in little stalactic drops, and is the concrete juice of a tree known here by the name of ash, or white bastard gum. In Sicily, according to Captain Smyth, the manna is produced from the *fraxinus ornus* by horizontal incisions in the bark at certain seasons of the year. It is said to be cathartic; but is found in the Bathurst country in quantities very inconsiderable and is merely a curiosity. One feels curious to know if this were the manna of the ancient Iraelites; and if so, how its peculiar medical qualities were overcome. According to subsequent observation near Bathurst, I felt satisfied no tree could yield daily more than one tablespoonful, even in the height of the season, which is in the three months of autumn; therefore I am of the opinion it could not have been an Australian ash, that afforded the Jews of old such a wonderful supply, who, according to Scheuchzer, consumed 91,466 bushels every day, for forty years, and as no manna fell on Saturdays, they would have to collect on Fridays twice the quantity, or 188,932 bushels, of which, at 56 lbs to the bushel, would be 4,723 tons; certainly a very large produce. This is not the place, however, to pursue the enquiry. After passing Jock's Bridge, and Antonio's Creek, about 25 miles of fatiguing ride, we left the high road, for the purpose of giving the horses a bite of grass, on the bank of the Fish River, and a very pretty spot we found, the first of the kind we had seen all the day. We lay down on the sward, and enjoyed our hour's rest and luncheon as much as the horses did theirs. If I had been inclined to give a sermon in reverence of the day, I certainly would have chosen for the text, that beautiful poetic verse of the 23rd psalm –

He maketh me to lie down in green pastures;
He leadeth me beside the still waters.

We still had 25 miles to ride to Bathurst, and therefore, as soon as we had rested our little hour, the saddles were adjusted, and we crossed the rapid Fish River through the ford, the old bridge having been here also carried away, and become unserviceable some years, apparently. There is a road party stationed here; it is always with a feeling of pleasure that I pass these useful hands. In my frequent excursions through the Colony, the utmost order and respect has been observable, in whatever direction I have fallen in with them. – The Fish River Hill is the worst hill from Sydney to Bathurst. We began to ascend immediately we left the ford; and never having been at Bathurst before, I could not help saying to myself *"this Bathurst ought to be a fine place to come all this dreadful way to see it!"* The sight of a four-rail fence, in Sidmouth Valley, after this weary hill, was the first symptom of humanity, for nearly *ninety* miles, and gave me unfeigned pleasure. We had now passed the Blue Mountains, and were in a tolerable country – thinly timbered, but hilly – affording good pasture on the high grounds for sheep, and presenting in the valley a vegetable mould, ten or twelve feet deep, as black as jet, resting on yellow ochre, dry and friable, containing mica and iron pyrites. A crop of excellent wheat had not long been off the ground and it was pleasing to see this first settler, upwards of 80 miles from Emu Plains, with a beautiful new cottage and substantial barns, outhouses, fencing, etc. The adjoining farm, of 4,000 acres, is the property of a respectable merchant in Sydney, and has a very large commodious cottage on it, with good out-buildings, etc. The country now improves every mile, and seven or eight miles on this side of Bathurst Plains you might suppose yourself once more in Leon or Estremadura. *Downs* would give you a better idea of this country in the neighbourhood of Bathurst, than the word Plains. There is said to be 30,000 acres of this open exposed country upon which there is not a tree or shrub as high as the candle by which I am writing. It is far, however, from being a plain country, as it rises in numerous swelling hills, of a dry silicious earth, by no means deep, bearing a sweet but scanty grass, which at this hot season of the year, and after an unusual drought, was a good deal burnt up. The farms of the Messrs Lawson, Cox and Hassal appeared all to great advantage, and with those of Messrs Street, Mackenzie and West, are calculated to impress the visitor with a very favourable opinion of Bathurst. If a man could be put down here in a balloon, or find some royal road to the country, without having anything to do with the Blue Mountains, he would hug himself with a constant satisfaction, and desire to know no more. The road was good enough for a coach and four, some miles before we arrived at Bathurst; the country resembling, I thought, the unenclosed wheat lands in the Isle of Thanet. On our right was Wimborne Dale, and the lofty well clothed mountains called the Ridge, where the settlers procure most of their timber for building, fencing etc. The greatest number of respectable settlers are found in this direction. On the left of the road are a number of small thirty and fifty acre farms, belonging to small settlers, formerly prisoners, whose white-washed houses and glazed windows, good gardens, and golden coloured stacks of wheat indicate a degree of industry and ease that was pleasing to contemplate. The river Macquarie ran close to us, at the bottom of these little farms, broad, clear, and rapid, and excited the most lively sensations, like the Niger of Africa, by reason of its unknown course. The fatigues of the journey were now over, and we were really in a christian country – the climate mild and delightful – the prospect cheerful and extensive – the sheep returning to the fold seemed healthy and happy, and awakened thoughts of abundance – of content – of thankfulness. The gorgeous sun was settling in a robe of gold, over that undiscovered country west of the Macquarie, and the scene was altogether worthy of a Claude. Here finishes, as this celebrated river, this modern Jordan, the fine property of the settlers; all beyond is the Government's! which has hitherto been considered too good to give away. You may look at the heavenly country, but touch not! taste not! handle not! has been, 'till the present moment, the tenor of all the General Orders upon this subject. The settlement or *city* is on the Government side of the river; and is the most paltry, contemptible thing imaginable. "Where's Bathurst?" I frequently enquired, and when we crossed the ford, where so many men have been *drowned for the want of a bridge*, and was told "this is Bathurst", I positively burst out laughing. Is the Majesty of Great Britain reduced to this?" "Oh! tell it not in Gath, mention it not in the streets of Ascalon! lest the ungodly triumph! lest the uncircumcised rejoice!" After hearing and reading so much of Bathurst, eight or nine years ago, at various bibliopoles, in *guid Auld Reekie*, I did not expect in the year of 1827 to find it something more than the mere "*magni nominis umbra*". My surprise equalled that of Tityrus, although very differently excited.

Urbem quam dicunt (*Bathurst*) Melibœe, putavi
Stultus ego, huic nostræ similem –

but I was greviously mistaken, the mere spot properly called Bathurst, or the settlement, being the wretchedest place in New South Wales, whereas if given out in allotments to settlers, it might soon become one of the finest. – In justice to the present government, however, it must be admitted, that the supreme folly of these overgrown government establishments, *in the heart of the settlers*, is not to be laid at their door. The system was a favourite one with Macquarie, and has extended its withering influence, like the Sirocco, all the way from the coast to this western country. I am happy to say, it never extended to Hunter's River. If these establishments were broken up as the settlers extended, and arrived, and the government marched off two or three hundred miles into the interior wilderness, like General Boon in the backwoods of America, the system would be excellent; and I would fain hope it will be adopted, under the present administration. I have told you before, and I now tell you again, that for so limited a population, there is not a shrewder or a richer people in the world than the people of New South Wales – more enthusiastically fond of the liberty and institutions of their fatherland; and where the foundations are being laid, quietly but certainly, of such numerous and princely fortunes from the growth of wool. Like Madeira wine, the voyage tends to improve all emigrants to this country, added to which, when here, you find so many men cleverer than yourself, that the mind is compelled to reflection, and we are glad to ask advice. In Bristol 'tis said men sleep with one eye open. "I'se York," is an old caution – and "there's only one to take in, after *doing* an Aberdeen man," is a common saying; but I assure you, these are all children; *this* is the *finish*, and without any jocular allusion, I speak it to their praise. No wonder then that, politically speaking, the people here have hitherto been always *in advance* of their government; though, we flatter ourselves, the day is now arrived when the government will be *in advance of them* – The settlers at Bathurst are all doing well, notwithstanding the disadvantages of their great distance, and mountain road. How can it be otherwise in a country so peculiarly adapted to the growth of fine wool as New South Wales. – But I must defer any further details 'till the next vessel. In the meantime, in laying these hasty scrawls before the respectable society, who have done me the honour, by your letter of the 10th of Jan. to elect me an unworthy member, you will apologise for their having appeared in our only *readable* Colonial paper, *The Australian*, and say my motive for so doing was two fold; first, that it might incite others in the Colony to follow the example; and, secondly, if any few grains of wheat might be mixed up in so much chaff, they might be the more readily found by being in print.

Richard Rowe

A TRIP UP THE HUNTER

How I Started for Muswellbrook and Only Got to Maitland

"Not there, not there, my child." – Mrs Hemans.

Up and down the steep, dimly-lighted streets that lie between Wynyard Square and the water, my cab goes blundering like a huge humble, – or, as I would rather write it, *Bumble*-bee – that beadle amongst insects. Cabmen are generally supposed to be well acquainted with the ins and outs of Sydney – some of them, unfortunately, are *too* well acquainted with the *inns*, and my driver is one of this description. In a glorious state of topographical uncertainty, hither and thither he jerks and lashes his horses; not infrequently bumping his pole against dead walls in vain attempts to find previously undiscovered passages to the wharf through *culs-de-sac*.

I begin to fancy that I shall have to pass the night in wandering along rows of houses that seem as fast asleep as their owners (their closed shutters reminding one of eyelids sealed), – in watching dissipated cats out upon the loose, and wearing the half stealthy and ashamed, half swaggering and independent air that marks their human congeners, young gentlemen with latch-keys; homeless dogs, hungry and fierce, foraging for garbage; hulking fellows as fierce and ravenous, without the dogs' excuse of homelessness and hunger; and the slow-footed Erinnyes in shiny hats, great coats, and oilskin capes, who have *not* their eyes upon these scoundrels, – when, suddenly inspired, my jarvie pulls up at a dark archway.

A lazzaroni-horde of ragged porterkins issue from the gloom, and squabble for my carpet-bag like a swarm of demons for the soul of a Don Juan who has craftily made a separate bargain with each individual imp. Guided by their howls, I follow the young devils through the darkness, reach the boat, and recover my baggage.

I like to leave Sydney at night, having a taste for the Dantesque. All cities, when viewed *en masse*, have then so *hellish* an aspect.

Rattle along the Greenwich Railway when the red-hot cinders light up the murky air and strew the road with smouldering *scoriæ*, as they whiz from the funnel or fall from the ash-box; and when the gas-lit rails seem glowing ploughshares on which, in horrible ordeal, the locomotives, with glaring eyes and shrieks of anguish, are doomed to rush along for ever. Look down upon the myriads of chimneys right and left, belching forth their hateful smoke into the already over-burdened atmosphere – upon that wide-spread, gloom-canopied plain of brick-and-mortar: of what text does the whole scene remind you?

Sydney tonight looks scarcely less infernal. Its smoke goes up to heaven, the sprinkled lamps serve but to intensify the circumambient blackness, the Gas Works jet forth their sultry column of lurid light, dark figures flit, blaspheming, before the cresset-fires upon the wharf.

And yonder gloomy, silent bush seems a dreary Hades, peopled with ghosts condemned, awaiting, within sight of hell, *Dies iræ, dies illa*, when, in Mephistopheles's fiendishly graphic phrase, they shall come shuddering up to judgment!

Judex ergo cum sedebit,
Quidquid latet adparebit,
Nil inultum remanebit.

Quid sum miser tunc dicturus?
Quem patronum rogaturus?
Cum vix justus sit securus.

The squalls of Sussex-street *pigs* in torment dispel these moody thoughts. It is on no *Inferno*, but merely a porcine purgatory, that I look.

Let me paint more minutely my surroundings.

The bull's eyes in the deck twinkle knowingly when I tread upon them, as if they saw that my boots, so swellish in their upper leathers, stand sadly in need of soleing, and chuckled over the discovery. The wheel – its brazen centre just revealed by the glow of these impertinently inquisitive little lights – gazes at the binnacle with its queer bell-crowned hat, like Polypheme ogling Mother Hubbard by mistake for Galatea, and – marvelling that Galatea should have all at once become so *passee* – *contenting* himself with gazing. The quarter boats creak lazily upon the davits. The funnels, with their cauliflower-heads of rising steam, look like gigantic pots of foaming beer.

Figureheads of neighbouring vessels peer in upon me: bowsprits point at me, as if festered fingers extended from the noses of the said figureheads in contemptuous "sight". Like the very spectres of ships – craft such as that which crossed the Ancient Mariner's track on his wild, lonely voyage – lie the more distant vessels, with shadowy hulls and dimly towering spars. Warehouses, commonplace enough by day, mere prosaic receptacles for "produce", loom through the murk awful as haunted castles. The crane looks fearsome as the tennanted gibbet upon a "barren moor", beneath which a benighted wayfarer suddenly finds himself – "drearily withering" around him.

> – – – – – the undescribëd sounds
> That come a-swooning over hollow grounds.

Here and there a glimmering lamp pries into the secrets of the black waters, with light all trembling as if it fell upon a corpse's face, – the putrefying features and stony-staring eyeballs of a murdered man.

A cable rattles, like a cart-load of cannon-balls, through the hawse-holes of yonder anchoring brig; and a voice cooeys, but cooeys long in vain, for a shore-boat. The watermen – choice spirits that they are – are in the public-house, and will not come until they have finished their grog, however loudly, my pea-jacketed Glendower, you may be pleased to call for them. At length, a boat shoves off, and, at each stroke of the oars, the silent water gives forth a phosphorescent gleam, like the glance of anger from a dumb man's eye. A wake of golden-white foam marks the swift wherry's course. Far away sounds the "melancholy-merry song" of mariners pumping at the patent-windlass: *click-click-click* sobs the "camel of the sea", as she pulls at her tether-pin. Ship-bells, in every key from deepest bass to shrillest treble, remind each other of the passing hours.

Presently a bell rings with impatient clamour, and all in a fret and fuss, with hissing steam, panting machinery, and splashing paddles – angry, as it were, at having been detained, and fearing that she will find no one up to welcome her – a belated Wollongong packet works her way up the harbour. Her red light turns its waters into wine, her flapping floats churn them into cream: thus mixing a beautiful syllabub – beautiful, but fit only for Barmecide banquets. With as much ado as the biggest mail-boat would make, the little vixen bustles into her berth, disembarks her draggletailed, cheese-complexioned passengers, and then snores herself off to dreamless slumber – i.e., blows off her steam.

The moon – long waited for by her patient handmaidens, the silvery stars – arises in full-faced beauty, paving the waters with a road of trembling gold. A less romantic arrival is contemporaneous with hers. Going below, I find that the mail-bags have just been brought on board, – the official who brings them looking very sulky when he beholds upon the cabin-table the luggage of a fellow-clerk, who – he for the first time learns – has obtained a few days' leave of absence, which, I presume, will double grim official's duties. Grim official, however, solaces himself by demanding a cigar of the civil black sub-steward, for which, in his perturbation of spirit, grim official forgets to pay; but, lighting it at the wrong end, stalks stiffly up the companion-staircase, crushing his hat with an appalling smash – as men wrapped up in their own wrongs are apt to do, when passing through low archways – ere he emerges in indignant majesty upon the deck. Civil black sub-steward loses his civility; an inebriate consigner of cargo persisting in looking for it in the steward's pantry. The Ethiop, provoked beyond endurance, calls him a "half-gentleman", and bids him hold his jaw. "Lucky for you that you're not in the States, my fine fellow," I think within myself. At the same time I feel proud that here all men *are* "free and equal", one can put up with a little free-and-easiness to be able to boast that blessing. The dapper obliging little steward – what a peculiar, pale-faced people, zealous (for a consideration) of good works, are the whole tribe of stewards – and the dainty obliging little stewardess flit about like Cock Robin and Jenny Wren amongst a lot of rooks; for gruff croaking is the dominant tone amongst the passengers who now are pouring in – lost parcels and pre-occupied berths being the grounds of their complaints.

Attendant friends, having imbibed valedictory nobblers, rush on deck at the cry of "Who's for the shore?" and I follow them. The boat is cleared of all but crew and passengers, the moorings are cast off, the gangway is drawn back with a jerking pull upon the wharf, and away we go: – past huge, anchored ships, with lights blinking drowsily alow, and brighter lights aloft, making their gaffs seem Aaron's rods bursting forth in golden blossom, – past bobbing buoys that look, with their long streaming locks of dripping tangle, heads of sea-monsters (submerged during day), come up to dry their manes, and breathe the cool night-air, – past Dawes's Battery, stronghold of infantry and pretty nursemaids, – past Fort Macquarie, shimmering ghostly-white in the moonlight, – past Woolloomooloo's avalanche of hovels, – past villa-gardens, where the moonbeams glint from lustrous banana-leaves like love-glances from Spanish eyes, and make the pale-blue aloes doubly pale – the very ghosts of *Agavæ*, and shadow morning-hours upon the solitary lichen-spotted sundials, as old men are visited in dreams by memories of youth, – past Rose Bay's reach of milkwhite sand, – past the Lighthouse, winking to itself as if it knew a thing or two that the Ocean wanted to do in the wrecking line, but didn't mean to let him, – past the dazzling Lightship, – past the Heads, looking over at each other sadly stern, recalling Coleridge's sweet lines on sundered friends, – out into the black, white-crested, surging, hissing waves, coming on, on, on, for ever and ever, and swept over by that lonely, *homeless* sea-breeze – half mournful and half fierce – that always makes me think of the wasted girls with hopeless eyes one sees in London streets at night, hurrying along wind-like – none knows whence, none cares whither.

Swaying from side to side like a sea-bird, the *Illalong* skims along the billows. From each funnel flutters a smoke-streamer spangled with glowing sparks. Far behind stretches a line of seething, creamy foam. Contrasted with the wild welter of the waters, how peaceful seems the pearly sky! And yet, in that calm heaven, a radiant rushing is really going on, that makes man's fastest, machinery-aided speed far, far less in comparison, than, beside *that*, appears the slowest snail's pace. Where we see only the fin-poised repose of sleeping goldfish, mighty masses are thundering through Space with more than a hurricane's impetus. So much for the "silent stars".

The moonbeams fall upon a passing vessel's swelling sail. White as Alpine snow it glistens in their tranquil light, and carries my thoughts back to that far-off night upon a distant sea when we were boarded by the ruthless pirate, Death – who cometh without nail, selects his victim, and then, unmarked, goes over the side again, in quest of other prey on the wide ocean.

We were becalmed in the tropics. The reef-points pattered on the idle sails like rain, as the ship, frosted with silver by the gorgeous moonlight – deck, canvas, cordage, spars, one blaze of lovely light – lazily rose and fell upon the heaving billows. But in that beauteous sea, round and round the ship, like a sullen sentinel, a grim shark kept his watch. I went below to the "hospital berth". A flickering lamp cast its sickly gleam on the sick man's pale and clammy brow, as he tossed in his narrow bunk; talking deliriously of scenes and faces far away, and petulantly asking why they should chain him there – when would the ship move on? A breeze sprang up a little after midnight; on went the ship, and the shark followed her. At sunrise, gasping forth some message to his mother – fated never to reach her, for none on board knew aught of her or him – the sick man died. Wrapt in the Union Jack, we laid him on the long-boat; and at evening, when the setting sun was tipping the foaming waves with crests of fire, the solemn words were read; the sails shivered as the ship was luffed up into the wind; there was a leaden plunge: a snowy sea-bird flew off to the horizon, like a liberated soul; the sails filled again; the ship went swiftly on, and far astern the moonbeams played above the stranger's lonely grave.

But it is time to turn in. A boisterous gentleman opposes my purpose, when I descend to carry it into execution; inviting me to partake of brandy and water with him instead, and asserting with swaggering emphasis that he is "Ocean's child", and considers "the delightful motion of the boat to be the rocking of his natural cradle". I observe, however, that "Ocean's child" cannot eat the ham sandwiches he orders. He soon grows very white about the gills, and disinclined to talk; and, at length, makes a precipitate retreat to his berth, beside which the black sub-steward (whom he has been chaffing), exulting at his discomfiture, hangs one of those queer little buckets like birdseed holders, and, grinning, leaves him to be lulled to sleep by the "rocking of his natural cradle".

Unfortunates, in various stages of the *mal de mer*, startle the night with moans and hideous uproar. Being pretty well sea-seasoned myself, of course, I am disgusted at their conduct. By-the-bye, is not this the way in which most of us treat a certain *moral* infirmity, also? Happening, from difference of temperament, to be proof against the particular temptation – perchance, preserved by strength of constitution from exhibiting the ordinary symptoms of having yielded to it – how we cry out against our peccant brother who has both eaten of the forbidden fruit, and manifestly has the stomach-ache in consequence! It costs many men nothing to be teetotallers, and yet they plume themselves upon their abstinence as though it were a sun-bright virtue. Others again, who have each drunk as much in a night as the object of their scorn would drink in a fortnight, turn up their noses at a poor weak-headed fellow who succumbs to a glass or two, in most ethical disdain. It is edifying to listen to their lectures upon sottishness.

When I wake the next day – a cool and showery Sunday – we have passed Newcastle, and are steaming up the river. *This*, then, is the far-famed Hunter – muddy as the Thames, with banks as flat as Essex marshes! True, there are some pretty hills in the distance just before you come to Hexham, but, as a whole, the lower part of the Lower Hunter appears to me about as lovely as a plate of soup.

* * *

I land at Morpeth, and proceed to Maitland, intending to go on at once by the mail to Singleton. At the inn from which the machine starts, I fall in with a friend. The sinner enticeth me, and I consent.

I wake next morning to find that my friend is gone, my money, too: an inconvenient state of things, since I remember enough of my pridian experiences to be aware that latterly I imbibed on tick, that my friend was impecunious, and that, consequently, an hotel-bill remains unsettled.

There at Last

Forsitan hæc olim meminisse juvabit.

To slope from the inn in which you have very unceremoniously taken your ease, without settling your account – even when you leave your luggage as security for ultimate payment, – is not the most gentlemanly mode of procedure in the world. It is, however, the course that I am compelled to adopt; for my wealth consists but of a shilling or two. I know no one in Maitland, and fear that if I disclose the state of my circumstances to my landlord, he may have me apprehended as a swindler who has obtained good liquor under false pretences.

Not belonging by any means to the *Pachydermata* of moralists in matters of this sort, I look so conscious of fugitive intentions when I descend the staircase of the "Northumberland" (an hotel, by-the-bye, that I can safely recommend to more immediately remunerating customers than myself), that I wonder the barmaid does not lay violent hands on me, and demand, on behalf of her master, the liquidation of my little bill. But she is flirting with an early nobbleriser, and suffers me to pass her yawning window unchallenged, and depart unheeded on my road to Singleton.

Travelling in Australia is sadly monotonous. The highways are all fashioned in one model. Everywhere you see the same grey or red rail-fences; the same ragged gum-trees, reminding you of men with dirty, tattered shirts; the same tall, bare, white boles, extending their arms like skeletons about to break forth in sepulchral oratory, or "set" in a "Dance of Death", the same charred, prostrate trunks like blackfellows knocked down in a drunken squabble (felled trees in other countries look like heroes o'ermastered in Homeric strife); the same black, jagged stumps, like foul, decaying teeth; the same distant verdure – verdure *a non virendo* – like piles of dry mud and soot, the same scrub close at hand, with dingy foliage that looks like Royal Mint-street clothing half hopelessly hung out for sale (even leaves in Australia possess "colonial experience", and are anything but green); the same not grass, but graminaceous scurf, as if the earth had got the ringworm; the same bark-roofed slab-huts, not so respectable as English pigsties; the same ramshackle, rambling roadside inns, with canoe-like water-troughs; the same execrable road, in dry weather a field abominably ploughed, over whose furrows the mail-cart goes *bump-bump*, *lurch-lurch*, churning all milk of human kindness in the new chum, polishing his pants on cushionless seats or subjacent post-bags, into anything but butter for the constructors of the accursed tracks on which the stay-at-home writers of Australian Guide-books have bestowed such lying eulogies: in wet weather a Slough of Despond no modern Christian ought to be called upon to pass, a channel of mire dotted with bogged drays, with drivers seated on their loads, like sailors in the tops of wrecks and foundering ships, smoking with the grim resignation of despair. "The roads of Australia *proverbial*!" Verily, they *are* proverbial – but in no fundatory sense!

To resume my catalogue of identities: – Everywhere you are oppressed by the same long miles of loneliness, relieved only by the same bullock-drays, with barking dogs jingling bells, kegs slung beneath, and pots and pannekins swinging behind; by the same flocks of sheep, herds of cattle, mobs of horses (their drivers – straight and thin as ramrods, lank-haired as Indians, sallow as mummies – sitting stately in their saddles, now cracking their stockwhips like so many rifles, anon resting the handles sceptre-fashion on their thighs, with the lashes looped in loose coil like tame serpents round their arms); by the same female equestrians, remarkable for short habits and substantial ankles, carrying all sorts of things, from a feather bed to a pumpkin-pie, dangling at their saddle-bows; and by the same Chinamen, with silken nets hanging veil-wise from their cabbage-trees, and balancing poles like milk-yokes on their shoulders, from the ends of which depend their blanket-bundles and umbrellas – whoever saw a vagrant Celestial without an umbrella?

Natives, when in the company of immigrants, are in the habit of trumpeting the beauty of their country about thirty times an hour. Now, for my own part, I always suspect everything, except a king or queen, that requires to be proclaimed; and remembering that most Australians, like the mouse in the fable, have had but scanty opportunities of comparison, and call their own land a fine one just simply because they have not seen any other, I make a point of never saying "Amen" to these fulsomely reiterated praises. I *don't* say it, because I *can't* say it. Of all the lands that ever *I* saw, Australia appears to me to be the ugliest, shrivelled and sulky-looking as the most ancient and hopeless of old maids.

* * *

The Dutch measure their distances by pipes: Charles Lamb used to measure his by pints. In emulation of that great *public* benefactor, I make my milestones nobblers. The consequence is that in the bush my miles are often somewhat lengthy. Scotch miles with very big bittocks. It is evening, and I recall, with melancholy appreciation, a derivation of the word *Spes* on which I stumbled once upon a time, whilst turning over the leaves of a German Latin dictionary: – "SPES; Sanscrit *bhâs*, akin to the Greek φῶς, light, – a light in the distance towards which you look and long." The light in the distance *for* which I look and long, is a public-house lamp, for I am footsore, fatigued, famished, and very thirsty; but none such can I discover. So, first drinking, or rather lapping up, and then bathing face, hands, and feet in, some water of the colour and consistency of coffee-grounds (using the gritty sand that circles it as soap – *very* Brown Windsor), I pick the grassiest spot I can find to camp out in, and lay me down to take my rest, with my paletot wrapped around me. The stars come out one by one, and look down on me like loving sisters' watchful eyes. Presently the moon rises over the dark trees. I don't relish her full light so much. I fancy that she is comparing me – not to my advantage – with Endymion.

She is "dropping down the sky all silently", when, after a wretched mosquito-haunted night, I wake for good. A rich aroma – there is some good even in gum-trees – fills the fresh morning air, as I push on to the next inn for breakfast; and cheerfully curls the blue wood-smoke from the encampments of the bullock-drivers, preparing for their day's journey. After a *dejeuner* SANS *la fourchette*, of bread and cheese and my pet beer, at a wayside "public", I descend upon Patrick's Plains, and hobble into Singleton – a town composed, apparently, of inns, mills, and tabernacles. In a small place the divisions of sect look almost ludicrous; it seems so strange that half-a-dozen people should want half-a-dozen different roads to heaven. Going to one of the mills to get a boat to cross the river, I overhear a Methodist expounding the peculiarities of his creed to his floury fellow-workmen. Instead of sneering, I somehow respect him for it. We southerners are such a set of Sadducees, or, if we have any religion, make it so exclusively a "thing of synagogues and Sundays" – locking it up, as it were, with what Sam Slick calls our "go-to-meetin' clothes", that this weaving of it into the warp of common workday life seems to me – to say the least – an interesting phenomenon. It makes me think of the old Apostolic times, when those who pulled the oar and hauled the net, were, also, fishers of men; of the old Puritan times, when, in Carlyle's phrase, the English squire wore his belief in God about him like his shot-belt.

Failing to obtain a boat, I return to the crossing-place; passing on the road a candidate for senatorial honours who is on a canvassing-tour. He folds his arms and knits his brow, striving, as he paces the veranda of his hotel – planting his little feet with all the ponderosity of which they are capable (and that isn't much – the lead lies in the opposite extremity) – to look the very Zeus of booksellers and statesmen, I need not say that he fails most deplorably in his attempt. It's no use trying, little Pid! Thou wast not meant to be majestic. – For want of a more dignified conveyance, I am constrained to mount a water-cart, and cross the river sitting, like a sign-painter's Bacchus, astride upon a tun.

A hot, dusty, tiring, thirst-provoking day – I meet an old pupil. He seems somewhat surprised to see his former "guide, philosopher, and friend", plodding through the bush, in shirt-sleeves and with upturned trousers, like a tinker on the tramp; but nevertheless – young scoundrel that he is – he offereth me not a horse. I wander through a wilderness of trees springing from soil so sun-scorched that one marvels that even an Australian forest can grow there. As the road winds, I catch glimpses of gloomy hills, with solemn Dead Seas of sombre foliage in the intervening gullies. Towards evening I reach

Glennie's Creek, and see, for a wonder, a little rural "bit" worthy of the pencil of a Gainsborough. The sun is low in the cooling sky. The grass gleams like burnished bronze. The leaves of the eucalypti are tipped with gold. A flock of bleating lambs are descending to the stream, followed by a bevy of barefooted children – just let out of school – as noisy and as gamesome. In front of an English-looking inn, stands an English-looking landlord, lazily watching a wool-dray which has just been upset on the other side of the creek, within shadow of the pretty little white stone church. To right the overturned dray, a team has been borrowed from the dray behind. One of the bullocks shams faint, and is liberated from the yoke; whereupon Strawberry knowingly whisks his tail, and rushes into the water with a broad grin upon his bovine nose. After sundry remarkable displays of engineering – mechanical science in these parts appears decidedly to be in its infancy – the wain is set upon its wheels once more, crosses the creek, together with its companion, and the drivers and their local allies celebrate their triumph with copious libations.

Another night of camping out. No sleep. The bull-frogs croak, like their human analogues, with a detestable tone of enjoyment. The parrots chatter like schoolgirls in their bedroom, when the governess on duty has gone down to supper. High up in the trees my little namesakes send forth their indescribable cry. Countless crickets hiss in chorus. Lukewarm rain falls ever and anon. Flies cluster on my face, making it look – if there were any one here to see it – a very liberally fruited currant-dumpling. Above all, those d–d mosquitoes – I can't help it, I *must* swear – jostle with the flies for the possession of my nose, and turn my hands into a pair of pink, perforated cards. I am a Pythagorean, and firmly believe that the souls of unpaid creditors migrate, on their decease, into mosquitoes, and in that form continue to torment their unfortunate debtors. That last dig came from a departed snip. This under which I at present wince, is the spiteful bite of a dead landlady. Would that I had bled honestly in metaphor, and thus avoided this vile literal phlebotomy!

Morning comes at last. A miserable breakfast, and a miserable day – spent in crawling along like a wounded snake, lying down in the Brummagem shade that Australian trees afford, and seeking for and drinking muddy water. Everyone, they say, must eat a peck of dirt in his lifetime. I am sure that I have taken my quantum, diluted, a dozen times over, in this trip of mine. Now, however, I can find no water, however muddy. Every moment I am tantalised by the fancied sound, the fancied sight, of running streams. I might as well hope for them in Sahara. Dead beat, with a hundred pulses throbbing in my head, I drop upon the ground, muttering, *Hibernice*: "It's all up with me!" When, lo! suddenly the sunlight fades, the wind rushes moistly past, and in a few minutes the lightning writes its blinding zigzags on the blackened heavens, and the awful thunder crashes and rumbles through the gloom. Down comes the rain, in sheets, not drops; I drink at every pore, and freshen like a plant.

The sun is shining again, in a blue evening sky, when, splashed to the eyes, at last I enter Muswellbrook. The wet shingles flash back his dazzling rays, and every leaf is decked with quivering brilliants.

Louisa Atkinson

CABBAGE-TREE HOLLOW, AND THE VALLEY OF THE GROSE

"Many a cloudy morning turns out a fine day," says a hopeful adage, which, in these misty and rainy times, it is very pleasant to believe. The day arranged for our excursion was a confirmation of its prediction, and though the ride from Fernhurst to the foot of the hill at Wheeney Creek was performed under a cloudy sky, with dewdrops sparkling on the branches by the wayside, it was soon evident that the rains of the preceding day and night were not about to return again so shortly.

The South Kurrajong is a series of undulations, extending from the foot of the higher portions of the range towards the Hawkesbury. Much of this tract is under cultivation, and offers such cheery, smiling, trite home pictures as might tempt the artist to portray: cottages nestling among the dark foliage of the orange, the higher branches of the acacia and bean-tree, or the kurrajong (*Hibiscus heterophyllus*), now starred with its white blossoms; green slopes, where sleek cows feed and horses roam at liberty, or corn, and the golden wheat, vary the hues. The plentiful moisture of the past season has added those lively greens and luxuriant tints which are so essential to such scenery. The high-wooded mountains on one side, and the glimpses of the low lands of Cumberland are accessories of great value to our picture.

Two or three miles of such scenery brought us to the forest land; the road was still good, the grass green, the trees fine and umbrageous, and the transition was from one style of beauty to another only. The owner of "Cabbage-tree Hollow" has constructed an excellent road to his property, which winds along the side of a hill crowned with beetling masses of sandstone, fretted and excavated by the atmosphere, while below the road lies a vale through which a small stream flows, bearing its waters onwards to join the Grose River. The extreme luxuriance of the vegetation attracts the attention no less than the greenness of the leaves and the superabundance of the ferns.

The deep shade, only broken by flecks of sunlight, or occasional gleams thrown across the road, rendered the ride particularly pleasant, and became doubly grateful as the sun gained power and poured a fiery glow upon the earth. Many little streams trickled down the hill side and, crossing the path, added their tributary waters to the brook in the glen below; altogether keeping up that pleasant cool sound which only running water can make.

Man's industry has already levelled some acres of the dense brush, and we found an embryo farm and orchard in the vale. The labour of the harvest field was in progress, and the slope of a hill was dotted with shocks standing amidst the stubble.

At the cottage we alighted, and our horses were secured while we proceeded to investigate the course of the stream by which we had ridden for the last mile, and another which joined it. Having been led to this spot by what an amusing modern writer is pleased to designate the *Pseromania*, the most ferny spots had the greatest powers of attraction. By more than one fallen tree did we cross rills hastening through the wheat field between their steep high banks, till the paling fence was reached. Here for a while bidding adieu to my companions, I left the comparative civilisation of the farm for the unbroken solitude.

Rocks, impeding the course of the stream, lashed the water into puny wrath, now leaping exultingly over an obstacle, again creeping beneath it – a curious churning, gurgling sound was the result, fit music for these sylvan solitudes, sombre with heavy shadows. On the edge, and even in the stream, grow *Alsophilia Australis* and *A. offinis*, *Todea barbara*, etc., with numerous lesser ferns, which cluster beneath their arborescent compeers, while the stones are green with *Hymerophyllum* and *Jungermannia*.

The stems only of the large cabbage-trees remain, but numerous small palmate leaves indicate the presence of young trees. Pensile moss-woven nests, attached to the extremities of the branches of trees or creepers, swayed above the stream, and their little builders flitted about them in all the importance of nesting season. The walk through the harvest field was varied by a rather large black snake crossing the path, which little interlude kept the attention awake till we remounted.

A rather abrupt and rocky path led up the hill, and we soon passed from the luxuriant and pretty vale to the thick scrub of a sandstone range. Here the advantages of a guide who thoroughly knew the country, and who could appreciate fine scenery, was experienced.

Pursuing the top of the range I presently descried with satisfaction the fine species of dwarf palm which obtains on the Shoalhaven River. While our obliging guide was seeking for nuts, some lyre birds (*Menura superba*) were disturbed, but continued to whistle and flutter about in much agitation till we resumed the order of march. Suddenly the thick scrub gave way, and the summits of distant mountains appeared. Hardly were the words uttered "We will alight here," before the ground was trodden, and eager steps pressing forward to the edge of the valley of the Grose.

There are scenes which baffle description when we can only feel like

> – – stout Cortes, when with eagle eyes
> He stared at the Pacific, and all his men
> Looked at each other with a wild surmise,
> Silent upon a peak in Darien.

Something of that hushed wonder for a moment held us spellbound, and then came the deep heartfelt, "Beautiful, how beautiful – how grand."

We stood on a rock looking down into the deep gorge, through which flowed a turbulent stream, yellow and froth-laden from recent inundations, while tributaries, which in their course clove asunder the mountains, dashed down the steeps. The heights are wooded to their summits with grand masses of yellow sandstone varying them, and the rich greens of *Backhousia myrtifolia, Pittosporum*, and *Tasmania aromatica* indicating the course of the various rills. After having brought the sketch book into requisition, we mounted our horses and rode through a scrubby piece of country, not without interest to the botanical student, to another spur of the mountain, from whence we again obtained a fine view of the Grose, perhaps hardly so striking as the first point of view, or else the repetition of the scene had lost its first startling effects.

Down the right-hand ranges fall the waters of Burrolow, and to the left is Springwood; through the furthermost part of the gorge we catch a glimpse of a distant cone – Mount Hay, perhaps.

On our return we did not descend to the lovely Cabbage-tree Hollow, but, pursuing a marshy stream, turned from thence across to a surveyor's road leading through a casuarina country till we re-entered the farmlands, and exchanged the grandeur of the vast scenes, the great depths and dense woods of the other localities for the sunny homes of the South Kurrajong. – As we purposed to devote the remainder of the day to further explorations, the kind invitation of one of our companions to dine at her house, was cordially accepted, and, having been in the saddle almost uninterruptedly from nine till after three o'clock, her hospitality was well appreciated. Quite refreshed and in excellent spirits we started up the mountain, and again bade soon farewell to the homesteads of man, and turned our backs on orange groves and vine-covered porches to pursue a shady road, which quickly led us up the range. The road, being in use to draw timber from the mountains, is broad and good, and offers a pleasant riding ground. Numerous bellbirds made the brush vocal.

After reaching the summit, the road leads over and along the opposite decline; from hence it is not in use for wheeled vehicles. It was originally cut by the former proprietor of Burrolow, and is the only means by which vehicles can gain access to the valley. The scene gains in interest as we proceed, high rocks rising on one side, Pipeclay is found in the road, and extolled as very pure, an old woman who was collecting it for the use of the cleanly housewives of the Kurrajong was recently lost, and exposed to a wet night.

The atmospherical effects upon the rocks increases in interest. In one place a mass has fallen from the cliff, and rolling so close beside the path exhibits an aperture about eighteen inches in diameter, which communicates with an extensive cavity occupying the centre of the boulder.

During a great part of this ride the forest is very dense, and the path is over arched with luxuriant vegetation, the trees being so festooned by creepers as at times to threaten to put a stop to further progress. Some rills of water cross the path, and the whole place is very humid and shady. When expecting shortly to descend into the valley, this path was found impeded by a fallen tree, and, therefore, leaving it, we wound through the scrub to the margin of the stream – the same which, much augmented, we had traced with the eye in its headlong course into the Grose. Many beautiful flowers adorn this portion of Bunolone. The vale is here contracted and wooded, but a short ride led us to the more clear land and ruined dikes – the evidences of what had been – and thence, by the usual narrow stony path, we wound up the hill, leaving the valley already grey with evening hues, though the sun shone brightly on the mountain tops.

A NIGHT ADVENTURE IN THE BUSH

A lady, her family, a friend, and several servants, among others a black boy, had occasion to perform a journey which, though not long, was rendered tedious by the nature of the ground traversed. So steep were the mountains, so unbridged the streams, that no vehicle could cross them. Goods were therefore conveyed on pack-saddles placed on the backs of bullocks trained to the work. The party, excepting the drivers, were mounted on horseback. The first fifteen miles accomplished, not without great fatigues, dangers, and delays, the cavalcade reached the descent of the M– Mountain. The pass had been improved by cutting steps down the face of the rocks, and the oxen, accustomed to such scenes, stumbled down as they best could, while the horses groaned audibly, trembled, and even in some instances sunk powerless on the dangerous declivity, not encouraged by the sight of the gully yawning at the side of the narrow road.

Coaxing, shouting, and other exertions of will surmounted this difficulty, and the party proceeded briskly, leading their horses; the pack bullocks and their drivers soon falling into the rear. The nature of the country had entirely changed, the barren sand had given place to vegetable mould; the flowering scrub to a dense semi-tropical thicket; the sun's rays were obscured by the over-arching branches, or fell like mosaic upon the moss green stones and ferns. The cabbage-palms stretched their slender stems above the tangled copse and looked up at the face of heaven; the tree ferns, elkshorn and birds-nest ferns revelled in the humid shades. The shrieks of the blue mountain and king parrots gave life to the green wood, and every stream was occupied by frogs which vied with each other in their shrill-toned croaking.

Onward trudged the travellers, hastening to the foot of the mountain where they were to encamp for the night. Darkness gathered round early in that deep narrow vale, where mountains rose abruptly on either side of the creek. Persons who travelled these parts with stock had erected a yard near the little stream on a small level, to secure their cattle in during the night, and near this the party sat them down, after lighting a fire, awaiting the arrival of the tents, provisions and servants, for only the black boy Charley had accompanied them. But total darkness closed above them, and the absentees came not; all ears were strained to catch the first sound of them; conversation had flagged, then ceased.

During this anxious hush the fire had died down – it was a darkness which could be felt – when suddenly appeared a small light, scarcely larger than a spark. "Charley, what is that?" enquired several tremulous voices.

"Debel debel, I believe," returned the lad in a tone as if his teeth were chattering. On came the light, about two feet from the ground.

"Nonsense, Charley; what can it be?"

Charley again hinted the possibility of the presence of his Satanic Majesty – while the little luminous speck crept cautiously onward towards the horror-struck group.

"Can it be a bushranger?" whispered the lady. "I believe so, missus," returned the aboriginal.

A bushranger with a lighted pipe in his mouth, about to fire upon the helpless victims, rendered visible by the flickering of a tongue of flame in the fire, while darkness concealed *him*, and goodness knows how many more! All this presented itself to the assembled imaginations. The lady fainted, the young people were panic-struck, Charley equally so. The gentleman who was recently from England, and entirely unused to bush life, although then on his way to inspect a station, prior to entering on possession, entered into the general alarm, but surmounted it so far as to throw some dead branches on the almost expiring fire. A bright blaze shot up, illuminating the surrounding scene – not revealing a band of brigands, but setting the light flickering in a way that bore evidence of its insect origin.

Inspired by new courage, active exertions were made, and a small brown beetle about three lines long captured; the light appeared to be emitted from a pale yellow spot on the under part of the body.

Still the men and the pack bullocks did not arrive; the chill dews of evening were falling, and no tents erected, no supper to refresh and invigorate the weary travellers. There is nothing like sitting in the dark watching, and listening, to provoke or evoke fear. Spite of the bushranger turning out a little beetle, fear held possession of all hearts, when presently was heard the tramping of heavy feet; one of the pack bullocks was running wildly down the mountain, dragging behind him a heavy body.

Again the black was applied to, as being better provided with bush lore, not courage, for he was overpowered by cowardice and superstition. In reply to a volley of questions he expressed an opinion that the bullock had killed his driver, and was dragging his lifeless body behind him. The ghastly suggestion was received in all faith, everyone being too horror-struck to reflect that as the driver was in no way attached to the bullock's harness, he would not be dragged.

On rushed the animal, concealed by the darkness, plunged into the creek, and hurried to the stockyard where it was in the habit of being released from its load. There was a pause, as of death – again were heard hurried feet, and again. The three pack bullocks had assembled at the yard, each dragging something behind them – their loads, suggested some one; and so it proved.

Now came the drivers and related the cause of their detention. A bright fire, warm cup of tea and the snug canopy of the tent, disposed the travellers to acknowledge "that there is but one step from the sublime to the ridiculous".

As the family, who formed the greater number of the party, were intending to make rather a lengthy stay when they reached their destination – a cattle station – they had brought with them a very important member of the household, no less a one than a *pet bear*. This rather portly gentleman had been accommodated with a seat in a pannier, and swung on one side of the pack saddle, while, "to make the balance true", a hamper of earthenware and a writing desk were suspended on the other side.

Whatever were Master Maugie's thoughts on this occasion, he had manifested that philosophy which usually marked his actions and given no expression to them, till he found his bearer descending the steep mountainside. This was too much for any choleric gentleman, who had nerves. Maugie waxed wrath, and stuck his long claws through the wicker-work into the bullock's back, no doubt intending "to make assurance doubly sure," but such a one-sided arrangement did not suit the ox; he began to run, the shaking causing Maugie to roar aloud, much to the horror of the bovine trio, who thereupon ran away, scattering such of their load as was insecure along the road, breaking the fragile, to wit, the earthenware, and releasing the bear, who speedily made his way up a tree. The drivers being unable to coax him down, felled it – a work of some time, trusting to the bullocks keeping the right road, and then had to secrete such of the loads as were scattered about, by which time night had closed in.

The bear, it must be understood, was neither the great polar, nor the Russian black, the Californian brown, or the North American grizzly bears, but only a *phascolarctus fuscus*, of leaf-eating habits, not given to hugging its prey, and a drug in the bears-grease market. And thus ends this "o'er true tale".

Edmond Marin La Meslée

[TOURING IN QUEENSLAND]

On the morning of the third day out from Sydney, the *Alexandra* steamed into Brisbane River. The day was perfect: not a cloud in the sky, just hot enough to be pleasant and just enough breeze to give a delicious freshness to the air. Such weather exists only in a tropical winter and, with the natural beauty that surrounded us, it made one think spontaneously of an earthly paradise.

From its outlet into Moreton Bay right up to the capital, the Brisbane River flows through relatively low-lying country. The vegetation was quite different from that in the southern colonies. Mangrove trees grew in the water to some distance out from the banks, and everything proclaimed that we were arriving in a tropical country. Wherever the land had not been cleared, the trees were interlaced with an absolute tangle of liana creepers. Here and there rose some *free selector's* hut, always surrounded by banana trees whose huge leaves had been slashed by the wind. It was clear that these trees grew here only with some difficulty, the climate not being hot enough to suit them completely.

The river wound along through the rich alluvial flats in which it had dug its bed: not until its junction with Breakfast Creek did the first signs of rising ground appear. On a little knoll where the two streams joined stood a charming country house, built in the colonial style with wide verandas on all four sides. Magnificent green lawns stretched right down to the water's edge and a pleasure boat was moored to a little stone pier. Two small children, a boy and a girl, gambolled about on the grass or let themselves tumble down it together to the foot of the hill. From here on to Brisbane the river's course became more tortuous: as it was only two hundred yards wide at the most, our experienced officer needed all his skill to pilot our 800 ton steamer safely to the Company's wharf, where we tied up at about eleven o'clock in the morning. A cab took us to the *Imperial Hotel* in George Street, where a good English-style dinner awaited us.

There are good reasons why Brisbane is by no means such a large and prosperous city as Melbourne or Sydney. From a commercial viewpoint, it is not very well situated. Standing on a bend in the river that bears its name, about thirty miles from the sea, it cannot be reached by large modern ships. The depth and breadth of the channel are not great enough to accommodate vessels of more than about twelve hundred tons. Consequently port charges are high, for sailing-ships must be towed up the river from Moreton Bay and big steamships have to unload their cargo at the river's mouth, whence it is carried to Brisbane by lighters.

In 1825, when Sir Thomas Brisbane was Governor of New South Wales, Brisbane was founded as the headquarters of the Moreton Bay penal establishment. Until Queensland was separated from the mother colony and opened its doors to free immigration, Brisbane was scarcely anything more than a convict depot. Since then it has grown steadily as its immense hinterland has been opened up and developed.

Immediately behind the town rises a very fertile tableland called the Darling Downs. Today it produces millions of sheep, thousands of cattle, quantities of wheat and of all the other cereals and fruits that flourish in temperate climates. Brisbane's prosperity depends largely on the Downs, with which it is now connected by rail. This line, which penetrates more than a hundred leagues inland to the centre of the pastoral district of Maranoa, forks at Toowoomba on the highest part of the plateau, and ships to Brisbane all sorts of products from the huge area it serves.

At the present moment the city and suburbs contain a population of about 35,000 people. As in Sydney and the other colonial cities, no one lives in the business centre: the suburbs extend in all directions, along the riverside and over the surrounding hills and valleys.

For a good view of Brisbane, people climb to the summit of Spring Hill near the observatory. From this vantage-point there is a superb panorama. The town is spread out below on a bend of the river which snakes across the plain. At your feet lies the aristocratic suburb of Kangaroo Point, joined to the city by a *ferry*, which crosses the river at Petrie's Bight near the Government wharves. Farther away a large bridge connects the city with the important suburb of South Brisbane. To the right the line of the horizon is etched by the blue peaks of the great coastal range, and to the left the suburban houses of Farm Valley cover the plain. The elbow of the river is partly hidden by the trees in the Botanical Gardens and in the adjoining reserve where Government House stands. Nearby a great domed building dominates a park which is, in some sort, a part of the Gardens. That is the Parliament House of the independent colony of Queensland, independent not only of the neighbouring colonies, but equally of the metropolitan country itself, which is content merely to send out a Governor to whom Queensland pays the salary of a hundred and twenty-five thousand francs a year.

* * *

The city's main thoroughfare, Queen Street, is already becoming rather crowded with business activity, and the shops are gradually invading the parallel streets nearby. In years to come the business quarter of the city will cover the whole area between the Botanical Gardens and the foot of Spring Hill. Some people are already predicting that the beautiful Gardens will have to be destroyed, in order to widen the river and build wharves in their place. It is to be hoped that the economic benefits to Brisbane, from such an act of vandalism, would be small enough to prevent its being committed. During our stay of nearly six weeks in Brisbane we often visited the Gardens, and it was always a fresh delight to walk along the great avenue of *bunya-bunyas* that borders the river. There too I met again those old acquaintances from Mauritius, flame-trees, with their exotic scarlet flowers that for a whole season of the year replace the leaves, and create such a beautiful effect among the surrounding greenery. I noticed also, growing beside some tree from New Zealand, a specimen of the traveller's tree, the *Ravenala* of the botanists, which is a native of Mauritius. This tree, which is provided with a little store of water at the base of its leaves, never has, despite popular belief, saved the life of any traveller dying of thirst in the desert. On the contrary, it grows in swampy country and is never found in arid lands.

In any city, except Paris, Rome or some other great metropolis with innumerable attractions, a visitor with no great business to attend to cannot fail to be bored after quite a short time. Brisbane is quite a pretty town, it is true, but it bores you to death.

We resolved to get out of it for a few days and next morning we left the *wharf* on board the *Emu*, a reasonably comfortable paddle-steamer of the American type, which I saw again some years later on the run between Manly Beach and Sydney. Having rounded the point formed by the Botanical Gardens, we sailed under the arches of Victoria Bridge and up the river, whose banks were dotted with pleasant villas and plantations of maize and sugar-cane. Everywhere the soil was extremely fertile and the vegetation luxuriant. The climate is not quite hot enough to be ideal for sugar-cane, but some small growers have done well with it in the neighbourhood of Brisbane. It can be seen at its best in the northern districts of the colony, where it grows prolifically and forms the main crop.

Early attempts at cane-growing were not very successful. Probably they were made by people who understood nothing about this kind of agriculture, and even less about the process of sugar refining. The unhappy results of these first efforts inhibited the progress of the industry for a long time afterwards. It was not till after our visit that sugar-growing really took its place among the staple industries of the colony. Profiting by past experience, those who had managed to survive the early disasters appealed for help to the authorities in Mauritius and the West Indies, and the situation was quickly transformed.

Today several companies have been formed in Melbourne, principally to exploit the alluvial lands that flank the northern rivers. In the southern part of the colony, as on the north coast of New South Wales, sugar-mills have been built on the main water-courses and *free selectors* have begun to take up farms around them. The farmers grow the cane and the mills turn it into sugar. According to well-informed opinion, this system gives the best results. The farmer is not obliged to find the considerable capital required to install crushing machinery on his own farm – something that only those rich enough to maintain a great plantation can afford. Each small working-owner of a twenty-acre block can thus grow his own cane without crippling overhead expenses. The mill buys his crop, at so much per ton of cane, or according to the richness of the *cane-syrup*, and his expenses are reduced to the simple costs of farming – something to which he must give all his time and care. If it were otherwise, cane-growing would be impossible for small farmers: only large companies could undertake it with any chance of success. On the river flats of North Queensland the industry is organised in this latter way; but in New South Wales and on the banks of the Brisbane River small farming is the general rule.

Our steamer continued its leisurely course towards Ipswich: the river meandered capriciously back and forth across the plain. But as we advanced, the countryside changed in character and cultivated land disappeared. A forest of huge trees, entangled with lianas, began to clothe the banks of the river and, rounding a sharp bend, we came upon a great, walled establishment resembling a convent or a monastery. It was, we were told, the lunatic asylum and bore the euphonious name of Woogaroo, a word borrowed from the dialect of the first inhabitants of the district, the Australian blacks. Here, as everywhere else, the native people have disappeared before the white invaders, leaving no trace of their existence other than some sonorous place-names which the newcomers have respected and retained. The Woogaroo Asylum is built in absolutely virgin country on the right side of the river, whose high banks at this point protect the institution from the terrible floods that sometimes ravage the area.

After steaming for thirty miles through this beautiful scenery, we reached the junction between the Brisbane and the Bremer rivers, on which latter stream the town of Ipswich stands.

To reach it, we had still to sail fifteen miles up the Bremer. This river was narrower than the Brisbane, the forest coming right down to the water's edge. Here and there a block of brilliantly coloured little parrots, blue, red and green, flashed across our path and perched in the trees, making the air ring with their discordant cries. These birds are very beautiful, and they do much to enliven the landscape; but their call is so piercing and disagreeable that one would cheerfully dispense with their presence. The river, already narrow, grew still more so as we approached Ipswich, where it was no more than a deep stream which our boat could navigate only because it was fitted with a rudder at both bow and stern. We reached the wharf at three o'clock in the afternoon, after a journey of fifty miles, perhaps a little less than eighteen leagues.

Some years ago Ipswich was a very important town, but it has been declining almost daily since the railway connected it with Brisbane. Up till about ten years ago, all up-country trade was funnelled through this town: wool, wheat, hides, everything was loaded aboard the small boats that tied up at its wharves. But since these products can now be despatched direct to Brisbane, Ipswich's trade is gradually dying. However, its population has not declined: the agricultural resources of the district still maintain nearly six thousand people in a condition of relative prosperity.

After strolling round the main streets, we set out for the railway station; but we missed our way and found ourselves at the foot of a hill on which stands the lycée of Ipswich, *Ipswich Grammar School.* Tired of walking, we stopped where an old woman was knitting, on a flight of steps leading into a house. We asked her permission to sit down for a moment and began chatting. In a few minutes she was interrupted by the arrival of an old gentleman, who wished us a friendly good-day.

These old inhabitants of Ipswich had been in the country for thirty-five years. They had come out at a time when the district was peopled only by fierce, man-eating tribes of Aborigines who have since disappeared. The old man told us how one day the cannibals attacked the village, then inhabited by only about twenty settlers, who defended themselves energetically. After a struggle that raged throughout the whole day, the miscreants succeeded in taking prisoner a very fat settler. Many others perished at the hand of the savages during the fight.

On the evening of the battle, the blacks took their prisoner to the top of the hill where Ipswich Grammar School now stands. They killed, roasted and ate him, in full view of the horrified colonists who could do nothing to save him.

"We saw them dancing round their victim," the old Irishman told us. "We heard them chanting their savage yells, as they argued with each other over the tit-bits. But what could we do? There were four hundred of them, and only ten of us left."

Recounting the story, with the enthusiastic corroboration of his wife, seemed to excite the old man; and he appeared to enjoy telling us about his early struggles, and painting a picture of the success which had crowned them.

"I came here a full thirty-five years ago, not worth a penny, and for the last twenty years I have been married to the good mate you see before you," he added, pointing to the old lady who smiled at her happy memories. "Well, I took my pick and shovel and went into the wilderness, for that is all it was in those days. I sowed, planted and ploughed. Later I was able to buy a plough and my crops grew heavier. I always had a good market at the Moreton Bay convict establishment. Over the years other settlers arrived: the land around me was cleared, and one day I saw the railway line pass by my front door. That was fifteen years ago now. Today all the land you see on both sides of the line is mine. My children are well established and, at the age of eighty-five, I can still walk three leagues in a day without becoming too tired. I have worked hard, and today I am much better off than I ever dreamed of being under my father's roof, when as a boy I used to mind our animals in the fields of old Ireland."

Could anyone help admiring the energy of this hardy race, for whom twenty years had been almost enough to snatch from barbarism these countries destined to a limitlessly expanding future?

We returned to Brisbane as night fell, and a few days later a new excursion was mooted; but this one would have been better described as a journey, since we were thinking of nothing less than a visit to Toowoomba, about a hundred miles from Brisbane. The Count planned to push on from there to the flourishing little town of Warwick, in the centre of the Darling Downs, and thus to visit all that part of the colony which is reputed to constitute one of the richest districts in Australia. At that time the railway did not go beyond Warwick, but today it extends to the Queensland border, a few miles from the New South Wales town of Tenterfield. This line, however, is only a branch of the great western railway which runs inland from Toowoomba. At the time of our journey in 1876 the main line terminated at Dalby on the Condamine River; but since then it has been pushed forward vigorously and the iron road now connects the prosperous little township of Roma, centre of a pastoral district, with the capital of the colony. From Roma it must swing north to the township of Blackall in the Mitchell district, to form the first section of the great transcontinental line mentioned above.

Twenty-five years ago at most, the vast stretch of land crossed by this railway was a wilderness, as wild and desolate as the country in which the ill-fated explorers, Burke and Wills, perished from the torments of thirst. A few native tribes wandered over it, leading a miserable existence in summertime, and living by hunting the kangaroos and opossums that infest it. A few years have sufficed for the tough and industrious squatters to transform the whole countryside. Today the finest cattle stations in all Australia are found there. The squatter reigns as absolute sovereign over his innumerable horned subjects, wandering at will over stations any of which is as large as one of our French departments.

To reach the tableland, the railway runs for some thirty miles through the rich alluvial plains watered by the Bremer and Brisbane rivers. After passing Jimbour Station, one of the most celebrated properties in the whole of Australia, it climbs the steep escarpment of the Little Liverpool Range. Construction of a railway up such a steep slope does honour to the engineers who were responsible for it. The iron ribbon snakes around spurs and along the face of cliffs and hillsides, which plunge downwards into deep gullies where gigantic eucalyptus grow far below. One wondered how the engine could pull the long string of carriages up such steep grades.

Thus we reached an altitude of nearly 3,000 feet above sea level. From this point we looked out over a magnificent panorama of heavily timbered country. The views were wonderful: nothing could equal the natural grandeur of these mountains. The trees towered to a height of 260 feet above the valley floors, and in the distance we could see the plains we had just crossed. To the south a rich valley, where sugar-cane and tropical agriculture make fortunes for the *settlers*, lay at the foot of the mountains. The rivers looked like long silver ribbons, strewn haphazardly on a green carpet. Unhappily, this superb vista was revealed to us only at intervals through breaks in the clouds. As we climbed higher a thick mist, soon to be transformed into torrential rain, formed around us. The nearer we got to our destination, the worse the weather became, and in another hour we were engulfed in a veritable deluge which robbed us of the finest views.

At Toowoomba, where we arrived at about four in the afternoon, the rain had preceded us and had converted some streets into torrents and others into absolute rivers of thick, red mud. It was urgent to shelter in some hotel and we were directed to one near the station, the Royal Hotel, said to be the best in the town. We reached it in an unspeakable state: soaked to the marrow, and bespattered with mud to the eyeballs. We were frozen into the bargain, for it was bitterly cold. We were shown into a little room where someone had hurriedly lit a good fire, but it took a long time for us to get warm.

Outside, it sounded like one of the forty days of Noah's flood.

Shivering by the fire in the chimney corner, Madame X— passionately declared that this was the last excursion she would ever make in Queensland. The good lady was afraid of catching a fever. As for her son, though he was already steeped to his ears in mud, he hankered for more, rushed out into the hotel yard, and came back five minutes later, unrecognisable. He had been inspired to roll on the ground, and he came in again wrapped in a veritable cocoon of red slime. It was not in his nature to do otherwise.

While the Count and I were trying to revive our spirits a little before dinner, and Madame X— was cleaning up her son, there was a knock on the door and the landlady came in. She was a thin Scotswoman, five feet eight tall and with a very dry exterior. The inner woman was of quite a different character for, unless appearances were deceptive, she probably applied herself most liberally to the bottle.

"Sir", she said to the Count in a husky voice, "there is another French count in the next room, who wants to know if you would like to see him."

"Good heavens," said Monsieur de Castelnau, turning to me, "I swear, by Noah's flood, it is raining French counts in this hole of Toowoomba! Who can this stranger be?"

"Show him in."

A moment later a tall, well-bred young man, dressed in bush fashion with sturdy riding-boots, made his entry.

"Be so good as to excuse the picturesqueness of my costume, Monsieur de Castelnau," said he, "but you see me as I have just arrived from Woodstock Station. In the *bar-room*, where the weather forced me to seek shelter, I heard it said that a French gentleman had just arrived at the hotel. Knowing of your visit to Brisbane, I immediately wondered who the traveller might be. My slight doubt was dissipated when the landlady, in speaking of her new guest, let slip the words '*French Count*', and I took the liberty of announcing myself.

"I am Count Pierre de B—."

"Well, please dine with us Monsieur de B— and we shall have plenty of time to talk, for we are all dying of hunger, and I imagine that your ride in the rain must have given you an appetite."

Monsieur de B— needed no urging: he was a charming conversationalist, full of gaiety and not lacking in spirit. He was in Australia for his sins, which, it seemed, were many and great; and he was now a *boundary-rider* on P. A. Jennings' Woodstock Station. An excellent horseman, endowed with considerable energy, he had taken to this free life and was quite happy, he said, among the sheep.

After chatting for about two hours, he left us and rode off again into the rain.

This chance meeting, in the depths of a lonely country, with a cheerful and friendly French gentleman, made us forget the vile weather, which looked as though it had come to stay. We left Toowoomba next day without going any further.

It was written that Queensland should be a land of unexpected meetings for all of us. Scarcely had we returned to Brisbane, when a distressed French ship entered the river. She was the *City of Lille*, commanded by Captain X—, whom I had known in Mauritius. While being very concerned for the poor captain, whose ship in all probability was about to be condemned, I felt very happy at the circumstances which had brought us such pleasant company: Monsieur X— was a first-class musician.

For some days there had been another French vessel in the river, the *National* out of Havre, a fine ship of 800 tons, skippered by a little dark man who was a *bon viveur* and very good company.

I went aboard the *National* the day after our return from the rain-soaked expedition to Toowoomba. The captain bade me stay to dinner and informed me of the *City of Lille's* arrival – something of which I knew already. The captain of the disabled ship came aboard while we were still at table.

He was not a little astonished to be greeted with the words: "Tell me, Captain X—, do you realise how small the world is? How are you?"

"What, it's you!" he replied, recognising me at once. "What are you doing here, then? Things are not going very well with me, as you can see!" And even while shaking me warmly by the hand, he could not repress a cry of pain. During the storm which had reduced his ship to the condition of a hulk, a wave had hurled him, with unheard-of force, against the cabin wall and almost broken his leg. He had stayed at his post till the end, however. Only when the ship and her crew were safe and sound in the river did he think of his wounded leg, which by then was all puffed-up and hurt horribly.

I stayed on for more than a month in Brisbane, devoting the days to my young pupil, who became more and more incorrigible in proportion as he was more and more spoilt, and spending my evenings aboard the *National*. There the time passed quickly, too quickly, for these gentlemen were both excellent hosts. Sometimes we left the poor invalid, whose leg was recovering only slowly, on board, and went to waste an hour or two in a room in Elizabeth Street which had been dignified by the title of the *Queensland Theatre*. Shakespeare's masterpieces were performed on a stage three yards square, and the ghost of the King of Denmark could be seen making his exit behind a backdrop representing Mount Vesuvius in eruption. Hamlet, dressed like an undertaker's mute, philosophised on the vanity of the human condition, while contemplating a hollowed-out pumpkin, in which an artist had cut out the jawbone, the nose and two huge round eyes. Other performances were in keeping with this. At last winter drew to an end and we left the capital of Queensland on board the steamship, *Governor Blackall*, which landed us in Sydney.

David Blair

DOTTINGS FROM THE DIARY OF A TRAVELLING TECHNOLOGICAL COMMISSIONER

From Melbourne to Albury

1887. May 18

At 4.55 p.m. bade farewell to Flory (who came with me to the train) and started for Albury. – In the carriage, besides myself, were an elderly gentleman, a young man who looked like a bank clerk, a very handsome young lady of 28, and a little girl of 10. – Fell into a train (an abstract, not a railway train) of melancholy musing – then into a doze – wakened up by guard shouting out, "Twenty minutes here for refreshments." – Found I was at Seymour – went into refreshment room, and had tea and bread and butter: paid 1s/6d for same. Got into train again, and away we went. – Fell into conversation with old gentleman – talked 16 to the dozen on political, social, personal etc. etc. topics – Old gentn. very intelligent and well informed – After a long talk told him who I was – expression of great surprise and pleasure at meeting the far-famed Journalist and Historian of Australasia – he said he had been hearing of me, reading me, and talking about me for 30 years – told me he was Mr Beeby, a saw-miller of Corowa in N.S.W. – Gave me a hearty invitation to go and stay with him for a month – plenty of good shooting etc. etc. – Promised him I would go when I could find time – Beeby got out at Wangaratta.

All this time a violent flirtation going on between young lady and gentleman – took them to be a newly married couple out for the honeymoon – little girl asleep, I having made up a bed for her with the rug – after a while discovered that the young flirts had quarrelled – he went to one side of the carriage and stuck his head out of the window, she came over and sat down by me – began to abuse young gentn. as being a brainless fellow, very conceited etc. etc. – said she had been listening to my conversation with old gentn. – began to pile on the flattery – said I did not look more than 50, and would never believe I was 75 – hinted that she was not married, and would be only too happy to have a gentn. for a husband of exactly my age, appearance, and size – said she thought a Travelling Technological Commissioner must be a very high and mighty Personage, with more to the same effect – ended up with fairly popping the question to me!!! – I was in the very act of telling her I should give the question into my most serious consideration, when the train came to a dead-stop and guard shouted "Albury" – awfully glad to hear the sound – shook hands with my ardent admirer (whose name I never asked), took up my traps and bolted – train started – and my fair postulant vanished with it into space – Walking to my hotel recollected that she had never enquired whether *I* was married or single! – Taken all round, this was the most surprising illustration of feminine bashfulness and reserve I have ever encountered in all my life – Got to my hotel (the Globe) and so to bed.

* * *

Albury to Sydney

May 20th

Wrote up my diary, and posted it, with the 2 newspapers containing the puffs, for home – had much pleasant talk with Mr Plouskowski and a young squatter (married and from Melbourne) named Johnson. – At 2.45 started in the slow train for Sydney.

With a resolute purpose of escaping the importunate flattery and offers of marriage of handsome young ladies of 28, who may be running about in railways in search of matrimony, I got into the smoking carriage, first class. – *Memo.* As my free pass had not come, the polite stationmaster at Albury wired to his Superintendent for leave to pass me on, and passed on I was accordingly. – Several civil fellows in the carriage with me, who got out at intervals at passing stations, and were replaced by others equally civil – much talking, some joking, not very much smoking.

Country travelled over before dusk rather uninteresting, and too well known to require describing afresh – was almost startled when I found myself crossing the Murrumbidgee.

* * *

As night came on, talk slackened and smoking increased – to keep up the sociality I rattled off no end of jokes and anecdotes, mostly drawn from the old and well-worn lecture on "National Wit and Humour" – never heard fellows roar with laughter as they did, the jokes being evidently new to them – towards midnight wrapped myself in the rug – night not very cold – dropped asleep at 1.30 and awoke, feeling strange and chilled, at 5.30 – raw morning after a rainy night – everything seemed confused when, about 7.30 we reached Sydney – genial fellow-passenger hired a hansom cab (there seem to be none but hansom cabs in Sydney) and took me and my traps to the Metropolitan Hotel in Castlereagh Street (corner of King St) – had breakfast, a wash, and so to bed.

Got up at 11.30 – dressed and went out to have a first look at Sydney – did not at all recognise the old Sydney which I knew in 1850–51 – was struck at once with the stamp of inferiority to Melbourne in everything: streets, people, buildings, etc. – city seems to have been stuck down "every which way" – no regularity, no straight lines of grand buildings as in Melbourne – people all common-looking – could not see the pretty faces that were common enough when I was courting Mamma in 1850 – some of the public buildings very fine, but all in such bad situations that they don't show out to advantage.

* * *

After dinner went for a stroll through the city until tea-time – resolved, as it was Saturday, and I was still in a rather limp condition from the 16½ hours in the railway train, that I would not show myself to any of my grand friends till Monday morning – Nesbit went with some friends to the Agricultural Show at Moore Park, so I was alone – did not meet a soul I knew, except the lad who shaved and trimmed me up generally in a barber's shop in George Street, who knew me well in Melbourne – paid 1s/3d for the barbering – told the barber that the last time I paid 5d. for a shave in the same shop (or one near it) in the same street was in Decr. 1851 – Barber stared at me as if I had two heads on me – came across a mean and shabby place called the Haymarket, where a very poor sort of a Paddy's Market was going on – everybody looked poor and miserable, not jolly and happy as in the Eastern Market in Melbourne on a Saturday night.

Strolled along George Street, which I could not recollect – admired the English cathedral and Town hall, but both badly situated – was deafened with the noise of the tramcars and omnibuses – tried to find the spots (sacred to memory!) where I first saw, walked with, preached to, courted, and proposed to, Mamma: but could not find one of them – returned to tea at 6 – found Nesbit awaiting me – after tea sat in the smoking room chatting till 9, when he went – encountered my old acquaintance, Habbe the scene painter – had a long talk with him – he had with him a Dane (who talks good English) who is going to England to give evidence in the case of the Claimant, he (the Dane) having sailed with him in the *Osprey* in 1852 – to bed at 12, in good health and spirits, thanks to God!

In Sydney Once More

May 22nd – Sunday

A glorious morning, all Australian sunshine and balmy airs – awoke wonderfully refreshed after a good night's rest, and feeling as young as I felt 37 years ago in this very same Sydney – can it be that I am actually an "old fogey" of 67?

* * *

After dinner went down to the quay and went on board the Clontarf steamboat for a trip round the harbour (ticket 1s.) – fell into conversation with an old sea-captain from Cork – he pointed out to me all the notable spots in the harbour; e.g. the spot where O'Farrell shot the Duke of Edinburgh, the old captain being at the moment in the marquee into which the Prince was carried; the place where the *Dunbar* was wrecked; Wentworth's house at Vaucluse, Dalley's house at Manley Beach, and other notable mansions – old sea-captain said he had seen all the fine harbours in the world, and that Port Jackson is, out of all sight, the finest. I fully believed him. Viewed simply as one of Nature's works, it is a masterpiece – I should dearly love to explore it in company with all my loved ones at home, Dr Bevan, and John Ruskin. [*Mem.* – Perhaps I shall some day.]

After tea wrote up diary and composed a sonnet – meditated deeply over my past life, which really began here in Sydney in 1850, and ended on the mournful 24th January 1887 – In this subdued but serene frame of mind went quietly to bed – have thus been two whole days in Sydney, and as yet have not met anybody from Melbourne.

May 23rd

Another splendid morning – after breakfast went to call on Sir Henry Parkes at the Treasury – found the old man, with his lion-like head and shaggy gray mane, seated at the Premier's table, with a wilderness of papers and official documents scattered about him – had a hearty reception from him, but only stayed a few minutes, as he was in the full swing of work – left him and walked about the city till dinner time – Wynyard Square very fine as a small city park – amazing expansion of the city since I left it in Decr. 1851 – recollect the site where Wynyard Square now stands an open waste, dirty and cheerless, surrounded in part by ranges of filthy old shanties fallen to ruin, which were, I believe, a female penitentiary in the early days – the change is from a pigstye to a palace.

Dined, and then dressed for the levée – a great crowd there, as I thought, but newspapers reported it a small number only – the usual display of showy official costumes; officers, naval and military, University dons with trencher caps, judges in horsehair and ermine, barristers and clergymen, aldermen in knee-breeches and silk stockings, and some hundreds of common citizens in swallow-tail coats (myself one of them) looking as dignified as they each knew how – had a pleasant smile and hearty shake of the hand from Lord Carrington, a bright-looking, handsome man in gorgeous apparel – thought he looked at me and pressed my hand as if he meant to say, "Mr Blair, I have heard your distinguished name before." But this is only my own egregious vanity, of course – met at the levée only two persons who recognised me; many persons looked at me dubiously, as much as to say, "Think I have seen *you* before, somewhere." Well, I have been there, once or twice, in my time.

At the levée shook hands with the Premier, and walked with him and the Ministry to the Treasury, an imposing building just outside the gate of Government House – Premier introduced me to two of his colleagues, Mr Roberts, Post-Master General, and Mr Abigail: the former, a youngish, good-looking man, with a cheerful face; the other a small, limping man, with a keenly intellectual face, but not in any way notable – both very civil – Noticed at the levée the gorgeous liveries of the footmen: crimson plush breeches, white silk stockings, blue swallow-tailed coats with enormous buttons etc. – were I to meet one of these Magnificent Personages alone by himself walking along the streets, I should take him to be the Lord High Admiral of Corea at the very least – walking back from the levée admired the beauty of the matchless situation, with the superb views of the Harbour, the luminous skies, the ultramarine tint of the water contrasting with the deep green of the brushwood on the shores – Garden Island, Pott's Point, Fort Denison, etc. etc. – "Where all, save the spirit of Man, is divine" – not that the Sydneyites are any worse than their neighbours.

* * *

May 24th

Queen's birthday: all Sydney keeping holiday – weather divine – rambled about after breakfast, admiring the bunting-covered ships in the harbour – cannons firing – street thronged with people, but the crowd much more commonplace in appearance than the Melbourne one – soldiers marching, with bands playing, to grand review at Moore Park – called in at Treasury – found that Parkes had gone to review with Governor – sat for a while in Chief Secretary's library dipping into some of the new books – stood on the balcony outside admiring the superb scenery – went over the Executive Council chamber: very fine, with splendid ornaments, statues, vases etc. etc. – sat in the Governor's and the Chief Secretary's chairs – Treasury chambers really grand, as the work-rooms of a Government ruling a great nation ought to be.

Left the Treasury and walked into Hyde Park – magnificent change since I lodged here, at this house, No.1, Burdekin Terrace, in 1850! – I was then a bachelor, very enthusiastic, deeply religious, full of intellectual and religious fervour, an omnivorous reader, utterly careless about worldly affairs or personal prospects, taking Our Blessed Lord's injunctions to His disciples in all their literal meaning. Yet I have survived through 37 years of the battle of life!

And here it was I first met Annie, and fell, at once and for life, deeply in love with that beautiful girl with the loveliest face I ever saw in my life, and who for 36 years (time of courtship included) was my more than other self; for whom alone I lived, and, having lost her, have lost all desire to live. Here is the very green sward upon which we were wont to walk upon sunny afternoons and moonlight nights, talking of life, and love, and God, and Heaven. *There* is the street up which I was accustomed to turn my steps, as, regularly every evening I set out from my solitary room to visit the cottage on the Surry Hills. *There* still stands the side-wall of the cottage that marked the corner of the street in which lived my Annie – *my* Annie even then – and by which waymark I could find my road on even the darkest nights. But the cottage itself is no longer there, and the spot is altogether changed in aspect. A new world, and I a solitary lingerer from the old world that has vanished for ever! *Here* was the very spot, then the little garden of the cottage, in which I first declared my deep passion, and was accepted, and the first kiss of engagement was given and taken! Ah me! What a throng of memories crowd upon my mind, whilst on this sacred spot I stand and meditate of times and joys departed! Two things only stand conspicuously out amidst the thronging multitude of recollections: the first is, how amazingly beautiful *She* was; and the second, how passionately I loved Her. Dear and sainted Annie! Never did I meet a second woman in all my long life who awoke in me even the semblance of the same deep, absorbing passion, nor a woman whom, as I have always felt since first I looked upon your lovely and lustrous countenance, I should have asked to be my wife. The universe, for me, possessed only one Annie Grant; and there never was, nor will be, another.

But these thoughts are too deep and too sacred for utterance in words. Silence and Thought alone are fitting here. Ah me!

In the afternoon I calmed my mind by taking a second trip round the Harbour, in company with Mr Callaghan of Melbourne, whom I met on the quay: and so, back to the hotel to dinner, and to bed.

Wrote up my diary in the morning and posted it – After luncheon went to the Treasury and had a long chat with my old friend Parkes. He gave me a commission to visit all the public institutions in N.S.W. and asked me to come and dine with him next day at his house in Parramatta. Stopped with him – he putting off all public business and refusing to see any of his numerous callers, for, as he said, the pleasure of talking freely with D.B. – Left him setting to work again at 4.30 p.m. – Strolled about the domain (an unrivalled park!) – Mused on the glorious afternoons long, long ago, when I wandered here, enraptured, in company with *Her*. – After tea went to the old School of Arts, where I lectured in 1850, and read till 10 o'clock – [*Memo*. The old institution is still substantially the same primitive place it was 37 years ago. The Sydneyites are not now, and never were, an intellectually cultured people.] – back to hotel, and to bed.

Ernest Giles

[CROSSING THE DESERT]

From 2nd April to 6th May, 1875

On the 2nd April we departed from this friendly depot at Wynbring Rock, taking our three horses, the two camels and the calf. The morning was as hot as fire; at midday we watered all our animals, and having saddled and packed them, we left the place behind us. On the two camels we carried as much water as we had vessels to hold it, the quantity being nearly fifty gallons. The horses were now on more friendly terms with them, so that they could be led by a person on horseback. Old Jimmy, now no longer a guide, was not permitted to take the lead, but rode behind, to see that nothing fell off the camels' saddles. I rode in advance, on my best horse Chester, a fine, well-set chestnut cob, a horse I was very fond of, as he had proved himself so good. Nicholls rode a strong young grey horse called Formby; he also had proved himself to my satisfaction to be a good one. Jimmy was mounted on an old black horse, that was a fine ambler, the one that bolted away with the load of water the first night we started from Youldeh. He had not stood the journey from Youldeh at all well; the other two were quite fresh and hearty when we left Wynbring.

By the evening of the 2nd we had made only twenty-two miles. We found the country terrific; the ground rose into sandhills so steep and high, that all our animals were in a perfect lather of sweat. The camels could hardly be got along at all. At night, where we were compelled by darkness to encamp, there was nothing for the horses to eat, so the poor brutes had to be tied up, lest they should ramble back to Wynbring. There was plenty of food for the camels, as they could eat the leaves of some of the bushes, but they were too sulky to eat because they were tied up. The bull continually bit his nose-rope through, and made several attempts to get away, the calf always going with him, leaving his mother: this made her frantic to get away too. The horses got frightened, and were snorting and jumping about, trying to break loose all night. The spot we were in was a hollow, between two high sandhills, and not a breath of air relieved us from the oppression of the atmosphere. Peter Nicholls and I were in a state of thirst and perspiration the whole night, running about after the camels and keeping the horses from breaking away. If the cow had got loose, we could not have prevented the camels clearing off. I was never more gratified than at the appearance of the next morning's dawn, as it enabled us to move away from this dreadful place. It was impossible to travel through this region at night, even by moonlight; we should have lost our eyes upon the sticks and branches of the direful scrubs if we had attempted it, besides tearing our skin and clothes to pieces also. Starting at earliest dawn, and traversing formidably steep and rolling waves of sand, we at length reached the foot of the mountain we had been striving for, in twenty-three miles, forty-five from Wynbring. I could not help thinking it was the most desolate heap on the face of the earth, having no water or places that could hold it. The elevation of this eminence was over 1,000 feet above the surrounding country, and over 2,000 feet above the sea. The country visible from its summit was still enveloped in dense scrubs in every direction, except on a bearing a few degrees north of east, where some low ridges appeared. I rode my horse Chester many miles over the wretched stony slopes at the foot of this mountain, and tied him up to trees while I walked to its summit, and into gullies and crevices innumerable, but no water rewarded my efforts, and it was very evident that what the old black fellow Wynbring Tommy, had said, about its being waterless was only too true. After wasting several hours in a fruitless search for water, we left the wretched mount, and steered away for the ridges I had seen from its summit. They appeared to be about forty-five miles away. As it was so late in the day when we left the mountain, we got only seven miles from it when darkness again overtook us, and we had to encamp.

On the following day, the old horse Jimmy was riding completely gave in from the heat and thirst and fearful nature of the country we were traversing, having come only sixty-five miles from Wynbring. We could neither lead, ride, nor drive him any farther. We had given each horse some water from the supply the camels carried, when we reached the mountain, and likewise some on the previous night, as the heavy sandhills had so exhausted them, this horse having received more than the others. Now he lay down and stretched out his limbs in the agony of thirst and exhaustion. I was loath to shoot the poor old creature, and I also did not like the idea of leaving him to die slowly of thirst; but I thought perhaps if I left him, he might recover sufficiently to travel at night at his own pace, and thus return to Wynbring, although I also knew from former sad experience in Gibson's Desert, that, like Badger and Darkie, it was more than probable he could never escape. His saddle was hung in the fork of a sandalwood tree, not the sandalwood of commerce, and leaving him stretched upon the burning sand, we moved away. Of course he was never seen or heard of after.

That night we encamped only a few miles from the ridges, at a place where there was a little dry grass, and where both camels and horses were let go in hobbles. Long before daylight on the following morning, old Jimmy and I were tracking the camels by torchlight, the horse-bells indicating that those animals were not far off; the camel bells had gone out of hearing early in the night. Old Jimmy was a splendid tracker; indeed, no human being in the world but an Australian aboriginal, and that a half or wholly wild one, could track a camel on some surfaces, for where there is any clayey soil, the creature leaves no more mark on the ground than an ant – black children often amuse themselves by tracking ants – and to follow such marks as they do leave, by firelight, was marvellous. Occasionally they would leave some marks that no one could mistake, where they passed over sandy ground; but for many hundreds of yards beyond, it would appear as though they must have flown over the ground, and had never put their feet to the earth at all. By the time daylight appeared, old Jimmy had tracked them about three miles; then he went off, apparently quite regardless of any tracks at all, walking at such a pace, that I could only keep up with him by occasionally running. We came upon the camels at length at about six miles from the camp, amongst some dry clay-pans, and they were evidently looking for water. The old cow, which was the only riding camel, was so poor and bony, it was too excruciating to ride her without a saddle or a pad of some sort, which now we had not got, so we took it in turns to ride the bull, and he made many attempts to shake us off; but as he had so much hair on his hump, we could cling on by that as we sat behind it. It was necessary for whoever was walking to lead him by his nose-rope, or he would have bolted away and rubbed his encumbrance off against a tree, or else rolled on it. In consequence of the camels having strayed so far, it was late in the day when we again started, the two horses looking fearfully hollow and bad. The morning as usual was very hot. There not being now a horse a piece to ride, and the water which one camel had carried having been drank by the animals, Peter Nicholls rode the old cow again, both she and the bull being much more easy to manage and get along than when we started from Youldeh. Our great difficulty was with the nose-ropes; the calf persisted in getting in front of its mother and twisting her nose-rope round his neck, also in placing itself right in between the fore-legs of the bull. This would make him stop, pull back and break his rope, or else the button would tear through the nose; this caused detention a dozen times a day, and I was so annoyed with the young animal, I could scarcely keep from shooting it many times. The young creature was most endearing now, when caught, and evidently suffered greatly from thirst.

We reached the ridges in seven miles from where we had camped, and had now come ninety miles from Wynbring. We could find no water at these ridges, as there were no places that could hold it. Here we may be said to have entered on a piece of open country, and as it was apparently a change for the better from the scrubs, I was very glad to see it, especially as we hoped to obtain water on it. Our horses were now in a terrible state of thirst, for the heat was great, and the region we had traversed was dreadfully severe, and though they had each been given some of the water we brought with us, yet we could not afford anything like enough to satisfy them. From the top of the ridge a low mount or hill bore 20° north of east; Mount Finke, behind us, bore 20° south of west. I pushed on now for the hill in advance, as it was nearly on the route I desired to travel. The country being open, we made good progress, and though we could not reach it that night, we were upon its summit early the next morning, it being about thirty miles from the ridges we had left, a number of dry, salt, white lagoons intervening. This hill was as dry and waterless as the mount and ridges, we had left behind us in the scrubs. Dry salt lagoons lay scattered about in nearly all directions, glittering with their saline encrustations, as the sun's rays flashed upon them. To the southward two somewhat inviting isolated hills were seen; in all other directions the horizon appeared gloomy in the extreme. We had now come 120 miles from water, and the supply we had started with was almost exhausted; the country we were in could give us none, and we had but one, of two courses to pursue, either to advance still further into this terrible region, or endeavour to retreat to Wynbring. No doubt the camels could get back alive, but ourselves and the horses could never have re-crossed the frightful bed of rolling sand-mounds, that intervened between us and the water we had left. My poor old black companion was aghast at such a region, and also at what he considered my utter folly in penetrating into it at all. Peter Nicholls, I was glad to find, was in good spirits, and gradually changing his opinions with regard to the powers and value of the camels. They had received no water themselves, though they had laboured over the hideous sandhills, laden with the priceless fluid for the benefit of the horses, and it was quite evident the latter could not much longer live, in such a desert, whilst the former were now far more docile and obedient to us than when we started. Whenever the horses were given any water, we had to tie the camels up at some distance. The expression in these animals' eyes when they saw the horses drinking was extraordinary; they seemed as though they were going to speak, and had they done so, I know well they would have said, "You give those useless little pigmies the water that cannot save them, and you deny it to us, who have carried it, and will yet be your only saviours in the end." After we had fruitlessly searched here for water, having wasted several hours, we left this wretched hill, and I continued steering upon the same course we had come, viz. north 75° east, as that bearing would bring me to the north-western extremity of Lake Torrens, still distant over 120 miles. It was very probable we should get no water, as none is known to exist where we should touch upon its shores. Thus we were, after coming 120 miles from Wynbring, still nearly 200 miles from the Finniss Springs, the nearest water that I knew. It was now a matter of life and death; could we reach the Finniss at all? We could neither remain here, nor should we survive if we attempted to retreat; to advance was our only chance of escape from the howling waste in which we were almost entombed; we therefore moved onwards, as fast and as far as we could. On the following morning, before dawn, I had been lying wakefully listening for the different sounds of the bells on the animals' necks, and got up to brighten up the camp fire with fresh wood, when the strange sound of the quacking of a wild duck smote upon my ear. The blaze of firelight had evidently attracted the creature, which probably thought it was the flashing of water, as it flew down close to my face, and almost precipitated itself into the flames; but discovering its error, it wheeled away upon its unimpeded wings, and left me wondering why this denizen of the air and water, should be sojourning around the waterless encampment of such hapless travellers as we. The appearance of such a bird raised my hopes, and forced me to believe that we must be in the neighbourhood of some water, and that the coming daylight would reveal to us the element which alone could save us and our unfortunate animals from death. But, alas! how many human hopes and aspirations are continually doomed to perish unfulfilled; and were it not that "Hope springs eternal in the human breast," all faith, all energy, all life, and all success would be at an end, as then we should know that most of our efforts are futile, whereas now we hope they may attain complete fruition. Yet, on the other hand, we learn that the fruit of dreamy hoping is waking blank despair. We were again in a region of scrubs as bad and as dense as those I hoped and thought, I had left behind me.

Leaving our waterless encampment, we continued our journey, a melancholy, thirsty, silent trio. At 150 miles from Wynbring my poor horse Chester gave in, and could go no farther; for some miles I had walked, and we had the greatest difficulty in forcing him along, but now he was completely exhausted and rolled upon the ground in the death agony of thirst. It was useless to waste time over the unfortunate creature; it was quite impossible for him ever to rise again, so in mercy I fired a revolver-bullet at his forehead, as he gasped spasmodically upon thc desert sand: a shiver passed through his frame, and we left him dead in the lonely spot.

We had now no object but to keep pushing on; our supply of water was all but gone, and we were in the last stage of thirst and wretchedness. By the night of that night we had reached a place 168 miles from Wynbring, and in all that distance not a drop of water had been found. We had one unfortunate horse left, the grey called Formby, and that poor creature held out as long and on as little water as I am sure is possible in such a heated and horrid region. On the following morning the poor beast came up to Nicholls and I, old Jimmy being after the camels which were close by, and began to smell us, then stood gazing vacantly at the fire; a thought seemed to strike him that it was water, and he put his mouth down into the flames. This idea seems to actuate all animals when in the last stage of thirst. We were choking with thirst ourselves, but we agreed to sacrifice a small billyful of our remaining stock of water for this unfortunate last victim to our enterprise. We gave him about two quarts, and bitterly we regretted it later, hoping he might still be able to stagger on to where water might be found; but vain was the hope and vain the gift, for the creature that had held up so long and so well, swallowed up the last little draught we gave, fell down and rolled and shivered in agony, as Chester had done, and he died and was at rest. A singular thing about this horse was that his eyes had sunk into his head until they were all but hidden. For my own part, in such a region and in such a predicament as we were placed, I would not unwillingly have followed him into the future.

The celebrated Sir Thomas Mitchell, one of Australia's early explorers, in one of his journeys, after finding a magnificent country watered by large rivers, and now the long-settled abodes of civilisation, mounted on a splendid horse, bursts into an old cavalier song, a verse of which says:

> A steede, a steede of matchless speede,
> A sworde of metal keane;
> All else to noble mindes is drosse;
> All else on earthe is meane.

I don't know what he would have thought had he been in my case, with his matchless "steede" dead, and in the pangs of thirst himself, his "sworde of metal keane" a useless encumbrance, 168 miles from the last water, and not knowing where the next might be; he would have to admit that the wonderful beasts which now alone remained to us were by no means to be accounted "meane", for these patient and enduring creatures, which were still alive, had tasted no water since leaving Wynbring, and, though the horses were dead and gone, stood up with undiminished powers – appearing to be as well able now to continue on and traverse this wide-spread desert as when they left the oasis behind. We had nothing now to depend upon but our two "ships of the desert", which we were only just beginning to understand. I had been a firm believer in them from the first, and had many an argument with Nicholls about them; his opinion had now entirely altered. At Youldeh he had called them ugly, useless, lazy brutes, that were not to be compared to horses for a moment; but now that the horses were dead they seemed more agreeable and companionable than ever the horses had been.

When Jimmy brought them to the camp they looked knowingly at the prostrate form of the dead horse; they kneeled down close beside it and received their loads, now indeed light enough, and we went off again into the scrubs, riding and walking by turns, our lives entirely depending on the camels; Jimmy had told us they were calmly feeding upon some of the trees and bushes in the neighbourhood when he got them. That they felt the pangs of thirst there can be no doubt – and what animal can suffer thirst like a camel? – as whenever they were brought to the camp they endeavoured to fumble about the empty water-bags, tin pannikins, and any other vessel that ever had contained water.

The days of toil, the nights of agony and feverish unrest, that I spent upon this journey I can never forget. After struggling through the dense scrubs all day we were compelled perforce to remain in them all night. It was seldom now we spoke to one another, we were too thirsty and worn with lassitude to converse, and my reflections the night after the last horse died, when we had come nearly 200 miles without water, of a necessity assumed a gloomy tinge, although I am the least gloomy-minded of the human race, for we know that the tone of the mind is in a great measure sympathetic with the physical condition of the body. If the body is weak from exhaustion and fatigue, the brain and mind become dull and sad, and the thoughts of a wanderer in such a desolate region as this, weary with a march in heat and thirst from daylight until dark, who at last sinks upon the heated ground to watch and wait until the blazing sunlight of another day, perhaps, may bring him to some place of rest, cannot be otherwise than of a mournful kind. The mind is forced back upon itself, and becomes filled with an endless chain of thoughts which wander through the vastness of the star-bespangled spheres; for here, the only things to see, the only things to love, and upon which the eye may gaze, and from which the beating heart may gather some feelings of repose, are the glittering bands of brilliant stars shining in the azure vault of heaven. From my heated couch of sandy earth I gazed helplessly but rapturously upon them, wondering at the enormity of occupied and unoccupied space, revolving thoughts of past, present, and future existencies, and of how all that is earthly fadeth away. But can that be the case with our world itself, with the sun from which it obtains its light and life, or with the starry splendours of the worlds beyond the sun? Will they, can they, ever fade? They are not spiritual; celestial still we call them, but they are material all, in form and nature. We are both; yet we must fade and they remain. How is the understanding to decide which of the two holds the main spring and thread of life? Certainly we know that the body decays, and even the paths of glory lead but to the grave; but we also know that the mind becomes enfeebled with the body, that the aged become almost idiotic in their second childhood; and if the body is to rise again, how is poor humanity to distinguish the germ of immortality? Philosophies and speculations upon the future have been subjects of the deepest thought for the highest minds of every generation of mankind; and although creeds have risen and sunk, and old religions and philosophies have passed away, the dubious minds of mortal men still hang and harp upon the theme of what can be the Great Beyond. The various creeds, of the many different nations of the earth induce them to believe in as many differing notions of heaven, but all and each appear agreed upon the point that up into the stars alone their hoped-for heaven is to be found; and if all do not, in this agree, still there are some aspiring minds high soaring above sublunary things, above the petty disputes of differing creeds, and the vague promises they hold out to their votaries, who behold, in the firmament above, mighty and mysterious objects for veneration and love.

These are the gorgeous constellations set thick with starry gems, the revolving orbs of densely crowded spheres, the systems beyond systems, clusters beyond clusters, and universes beyond universes, all brilliantly glittering with various coloured light, all wheeling and swaying, floating and circling round some distant, unknown, motive, centre-point, in the pauseless measures of a perpetual dance of joy, keeping time and tune with most ecstatic harmony, and producing upon the enthrallëd mind the not imaginary music of the spheres.

Then comes the burning wish to know how come these mighty mysterious and material things about. We are led to suppose our own minds and bodies progressively improve from a state of infancy to a certain-point, so it is with all things we see in nature; but the method of the original production of life and matter is beyond the powers of man to discover. Therefore, we look forward with anxiety and suspense, hope, love, and fear to a future time, having passed through the portals of the valley of death, from this existence, we shall enjoy life after life, in new body, after new body, passing through new sphere, after new sphere, arriving nearer and nearer to the fountain-head of all perfection, the divinely great Almighty source of light and life, of hope and love.

These were some of my reflections throughout that weary night; the stars that in their constellations had occupied the zenith, now have passed the horizon's verge; other and fresh glittering bands now occupy their former places – at last the dawn begins to glimmer in the east, and just as I could have fallen into the trance of sleep, it was time for the race of life, again to wander on, so soon as our animals could be found.

This was the eighth day of continued travel from Wynbring; our water was now all gone, and we were yet more than 100 miles from the Finniss Springs. I had been compelled to enforce a most rigid and inadequate economy with our water during our whole march; when we left the camp where the last horse died very little over three pints remained; we were all very bad, old Jimmy was nearly dead. At about four o'clock in the afternoon we came to a place where there was a considerable fall into a hollow, here was some bare clay – in fact it was an enormous clay-pan, or miniature lake-bed; the surface was perfectly dry, but in a small drain or channel, down which water could descend in times of rain, by the blessing of Providence I found a supply of yellow water. Nicholls had previously got strangely excited – in fact the poor fellow was light-headed from thirst, and at one place where there was no water he threw up his hat and yelled out "Water, water!" he walking a little in advance; we had really passed the spot where the water was but when Nicholls gave the false information I jumped down off my camel and ran up to him, only to be grievously disappointed; but as I went along I caught sight of a whitish light through the mulga trees partially behind me, and without saying a word for fear of fresh disappointment, I walked towards what I had seen; Nicholls and Jimmy, who both seemed dazed, went on with the camels.

What I had seen, was a small sheet of very white water, and I could not resist the temptation to drink before I went after them. By the time I had drank they had gone on several hundred yards; when I called to them and flung up my hat, they were so stupid with thirst, and disappointment, that they never moved towards me, but stood staring until I took the camels' nose-rope in my hand, and, pointing to my knees, which were covered with yellow mud, simply said "water"; then, when I led the camels to the place, down these poor fellows went on their knees, in the mud and water, and drank, and drank, and I again knelt down and drank, and drank. Oh, dear reader, if you have never suffered thirst you can form no conception what agony it is. But talk about drinking, I couldn't have believed that even thirsty camels could have swallowed such enormous quantities of fluid.

It was delightful to watch the poor creatures visibly swelling before our eyes. I am sure the big bull Mustara must have taken down fifty gallons of water, for even after the first drink, when we took their saddles off at the camp, they all three went back to the water and kept drinking for nearly an hour.

We had made an average travelling of twenty-eight miles a day from Wynbring, until this eighth day, when we came to the water in twenty-four miles, thus making it 220 miles in all. I could not sufficiently admire and praise the wonderful powers of these extraordinary, and to me entirely new animals. During the time we had been travelling the weather had been very hot and oppressive, the thermometer usually rising to 104° in the shade when we rested for an hour in the middle of the day, but that was not the hottest time, from 2.40 to 3 p.m. being the culminating period. The country we had traversed was a most frightful desert, yet day after day our noble camels kept moving slowly but surely on, with undiminished powers, having carried water for their unfortunate companions the horses, and seeing them drop one by one exhausted and dying of thirst; still they marched contentedly on, carrying us by turns, and all the remaining gear of the dead horses, and finally brought us to water at last. We had yet over eighty miles to travel to reach the Finniss, and had we not found water I am sure the three human beings of the party could never have got there. The walking in turns over this dreadful region made us suffer all the more, and it was dangerous at any time to allow old Jimmy to put his baking lips to a water-bag, for he could have drank a couple of gallons at any time with the greatest ease. For some miles before we found the water the country had become of much better quality, the sandhills being lower and well grassed, with clay flats between. We also passed a number with pine-trees growing on them. Rains had evidently visited this region, as before I found the water I noticed that many of the deeper clay channels were only recently dry; when I say deeper, I mean from one to two feet, the usual depth of a clay-pan channel being about as many inches. The grass and herbage round the channel where I found the water were beautifully green.

Our course from the last hill had been about north 75° east; the weather, which had been exceedingly oppressive for so many weeks, now culminated in a thunderstorm of dust, or rather sand and wind, while dark nimbus clouds completely eclipsed the sun, and reduced the temperature to an agreeable and bearable state. No rain fell, but from this change the heats of summer departed, though the change did not occur until after we had found the water; now all our good things came together, viz. an escape from death by thirst, a watered and better travelling country, and cooler weather. Here we very naturally took a day to recruit. Old Jimmy was always very anxious to know how the compass was working, as I had always told him the compass would bring us to water, that it knew every country and every water, and as it did bring us to water, he thought what I said about it must be true. I also told him it would find some more water for us tomorrow. We were always great friends, but now I was so advanced in his favour that he promised to give me his daughter Mary for a wife when I took him back to Fowler's Bay. Mary was a very pretty little girl. But "I to wed with Coromantees? Thoughts like these would drive me mad. And yet I hold some (young) barbarians higher than the Christian cad." After our day's rest we again proceeded on our journey, with all our water vessels replenished, and of course now found several other places on our route where rain-water was lying, and it seemed like being translated to a brighter sphere, to be able to indulge in as much water-drinking as we pleased.

At one place where we encamped there was a cane grass flat, over a mile long, fifty to a hundred yards wide, and having about four feet of water in it, which was covered with water-fowl; amongst these a number of black swans were gracefully disporting themselves. Peter Nicholls made frantic efforts to shoot a swan and some ducks, but he only brought one wretchedly small teal into the camp. We continued on our former course until we touched upon and rounded the north-western extremity of Lake Torrens. I then changed my course for the Hermit Hill, at the foot of which the Finniss Springs and Sir Thomas Elder's cattle station lies. Our course was now nearly north. On the evening of the third day after leaving the water that had saved us, we fell in with two black fellows and their lubras or wives, shepherding two flocks of Mr Angas's sheep belonging to his Stuart's Creek station. As they were at a water, we encamped with them. Their lubras were young and pretty; the men were very hospitable to us, and gave us some mutton, for which we gave them tobacco and matches; for their kindness I gave the pretty lubras some tea and sugar. Our old Jimmy went up to them and shook hands, and they became great friends. These blacks could not comprehend where we could possibly have come from, Fowler's Bay being an unknown quantity to them. We had still a good day's stage before us to reach the Finniss, but at dusk we arrived, and were very kindly received and entertained by Mr Coulthard, who was in charge. His father had been an unfortunate explorer, who lost his life by thirst, upon the western shores of the Lake Torrens I have mentioned, his tin pannikin or pint pot was afterwards found with his name and the date of the last day he lived, scratched upon it. Many an unrecorded grave, many a high and noble mind, many a gallant victim to temerity and thirst, to murder by relentless native tribes, or sad mischance, is hidden in the wilds of Australia, and not only in the wilds, but in places also less remote, where the whistle of the shepherd and the bark of his dog, the crack of the stockman's whip, or the gay or grumbling voice of the teamster may now be heard, some unfortunate wanderer may have died. As the poet says:

> Perhaps in this neglected spot is laid,
> Some heart once pregnant with celestial fire;
> Hands that the rod of empire might have swayed,
> Or waked to ecstacy the living lyre.

If it is with a thought of pity, if it is with a sigh of lament, that we ponder over the fate of the lost, over the deaths in the long catalogue of the victims to the Australian bush, from Cunningham (lost with Mitchell) and Leichhardt, Kennedy and Gilbert, Burke, Wills, Gray, Poole, Curlewis and Conn, down to Coulthard, Panter, and Gibson, it must be remembered that they died in a noble cause, and they sleep in honourable graves. Nor must it be forgotten that they who return from confronting the dangers by which these others fell, have suffered enough to make them often wish that they, too, could escape through the grave from the horrors surrounding them. I have often been in such predicaments that I have longed for death, but having as yet returned alive, from deserts and their thirst, from hostile native tribes and deadly spears, and feeling still "the wild pulsation which in manhood's dawn I knew, when my days were all before me, and my years were twenty-two", – as long as there are new regions to explore, the burning charm of seeking something new, will still possess me; and I am also actuated to aspire and endeavour if I cannot make my life sublime, at least to leave behind me some "everlasting footprints on the sands of time".

At the Finniss Springs I met young Alec Ross, the son of another explorer, who was going to join my party for the new expedition to Perth. My destination was now Beltana, 140 miles from hence. I got a couple of horses for Nicholls and myself from Mr Coulthard, Jimmy being stuck up on the top of the old riding cow camel, who could travel splendidly on a road. When I arrived at Beltana I had travelled 700 miles from Fowler's Bay.

Henry Lawson

LETTERS FROM BOURKE AND HUNGERFORD

Great Western Hotel, Bourke
21st September 1892

Dear Aunt,

Struck Bourke this afternoon at 5 and am staying as above. Will of course have no news until tomorrow. The bush between here and Bathurst is horrible. I was right, and Banjo was wrong. Country very dry and dull, but I am agreeably disappointed with Bourke. It is a much nicer town than I thought it would be. I got a lot of very good points for copy on the way up. Think I'll be able to hang out all night. Board and lodging £1 per week, and very good. Might take a job here if I see a chance. Had several interviews with Bushman on the way up. Most of them hate the bush. Had a great argument with a shearer about the number of sheep a man can shear in a day. I know nothing whatever about the business, but he did not know that. I have already found out that Bushmen are the biggest liars that ever the Lord created. Took notes all the way up. I will take time to write you at length this week. I took a stroll out to find the Darling but have not found it yet. There is a sheet of the *Bulletin* with my answer to Banjo here. Hope you will pull through. Keep up your heart.

Yours the same,
Henry Lawson

Great Western Hotel, Bourke
27th September 1892

Dear Aunt,

The paper you sent came to hand all right, though rather late. I saw it in the rack about two days after it arrived. You needn't mind sending any papers, as all the city papers come here sooner than you could send them. Thanks all the same. The private barmaids sent me to bed boozed last night, but they won't do it again, – no. They are a pair of ex-actresses and as cunning as the devil. I'm an awful fool.

This is a queer place. *The ladies shout*. A big jolly-looking woman – who, by-the-way, is the landlady of a bush pub – marched into the bar this morning, and asked me to have a drink. This is a fact; so help me Moses! She came in a wagonette.

I am doing a little work, *sub rosa*, for the *Western Herald*. Will send a copy tomorrow. The editor sent for the labour leaders to give me some points for a local political poem. The chaps have seen the proof and are delighted. Will make about £1 1s. this week. The editor wanted to give me a notice, but I preferred to keep dark for a while. There'll be a sensation when his paper comes out tomorrow. His brother is a very rich and very good-natured squatter near here. I gave him a show as a probable member of Parliament. Also the landlord where I'm staying. The labour men say that nothing hits like rhyme.

I'll get a billet on the station next week if something better don't turn up. I'm worried to think that you must be in an awful fix; but I think there will be better days for both of us soon.

I can get painting to do in town next week, but I won't do any good here. Everybody shouts. I must take to the bush as soon as I can. I am working up stuff for the *Bulletin* but – between you and me – I don't mean to sacrifice myself altogether. More next week.

Burn this.

Your affectionate nephew,
Henry Lawson

Hungerford, Queensland
16th January 1893

Dear Aunt,

I found your letter in the Post Office of this God-Forgotten town. I carried my swag nearly two hundred miles since I last wrote to you, and I am now camped on the Queensland side of the border – a beaten man. I start back tomorrow – 140 miles by the direct road – and expect to reach Bourke in nine days. My mate goes on to Thargomindah. No work and very little to eat; we lived mostly on Johnny cakes and cadged a bit of meat here and there at the miserable stations. Have been three days without sugar. Once in

Bourke I'll find the means of getting back to Sydney – never to face the bush again. I got an offer to go over and edit a New Zealand paper and wrote to say that I doubted my ability to edit but would take a place on the staff. They seemed anxious to get me, and asked me to state my own terms. Simpson is negotiating with 'em. You can have no idea of the horrors of the country out here. Men tramp and beg and live like dogs. It is two months since I slept in what you can call a bed. We walk as far as we can – according to the water – and then lie down and roll ourselves in our blankets. The flies start at daylight and we fight them all day till dark – then mosquitoes start. We carry water in bags. Got bushed on a lignum plain Sunday before last and found the track at four o'clock in the afternoon – then tramped for four hours without water and reached a government dam. My mate drank nearly all night. But it would take a year to tell you all about my wanderings in the wilderness.

It would not be so bad if it was shearing season – then, at least we'd be sure of tucker. But the experience will help me to live in the city for the next year or so. So much for myself.

I'm real glad to hear that you are still at North Shore (you may expect me there within the next six months – as soon as I get a few decent clothes). Sorry Don is dead.

I'm writing on an old tin and my legs ache too much to let me sit any longer. I've always tried to write cheerful letters so you'll excuse this one. Will tell you all about it when I get down.

And now for a lonely walk of 140 miles. Will write from Bourke.

Your affectionate nephew,
Henry Lawson

P.S. I'm going off the track to try and get a few weeks' work on a Warrego station. Will write from there if successful.

Bourke
6th February 1893

Dear Aunt,

I got back again all right, and am at work painting. Will no doubt be able to get down your way in a few weeks. It's hot as hell here – too hot to think or write. *Bulletin* hunting me up for copy, but they must wait till I get down. I have some work to do for a local paper here, the *Western Herald*, and so I'll be able to get together a pound or two and some clothes. A squatter who knew me gave me as much tucker as I could carry, when I was coming down, *and a pound to help me along*. Squatters are not all bad. My boots were worn out and I was in rags when I arrived here – you should have seen the hat I wore. I find that I've tramped more than 300 miles since I left here last. That's all I ever intend to do with a swag. It's too hot to write more. Send some news by return.

Your affectionate nephew,
Henry Lawson

IN A DRY SEASON

Draw a wire fence and a few ragged gums, and add some scattered sheep running away from the train. Then you'll have the bush all along the New South Wales western line from Bathurst on.

The railway towns consist of a public house and a general store, with a square tank and a school-house on piles in the nearer distance. The tank stands at the end of the school and is not many times smaller than the building itself. It is safe to call the pub "The Railway Hotel", and the store "The Railway Stores", with an "s". A couple of patient, ungroomed hacks are probably standing outside the pub, while their masters are inside having a drink – several drinks. Also it's safe to draw a sundowner sitting listlessly on a bench on the veranda, reading the *Bulletin*.

The Railway Stores seem to exist only in the shadow of the pub, and it is impossible to conceive either as being independent of the other. There is sometimes a small, oblong weather-board building – unpainted, and generally leaning in one of the eight possible directions, and perhaps with a twist in another – which, from its half-obliterated sign, seems to have started as a rival to the Railway Stores; but the shutters are up and the place empty.

The only town I saw that differed much from the above consisted of a box-bark humpy with a clay chimney, and a woman standing at the door throwing out the wash-up water.

By way of variety, the artist might make a water-colour sketch of a fettler's tent on the line, with a billy hanging over the fire in front, and three fettlers standing round filling their pipes.

Slop sac suits, red faces, and old-fashioned, flat-brimmed hats, with wire round the brims, begin to drop into the train on the other side of Bathurst; and here and there a hat with three inches of crape round the crown, which perhaps signifies death in the family at some remote date, and perhaps doesn't. Sometimes, I believe, it only means grease under the band. I notice that when a bushman puts crape round his hat he generally leaves it there till the hat wears out, or another friend dies. In the later case, he buys a new piece of crape. This outward sign of bereavement usually has a jolly red face beneath it. Death is about the only cheerful thing in the bush.

We crossed the Macquarie – a narrow, muddy gutter with a dog swimming across, and three goats interested.

A little farther on we saw the first sundowner. He carried a Royal Alfred, and had a billy in one hand and a stick in the other. He was dressed in a tail-coat turned yellow, a print shirt, and a pair of moleskin trousers, with big square calico patches on the knees; and his old straw hat was covered with calico. Suddenly he slipped his swag, dropped his billy, and ran forward, boldly flourishing the stick. I thought that he was mad, and was about to attack the train, but he wasn't; he was only killing a snake. I didn't have time to see whether he cooked the snake or not – perhaps he only thought of Adam.

Somebody told me that the country was very dry on the other side of Nevertire. It is. I wouldn't like to sit down on it anywhere. The least horrible spot in the bush, in a dry season, is where the bush isn't – where it has been cleared away and a green crop is trying to grow. They talk of settling people on the land! Better settle *in* it. I'd rather settle on the water; at least, until some gigantic system of irrigation is perfected in the West.

Along about Byrock we saw the first shearers. They dress like the unemployed, but differ from that body in their looks of independence. They sat on trucks and wool-bales and the fence, watching the train, and hailed Bill, and Jim, and Tom, and asked how those individuals were getting on.

Here we came across soft felt hats with straps round the crowns, and full-bearded faces under them. Also a splendid-looking black tracker in a masher uniform and a pair of Wellington boots.

One or two square-cuts and stand-up collars struggle dismally through to the bitter end. Often a member of the unemployed starts cheerfully out, with a letter from the Government Labour Bureau in his pocket, and nothing else. He has an idea that the station where he has the job will be within easy walking distance of Bourke. Perhaps he thinks there'll be a cart or a buggy waiting for him. He travels for a night and day without a bite to eat, and, on arrival, he finds that the station is eighty or a hundred miles away. Then he has to explain matters to a publican and a coach-driver. God bless the publican and the coach-driver! God forgive our social system!

Native industry was represented at one place along the line by three tiles, a chimney-pot, and a length of piping on a slab.

Somebody said to me, "Yer wanter go out back, young man, if yer wanter see the country. Yer wanter get away from the line." I don't wanter; I've been there.

You could go to the brink of eternity so far as Australia is concerned and yet meet an animated mummy of a swagman who will talk of going "out back". Out upon the out-back fiend!

About Byrock we met the bush liar in all his glory. He was dressed like – like a bush larrikin. His name was Jim. He had been to a ball where some blank had "touched" his blanky overcoat. The overcoat had a cheque for ten "quid" in the pocket. He didn't seem to feel the loss much. "Wot's ten quid?" He'd been everywhere, including the Gulf country. He still had three or four sheds to go to. He had telegrams in his pocket from half a dozen squatters and supers offering him pens on any terms. He didn't give a blank whether he took them or no. He thought at first he had the telegrams on him but found that he had left them in the pocket of the overcoat aforesaid. He had learned butchering in a day. He was a bit of a scrapper himself and talked a lot about the ring. At the last station where he shore he gave the super the father of a hiding. The super was a big chap, about six-foot-three, and had knocked out Paddy Somebody in one round. He worked with a man who shore four hundred sheep in nine hours.

Here a quiet-looking bushman in a corner of the carriage grew restless, and presently he opened his mouth and took the liar down in about three minutes.

At 5.30 we saw a long line of camels moving out across the sunset. There's something snaky about camels. They remind me of turtles and goannas.

Somebody said, "Here's Bourke."

IN A WET SEASON

It was raining – "general rain".

The train left Bourke, and then there began the long, long agony of scrub and wire fence, with here and there a natural clearing, which seemed even more dismal than the funereal "timber" itself. The only thing which might seem in keeping with one of these soddened flats would be the ghost of a funeral – a city funeral with plain hearse and string of cabs – going very slowly across from the scrub on one side to the scrub on the other. Sky like a wet, grey blanket; plains like dead seas, save for the tufts of coarse grass sticking up out of the water; scrub indescribably dismal – everything damp, dark, and unspeakably dreary.

Somewhere along here we saw a swagman's camp – a square of calico stretched across a horizontal stick, some rags steaming on another stick in front of a fire, and two billies to the leeward of the blaze. We knew by instinct that there was a piece of beef in the larger one. Small, hopeless-looking man standing with his back to the fire, with his hands behind him, watching the train; also, a damp, sorry-looking dingo warming itself and shivering by the fire. The rain had held up for a while. We saw two or three similar camps further on, forming a temporary suburb of Byrock.

The population was on the platform in old overcoats and damp, soft felt hats; one trooper in a waterproof. The population looked cheerfully and patiently dismal. The local push had evidently turned up to see off some fair enslavers from the city, who had been up-country for the cheque season, now over. They got into another carriage. We were glad when the bell rang.

The rain recommenced. We saw another swagman about a mile on struggling away from the town, through mud and water. He did not seem to have heart enough to bother about trying to avoid the worst mud-holes. There was a low-spirited dingo at his heels, whose sole object in life was seemingly to keep his front paws in his master's last footprint. The traveller's body was bent well forward from the hips up; his long arms – about six inches through his coat sleeves – hung by his sides like the arms of a dummy, with a billy at the end of one and a bag at the end of the other; but his head was thrown back against the top end of the swag, his hat-brim rolled up in front, and we saw a ghastly, beardless face which turned neither to the right nor the left as the train passed him.

After a long while we closed our book, and, looking through the window, saw a hawker's turn-out which was too sorrowful for description.

We looked out again while the train was going slowly, and saw a teamster's camp: three or four wagons covered with tarpaulins which hung down in the mud all round and suggested death. A long, narrow man, in a long, narrow shoddy overcoat and a damp felt hat, was walking quickly along the road past the camp. A sort of cattle-dog glided silently and swiftly out from under a wagon, "heeled" the man, and slithered back without explaining. Here the scene vanished.

We remember stopping – for an age it seemed – at half-a-dozen straggling shanties on a flat of mud and water. There was a rotten weatherboard pub, with a low, dripping veranda, and three wretchedly forlorn horses hanging, in the rain, to a post outside. We saw no more, but we knew that there were several apologies for men hanging about the ricketty bar inside – or round the parlour fire. Streams of cold, clay-coloured water ran in all directions, cutting fresh gutters, and raising a yeasty froth whenever the water fell a few inches. As we left, we saw a big man in an overcoat riding across a culvert; the tails of the coat spread over the horse's rump, and almost hid it. In fancy still we saw him – hanging up his weary, hungry, little horse in the rain, and swaggering into the bar; and we almost heard someone say, in a drawling tone: "Ello, Tom! 'Ow are yer poppin' up?"

The train stopped (for about a year) within a mile of the next station. Trucking-yards in the foreground, like any other trucking-yards along the line; they looked drearier than usual, because the rain had darkened the posts and rails. Small plain beyond, covered with water and tufts of grass. The inevitable, God-forgotten "timber", black in the distance; dull, grey sky and misty rain over all. A small, dark-looking flock of sheep was crawling slowly in across the flat from the unknown, with three men on horseback zig-zagging patiently behind. The horses just moved – that was all. One man wore an oilskin, one an old tweed overcoat, and the third had a three-bushel bag over his head and shoulders.

Had we returned an hour later, we should have seen the sheep huddled together in a corner of the yards, and the three horses hanging up outside the local shanty.

We stayed at Nyngan – which place we refrain from sketching – for a few hours, because the five trucks of cattle of which we were in charge were shunted there, to be taken on by a very subsequent goods train. The Government allows one man to every five trucks in a cattle-train. We shall pay our fare next time, even if we have not a shilling left over and above. We had haunted local influence at Comanavadrink, for two long, anxious, heart-breaking weeks ere we got the pass; and we had put up with all the indignities, the humiliation – in short, had suffered all that poor devils suffer whilst besieging Local Influence. We only thought of escaping from the bush.

The pass said that we were John Smith, drover, and that we were available for return by ordinary passenger-train within two days, we think – or words in that direction. Which didn't interest us. We might have given the pass away to an unemployed in Orange, who wanted to go Out Back, and who begged for it with tears in his eyes; but we didn't like to injure a poor fool who never injured us – who was an entire stranger to us. He didn't know what Out Back meant.

Local Influence had given us a kind of note of introduction to be delivered to the cattle-agent at the yards that morning; but the agent was not there – only two of his satellites, a cockney colonial-experience man, and a scrub-town clerk, both of whom we kindly ignore. We got on without the note, and at Orange we amused ourself by reading it. It said:

"Dear Old Man, – Please send this beggar on; and I hope he'll be landed safely at Orange – or – or wherever the cattle go. – Yours, –."

We had been led to believe that the bullocks were going to Sydney. We took no further interest in those cattle.

After Nyngan the bush grew darker and drearier, and the plains more like ghastly oceans; and here and there the "dominant note of Australian scenery" was accentuated, as it were, by naked, white, ring-barked trees standing in the water and haunting the ghostly surroundings.

We spent that night in a passenger compartment of a van which had been originally attached to old No. 1 engine. There was only one damp cushion in the whole concern. We lent that to a lady who travelled for a few hours in the other half of the next compartment. The seats were about nine inches wide and sloped in at a sharp angle to the bare matchboard wall, with a bead on the outer edge; and as the cracks had become well caulked with the grease and dirt of generations, they held several gallons of water each. We scuttled one, rolled ourself in a rug, and tried to sleep; but all night long overcoated and comfortered bushmen would get in, let down all the windows, and then get out again at the next station. Then we would wake up frozen and shut the windows.

We dozed off again and woke at daylight, and recognised the ridgy gum-country between Dubbo and Orange. It didn't look any drearier than the country further west – because it couldn't. There is scarcely a part of the country out west which looks less inviting or more horrible than any other part.

The weather cleared, and we had sunlight for Orange, Bathurst, the Blue Mountains, and Sydney. They deserve it; also as much rain as they need.

5

Floods, Flies, Fauna

EDITOR'S NOTE

This part is something of an extension of "Travelling", concentrating on some of the "typically Australian" scenes, creatures and natural events described by explorers, scientists and scenic and literary travellers in nineteenth-century Australia. In "Travelling", Henry Lawson's letters to his aunt recount the horrors of tramping in the bush, not least of which being the flies and mosquitoes. George Grey, Louisa Meredith and Frank Fowler swell the chorus of complaint. All three wax equally eloquent about the beauties of the landscape and the wonders of novel bird and plant life. The greatest animal novelty, of course, was the platypus. George Bennett provides a useful account of the initial European reactions to this strange creature as well as of his own research into its habits (and, incidentally, another picture of Aboriginal tolerance of the white strangers and their queer customs). Both Frank Fowler and W.H.L. Ranken describe the peculiarities of the Australian climate. Fowler's brief description of a corroboree may be compared with the ones given previously by Audrey Tennyson and George Gordon McCrae. Ranken also offers an interesting speculation about the possible fate of Ludwig Leichhardt.

George Grey

AT HANOVER BAY

December 4

To sleep after sunrise was impossible, on account of the number of flies which kept buzzing about the face. To open our mouths was dangerous – in they flew, and mysteriously disappeared, to be rapidly ejected again in a violent fit of coughing; and into the eyes, when unclosed, they soon found their way, and by inserting the proboscis, and sucking, speedily made them sore; neither were the nostrils safe from their attacks, which were made simultaneously on all points, and in multitudes. This was a very troublesome annoyance, but I afterwards found it to be a very general one throughout all the unoccupied portions of Australia; although in general the further north you go in this continent, the more intolerable does the fly nuisance became.

Sunrise offered a very beautiful spectacle; the water was quite unruffled, but the motion communicated by the tides was so great, that although there was not a breath of air stirring, the sea heaved slowly with a grand and majestic motion. On two sides the view was bounded by lofty cliffs, from three to four hundred feet high, lightly wooded at their summits, and broken by wide openings, into which ran arms of the sea, forming gloomy channels of communication with the interior country; whilst on each side of their entrances the huge cliffs rose, like the pillars of some gigantic portal.

In front of us lay a smooth sandy beach, beyond which rose gradually a high wooded country, and behind us was the sea, studded with numerous islands of every variety of form.

I was too much tired by the fatigues of the night before, to enjoy the scene with the full delight I should otherwise have done; the bruises I had received made me feel so stiff and sore that the slightest movement was painful; the rainy season was, however, now so near that it would not do to lose a single day of preparation. Directly after breakfast, therefore, whilst one boat went off to search for fresh water, and a convenient spot to land the stores at, I accompanied the Captain of the vessel in another up Prince Regent's river.

In general the openings to these rivers from the sea are very narrow, forming gorges which terminate in extensive basins, some fifteen or twenty miles inland; the levels of these reservoirs are subject to be raised thirty-seven feet by every tide through their funnel-like entrances, along which the waters consequently pour with a velocity of which it is difficult to form any adequate idea. By such a tide were we swept along, as we entered this river by its southern mouth.

On each side of us rose lofty red sandstone cliffs; sometimes quite precipitous, sometimes, from ancient landslips, shelving gradually down to the water, and at these points covered with a dense tropical vegetation.

At several such places we landed, but always found the ascent to the interior so covered with large loose rocks, that it would have been impossible to have disembarked stores or stock on any. The thickness of the vegetation made it difficult to force a way through, and whenever, in attempting to do so, a tree was shaken, numbers of a large green sort of ant fell from the boughs on the unhappy trespasser, and making the best of their way to the back of his neck, gave warning by a series of most painful bites, that he was encroaching on their domain. Yet it was sometimes ludicrous to see one of the party momentarily stamping and roaring with pain, as he cried out to a companion to hasten and assist him in getting rid of an enemy at once so diminutive and so troublesome.

We saw a great number of beautiful parrakeets, as well as a remarkable hawk of a bright cinnamon colour, with a milk-white head and neck. As there was no apparent probability of our finding hereabouts a spot suited to land our stock and stores at, we returned in the afternoon to the schooner, and found that the party in the other boat had been as unsuccessful as ourselves.

December 5

The long-boat was this morning despatched to the ravine where we had procured water on the first day of our landing, to bring a few casks for immediate use, and to examine the country again in that direction; whilst I accompanied the Captain to examine the inlet at which Captain King had watered in his visit to these parts, in 1821.

The approach to this watering-place was through a deep narrow channel, bounded on each side by high cliffs, against which our voices echoed and sounded strangely; whilst from the quantity of light which the cliffs excluded, a solemn sombre hue was imparted to the scene. Channels similar to the main one branched off on each side; they were, however, so narrow, that the dense vegetation which grew on their sides nearly met in the centre, giving them an appearance of dark and refreshing coolness; most of these terminated in cascades, now dry, but down which the water, in the rainy seasons, pours in torrents: at the foot of some of these cascades were deep cavities, or natural basins, worn in the solid rock by the falling of the water – and these were still full of the clearest cool water, in which sported small insects and animals, of kinds quite unknown to me.

As we were swept up the main opening by the tide and sea-breeze, its width gradually contracted, till at last we came to a small island bearing a single large mangrove tree, which we named "One-Tree Island". The shores now became thickly wooded with mangroves, from the boughs of which depended in clusters small but well-flavoured oysters, and soon after passing the island we found our farther progress arrested by large rounded blocks of sandstone, from amongst which fresh water came pouring in a hundred little cascades.

We here quitted the boat to enter a deep and picturesque ravine, of which the mean breadth was only one hundred and forty-seven feet, bounded on each side by perpendicular cliffs from one hundred and fifty to two hundred feet high; in the centre ran a clear stream, sometimes forming deep and extensive pools, sometimes divided into innumerable little rills which gurgled along through a dense and matted vegetation; and bordered on each side of the main bed by a lofty species of Eucalyptus, with a bark resembling layers of coarse white paper, and a foliage pendant and graceful; whilst the great height of these trees, for they raised their heads above the cliffs, contrasted strangely with the narrowness of the ravine in which they grew. The space between these trees and the cliffs was filled by a dense forest, principally composed of the Pandanus and wild nutmeg trees. Rich grasses and climbing plants occupied the interval and twined around the trees, whilst parrakeets of the most vivid colours filled the wood with their cries. Nothing could be more striking than this singular and novel scene; and we were all delighted as we wound our way up the beautiful ravine.

The same character continued for the next mile or two, whilst occasionally branch valleys of similar character ran off from the main one, giving it at these points a much greater width. The summit of the cliffs was found to be generally a rocky sandy table land, thinly wooded; and from what I had seen it appeared to me, that I was not likely to find a place better adapted for landing the stores than the main ravine.

On embarking to return, we could perceive no sign of One-Tree Island; and as we swept down towards the sea, the leafy top of a tree seen in the clear water under the boat was the only evidence of its existence; though a few hours ago it had formed so prominent an object.

The long-boat returned to the vessel half an hour after us, and brought eighty gallons of water; but the spot whence it was obtained had been found very inconvenient for the purpose. At the water-hole they had met Ranger, the dog we lost the first day; but he appeared quite mad, and without recognising any of them ran wildly away into the woods. The body of poor Ringhalz was also found, who had died on the spot where he fell.

Louisa Anne Meredith

[LIFE IN SYDNEY]

The market in Sydney is well supplied, and is held in a large commodious building, superior to most provincial market-houses at home. The display of fruit in the grape season is very beautiful. Peaches also are most abundant, and very cheap; apples very dear, being chiefly imported from Van Diemen's Land, and frequently selling at sixpence each. The smaller English fruits, such as strawberries, etc. only succeed in a few situations in the colony, and are far from plentiful. Cucumbers and all descriptions of melon abound. The large green water-melon, rose-coloured within, is a very favourite fruit, but I thought it insipid. One approved method of eating it is, after cutting a sufficiently large hole, to pour in a bottle of Madeira or sherry, and mix it with the cold watery pulp. These melons grow to an enormous size (an ordinary one is from twelve to eighteen inches in diameter), and may be seen piled up like huge cannonballs at all the fruit-shop doors, being universally admired in this hot, thirsty climate.

There are some excellent fish to be procured here, but I know them only by the common Colonial names, which are frequently misnomers. The snapper, or schnapper, is the largest with which I am acquainted, and is very nice, though not esteemed a proper dish for a dinner-party – why, I am at a loss to guess; but I never saw any native fish at a Sydney dinner-table – the preserved or cured cod and salmon from England being served instead, at a considerable expense, and, to my taste, it is not comparable with the cheap fresh fish, but being expensive, it has become "fashionable", and that circumstance reconciles all things. The guardfish is long and narrow, about the size of a herring, with a very singular head, the mouth opening at the top, as it were, and the lower jaw, or nose, projecting two-thirds of an inch beyond it. I imagine it must live chiefly at the bottom, and this formation enables it more readily to seize the food above it. They are most delicate little fish. The bream, a handsome fish, not unlike a perch in shape (but much larger, often weighing four or five pounds), and the mullet, but especially the latter, are excellent. The whiting, much larger than its English namesake, is perhaps the best of all; but I pretend to no great judgment as a gastronome. I thought the rock-oysters particularly nice, and they are plentiful and cheap; so are the crayfish, which are very similar to lobsters, when small, but the large ones rather coarse. I must not end my list of fish that we eat without mentioning one that is always ready to return the compliment when an opportunity offers, namely, the shark, many of whom are habitants of the bright tempting waters of Port Jackson. Provisions vary much in price from many circumstances. Everything was very dear when we landed in New South Wales, and at the present time prices are much too low to pay the producers.

The dust is one main source of annoyance in Sydney. Unless after very heavy rain, it is *always* dusty; and sometimes, when the wind is in one particular point, the whirlwinds of thick fine powder that fill every street and house are positive miseries. These dust-winds are locally named "brickfielders", from the direction in which they come; and no sooner is the approach of one perceived than the streets are instantly deserted, windows and doors closely shut, and everyone who can remains within till the plague has passed over, when you ring for the servant with a duster, and collect enough fine earth for a small garden off your chairs and tables.

Flies are another nuisance; they swarm in every room in tens of thousands, and blacken the breakfast or dinner table as soon as the viands appear, tumbling into the cream, tea, wine, and gravy with the most disgusting familiarity. But worse than these are the mosquitoes, nearly as numerous, and infinitely more detestable to those for whose luckless bodies they form an attachment, as they do to most newcomers; a kind of initiatory compliment which I would gladly dispense with, for most intolerable is the torment they cause in the violent irritation of their mountainous bites. All houses are furnished with a due attention to these indefatigable gentry, and the beds have consequently a curious aspect to an English eye accustomed to solid four-posters, with voluminous hangings of chintz or damask, and a pile of feather-beds which would annihilate a sleeper in this climate. Here you have usually a neat thin skeleton-looking frame of brass or iron, over which is thrown a gauze garment, consisting of curtains, head, and tester, all sewn together; the former full, and resting on the floor when let down, but during the day tied up in festoons. Some of these materials are very pretty, being silk, with satin stripes of white or other delicate tints on the green gauze ground. At night, after the curtains are lowered, a grand hunt takes place, to kill or drive out the mosquitoes from within; having effected which somewhat wearisome task, you tuck the net in all round, leaving one small bit which you carefully raise, and nimbly pop through the aperture into bed, closing the curtain after you. This certainly postpones the ingress of the enemy, but no precaution that my often-tasked ingenuity could invent will prevent it effectually. They are terrible pests, and very frequently aided in their nocturnal invasions of one's rest by the still worse and thrice-disgusting creatures familiar to most dwellers in London lodgings or seaport inns, to say nothing of fleas, which seem to pervade this colony in one universal swarm. The thickest part of a town, or the most secluded spot in the wild bush, is alike replete with these small but active annoyances.

One day we drove out to the lighthouse on the South Head, about eight miles from Sydney. Soon after leaving the town the road passes the new courthouse and gaol, and its handsome front, in the Doric or Ionic style (I forget which), is the only architectural building the "city" could boast when I was there, though I suppose that ere this the new Government House, a mansion in the Elizabethan-Gothic style, is completed. We began shortly to ascend a hill, the road being all sea-sand apparently, and nothing but sand was visible all around. Great green mat-like plats of the pretty *Mesembryanthemum æquilaterale*, or fig-marigold, adorned the hot sandy banks by the roadside. It bears a bright purple flower, and a five-sided fruit, called by children "pig-faces". A very prickly species of solanum also grew here, with large green spiky leaves, more difficult to gather even than holly, and pretty bluish potato-like blossoms. The universal ti-tree, and numberless shrubs which I knew not, adorned the sandy wastes in all directions. As we continued to ascend, the road became very rough, huge masses of rock protruding like gigantic steps, over which the wheels scraped and grated and jumped in a way that made me draw rather strong comparisons between the character of roads at home and abroad. As we approached the summit, the hollow formed by the road was suddenly filled by a background (forgive the paradox) of deep blue water; it was the open sea that gradually rose before us, seen over the rocks, and spreading out bright and blue, with small waves sparkling in the fervid sunshine, and the white diamond-crested spray dashing high against the iron-bound coast, here broken into a low craggy amphitheatre, into which the rolling waves came surging on, breaking over the groups of rocks, and forming bright little basins among them. On either side the rocks rose again in large masses, presenting a precipitous face to the sea, being part of the dark formidable cliffs we had seen in approaching the Heads by sea. The road, after descending the hill, turned to the left, through some sandy scrub, crowded with such exquisite flowers that to me it appeared one continued garden, and I walked for some distance, gathering handfuls of them – of the same plants that I had cherished in pots at home, or begged small sprays of in conservatories or greenhouses! I had whole boughs of the splendid metrosideros, a tall handsome shrub, bearing flowers of the richest crimson, like a large bottle-brush; several varieties of the delicate epacris; different species of acacia, ti-tree, and corraea, the brilliant "Botany-Bay lily", and very many yet more lovely denizens of this interesting country, of which I know not even the name. One, most beautiful, was something like a small iris, of a pure ultra-marine blue, with smaller petals in the centre, most delicately pencilled; but ere I had gathered it five minutes, it had withered away, and I never could bring one home to make a drawing from. Surely it must have been some sensitive little fay, who, charmed into the form of a flower, might not bear the touch of a mortal hand!

Numbers of parrots, those

> Strange bright birds, that on starry wings
> Bear the rich hues of all glorious things,

were flying from tree to tree, or crossing the road in chattering, screaming parties, all as gay and happy as splendid colours and glad freedom could make them. Often they rose close before us from the road, like living gems and gold, so vividly bright they shone in the sun; and then a party of them would assemble in a tree, with such fluttering, and flying in and out, and under and over; such genteel-looking flirtations going on, as they sidled up and down the branches, with their droll sly-looking faces peering about, and inspecting us first with one eye, then with the other, that they seemed quite the monkeys of the feathered tribes.

On nearing the lighthouse, after ascending one or two slight hills, we passed several small houses, and others were building; the views from thence are doubtlessly very grand, but it must be a most exposed situation, with nothing to break the force of the strong sea-breezes, and but little vegetation to moderate the glare of the sun.

The view from the cliffs is indeed grand,

> O'er the glad waters of the dark-blue sea;

and looking down over the dizzy height, the eye glances from crag to crag, till it catches the snowy puffs of foam flung up from the breakers that roar and dash in the cavernous chasms below, booming among them like subterranean thunder. As I fearfully gazed down, something leaped between me and the dark water – it was a goat, and there were some half-dozen of the agile creatures far down the slippery precipitous crags, leaping, jumping, and frolicking about, with scarcely an inch of foot-room, and only the boiling surf below.

Opposite to us rose the corresponding cliff, called the North Head, bluff and bare, and wearing on its hoary front the hues with which thousands of storms have dyed it. Myriads of sea-fowl were soaring and screaming around, and several vessels in the offing, and nearer shore, were apparently shaping their course to the port, but too distant for us to wait their entrance through these most grand and stupendous gates. The lighthouse itself is not in any way remarkable; close by is the signal-staff, by means of which the intelligence of vessels arriving is speedily transmitted to Sydney and Paramatta.

We drove back by a different road, nearer to the port, and less hilly, but equally beautiful with that by which we came. It led us through a moister-looking region, with more large trees, greener shrubs, and more luxuriant herbage, and commanding most lovely views, that appeared in succession like pictures seen through a natural framework of high white-stemmed gum-trees and tall acacias. Here and there peeped forth a prettily situated residence, with its shady garden and cool piazza, looking down into one of the small bays I have before mentioned, and beyond that to the estuary.

On one large dead gum-tree a whole council of black cockatoos was assembled in animated debate, sidling up and down the branches, erecting and lowering their handsome gold-tipped top-knots, as if bowing to each other with the politest gestures imaginable; and accompanying the dumb show with such varied intonations of voice as made it impossible to doubt that a most interesting discussion was going on, all conducted in the most courteous manner: perhaps a reform of the grub laws was in agitation, for the business was evidently one of grave importance, and we respectfully remained attentive spectators of the ceremony until "the House" adjourned, and the honourable members flew away. These birds are by no means common in the neighbourhood of Sydney, nor did I see any more during my stay in the colony.

The same deep sandy road continued: it appeared to me that this part of the country must have been gradually elevated from the sea, and a long succession of beaches consequently formed, and left inland by the retreating waters; for the prodigious accumulation of true sea-sand here seems difficult to account for in any other way. In the Domain, too, and many other situations, are raised beaches, consisting wholly of sea-sand and shells (recent ones, so far as I examined them), above which, in a thin stratum of soil, great trees are growing; so that, although these beaches have formed part of the dry land long enough for a body of soil to be deposited upon them, and for aged trees to have grown in that, they are still of modern elevation.

Sydney boasts her "Hyde Park"; but a *park* utterly destitute of trees seems rather an anomaly. It is merely a large piece of brown ground fenced in, where is a well of good water, from which most of the houses are supplied by means of water-carts. There is also a racecourse between the town and Botany Bay, racing being a favourite amusement among the gentlemen of the colony, and sometimes among the ladies, for I was told of a race somewhere "up the country", in which two "young ladies" were the riders, the prize being a new side-saddle and bridle, which was won in good style by one of the fair damsels; the horse of the other receiving a severe castigation from his gentle mistress, for having swerved and lost the race.

Most of the country gentlemen near Sydney, and for many miles round, are members of the "Cumberland Hunt"; they have a tolerable pack of hounds, and the destructive native dog, or dingo, serves them for a fox. So long as they hunt the really wild ones, the sport is certainly useful; but when, as frequently happens, a *bagged dog* furnishes the day's amusement, I cannot but think the field of mounted red-coats as something less than children. Dinners and balls of course form a part of the arrangements for the races and hunts, and everything is conducted in as English a manner as can be attained by a young country imitating an old one.

Frank Fowler

[SOME AUSTRALIAN NUISANCES]

Another colonial nuisance is the abundance of insect life. Flies – black, blue, bumble, and blow – musquitoes, cockroaches, spiders, tarantulas, and even centipedes, annoy and terrify the new arrival. The musquito is a beast. It comes buzzing against your cheek, with a drowsy singsong *whir*, fixes its suckers into the flesh, and bounds off with another song – a kind of *carmen triumphale* – leaving a large red mark behind it, which is far more irritating than a healing blister. While I am writing this little book, our ship is in the neighbourhood of Cape Horn, and my hands and feet are covered with chilblains. Still, I can safely say, never did chilblain – in its frostiest and most abandoned form – vex like the bite of a well-trained and experienced musquito. They use in the colony what are called musquito curtains; but so far from these keeping away the insects, I never found them of any other use than in imprisoning the little fiends who had sneaked in during the process of bed-making. Some nights they have driven me almost mad, forced me out of bed, and compelled me to dress myself, even to the putting on of gloves, in order to protect my skin. They have a great relish – being epicures in their way – for the round, fat, mottled part of the hand ridging the off-side of the palm. In about two seconds one will sow it with bumps and blisters from the wrist to the little finger. Strange as it may read, I used to let my beard grow in order that I might rub this part of my hand against my serried chin, and thus allay the irritation. If I slept in gloves, they punished my legs; if I slept in stockings, they riddled my hands; if I tried both, they punctured the edges of my ears. The walls of my bedroom were stencilled with their corpses; for whenever I was driven from the sheets, I used to go round with a slipper and – with intense satisfaction – settle hundreds of them as they stood stropping their stings upon the wall. They, too, especially hate and harass the new-chum.

Having thus given an outline – somewhat hard and dry, I am afraid – of the everyday doings and ordinary aspects of Australia, let me here frame the *coup d'œil* with one or two little bits of description calculated to convey an idea of the natural beauties and peculiarities of the country. Australia is not the level and unvaried waste that some have represented: its trees are not all gums, its flowers are not all scentless. I have gathered posies in the wild bush which, for beauty and perfume, would have delighted the most fastidious lounger at Chiswick. I have seen twenty different kinds of trees of twenty various shades of foliage, growing naturally in the space of about an acre; I have walked through rich and ever-changing scenes – verdant valleys, zoned with blue-capped hills – and, but for the somewhat dusty foliage, the ring of the cicada, the guffaw of the laughing jackass, or the rattle of the snake†, might have imagined myself in the fairest and fairyest spots of the Mother land.

The evenings in Australia are singularly beautiful. I have often read a newspaper by the light of the moon. The stars are very white and large, and seem to drop pendulous from the blue, like silver lamps from a dome of calaite. I used to visit a house a long way out of Sydney, for the pleasure of being lighted home by the stars. Generally, I did not admire the Australian climate – its sudden changes, occasionally of thirty or forty degrees in two or three hours, its clouds of dust, its awful storms, and its hot winds; but an Australian evening – especially in winter – in its serene loveliness, defies all attempts at description. I have looked from my little study window sometimes at midnight, and seen the harbour so brightly argent with the moon, that it seemed as though He had walked again upon the sea, and left the glory of His footsteps on the water.

Having mentioned, in passing, a hot wind, let me endeavour to convey some notion of what a hot wind really is. It is early morning, and as you look from your window, in the suburbs of Sydney, you see a thin white vapour rising from the far-off bush. The sheep out there in the distance are congregated beneath the trees, while the old cows

†Just after Christmas, last year, I was picnicing with some friends at Hen-and-chickens Bay, and was busy carving, or trying to carve, an antiquated fowl, when one of the party, a Dr P—, said, "Bring it to me, I understand its anatomy, and can manage it better than you." I stood up to carry the dish, when I was rather surprised to see I had been squatting on a large snake. In my astonishment I threw both fowl and dish at it, upon which it put out its tongue and wormed off.

are standing knee-deep in those clayey creeks of water that trickle from the headed-up rocks above. You have seen all this before, and know too well what it means. Before breakfast time, there will "be" a hot wind.

It comes. The white earth cracks as it passes over it, as though it were a globe of crystal struck by some invisible and mighty hand. The air is hot and murky, as the breath from an oven; and you *see* trees wither – the fruit shrivel and drop from the vines – as though the Last Seal were opened, and the breath of the Destroying Angel had gone forth. The cicadas seem to shriek (their shrill note is always shrillest in hot weather), and the birds drop dead from the trees. The dogs in the street lie down and hide their dry protruding tongues in the dust. Higher and higher rises the mercury in the glass, until now, at noon, it stands at 147°! You stop up every keyhole and crevice in your room to keep out the burning Sirocco, and endeavour, perhaps, to read. In a minute stars dance before your eyes, and your temples throb like pulses of hot iron. You allow the book to fall from your hands, and strive to drop to sleep. It is not much relief if you succeed, for you are safe to dream of the *Inferno* or Beckford's Hall of Eblis. There is only one thing you can do that gives relief. Light your pipe, mix your sherry-cobbler, and smoke and drink until the change arrives.

The "Southerly Buster", as this change is called, generally comes

> – sounding on,
> Like the storm-wind from Labrador,
> The wind Euroclydon,

early in the evening. A cloud of dust – they call it, in Sydney, a "brickfielder" – thicker than any London fog, heralds its approach, and moves like a compact wall across the country. In a minute the temperature will sink fifty or sixty degrees, and so keenly does the sudden change affect the system, that hot toddy takes the place of the sherry-cobbler, and your great-coat is buttoned tightly around you until a fire can be lighted. Now, if you look from your window in the direction where you saw that white vapour ascending in the morning, a spectacle terrible in its magnificence will meet your eye. For miles around – as far as the gaze can reach – bush fires are blazing. You see the trail of the flame extending into the interior until it grows faint and thin along the hilltops, as though a wounded deer had moved, bleeding, upon the road. Nearer, however, the sight is grand and awful, and hints of the Final Apocalypse when the stars shall fall like those charred branches that drop with a thundrous crash and scatter a cloud of glowing embers around them.

No matter where you live in Sydney, looking from your window across the harbour into the surrounding bush, you can always see sights like this after a hot wind. The reflection upon the water itself is very fine. The emerald changes into ruby – the water into wine. The white sails of boats become of "purple" and "their prows of beaten gold". Everything seems bathed in an atmosphere of romance, and, if the impression were not lowered by the idea, the sheets of flame in the distance might be taken for the crimson walls of Aladdin's palace gleaming through the woods.

Sometimes these hot winds last for two or three days, and then the effects are something lamentable. Scarcely a blade of vegetation is left in the ground – the sere leaves fall from the trees as in a blast of autumn. The same week that I landed in Sydney, a hot wind lasted for four days, on the last of which no less than thirty persons dropped dead in the streets. I remember I had a little garden to my house, and the white-starred jessamine was in full flower in front of the lower windows. Before the wind was over nothing remained but a bunch of dry sticks, kept to the wall by the pieces of cloth with which they were fastened. But I have witnessed other phenomena in Australia as remarkable – if not as terrible – as a hot wind, and I must therefore pass on.

Soon after my arrival in New South Wales, I went up the Paterson, a charming river watering some of the richest soil in the country. While here I saw that beautiful phenomenon, known as the Aurora Australis. Imagine, reader, an arch of palest gold built right across the heavens, and set along the top with rows of Gothic spear-like points, suffused with violet and tipped with burning crimson. Imagine further these lambent spears darting out a thousand varied coruscations until every tree around glows like the bush of Horeb, and the tops of the distant mountains flush with a pale uncertain consecration. Imagine, now, that the arch is first splitting into purple gaps, and now falling into molten fragments, mixed with a rain of many coloured stars – that the night is moonless, and all without the influence of the palpitating light as dark and sullen as the blasted strand of Erebus – imagine all this, and you will have a limning, faint and feeble enough, of one phase in the luminous existence of the Aurora Australis.

A leaf or two from my Up-Country Note Book, will not come in amiss here:

Monday

Nothing but gums and three-rail fences. Flies and parrots in abundance. Saw a flock of at least 500 paroquets, chased by a hawk. He caught one, and not being able to kill it on the wing, darted down to a gully, and held his little victim beneath the water until it was drowned.

Tuesday

Scenery improved. Fine dark hills clothed with verdure. At night I witnessed a "corroboree". About twenty naked blacks, painted hideously, with blue stripes along each rib and down each leg – white around each eye, and splashes of red upon the forehead – were dancing beneath the moon, and grunting all the while with a husky *hooh! – hooh! – hooh!* so as to keep a very *common* time. Five or six "gins", one with a little boy upon her back, were sprawled upon the ground, tomtoming on opossum rags, piling the fires with fresh logs, and occasionally breaking in with a wild chorus of

Corinda briár,
Corinda briarre!

prolonging the last syllable for nearly half a minute. Catlin would have given a little for the picture.

Wednesday

(I extract two brief paragraphs from a lengthy passage.) – A single fork of lightning struck the brow of a colossal rock rising from the waters along which we journeyed. A boom of thunder – low, rumbling, and long-continued – just wrinkled the face of the stream, and one or two large gouts of rain fell with a heavy plash upon the beach. There was a smell of balm wafted for a moment across the air. The atmosphere flushed suddenly to a pale lilac, and the water slept beneath its weight of lilies. The white leaves lay upon its surface like flakes of snow.

Fair prelude to the coming storm! In half an hour, black huddled clouds came sweeping up the sky, and presently *stream* upon *stream* of lightning (no other words will convey what I mean) began to pour down, until the air seemed saturated with the sulphurous vapour. The thunder appeared to shake the rocks, and the rain came upon us like a perfect deluge. It fell in water-spouts rather than drops, and we had to use our hats to bale the boat out. All nature seemed convulsed. Deep shadows moved upon the hills, and we could see the tallest trees upon their sides struck down, or rent in twain, by the half-blinding lightning. The storm, however, did not last long. In an hour the air was as clear as ever, and flocks of black wild-duck rose out of the cool reedy fens where they had taken protection, and went careering, with a hearty *caw-caw*, after their leader up the stream.

George Bennett

ORNITHORHYNCHUS PARADOXUS OR WATER-MOLE

Of all the Australian mammalia, none has excited so much attention as the Platypus or Water-Mole (*Ornithorhynchus paradoxus*, Blum.), both from its peculiar form, and the great desire evinced to ascertain the habits and economy of so singular a creature. It was in the year 1829, when I first visited the colony of New South Wales, that my attention was directed towards two points of natural science which at that time were objects of great interest – one, the mode of generation of the Kangaroo (to explain in what manner the young are brought into connexion with the nipple at a very early period of their existence, being then mere embryos); the other, the habits and economy of this paradoxical animal. Notwithstanding all the enquiries I made of persons long resident in the colony, I could get no correct information; I found then, as I have found during an extended residence in the colony, that the majority preferred forming theories of their own, and arguing upon their plausibility, to devoting their time to the collection of facts. At this time a scientific voyage to New Zealand, and among the islands of the Polynesian Archipelago, prevented me from devoting much attention to the elucidation of those doubtful points, and I left New South Wales, expecting that before my return to England some intelligent person resident in the colony would devote himself to the task, and determine them from actual observation. On reaching England, however, in 1831, I found that all the questions relating to these animals still remained in the same undecided state, excepting that my friend Mr Owen had succeeded in injecting with mercury the ducts of what at that time were only suspected to be mammary or milk-glands (for it was regarded as an impossibility that such a bird-like creature, without nipples, could secrete milk).

Perhaps no animal, on its first introduction into Europe, ever gave rise to greater doubts as to its classification, or excited deeper interest among naturalists (an interest fully maintained to the present day) respecting its habits and œconomy, than this enigmatical creature, which, from its external appearance, as well as internal anatomy, may be correctly described as forming a connecting link between the quadruped, the bird, and the reptile. When first a preserved skin was sent to England, it excited great distrust, being considered a fraud upon the naturalist (like Barnum's Mermaid), – an animal compounded of an old mole's skin, to which a duck's mandibles were attached; but subsequent specimens arriving, the creature was found to be real, and unexampled in its formation. It was first described and figured by Shaw in the year 1799, in the "Naturalist's Miscellany", vol. x., by the name of *Platypus anatinus*, or Duck-billed Platypus; and it was noticed in Collins's "New South Wales" (2nd ed. 4to, p. 62, 1802), where it is named *Ornithorhynchus paradoxus*, Blum., and described as an amphibious animal of the Mole-kind which inhabits the banks of the freshwater lagoons in New South Wales. There is a rude figure given of this animal in Collins's work, from a drawing by Governor Hunter, and evidently made from the usual elongated stuffed specimens. In the same work (p. 321) the native mode of capturing them is thus described:

> The natives sit upon the banks, with small wooden spears, and watch them every time they rise to the surface, till they get a proper opportunity of striking them. This they do with much dexterity, and frequently succeed in catching them this way. Governor Hunter saw a native watch one for above an hour before he attempted to spear it, which he did through the neck and fore-leg. When on shore, it used its claws with so much force, that they were obliged to confine it between two pieces of board, while they were cutting off the barbs of the spear, to disengage it. When let loose, it ran upon the ground with as much activity as a land tortoise, which is faster than the structure of its fore-feet would have led us to believe. It inhabits the banks of the lakes, and is supposed to feed in the muddy places which surround them; but the particular kind of food on which it subsists is not known.

The Ornithorhynchus is known to the colonists by the name of the Water-Mole, from some resemblance which it is supposed to bear to the common European Mole (*Talpa Europæ*, Linn.). By the native tribes at Bathurst and Goulburn Plains, and in the Yas, Murrumbidgee, and Tumat countries, I found it designated by the name of

"*Mallangong*" or "*Tambreet*"; but the latter is more in use among them than the former.

* * *

Although the following day was very showery, this did not deter us from ranging the banks of the river in search of Ornithorhynchi. The heavy rain in the course of the night and morning had swollen the stream considerably, and we saw only one specimen during the morning, which proved too vigilant for us, and consequently escaped. On our return home, however, along the banks, about two p.m., at a narrow part of the river, one of these animals was seen paddling about. We waited until it dived, which it did soon afterwards; and having made our preparation, on its returning to the surface, a short distance further down, it received the contents of the gun, which took effect; for although it immediately sank, it soon came up again, evidently severely wounded. It evaded capture by frequently diving, although in its wounded condition it was soon obliged to regain the surface of the water, and was evidently striving to reach the opposite bank (for when wounded they make for the land, either to escape into their burrows, or from being unable to support themselves in their weakened condition in the water); it moved tardily, with the greater part of the body above the surface, as is usually observed in these animals when they are severely hurt. It received, however, two effective discharges from the fowling-piece before it remained tranquil on the water and allowed the dog to bring it out. It proved to be a fine male specimen, and was not yet dead, but moved occasionally, making no noise except frequent deep expirations from the nostrils. When the fur of the Ornithorhynchus is wet, it has a sordid and far from attractive appearance, resembling rather a lump of dirty weeds than any production of the animal kingdom; indeed, were it not for their paddling motion on the water, these creatures would often escape observation; for their suppleness and colour, when wet, would cause them to be regarded only as masses of weeds, which are so often seen floating about the rivers. Such at least was their appearance when lying dead on the surface of the water, or when drifted by the current against the stump of a tree, or among the reeds and bulrushes which grew so profusely around.

A few minutes after the animal was taken out of the water, it revived and ran along the ground, instantaneously endeavouring to regain the water, but with an unsteady motion. In about twenty-five minutes from the time of its capture, it gave a few convulsive sighs and expired. This specimen being a male, and having heard so much related about the injurious effects resulting from a puncture of the spur, I determined to avail myself of the opportunity to ascertain the correctness of the assertion. The wounded state of the animal presented no objection to the experiment, as in one published account in which the poison is reported to have produced such terrible effects, the animal was also mortally wounded. As soon, therefore, as it became lively, I put its "poisonous spurs" to the test. I commenced by placing my hands in such a manner, when seizing the animal, as to enable it, from the direction of the spurs, to use them with effect; the result was that the animal made strenuous efforts to escape, and in these efforts scratched my hands a little with its hind claws, and, in consequence of the position in which I held it, with the spur also. But, although I seized it so roughly, it never struck the spur into my hand, nor did it even make an attempt to do so. As, however, it had been stated that the creature throws itself on its back when it uses this weapon (a circumstance that does not seem very probable to those who have any knowledge of the animal), I tried it in that position also; but, though it struggled to regain its former posture, no use was made of the spur. I tried several other methods of effecting the object I had in view, but, as all proved futile, I am convinced that some other use must be found for the spur than that of an offensive weapon†. I have had several subsequent opportunities of repeating these experiments with animals not in a wounded state, and the results have been the same. Some of the settlers consider the spur of the Ornithorhynchus as poisonous, not from any experience of their own, but in consequence of the aborigines saying (alluding to the spur), "It is very saucy," such being their English expression when they wish to imply that anything is hurtful or poisonous. They apply, however, the same expression to the scratching of the hind claws. It is also certain that they never seem afraid of handling the male Ornithorhynchus alive. When seen running along the ground, the animal conveys to the spectator an idea of something supernatural; and its uncouth form produces terror in the minds of the timid. Even the canine race (excepting those accustomed to bring them out of the water when shot dead) stare at them with ears erect, bark at, but fear to touch them, and the cats run from them immediately; still, although of such a "questionable shape", the creature is perfectly harmless: it is possessed, however, of a remarkably fidgety and restless disposition.

These creatures are seen in the Australian rivers at all seasons of

†In all the male specimens taken in the months of September and October, both in my early investigations and those made very lately, the *testes* were large, and in other months they had diminished to a minute size. On the 5th of October several males examined had them large; and in those examined on the 14th of September 1858, they resembled pigeons' eggs, and were of a pure white colour; they measured 1⅜ inch in length, and 1 inch in diameter; in others, examined at the end of January and beginning of February, they were not larger than small peas.

the year, but are most abundant during the spring and summer months, and I think a question may arise whether they do not hybernate. The best time for seeing them is early in the morning, or late in the evening. During floods and freshes, they are frequently perceived travelling up and down the rivers: when going down, they appear to allow themselves to be carried by the force of the stream, without making any exertion; but when swimming against the current, their muscular power is exerted to the utmost to stem its force, and generally with success. I recollect, however, seeing two make repeated and ineffectual attempts to pass a small waterfall in a rapid part of the river, and, after many persevering efforts, they were unable to attain their object. The opinion that so generally prevails that these animals must be shot dead instantly, or otherwise they would sink and not reappear, I did not find from my own observations to be correct. If missed, indeed, this is likely to occur; but if the animal is wounded, although it immediately sinks, it soon reappears on the surface of the water, some distance beyond the place at which it was seen to dive. Some require two or three shots before they are killed, or so severely wounded as to enable them to be brought out of the water; and they frequently evade being captured, even when wounded, by diving rapidly. Sometimes, too, unless the sportsman is very vigilant, they may come up among the reeds and rushes extending out from the banks of the river, and thus elude observation. I have no doubt, also, that some which sink after being wounded evade pursuit by escaping into their burrows, as, even when they cannot reach the bank, they may get access to the hole by the subaqueous entrance.

On the evening of the day on which the first specimen was shot we were fortunate in procuring a female. It was twice seen paddling about on the water, diving, and then rising again, but not sufficiently near to allow of its being fired at; the third time it dived, rising within good aim, it was shot. On being taken out of the water, it bled from the mouth, and it was found that the shot had struck it about the base and on other parts of the mandibles; it died almost immediately. The only indications of vitality which it gave consisted of a gasping motion of the mandibles and a convulsive action of the hind feet. This specimen differed from the last in the under surface of the body being of a much darker ferruginous colour; but, from subsequent observations of numerous specimens, I find these differences to depend merely on the age of the animal. In this individual the web of the fore feet was entirely black, but in many it is found mottled; the under mandible was nearly white, the upper of the usual colour. There was no spur on the hind foot; but in the situation which it occupies in the male, the female had a small impervious depression, which it is not improbable may serve for the reception of the spur of the other sex.

One morning I accompanied one of the aborigines named Daraga to the banks of the Yas River, to see the burrow of an Ornithorhynchus, from which he told me the young had been taken last summer. I asked him, "What for he dig up Mallangong?" – "Murrey budgeree patta" ("Very good to eat") was his reply. On arriving at the spot, which was situated on a steep bank, about which long grass and various herbaceous plants abounded, close to the river, my guide, putting aside the long grass, displayed the entrance of the burrow, distant rather more than a foot from the water's edge. In digging up this retreat, the natives had not laid it entirely open, but had delved holes at certain distances, always introducing a stick for the purpose of ascertaining the direction in which the burrow ran, previously to again digging down upon it. By this method they were enabled to explore its whole extent with less labour than if it had been laid entirely open. The termination of the burrow was broader than any other part, nearly oval in form; and the bottom was strewn with dry river-weeds, etc., a quantity of which still remained. From this place my sable friend said he had taken last season three young ones, which were about 6 or 8 inches long, and covered with hair. The whole of the burrow was smooth, extending about 20 feet in a serpentine direction up the bank. I may here mention, that when a half-civilised young native black accompanied me one day in search of Water-Moles' retreats, he expressly cautioned me against putting my hand into the burrow. "No put hand in, for he make smell hand." The burrows have two entrances – one usually at about the distance of a foot from the water's edge, and another under the water. It is no doubt by the entrance under the water that the animal seeks refuge within its burrow, when it is seen to dive and not to rise again; and when the poor hunted quadruped is unable to enter or escape from the burrow by the upper aperture, it has recourse to its river-entrance.

The discovery of a second burrow near the first afforded me an opportunity of witnessing the means the aborigines adopt to track these animals. Our black zoological collector pointed out to me, in the course of his peripatetic lecture, or rather demonstration of the whole art of capturing them, the distinct marks of the hind and fore feet of one on the moist clay near the river, and afterwards, inserting his hand up the burrow, brought from thence some lumps of clay taken from the under surface. These he closely regarded, and, placing them in my hands, pointed out recent impressions of the fore feet, which were distinctly visible. He then removed some other pieces from the interior of the burrow, on which there were further impressions indicative of the animal's recent presence, and it was therefore declared to be inhabited. I was anxious to explore it; but, as Daraga said that no "pickaninnies" (eggs were not mentioned by him) would be found there, nor "old women" either, I was overruled. Indeed, as respected the first, I was aware by the recent dissection of specimens that no young would be found at this early period of the season, and I depended on native accuracy for the old one not being in the burrow. This I afterwards regretted, for I subsequently procured a living female specimen by not relying on similar information given by the same native; and some time after, on exploring the burrow, I found it forsaken, the owner either having been killed, or having deserted her habitation.

Returning early one evening, there was time to visit the banks of the Yas River at Mundoona; and at six p.m. a female was seen, and a well-directed shot laid it, as if dead, on the surface of the water. When brought out, however, it was found not to be quite killed, and in a few minutes afterwards it revived, although severely wounded. By the time we had reached the house, the animal had partially recovered, and ran rapidly (with a sidelong motion, on account of its wounded state) about the room, and, dashing in its passage through the burning wood-fire, got much singed, but was not otherwise injured. It was extremely restless, and ran round and round the room, seeking some crevice from which it might escape. From the power which the animal possesses, by means of strong cutaneous muscles, of contracting its loose integuments, as well as its body, it can pass out of an aperture, which, to a person ignorant of these circumstances, it would appear impossible for it to force itself through. When I took it into my hand, it made strenuous efforts to escape from my grasp; and, from the flaccid nature of its skin, I found some difficulty in retaining it; but it made no attempt to bite, or otherwise inflict injury; indeed, its weak mandibles would be useless for such a purpose. As the animal was so very restless, I tied it up by a string attached to the hind leg; but it still renewed the efforts to escape from its place of confinement, scratching very violently, until it became exhausted, expelling the air from the nostrils, and uttering also a faint moaning noise. When I placed it in a bucket of water, it sank, but immediately afterwards came to the surface, expelling air from the nostrils. It appeared evident that in its wounded condition it was unable to support itself in the water; and in about two minutes, on taking it out, it was quite exhausted, and did not move again for several minutes. It died in the course of the night.

One afternoon the usual ramble was taken on the banks, to observe and procure specimens of these animals. As the native Daraga came to Mundoona this afternoon, he accompanied me, and I availed myself of his assistance in seeking for burrows. On a steep bank as one part of the river, the keen-sighted native pointed out to our uninitiated eyes the tracks of these animals on the moist earth close to the water, which tracks, being followed up the bank to a distance varying from 2 to 5 feet, the entrance of the burrow, concealed by long grass and shrubs, was soon discovered; the tracks had evidently a very recent appearance. Following the same method as he had adopted when the last burrow was discovered, the native placed his hand within it, and took from its lower surface pieces of clay, on which impressions of the animals' feet were distinctly marked; but, from the situation of these burrows, I regarded it as next to impossible to explore them. We had often during this excursion mistaken the holes of water-rats and other animals for those of the Ornithorhynchus; but my tawny companion always told me to what occupant they belonged, at the same time readily pointing out the differences.

Very late in the evening we watched two Water-Moles paddling about in a small pond of the river; but they eluded all the endeavours made to get a sufficiency near shot. I repeatedly heard a splash in the water at one particular part of the bank whenever I approached it, as if the animals had retreated to the land, but, unable to gain their burrow in time, had taken again to the water. As this occurred often about the same place, and as darkness was setting in rapidly, I marked the situation of the spot, and determined to examine it on the following day and ascertain whether I was correct in my supposition. My tawny friend Daraga remarked to me that it was of no use digging up burrows of Water-Moles now for "pickaninny", for "none yet tumble down from mother"; but that further in the summer season, in rather "more than one moon, plenty pickaninny tumble down from old woman". It puzzled him, however, why, with such abundance of cattle, sheep, etc. we wanted "Mallangongs".

On examining the cheek-pouches or the stomachs of these animals, I always observed the food to consist of *débris* of insects of the family *Nauceridæ*, very small shell-fish, etc. which were constantly found comminuted and mingled with mud or gravel. This latter might be required to aid digestion, as I never observed the food unmingled with it. The natives say that they also feed on river-weeds; but as I have never seen that kind of food in their pouches, I cannot confirm the correctness of the statment. The young are fed at first with milk, and afterwards, when sufficiently old, with insects, etc. mingled with mud. "All same you white feller," said one of the natives to me one day, when I asked him on what the young moles were fed by the "old woman". "First have milliken; then make patta (eat) bread, yam," etc.

W.H.L. Ranken

[CLIMATIC EXTREMES]

Floods generally follow droughts. On the coast, the more mountainous the country the more rarely are these extremes felt; but no part of the country is free from their visits. It is in the interior, however, that they have their home, and from that stronghold the forces which call the floods forth rule supreme, their power declining as they approach that of the ocean. Here, in the depression of the great plain, there is most probably only one long drought, or one long wet season; no seasons of a year, but years of a season. Wet seasons, like droughts, may last years; for the seas of shallow water, the innumerable lakes and marshes which some explorers in wet seasons have found north of Lake Eyre, may be years in evaporating, as frequent condensation must take place by the cold southern winds. And this milder inland climate will tend to mollify that of neighbouring regions. But these two extremes are overpowering; they make that interior almost uninhabitable, and they rule the character of the country, the produce, the people, and the history of the land.

The desolation of a drought is not less complete than that of a flood, and it perhaps has more effect upon the survivors. For years these droughts gather in force; they multiply their action before they are broken by the floods, and their termination is in a melancholy, awful landscape. For days and months the earth has been hot, parched, and cracked; for months the waters have ceased to flow, the trees have lived but not grown, and the sky has been cloudless. The never-green forest is browner, sadder, and still in the oppressive air; the plains are bare and dusty; the watering-places filled with dead; and the whole scene quivers before the eye by the great radiation of its heat. Daily the sun rises in a hazy sky, sails in a white heat through a cloudless course, and sets, a round red ball of fire, on the edge of a copper dome. A sullen dewless night follows the dreaded day. The leaves of the forest and the surviving grass of the field glisten like blades of steel in the glare of the mighty sun; there is no green thing, nor sound of life from bird, or beast, or tree, in the great noonday heat. – At length clouds mysteriously gather – daily they gather, and disappear at night – at last they form dense low masses, thunder breaks, and violent storms of wind sweep the plain; no rain. Again and again these storms break before the longed-for rain comes; and with it comes flood. Perhaps the rain, filling the northern streams first, floods the southern water-channels before a cloud is in their sky. But with the floods destruction to lingering life, no less than hope to withering vegetation, is brought down. Many a settler has been ruined by droughts; but many a flock which survived that ordeal has been silently, hopelessly, swallowed by the flood. Many a life has been lost thus; and here we may find a clue to the fate of Leichhardt.

He started to explore the interior. Having already defined much of the coast watershed, he desired to define the inland or southern drainage, and the nature of this vast inland plain; but from this expedition he never returned, nor have any trace or tidings of him been brought in, except of the very beginning of his journey. It has been conjectured that he was murdered by natives; that he perished in a drought, or for want of food; and that some of the party may still be alive. But each of these suppositions is weakened by the fact that no authentic information of such a fate has been obtained, while some might be fairly expected; for Leichhardt had the severest experience of bush-travelling before he started upon this trip. He was accompanied by chosen men, and he had horses, mules, and goats with him – all sagacious animals. And if want overtook him, he could, in all probability, meet it by his knowledge of the bush and of botany; if the natives attacked him, some of the animals would certainly have escaped and made homewards; and if any of the party still lived, some certain information would have been brought in of him. In either case some animal, some weapon, piece of cutlery, or part of their equipment, would have been found by later explorers, and have given a clue to the fate of the party; but no trace has been found. Had, however, one of these floods overtaken the party, weakened by a long drought, their total disappearance is quite accountable.

The reader can picture his party toiling over the white withering downs of the inland slopes, water becoming at every stage more difficult to find, – the grass becoming drier and scanter, the horses weaker, and the party more dispirited. Sometimes without water, always in a tropical heat, and without any sign of a change in the weather, they would be compelled to stay their progress, and to feel their way from one watering-place to another. This continual scouting would reduce the horses and exhaust the men. But the water-holes dry up, and they were forced to shift camp. At last they found a large lagoon, and determined to wait for rain.

Let us suppose this lagoon to be in an obscure river channel, 200 or 300 yards long, having grassy slopes leading into and out of it, and not a clearly-cut channel. It had steep banks, 30 feet deep, and some five or six feet of water in the bottom; it is in one channel of a northern stream, where it spreads over the plains, effecting a junction with another river – forming a network of channels and flooded flats. There has been no flood for some years, most of the channels are overgrown with grass and weeds, and patches of downs lie between the meshes of the net. Here the party camped, well knowing they were in flooded ground; but there was no other water. They hoped their horses would recover, that they would rest and gain strength, and with the first rain move on to a better camp. They dreamed of gigantic mountains and noble rivers, of plains well watered and shady forests, while all around was the most dreadful desolation. There is nothing so oppressive and utterly subduing as a drought. It is not a fierce calamity, nor a dreaded blow, nor any brief struggle; here, in the vast interior of Australia, it is a torturing Titan, overwhelming and resistless, but slow and monotonous in its destruction. Daily the same glaring angry sky, the same cracked, gaping, thirsty earth, the leaden ghostly foliage, the glistening few blades of grass – all quivering in the mighty heat. No green thing, no fresh colour, no breath of wind, no sound from earth or air of beast or bird or insect; all in silence – in a breathless appalling silence. Nightly the sun sets in sullen anger, and the moon rises in the cold distant ether. The firmament is clear beyond conception, the stars bright, the moon radiant; all cool, distant, dewless, pitiless.

They camped. Some life began to show itself; kites and crows watched their camp, and circled over them from daylight to dusk. This was some change from the circling whirlwinds which were the only other break to the dreariness of the scene. Then the air, in excessively hot spots, would silently gather into an eddy, gradually increase the sweep of its little circle, and ere it was observed, there would be a vortex of wind towering far into the sky, lifting up the withered herbs, the dry bushes, the dead reeds and grass, to scatter them – its fury spent – far over the plain. And at the sunset some more life enlivened the scene: flocks, clouds of pigeons came and drank at their water, then swept away into the dusk to roost upon the hot ground. – But ere they had been many days in camp, one sultry night they were surprised to find that most of the kites had left them, and that not one pigeon came to drink. It was strange, but stranger still that one of the party, as he returned from foraging with his gun, reported the main channel, about a mile from the camp, was running. Not a cloud in the sky, nor any sign of rain, but here was the proof of rain up the country.

At first they talked of their plans, of how they would travel up the river slowly; and so on. But this was the beginning of the end – they were caught in a net of floods. The last office of the night was to draw water; and in doing so they found that the channel upon which they had camped was running strong. Then began the struggle. Some went for the horses and animals; these were scattered over the plain, cut off from their camp by other rapidly-filling watercourses. Thus the men became separated; nor were the horses ever got together. Some horses, and even men, in the sudden knowledge of their fate, struck out wildly, purposelessly, for their lives, and perished. Others struggled at the camp to save some of their most valuable equipments and stores. They determined to make back to the high land they had left before they crossed a creek two miles back – it must be another river, and surely not impassable yet. It was midnight; the leader urged all on with what they could take; he would follow at daylight if necessary – surely their camp would not be flooded, and they might save their stores; they would save some horses; they would meet at the last camp; and so on. In the multitude of councils there is confusion.

But the floods came in torrents and volumes; they filled all the channels; they netted all the plain; they joined each with the other; they overflowed all banks, and swept the plain fifty miles wide. No man nor horse escaped that night, except the solitary man and a few bewildered animals that happened to gather up to the camp fire. All went before the torrents, drowned in the streams, or bogged in the muddy banks, separated, bewildered, and desperate; the waste of waters swept over all, buried the remains in sand and mud, or scattered them over 100 miles of plains. No vestige was left. Daylight came, and showed Leichhardt his inevitable fate; alone in a wilderness of water. A great sheet of flood spread over the landscape far as the eye could reach, to east and west, and north and south, one steady slow stream, its deepest channels only to be told by the tops of the river trees. No sign, no hope of any of his party; for he could see many miles of water on each side; he well knew he was in a net of watercourses.

Water, water, but no sign of life; no spot of dry land in sight; no hope. At the camp, his journals and charts, his comrades' saddles, raised another and a mightier flood in his mind. No friend, no comrade, save one or two terror-stricken animals; only overhead, upon a blasted tree, sat a carrion crow. Then the dumb animals, their feet now in water, drew up to the camp fire, and whimpered low their last sad appeal to friend and comrade. No guidance; and they turned and went with the flood, and sailed down the waters, looking to right and left for dry land. Last of all, as the waters sapped and drowned the camp fire, Ludwig Leichhardt strode into the flood, and passed away upon that exploration of which no traveller has reported.

* * *

All life is thus limited by the aridity and uncertainty of the climate. There is little rain over the great bulk of the continent; there is little vegetation, little animal life, only one beast of prey, and few, very few, human creatures. But the climate is not only niggardly on the whole, it is a most capricious tyrant, destroying at uncertain intervals what it has reared in a few milder seasons. No result is gained by a rich growth in the forest, if a drought comes and withers up all young or weak life. And the interior, which has so many features in common, is so extensive in proportion to the whole, that it impresses its characteristics upon every part of the country. It reduces tropical forests to exceptional patches in sheltered nooks; it encourages one type of animal everywhere, and has forbidden the immigration of the teeming populations of the adjacent tropical archipelago to its barren shores. Floods destroy some life, they may drown some young animals, but the increased production of all life which follows them more than makes up any decrease. Drought, dry seasons, and, more than all – that deadliest weapon of the tyrant – the bush-fire, reduces and selects the life of the country.

During the long dreary months of dry heat, without rain or dew, those broad-leaved trees and herbs, which expose a large evaporating surface and require a large supply of moisture, could not survive; only the hard, thick, narrow leaves of the Australian forest, glistening like steel when they cannot hold their edges to the glaring sun, come out of the trial. On the plains and downs the acacias cluster in thickets as if to shelter one another, or singly droop their scant foliage gracefully over the parched waste. On the flats and meadows the giant eucalypti rear gaunt stems and bare boughs. The hills are timbered, but shadeless; and even in the beds of the watercourses the melaleuca is ragged and wretched-looking. All have hard, rigid, narrow leaves, and few of those. The watercourses are drying up, and the animals struggle on from one death to another. The marsupials can live for long without water, but not so the dog. He, the only foreigner of the land, cannot live without frequent water; he cannot therefore always accomplish the journey from one water to another, as the holes dry up; and he cannot remove his young to water when it is an imperative necessity. No animals are so adapted to such a trial as the marsupials; and they survive. The trees having the smallest amount of foliage, and not dependent upon a regularly returning spring to reinvigorate them – an indeciduous shadeless forest – is another result.

Then the grass is withered white, it is dry and warm night and day, and one spark of fire sets all the landscape in a blaze. This widens over the plain, gathers air in its combustion, and becomes a hurricane of fire. It sweeps the plains, storms the mountains, and rushes irresistible over watercourses, to lick up withered grass on opposite banks. The seedlings are lost, the sapplings destroyed, the whole forest scorched, and every decayed giant of the wood is wreathed Laocoon-like in fire – scattering from his yielding limbs flakes and sparks on every side, from which fires spring hydra-like over the withered sward – to rise, to roar and rush on, and scale in rapid springs the grassy ranges. In the forest, it spares only the giant eucalypti, which have stems towering 30 feet without a limb, only scorching the smooth bark, which is shed and renewed annually; upon the downs, it spares only – as it lingers and lulls in the low grass – those hardy acacias which rise in iron-like columns beneath their thin graceful tresses; and upon the mountain, it spares only those eucalypti which have their veteran stems bound in an impenetrable coat of "iron bark". All the land is cleared except these selected trees. Hence the open forest of Australia; hence grazing and squatters and land-laws; hence wool and meat-growing are before everything else.

The jungles or "scrubs" are not touched, for they have not grass nor sufficient tinder to lead the fire into their masses; and when the country is stocked, and bush-fires carefully kept down by man, then thickets increase upon every side. If any tract be for some years free from the visitation, then the forest will thicken; and the trees which have the most inflammable bark, like "stringy-bark" and "peppermint trees", grow in poor ground, and grow thickly, where fires rarely penetrate, and then only to blast the whole forest.

The fire-storm sweeps over the land, and reduces the animal kingdom; all is subject. The smaller insects and animals in their struggles are followed by flocks of birds, who snatch their prey from the flames. The small game and reptiles flee before destruction, or perish in logs and other deceptive lurking-places; and the large rodents, who survive instant destruction, have to continue the struggle for existence – without any pasture on the plain, young or old – with only the hard foliage of the thickets. Desolation is doubly desolate; the desert is burnt black and lifeless. Life has almost to begin again in the lower vegetable kingdom, and even animals lose their young. The plain depends upon the deepest roots, and the hardest of the barbed and needle-pointed grass seeds buried in the soil, to grow another crop. The forest has lost its saplings, and must plant again; and the struggle is hardest and longest with the animals. The dog, far from shelter, cannot circumvent that furious sea of fire:

he cannot bound over the walls of flame and fields of cinders; nor can he remove his young, nor can they escape. If his lair is in a log upon the plain, or by the last water-hole in the valley, his life is almost worthless. The marsupial has a better chance than any other type of animal, for she can bound far over flames and scorching ground, and find a way through many fires. Her young has a much better chance; for, placed securely in its mother's pouch, it is carried high over the burning ground, over death and extermination to live, or at least to continue the struggle. The marsupials are the selected survivors; the one type of all the country. The dog has no enemy but the climate; he is not subject to any other beast of the field, and he has many varieties of victims utterly defenceless against his attacks, but is not the master. He would increase and gather into packs, like wolves and hyenas, under another climate, with the present natural stock of the country; yet he is a solitary exceptional stranger in the land. The marsupials have been selected, with hard bare trees, and all the peculiar types of the country, in that decisive struggle. And it may be conjectured that if the superior types of animals introduced by the colonists were left to continue the struggle alone, were the country at once depopulated, considering the great degeneration these animals immediately undergo if neglected, they would disappear from the climate of marsupials in a few thousand years.

6

Town and Bush

EDITOR'S NOTE

Many of the authors represented in "Town and Bush" were also travellers of one sort or another. Some, like William Howitt, stayed only briefly in Australia, but others remained for the rest of their lives. The two women, Rosa Praed and Mary Gaunt, both travelled in the opposite direction, going to Europe to achieve careers as successful novelists. Praed's "The Old Scenes", based on her return visit to Australia, is, however, the only piece concerned with actual travelling, opening with a shipboard arrival in Sydney Harbour, and then describing the long train trip to Queensland and the buggy ride from the railway to Murrum head station. Praed goes on to detail life at the station, introducing various "Free Selectors" and other bush characters.

The emphasis on human and social life in Australia, rather than on animals, the land and climate, is what sets the pieces in "Town and Bush" apart from those in "Travelling", and "Flood, Flies, Fauna". Richard Twopeny, after visiting Sydney, Melbourne and Adelaide, described various aspects of town life in Australia, ranging from food and shops to politics and religion, not forgetting "Dress", the chapter included here. Another visitor, Francis Adams, wrote on "Melbourne and Her Civilization, As they Strike an Englishman". Three writers who knew Melbourne more intimately and for much longer, offer contrasting, and detailed, pictures. J.E. Neild and Edmund Finn go behind the scenes at the theatre and other places of entertainment. Marcus Clarke's "Nasturtium Villas" anticipates many later exposures of life in Australian suburbia.

Other anticipations of later, and usually better known, authors may be found in the pieces concentrating on life in the bush. William Howitt's crazy shepherd would not seem out of place in the pages of Henry Lawson. A.J. Boyd's sketches of bush characters also anticipate Lawson's, particularly those narrated in the colloquial first person, such as "The Shepherd" and "The Fencer". Mary Gaunt's "Riverina", written at around the same time as Joseph Furphy's classic *Such is Life*, though published much earlier, also offers a number of interesting parallels as well as useful information on subjects taken for granted by Furphy but often quite unknown to readers today.

William Howitt

[A CRAZED SHEPHERD]

Bendigo Diggings
July 14th, 1853

Our road from the M'Ivor hither was alternately over plains and barren woodland ranges, scattered with white masses of quartz, and with the prickly acacia in flower. The roads, for the most part, were good, excepting a few miles on approaching the Campaspe. There we had several miles of the vilest crab-hole road, and a descent to the river horrid with masses of rock projecting from the hillside. However, we bounced and tumbled over it as well as we could, and were rejoiced to find the river of the classical name so low that we could drive through without wetting the stores in the cart. This small river rises often twenty feet in a few hours, and in rainy seasons is utterly impassable. Just above our crossing-place lay a horse, drowned only a few days before, when the river was running furiously bank-full, and when the rider, endeavouring to swim him across, only escaped with great difficulty. The river runs from Mount Macedon, and is often fullest here when there has been no rain in this neighbourhood, the rain having been at the mount.

The greater part of the way from the M'Ivor to the Campaspe the country was very fine and pleasant to look at, and the weather superb. We advanced over open plains, bounded on our right by downs, green, flowing in their outlines, and as free from trees as the downs in England. You would have said it was a cultivated sheep-farming country, like Wiltshire; but it was just as nature had left it.

The clear, soft swells, rising and falling like the downs, or the green hills of Derbyshire, in many places perfectly clear of wood, in others only thinly sprinkled, and the edges of the forest showing themselves round at a distance, had a most civilised look. All was as emerald green as England itself; and the great, broad, level meadows over which we passed, were traversed with a wandering stream, just like an English trout stream. But all this consists of mere sand, and in the very first approach of summer will be burnt like a desert. Green as it now is from the winter rains, it is delusive, for the grass is so short that the horses are nearly starved upon it, and, had we no corn with us, would be so.

The trees are nearly all of the box eucalyptus, which makes no dead wood, so that we are at our wits' end for fuel. The day after we left M'Ivor, you might have seen me sitting on a hill, overlooking this open, verdant, beautiful scene for miles round, M'Ivor in the distance, at the boundary of the diggings, standing finely aloft, in his dark garniture of woods. Here I sat, as I have done every day on our journey, waiting for the second load coming up. Beside me, a pile of goods under a tarpaulin, my steak cooking in the frying pan, or a slice of bacon frizzling on a pointed stick, and my tea boiling in a quart-pot, while I was busy setting up the tent, or, that done, preparing the dinner for the evening, when the party would arrive, or amusing my leisure, if I had any, with "Knicker-bocker's New York"; always looking very formidable, in case of any visit from bushrangers, by a revolver lying on a camp-stool at hand, and a bowie knife in my belt.

Our party now consists only of myself and my two sons; Mr Bateman having gone back to Melbourne.

The first evening we had a visit from a strange crazed shepherd; and I could not give a more lively idea of the intellectual condition of this class of unfortunate men, which I have often mentioned, than by simply stating what passed.

I had seen the man go by, while it was daylight in the afternoon. He was leaning forward on his stick, carrying a bundle on his shoulder, and talking aloud, as I supposed, to someone below the hill. But after it was dark, our dogs gave notice of the approach of someone, and a voice cried out from a distance, "Any danger?" We said "no", and soon emerged from the darkness into the light of our fire, this strange, insane man. He was dressed in a pair of those riding-trousers, which are covered on the seat and down the inside of the legs with doe-skin, looking very odd and piebald, partly coffee-colour, partly nearly white, the gift, no doubt, of some hard-riding squatter. He had a short, shabby drab coat, and an old greenish-gray wide-awake. His shoes were slit open, as to give ease to gouty feet, and his swag consisted of an old, dirty linen coat, tied together by the arms, containing only a little tea in a paper, and some bread and cheese.

He said that he had been some distance onwards to reach the station of Mr Patterson, a wealthy squatter, which, indeed, was conspicuous by day, on an opposite hill; but that it had grown so dark that he dared not proceed, lest he should be lost in the bush. He, therefore, begged leave to lie down by our fire for the night; and though, for obvious reasons, we rarely permit this to strange men, we permitted it to him, as he appeared perfectly harmless. We were just going to tea, and we made him sit down and partake of some capital beef-steak, fresh bread, and tea. The old man was delighted, and pronounced it beautiful!

As he had no rug to cover him, we made him a mimi of canvas in front of the fire, a bed of leaves, and lent him a horse-rug to protect him from the wind, which was intensely cold. The account that he gave of himself was, that he had been for years a shepherd, on the station of Messrs Hamilton and Riddell, near Mount Macedon. That, through being frequently wet for days together while out with the sheep, he was so cramped and stiffened with rheumatism, or rheumatic gout, that he was incapable of following the flock. That, therefore, Mr Maclelan, the overseer, had advised him to come up to Mr Patterson, who, he told him, could, no doubt, get him into the Benevolent Society.

This was clearly a crazy man's story, for Messrs Hamilton and Riddell could have done for him all that Mr Patterson could; and it would have been an absurd thing to send a poor, crippled, crazy man, nearly a hundred miles on any account, much less on one which was perfectly unnecessary, as it could have been done by letter. But this is a common phase of shepherd lunacy; the idea of something to be done a long way off, by which they are induced to wander from place to place till they frequently sink and perish in the bush. This, it appeared quite likely, would be the fate of this poor fellow. It was evident, from the state of his wardrobe, that he had been long wandering about. He had small features, dreamy eyes, such as I have often seen in old Australian shepherds; and his beard, though not his hair, was gray. He appeared sixty, but contended that he was only about forty. But his memory was obviously almost gone, probably from the effect of his ailment on his brain. He said that he came out from England so young that he did not remember what part he came from; yet he came to Melbourne direct; and yet Melbourne is only about eighteen years old, so that he ought not to be much more than twenty. Perhaps he did not wish it to be known where he came from; for his voice was that of an educated person, and I had a strange feeling that I had seen him before, somewhere in England; a feeling much strengthened by his frequent use of *thee* and *thou* in his conversation. From this and other circumstances, I had a very strong impression that in early life he had been a member of the Society of Friends.

This poor fellow was as visionary as any man could be. He said, that when he got down to the creek that night, he could see a log lying in the water, and he stepped upon it to cross, when, he could not tell how it was, but the land seemed all at once to go away from him, and the water to go "tinkle! tinkle!" oh, so beautifully, that he really thought he could rush in, and take it all round him. Then he gave a leap to get on the other side, and he was astonished to find himself again on this side. So he turned back, and seeing a fire near, he went towards it. The people were talking very loud all together, so he called out, "What are you people making all that noise for?" And they said, "Go along, old fellow, and never do you mind." So he came along to us.

He described his being first taken with his illness (insanity) with feeling all at once as if the world had stopped; and "my feet", said he, "were set fast to the ground, and they seemed as if they had a couple of blacksmith's wedges in them".

I asked him if he had any wife or children. "Oh, no!" he said; "a shepherd never thinks of marrying." "But," I observed, "it must be a very dull, monotonous life in the woods, always following a flock of sheep." "Oh! no!" he said; "it is really very amusing. The nature of shepherding" – he was always talking of the nature of things, and involving himself frequently in strange, tangled attempts at explanation – "the nature of shepherding is to take out your sheep in a morning. You take them out, play on the fife, the flute, or the fiddle;" – I very much doubt whether such a thing was ever seen in Australia. – "I think sheep are very fond of the flute. Some like the fife, some the fiddle, but the flute is the instrument that seems to possess the highest charm for them; – take out a book or a newspaper; take back your sheep at night; – and really it is very amusing. I never could follow anything but sheep; – I don't fancy anything else. The nature of a man assimilates itself to a thing; and that things works on the mind, and the mind works on it; and so nothing but that can please the man. It is the nature of things that it is so. There came a man to the station at the mount, and he said to me – 'Thee art a shepherd, and a shepherd thee must remain for ever.' And I said, 'What me?' and he said, 'Yes, thee; thee art a shepherd for ever.' He said this in the presence of Mr Maclelan, – and he was gone! – and I knew that it was true. I am a shepherd for ever.

"And really it is a very amusing life. I learned a great thing from Long John, the other shepherd. 'Long John,' said Mr Maclelan, 'is a much older man than thee, Harry, that is, Henry; so mark and learn of him;' and really I did learn a great deal in the nature of shepherding from him. Almost all shepherds follow after their sheep, but I observed that Long John did not follow his, but went away from them; and I saw immediately that it is the nature of sheep to go moving forwards if you follow them, and to stop if you go away from them; and I followed Long John's plan, and it really answered beautifully; for, instead of their rambling on and on, they staid and fed quietly in one place a long time together. I never could manage more than 3,000 sheep; some shepherds may, – Long John could, I dare say, – but 3,000 are my number. I could manage them, and no more. Once I came into a rough fuzzy scrub, and I really thought I should have gone mad, for here went leaping past 1,500 sheep: and another 1,500; and sometimes I could see them going! going! going! and sometimes I could not see them at all! No, 3,000 are all that I can pretend to take care of."

I asked him what books he had read. He said he had read Burns's poems and the Bible. And he had read some of Shakespeare. Two of Shakespeare's dramas that he had read were *Hamilton* and Macbeth. These were all he could remember. But he sometimes got a map to read, which was very amusing. To trace out the roads, and the places of market-towns, was very interesting. He complained much of the want of fruit in this country, and seemed to remember with a wonderful relish russet apples. "Oh! those russets! They are a beautiful fruit. I remember eating them somewhere in England; I don't remember where, but they were beautiful! A dumpling of them would fill you from morning to night. And do you know, I am very fond of currant cakes. As I came through M'Ivor Diggings I saw some, at a shilling a-piece. I ate two of them; two whole currant cakes! – I was astonished; – two shillings!"

Such is the childish condition to which these poor shepherds are frequently reduced by their life-long solitude. The merest trifles become wonders to them; the great events of their lives. Poor old fellow! he was singing and talking to himself most of the night; and in the morning he was very ill. He said he thought he should die, and we thought he would, too, upon the spot. I suppose the good supper, after much starvation, was too much for him. And he must have suffered immensely these cold nights from lying in the bush without fire or any rug or blanket to cover him. He had no doubt lost all these on the way; for his memory was gone, so that he could not remember Black Thursday, the 6th February, 1851, though the great bush-fire of that day had burned all round Mount Macedon, and on Messrs Hamilton and Riddell's station. "I had a rug; I had a blanket; I had a quilt," he said; "but they are all gone, I don't know how."

But it was easy to see how, – for that morning he was actually going away without his swag. It really gives one a miserable idea of shepherding, and of the little care taken of old, or insane shepherds, to see them thus wandering about. I never saw a man more racked with pains than he was that morning; and I heard him moaning to himself, – "What pains! what pains! It seems as if the end were coming, – that is my belief, and what I say is, the sooner the better. O Lord, take us! take us to thy glory, we pray thee, and we are tired of praying. Take us! take us!" And then again I heard him saying, – "Oh! what a world this is! what a world of trouble! No father, no mother, no brother, no sister, – all alone! Oh, what a world!"

We gave him some warm brandy and water, and urged him to get to Mr Paterson's as soon as possible, as we must move on; and we could not leave him to perish in the wilderness alone. But he sat to the latest moment with Charlton by the fire, and very much pitied me for thinking shepherding so dull a life. He said it was my misfortune. What a strange effect it is which this bush life has on these men: at once destroying their minds, and yet inspiring them with such a fascination for what is so dreary in itself, and which ends in such misery and desolation.

J.E. Neild

THE HIPPODROME

The Hippodrome is the name given to the last transformation of that extremely ugly and nondescript building which was, in the first epoch of its existence, known by the name of Tattersall's, and which has but lately served as a market for the sale of stale vegetables and meat of doubtful freshness. There was never anything attractive about the place: the concerts of its early days had a gaudy kind of squalor as their characteristic, and the balls had only more dust and confusion than the concerts. When it was devoted to its legitimate purposes it had an earthy, sephulchral smell, and its equine inhabitants seemed the most dismal of quadrupeds. As a produce market, it offered an interesting study to such natural philosophers as delight in investigating the decomposition of vegetable and animal tissues; and now that it has become a "Hippodrome", it is equally remarkable for moral foetor as it was erewhile for material mal-exhalations. Its contiguity to that *cloaca* of putrescent vice, Little Bourke Street, renders it most convenient as a reservoir wherein may flow that ever-moving stream of human loathsomeness which fills the localities hereabout; and hence Yankee 'cuteness has judged rightly for itself in believing that a certain kind of coarse, boisterous attraction would turn this current therein.

If there are any enthusiastic students of physiognomy who are not over-fastidious where they pursue their investigations of the human countenance, I recommend them to go to this Hippodrome, and they will see an assemblage of characters such as in few other places could be brought together. The place is approached with difficulty. I do not mean that the unsightly structure itself is not readily enough found, but there is requisite no little address to arrive inside. If any simple-minded individual should go thither with recollections of the entrance to the English Astley's, and expecting some kind of resemblance at least to the very brilliantly lighted and gaily decorated corridor which separates the doorway from the dress-circle at that temple of equestrianism, I should be glad to enjoy his discomfiture at the Hippodrome as he stumbles over the muddy uneven floor of its entrance, and gazes at the high wall of rough deal boards, through which some eyes are glowering at him from a hole, and upon which light is thrown from two or three flaring jets of gas. "Where do you want to go?" says a rough-looking man at his elbow, and in a tone extremely like that with which he was once accosted on a dark night on the Richmond Road, when he was requested to accommodate the speaker with all the loose cash he had about him. "Where do you want to go?" "Dress-circle," says the verdant visitor, with a start. "Pay there, and go along there," says the prize-fighting man, pointing with one hand to the eyes in the board, and with the other to a kind of passage at the end of which is a light. So he pays "there", and goes along "there", and having got to the end of "there", he is startled again by another man, roughly accosting him with "Now then, where's your check?" Having given up that instrument he is allowed to pass this Cerberus, who half fills up the narrow doorway as if he were expecting a violent rush and were prepared to resist it. Cerberus past, he finds himself upon an open platform, which seems to him to be intended for a stage, and he is convinced he has made some mistake; but, looking round, he sees benches filled by individuals who are apparently spectators like himself, for they are shouting at him to get out of the way, so he worms a passage through the crowd, gets into a corner and then looks round him. He sees a strange array of forbidding faces, but they are all turned in one direction: a coarse blowsy woman, in most scant petticoats, is jumping about upon a carpet spread upon the sawdust in the circle, and her gyrations excite the most tumultuous applause; she is led off by the master of the ring and the shouts of her admirers convince her she has distanced Fraulein Fannie completely. Band of wheezy wind instruments strikes up, and one of the "gorgeously-caparisoned steeds" enters. Following is one of the "world-renowned riders". The "world-renowned rider" mounts the "gorgeously-caparisoned steed", stands upon his back, and does some posturing. Presently comes in a clown, with a loud voice and stale jokes; having delivered some of his stale jokes, he assists several "tight"-habited individuals to hold coloured dusters after the manner of bridges, over which the "world-renowned" man jumps, to the frantic delight of the spectators. Encouraged by this approval, he attempts a somersault over one of the bridges, but, instead of coming down upon the back of the horse, he lands himself on his own back across the wall of the ring. He has more pluck than cleverness, however, for he tries again, and again, and again, and falls each time, manifestly to the delight of the audience, which seems composed of exactly the kind of people to enjoy a broken neck. But "world-renowned" cannot do the somersault, nor does he break his neck, and I am afraid he becomes in consequence unpopular.

To this failure of attempt at fracture and dislocation succeeds another, in a different way, by other performers. It consists in leaping from a spring-board over the backs of several horses. Neither horses nor men are damaged in this experiment, and the dexterity (which might be accidental) is accepted in lieu of the catastrophe. The comes a fellow with a pole which he plants on his abdomen, and another fellow climbs up it (not the abdomen – the pole), and apparently tries to singe his hair at one of the lights in the roof. Not succeeding in this attempt, he is seemingly seized with violent cramps, which occasion him to wriggle and twist in a manner which seriously embarrasses the lower man who holds the pole; having recovered from this spasmodic attack he slides down that piece of timber with a rapidity that suggests the possibility of his going down the throat of his companion. This feat of deglutition is not performed, however.

Comes in next a lanky man, who has by diligent practice succeeded in producing semi-luxation of the hip-joint, and who is thereby enabled to put his heels behind his neck, and his head out of sight; thus contorted he presents the appearance of a deformed frog on horseback. This hideous outrage upon ligamentous tissues is highly acceptable to the assemblage. He gives place to a man who jumps through papered hoops, and lastly through a kind of drum, in which have been placed some flags; after which he dresses himself as a Red Indian, and whoops and screeches like fifty devils in one. He shows how the Indian wields his club (the club being very much like a magnified carrot), and how he shoots his arrows. I was much interested to learn that the arrows used by the Indians are curved – for the purpose, I presume, of shooting round corners, like the fowling-piece of that historical Hibernian.

There is another clown besides the one first mentioned. He has a very Yankee accent, and his jokes are even more venerable than those of his companion. It was he who did the longest jump over the horses, and who did not, as he was manifestly expected to do, break any of his bones. There is more to be recorded, but it is all of the same kind – to wit, that of attempts to suffer breakage or laceration in some part of the body. For instance, the man who walks in stilts appears narrowly to escape dislocation of the ankle-joint; the man who hangs from the slack-rope also does his best to effect articular displacement of that joint as well as that of the wrists, and the maniac who allows himself to be dragged several times round the circle through the sawdust, is apparently some Indian Fakir, who has failed in being crushed by Juggernaut. So it will be seen there is very much at this Hippodrome to allay the craving for man-killing; and probably if the lovers of this kind of excitement go several times, they may most likely witness a genuine fatal accident, not to speak of the possibility of a fight in the pit or elsewhere, with a like termination.

The conductors of this establishment are evidently disposed to afford the freeest possible liberty to their patrons. Smoking is not disallowed, and the interchange of compliments in the shape of oranges and other delicacies between the occupants of the boxes and the pit is permitted without any gainsay whatever. If any *lady* should by accident visit the place, she will do well not to put on her very newest bonnet or cloak, as, to say nothing of the crushing and pushing to which she may be subjected, she will probably be undesirous of having those articles of apparel spoiled by an intermitting shower of tobacco-juice playfully spurted in the form of a salivary spray from the boxes into what is facetiously denominated the "dress-circle". Such persons, too, as are in the habit of carrying articles of value in their pockets will do well to button those receptacles carefully up, for, judging from the facial expression of a great number of the audience, the quality of digital appropriativeness must be one somewhat extensively possessed.

Marcus Clarke

NASTURTIUM VILLAS

Did you ever wonder where live the large-jointed men with the shining hats, the elegant trousers, the red neckties, and the big coarse hands twinkling with rings? I found out one day quite accidentally, through my friend, Joseph Wapshot. They live at Nasturtium Villas.

"Come down and have a chop on Sunday," said Mr Wapshot. He is a merchant of great respectability. "Me and the missus'll be at home. Nasturtium Villa on the Saint Kilderkin Road." I went at 1 o'clock – the "chop" was to be served at 2 p.m. – and found Mr Wapshot and his friends in the garding. "Ha, my boy," roared Wapshot, who was painfully clean, if I may be permitted the expression; "How are yer? Come in. 'Ave a glarse of sherry? Mr Baffatty, Mr Calimanco, Mr Blopp!" I bowed to three fat persons – who each wore a white waistcoat and elaborate watch-chain, a red necktie, and big coarse hands twinkling with rings – and followed Wapshot.

Joseph Wapshot is a good fellow – a very good fellow. He was, as you are aware, originally a clerk in the house of Hunks and Junks, the great Sandbank Ship Chandlers (Purveyors of Naval Stores they call themselves), and from that employment became a traveller for Dungaree Brown. Versed in the arts of the road, skilled in the pastimes of the commercial room, an adept at Yankee Grab, a noted hand at Loo, Poker, or "Selling the Pony", Mr Wapshot made his mark, and soon entered into business for himself. He married, became a father, bought a villa-allotment, and settled down into an honest tradesman and a gross feeder.

Mrs Wapshot was Miss Matilda Jane Harico (of Harico, Kidney, and Company), and is a sprightly, black-eyed young person with a round, plump figure, a profusion of ringlets not altogether innocent of curl-paper, and short, chubby fingers sparkling with rings. She is an excellent mother, a good housewife, a most unentertaining companion, and plays the piano with a voluble ignorance which enchants her husband.

Into this society on a hot summer afternoon I found myself entered. Evidence of wealth without taste was all around me. The drawing-room furniture, most expensive, and therefore most excellent, was green picked out with crimson. The curtains were yellow damask (Heaven only knows how much a yard at Dungaree Brown's!), while the carpet represented daffidowndillies, roses, and sun-flowers on a pink ground. The pictures on the walls were either chromo-lithographs, or – more abominable still – oleographs of the most glaring, hideous, yellow and staring nature. There was a bad copy of the Beatrice di Cenci – every house in Nasturtium Villas has a copy of the Beatrice di Cenci – and a Guido's Magdalen, simpering at a most indecent Titian's Venus. Birket Foster, with his golden-haired rustics, eternally meditating in gowns of coloured cotton with his impossible hedgerows, his marvellous clouds, his perpetual briar hedges, was pin-pointing to admiration in every chromolithograph corner. In the dining-room we had Martin and his Satanical Architecture; in the breakfast-room Poussin feebly mezzotinted, and Watteau – poor Watteau! – more feebly mezzotinted still. On the dining-room bookshelf was Cassell's Illustrated Bible, and on the drawing-room table Doré's pale reflections of the great Spaniard Goya. The house was, in fact, furnished according to Messrs Reachem and Bock's catalogue – "This splendid modern drawing-room; this dining-room replete with every convenience: sideboard, wine coolers, etc." Nothing was wanting, not even a stained glass window, with the device J.W., and the ancient arms of Wapshot akimbo beneath it.

It was worthy of endurance to see how Joseph has aped the manners of the class he detested. His servants obey him in fear and trembling – for Joseph rules solely by the terrible power of the purse. His "cut of mutton" was always admirably cooked. His "claret" cost him as much as the wine merchant could dare to charge. His clothes were from Bilton's – the only tailor in Fawkner's Town – who sneered in his sleeve as he measured the rotund good natured snob. His wife was amusing, and his cigars without peer. Do you wonder, then, that such fellows as Baffatty, Calimanco, and Blopp come and spend the evening with him? Do you wonder that Captain Phoebus, Major Busby, Jerningham Jinks, and Jemmy Jerboa are frequently found sucking-in Wapshot's wine, and leering at Wapshot's wife. If men will make their houses bachelor hotels, what other result is to be expected?

The dinner at Nasturtium Villa was an infliction under which all have suffered. Soup (*bad*), fish (*indifferent*), sherry (*very bad*), mutton (*good*), vegetables, own growing (*most excellent*), *entreés* of fowl and some other nastiness (*both infernally bad*), champagne (*that is to say moselle*), cabinet pudding, tarts, custards (*all good*), cheese (*colonial and so so*), dessert (*good*), wine (*tolerable*), cigars (*very shy, W. not being a smoker*), and brandy (*the most admirable which could be bought in the city*). This is the sort of dinner which one gets at all Nasturtium Villas, and the pure Bohemian feels inclined to say, "Sir, – you! I didn't *ask* to dine with you? We are not sufficiently familiar for me to condescend to take 'pot luck'. But if you want me to feed at your expense – give me a *dinner*, sir!" Had dear, good-natured Wapshot but offered us a saddle of mutton, some reasonable claret, some Stilton cheese, and some of the A1 Brandy, we should have gone home happy and satisfied. But his foolish efforts to emulate his betters, his silly assumption of rank, of good breeding, and taste not only reminded us of what he really was, but made us deem him to be a great deal worse than accident for a time had made him. In a jolly bachelor camp, in a pleasant manly meeting of friends frying a lamb chop, baking a damper, standing a drink, or uncorking a bottle, Joe Wapshot would have been excellent, charming, beneficent. But in a badly-furnished drawing-room, blocked up with a grand piano, a bird-cage, an indifferent plaster cast of the *Venus aux belles fesses* (*he* doesn't know it under that name!), and five spoiled chromo-lithographs of Der Günstumper's *Windelkind Gurken-salat*, he is much out of place. Mrs Joe, who would be delightful on a desert island, is simply an unobtrusive nuisance in her own house, and the three soft-goods friends are positively indecently stupid.

After dinner we went into the veranda, drank claret, and smoked "small Patchechos". I have never smoked small Patchechos before, and I never wish to do so again. They are bitter and meagre and unsatisfactory. I was obliged to have a pipe to take the taste out of my mouth. Yet poor dear Joseph, turning up his chin to emit the smoke in long, lingering puffs of delight, taking the filthy root from his mouth and passing the burning ash beneath his nose as if in paroxysm of chastened joy, sending smoke out of his ear and nostrils, and finally closing his eyelids in passionate abandonment as he had in the distance seen do the "swells" at the Podiceps Cornutus. The conversation was not brilliant. Baffatty related an anecdote about a sudden rise in the price of flannel, owing to a fit of the gout had by the Marquis of Welchshire. Calimanco spun a yarn concerning some ingenious swindling – broking he called it – about a shipment of tweeds, while Blopp told several old and admired spicy stories which sent the company into fits of knowing laughter. Then we went into the drawing room, and Mrs Wapshot sang "Constance" with great feeling, Mr Blopp obliging on the flute. Then Mr Calimanco tried "My

Pretty Jane", but failed rather we thought, and it was not until Wapshot had himself sung *"Gentlemen out! Turn out! Turn out! We'll keep these Roundheads down!"* that we expressed any large satisfaction at the melodies.

After the music we had supper, and this supper was the most entertaining part of the entertainment. Joseph forgot his grandeur, and took off his coat to carve with greater ease. Blopp churned his vinegar into his mouth with his knife. Baffatty unaffectedly picked his teeth. Calimanco swallowed onions like a true British tradesman, and Mrs Wapshot swilled porter out of a pewter pot until her red cheeks shone again. During the progress of this festive meal we abused everybody of whom we could think, except his Excellency the Governor, for the Wapshots make a loyal point of satisfying all the trivial social requirements which are needed to secure invitations to the At Homes and Balls of the Queen's Representative. We abused Miss Nelly Higgins, who, as you will remember, ma'am, was so forward at the masquerade given by Wrenchem, the dentist. We discussed the bearing in society of Mrs Hockstetter, whose name was well known in Great Carib Street years ago. We whispered how Bullion, the banker, had been seen climbing over the back-garden fence of Mrs De la Touche. We told o'er again the stale story of Bangalore's misfortune with the widow. We sniggered at the threadbare calumny concerning Parson Jesse Rural, and we admitted that Mr Clipperton was not married to Mrs Clipperton, or *"report spoke falsely"*. In fact, we conducted ourselves like genuine representatives of the class of dwellers in Nasturtium Villas, and abused infamously everybody above our own rank in life.

When supper was over, the gentlemen drank brandy and water – Wapshot struggling manfully with a small Patchecho – and the ladies strolled up and down the twenty yards of garden with their arms round each other's waists. Calimanco related more anecdotes of successful brokerage, and Blopp added four more spicy stories to our stock. When we wished to give a man the highest praise we spoke of him as being "well-in", or "having made his pile". When we desired to express our supreme contempt for him, we hinted that he was "rubbing along", that his "name stunk at the Bank" (this elegant metaphor was Baffatty's); or that he was "in" someone's "hands". In fact, having sacrificed to the only god we owned – our belly – we set up the only idol we worshipped – Mammon – and fell down before it. At a late hour I departed, meditating upon the curious phase of civilisation which I had discovered.

Here was a whole family – a whole tribe of human beings – whose only notion of their part in life was to obtain as much money as they could by any legal means scrape together, and spend it upon eating, drinking, and decoration of their persons. They have no aspirations and few ideas. They do not read, write, or sustain one ambition which a few bank notes cannot satisfy. Deprive them of their bank-balance, and they have no resources of consolation. Place them in any place where chaffering and huckstering are not the business of life, and they would starve. And yet – how kind is Nature! – they imagine themselves to be the salt of the earth – the only fortunate people worthy to be beloved by God and man.

A.J. Boyd

THE SHEPHERD

I'm a shepherd. That's so. I've been a shepherd for nigh on twenty-five years. And I've earned good wages, too, for all I look so ragged. I remember, in the good old times, when the shepherds was the bosses. That was at the time of the big rushes to the diggings. Money was plentiful then, and we used to have some tremendous sprees. Why didn't I save my money? There never was a chance to save. First of all, when we got our wages, the cheque wasn't a right cheque: it was an order written on flimsy or soft paper, on the nearest agent of the squatter, an' cashed by the nearest publican, who, of course, never handed over a cent. A man was compelled to stay there and knock his cheque down "like a man". Then if the order didn't happen to be drawn on a merchant close by, it was all the same. If it was drawn on somebody in Sydney, how could a poor devil get away to Sydney – perhaps a four or five hundred mile tramp, without a farthing in his pocket? A man was obliged to go to the publican to advance him some money, and once you took a drink (for you couldn't go away without taking a nip) it was all up with you. The liquor was hocussed, and you got mad, and before you knew where you were your cheque was spent – at least so the landlord told you, and he bundled you out neck and crop. If he was at all a decent sort of fellow, he would give you a bottle of rum to help you to recover from your spree, and you returned to the station in a few days penniless. I've no heart to begin to save. I was well-to-do once – had a station of my own; but what with foot-rot and scab, and not looking after my own place, I soon went to the wall, and I've been getting lower and lower, till at last I became a shepherd. It *is* a lonely life. I never see anyone but the ration-carrier once a week, and I've no books to read. I follow the sheep, and camp when they camp. I go to sleep sometimes and lose the run of the flock. But I've been pretty well broken-in to not going to sleep. I've been made to pay for lost sheep, so that for three years I hadn't a cent of wages to take. The native dogs and the blacks worry me. Many a night I watch all night to try and get a slant at the dingoes. I used to lay baits for them, but I had my best dog poisoned through taking one of the baits, so I've given it up now and shoot them when I've a chance. It used to be fine times at night when there was a hutkeeper, but now-a-days a man has got to be his own hutkeeper, and cooking, and washing, and watching at night, and shepherding all day, mending hurdles and shifting them, takes up plenty of time. It's not such an idle life as people suppose. There's always something to do. The idlest part of it is following the sheep out at grass. Lambing time makes it pretty lively for everyone. We see more people then, and get a bit of news. Would I recognise my sheep in a crowd? Of course I could. I know every face in the flock, and there isn't two alike. People are apt to think a sheep is a sheep. So is a child a child, but no two children are exactly alike, and no two sheep are alike. I could swear to every one of 'em. I don't think I shall shepherd much longer. I'm getting on in years. Sixty, close on. I'm thinking of saving my wages next year if the publican will let me, and taking up a bit of land. I could have a home then, and only take a job with a travelling mob sometimes, or else go to shearing at shearing-time, to keep one in tucker. I'd be obliged for a bit of 'baccy. The rations ain't due till to-morrow, and I'm clean run out. Thank'e, sir.

THE FENCER

"Five bob a rod! Things have come to a pretty pass, when a feller's only offered five bob a rod for a three-rail fence, slip panels included!"

Thus spoke old Bob, the veteran fencer of the district in which my penates were established. He was a queer fellow, this old Bob. I believe he was originally a confinee during Her Majesty's pleasure; in other words, he was strongly suspected of being a "lag". However that may be, he was the prince of fencers. He could use the mortising-axe as well as a carpenter the mortising-chisel. He trimmed the ends of his rails as if he divined by intuition the necessary amount of wood to chip off or to leave on. His posts were always upright, and no matter how long the line of fence, they were always exactly the same height out of the ground, and in a perfectly straight line. His corner and gate posts were marvels of solidity. He used to say regularly on ramming a gate post, "There, if that's knocked over I'll forgive the dray that did it." I had many conversations with this old fellow, and gleaned many particulars of his craft. "Splitting and fencing," he informed me, "generally went together. It was not usual for a fencer to do any other kind of splitting. You see we all has our particler work. We doesn't interfere much with one another. Many a tree as'll knock out five hundred or a thousand shingles ain't o' much use for rails, and I takes a good many trees as'll run rails but ain't no mortal good for shingles. I doesn't mind a bit of a wind in a tree, because I can mostly take out the wind in dressin' the rails; but it don't do to have a wind in a shingle. So it often happens, if I am working close alongside a shingle-getter, that we swops logs. Mine suits him, and his don't harm me. Logs with a bit of a pipe in suits me best. They ain't so hard to burst. Them as gets timber for saw-mills doesn't want no pipy logs, so we gets many a good stick out of them; likewise them from us. I onst got a log as a party of timber-getters left, and I knocked two hundred postesses out of it. I used to do all my own mortising, but it don't pay now. Timber's so scarce, one has to spend a long time looking for one as'll run. I gets men to mortise at twopence-halfpenny a post, and that leaves me free to go prospectin' for trees. How do I know a tree as'll run well? No, I don't take no chips out. That's done by fellows as isn't up to their work. They chops out a big junk of the sapwood, and they splits it. Of course it splits easy. 'Oh? that'll run like a match', says they, and down comes their tree, and they spends half a day tryin' to enter a wedge, and if it does enter they hammers it home, and the log don't budge, and they cuts their wedge out with the axe and goes to another. The sap ain't nothin' to go by. I've got many a score rails out of trees them fellows has passed. I judges by the bark. When it runs straight in long even furrows, and don't look interlocked, I says to myself it'll do, and I always look out to see if there's a hollow limb in the head. That's a sign of pipe, and I takes the tree and seldom makes a mistake. Big knots don't matter. They always stops on the outside slab. Some people likes knots in their fence. What timber does I like best? Why, flooded gum and iron bark is my fancy. Iron bark is bad to mortise and dress if it's left too long. Bloodwood makes the best postesses, and it's like butter to mortise. Takes a long time to punch the holes? Not a bit of it. A good man will do sixty or eighty three-rail postesses a day, and thirty panel is good puttin' up, with one to dig the holes and another to dress and ram. But that all depends on the ground. I was awful sold onst. I took a mile of fencin' to put up, and I went and looked at the ground, and I tried two or three holes in different places, and it was all fust-rate sinkin', so I takes it at six bob a rod for a two-rail with gates and slip-rails. Me and my mates sets to work and gets on fine for about a dozen rod, and then all of a sudden we come to hard rock six inches down. We thought it would only be a hole or two, but it kept on, and we had altogether over a quarter of a mile of pounding two-foot holes in solid rock, and when we'd doun the boss docked a shillin' a rod because the fence warn't as solid as if it was stiff clay. We was a long time pullin' up that. Yes, I've lost stuff in bush fires, but I'se generally too smart for the fire. I onst lost a whole stockyard as was all ready to be put up, and now I always burn the grass round a heap of stuff. Fencing don't pay now as it used to do. In old times timber was plenty. No need to hump the tools about half a day to find a tree. They was thick as bees. And fencers was scarce. Why, five shillings a rod for a three-rail ain't no more nor I used to get for a two-rail in the old times. Howsumdever, as it's you, and I've done pretty well on this here run, I don't mind sayin' as I'll take the job, but I won't take no dog-legs. I leaves them to the new chums. I doesn't mind a wire fence, seeing as it's all straight-on-end splitting, but I doesn't put up no wire fences with round stuff. That's new chum's work too."

THE BUSH BUTCHER

There be town butchers, and there be bush butchers; butchers professional, who, with marvellous precision, will slice off a steak which shall weigh a pound within a fraction, without the aid of scales; butchers non-professional, who are butchers by force of circumstances; and amateur butchers, who cannot for the life of them tell whether a sirloin be a portion of the neck or the hock.

My butcher is a conglomeration of these three. He is not solely professional, because he has but lately adopted the trade. He is not non-professional, because he gains his living by butchering; and he is not an amateur, because he dislikes the business, and only uses it as a means to an end.

The bush butcher generally starts his business as soon as there is sufficient population in an outside district to warrant his killing from three to four beasts weekly. He then sets up a spring cart and horse to run his beef round to his customers, and erects a smoking house, and a boiling down battery. He is now in full swing, and rapidly becomes one of the most important men in his district.

Of course he is a horsey man, and, consequently, is the first to initiate race meetings, at which he is invariably chairman. When races are to come off, he is always chosen, either as a referee, umpire, starter, or judge. He always seems to have command of money.

Whatever crisis may be impending, however badly off the neighbouring farmers may be (and they are almost always in a state of impecuniosity in a new district) – no matter, the butcher can rattle his dollars in his pocket.

There seems to be some connection, deep and mysterious, between cash and killing. Mysterious the whole thing is, for whoever knew a farmer who didn't owe his butcher a bill? The butcher never seems to get paid, and yet his pockets are never empty.

At horse sales, at pound sales, at the compulsory selling off of some poor neighbour, whose crops have not kept pace with his needs, the butcher is always to be seen, bidding for anything and everything, and paying down cash on the nail. I don't understand it, and I suppose no one ever will.

Did you ever watch a butcher buying cattle, by-the-by? Silently he sits on the stockyard fence, viewing the points of the beasts before him. He always wants that strawberry heifer run out of the corner. He is suspicious. If any particular beast is hidden behind others, he instantly sees in it a dark conspiracy between the seller and his men to blind him to the defects of that animal. He announces his suspicions in plain terms – too plain, perhaps. The seller retaliates. Mutual abuse, and the lordly butcher strolls off to where his pony is hitched to the fence. The seller, who sees ready cash moving off, gets off *his* high horse, and conciliates the butcher, who now has the whip hand. Well! he does not mind giving £6 all round. Seller can take it or leave it. He (the butcher) isn't particular. He adroitly throws in a hint about cash. Seller gives way, and butcher goes his way rejoicing. But this little scheme can only take place when our butcher has firmly established himself. At first starting he is not so exacting in his demands. He buys a beast here, and a beast there, and has to kill and sell them before he is in a position to buy more; but tallow, hides, horns, and bones, soon make ready money for him. He increases his business, and he keeps a boy to go round for orders. His first boiling down processes were carried on at his kitchen fire, in a kerosene tin. His parlour was the sanctum devoted to the salting of such beef as he had been unable to sell. Under his bed might be found salted tongues, and a few hams in course of preparation. But all this changes very rapidly. He has occasionally got into scrapes with his neighbours, by selling them beef at a time when he could not possibly have purchased cattle, and at the precise period when the said neighbours had lost some beasts. These little mistakes, however, are taken in good part (the neighbours have no evidence beyond their own suspicions), and our butcher's establishment swells. He has now large killing yards, which may be known by an odour of decayed offal, extending to a distance of thirty miles, more or less. This killing yard is a great resort for crows and hawks, likewise dingoes. These may be seen in scores, gorging themselves with the refuse of the yards. Pigs, of all sizes, colours, and degrees of dirt, wallow in the mire of the slaughter yard, and fight and struggle for the possession of the garbage of the place. These pigs are a source of great profit to our butcher. Costing him nothing to keep, they get coarse and fat on the abundant food they find in their favourite haunt. Arrived at a proper degree of obesity, they are sacrificed to the tastes of the public, and become bacon, ham, and pork. It may be noticed that the butcher never partakes of the flesh of his own pigs. They are for profit, not food. He has a weakness for the farmer's bacon.

There is one method by which the bush butcher swells the number of his customers, and at the same time realises great profits. Attached to the joints of meat, periodically left by the butcher's boy at the house of a customer, is a little strip of paper, with the name of that customer illegibly inscribed thereon. Now, raw meat is glutinous, and when several masses of raw meat are placed side by side, or heaped one on the other, the natural result is, that each one sticks to its neighbour; and, equally naturally, the little labels become detached from one portion of meat and attached to another. Thus it often happens that Mrs Jones's ticket (originally stuck on to a pound of chops) becomes detached, and fastens itself to a huge 14 lb joint of Bill Stumps, labourer, with eleven children; whilst B.S.'s ticket shows the said B. S. to be the destined proprietor of 1 lb of chops. The meat is delivered. Mrs Jones is aghast; but butcher boy drives off, and proceeds to leave Mr Stumps his chops. Stumps's partner in domestic felicity is irate, and butcher boy calmly receives a shower of loud invective. The butcher having been duly anathematised by Mrs Stumps, butcher boy gets a happy inspiration. Hadn't he better go back and get some more? Of course he had. Mrs Jones lives too far from the butcher to return her meat today, and next day the stupid boy forgets to call; the joint becomes doubtfully green; and Mrs J. equally green, eventually pays for it. Meanwhile, a second 14 lb joint has been despatched, this time to the right party. Stumps is appeased, Jones is resigned, and our butcher is jubilant; he has placed 29 lbs of meat instead of 15 lbs.

The police are often inconveniently troublesome to our butcher. He is sometimes required to produce hides from which the brands have unaccountably disappeared – before the beast's death, of course. But this is a trouble the bush butcher will steer clear of, if he wish to become a great man, and an oracle in his district.

His shop is never void of salt meat. Occasionally he has such a stock of this article on hand that he must have recourse to some subtle scheme to get it off. The most feasible and natural one seems to be the accidental straying away of his cattle. Some fine morning he canters through the most populous parts of the district, and lets the people know that there will be no fresh meat perhaps for three days, as the cattle have broken out of the paddock, and probably are in full trot for the station whence they came. Dismay of the inhabitants. If there any salt meat? Well, yes; butcher thinks there is a little left; but they had better be smart about getting it, as he doesn't think there's much. This is a very good scheme, and works excellently. He not only gets rid of his salted encumbrance, but he gains the sympathy of the people in his strayed cattle perplexities. The said cattle are meanwhile carefully "planted" in some far-away gully, "to be left till called for".

As time goes on, the bush butcher enlarges his borders, and probably takes unto himself a wife. Now he comes out in full force. He starts his buggy and trotting mare, with silver-plated harness. He and his wife may be seen riding out together in gorgeous costume. They are invited to dinners, both private and public. His opinion is taken in matters connected with stock and legislation thereon. Her advice is eagerly sought by thrifty housewives in connection with the curing of hams and the rearing of fowls.

Arrived at this point, we may find our butcher climbing the ladder of fortune in different ways. Some bush butchers have a taste for squatting, and eventually become station owners. Others are great in public houses, and probably end by owning two or three of these desirable tenements. Others, again, think that a horse bazaar expresses the sum total of human felicity. This particular business entails the necessity for our butcher having a taste for auctioneering. Accordingly, we find him glib of tongue, and quick of eye to catch a nod or a wink.

It occasionally happens that the horse bazaar leads to the hunt. He is now no longer the bush butcher. He slips the disguise, and disposes of the business to his right-hand man, who usually follows in his master's footsteps. He has served as a page and esquire, and now has earned his spurs, and is a knight of the Carving Block, a K.C.B. Our full-fledged bush butcher has cast his skin, and is now on the high road to fortune as a squatter, an auctioneer, or a house owner and landed proprietor. One remarkable feature of the character of the bush butcher is his peaceableness. It might naturally be supposed that he would be fierce and bloodthirsty; but the reverse is always the case. He is mild and gentle. His wife is, in most cases, the "better half". All his anger and wrath are expended on the beast that ejects him forcibly from his own yard. At home he is docile and meek; and, smart as he is in business transactions, he can always be brought, by the most shallow devices ever invented by the female mind, to see his domestic affairs in the light desired by the feminine despot who rules over the home and heart of the bush butcher.

Richard Twopeny

DRESS

I doubt whether in my preceding letters I have made the distinction between Melbourne and its sister capitals sufficiently plain. I shall perhaps best convey it by saying that Melbourne is quasi-metropolitan, while both Sydney and Adelaide are alike provincial in their mode of life. In the matters of which I have been writing, the difference has hardly been sufficient to warrant a separate treatment; but with regard to dress, it becomes so noticeable, that not to treat of Melbourne separately would convey a false idea. For in dress it is not too much to say that the ladies of Melbourne are luxurious – a charge which could scarcely be brought against Australians in any other particular that I can think of. And take them all-in-all, they do not dress badly; indeed, if one considers the distance from Paris, and the total want of a competent leader of fashion, they may be said to dress well, especially of late years. The highly fantastic and gorgeous costumes for which Melbourne used to be notorious are fast disappearing. Successful diggers no longer take their wives into a shop, and ask how much colour and stuff can be put into a dress for fifty pounds. Already outrageousness is confined to a few, and when I say that it is generally agreed to be "bad form", you will understand that its death-blow has been struck and the hearse ordered. Bright colours are still in vogue, but they are not necessarily loud or unpleasant beneath the austral sun, and the art of combining them is beginning to be understood. When one remembers how their houses are furnished, and what their general style of living is, it is astonishing to find Melbourne ladies dressing so brilliantly and yet with so little vulgarity.

But it is not among the *grand monde* – if the term be not ridiculous as applied to Victoria – that you must go to discover taste. I am not sure that, class for class, the rich do not show the least taste in their apparel. Many of them send to Paris for their dresses, and pay sums, which make one's mouth water, to be dressed in the latest fashion; but I fancy that the French *modistes* manufacture a certain style of attire for the Australian taste, just as the French merchants manufacture clarets for the Australian market. It is a compound of the *cocotte* and the American. Nor when she has got a handsome dress does the Melbourne *grande dame* know how to wear it; she merely succeeds in looking what a Brighton lodging-house keeper once defined to me as a "carriage-lady". A lady of the English upper middle-class dressed by a London milliner looks infinitely better.

There are some costumes worn by Victorian ladies which you will never see worn by any other ladies; but for all that, the middle and even the lower class are by no means destitute of ideas about dress. Compare the Melbourne with the Birmingham or Manchester factory girl, or the young lady in a Collins Street retail establishment with the shop-girl in any but the most aristocratic part of London; the old country will come out second-best. And why is it? It is no easy question to answer; at the bottom is undoubtedly that general love of display, which is almost as characteristic of Melbourne as it is of Paris. But then what is the cause of that? And a love of display, though it may be and is amongst the wealthy productive of grand dresses, as it is of grand dinners and grand furniture, does not make taste – *e.g.*, the Second Empire; and though it would be going too far to say that the ladies of Melbourne dress tastefully, it is within the truth to give them credit for a tendency towards taste. Throughout England the middle and lower classes dress hideously. Why should the first generation of Victorians show a disposition to abandon the ugly? I leave it to some æsthetic philosopher to find out the reason, and content myself with noting the fact. If I wanted to moralise, I have little doubt that the drapers' and milliners' accounts of these "young ladies" would furnish a redundant text, and that, although a large number of them make up their dresses themselves from paper patterns or illustrations in *Myra's Journal*. How they can afford to dress as well as they do, they and their mothers best know; but the bow here and the flower there are not costly things, and the mere fact of being able to cut out a dress so as not to look dowdy shows natural taste. It is the rarest of sights to see a real Melbourne girl look dowdy. Her taste sometimes runs riot: it is exuberant, and becomes vulgar and flash; but even then the vulgarity and flashness are of a superior type to those of her equals across the ocean.

Sydney and Adelaide are distinctly superior to English towns of the same size in the matter of apparel; but they will not bear comparison with Melbourne. On the other hand, gorgeous and flash dresses are very rare in the smaller cities. If they have not the talent of Melbourne, neither do they share its blots. They go along at a steady jog-trot, and are content to take their fashions second-hand from Melbourne, but with modifications. Their more correct and sober taste will not tolerate even many of the extravagances of which London is guilty – such extravagances, for instance, as the Tam O'Shanter cap, which was warmly taken up in Melbourne. But with all this good sense, they remain dowdy.

I have said nothing hitherto of married ladies' dress. When a colonial girl marries, she considers herself, except in rare instances, on the shelf, and troubles herself very little about what she wears. As a rule, she has probably too many other things to take up her time. She has got a husband, and what more can she want? He rarely cares what she has on, as soon as the honeymoon is over. There is no one else to please, and I fear that colonial girls are not of those who dress merely for themselves; they like to be admired, and they appreciate the value of dress from a flirtation point of view. Their taste is rather the outcome of a desire to please others than of a sense of aesthetics. It is relative, and not absolute. When once the finery has served its purpose, they are ready to renounce all the pomps and vanities of this wicked world. And if the moralist says that this argues some laxness of ideas before marriage, let him remember that it is equally indicative of connubial bliss. Once married, her flirtations are at an end – "played out", if I may use the term.

In another respect the Victorian is the direct opposite of the *Parisienne*. If you leave general effects, and come to pull her dress to pieces, you find that the metal is only electro, to whatever rank of life she may belong. The general appearance may be pleasing, but in detail she is execrable. Not but that the materials of her dress are rich enough, so that my electro simile will hardly hold water; but money does not make the artist. Let us being with the bonnet. Walk down Collins Street at the time of the block on Saturday, and I doubt whether you can count half a dozen bonnets which are both pretty and suitable to the face and head of the wearer. *Bien chaussée et bien gantée* might be Greek as far as Australia is concerned, and if by chance you see a stocking or any portion of the under-clothing, you will have your eyes opened. Whatever does not meet the eye is generally of the commonest. It would be thought a sinful waste of money to have anything particularly good or expensive which other people could not see. The light of Melbourne is never likely to hide itself under a bushel; external adornment is the *mot d'ordre*. Ribbons and laces, or anything that helps to improve the look of a dress, the colonial lady will indulge in freely and even extravagantly; but you must not penetrate her tinsel armour.

Owing to the climate, hats are much more frequently in use than bonnets, and if the merit of subdued tints is unappreciated, it is not often that the eye is shocked by the glaring discords to which Englishwomen are so prone. Fringes are much worn, and the hair is often parted on the side. In spite of the heat, *gants de suède* find very little favour; they look dirty, and with a 25 per cent duty cannot be renewed every day. The usual English fashions find their way to Melbourne in about eight months, and this is the more convenient, because your summer is our winter, and *vice versâ*. Spring and autumn we agree to forget; this is rather a pity, because practically nine-twelfths of our year are spring and autumn, and on a bright July or August day the dress which is appropriate to a London fog in December looks singularly out of place. Sealskins and furs are worn till you almost imagine it must be cold, which during daylight it hardly ever is in this country. In summer, suitable concessions become obligatory, and dresses are made of the thinnest and lightest materials. Pompadour prints and white calicoes reign supreme, and look better than anything else. It is then that the poorer classes are able to dress best, the material being cheap. Winter stuffs are expensive, and to a great degree their effectiveness is in direct ratio to their cost; but during quite half of the Australian year the poor meet the rich, if not on an equality, at any rate on much fairer terms than at home with regard to dress.

Servants, of course, ape their mistresses' dresses as in England, and generally manage to produce a delightful sense of incongruity in their attire; but for all that, they are much less dowdy than English servants.

So much for ladies' dress. Change the sexes, and the picture is by no means so pleasing; for thorough untidiness of person, there can surely be no one to beat the Australian. Above all must one beware of judging a man's position by his coat. It is impossible to tell whether the dirty old man who slouches along the street is a millionaire or a beggar. The older his coat, and the dirtier his shirt, the more the probabilities are in favour of the millionaire. Perhaps he thinks he can afford to dress as he pleases. The city men are more careful of their personal appearance, and have kept up the shadow and image of London. They wear shiny frock-coats and the worst-brushed and most odd-shaped of top-hats, and imagine they are well-dressed; at least I suppose they do, for they seem to have a sort of contempt for the spruce tweed suits and round hats of "new chums", and such of the rising generation as have followed their example and adopted that fashion. Can you imagine yourself wearing a black coat and high hat with the thermometer jogging about from 70° to 110° in the shade? If the coat were decently cut and of good cloth and well-brushed, and the silk hat well-shapen and neat, I might put you down a fool, but would admit your claims to be a dandy. But as it is, most of our city men are both uncomfortable and untidy. Their clothes look as if they had been bought ready-made at a slop-shop. The tie they prefer is a black bootlace; if not, it is bound to be of the most tasteless colour and pattern you can think of. A heavy gold watch-chain and diamond ring is *de rigueur*, but otherwise they do not wear much jewellery. Their hair, like their clothes, generally wants brushing, and hands and nails are not always so clean as they might be; but one knows that for the most part they tub every morning: this is a consolation.

The bushman, at least, dresses sensibly. When he comes into town, he puts on a slop-coat, but retains, if not a cabbage-tree, at any rate a wide-brimmed soft felt hat. Sacrificing comfort to ceremony, he generally puts on a collar, but he often kicks at a tie: he finds he must draw a line somewhere. But there is something so redolent of the bush about him, that one would not have him otherwise; the slop clothes even become picturesque from the cavalier fashion in which he wears them. Note that his pipe never leaves his mouth, while the city man does not venture to smoke in any of the main streets. He is a regular Jack ashore, this bushman. A bull would not be more out of place in a china-shop, though probably less amusing and more destructive. The poor fellow meets so many friends in town, that by the end of the day he has probably had more nobblers than are altogether good for him. It is a very hard life that he leads, and he takes his pleasure, like his work, hardly.

If the Adelaidians are perhaps the least got-up, they are certainly the most suitably dressed of the inhabitants of Australian towns. With them the top hat is comparatively of recent introduction. Silk coats and helmets are numerous still, though becoming more rare every day. Melbourne and Sydney think it *infra dig.* to allow themselves these little comforts, and Adelaide is gradually becoming corrupted. It must, however, be added that the Adelaide folk are the most untidy, as the Melbourne are the least untidy of Australians. Comfort and elegance do not always go hand in hand. Tweeds are beginning to come into use amongst the upper middle, as they long have in the lower middle and lower classes. Capital stuffs are made at Sydney, Melbourne, Ballarat, and Geelong; but the patterns are very common. In a dusty place like this it is impossible to keep black clothes clean, and tweeds give far the best wear and appearance of any stuff. For my own part, I wear them winter and summer.

The working-classes can, of course, afford to be, and are, better dressed than at home; for though clothes are in reality much dearer, they are much cheaper in proportion to wages. They do not often wear black coats in the week, but keep them for Sundays and grand occasions. Directly an immigrant has landed, he feels that his first earnings must be devoted to a Sunday go-to-meeting suit. His fellow-men all have one, and he does not like to feel himself their inferior, even with regard to a coat.

Francis Adams

MELBOURNE AND HER CIVILIZATION

It is difficult to speak of Melbourne fitly. The judgment of neither native nor foreigner can escape the influence of the phenomenal aspect of the city. Not fifty years ago its first child, Batman's, was born; not forty, it was a city; a little over thirty, it was the metropolis of a colony; and now (as the inscription on Batman's grave tells us) "*Circumspice!*" To natives their Melbourne is, and is only, "the magnificent city, classed by Sir George Bowen as the ninth in the world", "one of the wonders of the world". They cannot criticise, they can only praise it. To a foreigner, however, who, with all respect and admiration for the excellencies of the Melbourne of today as compared with the Melbourne of half-a-century ago, has travelled and seen and read, and cares very little for glorifying the *amour-propre* of this class or of that, and very much for really arriving at some more or less accurate idea of the significance of this city and its civilization; to such a man, I say, the native melodies in the style of "Rule Britannia" which he hears everywhere and at all times are distasteful. Nay, he may possibly have at last to guard himself against the opposite extreme, and hold off depreciation with the one hand as he does laudation with the other!

The first thing, I think, that strikes a man who knows the three great modern cities of the world – London, Paris, New York – and is walking observingly about Melbourne is, that Melbourne is made up of curious elements. There is something of London in her, something of Paris, something of New York, and something of her own. Here is an attraction to start with. Melbourne has, what might be called, the *metropolitan tone*. The look on the faces of her inhabitants is the *metropolitan look*. These people live quickly: such as life presents itself to them, they know it: as far as they can see, they have no prejudices. "I was born in Melbourne," said the wife of a small bootmaker to me once, "I was born in Melbourne, and I went to Tasmania for a bit, but I soon came back again. *I like to be in a place where they go ahead.*" The wife of a small bootmaker, you see, has the *metropolitan tone*, the *metropolitan look* about her; she sees that there is a greater pleasure in life than sitting under your vine and your fig-tree; she likes to be in a place where they go ahead. And she is a type of her city. Melbourne likes to "go ahead". Look at her public buildings, her New Law Courts not finished yet, her Town Hall, her Hospital, her Library, her Houses of Parliament, and above all her Banks! Nay, and she has become desirous of a fleet and has established a "Naval Torpedo Corps" with seven electricians. All this is well, very well. Melbourne, I say, lives quickly: such as life presents itself to her, she knows it: as far as she can see, she has no prejudices.

As far as she can see. – The limitation is important. The real question is, *how* far she can see? How far does her civilization answer the requirements of a really fine civilization? What scope in it is there (as Mr Arnold would say) for the satisfaction of the claims of conduct, of intellect and knowledge, of beauty and manners? Now in order the better to answer this question, let us think for a moment what are the chief elements that have operated and are still operating in this Melbourne and her civilization.

This is an English colony: it springs, as its poet Gordon (of whom there will presently be something to be remarked) says, in large capitals, it springs from "*the Anglo-Saxon race . . . the Norman blood*." Well, if there is one quality which distinguishes this race, this blood, it is its determined strength. Wherever we have gone, whatever we have done, we have gone and we have done with all our heart and soul. We have made small, if any, attempt to conciliate others. Either they have had to give way before, or adapt themselves to us. India, America, Australia, they all bear witness to our determined, our pitiless strength. What is the state of the weaker nations that opposed us there? In America and Australia they are perishing off the face of the earth; even in New Zealand, where the aborigines are a really fine and noble race, we are, it seems, swiftly destroying them. In India, whose climate is too extreme for us ever to make it a colony in the sense that America and Australia are colonies; in India, since we could neither make the aborigines give way, nor make them adapt themselves to us, we have simply let them alone. They do not understand us, nor we them. Of late, it is true, an interest in them, in their religion and literature, has been springing up, but what a strange aspect do we, the lords of India for some hundred and thirty years, present! "In my own experience among Englishmen," says an Indian scholar writing to the *Times* in 1874, "I have found no general indifference to India, but I have found a Cimmerian darkness about the manners and habits of my countrymen, an almost poetical description of our customs, and a conception no less wild and startling than the vagaries of Mandeville and Marco Polo concerning our religion." Do we want any further testimony than this to the determined, the pitiless strength of "the Anglo-Saxon race . . . the Norman blood?"

Well, and how does all this concern Australia in general and Melbourne in particular? It concerns them in this way, that the civilization of Australia, of Melbourne, is an Anglo-Saxon civilization, a civilization of the Norman blood, and that, with all the good attendant on such a civilization, there is also all the evil. All? Well, I will not say all, for that would be to contradict one of the first and chief statements I made about her, namely that "as far as she can see Melbourne has no prejudices," a statement which I could not make of England. *"This our native or adopted land,"* says an intelligent Australian critic, the late Mr Marcus Clarke, *"has no past, no story. No poet speaks to us." "No"*, we might add, *"and (thus far happily for you) neither, as far as you can see, does any direct preacher of prejudice."* And here, as I take it, we have put our finger upon what is at once the strength and the weakness of this civilization.

Let us consider it for a moment. The Australians have no prejudice about an endowed Church, as we English have, and hence they have, what we have not, religious liberty. As far as I can make out, there is no reason why the wife of a clergyman of the Church of England should in this colony look down upon the wife of a dissenting minister as her social inferior, and this is, on the whole, I think, well, for it tends to break up the notion of caste that exists between the two sects; it tends, I mean, to their mutual benefit, to the interchange of the church's sense of "the beauty of holiness" with the chapel's sense of the passion of holiness. Here, then, you are better off than we. On the other hand, you have no prejudice, as we last have, against Protection, and consequently you go on benefiting a class at the expense of the community in a manner that can only, I think, be defined as short-sighted and foolish. Here we are better off than you. Again, however, you have not the prejudice that we have against the intervention of the State. You have nationalised your railways, and are attempting, as much as possible, to nationalise your land.† You are beginning to see that a land tax, at any given rate of annual value, would be (as Mr Fawcett puts it) "a valuable national resource, which might be utilised in rendering unnecessary the imposition of many

† The remark is, of course, general. Most of Victoria, as we all know, is unfortunately definitely sold.

taxes which will otherwise have to be imposed". Here you are better off than we, better off both in fortune and general speculation. Again, you have not yet arrived at Federalism, and what a waste of time and all time's products is implied in the want of central unity! Now the first and third of these instances show the strength that is in this civilization, and the second shows a portion of the weakness, at present only a small portion, but, unless vigorous measures are resorted to and soon, this Protection will become the great evil that it is in America. There is just the same cry there as here: "Protect the native industries until they are strong enough to stand alone" – as if an industry that has once been protected will ever care to stand alone again until it is compelled to! As if a class benefited at the expense of the community will ever give up its benefit until the community takes it away again!

On one of the first afternoons I spent in Melbourne, I remember strolling into a well-known book-mart, the book-mart "at the sign of the rainbow". I was interested both in the books and the people who were looking at or buying them. Here I found, almost at the London prices (for we get our twopence and threepence in the shilling on books now in London), all, or almost all, of the average London books of the day. The popular scientific, theological, and even literary books were to hand, somewhat cast into the shade, it is true, by a profusion of cheap English novels and journals, but still they were to hand. And who were the people that were buying them? The people of the dominant class, the middle-class. I began to enquire at what rate the popular, scientific, and even literary books were selling. Fairly, was the answer. "And how do Gordon's poems sell?" *"Oh they sell well,"* was the answer, *"he's the only poet we've turned out."*

This pleased me, it made me think that the "go-ahead" element in Victorian and Melbourne life had gone ahead in this direction also. If, in a similar book-mart in Falmouth (say), I had asked how the poems of Charles Kingsley were selling, it is a question whether much more than the name would have been recognised. And yet the middle-class here is as, and perhaps more, badly – more appallingly badly – off for a higher education than the English provincial middle class is. Whence comes it, then, that a poet like Gordon with the cheer and charge of our chivalry in him, with his sad "trust and only trust," and his

> weary longings and yearnings
> for the mystical better things:

whence comes it that he is a popular poet here? Let him answer us English for himself and Melbourne:

> You are slow, very slow, in discerning
> that book-lore and wisdom are twain:

Yes, indeed, to Melbourne, such as life presents itself to her, she knows it, and, what is more, she knows that she knows it, and her self-knowledge gives her a contempt for the pedantry of the old world. Walk about in her streets, look at her private buildings, these banks of hers, for instance, and you will see this. They *mean* something, they *express* something: they do not (as Mr Arnold said of our British Belgravian architecture) "only express the impotence of the artist to express anything." They express a certain sense of movement, of progress, of conscious power. They say: "Some thirty years ago the first gold nuggets made their entry into William Street. Well, many more nuggets have followed, and wealth of other sorts has followed the nuggets, and we express that wealth – we express movement, progress, conscious power. – *Is that, now, what your English banks express?*" And we can only say that it is not, that our English banks express something quite different; something, if deeper, slower; if stronger, more clumsy.

But the matter does not end here. When we took the instance of the books and the people "at the sign of the rainbow", we took also the abode itself of the rainbow; when we took the best of the private buildings, we took also the others. Many of them are hideous enough, we know; this is what Americans, English, and Australians have in common, this inevitable brand of their civilization, of their determined, their pitiless strength. The same horrible "pot hat", "frock coat", and the rest, are to be found in London, in Calcutta, in New York, in Melbourne.

Let us sum up. "The Anglo-Saxon race, the Norman blood": a colony made of this: a city into whose hands wealth and its power is suddenly phenomenally cast: a general sense of movement, of progress, of conscious power. This, I say, is Melbourne – Melbourne with its fine public buildings and tendency towards banality, with its hideous houses and tendency towards anarchy. And Melbourne is, after all, the Melbournians. Alas, then, how will this city and its civilization stand the test of a really fine city and fine civilization? How far will they answer the requirements of such a civilization? What scope is there in them for the satisfaction of the claims of conduct, of intellect and knowledge, of beauty, and manners?

Of the first I have only to say that, so far as I can see, its claims are satisfied, satisfied as well as in a large city, and in a city of the above-mentioned composition, they can be. But of the second, of the claims of intellect and knowledge, what enormous room for improvement there is! What a splendid field for culture lies in this middle-class that makes a popular poet of Adam Lindsay Gordon! It tempts one to prophesy that, given a higher education for this middle-class, and fifty – forty – thirty years to work it through a generation, and it will leave the English middle-class as far behind in intellect and knowledge as, at the present moment, it is left behind by the middle-class, or rather the one great educated upper-class, of France.

There is still the other claim, that of beauty and manners. And it is here that your Australian, your Melbourne civilization is, I think, most wanting, is most weak; it is here that one feels the terrible need of "a past, a story, a poet to speak to you". With the Library are a sculpture gallery and a picture gallery. What an arrangement in them both! In the sculpture gallery "are to be seen", we are told, "admirably executed casts of ancient and modern sculpture, from the best European sources, copies of the Elgin marbles from the British Museum, and other productions from the European Continent." Yes, and Summers stands side by side with Michaelangelo! And poor busts of Moore and Goethe come between Antinous and the Louvre Apollo the Lizard slayer! But this, it may be said, is after all only an affair of an individual, the arranger. Not altogether so. If an audience thinks that a thing is done badly, they express their opinion, and the failure has to vanish. And how large a portion of the audience of Melbourne city, pray, is of opinion that quite half of its architecture is a failure, is hideous, is worthy only, as architecture, of abhorrence? How many are shocked by the atrocity of the Medical College building at the University? How many feel that Bourke Street, taken as a whole, is simply an insult to good taste?

"Yes, all this," it is said, "may be true, as abstract theory, but it is at present quite out of the sphere of practical application. You would talk of Federalism, and here is our good ex-Premier of New South Wales, Sir Henry Parkes, making it the subject of a farewell denunciation. 'I venture to say now,' says Sir Henry Parkes, 'here amongst you what I said when I had an opportunity in London, what I ventured to say to Lord Derby himself, that this federation scheme must prove a failure.' You talk of Free-trade and here is what an intelligent writer in the *Argus* says *apropos* of 'the promised tariff negotiations with Tasmania'. 'In America', he says, 'there is no difficulty in inducing the States to see that, whatever may be their policy as regards the outside world, they should interchange as between each other in order that they may stand on as broad a base as possible, but we can only speculate on the existence of such a national spirit here.' – These facts, my good sir," it is said, "as indicative of the amount of opposition that the nation feels to the ideas of Free-trade and Federalism, are not encouraging." – They are not, let us admit it at once, but there are others which are; others, some of which we have been considering, and, above and beyond everything, there is one invaluable and in the end irresistible ally of these ideas: there is *the Tendency of the Age – the Time-Spirit*, as Goethe calls it. Things move more quickly now than they used to do: ideas, the modern ideas, are permeating the masses swiftly and thoroughly and universally. We cannot tell, we can only speculate as to what another fifty – forty – thirty years will actually bring forth.

Free-trade – Federalism – Higher Education, they all go together. The necessities of life are cheap here, wonderfully cheap; a man can get a dinner here for sixpence that he could not get in England for twice or thrice the amount. "There are not," says the *Australasian Schoolmaster*, the organ of the State Schools, "there are not many under-fed children in the Australian [as there are in the English] schools." But the luxuries of life (and let us remember that what we call the luxuries of life are, after all, necessities; they are the things which go to make up our civilization, the things which make us feel that there is a greater pleasure in life than sitting under your vine and your fig-tree, whatever Mr George may have to say to the contrary) – the luxuries of life, I say, are dear here, very dear, owing to, what I must be permitted to call, an exorbitant tariff, and, consequently, the money that would be spent in fostering a higher ideal of life, in preparing the way for a national higher education, is spent on these luxuries, and the claims of intellect and knowledge, and of beauty and manners, have to suffer for it. Here is your Mr Marcus Clarke, for instance, talking grimly, not to say bitterly, of "the capacity of this city to foster poetic instinct", of his "astonishment that such work" as Gordon's "was ever produced here." He is astonished, you see, that the claims of intellect and knowledge, and of beauty and manners are enough satisfied in this city to produce a talent of this sort; he is astonished, because he does not see that there is an element in this city which, in its way, is making for at any rate the intellect and knowledge – an element which is a product, not of England but of Australia; a general sense of movement, of progress, of conscious power.

Free-trade – Federalism – Higher Education, they all, I say, go together; but if one is more important than the other, then it is the last. Improvement, real improvement, must always be from within outwards, not from without inwards. All abiding good comes, as it has been well said, by evolution not by revolution. "Our chief, our gravest want in this country at present", says Arnold, "our *unum necessarium*, is a middle-class, homogeneous, intelligent, civilized, brought up in good public schools, and on the first plane." How true is this of Australia too, of Melbourne! There are State schools for the lower-class, but what is there for the great upper educated class of the nation? The voluntary schools, the "private adventure schools". And what of education do *they* supply either in England or here? "The voluntary schools," says a happy shallow man in some Publishers' circular I lit on the other day, "the voluntary schools of the country" [of England] "have reached the highest degree of efficiency". This, to those who have taken the trouble to study the question, not to say to have considerable absolute experience in the English voluntary schools – this is intelligence as surprising as it ought to be gratifying. To such men, the idea they had arrived at of the English voluntary schools was somewhat different; their idea being that these schools were, both socially and intellectually, the most inadequate that fall to the lot of any middle class among the civilized nations of Europe. "Comprehend," says Arnold to us Englishmen, and he might as well be saying it to you Australians, "comprehend that middle-class education – the higher education, as we have put it, of the great upper educated class – is a great democratic reform, of the truest, surest, safest description."

"But there are many difficulties to be overcome – so many, that we doubt these abstract theories to be at present within the sphere of practical application. There is such a mass of opposition to the idea of Federalism. And, as for the idea of Free-trade, we can only speculate on the existence of a national spirit here. The thinking public is quite content with its State schools for the lower class, and cares little or nothing about State schools and a higher education for the upper class. They are much more interested in the religious questions of the day – the Catholic attitude, the conflict between Mr Strong and his Presbytery on the subject of Religious Liberalism or Latitudinarianism, as you may please to call it, etcetera, etcetera, etcetera." – All this is so, let us admit it at once, but it does not discourage us. We know, or think we know (which is, after all, almost the same thing), that these three questions – Free-trade, Federalism, Higher Education – are the three great, the three vital questions for Australia, for Melbourne. We know that, sooner or later, they will have to be properly considered and decided upon, and that, if Melbourne is to keep the place which she now holds as the leading city, intellectually and commercially, of Australia, they will have to be decided upon in that way which conforms with "the intelligible law of things," with the *Tendency of the Age*, with the *Time-Spirit*. For this is the one invaluable and, in the end, irresistible ally of Progress – of Progress onward and upward.

December, 1884.

NOTE. – No one, speaking of Free-trade and Federalism in Australia, can omit a tribute of thanks to the *Argus* and the *Federal Australian* for what they have respectively done for the two causes. The cause of Higher Education, however, still waits for a champion in the Press.

Edmund Finn

[THEATRICAL SHENANIGANS]

Attempted Abduction

"Catching an Heiress" most of us have seen acted at some time, but forcibly abducting an actress remains to be written. A dramatic burlesque of this kind was improvised on the evening of Saturday, 3rd September, during the rehearsal of the not inappropriate piece the "Wood Demon". Miss Sinclair, a lady *attaché* of the theatre, was possessed of some personal attractions, of which a Mr Montague Charles Greaves was terribly smitten. The fair one gave the cold shoulder to his addresses, and he determined to have her *vi et armis*, if necessary, or perish in the attempt. Taking counsel with a Mr William Raymond, a Justice of the Peace, they got together a small but "select party of roughs", and proceeded to besiege the theatre at a time when they were assured the lady was there. Getting round to the rear of the building they burst in a door, invaded the sanctity of the green room, and peremptorily demanded that Miss Sinclair should be surrendered to them.

Buckingham indignantly refused to be guilty of such unmanliness, and mustering his forces, called upon each

> To set the teeth, and stretch the nostrils wide,
> Hold hard the breath; and bend up every spirit
> To his full height;

And forthwith a brisk hand-to-hand encounter commenced. The theatrical people were in full force, and fought well, Davies showing himself a prodigy of valour; and after some smart pummelling the attacking party was ejected, and the lady so far preserved. The Greavesites then retreated to the *Prince Albert Hotel*, close by in Swanston Street, where an extensive "liquoring up" ensued, and several recruits were obtained; so the stormers, re-animated by "nobblers", and increased numbers, returned to the field of battle, re-entered, and the hammering re-commenced. The garrison had also secured reinforcements, stood bravely to its guns, and bouquets in the shape of black eyes and sanguinary noses were pretty equally distributed. Again the fortune of war favoured the theatricals, and the others were again repulsed, but so roughly that Greaves and Raymond, who were the last to turn tail, had to run for it; but in their exit, both coming together upon an old trap door, the fastenings gave way, and the two heroes disappeared into an infernal region, where they were trapped like a pair of rats, when the police appeared and marched them off to the lock-up. Next morning they were charged before the Police Court, but, through some unaccountable leniency, Raymond, the brother magistrate, got off with a half-a-crown fine, and a penalty of only 40s. was inflicted upon Greaves, who paid rather dearly for his whistle in another way, as he was dismissed from a clerkship he held in the Bank of Australasia.

* * *

To avoid a future digression, it may be convenient to introduce here one of the most grotesquely comical outrages imaginable, attempted on a dark night during the winter of 1843. It was nothing less than a wild Quixotic

Attempt to Capsize the Theatre

If a band of high or low-bred larrikins at the present day not only proposed, but attempted to impede a railway train freighted with a pleasure party, it would raise a thrill of horror through the community, and no punishment would be deemed sufficiently condign for such an outrage. Yet in intent, at all events, the meditated overturning of a performing theatre is no less heinous. In the attempt now recorded the project was not only preposterous, but impossible, and the whole thing eventuated in a most hair-brained *fiasco*. At the time I am writing of there was a remarkable tenement rearward of the now Australian Club House, in William Street, known as "The Crib", and hither invariably wended their way certain *habitués* of the Melbourne Club, when they attained to the stage of inebriety, pugnacity, or mischief-making, which unfitted them for quarters where even the line of licentiousness was never too tightly drawn. On the evening in question there was the unusual theatrical attraction of a black boy, or servant, brought from Sydney by Mr C. H. Ebden, and this darkey was A1 at singing a nigger song, or dancing a Yankee breakdown. It was thought he would draw a full house, though he did not, in consequence of the wetness of the weather.

About 10 p.m. there sallied forth from "The Crib" some dozen young swells, in the heyday of hot blood, and skin full of more pungent *spiritual* influences than are to be found patronising table-rapping *séances*. They were out on the "ran-tan", determined to signalise the occasion in some remarkable manner. Night-watchmen and "bobbies" they had already bobbed about to their hearts' content; door knockers had been abstracted, church bells had chimed, window shutters were removed, and such commonplace exploits found no further favour in their sight. Alexander sighed for a new world to conquer, and these night birds hiccuped out a desire for some unprecedented freak to offer, in which they might find some complete change of amusement. They held a council of war by the fence of St James's Church Reserve, and in a flash of lucky inspiration one of them suggested that to upset the old Pavilion would be "capital fun". The proposition was received with a hilarious shout of approbation, and instantly nominating a leader they started off on their madcap expedition. Approaching the scene of action, they slackened pace, and at the now Beehive Corner, settled the plan of campaign. They then separated, and approached stealthily to the theatre, when they got without difficulty through the foundation piles, and were placed at their several points of duty by the leader, who was to chaunt the heaving signal, in the manner of sailors working aboard ship. The *"generalissimo"* was either a stupid strategist, or when the wine, or something stronger was in him, the wit was out, for instead of posting his men all on one side, he distributed them promiscuously between the earth and the theatre flooring, so that when the tug of war came, it was a bootless trial of general strength, for each of the fellows practically counteracted what the others did, by virtually working on opposite sides. Of course, it was ridiculous to suppose that even were they a dozen full-haired Samsons, they could produce any effect; yet they succeeded in causing the superstructure to creak. They tugged, and shouldered, and hove away for some time, in obedience to the loud "yeo-ing" of their skipper, until some of the theatrical people, astonished by the loud intermittent uproar underneath, obtained the services of two or three constables, who secured the leader only. As he was, in appearance at all events, a gentleman, and doubtless well-known to them, he was spared the indignity of the handcuffs. At the intersection of Collins Street, then known as Cashmore's corner, there was a large pool of stagnant water, not sufficiently deep to drown a man, but quite sufficient to half do it. Just as they approached within a short distance of the water, the prisoner suddenly and firmly gripped a custodian at the back of the neck with each hand, and shot them both into it and took to his heels. Nothing further was heard of the matter, and there was no report of the affair in the Police books of the following day. Probably it was "settled out of Court" by the "squaring" process then so much in fashion. It did not even creep into any of the newspapers; and this almost incredible attempt to overthrow the first theatre in Melbourne, is now detailed to the world for the first time. I may add that my informant, no less a personage than the "Captain of the Guard" himself, is still alive and jolly, and laughs heartily when he recalls to memory the particulars of his idiotic escapade of over forty years ago.

Mary Gaunt

RIVERINA

It is curious that, with the river so close, boating is not one of the chief amusements at Deniliquin; but there are few boats, and still fewer people ever go on the water. About September the fishing season begins, and then Murray cod are fairly plentiful. These fish, if taken from the running water, and not from the muddy lagoons, are very palatable; and one fish is, as a rule, ample reward for the angler, for they weigh generally from seven to seventy and one hundred pounds, while even monsters that turn the scale at two hundred pounds are not unknown. The disciple of Isaak Walton certainly requires some little encouragement, for the mosquitoes down by the river are so numerous, so aggressive, and so voracious that life is only bearable to the most enthusiastic and devoted of fishermen.

The streets of Deniliquin, as we have said, are usually quiet even to wearisomeness. Occasionally a bullock-team toils patiently down the road, dragging some squatter's clip bound for Victoria, or stores for his station far out on the plains. Now the little mail-coach from Balranald or Jerilderie dashes up to the post-office with as much bustle and importance as if it were built to carry twenty or thirty people instead of six. A covered wagon, driven by a Chinaman, comes lumbering through the street; his household goods are behind him; his white wife, arrayed in a cotton gown and a sun-bonnet, is at his side; while the yellow faces of their numerous progeny peep over their shoulders and through the cracks and rents in the wagon-cover. John, too, is bound for some station out on the plains where he will be employed as a rabbiter. He is a well-to-do man, and probably has a snug little account at the bank, for the Chinaman has established himself as firmly in these towns far inland as on the coast. At Deniliquin is a Chinese camp on a small scale, and the Chinamen pursue their avocations as market-gardeners and rag-pickers.

About five o'clock in the afternoon the sleepy old town begins to show more signs of life, for the event of the day now takes place, namely, the arrival of the evening train from Melbourne. Then, apparently, the greater part of the population may be seen wending their way to the railway station, there to assemble on the platform to gaze upon the iron monster as if they had never seen a railway train before, and feared they might never have the chance again.

Once a year, however, the town wakes from its lethargy in real earnest, and holds high revel. This is in the middle of July, the depth of winter, though the term winter hardly conveys the right impression. Then are held the races and the sheep show, and from all the stations and towns around, with that blissful disregard of distance which characterises the Australian squatter, strangers pour into the town, till it is full to overflowing. The tradespeople reap their annual harvest from the pleasure-seekers, and the hotels are full; bar, passages, billiard-room, and dining-room – every corner that can hold a lodger who is not particular as to his personal comfort for a day or two is pressed into the service.

For a week the town is given over to pleasure; and balls, races, and picnics are the order of the day. The sheep show brings in squatters from the farthest back blocks on the Darling, and for one whole week the streets are full, busy, and bustling; then the strangers return to their distant homes, carnival week is over, and Deniliquin drops to its normal state of quiet.

After the arrival of the Melbourne train, the next daily event of any importance in Deniliquin is the setting-out of the Hay coach, which six nights out of the seven crosses the eighty miles of plain that lie between this town and Hay. Punctually every evening at seven o'clock the coach, with its five horses, leaves the "Royal Hotel", stops for one moment at the post-office for Her Majesty's mails, and then dashes on again (sometimes crowded with passengers and luggage, sometimes with but the driver and another man) down the road, across the bridge, and out on the trackless plains, to travel there all night till the morning's dawn shall bring into sight the river-belt of the Murrumbidgee, on the other side of which is Hay.

Road on the plains there is none; the stock-route is over a mile wide, and the crisp salt-bush crackles beneath the horses' hoofs as they swing along at an even, steady pace, the heavy coach swinging on its leather springs backwards and forwards with a troublous, uncomfortable motion, strongly calculated to produce sea-sickness in the uninitiated. It is a weary journey. One mile of plain by day is remarkably like another, and by night there is nothing to mark the passing of the hours and to break the monotony save the stoppages for fresh horses, which are changed every ten or twelve miles. There is something weird and strange in the notion of receiving one's mails and almost all the news of the outside world at dead of night, as the inhabitants of these lonely public-houses, miles distant from other habitations, do. By day an occasional drover, riding slowly behind his flocks, or a traveller who prefers to journey by day, are their only visitors; but regularly as clockwork every night come the coaches. A sound of wheels is heard from the distance, and the whole household is alert and ready; fresh horses stand waiting, the door is open, and a ruddy light streams out, the landlord stands hospitably in the glow, and the one or two women the shanty contains peep round the door-post or fidget over the table roughly laid for tea – for is not the event of the day, or rather night, about to take place? The sound of wheels comes nearer and is plainly heard on the dry, still air, the five great lamps are visible, and then the lumbering form of the heavy coach itself looms out on the darkness. The steaming horses stop suddenly in the lamp-light, and willing hands rush forward to unhitch them, the driver never relinquishing the reins till every strap and buckle is free. Then perhaps, if he is in a condescending mood (for the driver of Cobb's coach is an important personage on the road), he steps down from his lofty perch, strolls carelessly through the open door, warms himself before the glowing fire (for the nights in winter are often chilly on the plains), retails gossip in an affable manner to the admiring women-folk, patronises the obsequious landlord, deigns perhaps to partake of a cup of tea or a little "something hot", takes charge of a letter, and then – time is up – the great man strolls out again, climbs to his perch once more, gathers the reins in his skilful hands, gives a few directions to the lanky stable-helps standing round open-mouthed and envious – a shout of "All aboard", a crack of the whip, and the coach is off again for another ten-mile stage.

These little stopping-places on the plains all bear a strong family resemblance to one another. At "Pretty Pine", the first after leaving Deniliquin, there is a native pine-tree carefully fenced, from which the little inn takes its name. By night, of course, its beauties are not perceptible, nor do they appear specially remarkable by day, for to the ordinary observer the "pretty pine" appears a very common-place tree indeed – that is, if he come from forest lands. A dweller on the plains would probably be more lenient in his judgment. Wonganilla, on the Billabong Creek, the next stopping-place, is the only place between Deniliquin and Hay that can even be dignified by the name of hamlet. Here there are two public-houses, a store, and a blacksmith's shop; but, spite of this magnificence, the Pine Ridge, or Booroorban, as it is but seldom called, thirty miles from Hay, is the principal stopping-place. Here the coaches stay nearly half an hour, and passengers and driver of the Hay coach make a late supper, while those from Deniliquin have an exceedingly early breakfast – somewhere about three o'clock in the morning. There is no such levelling process as coach-travelling. No one, of course – not even the Governor of the Colony – could object to sitting down to supper with the driver; an ordinary individual feels it rather an honour than otherwise. He is far the most important personage for miles around. There is no second class – all must pay the same (and pay highly, too) for the privilege of riding in the coach, and all alike must sit at the same table, partake of the same fare, use the same black-handled knives, and drink from the same coarse white cups – be it dainty, fastidious Englishman, just fresh from the comforts of the Old Land, or lean, yellow Chinaman going to join his "cousin" somewhere out on the plains far beyond Hay.

Between Wonganilla and Pine Ridge the event of the journey ought to take place, for at "Trotting Cob" resides an Australian ghost. Every night, at twelve of the clock, a ghastly figure (its bloody head under its arm) may be seen trotting slowly round the little inn, mounted on a snow-white cobby horse. It is not on record that any of the passengers by the mail-coach have as yet seen this figure. That the ghost is there is, of course, an undoubted fact – for has not the place been named after it? And the driver, if he be in a communicative mood, will tell a long story of the cruel wrong and murder which led to the place being haunted. Unfortunately, it is out of our power to give the true story of this most authentic ghost, for it varies with the different drivers (sometimes even with the moods of the same driver), and, consequently, the history of "Trotting Cob" is lost in the mist of many journeys to and fro and much whisky and water.

After leaving Pine Ridge the coach crosses a portion of the Old Man Plain. It is well on in the small hours now, and the interest with which the passengers began their journey has given way to an overpowering desire for sleep. Perhaps this is as well, for here are no points of interest whatever. Wonderfully silent have they all become. Inside some are dozing in various uncomfortable attitudes. One has betaken himself to the boot, and is sleeping the sleep of the just in somewhat uneasy fashion on the mail-bags and luggage, while on the roof already more than one man has nodded so perceptibly that the driver feels constrained to call out a solemn warning that "only last week a gent as fell asleep on top of the coach fell off, and was picked up a stiff 'un". Very slowly the time seems to pass, and to every anxious question as to where we are now comes the same laconic answer, "Old Man Plain"; but at length the Sixteen Mile Gums are reached, the last stage is begun, morning dawns in the east, and there before the eyes of the travellers lies the dark winding river-belt of the Murrumbidgee bounding the horizon to the north, and the coach has very nearly reached its destination. Sleepily the passengers rouse themselves and compare notes, the driver puts on an extra spurt, the coach thunders across the bridge, dashes up the street (wakening with its clatter the sleepy town), and finally draws up at Cobb's Coach Office.

Hay in all its features remarkably resembles Deniliquin, and the description of the one town would do almost equally well for the other. And yet there are radical points of difference. Deniliquin, the terminus of the Victorian Railway, is essentially a Victorian town, having Melbourne for its capital, while Hay, on the other hand, belongs entirely to its own colony, is the terminus of its railway, and owns Sydney for its capital. Here, too, dwells the Anglican bishop, who, though he be Bishop of Riverina, makes Hay his headquarters; and, greatest difference of all, while Deniliquin is on the decline (or, at least, at a standstill), Hay, though as yet its population is but little over 2,000, is a rising town, destined, its people declare, to be the future capital of Riverina. The little town is due north of Melbourne, and a line drawn from Sydney to Adelaide not only passes through it, but is nearly bisected by it. It is situated in one of the most picturesque bends of the unpicturesque Murrumbidgee, and is a neat, tidy little place. Its streets are wide, and planted with trees – quaint currajongs, a species of eucalyptus (very like in form to the stiff wooden trees we have all played with in childish days); bright green pepper-trees, with their coral berries; and graceful grevilleas, which in the spring are gorgeous with orange-coloured blossoms, and promise to add greatly to the beauty of the town when they shall have grown to their full size in the years to come.

Hay nestles close to the river, hugging the waterside, while the railway station is half a mile away, surrounded by the bare blocks and pegged-out streets of the surveyed town, which as yet but few people have settled upon. There are some two-storeyed buildings in the town, but generally, as in Deniliquin, the houses are seldom more than one storey high, are built in cottage form with broad verandas, and are usually set in the midst of gardens – hardly trim English gardens (labour is too expensive and water too scarce for that), but pretty gardens, nevertheless, full of semi-tropical plants and fruits that require the warm sun of Riverina to bring them to perfection. The streets are lighted by gas, and so are most of the public buildings, but as yet it is so expensive that but few private persons indulge in the luxury. Water, as in Deniliquin, is pumped into a high water-tower (in this case an iron one), and is thence laid on to the town. The river here is navigable in the spring and early summer, when the snows have melted on the far-distant ranges where the Murrumbidgee has its sources; and the little steamers come up far beyond the town, carrying stores to the distant stations out on the plains, and returning again with the squatters' clip in closely-packed bales before the river has fallen to its summer level. The traffic on the river is always a source of excitement for the Hay people, a diversion which Deniliquin lacks, for the Edward is not navigable, being far too full of snags (fallen trees) and sand-banks. At Hay the state of the river is a constant topic of conversation. It is very low, it is rising, it is running a banker, and then the first steamer of the season has made her appearance – a little steamer, whose cabins and deck-houses apparently make her somewhat top-heavy, with a big paddle-wheel in the stern, and behind her she tows three or four barges destined to carry the wool. Eagerly is she watched as she comes puffing and panting to the long bridge, which seems at first to present an impassable barrier, but as she approaches the whole of the centre is swung slowly out on a pivot until it stands lengthwise in mid-stream, and there is ample room for her to pass on either side. Her crew consists of three or four men – namely, the skipper, his mate, and perhaps two deck-hands, who may be seen lounging over the railing, idly scanning the view as they pass.

A river-sailor's life can scarcely be counted a hard one. As long as the river is high enough its navigation presents little difficulty, and at night almost invariably – always, in fact, unless the moonlight is very brilliant – the little steamer is drawn close to the bank and firmly held there by a rope thrown round the nearest tree-trunk. Twenty years ago, when very few railways were open, the river-steamers were extensively used by passengers, especially by women and children, who dreaded, not unnaturally, the long and weary coach-journeys. In point of time, of course, the steamer took longer, for one hundred miles by river may mean but three by land; and this, with the nightly stoppages, made a journey in a cramped and crowded vessel one not to be lightly undertaken, more especially as the provisions were humble, not to say coarse, while the cookery was of an exceedingly primitive order.

Seldom – we might almost say never – do passengers travel by steamer now. The coach is generally preferred, even to reach the towns on the Darling in the far west, and the steamers, owing probably to the uncertain state of the rivers, are wholly given up to carrying cargo. There is no doubt that they carry an immense quantity of goods, principally station stores – flour and tea, kerosene and tobacco, blankets and leather, and, above all, pain-killer. The amount of this medicament consumed "out back" must be enormous. The bushman regards it as a sovereign remedy – the panacea which, whether applied outwardly or inwardly, cures all the ills that flesh is heir to. Far out, too, where, when the whisky has run out it is impossible to procure either that or any other stimulant at a moment's notice, there will sometimes come over a man a longing and craving for strong drink, which he appeases as best he may, and he will even toss off kerosene and water with great gusto. Under these circumstances it is not surprising that pain-killer, spite of its fiery nature, or perhaps on account of it, ranks high as a stimulating drink. The story is told out on the back blocks of a traveller who, arriving at a wayside shanty where they were out of liquor, called for a nobbler. He was promptly presented with a glass of pain-killer and water. "Surely," said he wonderingly, sipping at the milky-white liquid – "surely it's painkiller." "Shut up, you fool," cried the landlord, holding up a warning finger – "shut up! Why, man, they're drinking Farmer's Friend in the parlour." And, really, he should have been satisfied, for Farmer's Friend, seeing that it is only used for dressing wounds on horses and cattle, must be considered much lower down in the scale of drinks.

Rosa Praed

THE OLD SCENES

"Is that all?" said a pretty sick girl on our steamer, who had had her chair brought close to the bulwarks, that she might not miss the first sight of Sydney Harbour. "Oh, I don't call it much more than just pretty. Seems somehow as if the mountains had been forgotten."

She expressed it exactly. One does feel as if the Creator had forgotten the mountains. And yet, indeed, how beautiful Sydney Harbour is, though one begins to wonder whether it is as beautiful as the harbour of Nagasaki, or of Hong Kong, or even of Algiers, or of many other places one has heard less about. There is always the want of the background.

Strangely enough, I didn't seem to be steaming gently into Sydney Harbour in this big Orient boat, on this summer afternoon, but to have gone back – oh, ever so many years – to a certain wild morning, when the sea was all grey and dirty-white, heaving and growling after a great storm, in which a little brig – she was called *The Briton's Queen* I remember – had gallantly held her own, though the English mail steamer was in peril of her life, and more than one ship went down off the coast that night. Brave little *Briton's Queen*! I can scent now in my nostrils the briny freshness of that squally morning, and oh, the delight of it after a day and a night with hatches down in a cabin half full of water, and a smell – an unforgettable and intolerable smell – of decaying apples. *The Briton's Queen* was freighted with fruit, and we had been a fortnight in making the voyage from Tasmania. Nothing of that voyage remains in my memory but the smell of the apples, the gale, and the feeling of intense exhilaration, as our little ship, with her sails set, scudded over the waves on that tempestuous morning and passed between Sydney Heads into balmy peace.

There it was again – the break in the grey-blue line of cliff, the two huge profiles of rock – the boldest with a lighthouse upon it, and the ocean roaring against its iron rampart. A little boat with a reddish sail raced the big steamer round the North Head and won the race. And now we were in perfectly smooth water, a blue basin with sandy-beached bays curving in and out, and a flotilla of boats – it was Saturday afternoon – dancing about the points.

There flashed into my memory another entry into Sydney Harbour – this a night one – after a second voyage from Tasmania; and the thrill of hearing out of the darkness, as a boat pulled up to the steamer, the news that the Duke of Edinburgh had been shot by Farrell, the Fenian. Then, next day, the mingled excitement and horror of seeing Sydney placarded with posters offering "£1,000 reward for the accomplices of Farrell."

It is all confusing, terribly confusing; and the two lightning streaks of impressions are dead trees and hats. Were there always so many dead trees, and did Australians always wear such a bewildering variety of hats?

There are hard felt and soft felt, broad-brimmed and narrow-brimmed, sailor, Panama, Buffalo Bill, Jim Crow, cowboy, and cavalier; hats puggareed, hats bare, and even the white "Derby" chimney-pots. It is a nightmare of hats.

And the dead trees! They, too, have become half a nightmare, half a fascination. These are not the few scattered clumps of "rung" gums, which used to show here and there round a head-station or stockman's hut, in picturesque contrast with the mass of grey-green foliage. All along the railway line there are miles and miles, paddocks full, whole tracts of these livid corpses of trees, which stand bolt upright, stretching forth long naked arms, that twist up and down and interlace each other in weirdly human fashion. At first their deadness seems a mystery, and then one remembers that it is the Free Selector now and not the Squatter who rules the land; and that because of him is its greyness. For it is all grey, all the same dull, dead monotony of colouring – grey two-railed fences, brown-grey grass, green-grey leaves – where there are leaves – yellow-grey sawn-wood houses; grey shingles, grey skeletons, grey ashes, where the skeletons have been burned and the soil made ready for crops of corn and vines and millet and cotton, and all the other good things which the Selector eventually produces. But it takes a long time first to dispossess the gum-trees, which are the inheritors of the ground.

Oh the heat and glare of that railway journey between the skeleton-trees and the two-railed fences! Only here and there, a little township of weatherboard houses, bare and straight, with oblongs of windows, like the houses in toy boxes, and their zinc roofs blazing piteously in the scorching sun. It is a relief to see near the townships, beyond the aggressive newness of their stores and public-houses, some survival of an old slab-and-bark homestead, with its patch of pumpkin vines and a few willows and mulberries, and perhaps an orange-tree. That is on the higher land, near the border, where the air has cooled a little.

Here, in a certain region, the skeletons give place to queer grey boulders – everything is always grey – scattered anyhow, in shape of crouching beasts and altar-stones, and fat monoliths. Now, as we descend, steamy rain falls, and the heat is a clammy misery and a prickly aggravation. Night comes. At the different wayside stations friendly hands are stretched forth, and there's a ghostly feeling in the sight of familiar-strange faces – the faces of children grown to manhood and womanhood, and of the middle-aged become old and grey-haired. It is midnight, when at last the thirty hours' train journey is over, and I step into the clammy stove-house atmosphere, and know that, after twenty years, I am once again in mine own land, amidst mine own people.

Familiar-strange, too, those bush boys on unkempt bush horses, and with the real bush seat, an easy, slouching oneness with the beast beneath, who are waiting in a clearing of the scrub for the mail to be thrown out as the train passes.

Where are the old landmarks? Twenty years ago it took a good three days getting from the township to Murrum, and extra horses had to be sent along to pull the buggy through Doondin Scrub. Now it is a question of being three or four hours in a railway carriage, and of a fifteen-mile drive over the range. But how much more exciting it used to be! The plunge into the gloom of the scrub, the toiling on foot down leafy gullies and up steep muddy pinches, the jibbing of the horses, the shoutings of the blackboys, and all the buggy-breakings and mendings, and the uncertainty as to ultimate possibilities! Very little remains of the scrub, only a few belts of glossy green, and some of the old bottle trees, which are like historic monuments of some strange order of architecture. So that one might fancy Lemurian builders had raised pillars of a grotesque topsy-turviness, with bulging middle, base tapering inwards and over-loaded capitals. All the way are Selectors' homesteads, set in gardens and orangeries, and where once was dense forest, homely German settlements with schoolhouses, stores, and plantations of maize, cotton, arrowroot, and even tobacco.

The Selectors in these parts have long passed the skeleton and grey stage; and all over the hills and on the plains where the scrub used to be, are vivid patches of green and yellow and the red-brown of millet. The clearing of the forest has brought the mountains into view, and it is such a satisfaction to find that years have not dwarfed their outlines, nor imagination magnified their beauty. They are all just as memory painted them – tiers of blue peaks – the border range in the far distance, and the Jerra Crag, with its encircling precipice and turret top, rising between the Murrum hump and twin-peaked Kumbal – as real and good to look at as the Southern Cross and many other things that were of old.

There is with us a little English artist girl, who has lived all her life in London, and an English boy called Rothwell, going to do "colonial experience" at Murrum. The three "M's", Meg (that is the English girl), Marge, and Mena, make as charming a nosegay of maids as could be seen. And there is Cousin William, outrider to the buggy just then, a miner by profession, and self-appointed instructor-general to Meg on things Australian. And there are Terry, Fulvia, and the doctor.

"He's a young one," Terry said, apologetically, as the near horse shied at a stump and tilted Meg almost into the Flagstone Creek. "Only tackled this summer. Never had a better puller . . . . But this won't do. Must attend to my business and not talk. Look out! Here we are coming to a bit of corduroy."

And we found out that "corduroy" meant a road made of little gum trees, and that it jolted exceedingly.

Two men with their blankets rolled into swags were boiling their billy of tea in a gully by the roadside.

"They're humping bluey," explained Cousin William.

"What does that mean?" asked the artist girl.

"They're on the Wallabi track," further explained Cousin William.

Meg asked no more, but later on she made a sketch of "Humping Bluey".

Meg has the air of one to whom no surprising experience can now be a novelty. She has been given tea for breakfast, luncheon, and dinner, at five o'clock and also at eleven a.m. A monstrous frog stared at her out of her washing basin this morning, and she was shown a corrugated black fellow in a ragged shirt and abbreviated trousers, with a brass plate – symbol of sovereignty – on his tattooed breast, and told that he is a king.

We stopped on the shoulder of the dividing range – not the great Border range, but a little one between Cuchin and Murrum. Below stretched the Cuchin plain with its water-hole, the Crag beyond, and the head station on a green promontory jutting out into the sea of tall grey-green grass. Now it is "eucalyptic cloisterdom" once more; and we seem as we descend, to be passing through interminable aisles of red-gum trunks and fretwork of bough. Locusts whirr intermittently.

Never was such rich grass as grows in the furrows of the hills. Meg takes her revenge on Cousin William by drawing his attention to the fine blot of colour which a herd of red cattle make on the grey-green. She wishes him to understand that if he can talk Australese, she can talk Art jargon!

Some of the gums have grotesque protuberances – these are what the shepherds and stockmen used to make *coolimans* out of in the old Bush days; and there are grass trees with spears and tufts, and great brown ant-heaps like queer shaped tombstones.

Then comes a splash through the river at Cuchin crossing, which is close by Murrum stockyard; and – is it the cornshed of memories? . . . The paddock is clearer than it used to be, and the river fringe of ti-tree and she-oak has been broken, and there's a grand new Selector's homestead that was not there long ago. The dogs run out barking, Fulvia, young Marge, and Mena, and the St Bernard, and the cockatoo are at the garden fence – how the lagerstromia and the creepers have grown! – and three peacocks give screeches from the roof of the kitchen gangway. They are moulting, poor things, and terribly ashamed of their draggled tails, but a sense of family obligation and of the dignity of the occasion does not permit them to retire altogether as, for the next week or so, they consistently do.

It is a funny little cluster of wooden cottages, Murrum head station, joined together by gangways which are covered with bougainvillea, bignonia, rinkasporum and ever so many other creepers. There are bowery nooks between the verandas filled in with plants set in stumps and with stag-horn and bird's nest ferns growing upon walls and posts. Here Mena makes a pretty picture in the mornings, learning her lessons, with the St Bernard panting in the heat at her feet. Inside, the walls are of cedar – it isn't the old drawing-room, but a new room altogether, with windows at the end giving peeps of the Jerra Crag, and the Kumbal peaks, and showing the old mandarin orange tree and quince orchard and the prickly pear hedge. Outside there is a veranda like the deck of a ship, where everybody lounges in cane chairs and the hammock, and eats grapes and water melons, and where we spend the long hot evenings looking on the dim semicircle of mountains and watching the Southern Cross mount from behind Mount Murrum.

Alas! It is the time of the rains, and for five days and nights the heavens have poured forth water. A blanket of steam has covered the mountains. The air is a vaporous oppression, and over all broods a clammy stillness, broken by the crashing downpour upon a zinc roof, and the spattering upon the window-panes and rebound upon the floor of the veranda. Mena's bower is no longer inviting. The ground is strewn with sodden bougainvillea petals, and the fern tongues drop wetness. The grey stumps in which a little while ago colcas and calladium plants flourished joyously, are now black with moisture, and all the slender stalks are bowed and the downy leaves torn to shreds and drooping and flabby. Mena's magpie is taking a bath in one of the stumps. Now he perches on the hedge, spluttering and spreading his wings with his head cocked on one side, and a wicked look in his little eyes. The Galah parrot toddles up and down disconsolately. There is a soft swish of rivulets blending with the hushed murmur of insects. At night, the frogs and crickets are deafening and the roar of the river grows deeper.

The nasty creeping things come out. A fat tarantula crawls up the curtains, and there's a hundred-legged spider between Meg's blankets; and ants run about in myriads, and get into the jam and sugar, and drop their wings uncannily on the tablecloth. We have no joy now in the veranda, though we draw the cane chairs close to the wall to avoid driving drops, and the doctor and the man from the next station and Cousin William tell grim stories of the bush. The fruit is sodden; the beast which has been killed has gone bad; the wood is too damp to burn in the kitchen. Fulvia enters tragically, in her arms a bundle of fine damask, black with mildew, and a snake is killed in the bush house.

That evening the doctor, the man from the next station, and Cousin William tell snake stories, and Meg dreams evil dreams.

The man from the next station has only nine fingers. When he was a little boy, he and his brother went out into the bush with their tomahawks to play at finding 'possums. As he moved a bit of dead wood a black snake bit his forefinger. The man from the next station put his finger straight out on a stump, and told his brother to chop it off, low down, with the tomahawk that very moment. The boy chopped, and then they sucked the sound, and that's how he comes to have only nine fingers.

The doctor too had his snake experience. One night he camped in a newly-built but deserted hut. A sheet of bark was on the ground, he spread his blanket over it and laid him down to sleep. Several times during the night he fancied that the bark heaved beneath him, but he was too tired to take any serious notice. In the morning when he had rolled up his blanket again, he kicked away the piece of bark and saw a great black snake coiled under it.

Cousin William knows a man on the diggings whose nerve broke after the gruesome adventure of one night. The man was travelling alone, and that evening he had camped in the open under a gum tree. It was bright moonlight. Suddenly, in the very small hours he awoke, feeling something moving over his chest – he was lying on his back barely covered with his blanket, for the night was hot. As he awoke, he saw that a brown snake had coiled itself upon his chest. Now, a brown snake is deadly; and the man had no brandy nor ammonia, nor anything which would save him if he were bitten. For long hours he lay watching. He dared not move, he scarcely dared to breathe. He nursed the loathsome Thing, a thin shirt only between him and its fang. Cousin William related how the man described the stillness of the night; his horror of a puff of wind, of a falling leaf or twig, and his dread of the approach of animal or bird which might startle the Thing. Then the breaking at dawn, and the twitterings and callings, and all the rousing of the bush. He was afraid lest his horse should come and sniff, and yet longed that it might come, as perhaps the noise might frighten the Thing away. And as the light grew he saw that there were soldier ants close by, and knew that if they crawled on him he must let himself be stung till it should please the Thing to move. He studied the flat head of the Thing and its triangular markings, and thought he must go mad. At last, when the sun was high the snake uncoiled itself and crawled away. And the man got up, shaking as if with palsy. "And Lord," added Cousin William, "you wouldn't have known that chap when he got to the diggings next day. He was trembling all over and couldn't sleep for weeks. And as for his nerve, which was like iron before, it clean broke into little bits."

"It's only some magisterial business," says Terry, getting up. "I'll be back in five minutes," and presently he is heard calling, "Bring me a Bible, dear," and young Marge runs off with the Bible, remarking, "Some of the Free Selectors come to swear."

When they had "sworn" and gone, Terry explained the matter. "You see, the conditions of their being allowed to own their 160 acres – or less, according to what they take up – are that they must reside on the selection for five years, but most of them after they have put up a hut, leave their wives and children to fulfil the residence condition, and hire themselves out on the job. Then they must pay sixpence a year – five sixpences in all – and must make improvements up to the value of ten shillings an acre, and at the end of the five years they have got to bring along two witnesses and swear before a magistrate to the residence and the improvements, after which they can get a free title. That's what those fellows were doing."

"Seems an easy way of becoming a landed proprietor," said Rothwell, the English boy.

"If they want to become bigger landed proprietors still," says Terry, "they can lease extra land up to two thousand acres, at a rent of threepence per acre; only, to fulfil the residence conditions, it must be within fifteen miles of the original selection. They must put a fence round the extra bit within four years, and when that's over, they can buy it at a price fixed by the Land Boad."

Fulvia came along the veranda carrying a silver tray and the teapot, Marge and Mena following with cakes and grapes. The lace frills of Fulvia's pretty blouse were tucked up towards her shoulders.

"Please forgive my bare arms. They've been up to the elbows in flour. I'm making bread." Fulvia was very hot, and very tired, though she contrived to look remarkably dainty in her white cooking apron.

Three days ago Fulvia's cook and parlourmaid had found themselves in bad health and requested to be driven to the Doondin terminus. Then it was suggested that the three Ms should forage among the Selections and see if they could find anyone willing to make the bread and wash for Murrum station.

They make quite a colony, the Selectors, along this side of the river, and slab cottages climb up the slope where scrub used to be. All the wilderness of the river is gone. There are millet and lucerne and Indian-corn patches by each bank, and men were ploughing as we passed. The ti-trees have lost their beauty. Of the two great cedars on the Mulgam flat under which we used to boil our afternoon tea, one has been felled and the other is naked and dead; and there are deep wheel tracks down to the arum pool where the Selectors' water-carts go to be filled. The settlement having got the number of children required by administrative powers, and having built the schoolhouse with the cracked bell, which is planted lower down among the gums, the government provides at a stipend of £80 a year, a schoolmaster, who lives in a weatherboard hut on the border of the scrub. The debating club sits too in the schoolhouse; there the balls take place, and the Sunday services, when a clergyman comes along; and there the election meetings are held. On the whole, the community seem to have a pretty lively time.

Mr Hindmarsh, whose wife Fulvia considered a hopeful resource in emergency, was at work among his crops by the creek.

"And how are you getting on with your maize, Mr Hindmarsh?"

"Bad, bad," answered Hindmarsh, mournfully. "Three hundred bags."

"Done well?" asked the doctor. "Tenpence halfpenny, eh?"

"Elevenpence," returned Mr Hindmarsh. "Times are wretched. It ain't only the squatters that has got cause to complain. What the country's coming to *I* dun-'now."

"It's bimetalism that's at the root of everything," said the man from the next station, "and until silver is acknowledged payment again, and forty shillings instead of twenty given to the pound, the country will never come to any good."

Mr Hindmarsh couldn't see how that could make a difference, and another Selector called Bascomb, who seems a serious person, and is, I hear, chief spokesman at the debating-society meetings, disagreed with him.

"You see, it's this way," said Mr Bascomb. "If all the produce in the world was put on this side" (prodding the ground with the butt of his bullock whip), "and all the gold in the world was put on the other side, why, there wouldn't be gold enough to buy the produce. For those that have the gold it don't matter; and for those who haven't it's a bad job."

"That's about it," said the man from the next station.

Mr Hindmarsh changed the conversation. "My word! it's been terrible hot today . . . . The missus did you say? *I* dun-'now. Most like you'll find her up yon'." His long upper lips puckered down over his teeth; and he jerked his thumb in the direction of a slab house with a veranda, set in a garden of stumps and some pumpkin vines, on the side of the hill.

Fulvia felt a delicacy in pressing enquiries. Hindmarsh was known as "a quiet man but given to sulks, and awful bad to put up with". His neighbour Garstin, who was helping him, was loud and masterful, and only that morning Garstin, up at the station on business, had related how the Hindmarshes had had a difference, and had given it as his opinion that a chap "mum in his tantrums" like Hindmarsh was more aggravating to a female than the most raging of devils, and that, therefore, Mrs Hindmarsh might not be unwilling to distract her thoughts by a day's baking. "But Lord! I says to Hindmarsh," continued Garstin. "You doan't know how to take the women, Hindmarsh. Why, you mun give 'en a kick and knock 'en down, and they'll coom all right after a time or two. Doan't crush 'en with silence"; which became a family saying at Murrum, and when anyone nursed his grievance in dignified aloofness it was customary to remark, "Doan't crush 'en with silence."

Mrs Hindmarsh, who is a big woman with great black eyes and crinkly hair, did not look in the least crushed, as she came up from the pumpkin patch with a huge pumpkin under one arm and a baby under the other. She had got a batch of bread coming out of the oven that very minute, she said, and if we liked we could take it over.

"I am ashamed to ask you into such a dirty place. I've been cleaning after the rains. The bread don't look as nice as it might, for it's baked in a camp oven; if there's a cake-tin or two to spare at the station I'd make the loaves a better shape for the table . . . . No, I wouldn't come to do the washing at the station, you'd best get someone else – there's Mrs Garstin perhaps – but *I* don't know . . . . You've had a deal of trouble I hear in the kitchen. If you want your moleskins washed, Mr Rothwell – or the doctor – tell him I'll do 'em if you send 'em over. There's funny things goes on in the kitchen with them girls, ain't there, Mr Rothwell?"

"There's plenty of funny things in Australia, seems to me, Mrs Hindmarsh."

"Yes, they're queer, those servant girls. They objected to the moleskins. I heard the word; you send them over, Mr Rothwell."

"Well, if you've time, Mrs Hindmarsh."

"Oh, I'll make time – at threepence the pair . . . . So Hindmarsh is going to take a job with the cart up at the station?"

Mrs Hindmarsh was informed that such was the arrangement.

"Hindmarsh hadn't always come down to going out on the job. We were in South Brisbane once, in a house of our own; it's the bad times has brought us low. He has lost £800, has Hindmarsh." And Mrs Hindmarsh announced the fact as cheerfully as though she were putting forward a claim to distinction.

We made a little round of calls that afternoon. Rothwell and Meg had already established friendly relations with the Selections, and had brought a camera, which hung on the pommel of Meg's saddle.

"We've got two plates left, Mrs Garstin, and Mr Garstin says he'd like you and the little girl to be taken; and we'd like to photograph the house if we may."

"Garstin said as he'd like the two children done," said Mrs Garstin. "It's seventeen year now since I was took – didn't like to, somehow. But I'd be pleased to have the children. Garstin, he wanted to have little 'Liza done last year, but I said (with a smile at the infant), wait a bit and get in two of 'em."

Mrs Garstin was the mother of a large family. The doctor joined us while the photographing was going on, and Mrs Garstin had much domestic intelligence to communicate.

"Jimmy was nearly dead, doctor, since you was here last. Johnny come down from the scrub and says, 'Mother I want some eucalypt stuff.' 'What for?' I says. 'Jimmy's had a hurt,' says he; and sure enough there was Jimmy lying onsensible . . . . But I'm that used to their getting hurts, I don't feel frightened. There was Jo broke his leg, and I pulled the bones together, and bandaged it, and set it in splints; and the doctor there told me he couldn't have done it better himself . . . . Lift up yer trouser, Jo, and show the doctor and the ladies your leg . . . . And there was Harry as chopped off his fingers – two of 'em hanging by a bit of skin; and Garstin says, 'Give us a pair of scissors, and have done with 'em.' But I says, 'No, I ain't going to have my boy short of fingers if *I* can help it.' So I sets the fingers back again, and binds them up; and they're as good as the others this day. Show the doctor your fingers, Harry. And I had to go to Murrum station for sticking plaister and hump him all the way; and Lor'! I don't know how I done it!"

After the rains came a great freshness. Higher up the Ubi is a gorge where in old days we always rode after rains to see the spring swollen into a waterfall. There was a question whether the river would be crossable – it was still a brown, turbid torrent. "I don't think we can manage it," said the man from the next station.

Cousin William spurred his horse on. "Keep up," cried Terry.

But Cousin William got through all right, and the rest followed even to little Mena in her holland knickerbockers, riding man-fashion. The horses swayed unsteadily with the current. The little one couldn't guide hers, and he went down slantways with the stream.

"Baby, keep up," screamed Fulvia. "Keep up, baby." Then Cousin William dashed back and took hold of Mina's bridle, turning her up-stream.

"You should never shout to anyone in a flooded creek," said the doctor. "It makes a fellow lose his head – like the mailman on the Jerra the other day, who was as near as possible carried down. They kept calling out from the bank, 'Keep up! keep up!' till the chap trembled and turned white, and at last got so confused that he let the reins drop helplessly and said, 'Which *is* up? I can't tell.' "

We follow a creeklet fringed by she-oaks, and bordered on each side by stony ridges. On the top of the ridge, the dark, distinctive line of scrub stands up like a wall from the blady grass and bracken. By-and-by the ridges swell into high hills and come close, blocking the foreground as the valley narrows. The she-oaks thicken, and the whispering among their needle points sounds fuller. There is a great side cleft in the hill, and a white torrent comes foaming down among the grey-black boulders which are scarred and patched with lichen. Terry and Cousin William drag logs and make a bridge over the torrent, the horses are hitched up, and the glen swallows those of us who walk foremost.

It is just a chasm torn out of the mountain side. The grey walls of rock overhang it, making jagged ledges, from which drop ferns and rock lilies – I remember the lilies' feathery plumes in spring, but they are not in bloom now – and there are thick withes of hoya festooning the cliff. High on the top, native bears and opossums and wallabis have their unmolested dwellings. Slanting outward from the cliff are slim trees of the red-barked mahogany, and of mountain ash, as well as a fleshy-leaved shrub giving out an aromatic perfume. Down in the bed, the torrent roars along the channel it has cut, over worn stones and between great grey rocks. It rushes out of a deep pool, dark, mysterious, and still, except where another stream, falling from a gully at a higher level churns the pool into brown foam.

This is not much of a waterfall. The children climb up the rock ledges close to the fall, and are wetted by its spray. And then there is a rare clamber to the upper ravine, sacred to the memories of twenty years back; and young Marge comes down presently, her arms full of native geranium and red berries off those same plants from which we elder ones used to gather them long ago.

So we went back to the old scenes – went back to the old scenes!

Do we ever, indeed, get away from the old scenes?

7

Friends, Lovers, Sexual Commerce

EDITOR'S NOTE

Charles Harpur's letters to Henry Parkes chart the waxing and waning of a friendship, begun with a shared enthusiasm for poetry and the ideals of human brotherhood, continued during a period of agitation for political and social reform and ending in bitterness over money. By the time of the last letter, June 1866, Parkes was New South Wales colonial secretary. Harpur, his poetical achievements still unrecognised, was, as often, short of money and unemployed, having just lost his job as goldfields commissioner.

The marriage anticipated in David Blair's love letter to Annie Grant took place in 1852 and produced four daughters and two sons. Though eleven years younger than her husband, Annie Blair predeceased him, dying on 24 January 1887, as one learns from the earlier extract, Blair's "Diary of a Travelling Technological Commissioner".

Whatever Blair's attitude to Annie Grant, many nineteenth-century Australian women were not placed on pedestals and worshipped. In 1858, Cora Ann Weekes, who had herself been persecuted in America because of her gender, presented a lecture in Sydney on the need for "Women's Rights". Anticipating the usual objections, she is careful to begin by stressing that women must remain virtuous, honourable, kind and loving to their children and husbands. But, given this, there is no reason why women should not, like herself, lecture in public or, more importantly, have the opportunity to earn a respectable living. She implies that many women turn to prostitution because there is no other way in which they can earn money. The growing concern over prostitution in Australia is also reflected in Daniel Deniehy's "The Social Evil". For Marcus Clarke, as for the other literary men and men about town who appear in James Smith's diary, extracted later in this book, prostitutes and brothels were an accepted part of Melbourne night-life.

The double standard – particularly in relation to women and sex – is also revealed in the remaining items in this part. J.E. Neild, an eminent theatrical and medical man, in reviewing Ibsen's *A Doll's House*, can only conclude that the heroine, Nora, must be mad. (James Smith thought that the play's ending should be changed, so that Nora came back to her children!) Louisa Lawson's struggles to achieve the kind of Women's Rights advocated by her sister editor Cora Weekes eventually resulted in her breakdown. But sense and logic shine through her editorials on women's suffrage and how best to cope with housework, while her strength and humour are apparent in every line of the interview given to A.G. Stephens. Stephens's diaries hint at the dirty talk and sexual gossip male friends indulged in privately, when women were absent.

Charles Harpur

LETTERS TO HENRY PARKES

Jerry's Plains
11th August, 1843

Dear Sir,

I have just had sight of your beautiful sonnet addressed to me as author of a series of poems in the "Australasian Chronicle". To attempt to express the feeling of gratification and pride with which I read it, were about as vain in me as to aim at rivalling the generosity of which it is a noble manifestation. Indeed, to enwreath the brow of one so clouded up in obscurity, with so fragrant and blooming a garland, merely because you believed him to possess poetical merit, is what could only be expected of one imbued with the rarest spirit of human kindness: and believing this, I do, and shall ever, set a higher value on your applause and kind wishes, than upon those of any other literary man in the colony.

I would mention also, how flattered I was by your having addressed the sonnet simply to "Charles Harpur". This substantiates in my mind the fact of your thinking highly of me. If a name be anything in itself, what need is there for prefixing "Mr"; or adding "Esq." to give it weight? Who, for instance, with any soul, ever thinks of Byron as having been a Lord – of Shelley as a man of fortune – or of Milton as Latin Secretary to a Government? I know you will not attribute these remarks to mere vanity. In making them I am only elucidating what appears to be a principle of feeling in myself – and in you.

Again thanking you for your most generous notice of me and my *Harp*,

I beg to subscribe myself
Yours fervently,
Charles Harpur.

Jerry's Plains
21st March, 1844

My dear Sir,

I hasten to acknowledge your kind present of Mrs Shelley's edition of her illustrious husband's poems, which has only just come to hand. The letter accompanying the books, for which I am also sincerely thankful, is dated, I perceive, as far back as Nov. in last year. The delay in the conveyance which has evidently taken place, makes me very anxious lest you should attribute my silence since to any other than the true cause – my not being aware of your having again manifested in so flattering and substantial a manner your disinterested regard for a brother poet whom you have never seen – and merely because you believe him to be a true child of Song. I say *substantial* above with reference to the beauty and rareness of your present – but assure you, at the same time, that even a pin from you, given in token of good will, would be as gratefully received – aye, and as highly prized, in as far as the commercial value of articles constitute a consideration. In nothing do I feel more honoured and assured of my merit as a poet, than in the respect and attention with which you have from time to time gladdened my solitude. Accept then in return, all that I have at present to offer, the grateful friendship of a heart, which, though something less warm and trusting perhaps than it has been, is yet, I believe, true in its affections, and unspotted by the selfishness of the world.

As far back as in Jany. last, with a view of re-filling the "cup of kindness" that had passed between us, I composed the following Sonnet to you, intending to publish it in the "Register"; and I delayed to do so only, because my pieces latterly have been so fearfully misprinted therein, that I have felt quite savage while glancing them over – and I would not for a good deal that this Sonnet to you should meet a similar fate. However lamely expressed, I know you will give me credit for sincerity in the feeling it unfolds –

Sonnet to Henry Parkes

Dear Henry, though thy face I ne'er have seen,
Nor heard thy voice – albeit that beams, I know,
With goodness, and that this at times can flow
Melodious as a mountain stream – between

The waters of Port Jackson, and the scene
Where now I muse, of rich, poor, high or low,
There dwells not one that I so far would go
To talk with through the evening hours serene.
And when we yet shall meet, say, shall not we
Be as old friends at once? and sit, and pour
Our souls together? which, so mixt, shall be
A brimming draught of thought-thick poesie –
Even such as young Keats reel'd with, gazing o'er
The wondrous realms of Homer's minstrelsy.

You will see by the above, that I was not willing that the kindly feelings which had sprung up between us, should pass away with the blossoms of the Spring. No: I trust that they will ever continue to strengthen – and whenever my regards are turned Sydney-ward, I love to promise myself that they shall furnish the fruit of many an intellectual feast throughout the summer, and even the winter of our mortal days.

I am exceedingly gratified by the selection you have made in your present. Shelley is a great favourite of mine; and besides I never saw the whole of his poems before. I had heard that Mrs Shelley was giving or had given to the world a completed editon of her husband's works, and longed particularly to see it – guess then the pleasure I was master of, or rather was mastered by, on receiving the same work in testimony of a friendship I value so much – and which envinces to me the fact, that disinterested literary kindness departed not the world with that most benevolent. I love Shelley intensely; and yet I am not blind to his faults. If we would attain to highest excellence we must exercise the judgment with a rigid and resolute will, maugre our feelings to the contrary. Shelley has great faults, or rather great wants. His poems, though brilliant and beautiful as the splendours of sunset, are, I fear me, as unsubstantial as those fleeting hues. Not that I complain of their extreme visionariness; but that there is not enough of solid humanity wrought up with it to add strength and flavour. Even in the "Revolt of Islam" the human interest is damaged by the airy-nothingness of the characters, and the impossibility of many of the incidents. Modern Ideality and Wonder, however wandering and willing, are yet, when over tasked, very apt to grow skittish, and to fly off at a tangent, with an appeal to Reason. Still Shelley is perhaps *my* greatest favourite; and though I may seem just now to be much "critic-bitten", I have been throwing out such objections as I *apprehend*, rather than such as I *feel*. As a proof of this, it is scarcely an hour since I was gloating over the pages of your fine present with inexpressible satisfaction.

The generous object of your letter is, I take it, to incite me to renewed efforts. I also found a pen in the packet, which I understand to mean *write away*. I will obey in as far as I can; but I have to care so much for the mere crusts of life, that I am not often now in right tune for song. You letter has, however, somewhat revived the "bard in my bosom". Whether anything worth recording will be the result I cannot pretend just now to say. But we shall see. I sometimes feel it hard to have written so much as I have already written with the power of publishing so little. Those sustained efforts upon which I would peril my poetic claims with considerable confidence I have not been able to give to the light at all. But perhaps all is for the best.

I hope you have not abandoned the Muse. I promise myself a treat, when I shall some day *forgather* with you, in pouring over the MSS of your late and more sustained pieces. Let me not be disappointed. You have the power if you have the will.

In conclusion, accept again my pledge of friendship, and allow me to solicit yours. Let us determine from this day, to be resolute so as to overcome whatever may tend to chill or diminish the brotherly feelings and kind wishes that have grown up so singularly between us. This is my firm resolve, and I assure myself that it will be yours – and

I subscribe myself therefore
Your friend and brother,
Charles Harpur

Excuse haste!

Jerry's Plains
Decr. 4th, 1848

My dear friend,

What could possess you to think me positively offended with *you* – and to talk about being the "first to humble"? To me? God forbid! If there be any sin against the spirit of friendship between us, *it must be on my part*.

The truth is, where I love much I am somewhat disposed to *jealousy* – I cannot help it: and under some morbidity of this sort I wrote to you a letter which I would fain have recalled the moment I had despatched it. But it was *too late* – and you replied to it a *little reproachfully*. Still all you said was just – I felt that it was; and intended to have answered you immediately in a becoming and atoning spirit; and have been delayed doing so by the sole fact, that my wandering foot has been ever since lifted as it were, in the act of paying you a visit in person. Have I said enough? I trust I have; and that the piece of womanish jealousy *on my part* above confessed to – being forgiven, will forever henceforth be but a *"by-gone"* between us.

Believe me, there is nothing in fortune could afflict me more, than to have to look back upon your friendship as amongst the good things I have lost: some through my own folly, and some through the folly of others; some wantonly, and some fatally.

Do you know that for the last 18 months I have been living the life of a hermit – utterly alone, day and night, in a sad looking house, with Mount Kobaubonia in the distance, and a loveless, gainless, hopeless, bookless solitude all between and around me. I see my brother about once a week, if so often, and two or three other persons on post-office or pound business (mere pigs) twice or thrice in the same time. I wash, bake, cook, and mend etc. for myself, the profits of my agency not yielding more than what will barely clothe me. Can I be so very thin skinned then? *Hardly*; and could I but once stand fairly before my countrymen, I could well submit ever afterwards even to such a condition as this. I should be quite content, could I but once say to them, in my entirety, through the press, "I am a solitary prairie tree, but I have borne fruit in my solitude: behold it; gather it; taste; and *know me aright*." – But I must jump out of this egotism.

I read your little Leader in the "Atlas", and like both the spirit and style of it. And I am glad to hear the "Atlas" is now in such worthy hands. I had not failed both to perceive and admire a very marked improvement in it for some time.

I saw notices in the paper of the association you speak of. There can be no question but that such an association is greatly needed; and I should like to see similar ones forming in every populous district: for in the present state of society, your only efficient political battering-ram, is an *Association*.

Leigh Hunt's answer to *What is Poetry*? is all light. What a fine old fellow it is! with his spirit still as bright as the face of the Beautiful, and his heart as fresh as a rosebud. I cannot help fancying, how the heart of the old boy must sometimes indulge in a pleasant laugh at the expense of his grey head – being itself so juvenile. What would I not give to shake hands with him; – and sit in his actual presence, as at the feet of my poetical Gamaliel, *once* at least, before he is called out of Time, to join the Immortals in Eternity. But that cannot be.

You will be glad to hear that I am very temperate. Even when my means are a little flush, I never exceed in any respect. That is, I have not exceeded, for a long time. "Wisdom", you know, "(curse on it) will come soon or late." I am actually getting wise! – that is to say, (perhaps), *wiser*.

I have a world-full of questions to ask you – but I defer them, first, for want of space (as you see), and secondly, because I intend (God willing) to visit you about Christmas. I cannot positively say that I will see you at Christmas, but about that time, or shortly after, I certainly will, God willing, as I said before. I suppose you will be more at leisure then than usual – and won't I dose you?

Remember me to Mrs Parkes, and to Clarinda the younger, and to

Sydney the first, whom I calculate to be a booming rogue by this time. – And believe me yourself, yours wholly,

Chas: Harpur

* * *

Euroma, via Bodalla
28th June, 1866

My dear Sir,

I am in receipt of your favour of the 21st. instant; and at another time, I intend to write to you an answer to it in full – in which, I doubt not, I shall be well able to show you that the ex parte statements of volunteer informers and self-constituted spies are in no wise to be depended upon, but rather that the reports of such characters – always base and detestible – are to be ever taken with much salt; that the "freaks" you speak of as being all known in Sydney, were either sheer lies, or mere minor matters of morals and manners that have been most egregiously distorted into enormities, or invidiously magnified out of all life-likeness: and with which in fact the Government had properly nothing to do.

But in the present note I intend to touch upon nothing but the Superannuation Fund. You [tell] me that I have no claim upon that Fund. Why, when a common constable is turned adrift, he is allowed a month's pay for every year of service. And such was the rule, I believe, throughout the whole civil service, previous to the passing of the Superannuation Act, which was to make all Officialdom more easy in mind as to the future, and which to that end has exacted from me monthly ever since it came into operation the sum of £1-3-4. For what, as it turns out? To provide a comfortable retiring allowance for a few favoured old fogies some twenty years hence – and who, all of them, will, until then, have been comfortably lapped – not in superannuation lavender, but in what is nearly as good – big and constant pay: not a mere pittance which at a dear outpost was barely a living! This surely is not just. And I think Mr Martin (being a logical lawyer) will at once see that it is not.

I remain, dear Sir,
Yours very truly
Chas: Harpur

P.S. As this is the last letter but *one*, which it is likely I shall ever write to you, perhaps you will do me the favour of answering it.

David Blair

[A PROPOSAL OF MARRIAGE]

June 17th, 1850

My Dearest Annie,

There are many things which I wish to say to you, and which I *ought* to say to you, which nevertheless are better put upon paper than spoken directly. Grave long speeches are not the kind of intercourse that I like, any more than (I am sure) you would. Besides, it is not easy to be *very* sedate while sitting beside you, with your beautiful sunshiny countenance and most pleasant smile, and the delightful feeling of quiet happiness I have while talking to you. I am altogether too light-hearted when beside you, to put on a grave face and talk like – what I am – a philosopher. So I have been meditating about you (as usual) here in my attic for the last couple of hours; and so I shove away the tiresome books, and begin the agreeable task of talking to you on paper.

That I do most truly and most entirely love you – as I never before loved a woman; as I never again can love a woman – I know you believe. However surprised you may have been at first, you fully believe this *now*. You have accepted all the love I had to bestow – valueless as I feel the gift to have been – and I *know* you have given me the priceless treasure of your true love in return. If we were less formal and less dilatory in settling this most delightful business than others are, at least we were fully as cordial and sincere as any others *could* be. Next to the happiness which I feel in possessing your affections, is the happiness springing from the feeling that you bestowed them upon me spontaneously and most willingly. I am perfectly satisfied and happy. The love of one such puresouled and affectionate girl as you are, was all I asked. I have found it, and I am content and more than content. You are satisfied with me, I know. You know me, short as our acquaintance has been, very thoroughly. You have seen all my character. There is nothing more to let you know, and nothing concealed from you. I am simply the book-loving, intellectual, earnest man, with fluent (sometimes eloquent) speech, and high thoughts, which you see me to be. I have no money, no friends, no "prospects", no hopes of a "situation under government". But I have a strong belief that a man's life consists in quite other things than fine house, splendid dinner parties, carriage, and all that. I carry this idea so far that I don't care much about these things – nor about the people who have them. I have a soul, and a Bible, and a splendid sky above my head, and a magnificent vision forever floating before my mind of a glorious Heaven where all is light, and love, and joy. I actually *do* believe in God, and the Bible, and in the immortal destinies of the human Soul. And I intend living – whether I am single or married – in the clear belief of all these things. I intend not merely to *say* I believe them, and preach about them, but I do really and actually mean to live every day in the fullest realisation of them. Withal, I believe that man, being human and not angelic, must live as a man, and fight the Battle of Life bravely, taking joyfully the blessings God sends him, and bearing meekly the trials God sends him. In a word – and in all seriousness – I am a Christian, and mean to live as a Christian, with the help of God . . . .

Now, Annie Grant, what do you say to *that* portrait of an actual Lover, and possible Husband? Think over the whole affair, seriously. Look at both sides of the picture. And say whether you would choose to link your fortunes and your happiness with such a man, than take the probable chance of a Life Companion much handsomer, much younger, much richer, and much more what the world calls "respectable". For, a thousand to one you will get *that* if you "wait a little longer". But, I beg a thousand pardons for the bare supposition. I do most entirely trust in your faithful love for me. Only I write in a wild kind of way to awaken in you deeper thoughts and feelings than you might be disposed to cherish, under the excitement of feeling produced by a fervent attachment (as I believe yours to be).

I have drawn a picture of my "inner man" which – upon looking it over again – is too flattering. I have faults – lots of faults. I know it well. But I do honestly say that I have no fault of a kind to mar the happiness of a lovely girl who trusts her all of earthly good to my keeping. I know that I am *not* capable of any meanness or pettiness of feeling – any paltry jealousy – any miserable personal vanity. I have *no* fault which would be the means of giving pain to a gentle and affectionate Wife. Where I loved, I should be trustful, tender and constant. I am sure I should be generous and tender even to the little failings – for we are all human – of the One I loved. I never could be vindictive, nor irritable about trifles, nor morose or sullen, to Her. O no! I would aspire to make the pure passion by which I was bound in heart and soul to Her, a worthy and exalted passion, as free as might be from all gross and sordid taint. I should try to live a noble and dignified life; happy myself, and making others happy; and thus tasting in all its exquisite sweetness

The joy of loving and of being loved.

To me, all that life can give of peace and happiness, and perennial comfort and consolation, would be summed up in the one sweet word Wife. I should have Home, however humble it might be, the sanctified abode of Love and Peace and Purity, so that (like the Patriarchs of old) I might be able to entertain angels if a stray one ever visited our quarter of the world again. This is *my* Ideal. O Annie Grant! how far could *we* go in making it the Real?

There is one point which I am somewhat dubious about, after all. I don't think I ever told you – or you ever asked me – the important question which relates to my *age*. My conscience gives me a fillip about this. I *ought* to have told you: for *I* think *you* think I'm younger than I am. Don't be startled – still less shocked – least of all awfully frightened – if I tell you honestly that I have reason to believe I am – guess! – no, not 26, nor 27, nor 28, nor 29, but – actually 30!!! That's too bad, isn't it? But really I'm not to blame. In the first place, I can't help my age. In the second place, I thought – forgive this very ungallant avowal – I really *did* think you were more than 18¾. I thought – from your beautiful feminine grace – your thoroughly developed womanly beauty – that you were about 21. And I thought (thinks I), "well 9 years are not so frightful"; but eleven *is* too bad. However, I can only say – as I said before – that *that's* your business. If you take me, you must just take me as I am, "with all my imperfections on my head" (as somebody says somewhere.) You can't reasonably expect an angel complete, can you now? In fact, *you* have all of the angelic kind that there is in both put together: there's none left for me to have: you have your own share and mine (or what should be mine) also.

Well, but you will say, if I am so old a soldier, why didn't I pitch my tent before now? There's the very point. Well, you see, Annie Grant, I found it so difficult to carry the Ideal into actual everyday practice, that I had to wait until the Beau Ideal – the beautiful Realised Ideal – should come. To say truth – what with my lecturings and verse-scribblings, I have more than once had meaningful glances from bright eyes in the heads of pleasant countenanced young ladies cast upon me. Nay, I have even sat at tea, or at supper, or gone to picnic parties, with decidedly very loveable young ladies – who were so very condescending as to smile when I spoke to them, and to talk of my "talents", and all that, and to wonder why I was so very self-absorbed, a bachelor, and so forth. But somehow there was sure to be something or other that whispered me that *here* I could not give my heart safely, and *there* it would not be altogether wise to plunge lip-deep [by the bye, that's just the depth people *do* go] in love. [Note: if people went deeper than lip-deep in love, how could they manage to speak to each other, never to speak of kissing each other?] So I have escaped Scotfree from England. And here in Surry Hills, (Sydney, NSW) I find the true living Ideal-Real at least. All that I ever dreamt of loveliness, and all I ever sighed for in pure affection, and innocent-heartedness, I find summed-up, concentrated, embodied, personified, realised, in the pleasant, attractive, agreeable, delightful, lovely, fascinating, bewitching, enchanting Annie Grant!! And so good night, my sweet love! I kiss you a thousand times. God for ever bless you!

Ever your faithful and devoted,
D.B.

Cora Ann Weekes

FEMALE HEROISM IN THE NINETEENTH CENTURY

I would have begun to address you, ladies and gentlemen, with a great and holy thought of Elizabeth Barrett Browning's, which embodies that illustrious lady's ideas of Woman's duty as a member of the Commonwealth – had not a remarkable passage from the Book of Books, occurred to my mind. I may, without irreverence or pedantry, read you the passage, which is so full of wholesome truth and rich poetry. It is taken from the Book of Proverbs, and reads thus:

> Who can find a virtuous woman? for her price is far above rubies.
> Strength and honour are her clothing; and she shall rejoice in time to come.
> She openeth her mouth with wisdom, and in her tongue is the law of kindness.
> She looketh well to the ways of her household; and eateth not the bread of idleness.
> Her children rise up and call her blessed; her husband also, and he praiseth her.

Now we have here, from the mouth of ineffable wisdom itself, the characteristic traits of the greatly good woman. We have immaculate purity; exquisite sensibility; indefatigable industry; and strength of mind and purpose. In proportion as a woman – no matter to what sphere of duty called – possesses these qualities – in proportion as they give shape and colour to her mortal nature – so is she good; great; pre-eminent; heroic! [Applause.] Fling upon her all fame and glory – hail her genius, her devotedness, her enthusiasm – bow before her surpassing beauty and exquisite grace – worship her queenly presence and her lightning wit; still, if she lack the four normal attributes referred to, she is no heroine, as I understand the term. [Applause.] She is of the earth, earthy. She is an ephemeral divinity! – the gilding will soon fade and the glory depart! But if on the other hand, she be possessed of these four cardinal virtues, then indeed shall the words of the wise man be verified – "Her children shall rise up and call her blessed."

I have made these preliminary remarks because I intend presently to meet an objection and attack a prejudice. There never was a great social or civil reform that did not create opposition and excite enmity. This is a consequence, and consequently a natural result, of our poor, weak, fallible nature. Honest efforts at great civil and social reforms, then, causing commotion as they do; arousing enemies and enmities; exciting jealousies; alarming weak heads and craven hearts; – are sure to be misrepresented – they are overlaid with falsehoods and calumnies, so that it takes time and requires patience, courage, and a good conscience, to effect a happy result.

During the last thirty or forty years, a movement has been made to remove certain social disabilities of Woman – to elevate her position in the commonwealth – to enfranchise her with certain moral privileges – and to enlarge the sphere of her activity and usefulness. The effort was an honest and an honourable one. Discussion ensued, and the best of the argument lay on the side of the weaker sex, while all or most of the wit and humour was with the stronger. A joke may contain a reason, although the chances are sadly against any such gold veining the quartz. But it is no joke to scout and flout fair, straightforward, logical reason out of the field by jokes – some of them pointed – others very blunt; some possessing attic salt – others very unsavoury – some very piquant and peppery – others very flat and flippant.

One of the greatest literary caricaturists of the age has made the question of "Woman's Rights" as ridiculous as a vivid fancy and a fine eye for contrasts could make it. He has created the absurd and improbable character of Mrs Jellyby.

* * *

Now this description is all very funny, and may have been provoked by certain eccentricities of certain ladies who felt themselves "called to perform missions"; – but that this sketch should be flung in the face of every earnest woman who makes an effort to elevate the condition of her sex, is as absurd as it is unjust. These Mrs Jellabys are not the women who will do anything greatly good. They want one or more of the prime conditions laid down at the very outset of my remarks. They forget their domestic obligations – they forget their most obvious responsibilities – they do not possess that particular sort of industry which alone is recommended by the "wise man". In the Female Heroism which I commend, and on which I propose to talk with you for a half-hour tonight, you will find none of their extravagance. You will find no moral or domestic duty neglected – no personal responsibility laid aside. You will see that women can go earnestly and directly to a good work, with the same bravery and loyalty as men. You will find nothing absurd, nothing unfeminine, nothing unbecoming the co-operation of every true Christian patriot, in that species of "Woman's Rights" which I am here this evening to advocate.

But inasmuch as I have given you Mr Charles Dickens's idea of "Woman's Mission", in the ridiculous character of Mrs Jellyby, perhaps you will permit me to quote a few lines from the pen of a dear friend, a noble example and shining light to her sex. Let us see how a woman's idea of "Woman's Rights" compares with Mrs Jellyby's practice. The passage runs thus:

The Rights of Women! what are they?
The right to labour and to pray!
The right to succour in distress –
The right, when others curse, to bless!
The right to smooth the brow of pain –
To lift the fallen up again!
The right to suffer and forgive!
The right to teach men how to live!

[Loud and long contained applause.]

O, my friends, these are woman's true rights! These are the glorious duties which it is our high mission to perform! These are the heroic achievements that the true women of the Nineteenth Century are expected to accomplish! These are the labours which have written the name of Miss Dix on a million hearts – these are the deeds which have encircled, with a halo of imperishable glory, the honoured names of hundreds of English heroines. [Sensation.]

Before proceeding further with my discourse, it may not be impertinent to the general question at issue, to answer a personal charge that may be made. The general reasoning that I shall adduce would, indeed, be a sufficient answer to the particular charge, but I will take the objection up for a moment in a more direct manner. Why am I doing so unusual a thing for a lady – why am I attempting to lecture tonight? To this I have two answers to make: First, as the Editor of a public journal, I am in the habit of addressing myself to the general public. There is no conclusive reason, why, if I can amuse or instruct the public in that capacity, I may not in this. [Cries of hear! hear!] I have another answer. I am here – although perhaps some will be ungenerous enough to doubt the assertion – I am here, really, and positively, this night, *to do good*! [Applause.] How that good may be accomplished, I shall presently attempt to explain. There never was an age in the world's history in which woman did not, by her life and actions, demonstrate that divine gifts had been bestowed upon her, the queen, as well as upon man, the lord of creation. From Judith to Joan of Arc – from Joan of Arc to Elizabeth of England – from Elizabeth of England to Maria Therese – from Maria Therese to our own sovereign lady, Queen Victoria – fame and glory, or rather the glories of bright fame – like a radiant atmosphere surround and encircle them. They each have niches in the temple – a halo round their heads – places in the annals of human greatness – and they are memorable examples for all time to come. [Sensation.] And if woman has adorned the crown and the diadem – if she has stood in regal pomp at the head of mighty nations – if her virtues have added grace and dignity to the sceptre – if her beauty has dazzled amid the glittering pageantry of court and state, so also has her presence, like the sun-rays that burst from the Eastern hills, shed bounteous blessings in every scene of life. Go to yonder humble cottage-home. See the poor young wife – she whose whole wealth is the wealth of a pure conscience and a loving heart! See how her gentle assiduities console and comfort her husband, who has just returned home after a day's struggle with the great, selfish world. See how her home smiles with beauty – how flowers just bursting into blossom, carefully tended and nurtured by her hand, add fragrance and loveliness to all – till even Poverty himself, ever intruding where he is not wanted, slinks away, and hides his diminished head! [Laughter and applause.]

But it is not to eulogise the achievements or dwell on the renown of my sex, that I address you. I prefer rather to call your attention to the fact, and, if possible, make you converts to my opinion – that there is a finer, more vigorous, more healthy development in woman's efforts to accomplish the great and good – that is, the heroic – in this Nineteenth Century, than has hitherto manifested itself. I will not read you biographies of illustrious heroines; but I will in the course of my remarks, adduce shining instances of their high ambition and good work done, as illustrations of the justness of the position I take.

But before I proceed, I wish to call your attention to one important point. *It is the imperative duty of society to find, immediately, additional means of honest and respectable employment for females!* Old Europe, full of inhabitants and full of prejudices, must sooner or later suffer great disasters, unless the means of earning a virtuous livelihood, is found for every adult female. And Australia, the fairest child of an august parent, must share in the disasters, as well as the blessings, of the fatherland. The sneers and jokes about women in the senate – women in the army – women at the bar, in gown and wig – are mere subterfuges – a mean shrinking of the knotty question at issue. We do not look for, nor desire, employment in the army, the navy, the bar – and why? Because as Dr Wharton of America would say, because we are WOMEN! He writes:

> Physiology points us to the grand fact of sex. It tells us what that means. It tells us that Woman is human, but not Man. She is Woman! The vine and oak both spring from a common source, the earth. They both grow, and flourish, and decay. They have elements and laws in common. But they have elements and laws not common, those namely, which constitute one a vine, and the other an oak, which makes one tall and strong, the wrestler with the storm, which makes the other dependent, graceful and ornamental. Both were planted for ends, by the Creator; and to compare the ultimate utility of those ends, or to murmur because they are not the same, is to shame the thoughts of Deity and denounce him as an imperfect being.
>
> The sex of woman has entailed upon her a weaker constitution, generally. Her muscular system is of slighter texture. She is liable to injurious fatigue from violent exertion. Exercise cannot bring her up to the physical level of man, and while it thus fails, it renders her less feminine. The women of Sparta were the least attractive of those of Greece; and the youths who contemplated matrimony, turned from the gaunt Amazons to the romantic and fascinating maidens of Athens. Yet, in contending for the participation of women in all the political privileges of men, you would metamorphose our fair Athenians into ungainly Lacedemonians; for privileges are never unaccompanied with duties, with laborious conditions preliminary to their enjoyment. In effect, you would establish a more barbarous rack than that of Procrustes, for women would be its tortured victims.

Now these remarks have not been contravened by any true, heroic woman of the age. They are true to nature, and therefore just. But is this any answer to the general charge, that women are not experiencing the blessings of advancing civilisation, in proportion as men are? How many situations in life are open to industrious young women? Are they employed in printing houses, in jewellers' shops, in studios, chemists' establishments, and other light occupations? No! They are only dressmakers, or school mistresses, or drapers' assistants, and no more! They are driven in hundreds – yea, thousands and thousands – through the force of circumstances, often through actual want and the inhuman thoughtlessness of men, to live for ever in the violation of God's holy law! The days of gloomy superstition are past and gone. The dull, dark cloud, like a heavy nightmare, no longer rests on the enlightened soul. The forest is no longer full of fears – the old hall no more the home of terrors – the earth and air are no longer contaminated by the presence of the unhappy dead. "We no longer believe in ghosts", cries out Hans Christian Anderson, "and no longer believe that the dead in their white garments, appear to be living at the hour of midnight. Ah! we see them yet in the great cities. By moonlight, when the cold north wind passes over the snow, and we wrap ourselves closer in our cloaks, we see white-garmented females, in light summer dresses, beckoning, float past us. The poisonous atmosphere of the grave breathes from their figures – trust not the roses on their cheeks, for the death's head is painted there! Their smiles are the smiles of intoxication, or of despair! They are dead – more horribly dead than our deceased ones. The soul is interred – the bodies wander, like evil spirits, hither and thither! They are horrible, unhappy ghosts, which do not sink into the graves by the morning twilight! No, for then they are followed home by the dreams of despair, which sit like nightmares on their breasts, and tell them of the scorn of men, of a better life – of a terrible, terrible hereafter! 'Save me! save me!' is oftentimes the cry of such unhappy being. But everyone flies away horrified who hears the voice out of the grave, till she has no longer strength to throw from her the coffin lid of her circumstances, and the heavy earth of sin!"

O, my good friends, is not this terribly truthful, and truthfully terrible? Think of these midnight ghosts of the Nineteenth Century – think of these creatures with the tainted atmosphere of death surrounding and around them. Think of all this, and then ask your conscience, each one of you. "Have I done ought to bury these unholy ghosts, that not only haunt us by night, but flout the heavenly sun by day!" [Sensation.]

In proportion as civilisation advances, the temptation to live on the bread of sin and death seems to be brought nearer day by day to thousands of our sex. But as in the first French Revolution, we find the most heroic virtue as well as the most atrocious profligacy – the loftiest patrotism as well as the most wretched treachery – the sincerest piety as well as the most shameless neglect of God and all holy things; so in this corruption of the age, in this wide dishonour to our common humanity – side by side with the evil, a great and glorious good has arisen. Women – brave, noble, energetic women, have gone forth clothed in purity brighter than raiment made from the sunbeams – crowned with Charity, a more radiant diadem than the stars of God – walking strongly in Faith, with the simple majesty of Eve in Eden before the fall – inwardly illumined with Hope, a light from the luminous centre above; they have gone forth, I say, with the invincible and impregnable armour of a pure intent, to do battle with the dragon – to wage war against the hydra-headed monster that destroys and desolates so many homes. They have spoken in their prayerful, powerful might, and the demon

Intemperance has spread his dark wings and soared away; they have stooped to lift from the dust of death their sin-stained sisters, and God has blessed them in their good work – they have founded "Female Hospitals", "Magdalen Retreats", and "Houses of the Good Shepherd". And the women who engaged in the good cause – who sacrificed many of the most obvious joys of life for the sake of humanity – were of the high and noble of the earth. Their example is indeed bright and memorable. Their heroic deeds are worthy of man's reverence and man's love! [Deep sensation.]

Thus it is, ladies and gentlemen, that we find woman's beneficent influence permeating and pervading, like an atmosphere of light and fragrance, all climes, all countries, and all nations. The proud and mighty bow to her – the lowly pay her homage. She was honoured above all – she was the mother of that great Architect who has designed for fallen man a path – more beautiful than Jacob's ladder of old, which reaches from earth to heaven! She was the follower of that great Teacher who went about doing good! She lingered at the foot of the cross, when its heavenly Victim suffered – she mourned at the door of the sepulchre, till the grave gave up its dead, and Immortality appeared, robed in glory, to display its mighty triumph over death! [Sensation.]

But perhaps you will tell me, that while all these remarks are just and eminently true, they are not pertinent to the question at issue. You will tell me that woman is and will ever be, respected in her own proper sphere. You will tell me that woman is born to be the light and the blessing of home – that whenever she steps aside from the duties of domestic life, to face the world in public capacities, she becomes in some sense a gladiator. That the Editor's chair, and the lecturer's desk, are not within her proper sphere. Well, my friends, I have but one answer to make to these objections. The surest standard by which to judge of man's fitness for his profession, is just this – *his success*. And should not the same rule apply to my own sex? Can I not point you to a hundred shining instances wherein women have succeeded as public teachers? Who today stands at the head of the literary press of America? A WOMAN – Mrs Stephens. [Applause.] Who has for many years maintained an honourable position in the literary press of England? A WOMAN – Eliza Cook. [Loud applause.] Who has even penetrated to the country of the Celestials, and taken her place at the head of the literary press, to teach the Chinese barbarians respectable English? A WOMAN – Mrs Beecher. And may not I, less gifted and more humble than these whom I have named, strive to emulate their good works in this fifth division of the globe? I challenge my opponents to give one good and substantial reason why I should be denied this privilege.

But I must hasten to give you one or two illustrations of Female Heroism in the Nineteenth Century. I might dwell on the deeds of

Grace Darling and others; but I am rather anxious to point you to deeds of moral, not of physical greatness. And perhaps, in this connection, it may not be out of place for me to relate to you an anecdote – an incident in the life of my good friend and sister, Miss Dix of America. You have all doubtless heard of this lady. She was born in the city of Boston, United States. She was the child of opulent parents, and during her early years, she was surrounded with all the refinements and luxuries of a patrician home. But she had a heart which could feel for the woes of her fellow creatures. She knew that God had given her talent, strength of mind, warm sympathies. She asked herself – "Shall I waste my years in indolent pleasure at home, while lacerated hearts and desolate hearths are all around me? No! I will go out into the world, and faithfully perform the duty which God has given me to do."

She turned her attention to prisons, and prison discipline. She visited every jail and penitentiary in the United States. She entered the convict's cell, and carried light and blessings with her. The condemned in his dungeon, all chained as he was, fell on his knees and kissed the hem of her garment, when she told him of that mercy which is vouchsafed to the contrite in heart. Thus, year after year, did that heroic woman travel up and down the land, introducing reforms in prison management, till at this hour, through her instrumentality, the prisons of the United States are changed from their former horrible and disgusting condition, to be the most perfectly managed establishments of the kind in the known world. [Cries of hear, hear!]

On one occasion, Miss Dix was the only passenger in the mail, through a wild and unsettled country. She noticed that the guard had provided himself with a huge pair of pistols, and that his conduct was somewhat singular and constrained. She asked him why he carred those weapons? "Because, madam," he replied, "this is a very dangerous road. The mail has been robbed more than once in this forest, and it is well to be armed." "Give me the pistols!" she exclaimed, "I will protect the mail." He did so very reluctantly. Soon after, a powerful man sprang from the bush, seized the horses, presented a revolver, and demanded the money and valuables of the party. She looked out from the window, and said to the highwayman. "Sir, would you be so unmanly as to rob a woman? I am the only passenger in the coach. I have but little money, and what I have I intend to give for the benefit of the prisoners confined in jail at the next town. Still, if you are suffering, I will give you half!"

He listened to her words, relinquished his hold of the horses, and approached the carriage window. "That voice," he exclaimed, "I think I know that voice. Are you not Miss Dix?" Before she could reply, he had caught a glimpse of her face. He threw his revolver from him and fell on his knees. "God forever guard and bless you, Miss Dix," he cried, as great tears streamed down his swarthy face. "I was a prisoner in the Philadelphia jail, condemned to death. You visited me – you wept with me – you prayed for me. I escaped from prison, and I am now a fugitive, obliged to hide in this forest, and to get bread by robbery. But never, so help me God, would I wrong the woman whose lips have breathed a prayer for me!" [The sensation and applause was here so long continued as to occasion a considerable pause in the discourse.] Saying this, he plunged into the depths of the forest, and disappeared.

Now, my friends, will you tell me that woman has no right to step aside from the duties of domestic life? Will you tell me that her place, and her only place, is at home, a puppet in the chimney-corner, or a drudge in the kitchen? Will you tell me that she ought not to have a soul above puddings and pastry? – that she is only competent to darn stockings, and sew on buttons, on the one hand, or to gossip or gad on the other? Heaven forbid that we should be deficient in the culinary department; and I sincerely advise the gentlemen never to take a wife till she has served at least a short apprenticeship to pies and puddings. [Loud laughter and cheers.] But if she can not only make a tart well, but accomplish the higher and more important duties of life well, there is no earthly reason why she should not be allowed to do so. [Hear, hear.]

But it is not only in high moral warfare that the women of our age have won imperishable renown. In a more appalling field of heroic enterprise they have brought away honours far beyond trophies and laurel crowns. When the flame of red war, fanned by the black wing of the eagle of the North, lit all the heaven, east and west – when men rushed madly to the strife and the conflict, rage in their hearts and blanching words on their lips – when the cannon awakened the echoes and the trumpet sounded its shrill notes of danger – there was a soft presence in the midst of the fierce warriors – there was a heavenly light streaming along, and if I may be allowed the expression, silver-lining the lurid clouds! Woman – mild, beneficent, devoted, and heroic woman – was there; – yes, was there to avert, as far as might be, the horrors of the strife – to attend the sick, and wounded – to comfort the bereaved – to counsel the weak – to do, in her own gentle, but energetic way, the great work of God. O, my hearers, you know as I know, and you value as I value, those pale-faced Sisters of Charity who, during the horrors of that memorable Crimean winter, flitted from camp to camp, blessings on their lips, charity in their hearts, loving kindness and human kindness vibrating through every chord and fibre of their natures. And you remember, as I remember, and you reverence as I reverence, the radiant moon that rose up among those virgin stars. Nobler than all in goodly presence – higher than all in queenly grace – equally single-minded, enthusiastic, and devoted – she illuminated that dark epoch of history, and banished half its night away. Yes, you remember as I remember, and you reverence as I reverence, that name first and highest among holy names in the Nineteenth Century – that heroine so far above all heroes – that mortal so far above mortality – that name which you cannot utter without heaving hearts and swimming eyes – that name written in immortal characters among God's high and noble ones – the name of Florence Nightingale! [Immense applause.]

Here I might well pause. My sex is vindicated. I need speak no more, and still this audience would retire more than satisfied. They have listened to my illustrations of the greatness, the heroism of my sex. O, my sisters, be proud! Bow not your heads – falter not your hearts. Remember the watchword before you. See how history is bright with our names. Read of Sarah, the wife of Abraham's old age – of Ruth, the gentle and loving – of MARY, the follower of Jesus – then come down through the night of ages, and on to that long line of English heroines who have given the British nation its strength and virtue. I tell you, my sisters, we may hold high our heads with a lofty and a holy pride, when we think of these. When I think of them, I am constrained to bend the knee in thankfulness to God that I am a woman. [Applause.]

On the achievements of woman in art and letters in our day, I fear time will not allow me to dwell. The traces of her progress in these departments, however, are so remarkable, that no one will deny she has in some of their highest walks, excelled her male rivals. Who will deny that Elizabeth Barrett Browning is a great poet; that she is imaginative, reflective, bold, real, and impassioned. Tell me the poem of Tennyson's you can compare with her "Aurora Leigh"; or the piece of Longfellow's you will put alongside her sublimely shadowed "Exile". Tell me the prose writer in fiction you will compare with that wonderful Charlotte Bronte – the "she Carlyle", to use the somewhat too vigorous language of a literary friend of mine. For downright, steady, practical common sense, put into bold, thorough English, – the fine old English our ancestors spoke three hundred years ago – who can excel the earnest, heroic, Harriet Martineau? And then there is in France that wonderful Madam Dudevant, and there has been in Germany the thoughtful de Stael, and there is in the cold North, Frederica Bremer, and there has been in Ireland Maria Edgeworth; and in every European country, within the last fifty years, there have been great, hardworking, virtuous, heroic Women.

And, now, a few words in conclusion. What is the moral of all I have said? What will be the result of this great heroic demonstration on the part of woman? What is to become of the thousands and millions of our sex, who, less gifted than these, are obliged to tax their physical rather than their intellectual qualities? My observations have tended to this point – a point to the realisation of which I fearlessly tell you I have as far as in me lies, devoted my humble life – namely, to give equal facilities to women as are possessed by men towards earning as honest livelihood. O, if men are men, if made of sterner stuff than women; if the great Creator in his ineffable wisdom hath given them larger bone and stronger muscle – if they have higher wisdom and superior inventive faculties – surely they can leave a larger field of productive labour open to the weaker, feebler, less gifted sex; and betake themselves to rougher labour and severer toil. We must have more means opened up to us of living honestly. The necessities of the world cry out for it. The destinies of society demand it. Therefore I ask you, gentlemen, to weigh this moral problem well – to tax your conscience on the duty you have to perform. And to you, ladies, I address myself. Many of you have already practised yourselves in the art of binding up wounds – of cooling the aching head – of strengthening the feeble heart – of illumining the darkened soul. O, do not forget the exigencies of the times – the terrible condition of thousands of your sisters. Many of you are only walking in the first soft downy path of life. To you the world is young, and bright, and fresh, and fragrant, and musical. Nature smiles upon you with smiles of intense enchantment. The beauty of earth and the glory of heaven hold your souls in a divine enthralment. I say to you, as you value the blessing of a long life without a stain – as you value the treasure of a happy memory – as you thank God that he gave you soft hearts and kindly nature – I ask you to co-operate in every movement for the elevation of your sex. The new year is at hand. God grant that through your instrumentality, it may be a happy new year to many of the tempted and erring of your sisters. [Applause.] But not alone on myself, nor on yourselves, do I rely for the accomplishment of the great moral work – not alone in the human will and human arm do I confide – but on the might and power that never falters – on the love that never fails – on the goodness that is infinite – on God, the Father of us all!

D. H. Deniehy

THE SOCIAL EVIL

A public meeting was some time since held in the metropolis for the purpose of considering the best means of dealing with that most wretched and hopeless of all questions, the name of which, in the periphrasis of the publicists, stands at the head of this column.

A great deal was said on the occasion, a good deal of sympathy, and much spasmodic speechifying. But nothing pertinent was suggested, and nothing practical was done. A great many of the gentlemen present were very admirable in their way, very admirable indeed; but scarcely, we suspect, the sort of men to grapple with this question. It was a matter of pitch, and they had gloves on, very white ones, too.

It may do excellently well for a number of reverend ministers of the Gospel to appear upon a platform and pronounce on the horrors and the woes, the curse and the corruption, of body, and soul in this lowermost abyss of human misery. But that affair of preaching has been going on for centuries; and on this peculiar question, in the hearts of those most concerned, there lurks a grim satiric sense of differences between the world's talk upon the subject and the world's practice. And there is no use burking or shirking the matter. There are terrible psychologic difficulties surrounding the question which none other, not even drunkenness itself, presents, and which homilies and advices by themselves, even from the lips of angels, will not affect. All the preaching since the days of Him who dealt mercy to the woman taken in adultery never brought back an erring female to the forsaken path.

Preaching on the subject is simply preaching, whether the thing be worked up in the best infernal patterns and coloured with brimstone, or full of sympathies and sentiment and graceful mournings for what is the holiest and loveliest in woman. Very few of the preachers know the pathology of the frightful disease they pretend to treat. They do not, and for obvious reasons they ought not. Their prescriptions for the evil are, therefore, in the main, practically idle. Whoever attempts to deal with it must know something about it practically and thoroughly, dark though the price which was paid for the knowledge, bitter as the curriculum of the loathsome study may have been.

There are two points of view from which the question is to be regarded – as it concerns the individual, and as it affects society at large. The latter point, the only one upon which legislation and the exercise of statesmanship is demanded, because the only one upon which they can be practically effective, has been pushed out of sight and persistently ignored in British communities. Unfathomable and immeasurable in some directions is the cant and hypocrisy of English social opinion and practice. Horrors such as the cities of antiquity and the vastest abodes of barbarians presented scarcely a shadow of, are allowed to fester and rot in English society under the pure eyes of cherished and guarded English maidenhood, simply because English masculine ears must not hearken, even in the service of God and God's most forlorn creatures, to anything that savours of what is "naughty". And then, of a surety, honourable members of the legislature, virtuous husbands and fathers, keep no "mistresses", and only sneak under cover of night into the verandas of a brothel.

This goes on in this eminently practical nineteenth century, in supremely practical British communities, where practical men look upon the economics of public health, sanitary legislation, as the most practical of things. Ventilation in public lodging houses must be provided for by special Acts of Parliament, and fifty other matters which range themselves round the salubrities of sinks and sewers. But on matters that far more deeply and insidiously affect the health of the people, there the national Mr Pecksniff, and the national Mrs Grundy, and the Decencies of Society, all *dimanché* and in white neckcloths, meet one inexorable and impracticable, "a melancholy train". God help us; and the father with eyes too arid in their hopeless woe for a tear to wet the sockets, gazes on his son dropping piecemeal before him, a mass of hideous syphilitic carrion, the victim of some error in the climacteric of youthful passions which the Decencies of Society never committed in the calends of their youthful adolescence.

On the pavement beside the house, walks with those fresh cheeks and the full eyes of childhood, which Jeremy Taylor so touchingly speaks of, offspring cursed with the curse which will bask and warm its hateful life in the blood of the unborn, the children of those doomed little ones. The pretty little maiden but three months ago in honest service is "on the town" tonight, where she never would have been had she not seen Betsy This, or Nelly That, flaunting in King Street, in hat and mantle, satin flounces, and lavender boots, doing what the law seemed to take no notice of, and everybody looked at as a matter of course. Law, this, which with all the disgrace of police-office inquisition, and the heavy checks of large pecuniary penalties, and gaol confinements in default, meanwhile puts down the slightest approach to irregularity in the sale of spirituous liquors. British, and, therefore, Colonial law has, by the way, a logic of its own on this head. The wretched woman shall expose herself as ware for sale in the streets, nay, call attention by some horrible process of devices akin to those of the hawker and the chapman, and the law does nothing, and has power to do nothing the while. But when the interests of public decency and the open scandal of the thing cease, and the abomination of it is about to be completed in secret, then the constabulary impersonation of the law dives into "houses of ill fame", then the majesty of Quarter Sessions is invoked, and the culprits punished much in a Spartan fashion, not for anything done, but for being found in places which the law regards as objectionable. How the creatures who ply their wretched trade on the streets try to reconcile this obvious contradiction in the regulation of things, if they do at all, we know not. Their opinion upon legislation and legislators, roughly and readily in their own simple and unthinking way arrived at, gives a practical result perhaps not very different from that of persons who have set themselves the task of watching parliamentary men and parliamentary proceedings.

"Hideous disorders", says one deeply learned in the dismal statistics of this province of human shame, Dr McCormack, "attend the unlawful commerce of the sexes, blighting the infant unborn, inducing inevitable ruin and decay. The skin, throat, bones even do not escape. The beautiful structure of the eye is doubly implicated, first in syphilitic iritis, and then in gonorrhoeal ophthalmia, that wretched malady which, as I conceive, has housed itself in Egypt, and infects our race. These diseases are at once acute and chronic, nor does one attack yield exemption from another. The evil is urgent, the very remedy is dire. Medical writings are rife with details only to be surpassed by the yet more horrible reality. Very children even are found in the Lock hospitals of great cities, while millions, it may be affirmed, are lavished on the wages of debauchery. In Edinburgh, he counts one-fourth of the annual mortality as amongst the female victims to prostitution, this so brutish vice and utter violation of the loftier destinies of our kind. Brothels, and low lodging-houses, if possible worse, subsist in all our larger towns, and there prostitution and syphilis, the sin and the soil, go hand-in-hand. Forty thousand illegitimate children, according to the Registrar, are yearly born in England, besides those who perish, sometimes mother and child together, through the execrable arts of hired aborters. In London alone, two thousand women, it is said, annually replace those who die in their sin and misery."

Something more must be done, then, than preaching and making speeches. Upon this matter, as on all others which prejudice or are likely to prejudice its interests, society has a right to legislate on the grounds of self-protection. The affair from this point of view is simply one of police *correctionelle*. As things in this world just now are, and are long likely to be, it makes one's heart ache to think how long, to put down prostitution is impossible. But it is not impossible to keep it in check, and impose upon it those regulations which will protect the morally untainted from the terrible scandals and temptations hourly paraded in public places before the eye, which will to some extent guard public decency, and while doing this, act as a discouragement to the wretched trade itself, by denying it the open facilities that at present obtain for pursuing it with success. One step, simple, summary, and easily taken, would, we think, in the course of a year revolutionise the abomination, in some of its most public and, therefore, most dangerous characteristics. Remove by law from the thoroughfares and highways all women of abandoned character, or whose demeanour or habit of loitering in the streets makes it fair to believe them abroad for improper purposes, and you will do it is impossible to say how much in the right direction. Without mentioning that portion of King Street adjoining the Prince of Wales's Theatre, or the neighbourhood of the Victoria Hall, there is one spot in this city which for everything that can disgust and demoralise and be a disgrace to a civilised community, is unparalleled by any locality in the world used as a public promenade, – the walk in Hyde Park. And often as we hear and have heard pretty lavish praise given to our police authorities, we have marvelled, as they were so admirable, with whom the blame of this crying evil lay.

We presume we ought not to be above taking some hints here and there from what French statesmen have thought and done upon this subject, especially as the results are very satisfactory evidences of the wisdom and the benefits involved. An immense amount of vulgar and ribald persiflage is talked in English society upon French police administration in this matter. But all honour, say we, to the brave and enlightened legislation that has dared to cope, for the benefit of society, with this darkest and wildest of all the evils that encompass it. Here are the regulations of the French authorities, and we put it to every sensible and reflecting reader, how much, by even a partial adoption of them, might be checked and diminished the present abominations left to welter and riot in open carnival of debauchery amongst ourselves, with a *nonchalance* on the part of our law makers that cares neither for the prostitute nor the victim:

"Brothels are suffered, by licence, to exist in certain quarters; but at and from the period of their establishment, they are placed under the entire management of a servile yoke of a portion of the police, whose office is to guard *attentas aux mœurs*." What a check this of itself would be on visitants of a certain class, is sufficiently obvious. "Such places are not permitted in the vicinity of a public school or a church, or, indeed, of any public institution whatever. The keeper of the brothel is bound within twenty-four hours to forward to the Prefecture of the Police the name, for the purpose of registration, of every young woman who may seek to reside in the house. Immediately after this formality, it is necessary that the woman should appear before the authorities; she is then cautioned and warned that if she enter on that course of life, she is under the surveillance of the police, and told her name, once entered as *une fille inscrit*, that name must always remain as a lasting record of her degradation. If her youth be remarkable, she is sent to the Hospital of St Lazare, where she is employed in needlework; and if she be from the provinces, her parents or the mayor of her locality are written to for the purpose of interposing to induce her to return home. If she be friendless, she is received into the Hospital of St Lazare. If this fail, she is then suffered to place her name upon the roll, and her residence is numbered in the books of the prefecture. She is forced to carry with her, and to produce to any person when required, a ticket showing the weekly medical report of her health made by the physician appointed to inspect houses inhabited by persons of her class, and those who dwell with them. Women of this kind are prohibited from wearing showy dresses, and (at Paris) from appearing in the Gardens of the Luxembourg, of the Palais Imperial, or the Tuileries, or other public promenades, and they are not allowed, upon any occasion, to appear at the windows of the houses they inhabit. For a breach of any one of those regulations, the penalty is two months' imprisonment. Those who live quietly in a similar course of life have also the eyes of the law upon them; even the *fille isolé* is tracked through her course of sin; and, in fine, upon the French prostitute every indignity that woman can suffer is inflicted by an active and vigilant police." Whether the best interests of society and those of the wretched women themselves are most consulted by English non-legislation or French law, we leave the intelligent reader to judge for himself.

How far some system, which for the female herself would render the walk of infamy an intolerable and odious road, shorn of the glaring riot and excitement which make its fascination and its reckless licence, would drive her to some other calling, may not be unworthy of attention. People who, with the very best intentions in the world, talk of voluntary reform in Magdalens and asylums, forget the terrible physical change a course of prostitution makes in women; and of whatever worth this may be in the individual, it is too fragile and too precarious a matter, as far as society's own interests are concerned, for it to trust to.

Marcus Clarke

MELBOURNE STREETS AT MIDNIGHT

The rapid progress of Melbourne has long been proverbial, and nothing shows it more strongly than the night life of the city. The scenes in Melbourne streets after dark are of a very different nature to those which took place some fifteen years back. One no longer sees diggers, temporarily rich in some two or three hundred pounds, reeling from from tap to tap, or hears of "a body" found with "two knife-wounds in the breast, and the pockets turned inside out". Diggers have given up watering their horses with champagne and bathing their brawny arms in the vintages of Burgundy and the Rhine. We no longer hear of ruffians with a taste for jewellery ordering barbarous *bijoux* of fine gold to be made for them by a certain day, paying for them, and then disappearing forever, being "knifed" in some drunken frolic. The good old times are happily over, but some curious sights are yet to be seen under the gas-lamps.

Perhaps, for its size, Melbourne is as vicious a city as any in the southern hemisphere, but the artificial impetus given to crime by the outbreak of the gold mania is subsiding, the permanent settlement of a large number of industrious persons having in a great measure absorbed the floating criminal population. The dens of infamy and vice, which were for a long time the disgrace of the city, and which were used as schools to train the young of either sex for the gallows and the hulks, are rapidly being destroyed by the demand made upon house-room by the respectable working population. There is little open violence, and the criminal class prefer to keep to themselves, and as much as possible avoid thrusting their miseries before the public. The smallness of the city forbidding the existence of a race of social Arabs, like the floating street population of Paris or London, those who habitually frequent the large streets after dark are all of a better class, and the most degraded and utterly criminal confine themselves strictly to their own narrow rights-of-way and lanes, never, unless for some urgent reason, appearing in the public thoroughfares. We have recently, with the assistance of the police, penetrated into all these places, and we propose to lay the result of our observations before the reader. The most startling and interesting details were gathered in the least public places, and will be given in their due course. In this present article it is our intention to give only a general outline of the appearance of the large thoroughfares at midnight, reserving the lanes, "rookeries", and rights-of-way for another opportunity.

The large streets present no spectacles of extreme poverty or extreme vice. They are the haunt of the "upper ten thousand" of Bohemia only, while, owing to the rapid rise of the city, and the natural tendency of a young population to centralise, the theatres and casinos are nearly all in Bourke Street, which thoroughfare is filled nightly to overflowing, while the other streets are almost deserted. Bourke Street at midnight is something very little better than the Haymarket (London) at two in the morning, and from nine p.m. to one a.m. presents a scene of the most varied kind. There is not perhaps that excess of vicious brilliancy that an older city would show, but some of its features are peculiar to itself. Let us take the Portico bars for example, which at the time of our commencing our "round" will be in the full heat of business.

Passing through the iron gates, we find ourselves in a large hall, open at one end to the street, and closed at the other by the pit and stall entrances to the theatre. The curtain has just fallen upon the piece of the evening, and the crowds from gallery, pit, and stalls are refreshing themselves before the farce. On each side are covered bars, where some twenty or thirty girls dispense, with lightning rapidity, the "brandies hot", "glass of ale", "cold without", "colonial wine", "nobblers for five", "whiskeys hot", "sherry and bitters", "two glasses claret", "nobblers for two", "dark brandy", etc., which expectorating crowds of men and boys call for on all sides. White-coated waiters shoot like meteors through the mass, bearing coffee to some of the more quiet frequenters of the place. These sitting at little marble tables drink and smoke philosophically. At the furthest table from the door sits a knot of Government clerks – young Piffins, of the Treasury, and Biffins, of the Chief Secretary's office; beside them reclines in drunken slumber Tom Bambury, of the Customs. Some two more friends of the group coming up, and commencing a fight with sticks over the inebriate's head, he is at length roused to a sense of his position, and staggering up, passes into the little door where a woman in blue silk and white lace is standing. That door leads to the "ladies' refreshment-room", but is known to its fast frequenters by another name. The women who assemble there are well dressed and orderly. They live for the most part in adjacent streets, paying a high rent for their houses, which are usually leased and kept in order by some old woman, who is too old to attract; and the less public of them frequent the theatres more for their own amusement than with other designs.

A notable feature of Bourke Street, from nine to eleven, is the number of sewing girls and milliners' apprentices that haunt its pavement. These girls, neatly and sometimes handsomely dressed, will pass and repass for hours, either for amusement or for the purpose of making assignations. There are nearly 2,000 girls, from the ages of fifteen to twenty-five, employed in Melbourne, and in their manners and mode of life they are daily assimilating themselves more nearly to the Parisian *grisettes*. Walking up the street, we meet a knot of station-men from the Murray with cattle. They have just put up their horses preparatory to "goin' on the bust", and walk down the pavement four abreast, all booted, breeched, and smoking violently. Reeling after them are some half-dozen sailors from a passenger ship now in harbour; these are evidently "on pleasure bent", and with vehement addresses as to everybody's eyes, limbs, and internal anatomy, lurch into a convenient bar for drinks round. A cab, loaded fore and aft with a still more drunken and melodious crew, goes flying over gutters and round corners, *en route* for Sandridge and the harbour. Presently we come upon a group of Celestials, pigtailed, blue-coated, and mandarin-capped, chattering in their teeth-breaking lingo. "Well, John, how goes it?" "How-yeh! Yoh! Aaaah! G'night!" and a burst of gutturals drowns the remainder of the greeting. These turn down Little Bourke Street into an opium-house, and will probably spend the remainder of the night in gambling away their hard-earned gains. The pavement is crowded with people. Piffins and Biffins pass arm-in-arm up the street, the former peering under the bonnet of every woman that passes, in the hope that he may meet a girl with whom he has an assignation. Ha! – he has met her at last, and they cross the road to one of the numerous public-houses, which, under cover of a "bar trade", do a most lucrative business as receiving-houses and bagnios. The pavement is crowded with persons, all strolling quietly on as though it was a public parade. What Collins Street is from three to six, so is Bourke Street from nine to twelve, with this difference, that respectability is at a discount in the latter. It is the seamy side of Collins Street and its "humours" are all of the grosser sort. In the gutter a purple-faced man, with sodden eyes and unsteady gait, gasps forth the last notes of a ballad, and an itinerant "seller of songs", a little higher up the street, is screeching in humorous conjunction the titles of some of the "noo and fav'rite" melodies that float yard-long from his stick. The coffee vendors have already erected their stalls, and are thinking about commencing their night's work, while the man with the telescope, who shows Saturn's rings for a penny and describes Jupiter's moons for a glass of gin, is putting up his machine, and preparing for home and bed. At the corner of Bourke and Stephen Streets, a crowd is assembled round a "street-preacher", who, with hat off, and his hand upraised, is giving out the first verse of a hymn. Numerous persons join in chorus; meanwhile, three little boys have been busily engaged picking pockets, and, before the strain is finished, sneak off with their booty into the convenient sanctuary of Little Bourke Street. Dirty and draggle-tailed women begin to appear at the ends of right-of-ways, and the popular music-halls have just vomited forth a crew of drunken soldiers, prostitutes, and thieves. There is a masquerade at one of the casinos, and the entrance is crowded with fast men and "gay women". The brass band at the window of the Waxworks Exhibition is vigorously playing the "Last rose of summer", previous to going home for the evening. Cabs commence to draw up against the doors of the refreshment places into which bevies of *lorettes* and their attendants are going for supper. The cabs are drawn up close against the kerb, awaiting the orders of their hirers. Cabmen are frequently in league with prostitutes, and if an unsuspecting individual hires the vehicle the woman is taken up as a passenger, and frequently succeeds in inveigling the pigeon into her house. On one line of road, indeed, this practice is notorious, many cabmen living as the "fancy men" of the women of the town, and assisting them in robbing the sailors whom they have in tow.

Coming down the street are four young thieves. One of these, "Nosey Samuels", is a Jew boy, and has already done four years' imprisonment, or, as he terms it, "four stretch", for a robbery of jewellery. They are on the loose tonight, and will probably finish the evening in one of the numerous dens in Romeo-lane. The theatres are closed by this time, and from the stage-doors the wearied supers and scene-shifters are issuing; but the casinos and dancing halls still give forth beams of light. Tobacconists still are ablaze with lamps, and anyone who took the trouble of watching the doors closely would see many persons enter and not come out again. A great many of these shops are "blinds". The real trade of the place is done upstairs. The upper rooms are fitted up as gambling saloons, and the arrangements for communication with the shop below are so perfect that on a stranger attempting to enter the *penetralia* the "office" is at once given by means of a wire, and all signs of the occupation removed. Not long since a raid was made upon two of these places by the police, and nearly thirty persons captured; but the affair was a long time in arranging, a detective having been employed for some weeks in insinuating himself into the good graces of the proprietor, and obtaining admission to the upper rooms. Turning round into Stephen Street we come upon a new phase of life. Pawnbrokers' shops abound, old furniture shops and old bookstalls are rife, while from out the villainous dens whose lighted windows shine dimly at the bottom of the rights-of-way the sounds of a cracked fiddle and the discordant laughter of the miserable women who inhabit them fall upon our ears. At the door of one of the pawnshops stands an old man, with a face like a caricature of Ernest Griset's. He might pass for the ancient dealer in curiosities who sold Balzac the shagreen-skin. That is Jacob —. He is a Dutchman, and still talks pathetically of Rotterdam and the Boomjees. He is the most knowing and artistic "fence" in Melbourne. Like Shakespeare's apothecary, his shop shows but a beggarly account of empty boxes, but he has store of wealth somewhere hidden. His shop has a back entry, where many a case of jewellery or watches has entered, never to return again. Old Jacob is "friends", to a certain extent, with the police; and his old wife – a Tasmanian Jewess – professes much affection for the members of the D division. Night-cabs, with gorgeous-hued dresses swelling over the foot-rails, rattle past. In "shy" houses lights glimmer through the shutters, while in some of the doorways flaunting but shabbily-dressed women peer forth, like spiders from their webs, on the lookout for prey. Most of these women are thieves as well as prostitutes; and in the fetid and dingy back premises lurk ill-looking ruffians, who are prepared to silence any opposition on the part of the not sufficiently stupefied victim. Coming up the street with leisurely step is Detective Fox. A robbery of £30 from a sailor has been reported, and he is taking a stroll around the "cribs". The woman at the door enquires "Am I wanted, old son?" and being answered in the negative, gives herself a defiant shake, and requests a "shout" instanter. A little further up the street Fox stops to speak to an orange woman. This personage is termed "Dandy Sal", and is a sort of hanger-on of the police. She is much above the average of others of her class, and how she came to her present position is a mystery. She has travelled through the greater portion of the Continent, and speaks French and German fluently. Her son is the companion of young thieves, and often extracts much information, which his mother duly reports in proper quarters. There seems to be nothing particular to communicate this evening, for Fox, after a brief consultation, strolls leisurely on. At the corner of the street he comes plump into the middle of five men, who, recognising him, chaffingly ask after his well-being. These belong to a notable class of street-walkers. They are "magsmen", and their occupation, as Fox tersely puts it, is "kidding on the flats". They will follow a man from up the country, and engage him in cards, drinking, or betting, and end by fleecing him of his money. The big man, with the "mouse mark" on his cheek, is Luke Isaacs, the Jew;

and the one next him, who wears a velvet waistcoat, and looks altogether not unlike our old friend Mo' Davis, is Cornstalk Charlie, who has just come from Randwick Races, and is on the lookout for a man who "owes him a pot, s' help him!" The little one at the end is named "Slipslop Joe", and has only come out of gaol a week back, where he had been rusticating for three months for winning £19 from a sailor by the "dog-collar touch". They have got a "flat" in their toils now, and are off with him to some friendly drinking-house.

It is now half-past two o'clock, and the shops are all closed. The streets are tenanted only by a few wretched creatures, who still wander disconsolately up and down, on the lookout for some stray victim. A few "bar loafers" are shudderingly creeping down into the back slums, and wondering if they can get another "nobbler o' P.B." shouted, before they finally turn in to their private gaspipe for a night's repose. The "coffee stalls" are nearly deserted, and their owners are taking a snooze, preparatory to their "early morning's business". Two or three cabs still hover about, but the policeman reigns supreme, and even the itinerant trotter-seller is going home to his hovel. The shutters are up, and the lights in the newspaper offices are the only signs of industry. Melbourne is asleep, and street life is over for one night.

J.E. Neild

REVIEW OF IBSEN'S *A DOLL'S HOUSE*

Ibsen's play, of which so much has been heard of late, is a new departure in stage-presentation. It is a play with a purpose and a moral. The author appears to have had in his mind the evil of treating women as children or dolls, rather than as thinking beings. Hence the title, "A Doll's House". The heroine of the story is a woman who has been the petted, spoiled child of the father, and who, up to the opening scene of the drama, has been petted and spoiled by her husband. But she has not only been indulged in all her whims and fancies, but her moral principles have been neglected. She, consequently, has only a limited perception of the duties of truthfulness and honesty. In effect, she lies whenever she finds it convenient to lie; and she has committed a forgery which, until she discovers that the consequences are going to be inconvenient to her, does not lie heavy on her conscience. Perhaps it may be convenient here to remark that in this disregard of the commoner ethical obligations, she does not differ greatly from the current practice of society. But this is by the way. She, however, finds herself in the power of a man who threatens to expose her to her husband and to the world unless she complies with certain demands. In ordinary novels and plays such demands would imply the possession of her person and the surrender of her chastity. But Ibsen does not comply with the common custom of dramatists in the method of ransom. The doll's husband is a banker, and the price insisted on by the villain for the redemption of the forged document, is his retention in the bank from which it has been determined he shall be discharged. And it is at this point that the strong interest of the play begins. In the early scenes we behold the doll-wife, happy, careless, living unconscious of the sins she commits, dwelling in an atmosphere of fragrance and brightened with unclouded sunlight. Then in contrast to all this lotus-eating life comes the surprise, the bitterness of reflection. It dawns upon her that, with all her gaiety and butterflyism, she has not the attribute of innocence, and when it is made clear to her that she has brought herself within the hard grasp of the law, notwithstanding all the airyness and faëryness of her life, the revulsion is terrible. It is made more terrible still when her husband discovers the facts of her crime, and not unnaturally reproaches her for the disgrace she has brought upon his good name. To an ordinarily well-balanced mind the explosion of marital anger is sufficiently explained and quite pardonable, but to the mind of the dramatist as expressed by the heroine of the story there is no justification for it. And in accordance with this conclusion the frivolous, wicked little creature overwhelms her astonished husband with reproaches for not having attended more carefully to her moral education, and at a late hour of the night and in very severe weather she quits her comfortable home, forsakes her indulgent husband, and abandons her three dear little children. She goes out into the night and into the world, to enter upon the study of ethics, and her husband, accepting her decision as irrevocable, sinks into a chair, and remarks that the situation is a miracle. And so the curtain comes down. No doubt the play represents a new departure, but does it represent a truth or a principle, or is a picture of real life? It is true one never can quite say what particular form insanity may take, but it is certain that to any competent psychopathologist the circumstance of a woman quitting her home at midnight to study ethics, would supply a substantial reason for certifying to her unsoundness of mind. Henrik Ibsen may be a philosopher and a poet, but if he persists in declaring that such a woman is a rational being, he is as mad as she is.

Miss Janet Achurch, who, in sustaining the character of this eccentric person, made her first appearance in Australia, is an actress of remarkable power and naturalness. Her manner, indeed, was so entirely free from affectation or stage artifice, that she almost caused one to forget how unreasonable itself the character is. But for her acting, which fully deserves to be called powerful, the play would be a very dull play. It has hardly any telling situations, and the dialogue is often unbroken during a long level of colloquial interchanges. But the intense earnestness of Miss Achurch's manner, all through, compelled the attention of every thinking person in the audience. It was impossible not to be interested in the subject for all that there was really very little story to be told. She made one feel a kind of compassion for a woman whose mental obliquity was so complete as to cause her to act with such a preposterous disregard of commonsense. She carried out most conscientiously the intention of the dramatist, and therein demonstrated how entirely she can identify herself even with a morbid dramatic creation. She sought no aid from the attraction of costume or make-up. She seemed as if she disregarded all such adjuncts as unnecessary or incongruous. Else surely she would not have neglected the opportunity of a picturesque costume for the fancy ball to which her husband takes her, nor in respect of her other dresses would she have lost sight of the incidental attraction they could have procured her. There are times when an actress has to compel herself to a good deal of self-sacrifice, but in this case it was surely not required.

On this same occasion Mr Charles Charrington made his first Australian essay in the part of the Doll's husband. He showed therein a large measure of intelligence, and never lost sight of the purpose it was his duty to carry out. In the scene where he discovers his wife's criminality he rose to the height of genuine tragedy, nor less so in the after situation, where he entreats her not to carry out her insane purpose of studying abstract ethics in the depth of winter, and at midnight, out of doors.

Louisa Lawson

THAT NONSENSICAL IDEA

"I am utterly opposed to this nonsensical idea of giving women votes," said one of the Members of Parliament commenting on the proposed Electoral Bill. So are we opposed to it if it is nonsensical, but as so many reforms and discoveries of incalculable value have at first sight been declared idiotic and absurd, we may as well look at the foundation facts and see if this proposed Bill contain the essence of foolishness or whether it does, as some claim, bring us as near to pure justice and absolute freedom as any human law has yet approached.

We are a community of men and women living in one corner of the globe which we have marked off as our own, and since the business of so many people cannot be managed by all, we select a hundred and fifty men to make laws for us and manage our public offices. The laws made by these deputies are binding on women as well as men, but the women have no advocates or representatives in the Assembly, nor any means of making their wishes known. The life and work of every woman is just as essential to the good of the community as that of every man. Her work and the character she bears raise or depress the standard of the state as much as does the life of any individual man; why is she set aside and disabled from expressing her opinion as to what should be done by this community of which she is a member. Why are her rights less than her brothers. She bears a full half of the trouble when the affairs of the state are depressed, an unjust law or the lack of law brings to her life care or hardship or injury as it does to men, yet none of the deputies ask what she wishes – why should they, she has no vote. She belongs to the better behaved sex – for women only contribute one-fifth to the criminal class (four-fifths are men) and it would therefore seem likely that her opinion would be worth having, yet she is expressly discouraged from the formation of opinions, they are declared ineffectual by the other half of this community of people. It does not seem so nonsensical after all, this idea that a woman's opinion as to the fitness of a deputy may be as just and right and worthy of weight as a man's opinion.

Supposing

There are two views of the woman's suffrage question commonly discussed, the justice of the measure, and its expediency. Few doubt its justice, many question its expediency, and yet, being just, what does all else matter?

Suppose that the right to vote lay with women only, and that the progress of the world was bringing expansive thoughts and hopes of a happier future into the minds of men. When men perceived that this right was unjustly withheld from them, and felt that their individual manhood was title enough to this right to a voice in decisions affecting all, would they tolerate discussion as to the expediency or wisdom of the measure. Would they stand by and hear the women conjecture how men might perchance misuse the concession if granted, would they quietly wait while political factions summed up the chances of the support of the new voters? No, they would say "Curse you – it is my right. What business is it of yours how I use it?"

Her Proper Sphere

As to expediency the arguments have been so often repeated that it seems foolish to reiterate them especially as nothing cogent is brought forward on the opposing side. In Parliament such old phrases as these were used, viz: – that "woman should be kept in her proper sphere" and "women have duties quite outside the political arena". One would think the political arena consisted of the Parliamentary Refreshment Room, they are so sure it is not a desirable place for a woman to be seen in. In the minds of these objectors "politics" seem to consist of the petty animosities and personalities which the law making business now gives rise to, but "politics" in reality cover nearly all questions which a thinking man or woman do now consider and form opinions upon. Laws are made upon divorce, the sale of liquor, factory regulations, the employment of children, gambling, education, hours of labour, and scores of subjects upon which women do think and respecting which they ought to have the power of giving effect to their wishes by the selection of men representing their shade of opinion. And if women do not also at once enter the "political arena" so far as to care greatly about the land laws and mining acts, pray do men voters come to an intelligent decision on every possible subject of legislation before casting a vote? Most men do not seriously consider and decide in their own minds upon more than two or three of the many subjects which come within the wide circle of "politics", and it would not therefore take women long to reach equality in that respect. We are inclined to believe that a woman can form as good an idea as to the best man among Parliamentary candidates as the average man voter.

More Logic

But say some people, women do not want the vote, most of them would not use it if they had it. What will happen after they have the vote may be left to the prophets to say, but if A and B do not want something is that a reason why C who has a just claim should be denied?

Prematurity

In the debate, Mr Traill, who said he was in favour of woman's suffrage, urged that the measure would be premature; that women should be first educated to the use of a vote by possessing the suffrage under a Local Government Act. "Then," said he, "if found to be using it well they should be permitted to influence Imperial questions."

This would be kind indeed, but this is not the method hitherto employed when new classes have been admitted to the franchise. We have not first put them through political schools; we have taken the raw material, and under the influence of its new liberty and swayed by the responsibilities of its new standing, the raw material has developed, but where has any government ever had raw material so certain to act conscientiously, so prepared already with intelligence and with a strong bias towards moderation, peace, steady reform, and moral purgation? Probably it is because they know that with women voting the men of bad character would have little chance of future election, that makes men so fearful that women "might not use it well".

Women Members

Many of the speakers in the House contended that if women received the right to vote they should also logically have the right to sit in Parliament. This is not asked for and need not at present be decided. Few women would care for such a post, but it may be safely said that if exceptional women spring up such as the world has hitherto had some examples of, they could not fail to raise the tone of the House and fill a place worthily. It is to be remembered that men will not cease to vote when women have the suffrage, and that women are decidedly critical of their own sex. She would need to be a remarkable woman who could win the confidence of a mixed constituency of men and women. A young married woman is the usual illustration taken to show the absurdity of a Woman Member and a woeful picture is drawn of her deserted babies and dinnerless husband, but these pictures only show the speaker's ignorance of women, for there is no woman who would not think of her baby and the happiness of her home long before she desired in her wildest fancies the barren honour of a Parliamentary seat. She would not be likely to be asked to stand, and she would not consent if asked.

Some members treated the question in the old semi-facetious way, conjecturing the effect of pretty women in Parliament and the power of a lovely woman Premier to win susceptible opposition members to her side. This presupposes that the political convictions of men are but wavering undecided beliefs, and easily unseated, and forgets this fact that a woman of such attainments and character that a mixed constituency of men and women esteemed her a fit Parliamentary representative, would by her very nature, her modesty and quiet sense, make this silly gallantry impossible, and she would so scorn adherents won only by beauty that they would probably begin under her influence to form their opinions firmly and honestly. Another member alleged that his brother members would do no work if ladies sat beside them. If men are indeed so silly that in a place of business they must inevitably be simpering to women, it will not be so nonsensical to give a vote to a class undoubtedly not prone to publicly exhibit their weakness or their foolishness.

METHOD

No one who is the habit of reading any of the many journals devoted to the interests of women, can have failed to be struck by the cry of overwork and overpressure which goes up from the hearts of women. From all parts, in varying accents and in different words, but with ever the same sad refrain comes the cry, "My burden is greater than I can bear; the ceaseless hurry and turmoil of my life is crushing me." And the pathetic part of it is that this is no complaint of idle, lazy women, but the expression of house mothers, workers, leaders in great and good works, whose energies are spent for the good of their families and of humanity at large, and who only desire that their burden may be lightened that they may do their work more faithfully. The cry goes up not alone from the poorer classes, it is echoed by women in every rank, through the length and breadth of the whole continent. That there is overpressure, is sadly and abundantly proved by the increasing numbers of women who are incapacitated by diseases of the nervous system, or who swell the roll of those poor souls who find an asylum within the walls of our hospitals for the insane. Mr Bellamy has done what he could to stem the rising tide of household difficulties or rather to abate the flood which threatens to overwhelm so many homes, but women must understand that the real remedy lies with themselves.

Greater simplicity of life, dress, food and surrounding would at once mitigate, if not abolish the evil, and we may be very sure that men will not raise any strong objections if we lead the way. Indeed there are many who will welcome gladly the emancipation of their women-folk, and if we are honest with ourselves we shall at once own that most men prefer simplicity in dress, and that whatever may have been our reason for sitting up late, with aching back and eyes to put those two frills on little Irene's skirt or goffer our own flounces, it was certainly not to please the good man, who, though he likes his wife and children to look well dressed, is always on the side of plainness. So long as we all strive to live in the same style and to present the same appearance as our wealthier neighbours, so long will the house-mother have a tired face and a sharp or a weary tone in her voice, and the house-father but a small bank account. However as we cannot hope to hew down and root out in a few days or weeks the Upas tree of vain competition which has so long been growing in our midst, it may not be amiss to offer here a few suggestions which may prove useful to the overworked who see no way to lessen their labours.

After all, it is not the physical weakness which is the hardest to bear, but the constant strain on the memory that nothing shall be omitted and the continual attempt to do and think of two things at the same time. And here my suggestions may prove helpful. To ease the overburdened memory, try this simple plan; carry always in your pocket a small notebook and pencil and write down anything you want to remember to do, immediately you think of it, instead of turning your ring, or tying a knot in your handkerchief, or asking someone to remind you of it. Every morning as you dress have your little notebook open on the toilet-table and see what are the things to be done that day; like a wise general, plan your campaign before starting for the day's march. Train yourself to look in the little book when you have a few spare minutes, that you may see what is the most urgent duty.

Be sure to put down *everything* you wish to remember, letters to be written, visits to be made, little jobs of needlework or about the house, matters about which you wish to consult your husbands, orders for your servants and trade-people. Notes of invitation, etc., should always, when possible, be answered at once, so they will not need to be entered in your book.

No woman with a bad memory, who has not tried the notebook system, can imagine the satisfaction it gives to run one's pencil through some line in the book and think comfortably "That is done and finished with." I do not propose the notebook as a panacea for all the troubles of overworked women, but it will certainly ease their labours to do their work more systematically. We should do well to lay to heart the precept of old George Herbert, whose wise and godly poems are not read half so much as they deserve to be, "Sum up at night the things that thou hast done, and in the morning what thou has to do."

If you have servants, write down on a slate the *menu* for the day, it helps them to remember and there can be no mistake. If you have no servant, still write out the *menu* and look at it as you prepare the meals, that you may have the things planned. It is well, in a spare half-hour, to gather together all one's cookery books and plan out the meals for a week; they can be modified afterwards to suit the contents of the larder and it simplifies the marketing and reduces the butcher's bill: there are so many inexpensive little dishes that are a welcome change from joints, chops and steak, but the existence of which one is apt to forget unless reminded by the cookery book.

If you have many garments to repair and not much time to devote to them, try the plan of giving one hour to preparing your work – matching materials from your piece-drawer, tacking on patches, cutting out, setting tucks, etc., then fold the prepared work neatly away, to be taken up at any moment, when chatting with a friend, when your husband is ready to read aloud to you in the evening or when you have a few minutes to spare. Much can be accomplished thus when it would be out of the question to devote the time and attention requisite for fixing the work. Look carefully over all linen which comes from the laundress and put aside all that requires mending, remember that the stitch in time neglected for one week often means two or three hundred the next.

Procrastination is not only, as we learned in our copy-book "the thief of time", it is also a chief factor in the sum of weariness, which oppresses many women. The writer having a natural tendency to that failing, knows from experience that the letter which should have been written and was not, the visit which was neglected in the proper time, tire one far more than letters written and visits paid. Here is one advantage of the notebook, it will not let one forget, and shames one into doing one's duty.

A.G. Stephens

A POET'S MOTHER – LOUISA LAWSON

Many gifted men have had remarkable mothers, and Henry Lawson's mother, Mrs Peter Larsen (better known as Louisa Lawson), is in many ways a remarkable woman. Born at Guntawang, near Mudgee, New South Wales, she has suffered all her life from that craving for knowledge and culture which one sees in so many bush girls – often suppressed in deference to their not understanding men-folk, sometimes fighting hopelessly against the round of trivialities in which Custom circumscribes a woman, rarely succeeding to reach an enlightened plane of thought or performance. Louisa Lawson's mother burnt her books; her husband, a clever, capable man, frowned down her impulse to imaginative work; friends and relatives looked askance at her "queer ways". The energy of a magnificent physical constitution enabled her to struggle on. She read, and wrote, and occasionally talked. When she came to Sydney a dozen years ago, a poor little wooden cross marked the grave of poet Kendall in Waverley cemetery. Maybe the sentiment was a foolish one, for Kendall's monument is in his work, but Mrs Lawson initiated a movement which replaced the shabby little cross with a handsome monument. Then she started *The Dawn*, a journal for the household, edited, printed, and published by women. The paper is living yet, and in its heyday spoke many brave and true words. Then she organised the first Woman's Suffrage League established in Sydney. Then she was chosen a member of Sydney School of Arts committee, and for several years her strong sense was a force in its deliberations.

Recently she has become a Government contractor – and inventor. For twenty-one years New South Wales mail-bags have been fastened with a strap, sealed by a device invented by Superintendent Davies. Mrs Lawson took a contract for supplying these straps, and it struck her at once that the contrivance for fastening was slow and cumbrous. So it was, undoubtedly; the astonishing thing is that in twenty-one years the consensus of male wisdom among postal officials should not have bettered it. In odd moments Mrs Lawson thought out an improved buckle, had a model made from her description, and took it to the Post Office authorities, who instantly recognised its ingenuity and adopted it. It saves two-thirds of the time formerly needed to fasten the bags, and many hundreds of pounds annually in value of string and wax. Mrs Lawson's portrait in another part of this issue barely does her justice. The expression is too hard. Despite all, Louisa Lawson is essentially a womanly woman, of a characteristically feminine type. Her nature is the groundwork of her son Henry's; but there is in him the additional element of restless male intensity. And now Mrs Lawson may speak a little space for herself.

"Something about myself? Oh, dear! Won't it look very conceited? Well, if it does don't blame me. Are you sure *The Bulletin* wants it? Do you know, I'd much rather not.

"I'm forty-eight. But you don't want to tell the people my age, do you? I was married when I was eighteen – and what I've gone through since then! It would fill a book. You know my husband's name was Peter Larsen, but Henry's name is really Lawson – he was registered Lawson – that was the way people always spoke of my husband.

"He is dead years now. Of the children, I think Bert takes after him more; Henry is like me: Gertie is more like my mother. You have heard how clever Bert is at music? And everybody knows Henry. Gertie is with me now, working on *The Dawn*. Henry and Bert are in Westralia.

"My father is alive still – such a fine old man! – he must be about seventy-five now: mother died only the other day. Father's father and mother were such good old people – that's my grandfather and mother – Henry's great-grand-parents. The old lady – she had worked hard all her life, poor soul! – she could reap her three-quarters of an acre of wheat in a day – and when she felt herself going to die she got out of bed and washed herself, dressed in clean clothes, lay down again, and folded her hands on her breast – 'so as not to give trouble', she said.

"Father is a born poet; they tell me I take after him. You can see the likeness in this portrait: Henry is the same. He is a good old Kentish yeoman, is father; a big, strong, handsome man. You think I'm handsome? Do you really? I suppose I am taller and stronger than most women: I'd need to be, for what I've gone through.

"And why shouldn't a woman be tall and strong? I feel sorry for some of the women that come to see me sometimes; they look so weak and helpless – as if they expected me to pick 'em up and pull 'em to pieces and put 'em together again. I try to speak softly to them, but sometimes I can't help letting out, and then they go away and say, 'Mrs Lawson was so unkind to us!'

"And whose fault is it but men's? Women are what men make them. Why, a woman can't bear a child without it being received into the hands of a male doctor; it is baptised by a fat old male parson; a girl goes through life obeying laws made by men; and if she breaks them, a male magistrate sends her to a gaol where a male warder handles her and looks in her cell at night to see she's all right. If she gets so far as to be hanged, a male hangman puts the rope round her neck; she is buried by a male gravedigger; and she goes to a Heaven ruled over by a male God or a hell managed by a male devil. Isn't it a wonder men didn't make the devil a woman?

"Run down the men? Don't you go away with that idea. Men are gods – and women are angels. And do you know what you make them suffer? I declare, it's the most pitiful thing in the world. When I come sometimes to a meeting of these poor working women – little, dowdy, shabby things all worn down with care and babies – doing their best to bring up a family on the pittance they get from their husbands – and keep those husbands at home and away from the public-house – when I see their poor lined faces I feel inclined to cry. They suffer so much.

"And listen to their talk! So quiet and sensible. If you want real practical wisdom, go to an old washerwoman patching clothes on the Rocks with a black eye, and you'll hear more true philosophy than a Parliament of men will talk in a twelve-month.

"No, I don't run down men, but I run down their vanity – especially when they're talking and writing about women. A man editing a ladies' paper! Or talking about a woman's question in Parliament! I don't know whether to laugh or cry: they know so little about us. *We* see it. Oh, why don't the women laugh right out – not quietly to themselves; laugh all together; get up on the housetops and laugh, and startle you out of your self-satisfaction.

"Men are so self-satisfied. Why, would you believe it! I was talking a while ago to a member of Parliament and sympathising with him about his wife – he's separated from her, poor thing! – and saying how hard people were on a woman that's alone, and he looked up at me so innocently and said, 'I'm not in the market, Mrs Lawson.' The fool thought I wanted to marry him! And to this day I believe he thinks he had a narrow escape. Poor men!

"*Did* you ever think what it was to be a woman, and have to try to make a living by herself, with so many men's hands against her. It's all right if she puts herself under the thumb of a man – she's respectable then; but woe betide her if she strikes out for herself and tries to compete with men on what they call 'their own ground'. Who made it their own ground?

"Why, when I started out ten years ago to make a woman's paper – *The Dawn* – this is the last number of it – the compositors boycotted me, and they even tried to boycott us at the Post Office – wouldn't let it go through the post as a newspaper. I knew nothing about printing, but I felt I could write – or, anyhow, I felt I could *feel* – so I scraped a few pounds together and got a machine and some type, and I and the girls began to print without knowing any more about it than Adam.

"How did we learn to set type and lock up a forme? Goodness knows! Just worked at it till we puzzled it out! And how the men used to come and patronise us, and try to get something out of us! I remember one day a man from the *Christian World* came round to borrow a block – a picture. I wouldn't lend it to him; I said we had paid a pound for it, and I couldn't afford to go and buy blocks for other papers. Then he stood by the stone and sneered at the girls locking up the formes. We were just going to press, and you know locking-up isn't always an easy matter – particularly for new-chums like we were.

"Well, he stood there and said nasty things and poor Miss Greig – she's my forewoman – and the girls, they got as white as chalk: the tears were in their eyes. I asked him three times to go, and he wouldn't, so I took up a watering-pot full of water that we had for sweeping the floor, and I let him have it.

"It went with a s-swish, and you should just have seen him! he was so nicely dressed – all white flannel and straw-hat, and spring flowers in his button-hole; and it wet him through – knocked his hat off and filled his coat-pocket full of water. He was brave, I'll say that; he wouldn't go; he just wiped himself and stood there getting nastier and nastier, and I lost patience. 'Look here', I said, 'do you know what we do in the bush to tramps that come bothering us? We give 'em clean water first, and then, if they won't go, we give 'em something like this.' And I took up the lye-bucket that we used for cleaning the type: it was thick, with an inch of black scum on it like jelly, that wobbled when you shook it. I held it under his nose, and said: 'Do you see this?' And he went in a hurry.

"Did Henry help me? He did that. His father thought a lot of Henry; he used to call him a tiger for work. Poor boy! when we were starting *Dawn* he used to turn the machine for us; he would just get some verse in his head and go on turning mechanically, forgetting all about us. He didn't like to be interrupted when he was thinking, so often when the issue was all printed off we would go upstairs to supper and leave him there turning away at the empty machine, with his eyes shining.

"Are you married? I am glad: a bachelor is only half a man. But so many of you think that a wife is bought by a wedding-dress and a ring. No! a woman is bound to a man only by her love for him, her respect for him, to the extent of her trust and faith in him. O, if men would permit us to trust and honour them! We do so wish to."

BULLETIN DIARY

3/6/96

Holdsworth called today Milton Terrace – gave him tea & sardines for lunch, cigar & whisky. He professed not to mind Bohemianising but seemed ill at ease, not very hearty in his relish.

Asked him to write missing verse in Kendall's "Orara": he didn't care to, though he repeated it. I didn't quite catch.

It might have been different, I might have been human
If the woman I loved had been more of a woman
. . . forbidden
. . . hidden
The past is the past: let the word be unspoken
That would wound a whole heart for heart that is broken.

I have had 3 yarns of his to read – a rather amusing (for reading aloud) sketch of a musical neighbour who sang till 2 a.m., and whom he "killed" by hiring a trombone player to go on from 2 a.m. to daylight. (This Holdsworth says was J. C. Neild, M.P., formerly neighbour to him at Woollahra, who used to chant Italian Opera till 2 or 3 a.m. then chop wood, then water his plants. When the sketch first appeared (? 10 years ago) in some local annual, Neild threatened legal proceedings, & Holdsworth came home & found his wife in tears over a threatening missive. Nothing came of it.) A commentary on Shakespeare giving new readings (one – "My May of life has fallen into the sere, the yellow leaf" – struck me as happy, and Holdsworth thinks it's original, but wouldn't let me publish it as his, so I suspect he's cribbed it); & a third ghost story, not much. They're all clever in a way, but over-laboured & ornamented – like his verse. Holdsworth asked me if I thought good enough to print in book form: I hesitated, & I could see he didn't like it. He can take a lot of flattery, evidently.

Holdsworth told some fair Parkes stories.

"Julian Ashton, artist, called just after birth of Cobden Parkes, 3 years ago (1893), when old man 78. Parkes said in his squeaky voice: 'We've just decided on a name – Cobden.' Ashton: 'But think how awkward when the boys call him Cobby at school. Cobby Parkes isn't nice. Why not call him after some American patriot – Washington,

Lincoln, Garfield?' 'Mr Ashton, Lady Parkes and I have thought of those names, and we are keeping them for the *next* three boys.'

"At a dinner given by Major Z.C. Rennie at the Hotel Australia, Editor Curnow, of *Sydney Morning Herald*, remarked 'These oysters are good.' Parkes: 'Mr Curnow, I don't need these adventitious aids. Lady Parkes and I until quite recently have been in the habit of having connection 17 or 18 times every night, and we now have connection 10 or 11 times.' Curnow was very quiet for the rest of the dinner (this was said out loud before all the table); but Parkes later, proposing or replying to the toast of 'Federated Australasia' made a splendid speech, full of elevated thought and moving language.

"Parkes on one occasion travelling up to Faulconbridge in train with W.R. Piddington of Mt Piddington. 'Ha! Piddington, are you off up to the mountains?' 'Yes, Sir Henry, I'm going to my little place from Saturday to Monday – must fulfil residence conditions you know.' Squeak: 'And may I ask what you have in that basket, Piddington?' 'In this basket, Sir Henry? Oh, sandwiches.' 'Will you let me see those sandwiches, Piddington?' 'Certainly, Sir Henry,' and Piddington opened the basket. 'Ha! a bottle! What is in that bottle, Piddington?' 'Hock, Sir Henry.' "Ock! Dear me. Now, I wonder have you a corkscrew with you.' 'Yes, would you like a glass, Sir Henry?' 'Piddington, since you press me, I will,' and while Piddington was opening the hock, Parkes ate the sandwiches. 'Ha!' holding the glass up, 'this looks good 'ock.' Drinking it & taking the bottle. 'Piddington, this is good 'ock.' And he finished the bottle – the sandwiches were gone! 'But I perceive you have another bottle Piddington. What is in that bottle, Piddington?' 'Claret, Sir Henry.' 'Well, if there is a wine I prefer, Piddington, that wine is claret.' And the claret followed the hock. 'But what is that you have in that parcel Piddington?' 'Oh, a little bit of cake, Sir Henry.' 'Cake! Dear me!' And the cake followed the sandwiches. 'Piddington, I thank you for your hospitality. I could wish that we travelled together oftener, Piddington. Goodbye Piddington.' And the old man got out."

A typical Parkes yarn (his own): "I remember, Piddington, hearing of a delicate young lady who was travelling from Sydney to Penrith, Piddington, and on the way she found, if you'll excuse me, Piddington, that she could not restrain her natural functions further – in other words – whether you'll excuse me or not, Piddington, she wanted to pee, Piddington. Now this delicate young lady, Piddington, being placed in this extremely delicate position – what was she to do? She was in great distress, and at last she decided to pee on the floor of the carriage, Piddington, and she did Piddington. So when she came to Penrith, Piddington, this delicate young lady called the guard, and she said, 'Guard, I hope you'll excuse me for making this mess, but the fact is I spilt a bottle of wine, and it went all over the floor of the carriage.' The guard put his finger in the liquid, Piddington, and raised it to his nose: 'Ah miss,' he said, 'I think I have a cork to fit that bottle!' "

"A civil servant made a claim on Parkes for overtime, and sent in a letter saying he had frequently been up from 5 p.m. to 2 a.m. copying documents. Parkes sent for him & squeaked. 'Good-day Mr –, sit down. Did I ever mention to you that I knew your father? I was also very friendly with your mother, and I had some acquaintance with your aunt. Dear me! I see that you here claim overtime for copying documents. Is it not very unusual to claim overtime for copying documents?' The c.s. was getting nervous. 'N-no, I don't think so, Sir Henry.' 'Dear me! Mr —, I don't know whether I should mention that I have a kind of affection for you – I take a great interest in you – owing to the fact, as I say, that I knew your father, and was on intimate terms with your mother, and had some slight acquaintance with your aunt – a most estimable woman.' (The c.s. quaked: 'What's coming? What have I done?') 'And may I ask, Mr —, *where* you copied these documents?' 'At home, Sir Henry. I took them home after I had finished my day's work.' 'Dear me! Mr —; this is very sad, and your aunt such an estimable person. (Sternly) Are you aware, Sir, that under the Public Documents Act the penalty for taking public documents away from the Treasury is two years' imprisonment with hard labour?' 'N-no, Sir Henry; I n-never knew that.' 'Well, Mr —; as I have told you, I had a great esteem for your father, not to mention your mother & your aunt; & don't you think you had better withdraw this claim under the circumstances?' 'Oh, yes, Sir Henry,' said the relieved c.s., 'certainly, Sir Henry.' 'I am glad for your father's sake that you agree with me, Mr —. Good morning.'

"One Jones, of Lithgow, took a £5 ticket in Parkes's Art Union – so many members at £5 each – the prizes: Parkes's books, statuary, &c., at Faulconbridge in the Blue Mountains. (?This art union was never drawn & Parkes stuck to the money.) Some 8 or 9 months after Jones had to compound with his creditors, and, needing money badly, thought he would call on the old man & get his money back. He did so, at the Treasury Building. 'Oh, good morning, Sir Henry, I've called . . . ' 'I beg you pardon, sir,' said Parkes, who must have known the man perfectly well & suspected his errand, 'but you have not told me your name.' 'My name – oh, yes, Sir Henry – my name is Jones. You remember that I took a ticket . . .' 'I beg your pardon, Mr Jones, but you have not told me your address.' 'Address? – oh yes, – my present address is 214 Cleveland Street, Redfern. You will perhaps remember, Sir Henry, that I took a ticket in the Faulconbridge Art Union, which has not been drawn yet, and I understand is not likely to be drawn for some considerable time. And, as I have since had very heavy losses, and am extremely hard-up, I thought I would call,

Sir Henry, and ask you to be so good as refund me the price of my ticket, Sir Henry.' 'Mr Jones. Hare you haware that by the recent decision of the Hattornies General Hart Hunions hare declared hentirely hillegal? Hi ham sure you will see the himprudence of hengaging me to hassist you in hany hillegal transaction. Good morning, Mr Jones.' "

Holdsworth thinks decidedly Parkes had "intellect".

He tells some yarns of "old Jack Robertson" (nasal twang).

"On one occasion a dashing member of the demi-mode called to complain that the police were harrying her. Jack was Colonial Secretary at the time; and at no time could he resist a woman. She was a real bouncing, vital highstepper. Jack promised to turn the police off, and turning with a glance of admiration to Chrichett Walker (Under-Secretary) as she was leaving the room: 'I say, Walker! What a damn fine other fellow's wife she'd make.'

"Jack was coming out of the Reform Club as his wife was passing on the other side of the street. In the act of raising his hat he tripped on the mat and just escaped a bad fall. Then, to the waiting cabman: 'Humph! Cabby! See that? Just because I raised my hat to my wife. Wonder if I'd raised my hat to somebody else's wife would I have tripped over that bloody mat?'

"After hearing a number of country deputations clamouring for new post and telegraph offices Jack lost patience, and to the last of them: 'See here, Mister bloody Mayor: if you think I'm a bloody spider to go and spin wires out of my bloody arse you're bloody well mistaken, that's all.'

"Some Victorian parsons, delegates to a conference, being entertained by the Ministry. Jack drove them round the Domain. This in the days when sewage went into the harbour. Jack couldn't hear a word said against the harbour especially by 'a bloody cabbage-garden cove' (as he labelled Victorians). Wherefore, one of the parsons asking at Woolloomooloo Bay: 'And is this the place, Sir John, where the city sewer disembogues?' 'What's that – disemb –?' 'Where the mouth of the sewer is, Sir John.' 'Oh yes, disembogue – yes, this is the place.' 'I suppose there must be a great nuisance caused by the effluvium Sir John.' 'See here, Mr Bloody Parson, if you put your nose up my arse I don't deny you'll get a sniff, but will you say I stink?' "

Bulletin contributor's point (improved): "Missionaries: the children of God and the fathers of half-castes"!

7/9/96

At Archibald's suggestion addressed to N.S.W. Public Service Board an application for the Government Printership on same terms and same salary (£800) as present occupant (Chas. Porter), who is over 60, and (so the Board appears to think) antiquated.

11/9/96

Received acknowledgment of Government Printership application from Public Service Board. Apparently Macleod is their consulting authority in matter. He & I have never chummied together – he is a little inclined to be suspicious, & has a trace of the dictator in his manner sometimes (though punctiliously courteous) & I am independent & my nerves are on edge through continual overwork. So being conscious that in the matter of "tact" I have left a bad impression on him, don't know whether I'll get his suffrage.

Received today a large packet of late B.H. Boake's papers, MS, etc. from his father B.C. Boake, photographer, Albert Street, Daylesford, Victoria. Have undertaken to edit Barcroft Boake's poems for Angus & Robertson, & supply memoir, fee 20 guineas; work on illustrations extra as arranged. *Bulletin* permits A & R to reprint, making me representative – putting me, in fact, in Boake's place. *Bulletin* right of reprint reserved. Acknowledgment of *Bulletin* cession of rights (my stipulation) to preface volume. Terms: half net profits to author. A & R told me that reckoning net return from 5/- book (say "Banjo's" poems) at 3/-, there was 1/6 profit – 9d. to author – per copy. This even in the 1st 1000 – rather more after. Books must be printed & bound very cheaply.

Busy today on article on case of Thomas Suffield, given 10 years penal servitude by Judge Windeyer in 1891, at Maitland, for raping a servant girl named Annie Chambers, at Lambton, near Newcastle, N.S.W. There is certainly a strong case for Suffield's innocence – or at any rate for the non-proof of his guilt. Windeyer seems to have jumped to conclusion in favour of woman as usual, & dominated country jury. Archibald very bitter, as usual. Windeyer must have personally insulted him in the past, surely. Vicarious sympathy would hardly account for his overmastering hatred of Windeyer, which throws his mind almost entirely off balance as to value of evidence & proportion of matter.

W.H. Traill lunched with me at Dawes Point this day week (4/9/96). A big Scotchman, plenty of vitality & force, inclined to domineer, not much *essentially* literary capacity, I should think, but a good deal of sledge-hammer rough & tumble journalistic power.

Talk essentially dirty – dirty books – dirty lines – dirty pictures. Described a Memoir of Casanova which he had – fine & dirty.

"I brought my wife down here to a lodging-house which used to stand almost at the back of this place (Milton Terrace) the second night after we were married. I remember the landlady taking me aside next morning & saying 'Would you mind closing the door of your room tightly, sir. Your poor little wife – we heard her crying out last night' A young man is merciless", added Traill with a leer.

Apparently he killed her so, for he now has No. 2. See *Discords* for the marital torture of a delicate woman with a husband gross, strong, well-nourished & stimulated. It must be Hell. Ugh!

Reminds me of Cox (?) who took my place as editor of Cairns *Argus*, and had to sue W.G. Henderson for his salary. He had no children & said: "My wife & I are like the fishers of Galilee. We toil all night & catch nothing." He was proud of it too. "You haven't heard that before, have you?"

Traill: "For five years & four months I controlled the *Bulletin* – laid its foundation. It would have died over & over again but for me. I found Hop & Phil May. (Archibald comments: 'The most wonderful piece of luck that ever happened to *Bulletin* – to go & pick up two such men one after the other – & Traill had no special aptitude in selection.') I'm not a Jew, but I would never have let Phil May go to England. He was always clamouring for an advance: I would have given it to him and held him by it.

"Hardly anybody knows what I did for that paper: it nearly killed me. Things weren't like they are now: I had to *create* them – create my machinery as I went along. I put that big machine up, & there was nobody in Sydney that could work it for me. I used to stand over it hour after hour, and watch it tearing sheet after sheet of paper on the rollers. We got it going at last, a little bit at a time – week after week pegging away. I used to write the leader & most of the 'Plain English', and answer most of the correspondence – I had the whole business on my hands, too – I was managing director, editor, printer, and everything else – spend the day in the office, go home & get through a batch of correspondence, have a few hours sleep, and be down again early next morning laying over the machine with a spanner, and breaking my heart to hear the swish-h of the paper tearing on the rollers, and the office besieged by runners – a machine that ought to print (?) 2,000 an hour doing 600 or 700.

"And then I'd snatch an hour to go up to Darlinghurst & keep up Haynes's and Archibald's spirits – they were very nervous – Haynes was a particular nuisance – Archibald was better.

"I invented the title 'Plain English'. Archibald had an idea of 'The Stockwhip' and it went as that for two or three issues; then I put 'Plain English' in. I used to write a different kind from what you have now: my idea was to get the simplest possible expression of opinion on a public question, simple & strong, & throw it at their heads so that they couldn't help understanding it."

8

Rituals and Celebrations

EDITOR'S NOTE

Many European rituals were imported into Australia with the First Fleet. "Rituals and Celebrations" includes examples ranging from murder trials, funerals and sermons to the celebration of Christmas and the New Year. The *Sydney Gazette*, Australia's first newspaper, began publication on 5 March 1803. From the beginning, court reports were prominent with, as nowadays, murder trials being reported at particular length. A special supplement to the *Gazette* of 14 September 1811 was required to carry all the sensational details of John Donne's brutal killing of Mary Rowe. Most nineteenth-century Australian magazines and newspapers also carried regular reviews of local publications and theatrical performances. In the second half of the century overseas books were regularly reviewed. Most of these reviews are now of interest only to specialists in theatre or literary history. Accordingly, the detailed discussion of the performance of Thomas Morton's *Speed the Plough* has been omitted from the account of the opening night of the Theatre Royal at Hobart. The Royal is the only early Australian theatre still in use, though considerably changed from the house described here. The *True Colonist*'s allusion to the function of the dark passage at the back of the Theatre Royal's boxes would have been readily understood by contemporaries. Theatres and nearby streets were favourite haunts of prostitutes, as D.H. Deniehy observed in "The Social Evil", included in part 7, "Friends, Lovers, Sexual Commerce".

The next three extracts relate to various rituals and celebrations enacted in Melbourne between the middle and the end of the century. The colony of Victoria was not formally established until 1850, with great festivity and rejoicing, as Georgiana McCrae describes in her journal. But the discovery of gold shortly afterwards meant a very rapid growth in population and prosperity. Melbourne became the major Australian city, centre of literary as well as economic life. James Smith was one of its leading literary men, though he is now remembered, if at all, for being wrong about the painters of the Heidelberg school, in a review included here. His private diary for 1863 provides fascinating glimpses of the higher, and lower, life of Melbourne at this period. He writes of art exhibitions and theatres, the last rites given the bones of Burke and Wills and all the gossip and scandal of the day. Smith even went to Pentridge Prison to read Dickens's *David Copperfield* to the assembled convicts. It is interesting, too, to compare the different styles Smith used when writing in his private diary and when writing for publication, as in "An Impressionist Exhibition". Since the Melbourne Cup was established in 1861, one might have expected to find a mention of it in Smith's diary. By 1876, all Melbourne appears to have gone to it, as one sees from "The Vagabond's" account.

Towards the end of the century, the centre of Australia's literary life, which at this period meant its journalistic centre, shifted back to Sydney, largely because of the rapid rise in popularity of the *Bulletin*, a magazine established in 1880. In the early days, the *Bulletin* was highly iconoclastic, radical and republican in its politics and bitterly opposed to the 1888 centenary celebrations of the founding of white Australia. On 21 January 1888 it printed its parodic "Centennial Oration", speeches that would definitely not be given at any official dinner five days later. To the *Bulletin*, 26 January 1788 was "the anniversary of a loathsome tyranny", and the day Australia ought to be celebrating was 3 December 1854, the anniversary of Eureka Stockade, the first major protest against British authority. Two of the *Bulletin's* radical heroes, J.D. Lang and Peter Lalor, appear in part 9 of this book. So does Henry Parkes, though the *Bulletin* sees him as a mere toady and a groveller to the imperial powers.

Few ordinary Australians in this period would have shared the *Bulletin*'s republicanism and rejection of ceremony. For Jane Watts and her family, it was a great honour to have the governor to dine though, in the South Australia of 1838, quite a struggle to find a suitable meal for him. Many, as Nat Gould records, ignored the seasonal differences to rejoice in all the traditional trappings of Christmas and New Year. Others, like Catherine Helen Spence, took comfort from religion though Spence, as a Unitarian, rejected many of the old conventions. In this sermon, she even attempts to come to terms with the theory of evolution.

Sydney Gazette

TRIAL FOR MURDER

Yesterday the Court of Criminal Jurisdiction assembled at 10 in the forenoon; and proceeded to the trial of *John Donne* alias *Dun*, a foreigner; *Thos. Welch*, and *Ann Wilson*, for the wilful murder of Mary Rowe, at Parramatta, on Sunday the 25th of August ultimo. The indictment charged *Donne* as the perpetrator of the crime, and under three counts charged *Welch* and *Wilson* as accessories to, before, and after the fact.

Several witnesses proved the state in which the body of the deceased was found on Monday morning the 26th, and stated generally, that the deceased lived with one Charles Wright, whose dwelling is situated between the back of Mr Ward's premises, at Paramatta, and the stone quarry, a situation lonely, retired, and obscure; that on Monday morning, a child of Mr Parrott's went into Charles Wright's to purchase milk, as was her custom; and returning homewards, related, that Mrs Rowe was lying dead and mangled on her own floor: that the alarm immediately reached Mr Chief Constable Ward's, who exerted himself in a manner becoming his office in the development that followed; that the body and limbs of the deceased were dreadfully mangled; a part of the flesh of her right thigh brutally cut and torn away; her cloaths rent piecemeal, and that the murdered body was found on the floor in a doorway, her legs in the front room and her head and body in the back room, where she had always slept. That Mr Surgeon Luttrill was called in to examine the body; who deposed to the following effect, viz; that at 9 on Monday morning he was called upon to view the body, and immediately obeyed the summons; that upon entering the house he found her lying as above described, and that her face was much bruised and disfigured by blows; that a shawl was twisted about her neck, as if designed to strangle her; beneath which, when taken off, there appeared a livid circle round the neck, about two fingers in breadth; that the breast was a good deal scratched and lacerated; and that a most ghastly wound extended from the upper part of the thigh down to the knee, which was not merely an incision, but that evidently a part of the flesh had been cut or torn away, and the bone left bare; that her death had proceeded from strangulation, and not from this ghastly wound, which though sufficient to have occasioned death, independent of any other cause, yet had undoubtedly been inflicted after death, as little or no blood had issued, whereas the infliction of such a wound upon a living subject would have produced a very large emulgence. This Gentleman also gave it as his opinion, that the body had been lifeless 12 or 14 hours before he viewed it, which was about 9 in the morning.

John Welch, a boy about 14 years of age, son of the prisoner at the bar *Thomas Welch*, was then called as an Evidence for the Crown, and seriously admonished by the Judge Advocate on the critical position in which he stood; as upon his truth and candour depended not only his present enlargement, but his salvation in a future state. – This evidence being then sworn deposed, that he lived at Parramatta with his father, with whom the prisoner at the bar *Ann Wilson* co-habited, and that the other prisoner at the bar, *John Donne*, lodged in the same house when in Parramatta, he being employed on the roads by Mr Harrex, the Road Contractor. – The deponent knew the deceased very well, as she was his father's next door neighbour; and proceeded to state, that about ten on Sunday morning *Donne* went home to his the deponent's father's, with half-a-gallon of spirits, having two women in his company, whose names were *Catherine Murphy* and *Bridget Bryan*, all parties sober; that the prisoners *Welch* and *Wilson* were absent from home, having gone to Mr Martin's farm at Seven Hills, a distance of about 7 miles from Parramatta; – That *Donne*, the two women, and the deponent drank the whole of the spirits, and about two o'clock the women went, *Donne* shortly after following, but returning at half past three, asked in a familiar way if the deponent thought their neighbour, Mary Rowe, who lived not more than 18 or 20 yards distant, was possessed of money? To which the deponent answering that he could not judge, *Donne* rejoined that *he would see*; and added, that he had given her a pint of rum, which had operated powerfully upon her; that she might be robbed without danger, and that he would kill her if she did not immediately give her money up: – That the deponent attempted to advise him against the crime, but finding him inflexibly bent upon the project, bade him take his own course, for that he would have no part in it; dissatisfied with which resolution, he assured the deponent that unless he assisted in the robbery *he would serve him in the same way*; that he again absented himself, and returned at 4 o'clock, by which time *John Welch* and *Ann Wilson* had also returned home; that deponent did not acquaint either of the two latter with *Donne's* project, or with his menaces towards himself; that *Donne* told him, privily, that Charles Wright, with whom the deceased lived, was not at home, that he, *Donne*, shortly afterwards called *Thomas Welch*, deponent's father, towards the threshold, and wanted to borrow his axe, which was behind the door of his own house, saying to him also, that he had been trying to open Mary Rowe's box, but could not effect it, for which purpose he wanted the axe and that his father, *Thomas Welch*, answered that he should not have it, asking at the same time *if he was tired of his life, and wanted to be hanged?* to which *Donne* made answer that *there was no danger*. *Donne* took up the axe accordingly, but *Welch* the father took it from him; that they all sat down to supper between 7 and 8, during which Mrs *Rowe* knocked at the door, which being opened by *Donne*, she exclaimed *My good man, how dare you take the liberty to break my bedroom window open? if Wright had been at home you would have had a blunderbuss blown through you?* to which *Donne* made no reply, but followed the woman, she going directly homewards, and he desiring deponent *Welch* to accompany him, which he did at a small distance. That *Donne* was nearly close to Mary Rowe when she entered the house, near to the inner door of which deponent saw him grasp her round the neck with both his hands, and after choaking her for about ten minutes she fell, without a struggle, lifeless! That *Donne* then proceeded to plunder the house; and with an axe he found therein broke open a box, from whence he took, in presence of deponent, a tea-kettle full of copper coin, a bag, and a piece of cloth containing coppers likewise; deponent could neither account for the shawl being twined round the neck of the deceased, nor how her cloaths became torn, as he did not see Donne do either. That both returned to Welch's house, Donne taking thither the plunder, and found Welch up, and Ann Wilson abed, and asleep, as he believed. That as soon as they entered the house, Welch, who either heard or saw the spoil brought in, ordered *John Donne* to go and take the same away and secrete it, as it would not be advisable to leave any part in the house. That Donne attended by deponent, took away the kettle, bag, and cloth that held the money, and buried the whole in the sand near the quarry (where by the deponent's information they were next day found): That they returned home, and at Donne's wish went to procure a pint of spirits at the house of one Clowers, who having none, Donne paid to him two half-crown bills on a former account, and they next went to Mr Beldon's, where they drank two pints, of which several other persons partook, and a third they took home. That they were admitted by Welch, who had gone to bed, from which he arose, and afterwards drank of the spirits: Ann Wilson was awakened by Donne, to partake of it likewise, but she refusing, Donne threw part of it over her. That Donne and deponent again went to the house of Charles Wright, from whence D. conveyed the dead body to the bottom of the garden, and there left it, having first made the dreadful incision down the thigh with his knife, from an apprehension that she might not yet be dead. That they then went back to Welch's: he was up: Donne told him what he had done with the body, and Welch objecting to its being out of the house, advised D. to take it back: to accomplish which they all three went to the spot, from whence Donne reconveyed the lifeless body into the house she had scarce an hour before been mistress of. That deponent went in with Donne, and Welch the elder remained outside. That they searched for further spoil, and found two books, containing bills, which they took home; D. searched the books in presence of deponent and his father, took out the bills, and burnt the books: That Donne and deponent after this went back to pillage the place, namely about 11 o'clock, and finding a few more bills, went home, and went to bed! The deponent, having thus ended his narrative of the horrible night's adventures, added that Donne left his father's house before sun-rise: he, the deponent, went out at 8 to tend a herd of cattle, which was his avocation; and at about half past 12 he was apprehended on suspicion, half a mile from Parramatta, very much intoxicated, as had been declared by Mr Ward, to whom he first disclosed his knowledge of the murder.

The testimony of the Crown Evidence was closely corroborated by witnesses to the minor facts, which tended to connect the chain of circumstances, and stamp his evidence with a degree of credit, to which, divest of such auxiliary support, it might not have appeared entitled.

Thomas Clowers, who in his evidence to the Coroner produced the two half-crown bills paid to him by *Donne*, and one of which had been deposed to by Charles Wright as making part of the sum stolen from his house on the night of the murder, could not now identify the bill, but stated that Donne & Welch the younger were together, and that it was about 8 at night.

Mr Beldon, a publican of Parramatta, in his evidence corresponded with the boy's; namely, that they went together to his house, drank two pints of spirits there in company with persons who were already there, and took a third away, for which Donne settled: – this deponent adding, that in part payment he had tendered two bills, one for 2s. 6d. the other for 5s. both which being somewhat scrupled by Mrs Beldon, were instantly committed to the flames by Donne, to whom the boy remarked that he had no need to pay in bills as he had plenty of *coppers* at home; to proceed whither he went out, and returned in ten minutes with 10s. 3d. of copper coin. At nine they left deponent's house.

Mr *Owen Martin* proved, that the prisoners Thos. Welch and Ann Wilson were at his farm that day, and staid there till he supposed to be about three o'clock.

The two women who had been with Donne at Welch's house in the forenoon of Sunday, and partook of the half gallon of spirits, both substantiated that part of the evidence; and Mr Harrex stated that he that morning gave half a gallon of spirits to Donne; together with 7s. 6d. in bills, he being a labourer in his employ; and that his character was that of an industrious, mild, deserving man.

The whole of the evidence being gone through, the prisoners were put upon their defence.

John Donne denied the accusation generally, and stated that he had gone alone to his master's (Mr Harrex) between five and six in the evening, and was absent half an hour or more; that upon his return to Welch's, it being then about dark, he found the house shut up, the place in darkness, and an entire silence prevailing; that he cast his eyes around, and saw the boy John Welch hovering in silence about the house in which the deceased resided; and on enquiring what he was about, received for answer that he was looking for *him*. At *that* juncture he was persuaded the murder had been effected; both as to any circumstance that took place after his conversation with the boy; how they passed the evening and night; or what became of the prisoners Welch and Wilson, in whose hut, which is represented as a single apartment less than 12 feet square, he slept, he gave no account; nor did he account for the money he had spent; but admitted that he had burnt the bills, because he had been informed that they were bad.

Thomas Welch also declared himself innocent, and accused his unhappy son of having advanced falsehoods to his prejudice, and "sworn HIS life away!!!" . . . . He solemnly protested, that when the deceased came to his door and challenged *Donne* with the breaking open of her window, he was totally unacquainted with the nature of the fact; that the boy followed Donne from a signal he must have given, as he did not hear him speak at the time, nor did the woman, though the boy sat between the two; that after Donne and his son had been away a length of time, he went to bed – the woman had done so likewise; that what Donne and his son were about he knew not, as he had never arose from bed from the time of his going in to that of his rising in the morning, or until he let them in – which of the two was the assertion we did not distinctly hear.

Ann Wilson rested her defence upon her original plea, *not guilty*, and threw herself upon the opinion of her impartial Judges. –

– The Court was directed to be cleared, and after an hour and a quarter's exclusion, the prisoners were recalled to the bar, and the auditory re-admitted.

The crisis of expectancy being arrived, the Judge Advocate communicated to the prisoners severally the Verdict of the Court, which without a shadow of doubt had convicted the prisoner Donne of wilful murder, and the prisoner Thos. Welch of being an accessory *after the fact*, which extended to him the Benefit of Clergy. Ann Wilson was pronounced *Not Guilty*.

The Judge Advocate finally proceeded to the awful Sentence of the Law against John Donne, otherwise Dunne, which doomed him to suffer Death on Monday the 16th of August instant, and his body to be afterwards dissected and anatomised.

And as Thomas Welch was already a prisoner for life, and the nature of the offence of which he had been convicted differed in its shadowing but little from that of the condemned culprit, the Court had thought proper to sentence him to 7 years confinement to hard labour wheresoever it should be the pleasure of His Excellency the Governor in Chief to direct.

The Trial lasted from ten to five, at which hour the Court adjourned *sine die*.

True Colonist

THE OPENING OF THE THEATRE ROYAL, HOBART

On Monday night we went to see the opening of the New Theatre, but we were prevented from getting there until the performance had commenced. We understand that Mr Cameron spoke an address, of which we have not, at the period of this writing, been able to obtain a copy. He also apologised for the absence of four of the performers who had been announced in the bills. The upper boxes were quite full, as also was the gallery, and there was very little spare room in the pit or in the lower boxes, which last were all occupied by respectable people. The whole appearance of the house will be very elegant when properly lighted. The scenery is equal to any in any theatre in Britain out of London. The drop scene is particularly beautiful; it is copied from a print (in one of the Annuals) of Byron's Dream, and looks really like a highly-finished oil painting. The scenery was not well worked, which in some parts spoiled the effect. The audience part of the house was very badly lighted by a temporary affair, composed of several concentric rings of iron in the shape of something like an inverted cone with the apex cut off; these rings being stuck over with tin lamps and glass chimneys, but no globes. This house can never be properly lighted without bracket lamps all around the box circle. We would here suggest to the proprietors whether it would not be to their advantage even in a pecuniary point of view to light the house with gas – the *convenience* of such an arrangement, especially for the stage lights cannot, we apprehend, be questioned. The apparatus could be furnished by an ingenious artisan of Hobart

Town at a reasonable cost. The pillars of the proscenium are tastefully gilt, and the whole surmounted with an escutcheon of the Royal Arms. Opposite the proscenium is a motto in Latin, *"mores mollit"* which our "Little Particular" translates *"mollify your morals"*, for which purpose the managers and *moral protecting* magistrates have very considerately licensed the *"Shades below"*, where all sorts of stimulants, the use of which is so well adapted for *"mollifying"* any *rigidity* of *"morals"* the play-going youth may possess, are to be had in abundance. The saloons being also part and parcel of the licensed house, all the means necessary in the shape of liquors for inflaming the *passions* and destroying the *reason* are to be found there. We believe that this is the only theatre in the British dominions that has attached to the same building a licence to *sell spirits*. Now it was generally understood that the object of the proprietors of the new theatre was to *soften the manners*, and to render more rigid, not to *"mollify"* the morals. We question much whether this *grog selling* in the Theatre will not have an effect directly opposed to that which the shareholders *professed* to have in view. We would recommend the managers to place lights in the passage at the back of the lower tier of boxes; we have heard some very equivocal remarks about the purpose for which this passage was (said to be avowedly) kept in darkness. Smoking in the saloon ought not to be permitted – let this indulgence be entirely confined to the *"shades below"*; we like our cigar as well as any of the *swaggering* smokers, but we could never think of indulging in it where the fumes must annoy one person, much less when they annoy some hundreds.

The acting was on the whole decidedly below mediocrity; but the novelty and beauty of the house kept the audience in good humour throughout the evening. Mrs THOMPSON, the *star* of the night is, we understand, a newcomer, but very respectably connected in the Colony. We understand that in her early youth she was a favourite performer on the London boards, and at the period she would no doubt have made a very pretty interesting "Little Pickle," but when she tried that character here on Monday night, she must have forgot that she is not now so young as she was twelve years ago . . . . We make every allowance for the *first* performance in a new house, and as we have said before the beauty of the house, scenery, and decorations will for a time take attention off the failings of the players, but the Committee must get Meredith, or they cannot get on while he keeps his little theatre open, for any person who likes to laugh at a play must enjoy one hour of Meredith's acting more than all the vapid *entertainment* of seeing and hearing his substitutes at the new theatre, with all the advantages of a really elegant house and excellent scenery.

We would recommend *gentlemen* to walk in the box doors in place of jumping over the back partition, and wiping their dirty boots on ladies' silk dresses. The public expect some regard to decency and good manners in persons who occupy the dress circle, they must *learn* to behave themselves or seek associates of a more congenial habit, in the "dark corners" of the house. The press will soon drive them out of the dress circle if they cannot behave themselves.

Georgiana McCrae

[VICTORIA CELEBRATES SEPARATION]

Jolimont, Sunday, November 11th, 1850

At dinner Mr Harding was telling us about plantain leaves used for plates in India, when there came the sound of wheels grating on the carriage-way followed by the noise of at least two sticks hammering on the door. Mr La Trobe sent his servant to answer the summons, and, while he arranged his neckerchief, hinted at the possible arrival of a new governor in search of a night's lodging! Enter the mayor, Nicholson the grocer also, the ex-mayor Augustus Frederick Adolphus Greeves . . . Nicholson, with one of his fingers tied in a rag, holding an Adelaide newspaper.

"Your Honour, allow me to draw your attention to the fact that the Separation Bill has passed through both Houses. The news is spreading quickly, and I shall be unable to restrain the people –" Here Augustus Frederick coughed, as though *he* would like to add something, when Mr La Trobe quizzically remarked "The Bill is incomplete until it has the Royal Sign Manual." Nevertheless, he gave the required permission to celebrate that night, and the mayor scuttled off to light his private bonfire which is to be the signal for general jubilation.

12th

The Prince's Bridge to be opened on Friday; the ball to take place on this day fortnight.

13th

Another sitting from Charlie, but not a good likeness. Indeed, I fear the excitement of the Separation doings has had an unsettling effect upon me. Also, Master Charlie himself has grown restive since he heard that a royal salute is to be fired at one o'clock, and jumped about like a mad thing when his papa invited him to come and "see the smoke!" Arrangements for the illuminations are well in hand, stands are being built, and a hundredweight of candles has been ordered from Jackson and Rae's, and now it is whispered abroad that one of the Bishop's men-servants has composed an ode – or is it only a congratulatory address? – to be read to "The First Governor of Victoria".

14th

A sitting from Charlie, who has assumed the airs of a man-about-town since he was allowed to eat the mustard Mr Bell had put upon his plate!

16th

A day full of surprises and excitement. At 6 a.m. the saxhorn band began to play a reveillée outside "The Châlet": a performance which had been kept secret even from Mr La Trobe himself, who now appeared in a flowered dressing-gown, straining his eyes at the window. He held my sleeve while some of the gentlemen put down their horns to sing "Hark, Hark the Lark!" in a key that was too high for them; yet it sounded better than the French *aubade* which immediately followed. After this they recovered their instruments and gave us stirring polka tunes, although poor Madame, who had one of her neuralgic headaches, would gladly have forgone that part of the programme. Mr La Trobe then walked out on to the veranda to put an end to the music, but with the opposite effect, for, no sooner did the performers behold him, than they joined, some with voices, some with saxhorns, in a tremendous rendition of the national anthem. His Honour bowed, and they would have gone through it again had I not led him into the house . . . . So they marched away, still playing polkas.

Upset by the saxhorn band, and fearful of any cannonading, Mrs La Trobe appointed me her deputy at the opening of the bridge, an arrangement hardly completed, when Mr Edward Bell blew a bugle to announce his arrival in a carriage and pair.

Behold me now, equipped in Madame's black satin polonaise jacket, trimmed with Australian swansdown (a present from Mr Cowper, of Sydney), and my own grey silk bonnet! The Superintendent, having first of all handed me into the carriage, entered it himself followed by Agnes, Nellie, Cecile, Charlie, and Mademoiselle Beguine. Adolphe de Meuron sat on the box, beside Mr Bell, and thus snugly packed together, we came to the Treasury, where Mr Bell changed places with His Honour who drove us, more slowly than his predecessor, to the corner of Swanston and Collins streets, and thence, after a view of the procession, to our proper stand – beside the Bishop's barouche – in front of the Prince of Wales Hotel. From this point of vantage, we had a clear sight of the hill, with its tent and a few field-pieces, opposite, while constantly moving banners, very small in the distance, glittered and went out again, according as the phalanxes changed places in the sun. Horsemen had hard work to keep onlookers from trespassing on the field, and we witnessed many rushes, but none which broke the line. For want of control, the cheering was ragged, and, no doubt, if the two lots of instrumentalists that followed the saxhorn band had been more *d'accord*, the music would have been better.

At 12 a.m. Mademoiselle Beguine, who had been observing the hill through her *lunette d'approche*, exclaimed that she saw smoke, and, on the instant, there arose a prodigious noise of guns, the signal for us to set out for the bridge. Mr La Trobe gathered up the reins and we proceeded at a majestic pace until we reached the middle of the arch, 75 feet from either bank; here His Honour stopped, and merely saying "I declare Prince's Bridge open", drove to the opposite side. During our progress thither, we were passed by a procession of Freemasons, and each man, as he went forward, ducked his head to "Madame", whose double in the black satin jacket replied with the most gracious salaams. At the summit of the hill, Mr La Trobe alighted, and, standing by the flap of the tent, spoke a few words suitable to the occasion. Mayor Nicholson said something supplementary, after which the Superintendent proposed the Queen's health, this being drunk off in small ale drawn from a barrel under a cart where it had been placed to keep cool.

His Honour then returned to us, and we accompanied him (walking) to the Botanic Gardens, where two thousand buns were distributed to children of all denominations; deduct from these, two begged by Mr Eyre Williams for his little boy, and one each to Charlie, Cecile, and Nellie La Trobe.

Mademoiselle and myself were so hungry, we felt we could have eaten the whole two thousand between us!

The Superintendent drove us back to Jolimont, Charlie beside him, carrying the ceremonial sword. On the journey, a few spots of rain made me anxious on account of Madame's best jacket which had already been stickied by Nellie's saved-up bun. Then, when we arrived at "The Châlet", the wind blew through the house, throwing the doors open, and the children made so much noise shutting them again that poor Mrs La Trobe retired to her bed. The servants were still absent, but the gardener's old helping-man, who had stayed at home, brought in a round of beef with vegetables, and on these we dined *en famille*, most heartily.

17th

Yesterday's procession is said to have been three miles long, and Mr La Trobe estimates the number of people assembled on the hill at twenty thousand. (Mr J.B. Were informs me that a ship was to sail from London on August 10, by which time the Act of Separation would probably have received the royal signature.)

James Smith

[SOME MELBOURNE RITUALS]

Thursday 1 January

Last night the bones of Burke & Wills were deposited in their metallic coffins. The skull of Wills & feet of both had disappeared. Burke's skull a very fine one. In taking a cast of it some of the teeth dropped out which I procured. The woollen shirt of Wills still hung in tatters round his ribs. Mrs Dogherty (Burke's nurse) who had "stretched" his father & his mother, performed the last sad office for her darling, wrapping the cere-cloth round his bones & placing a little pillow beneath his skull. The room (the Royal Society's Hall) hung with black & dimly lit, with a catafalque & baldacchino in the centre, had a sombre & solemn effect. Wrote a species of requiem for performance at the Theatre Royal on the evening of the funeral. To the Exhibition of Fine Arts. The best local pictures are the "Weatherboard Falls" by E. von Guerard, a Canadian lake scene by M. Sonntag, and "Tea Trees & Creepers" by N. Chevalier, whose "Waterfall on the Parker River" has many fine points about it. But, alas for art in this colony! Guerard – the ablest, most conscientious & most industrious of the painters told me that his whole earnings last year were only £120 – less than the wages of any artisan. To the Theatre Royal in the evening – Akhurst's pantomime. Introduction very tolerable. Scenery poor. Chas Young as an oriental Dundreary excellent. Sang a clever burlesque of "Piff Paff" (Riff-Raff); the ballet girls have a clever imitation of the Maoris. *Toute pensée traduite en personnages et en action*, says Auguste Vacquerie, *est drame, dans le sens large du mot*.

Friday 2 January

To the Princess's last night – "Wives as they Were", and the "Conjugal Lesson". Jefferson's drunken man is one of the best I have ever seen on any stage. The dull lack-lustre eye, the immobility of the mouth, the thickness of utterance, the limpness of limbs, the maudlin tones of the voice, the confusion of time, place & person in the memory, the dim sense of humour lighting up the foggy condition of his mind generally, the vague motion of the hands & the imbecile good humour of the man, are points of detail, each of which challenges a separate tribute of admiration. One special merit of Jefferson's acting is that he is absorbed in & by the character he sustains for the time being. To quote a favourite expression of his own, he never "travels out of the picture". He appears to be unconscious of the presence of an audience, & therefore never plays at them. When he is not taking an active part in the business of a scene, he fixes his eyes on those who are speaking, and does not endeavour to divert attention from them, or to defraud them of their legitimate applause, by the introduction of impertinent bye-play. In addition to which, he is scrupulous in "giving the stage" to the principals in the dialogue.

* * *

Wednesday 21 January

Public funeral of Burke & Wills. All business suspended. The procession about a mile in length, started from the Hall of the Royal Society, passing through Spring Street, Bourke St & Elizabeth Street to the new Cemetery. The footpaths lined with spectators, who also clustered on the housetops, on the awnings, at the windows, on cars, coaches, carriages & wagons, & wherever a view of the cortege could be obtained. From all the suburbs of Melbourne, & from the country districts people had been pouring in all the morning, & I should compute the number of persons who witnessed the imposing spectacle at not less than one hundred thousand. I rode in the same mourning coach with Bourke's [sic] foster mother, Mrs Dogherty, & the survivor of the Expedition, John King. In the evening, at a crowded meeting in St George's Hall, the Governor presented the addresses I had written, to Ambrose Kyte, Commander Norman & Alfred Howitt. Dr Macadam made a successful speech vindicatory of the Committee. He was denied a hearing at first; but eventually carried the audience completely with him, & was congratulated by the Governor, the Chief Justice & the Bishop in having rehabilitated the reputation of the body to which he had acted as Hon. Secretary. At the Theatre Royal, a Musical Ode on the death of Burke & Wills, written by myself, & admirably set to music by Mr Reiff was sung by the company in mourning, Madame Lucy Escott, Miss Hodson, Mr Squires & Mr Wharton taking the solos. It was followed up by a tawdry *tableau vivant*, which had been better omitted. At the Haymarket, Richard Younge declaimed a Monody written by Dr Bowman, illustrated by *tableaux vivants*.

Thursday 29 January

A complete fiasco at the Theatre Royal. A young lady named Young whose appearance had been heralded by mysteriously worded puffs, made her debut as Amina, in "Sonnambula". Her voice was painfully thin, her execution tolerable, her action awkward, her stature short, & the experiment an utter failure. The house was crowded in every part, & at the end of the First Act, there was such a manifestation of displeasure as a Melbourne audience rarely indulges in. At length the Manager came forward & made an apologetic conciliatory speech, in which he stated that the young lady was an Australian (Farquharson says she was born in London) that he was induced to give her an appearance by the recommendation of some gentlemen who heard her at rehearsal, and concluded by soliciting a hearing for her in the next Act. This was accorded, but from what I heard in the course of ten minutes, it was apparent that her presentation to the public was a ludicrous mistake.

* * *

Thursday 5 February

Placed the correspondence in Aspinall's hands. To Lyndhurst in the evening to dine with Barden. The other guests consisted of Messrs Sasse, Duigan, Teale & Labertouche. After dinner our conversation happened to turn upon the sensual extravagancies of Martley (Solicitor General in a former Administration, who is married to a charming woman – a niece of Chas. Lever's). On one occasion Martley is said to have been found dancing, naked, in a brothel, surrounded by prostitutes. On another he gave the wretched inmate of one of those houses, situated in a right of way off Bourke Street, a cheque, which was dishonoured. The women of the house took away his clothes, & he was a prisoner for two or three days, until a brother barrister sent him a suit & released him. Someone observing that such a man ought to be castrated, Duigan said that he knew a lady (née Kate Featherstone) who, having detected her husband, a Major in the army, in an act of infidelity, actually excised his penis with a razor, from which he nearly lost his life. Sasse said that while he was residing at Montpellier a similar circumstance came to his knowledge. In this case a young girl had been seduced by & lived with a young man, to whom she became passionately attached. But on the eve of his marriage with another woman, his former paramour induced him to sleep with her & she performed the same horrible operation with the same weapon. After having thus mutilated him, she announced her willingness to marry him. He took her at word, & she became a most devoted wife.

* * *

Sunday 15 February

Dined at O'Shanassy's with H.W. [W.H.] Archer, Hugh Glass, P. Higgins, Quinlan, Julian Woods, Father Finn etc. Discussed the project of an Australian Quarterly Review, drawing its contributors from the whole of the Colonies in this group, circulating among all & endeavouring to build up a sound & healthy public opinion to discuss problems of political & social science with breadth and vigour, and to serve as a bond of union among the first class literary & scientific men in Australia. Woods, Archer & I offered to give our services for a year. Conversation turning on the approaching visit of Prince Alfred, the foundation of an Australian kingdom, with Prince Alfred as its sovereign was debated. O'S strongly in favour of monarchical institutions; observing that our future choice lay between them & petty ephemeral republics. We were rich enough & populous enough to constitute an independent kingdom, and the creation of a Court & aristocracy, surrounded with the elegancies of civilised life would have the effect of rendering the colonies more attractive both to those who are already here & to those we are desirous of alluring hither. The only difficulty anticipated was the agreement of the other colonies, seeing that Melbourne from its position & other circumstances would naturally claim to be the capital of the kingdom, and the seat of the Court & Legislature.

Tuesday 17 February

Aspinall tells me that the brothels of this city are under a police surveillance not altogether dissimilar to that which is practised in Paris. They are classified and those in which the visitors are liable to be robbed are carefully discriminated from those which are conducted on "respectable" principles. In some cases the prostitutes are serviceable as thief-takers, giving information to the police when notorious bushrangers & others pay them a visit. Captain Standish – my informant adds – is furnished with a report every morning of the number & the names of those who have spent the night in the better class of brothels. The record must be a curious one and calculated to lift the veil from the secret immoralities of many of the outwardly moral & respectable.

* * *

Tuesday 21 April

Parliament re-assembled. Duffy mentioned a smart repartee of Mr Moore one of the Irish members in the Imperial Parliament, who, referring to the dissensions among his own countrymen, quoted the current saying that if one Irishman was being roasted alive, you would always find another to turn the spit. An Opposition Irish member interrupted him by some inaudible ejaculation; whereupon he exclaimed "What was that? I didn't catch the remark of the honorable turnspit." The House roared. Another anecdote of Archbishop Whately who, at the time the Whigs were filling all the offices in Ireland with Catholics, was consulted by the Lord Lieutenant as to the most fitting man to appoint to a vacant bishopric. "Couldn't you find a respectable Caro-tholic?" was the sarcastic query of the Protestant prelate.

Introduced to Deniehy, of Sydney, one of the ugliest men I ever saw, short of stature, slovenly in attire, with unkempt hair, a fluffy moustache, small eyes obliquely set, very near his nose, & generally half close, & eyebrows rising diagonally from the root of his nose. Altogether his countenance resembled that of a withered monkey. Completed "Duke's Motto" and handed Fifth Act over to Kyte.

Tuesday 19 May

Festivities in honour of the marriage of the Prince of Wales to the Princess Alexandra of Denmark. A steady rain until 2 p.m. when it cleared up until midnight. The city and suburbs gay with garlands, triumphal arches, flags, banners and greenery. At night a brilliant illumination, the streets thronged with spectators, & the general effect impressive if not imposing. Transparencies innumerable were exhibited, & tons of Chinese crackers must have been exploded. In the Chinese quarter, in Little Bourke Street, so incessant was the discharge that it resembled a sustained fire of musketry, & was accompanied by the beating of gongs, tom-toms, & all sorts of discordant instruments. From the roof of the Library, the *coup d'œil* was magnificent. All Melbourne & its belt of suburbs, was visible. Bonfires were kindled on Mount Macedon, the You Yangs, Plenty Ranges, and at other points on the horizon, & showers of rockets were sent up from the Botanical Reserve. Coloured fires were burnt on the roof of the Melbourne Club, the Bank of Australasia & other elevated sites; two huge "A"s flamed in front of the University; a gigantic cross of light sparkled in front of St Patrick's & St Francis's Cathedrals; & a huge cresset blazed at the unfinished tower of the former. Looking down Bourke St the sight was very animated. The yellow light gleamed upon a dense mass of upturned faces, reaching from Spring Street to Queen Street, and through the midst of the crowd slowly wound a serpentine line of carriages, each with its pair of lamps, & looking, in the mass, like a monstrous snake with luminous scales. In most of the suburbs, oxen were roasted whole, & barrels of beer set flowing; while the poor and the inmates of the charitable institutions were universally regaled.

Thursday 28 May

Governor's Ball at the Exhibition Building

Frazer MLA got very drunk & on the way home quarreled [sic] with a cabman, who called in the police. He abused these as being either orangemen or papists, O'Shanassy's spies or Standish's pets. Eventually he was taken to the watch house, but was liberated on his own recognisances. About daybreak, accompanied by Dr Macadam, he knocked up the Mayor (E. Cohen) and entreated him to take the charge off the charge sheet. Upon the Mayor refusing to adopt such an illegal course, Frazer shed maudlin tears of penitence, wiped his greasy face with a skull cap (which he pulled out of his pocket instead of a hand kerchief) and presented a most ludicrously woebegone appearance; being half sober, and wholly dirty and demoralised in appearance. What makes his escapade the more amusing is that he is Chairman of a Legislative Committee, now sitting, to inquire into & report upon the organisation, discipline & management of the Police Force.

* * *

Friday 14 August

Kyte related to me an episode of colonial life. Some weeks ago a young lady called at his office to enquire if he had any rooms to let in Bourke Street, suitable for opening a school. Interested by the applicant he questioned her pretty closely & found that she possessed good testimonials; that she had been a governess in Sydney, where she was engaged to be married to a respectable young man, who died of disease of the heart a few days before the time appointed for their wedding. Her health & spirits having been shattered by this shock, she was recommended to come round to Melbourne, where she had formerly lived & where she hoped to obtain an engagement as a governess. Disappointed in this expectation, she was induced to apply to Mr Kyte, who having satisfied himself of the truth of her story, told her to call at his office for a weekly stipend, until she could obtain employment. A month afterwards, when confidence had been established between them, she told her benefactor that when she first called upon him she was penniless, had pawned all her spare articles of clothing, had been turned out of doors by her landlady, & had been without food for two days. She had therefore determined on committing suicide, but some vague impulse had induced her to apply to him. "What a glorious thing money is!" said Kyte repeating the incident to me. "I never felt so proud & thankful as when I found out that I had stept in between that poor creature and destruction."

Wednesday 21 October

To Guerard's in the evening. Good story of a Mr Horden who was the first to take cattle overland to Adelaide. Being looked upon as a great gun, he was invited to Government House, but was so much immersed in the business objects of his journey, that when Governor Gawler, at dinner, happened to inquire "What will you take, Mr Horden?" he replied, "Fourteen-ten a head all round & the calves thrown in."

Wednesday 11 November

The Governor declines to give his patronage to a performance at the Theatre Royal, for the benefit of the Benevolent Asylum, because Barry Sullivan is opposing Chas Kean, who, as the protégée of the Duke of Newcastle, Secretary of State for the Colonies, is necessarily an object of interest to a colonial governor.

After the first night of the Keans' appearance at the Haymarket, when the audience was neither excessive in number, nor immoderate in its enthusiasm, Mrs Kean observed to Coppin: – "If I were Ellen Tree, I would play once more, to complete the education of the people, & return to England forthwith."

Thursday 12 November

Gave some readings from Copperfield to about 400 prisoners at Pentridge. I felt that I never read so well or succeeded more completely in carrying the audience with me. It was interesting to watch the effect of the pathetic passage descriptive of Mrs Copperfield's funeral on that congregation of felons. The most profound silence reigned – broken only by the "sniffing" of the attentive listeners. Numbers dropped their heads, & were touched with a sympathetic grief, & at the end there was a general blowing of noses & clearing of throats. The humorous passages they appeared to enjoy hugely.

* * *

Wednesday 16 December

After three days heavy & incessant rain, we experienced a devastating flood. The Yarra rose 37 ft 6 in above its ordinary level & all was ruin & consternation on its banks. Houses were swept away, trees uprooted & crops washed out of the earth. The rise was so sudden & so incredible that numbers of persons living on the banks of the river were unable to save their furniture. In my garden the water nearly reached the edge of the flower beds about two hundred feet distant from the ordinary banks. A wide waste of water swept from the Custom House to the sea & boats traversed the interval. Emerald Hill rose like an island from the flood. Traffic on the Hobson's Bay Railway was suspended & communication with St Kilda cut off, except by a circuitous route. Numbers of small farmers in the rich valley of Heidelberg were ruined by the calamity; & market gardeners, brick makers & felmongers on the banks of the Yarra suffered severely by the inundation.

AN IMPRESSIONIST EXHIBITION

Such an exhibition of impressionist memoranda as will be open today at Buxton's Art Gallery, by Messrs Roberts, Conder, Streeton, and others fails to justify itself. It has no adequate *raison d'être*. It is as if a dramatist should give a performance on the stage of such scraps of dialogue, hints of character, ideas for incidents, and suggestions of situations as had occurred to him while pondering over the construction of a play, or as if a musician should invite people to listen to crude and disconnected scraps of composition, containing the vaguely indicated themes for a cantata, a symphony, or an opera; or as if a sculptor should ask us to inspect certain masses of marble from which he had just blocked out the amorphous outlines of various pieces of statuary. None of these is to be regarded as a work of art. Neither is a painter's "impression". It is simply a record in colour of some fugitive effect which he sees, or professes to see, in nature. But, like primeval chaos, "it is without form and void". To the executant it seems spontaneous and forcible. To the spectator it appears grotesque and meaningless. The earliest impressionist of whom we have any knowledge was Piero di Cosimo, and he had "a bee in his bonnet". Vasari tells us that "he would sometimes stand beside a wall against which various impurities were cast, and from these he would image forth the most singular scenes, combats of horses, strangely ordered cities, and the most extraordinary landscapes that ever were seen". The modern impressionist asks you to see pictures in splashes of colour, in slap-dash brush work, and in sleight-of-hand methods of execution leading to the proposition of pictorial conundrums, which would baffle solution if there were no label or catalogue. In an exhibition of paintings you naturally look for pictures; instead of which the impressionist presents you with a varied assortment of palettes. Of the 180 exhibits catalogued on the present occasion, something like four-fifths are a pain to the eye. Some of them look like faded pictures seen through several mediums of thick gauze; others suggest that a paint-pot has been accidentally upset over a panel nine inches by five; others resemble the first essays of a small boy, who has just been apprenticed to a house-painter; whilst not a few are as distressing as the incoherent images which float through the mind of a dyspeptic dreamer. Here is an impression, for example, entitled "Harrowing", which is quite true to its title. It represents a long-legged pig in company with two terribly deformed horses – or are they "creatures of the slime?" – struggling to get away from one of those scarecrows, which English farmers set up in their cornfields when the grain is ripening, and dislocating their legs – number uncertain – in the process. And here is a mystery, called "The Milky Way", consisting of two or three spots of positive colours on what appears to be a sheet of smoked brown paper. Here, again, is something bearing the title of "Orange, Blue and White", representing a hydrocephalus doll, with glass eyes, wooden hands and a broken nose, almost buried in a mass of white-lead. And there are landscapes and samples of architecture, belonging to some embryotic world, in which, as Pandulph says, "All form is formless, order orderless", and nature herself is either unshapen or misshapen. Some of the impressions, in which sufficient work has been put to entitle them to be spoken of as sketches, show that the artists are capable of much better things. Such is the clever "Looking over to Williamstown" of Mr R. E. Falls; the "Fisherman's Bend", "Evening in Richmond Paddock", and "Austral Summer", of Mr A. Streeton; the "Treasury", "Early and Damp", "Good-bye", and "Going down to Dinner", of Mr Tom Roberts; the "Dear Lady Disdain" and "Myosotis", of Mr Charles Conder, and the plastic sketches of Mr C.D. Richardson. These and a few others afford something agreeable for the eye to rest upon; but the exhibition, viewed as a whole, would leave a very painful feeling behind it, and cause one to despond with respect to the future of art in this colony, did we not believe, with Mr W. P. Frith, R.A., that "Impressionism is a craze of such ephemeral character as to be unworthy of serious attention."

J.S. James

THE CUP DAY – 1876

The Eve of "The Cup"

The gathering and festivities in honour of the Melbourne Cup are totally unlike anything else I have seen in the world. The show seems to me to be a mixture of a Fourth of July celebration, *Mardi Gras*, an Italian carnival, the Derby and Goodwood Race meetings, and the Agricultural Show at Islington. No purely race meeting in England will compare with it. The Derby is a mighty gathering, one of the grandest sights in the world; but Epsom is too remote from London to allow of the races there affecting that great centre in the manner "the Cup" festival takes hold of every part, and nearly every inhabitant, of Melbourne. The show on the Lawn may be said to resemble that at Goodwood; but there the meeting is attended chiefly by the upper ten thousand, and "the people" are in a minority. Cup Day here is not only a great sporting feast, it is a fashionable *fête* and public and national holiday, and its importance is intensified by the presence of the Governors and chief citizens of neighbouring colonies. It is a rejoicing unique in all its aspects, which Victorians may well be proud of.

For the past week a strong element of *rus in urbe* has been seen in the streets of Melbourne. The intercolonial and coasting steamers have been crowded. From the country districts, railroads and coaches have discharged their living freights. Besides ostensible pleasure-seekers, a large number of people have informed the partners of their cares and joys that they have a "little business down in

Melbourne". Such is the duplicity of man! The accommodation at the principal hotels is severely taxed, and young men from the country, carpet-bag in hand, were on Monday to be seen wandering about the streets in search of convenient or economical lodgings. The price of bed and board has risen considerably at minor taverns, whose proprietors wish to make their golden hay during the sunshine of custom of the race week. I am told, however, that this year the supply of accommodation is quite equal to the demand. The amount of bad liquor consumed during the past few days must have been enormous. At every public place, and in every private family, "horse" was talked. The Cup fever had seized on all Melbourne. From the vice-regal palace to the home of the artisan on Collingwood Flat, or rookery in Little Bourke Street, the one leading topic of conversation was, "who will win?" Something of this may be seen in London before the Derby, but the excitement there is very superficial. At clubs, places of business, and public resorts, people talk about the favourite because it is considered to be the thing, but the majority know nothing at all about a horse, and never bet. In Victoria, where sport, as well as work, seems the natural heritage of all (and I am thankful it is so), many really know something about the merits of horses, and take more than a mere cursory interest in racing. Perhaps, to a majority, the Cup Day is only a pleasant outing, but in this respect, I think, not to the same proportion as at the English Derby. Everyone, too, from the Governor to children at school, appears to have some interest in the race in respect of bets or sweepstakes. This is really a gambling community; men, women, and children seem to be affected alike, all wishing to back a horse or take a chance in a "sweep". On this occasion, and for once in a while, I am not going to quarrel with the popular folly. Because I am virtuous, I cannot and would not deprive the masses of "cakes and ale". Besides, backing one's opinion with a friend is a different thing to making a trade of betting, either as a bookmaker or owner of racehorses.

On Monday night Melbourne seemed given up to pleasure. It is true that, besides the life and motion in the principal streets, there was also a glare of light from shop windows, kept open until a late hour to catch the country custom. Even in the suburbs the stores did not close until midnight, and a considerable trade was done in white hats, veils, and fancy scarfs, the colours of the popular favourites. But I am afraid the outlay in gas did not in all cases meet with a sufficient return. The hotels and drinking establishments, however, did a roaring trade. This is a thirsty generation, and the beverages in vogue are not those recommended by the Total Abstinence Society. In this respect, the provision made in Melbourne is quite astonishing. In some quarters of London gin palaces are thick; my recollections of Hamburg are, that in certain streets every other establishment was a *café* or *gasthaus*; in the Bowery, New York, lager-beer cellars are numerous; but, in proportion to the population, I should imagine that in Melbourne there are more licensed drinking places than in any other large city in the world. In these, on the eve of the Cup Day, our country cousin was very conspicuous. The places of amusement were crowded, the presence of the trio of Governors at the Academy of Music attracting the upper ten thousand – or rather five hundred – of the colony. But the Theatre Royal, Opera House, and St George's Hall were equally attractive; and the Circus, the Boxing Match at the Princess's Theatre, and Mr Roberts's billiard-playing, "fetched" the less artistic and more sporting of the visitors. At the Albion, Goyder's, Garton's, and Tattersall's, the conversation was all about the Cup, and the "great pot" upset by the defeat of Newminster. In "the rooms" there was, so to speak, joy in Israel, the settling over the Derby putting thousands in the pockets of the members of the ring. Newminster, three days ago the hope of the backers and the feared of the layers of odds, the "grandest horse ever foaled in Australia", was now scorned by everyone – none would do him reverence. Mr Frank Dakin sustained a great deal of chaff. The fact of his tasting every drop of water before the horse drank was now held to be a capital joke. The revolver and bulldog business was excellent fooling. Mr Graham Mitchell was jubilant. Never mind, Mr Dakin, you did your work well; caution is always praiseworthy in a trainer, and you know your world. However, I was sorry to hear loudly-uttered suspicions by many outsiders of the good faith of late transactions at Point Cook. One gentleman from the country was very irate. "All that rot about the horse being poisoned, and the pistol business," said he, "I don't believe in it. The stable knew the horse had gone amiss, and they kept up all that secrecy, deceiving the public. Fools went on backing him, and the stable 'got out', and didn't lose so much after all. The public suffers, as usual." Now, I cannot say that I believe this; still I know that, in England, many like transactions have happened. It is one example of the ethics of the ring; and an instance of the decadence of the standard of honour induced by that institution which I have before lamented. If Sir Hercules Robinson can purify the Turf of New South Wales, he will do a far greater work than the useful sanitary exploit of his namesake.

As the night wore on the places of amusement disgorged their thousands, and everywhere there was a rush to the bars. Hansom cabs rattled up Collins Street to the club, which presented an unwonted lively appearance. Waiters and Hebes put on many airs, and would scarcely deign to serve anyone who had not the appearance of "a squatter", owning a few million sheep. I am afraid that, on the whole, Melbourne was not a moral city on Monday night. Certain supper-rooms, and the "saddling-paddocks" and the vestibules of the theatres, were crowded. The bars in these latter were open until midnight, the "paddocks" having put on fresh paint for the occasion. Many gentlemen explored the purlieus of Little Bourke Street, the Chinese quarter being quite a mine of wealth to certain police officers and detectives during the Cup week. I received a written invitation to join one of these parties, a dubious sort of compliment. At most of the principal hotels betting and drinking went on until a late hour in the morning, but wise men retired to bed early. Walking homeward along Bourke Street, I saw many sights which it is prudent not to record here. It is well that, after midnight, the proceedings of many of our country cousins should be carefully veiled. I am sure they will suffer enough from the amount of abominable drink they have concealed; why should I moralise over them?

The *Bulletin*

A CENTENNIAL ORATION

The undermentioned speeches will probably not be delivered at any Centennial banquet in New South Wales, or, if delivered, they will certainly not be reported by the slavish daily Press. For this reason they are printed here in advance, and when deep answers unto deep in the great ocean of lies and sycophancy, and New South Wales goes mad over the Centenary of its first gaol and its first gallows, we trust that at least a few genuine Democrats will try to forget the anniversary of a loathsome tyranny, and spare a thought for the day which Australia ought to celebrate.

The Day We Celebrate

On this 26th of January the people of New South Wales will be called upon to jubilate. This is as it should be. In this the "authorities", as in the past hundred years, arrange the festival and "command" the obedient enthusiasm of a nation of serfs. The 26th of January is the gala-day of Officialism – the ragamuffin stands without, cap in hand, to cheer a docile approval when the hired band within the banqueting chamber plays "God save the Queen" to the first toast on the list. One hundred years ago Governor PHILLIP landed in the little bight whereon now stands the city of Sydney. He named the cove after a viscount; the curse of official patronage began with the baptism of the settlement. He found "a fine run of fresh water stealing silently through a thick wood". The wood has vanished, the stream still flows, but polluted, subterranean and noxious. This is typical of our progress from the date of that eventful landing down to the present day. Our early history would disgrace the annals of an Ashantee sultan. The pages are stained with blood, with cruel, deliberate, but judicial murder. They smell of the gaol; they are marked with the rust-prints of gyves; they are bruised and branded with the lash. The day of the Centenary should also be the day of Atonement. The rulers of New South Wales – the administrative chain-gang of history which hands down the hated traditions and perpetuates the hideous memories of the past – not the people, should upon this day mourn fasting, with their hands upon their rotten hearts, like to those doomed ones in the dreadsome Hall of Eblis. Of the long list of the representatives of England's majesty and greatness is there one whose name is worth preserving from its fated oblivion? Not one! And what a list! From puling PHILLIP to society-leading CARRINGTON there is not a man who has for "his" colony done as much good as poor old Dr LANG, who, with all his aberrations of intellect, was a whole-souled, single-hearted, though somewhat eccentric hero. One hundred years are past, and we are still the fettered bondsmen of the taskmasters put in authority over us. And the fetters are the more galling inasmuch as they are not now in all cases so tangible. Those who rank as statesmen, like the officers of the ancient convict-guarding New South Wales corps, look across the ocean for preferment, and tyrannise over their fellows for a puppet-decorating gewgaw from the hands of those who keep watch over the sycophant-rewarding smiles of Royalty. In Sydney itself, that hallowed spot upon which first pressed the foot of manacled man, where first the dusky child of the forest heard the musical clink of the law-abiding leg-iron and the "whish" of the skin-abrading cat; in Sydney itself, in this lotus-land of loveliness, poverty is not unknown; in this God-given stretch of luxurious prosperity, this smiling, milk-blessed and honey-benisoned paradise, men have actually died of want. Here, on this historic ground, where first was poured that sacred libation of civilised and Christianised rum, nigh upon a hundred years ago, thousands have but recently gathered, and besought the red-tape Officialdom that brought them hither for work, or the coarsest fare that would keep aflame the spark of life. We have much to be thankful for. Where PHILLIP landed white men have had to fight with coolies and with Chinamen for the drudgery that will enable them to gain the pittance that buys the bread of dependence, while the descendants of those same historic rulers are quietly and luxuriously enjoying the unquestioned possession of noble stretches of the people's land. New South Wales has never been wholly emancipated. She drags a broken fetter at her heel. It was attempted to change the character of the settlement from bond to free by simply diverting the stream of convicts which once flowed into Sydney Cove. But the system remained unchanged. The old Officialdom, the men whose cradles were rocked to the tune the lash played on a man's bare back, whose infant rattle was a hand-cuff, whose teething pad was the link of a leg-iron; these were retained. One of the Chief Justices of the colony was ex-Attorney-General of a neighbouring penal settlement in its worst days of brutal tyranny. His son, bred in the atmosphere of Convictism, sits on the Bench of the Supreme Court. The gallows was one of the earliest institutions in the colony. It still thrives luxuriantly on the soil made rich by the spilt blood of judicial victims. It is said that among the first hangings on New South Wales soil was a boy of 17. We cling fondly to these loved traditions of our past. Only a year before this Centennial period we hanged two boys of that age and two but a couple of years older. We did it, too, as a blood-offering to the New Year. These early judges and gaolers were humorous men, and their spirit survives. The lash was also one of the earliest, if not one of the most popular, of English imports. We have been compelled to take many a hated institution from England during 100 years, but the lash was very salutary. We have been brought up under it. We have been flogged like the blackfellow's "gin" to "make us good". We ought to be very good! Spare the rod and spoil the child! Can it be possible that we should be spoiled after all that was done in loving kindness to reclaim our fathers? They used to drive them to church in those early days. Now they put the screw on with the same intent, albeit in a different fashion. The door of Science is slammed in the faces of the people, and a PROCTOR is commanded not to preach the Gospel of Nature, because it is the "Commandant's" desire that the "Sabbath" be not broken. A free man dare not moisten his lips on the day sacred to Cant, lest the ghost of some defunct convict chaplain be outraged. The "authorites" have a great admiration for the folk-lore of their prison-walled past. They strove to celebrate the last Christmas by flogging a man, and would have done so as in the good old times, but a legal technicality interfered, and the grand and antiquated ceremony somehow fell through, much to the disappointment, no doubt, of those same guardians of law and order. It was spoken of in the Legislature, too, that one judicial tiger recommended a man in prison to submit to a hideous mutilation, and in this free colony of New South Wales now celebrating its glorious hundredth birthday, fiends could be found to applaud. Women, hell-hags, fit to be the mothers of such a Caliban-begotten brood, smacked filth-stained lips with unction over the proposal. Some of these women will one day give birth to the men on whom we rely to hand down the splendid traditions of our proud heroic past. New South Wales has statesmen! – alas! that it should be so; would she had none – men who trail their country's honour in the dust, and solicit our alms with the unblushing effrontery of a courtesan. One of her "statesmen" recently quoted New South Wales as the "mother of civilisation in this part of the world." Unfortunately, it is true. New South Wales is the "mother of civilisation in this part of the world", and the word "civilisation" carries with it all those horrible associations of gyves, and gallows, and gaols – sycophany and lying toadyism, robber speculation and commercial theft, ignorant proletarians and remorseless labour-swindlers; rum and ruin and retribution. The 26th of January 1888, is a fitting conclusion to a disgraceful and crime-saturated period. It began with crime and crime stalks through it redhanded to the last hour of its blood-stained continuance. The sins of those it was sought to punish, and the tenfold more loathsome crimes of the gutter-fiends who acted as their gaolers, have eaten upward, and now with awful vengeance find a fertile breeding-place in the very hearts of the rulers of this people. Honesty is openly laughted to scorn; corruption rules in high places; the cardinal virtues are assessed at the rate of interest they will return; political purity was sunk outside the Heads many years ago, and there is no one left to mourn its death; the marketable vices fetch 200 per cent. in the stock exchange – usurer's ordinary interest – and the man most prominently connected with the history of the colony during the latter part of its first century is, fittingly enough, its Premier on its hundredth birthday. Beneath his rule we have written our name down on the annals of the world's progress in characters of shame and folly. At the end of his political life he brought all his power and craft and cunning to bear in order to fetter us to a policy of war and Imperial intrigue. This Machiavelli essayed also to celebrate this day of festivity and jubilation by a political burglary, and attempted to filch the common property of the Continent in order to ornament with an honoured, but rifled, name the period of his own dictatorship. This man, whom one of his own followers most appropriately describes as a "CAESAR of sand", displays his competence for the management of the affairs and finances of the country, whose misfortune it is to be ruled by him, by mismanaging and squandering his own, and at the close of a life of imbecile and spendthrift extravagance is saved from insolvency – for the third or fourth time – by the dole wrung by threats from unwilling civil servants, schoolchildren, and workmen of the humblest class slaving for a food-wage on Government relief works. Fill high your glasses, rave loudly of your independence, of your prosperity, of the broad-spreading future of the golden years fading away into the roseate mist of poetic farness; "let the kettle to the trumpet speak, the trumpet to the cannoneer without, the cannons to the heavens, the heaven to the earth"; wreathe your heads with chaplets of flowers, gorge like the Choctaws of the forest upon costly viands, swill like the Vikings of old of the red sparkling wine; let eyes flash with rapture and pulses thrill with delirium, until, like CIRCE'S hogs, you are happy in bestial enchantment – the salves echo among the tree-clad hills of Sydney Harbour, the glasses clink, the champagne gurgles down the throats of the fools who shout "Hurrah!" They did all just this 100 years ago!

The Day We Ought to Celebrate

On the 3rd December 1854, not 34 years ago, a deed was done, the influence of which in some genuine Australian hearts is felt today, and will be felt by increasing numbers for many days and many years to come. Whilst New South Wales was hanging boys and flogging virtue into the hides of hardened criminals, its young southern neighbour was springing forward with a wondrous nascent vigour in a race for first place, and the fondly self-styled "mother colony" was speedily left lagging in the rear. It has not yet caught up, though its age is three times that of its rival, and the area of its territory four. New South Wales brags loudly of the aid she has extended to her sister States, forgetting that the moribund institutions which she has patronisingly bestowed upon them have in nearly every instance been productive of wholesale trouble and acrid dissension. Is it necessary to cite the pro-convict faction fights of old Moreton Bay and the separation struggles of the past, or will that one instance of December 3, 1854 suffice? We all know its history; it is familiar as the names of the men who led the English van on Crispian's Day to those who fought at Agincourt. Victoria sprang into existence like Minerva, a perfect goddess clad in shimmering mail, fresh from the brain of Jupiter. There was no painful preliminary epoch of agony and death-torture. The convict-settlement notion of colonisation luckily failed through Judge-Advocate COLLINS' ignorance and impracticable red-tapeism. Victoria enjoyed a respite of 30 years. Then came a race of hardy adventurers, steady sturdy men with strong arms and a free look of liberty in their eyes. And New South Wales made haste to gather into the fold of official espionage the new-born settlement. Sydney's departmental under-strappers were despatched to keep the new outpost in regulation repair, and when Victoria grew too big to be governed from the vice-regal sentry-box at Botany Bay, England generously gave her a vice-regal sentry-box of her own, but of similar pattern, erected on the same plan, according to the same specifications, as that one overlooking the waters of Farm Cove. It answered for a little while, just so long – and no longer – as it took the new colony to assert itself, which it did on the 3rd December, 1854. When gold was found, all the brawn and brain of Europe flocked to the port of Melbourne. These were men who came in search of wealth 'tis true, but men who dared danger and death and loved adventurous enterprise, many of them, as much as they loved gold. They were not as the commercial thieves and titled spongers who visit the colonies in later degenerate days. These gold-searchers were the fathers of Victoria, and almost the first thing that happened after their multitudinous invasion was collision with the cut-and-dried system of government provided so generously by England and copied so slavishly from the fusty pattern furnished by the alleged "mother colony". The Victorian Legislative Council, composed partly of nominee and partly of presumedly-elected members, knew not the people – the diggers. Those sons of toil were not represented in the official-filled and squatter-bossed councils of the State. They paid an exorbitant fine for the privilege of working. They were hounded like dogs by the insolent brats who wore the Government uniform. Digger-hunting was huge sport. Miners were chained up by the 50 like a road-gang, and dragged to the police-court to be fined. Two days every week were devoted by the authorities to hunting for unlicensed diggers. By and by a man named SCOBIE was killed in a brawl at Ballarat, and his murderer was acquitted by the police magistrate who tried the case. The enraged diggers burnt down the assassin's hotel, and MACINTYRE, WESTERLY and FLETCHER were imprisoned for the act. A demand was made by their comrades for their release, and it was refused. The soldiers marched up from Melbourne to keep order and were harassed by the diggers who hung upon their trail. Then came the weekly hunt for unlicensed miners, with the red-coated rabble to support the police. The diggers resisted and enrolled themselves in a citizen army under the leadership of PETER LALOR, noblest of diggers and of opponents to the first manifestation of aggressive Imperialism in Victoria. On December 3, 1854 – the day we ought to celebrate – met this little representative Democracy and the paid bloodhounds of unjust authority. It was Sunday morning, the day upon which Officialism was wont to repair to church, and to pray with sycophanic snuffle for the evangelical replenishment of their most Sovereign Lady, QUEEN VICTORIA, and the prospering with all happiness of that multifarious entity euphemistically described in the church service of an obedient people, as "*all* the Royal Family". It was Sunday morning when a prayer was put up to Liberty by a digger, and the responses were sung by the rattle of side-arms and the whistle of death-dealing bullets. Two hundred and seventy-six men in the pay of a foreign power, including a strong body of cavalry, stole forward in the gray mist of morning to carry by assault the miner's frail embattlement. They fire alternately – the diggers and the docile instruments of military force. The men behind the stockade give a ringing cheer, and fire again. Then there is a dash on the part of the hirelings of authority and the first line of defence is crossed; the police rush the inner line, and uproot the flagstaff, and tear down the banner of rebellious Labour. On come the soldiers, close in the wake of the police, but Captain WISE, of the 40th, and Lieutenant PAUL, of the 12th Regiments, are wounded, the former mortally. The military rush headlong over the barricade, carrying the tiny redoubt at the point of the bayonet. But the insurgents behave gamely to the last. Thirty of them lie dead in the entrenchment, 125 are disabled, and taken prisoners; the district is placed under martial law, the tents of the diggers are burnt and razed to the ground. And all this happened while the good people of Melbourne were sleepily preparing to go to church, and pray for their Gracious Sovereign Lady, QUEEN VICTORIA! PETER LALOR, left for dead in the Eureka Stockade, escaped with the loss of his arm, and, like his lieutenants – VERN and BLACK – defied the cunning of the police, though a reward of £400 was offered for his capture, alive or dead. In the following year, Mr LALOR and Mr HUMFFRAY, also a rebellious miner, represented the Ballarat diggers in the Government of the country. The State had condoned rebellion, and was compelled to recognise the will of the people. Revolt is the parent of reform; and, though Eureka Stockade fades into insignificance when placed beside Bunker's Hill, the meaning and the impulse in each case of armed resistance were the same. In the dusky dawn, when the hired soldiers of Imperialism crept forward to take by storm the rude barricade erected by the insurgent citizens; when the ringing voice of LALOR thundered out upon the damp air of the morning; when, with the glistening dew beading their unshorn beards, the stalwart diggers gripped with brown hands or swung aloft with brawny naked arms the clubbed musket; then – then was heard in each heart an echo of the shot fired by the New England farmer which won a nation's freedom and gave mankind another lease of hope. Then was heard that voice in the crack of the miner's rifle that rang out in the lines of LANG when he wrote to EARL GREY with scathing invective, and warned him that for three years had that unwitting nobleman been knocking at the gates of Futurity for the President of the United States of Australia. The spirit of LALOR and of LANG is the spirit that we long for in our public men, but it is the spirit that seems to have taken flight with the men who gave it birth. LANG is dead; LALOR has retired from public life. As with America so with Australia. WASHINGTON, LINCOLN – CLEVELAND; LANG, LALOR – PARKES. In America of the past, heroes, patriots, farmers. In America of the present, capitalists and their human property. In Australia of yesterday, pioneers, diggers, Democrats. In Australia of today, toadies, grovellers, lick-spittles. The old impulse is not dead, however, though the land-thief and the labour-thief rig our markets and shark our estates; though our politicians sell us for an empty distinction and barter our birthright for a mess less than royal pottage. The people of Australia – the true, the genuine Democrats, the AUSTRALIANS – refuse to celebrate the landing of PHILLIP; they look across the Murray for the one representative act of their nationality; they look across the ocean for the one representative utterance which foretells their future, and they find their exemplars in the rebellious minor, LALOR, and the irritable parson LANG. The one, by his heroic action in heading the diggers in revolt against unjust and tyrannical authority, furnished forth a precedent to Australia, which all Australians worthy of the name should inscribe in letters of indelible print within the red-leaved tablets of their hearts. The other, by his magnificent pertinacity and splendid daring, snatched a grand territory from convict-loving Officialdom and gave it to the free settler. Their deeds will speak ever louder than tablets of brass or monuments of marble, but if there is one thing the people of Australia could, with beautiful propriety, perform, it is to place in the Fortitude Valley, Brisbane, in the very locality in which LANG's first free settlers took up their first abode, a memorial of this genuine worker and true Australian. The Ballarat monument still remains to be erected, but alas! the race of men in Ballarat of today are not the stalwart heroes of fifty-four. They huckster about a Stock Exchange, and their most magnificent effort at appreciation of merit is a statue to a GUELPHIC and foreign Sovereign. Let it pass. The men who fought for liberty are not of the brand to be pleased with flattery. Their deeds live on in default of tablets. The shouts of diggers are in the air, the ping of the rifle-butt is heard overhead, there is a clash of steel and a hurtling of arms; a flag with the insignia of labour – the pick and the shovel – flaunts proudly in the morning breeze above us . . . . 'Tis a memory of the day that Australia set her teeth in the face of the British Lion, December 3, 1854 – the Day We Ought to Celebrate.

Jane Watts

[A DINNER FOR THE GOVERNOR]

That night, while seated around the old-fashioned supper-table, they learned that Mr A. had received official intimation of the Governor's intention to land the next morning, to inspect the township and hold a levée. It was at once settled that he must be invited to dinner, together with his suite, and the captain of the Queen's ship, the *Pelorus*, as they were to sail again immediately, the gentlemen on the island being asked to meet them. Now this, it must be owned, was rather startling intelligence. For when it is taken into consideration that the family had only just moved into the house, which was in the greatest state of confusion, with not a room in order; and moreover that they were living in a place where frequently provisions of even the plainest description could not be procured for love or money, it must be admitted their position was a perplexing one. To provide, at only twenty-four hours' notice, a suitable dinner to set before twenty-four persons, was no easy task.

Fortunately, Mrs A. proved herself equal to the emergency, notwithstanding the ludicrous difficulties to be encountered. Her great ally on the occasion was a young man – one of the steerage passengers of the ship they came out in, who happened to be over from Adelaide at the time, on a visit to their maid servant to whom he was engaged to be married. He was a fine, hearty, good-natured young fellow, a sort of "Mark Tapley" in his way, delighting in difficulties, for the pleasure of overcoming them, and he agreed to start at daylight for the Farm on a foraging expedition. Another messenger was then told off to go to the township before breakfast, with orders to bring back anything in the way of provender he could honestly come by. This one speedily returned with the overwhelming intelligence that not one pound of meat was to be got upon the island, save a solitary loin of mutton, kindly sent by a friend, which, with four eggs, was all that could be had.

Matters now began to wear a very serious aspect. The morning was passing away. Mary, the cook, had finished her pastry, and was in a state bordering on distraction, for how she could be expected to have a dinner ready by six o'clock that night, and no material in the house to cook it with, seemed to her unsophisticated mind a problem impossible to solve. At length the happy thought occurred to Mrs A. of sending off to one of the ships, to see if the good natured Captain L–, of the *Goshawk*, would prove a friend indeed in this dire time of sorest need, and to the credit of humanity be it said, he "was all their fancy painted him", bountiful and generous as a prince – placing at their disposal, in the kindest manner possible a boat load of good things. There was a splendid ham, an English cheese, tins of soup, roast veal, preserved fruits, and hosts of other dainties, with some excellent light dinner wines – sauterne, hock and claret – all of which, with a sailor's generosity, he begged their acceptance of – refusing to take a shilling in payment.

Mark Tapley, too, returned in high glee, on the only "Rosinante" the island possessed, with a turkey dangling on one side of the saddle, a goose on the other, and, strapped before him a "wallaby" fat enough to make the old geologist's eyes twinkle with delight. Now their fears vanished in a trice! Cook, they knew, was admirable in her line of business, Patty neat-handed as a waiter, and Mark Tapley a host in himself, a veritable tower of strength, skinning that wallaby and plucking that poultry as if he had not done anything else since his birth, and then turning to and washing the vegetables with a skill and deftness worthy of the "old girl" in Dickens's "Bleak House".

After all their gloomy forebodings, when the dinner-hour came, and the guests arrived, everything was in readiness for their entertainment. The carpet had been laid down in the dining-room, curtains and pole affixed to the windows, pictures hung upon the walls, and with good napery, and a sufficiency of glass, silver, and wax lights upon the tables, as excellent a repast was provided as anyone not absolutely an epicure could possibly desire, the wallaby soup in particular being much enjoyed from its rarity. The drawing-room, though furnished, still wore a dismal look, from its new plastered walls and generally unfinished state; but "Rome was not built in a day", and no small amount of energy and pluck must have been exerted by those pioneers of civilisation in surrounding themselves with the comforts here recorded, so early in the colony's history as June, 1838.

Their visitors were pleasant, agreeable, gentlemanly men, and were evidently gratified at the efforts made to do them honour. The Colonial Secretary – afterwards Acting-Governor – was a good-looking, dapper little man, with light curly hair and whiskers, extremely fond of dress, and *small* in every way; he wore ladies' number fours in boots (if a droll skit of that day might be relied upon) and possessed various showy accomplishments. He danced well, sang soft sentimental ditties, such as "Love's Ritornella", "Come away Love", and other songs of that class, to the accompaniment of a guitar, adorned with blue ribbon, and was in fact what usually goes by the term of a "lady's man", with an abundance of small talk considered suitable to the feminine capacity!

Whether he was as great in more important matters as he was in etiquette and soft nothings will not be commented upon in this light, gossipy narrative, which only professes to skim the surface of things. His colleague, the Private Secretary, however, was a man of a very different stamp: in person, tall and powerfully made, not handsome in feature, but with a good, intellectual countenance and well-shaped head, and of undoubted talent, as to an eminent degree the newspaper he afterwards conducted showed.

But the observed of all observers, was, as may be supposed, the Governor himself – Captain (afterwards Sir John) Hindmarsh – who was of middle height, pleasant-looking, with frank, genial, affable manners, and every inch a sailor. There was one peculiarity though in his appearance which must not be forgotten, as it seemed to have a sort of irresistible fascination for one of the Miss A.s, sitting as she did, where she had a full view of him. His eyes were of the brightest blue; but whilst one of them moved here and there in every direction the other remained stationary in its orbit, and had a cold, unmeaning star, which puzzled her excessively. He asked her courteously to take wine with him, which she did, bowing with inward trepidation, it must be owned, to that awful eye! At last curiosity got the better of her so completely that she interrupted the young sailor at her side, in the middle of a poetical quotation anent the "dark-eyed Hinda", to beg of him, *sotto voce*, to tell her what was the matter with one of the Governor's eyes? In sephulchral tones, he uttered the one word "glass". That was sufficient, she was satisfied.

The dinner at length was over, the speeches made, and then Mr A. who never failed to show appreciation of real merit whenever it was in his power to do so, had jolly Mark Tapley summoned from the regions below, where he was solacing himself after the fatigues of the day with a little love-making. A glass of wine was given him, and he was introduced to the assembled guests as "an enterprising young Englishman" of excellent principles and character, who, by his industry, activity and energy, would undoubtedly prove a valuable colonist. Kind notice having been taken of as fine a young fellow in his sphere of life as ever came out to South Australia, Mark quickly made his bow and exit, only too glad to get back, we may be sure, to the more congenial society of Patty and her friend the cook, with whom he could talk at his ease over their plans for the future, arranging to return to the island to marry his fiancée as soon as a cottage could be got ready for her. And yet, in that self-same hour, when his prosepcts were of the brightest, and humanly speaking a useful, successful career was mapped out before him, little as they were aware of it, in the dim distance an ominous black shadow was approaching that would ere long envelope them both as with a shroud.

On retiring to the other room for coffee and music a capital comic song was sung by a clever little man present, describing in a ludicrous way the sore trials undergone by a bashful youth in his endeavours to gain the affections of some coy young maiden. The singer, at one part of the melody, assuming the character himself, startled Miss A. not a little for the moment – as evinced by her terrified look and blushes – for, gradually working himself up to the pitch of enthusiasm, and resolving with commendable persistency to throw bashfulness to the winds, and do or die, he suddenly darted across the room to where she sat, and suiting the action to the word demanded in impassioned strains the possession of her fair hand. The whole scene was so naturally and admirably acted, that it almost seemed to the lookers-on as if the performer had himself in reality gone through an experience of the kind portrayed in the song, until it was remembered that he had lately allied himself, at the age of five-and-twenty, to a lady possessed of no attractions whatever either personal or mental (though a good housewife) who would never see her fortieth summer again. It was therefore supposed, whether erroneously or not, that the difficulties in obtaining her consent to enter into the matrimonial state could hardly have been of so formidable or heartrending a nature as his love-lorn strain would have led the company to imagine.

The boat being now in readiness to convey the Governor and his suite on board the *Pelorus*, cordial adieux were made and a pretty effect was produced, as the sailors, each carrying a blue light, formed a line on either side to escort them to the beach, where they soon embarked, sailing that night for Adelaide.

Nat Gould

CHRISTMAS AND NEW YEAR

What a contrast Australia affords to the old country at Christmas! This festive season is just as much thought of under Australia's burning sun as it is amidst the snow and frost of England. I have spent Christmas in Queensland and New South Wales, and found it thoroughly enjoyable. On first acquaintance with an Australian Christmas, one can hardly imagine it is that season of the year. To indulge in roast goose and plum pudding with the thermometer at over ninety in the shade is making a toil of a pleasure. Christmas in the colonies is a great time for picnics and outdoor merry-makings. As a rule it is brilliant weather at this time of the year, and there is very little chance of being caught in a storm or compelled to abandon an outing owing to the unfriendly nature of the elements.

The Australians can therefore prepare to hold high festival without much fear of a disappointment. And certain it is that great preparations are made to give Christmas and New Year a fitting reception. For weeks beforehand there has been much fattening of poultry and a great making of cakes. Shop-keepers are alive to the fact that Christmas will bring in a lot of ready money, and that they will be able to dispose of goods that cannot be sold at any other period of the year. One of the first signs of approaching Christmas may be seen in the stationers' shops, where the times of the latest mails to arrive in London before December 25 are posted. Christmas cards for friends in the old country fill the windows, and many of them bring joy and delight when friends and parents receive them on the other side of the world. Some of these cards are of exquisite design. A bunch of Australian wild-flowers painted in true colours forms a fitting souvenir, or perhaps a view of some choice spot in the harbour or up the Blue Mountains. Thousands of these cards are mailed to England about six weeks before Christmas, and reach their destinations before the all-eventful day. Then come the pictures from the London illustrated Christmas numbers, and they arrive in ample time to be displayed before the end of December arrives. Some of these Christmas publications are published a long time ahead, and it would not be at all surprising to read that at Christmas, 1897, the annual for 1898 had just been issued.

If Christmas Day happens to fall on a Friday, the probabilities are no business will be done until the following Tuesday or Wednesday morning. They are wonderful people for holidays in the colonies. An odd day's holiday is not regarded as a special blessing. What the native requires is the day before to prepare for the holiday, then the holiday itself, and then the remainder of the week to gradually get over it. At Christmas time a little extra indulgence is permissible, and most employers of labour are only too willing to extend the holidays after the bustle and worry coming before them.

Of course the grocers make special displays. Mr James Kidman, an ardent sportsman, and likewise an extensive retail grocer, generally manages to collect a crowd round his windows in George Street and Oxford Street. Mr Kidman is great on cheese. He orders a couple from Bodalla, and each weighs two or three tons. These huge monsters he places on a couple of drays, and has them drawn in triumph through the streets by a team of bullocks, with black native drivers to look after them. They are afterwards placed in the shop windows, when it is a case of cut and come again at them by many people, in the hope of securing one or more of the numerous coins that are stated to be buried in the interior. This mode of advertising pays, and Mr Kidman is generally alive to the advantages of publicity.

Whether times are bad or good, there always seems to be plenty of money, and to spare, at Christmas. Most people manage to save up a few shillings for this particular time, and the rejoicing is universal. It is a bustling, busy scene in Sydney on Christmas Eve, but on New Year's Eve the young men of the period are abroad, bent on mischief and mad pranks. There is no busier time of the year than Christmas, and a roaring trade is done in hampers and all the picnic necessaries.

And what picnics they are! Monster organisations, some of them, others on a more modest scale. The harbour resorts are besieged, and picnic-parties camp so near to each other that the wonder is they do not amalgamate and combine the contents of their hampers. Somehow they generally keep in separate groups until one party runs short, and then a deputation of borrowers is sent round. The costumes of these merrymakers are in keeping with the climate. The young men start out arrayed in white flannels, and with broad-rimmed hats that would not be unlike Japanese sunshades if they had sticks in the centre. Collars are at a discount, just the usual turn-down on the flannel shirt, with perhaps a tie round the neck. A pair of white boots and a sash round the waist, and the male picnicker is complete. And the lady friends who are invited to the picnic are arrayed in the lightest of attire – gauzy looking white or coloured dresses that seem as though a puff of wind would float them away and leave their owners lamenting. And such hats! They would do credit to a florist, so tasteful are the decorations.

The Australian girl at a Christmas picnic is about as fairy-like a mortal as one would expect to see out of a pantomime. They go out in parties of ten or a score, or even more, and the prettiest spots in and around Sydney ring with their merry laughter. There is no shivering in the cold, no fear of getting chilled, no danger of rheumatics from sitting on damp grass. Nature has laid herself out at her best advantage for these Christmas picnics, and if it is a trifle hot – well, it is better than being choked with fog and damp, and half starved to death into the bargain. And if the shades of night fall fast, and daylight quickly fades into darkness, what matters when the evening air is as balmy as zephyr's breezes, and there is not a chill in the night wind? After the glorious sunshine of the day, the shades of night come as a welcome change. As these picnic-parties are homeward bound, the sound of music echoes across the waters of the harbour, and then comes a chorus of song. The day has been merry, and so let the night be.

If ever there was a place where peace on earth and goodwill towards men ought to reign supreme, it is in Australia at Christmas. And after some years of experience, I can safely say that such a state of feeling prevails at this season. There never was a lighter-hearted joyous throng than is to be found among the Christmas holiday-makers in the sunny South. All past feuds seem to be buried for the time, and although they may arise again when Christmas is past and gone, nothing is heard or seen of them then.

Boxing Day is the day of days for a grand round of enjoyment. From early morning until late at night, the holiday-makers throw care to the winds, and give themselves over to pleasure. Racing, cricket, yachting, bicycling, and sundry other sports and pastimes, find thousands of votaries. At Randwick the Australian Jockey Club hold their Midsummer meeting, and there is seldom a bigger crowd on this famous course than on Boxing Day. At the Association Ground there is probably a cricket match of importance going on either between England and Australia or between the inter-colonial teams. The harbour is alive with yachts, and regattas are being held in different parts of this splendid water.

At night there is a rush for the theatres, where pantomimes are produced under trying circumstances. Although the heat is intense, this does not prevent people from crowding round the doors early in order to be stewed for several hours in an atmosphere much like that of an oven. It is a far different thing to go to the pantomime on Boxing Night in Sydney to what it is in London. There is the same struggle to gain admission, but there is more chance of being baked than frozen, when waiting for the doors to open. Her Majesty's and the Lyceum are generally first in favour, and the pantomimes produced there would do credit to many London theatres. It is trying work for all engaged in the production of these pantomimes.

The large theatre is packed with people, and this adds to the already stifling nature of the atmosphere. With the heat so intense, the good fairies of the play must be comfortably cool in their scanty costumes. In the snow scenes, the "property" icicles hang down in a limp fashion, and it would not surprise anyone to see them drip, drip, drip, on to the stage. The snowballs seem inclined to melt and flow in a stream into the orchestra.

The demon of the play has a lively time rousing up the fire that is to consume the hero and his attendant sprites. The mere sight of flames makes the already perspiring audience mop their faces more freely with huge pocket-handkerchiefs. It is a curious sight to look from the stage at the crowded house when hundreds of pocket-handkerchiefs are being used as fans or towels. I have seen pantomimes before and behind the curtain in the colonies, and it is doubtful which is the hotter, the audience or the players. From seven till eleven, or later, this sultry kind of enjoyment goes on, and people seem sorry when the curtain falls on the final act of the harlequinade. Then as the crowds surge out of the places of amusement, night seems turned into day, and the streets are once more filled with a merry, laughing throng. It is long after midnight before many of these pleasure-seekers reach home, but it is surprising how fresh they are at the end of such a day.

On New Year's Eve the rougher element is let loose. Bands of youths, with more impudence than brains, parade the streets and make night hideous with unearthly sounds. Occasionally one of these "pushes" take possession of an arcade, and then law-abiding and peaceful citizens give them a wide berth in that particular quarter. The streets of Sydney on New Year's Eve are not pleasant places; half-drunken mobs of larrikins rush from place to place, clearing all before them, and smashing windows and lamps. This sort of thing is continued in the suburbs until an early hour on New Year's Day.

At midnight there is a great ringing of bells, the whistles of steamers in the harbour are turned on at full steam; tin trays are belaboured with rolling-pins, or any other weapon that comes handy;

dinner-bells are violently rung in private houses; doors are flung wide open to let the Old Year depart and the New Year come in; house-to-house visitations take place, and the callers are generally invited inside to toast the New Year. I have heard many discordant rows in my time, but, for a vertiable pandemonium of hideous sounds, give me Sydney on New Year's Eve.

After the adventures of the night, people rise refreshed and ready for action. But few ill effects of the midnight revels are noticeable, and New Year's Day is given a chance to wear them off.

Christmastide in Australia is a round of jovial festivities. The sun shines a welcome on all, and the clear blue sky adds a charm to the scene such as winter climes do not know. It is well worth while spending a Christmas in the colonies in order to see how the children of these sunny climes revel in the lightness and brilliancy that surround them on all sides.

Catherine Spence

EACH IN HIS OWN TONGUE

Acts II., vi. and vii. – "Each in his own tongue."

The mythical narrative which symbolises the spread of the Gospel through all lands, among all peoples, and in all languages, which is commemorated in the Roman, Greek, and Anglican Churches on the festival of Whitsunday, six weeks after the Resurrection feast of Easter, has been perhaps best fulfilled in the work of the Bible Society, which has translated the sacred books of the Hebrews and of the Christians into every known language.

It is evident that the story is not literally true, for although Paul writes of the speaking with tongues as one of the gifts or manifestations of the early Christian Church, he accounted it as the least of the gifts, because what the rapt speaker said was unintelligible to others, and needed a gifted interpreter. The speaker edified himself only, and contributed nothing to his hearers.

Some brethren indeed believed that they could interpret, but it was quite possible that they gave only their own ideas. The characteristic of the Pentecostal miracle was that the tongues were understood by people of various nationalities; but as Paul describes the gift it was like the Irvingite tongues in later days, a quite useless and bewildering manifestation of religious excitement.

The modern fulfilment which gives the Bible to all peoples does not always do the good that is boasted of at centenary meetings. Scattering a collection of books of various value over the world does not evangelise it. Sometimes, for want of wise guidance, these Scriptures have been regarded as fetishes, and instead of being read as the records of religious evolution during a period of thousands of years, they have been used to strangle the living inspiration which never leaves us, and to stereotype creeds and ceremonies that check the expansion, the purification, and the elevation of the religious sentiment, "Commit Thy Word, O Lord", not to written books only, "but to the lips of faithful men, and to the free winds of Thine invisible Providence" – the prayer in our Prayerbook – not to bishops or priests, not to kings or emperors, not to ecclesiastical councils or secular parliaments, not to printed Bibles or Prayer-books, but to the lips of faithful men and the free winds of Our Father's invisible Providence. This is a prayer for a Free Church.

Into every hide-bound law or custom or book, however grand and free it may have originally been, there creeps the dry rot of stagnation and the worse canker of bigotry. "Thus shalt thou believe and profess, and not otherwise. There is danger in doubt, there is destruction in schism. The Church's robe is in one piece, like the coat of Jesus. Woe to him who would rend it. The Church's fold is the only refuge for the weak and the sinful, the only sanctuary for even the best and the strongest of the human race." And even when dissent became imperative, and the voice of a Luther, of a John Knox, of a Wesley, called those who thirsted after a better righteousness than that of the Church of their fathers into a new communion, each sect claimed to be the true Church, and built a wall of separation, beyond which salvation was doubtful, if not absolutely hopeless. To each individual in each body of sectaries the Gospel was preached in his own tongue. He felt the light and the truth and the hope come home to his understanding and to his heart, as he had not felt them in the old outworn forms, uttered by conventional or indifferent or self-seeking clericals. And it is this which is the spiritual lesson of the marvellous tale of Pentecost. The Gospel appealed to all, and all felt they could claim it. In the full glory of the great Roman Empire a small band of poor men began a work that has outlived that empire, and is going on now. No wonder that tradition heaped marvels and myths round its crucified Head and His immediate followers; no wonder that it costs us some pain to sweep them away.

The modern rendering of my text, which I shall follow in these remarks, I find aptly and beautifully expressed in a poem by William Herbert Carruth, published in "Brotherhood", and it shows how we of all denominations can embrace all thinking and loving men and women in our fold with no separating walls. We need say, "Stand off!" to no one. "Let whosoever thirsteth come and drink of the water of life freely." This is the poem:

A fire-mist and a planet,
  A crystal and a cell,
A jellyfish and a saurian,

And a cave where the cave-men dwell.
Then, a sense of law and order,
And a face turned from the clod;
Some call it Evolution,
And others call it God.

A haze on the far horizon,
The infinite tender sky,
The ripe, rich tints of the cornfield,
And the wild bird sailing high.
And all over upland and lowland
The charm of the golden rod;
Some of us call it Nature,
And others call it God.

Like tides on a crescent sea beach,
When the moon is new and thin,
Into our hearts high yearnings
Come welling and surging in,
Come from the mystic ocean
Whose rim no foot hath trod;
Some of us call it Longing
And others call it God.

A piquet frozen on duty,
A mother starved for her brood,
Socrates drinking the hemlock,
And Jesus on the Rood,
And millions who, humble and nameless,
The straight, hard pathway trod;
Some call it Consecration,
And others call it God.

It naturally divides into four parts – Creation, Nature, Aspiration, and Consecration. And I shall try to take each in its order. It will do you no harm to repeat each division the weighty words contained in the eight lines which give the idea to be grasped –

A fire-mist and a planet,
A crystal and a cell,
A jellyfish and a saurian,
And a cave where the cave-men dwell.
Then, a sense of law and order,
And a face turned from the clod;
Some call it Evolution,
And others call it God.

I am old enough to recollect the first whispers of evolution, not, indeed, in the scientific world when Lamarck spoke to somewhat deaf ears, long before I was born, but in the forties, when Robert

Chambers published anonymously his "Vestiges of the Natural History of Creation", and later the works of Charles Darwin on the "Origin of Species", and of Herbert Spencer, Huxley, Wallace, and others. What a terrible thing it appeared to the man in the street, to the woman in the house, and, above all, to the priest in the pulpit, that anyone should dare to doubt, and even to contradict, the Scriptural record that man, full-formed and developed, perfect in mind and body, had been created by the fiat of the Deity out of the dust of the ground, and given dominion over all the lower living creatures and over the whole earth. But even the Biblical record did not claim that man had been created of nothing, any more than the earth. That was said to be without form and void, and darkness brooded over the face of the earth. It was created at first dark and empty and silent, with water above and water beneath. And God said, "Light be", and "Light was". This is the literal translation which the Greek critic Longinus admired so much, more sublime than ours. In six successive days all was made, and all was good. Hugh Miller and others tried to explain the days as ages or aeons with doubtful success, for the creation of the sun, moon, and stars in the midst of the marvellous week was a serious stumbling block.

The verses I read give in eight lines an advance of, I am afraid to say or to guess how many millions of years, and the steps between each degree of development are quite as sublime and noble as those in the magnificent hymn of "Creation" which the old Hebrew writer has handed down to us from oral tradition. No early literature comes up to it in its account of the origin of the universe.

A fire mist and a planet,

How long before the fire mist consolidated into a new planet? How long before the molten mass of elements, revolving round the central sun of our solar system, cooled into rocks of granite and crystal? And before the waters found their appointed places? Not for ever, as the Psalmist believed, for interchange of ocean and continent has taken place once, or more than once. How long was the crystal, the atom of the rocks, the only struggle towards organised life? How long before the cell, the primordial source of life, multiplied itself by fissure, and produced the lowest forms of animal existence, gradually rising through ascidians and jellyfish to creatures with bones outside, like crabs and shrimps, up to vertebrate fishes, up through many steps to the gigantic saurians who peopled this earth? Still on and upward life ascends, through the birds and mammals, with their love and care for their offspring, the beginnings of altruism and heroism – always higher, and, as a rule, more beautiful.

At last comes man into a world which he is to subjugate to himself, not through strength; the elephant, the lion, the bull, and hosts of other animals have far more strength than he. Not through natural weapons; he cannot rend with teeth and claw, he cannot gore with horn or tusk, he cannot trample to death with his weight the creatures with which the earth is filled. But the process of evolution, slow and sure, has enabled him to stand upright and look up as well as down, and on a level. The forefoot of the quadruped has developed into the marvellous hand that can fashion tools for work, and weapons for defence, and with regard to the wonderful grey matter in the brain, that receives and sends messages to eye and ear, and limb and trunk, more richly endowed than any of the creatures large or small by whom he was surrounded.

Is this an ignoble ancestry? Are we ashamed to think that we have real affinity with the lower animals, and have been advanced to be their lord and master; and, therefore, should be merciful and careful for them? Man has been proud of having been formed of the dust of the ground and made perfect. Alas! the perfection was of brief duration. He might more reasonably be proud, or, at any rate, be thankful, that he has been endowed with the power to make progress, and with the desire to do so. A great world was before him to shape to his needs. Some things he had to submit to, others to conquer, and the soul which acts through this wondrous grey matter has to decide which course to take.

A sense of law and order,
And a face turned from the clod.

When did this dim sense arise? How was it developed? Was it not by taking note of the regularity of day and night, of summer and winter, of vegetation, of growth, of birth, of death? It was a hard school our far-away forefathers were set into, but they learned their lesson. And it was the settled order of things that encouraged industry, that led to agriculture, to taming of domestic animals, to storing for the future. It was the irregularities, the storms, the earthquakes, the volcanoes, the floods that led them to that fear which is the beginning of all religions. Thank God it is not the end of them! What they could see and understand helped them. What they could not understand or provide against paralysed them, and gave rise to priestcraft and ritual, and ideas of Divine wrath and vengeance, to be propitiated by sacrifice, to be softened by prayer, to be warded off by praise. But the more we study the laws of nature the less there is of the unknown which is to the untrained mind the terrible, and the gradual evolution of religion towards love and trust in the Creator and Preserver of the Universe, and towards peace and goodwill towards men, is permeating the world of creeds and Churches.

This growth is not only natural; I think it is lovely. Would any parent among us desire to have his children come to him like full-grown men and women, little Adams and Eves? We know that before birth each human germ goes through the lowest form of the cell, up through every gradation of animal development till it reaches the perfection of child life; and after it opens its eyes on the world has to learn to see, to hear, to smell, to touch, to taste, and for the first few years of life has no conscious memory of the time when it was learning more and accomplishing more in proportion than in the same lapse of time ever after. Truly a grand commentary on the doctrine of evolution, and, to my mind, a conclusive proof of its truth. And it is not bodily or mental powers alone that are gradually evolved from the primal germ. How interesting it is to watch the evolution of the religious instinct in the old writings of the world, and especially in the Hebrew Scriptures. The pictures of Jehovah in the earlier records are material and partial and cruel, rising gradually to the grand conceptions of Isaiah and Micah and the later Psalms, of a God just and compassionate, who prized mercy above sacrifice, and honesty and charity above professions of devoutness to Himself. In reading Claude Montefiore's Bible for Home-reading for use in Jewish families, this gradual elevation and spiritualisation of the character of God is shown to have gone on till not only the Unity but the Fatherhood of the Deity was taught in temple and synagogue and home. It was not altogether a new doctrine when Jesus proclaimed it. The mission of Israel to be a light to the world, which we see, especially in the later Psalms, where the devout are called on to sing a New Song, showed the expansion of the idea of a tribal or national God to the conception of a God of the whole earth and of all peoples, "Each in his own tongue".

II. The second branch of my subject deals with Nature, the visible universe –

A haze on the far horizon,
  The infinite tender sky,
The ripe, rich tints of the cornfield,
  And the wild birds sailing high.
And all over upland and lowland
  The charm of the golden rod;
Some of us call it Nature,
  And others call it God.

How much or how little of this beauty was perceived or felt by the cave men or the lake dwellers we can only guess. The oldest literature does not deal in description of inanimate Nature, but in narratives of the actions of men, or the deeds of those magnified men whom they held as Gods. Indeed, the appreciation of natural beauty seems as much evolved and developed from small beginnings as the arts and sciences themselves. The haze on the far horizon was scanned only as portending the weather to come. The infinite tender sky, with its blue space flecked by sailing clouds, white or dark, by day and night, and gemmed with stars, which were only regarded as the little lamps which aided the sun and the moon to shed light on the great centre, the earth, were first watched for guides to steer by in the desert, or the forest, or on the sea before either their beauty charmed the eye, or their magnitude or their distance dawned on the intelligence. And even now there are but few of us who make the most and the best of the feast of beauty provided for us every day and every night, and at every season of the varying year.

Perhaps theology is answerable for giving a wrong direction to our thoughts, for all the ideas of celibate monks, of ritualistic priests, of devout puritans, were that the world in which we are placed was under a ban, and it was only by giving a spiritual interpretation to natural objects that we could please the Creator and Preserver of the world. I can scarcely give you a better example of what I mean than by quoting, as well as I can from memory of sixty years, some lines of John Newton's, the friend of the poet William Cowper, whose influence was not good for that great reviver of the love of Nature, who should have been encouraged to look outward, and not inward.

The lines are written on the seashore, a rocky, romantic shore of England –

In every object here I see
Something, my God, that speaks of Thee;
Firm as a rock Thy promise stands,
Thy mercies countless as the sands,
Thy goodness as the ocean wide,
Thy grace an ever flowing tide.

In every object here I see
Something, my heart, that tells of thee;
Hard as the granite rock, that stands
Barren, and shifty as the sands,
False and deceitful as the ocean,
And, like the tides, in constant motion.

This is the manner in which Newton would have liked Cowper to have looked on Nature; but for the benefit of mankind he looked at it otherwise, and saw in every freckle, streak, and shading of the wayside or the garden flower marks of God's unrivalled pencil; saw the grandeur of the ocean, first the barrier between nations, afterwards its highway for human intercourse; in the smooth sands worn down from what was once the steady rock, the way by which continents are built up and worn away; in the tides the ebb and flow of the vast ocean in obedience to the attraction of the sun and the moon.

The poem which is my text is American, no doubt, as it speaks of the charm of the Golden Rod; but all over the world, and particularly in Australia, yellow is the prevailing colour of the natural flora. In England we have the buttercup, the primrose, and the dandelion, the gorse, and the broom as examples of the exuberance of bright yellow flowers. Grant Allen quotes Darwin, Lubbock, and Müller in support of his contention that yellow is the primitive colour of all flowers, and that it is sure to predominate always, especially where the bee and the butterfly and other pollen-bearing insects are unknown or few. We have the charm of the yellow wattle and all the Mimosa tribe in our early spring, and the Cape marigold or dandelion lower down, and of the smaller flowers, whether bulbs or not, yellow is the colour of the greater part of all.

Garden flowers carefully cultivated have their infinite varieties of hue as well as of structure, dependent on selection and fertilisation, but the original gift of flowers to man is golden, all over the world.

An Australian poet has well expressed the feelings of joyousness with which we breathe sweetness and see the beauty of our early summer –

There is bloom on the golden wattle,
  And a fragrance fills the air
From the odours, rich and subtle,
  She shakes from her wavy hair.
From the quickened glebe is springing
  The green and the blended gold,
And the glen and the gorge are ringing
  With the hymns of the sylvan wold.

In a natural sense, and not in the spiritual sense of the poet who sees Horeb and Sinai in our daily life, we see

Every common bush aflame with God.

Mary Howitt says –

God might have made enough, enough.
  Enough for great and small,
Enough for food, enough for health.
  Without a flower at all.

Not without flowers of some sort, otherwise there would have been no corn or berry or fruit, but the dull green of the primitive flora was well exchanged long before man had eyes to see them for the golden flowers of the waste and the wild. When Mungo Park's heart was cheered by the sight of a little wildflower in the deserts of Africa it was not because it was an emblem of spiritual growth or heavenly bliss, but because he felt the great Creator, who had given this lonely plant existence, and let it bloom, would also care for him in his needs and his distress. And instead of writing and singing doleful verses about the falling leaves of autumn, emblematic of deterioration, decay, and death as a warning for us to be ready for the winter of death, we should hail the season of harvest, when the rich ripe tints of the cornfield give promise of food for man and beast, and the blossoms of spring have developed into ripe fruit, delicious and wholesome. God has made everything beautiful in its time – day and night, summer and winter, seedtime and harvest – has each its appropriate charm. Nature never did betray the heart that loved her, and no amount of mechanical invention and scientific discovery can check the development of the sense of beauty in our hearts. Each generation brings its own poets, each generation now brings its own painters to see and to express that sense of beauty. The early artists confined themselves to the human form and to grand architecture. At the revival of letters and arts it was humanity, not Nature, that was the subject of painter and poet, but gradually we are learning that what is seen and felt of natural beauty and of Nature's processes can be absorbed by the poet and the painter and expressed with a human interest added, which heightens the beauty of the poem and the landscape.

"Each in his own tongue" the poet, the painter, the man of science expresses God Himself when he reveals the living garment of God.

"Tell me where God is?" a somewhat cynical sceptic asked of a child. "Tell me where he is not," said the child, and indeed the sense of the omnipresence, of the all-pervadingness of the spirit of the universe is stronger now than it ever was. In the words of the greatest Psalm in the Bible, "Whither shall I go from Thy spirit or whither shall I flee from Thy presence. If I ascend up into heaven thou art there, if I make Sheol my bed Thou art there."

I may here quote from James Lane Allen in words which he puts into the mouth of an enthusiastic devotee of science: "Men used to talk of the secrets of Nature; there is not the slightest evidence that Nature has a secret. They used to speak of the mysteries of the Creator. I am not one of those who claim to be authorities on the traits of the Creator. Some of my ancestors considered they were such. But I do say that men are coming more and more to think of him as having no mysteries. We have no evidence that as the old hymn says, 'He loves to move in a mysterious way.' The entire openness of Nature and of the Creator – these are the new ways of thinking. They will be the only ways of thinking in the future unless civilisation sinks again into darkness. What we call secrets and mysteries of the universe are the limitations of our powers and of our knowledge. The little that we do know about Nature, how open it is, how unsecretive! There is nowhere a sign that the Creator wishes to hide from us even what is life. If we ever discover what life is no doubt we shall then realise that it contained no mystery. It was the folly and the crime of all ancient religions that their priesthoods veiled them; whenever the veil was rent, like the veil of Isis, it was not God that men found behind it; it was nothing. The religions of the future will have no veils. As far as they can set before their worshippers truth at all it will be truth open as the day. The Great Teacher in the New Testament, what an eternal lesson on light itself does He give to us. That is the great beauty of His Gospel. And His Apostles. Where do you find Him saying to them, 'Preach my word to all men as the secrets of a priesthood and the mysteries of the Father?' "

It is the tragedy of man alone that he has his secrets. Life is full of things that we cannot tell, because they would injure us; and of things we cannot tell because they would injure others. But surely we should all like to live in a time when a man's private life will be his only one.

Ah! and when, troubled and perplexed with our own secrets, and with those of others, which are often as embarrassing, how healing is the influence of Nature. We may call her unconcerned, for she may not sadden the world out of sympathy with us and our individual suffering, but her very calmness soothes us. I think it is rather an anthropomorphic idea that some good preachers express when they say that we grieve God by our sins, and gladden Him by our repentance. But as the manifestation of God in outer nature so often comforts us, helps us, inspires us, we may feel sure that in the inner depths of our souls, which are akin to the Divine, we have only to open ourselves to the light, only to seek guidance in perplexity, and strength in weakness, to receive from the Inexhaustible and the Infinite what we need.

9

Protest and Revolution

EDITOR'S NOTE

"Protest and Revolution" provides further examples of the complex interrelation between spoken and written English in nineteenth-century Australia. For example, the written reports of speeches by J.D. Lang, D.H. Deniehy and Robert Lowe use a more formal and standard kind of English than that found in either Ned Kelly's Jerilderie letter or Raffaello Carboni's *The Eureka Stockade*. The latter is a real literary curiosity, a heady mix of history, autobiography and polemic which combines chapter headings in Latin with direct addresses to the reader and other colloquial features. Embedded within the extract given here, too, are examples of other written forms of the period: the newspaper report, the letter to the editor, the diary entry, the government notice.

The items selected cover most of the major political movements and historical events of the second half of the century: the struggles for independence from Britain and for a more democratic system of government, the Eureka Stockade, the phenomenon of Ned Kelly, the federation of the Australian states. Both J.D. Lang and D.H. Deniehy argue against the colonial mentality. Although Lang's Australian League had little immediate success, one of its members, Henry Parkes, who had also been a leader of the anti-transportation movement, was to play a significant role in the achievement of federation. Deniehy, another supporter of the Australian League, managed through his famous "bunyip aristocracy" speech of 1854 to block W.C. Wentworth's plans for a colonial peerage, which would have given the New South Wales parliament a nominated upper house equivalent to the British House of Lords. Ned Kelly's Jerilderie letter was apparently composed with some help from Joe Byrne, another member of the Kelly Gang, and left to be printed at Jerilderie during the gang's seizure of the town on 8 February 1879. Instead, it was taken to Melbourne and survives in a copy made by a clerk in the Crown Law Department, now held by the Public Records Office of Victoria.

J.D. Lang

FROM THE COMING EVENT

Fellow Colonists of New South Wales, is it necessary, after these explanations, that I should now call upon you to join the Australian League, to give freedom and independence to your adopted country? There is clearly nothing else worth agitating for in our present circumstances, and be assured that if you do agitate for this great boon with earnestness and determination, you will certainly obtain it. So long as we continue a dependency of England, our condition will be that of a mere football, kicked about at pleasure by every underling in Downing Street, and condemned to utter insignificance as a community. [Strong expressions of assent.] But as a Sovereign and Independent State, our noble city would be the flourishing capital of a great and powerful confederation – a confederation whose representatives would be respected and honoured in every nation in Christendom, and which would ere long give the law to the boundless Pacific. [Much cheering.] As a mere colony we shall descend rapidly, as we are now actually doing, into insignificance and poverty, and be pointed at with the finger of scorn by all free nations; but as a Sovereign and Independent State, capital and emigration, enterprise and moral worth would again flow to our shores, the vast resources of our noble country would be rapidly developed, and prosperity would again revisit and cheer our land. [Loud and protracted cheering.]

Natives of New South Wales, it cannot surely be needful to call upon you to join a League for the achievement of the freedom and independence of your native land. You have hitherto, even in the estimation of Great Britain herself, been the tail of the world, and every brainless creature of blighted prospects and broken fortunes from England, with no personal merit but servility, and no intellectual qualification but toadyism, has been systematically placed above you even in this the land of your birth. Why, it is a rule of the service under the present *regime* that no native of the Colony, however able, talented and meritorious he may have proved himself, can be appointed by the Governor to any office under government with a salary above £100 a year. [Loud and indignant cries of Shame.] You have all heard, I doubt not, of our Public Educational Institutions going down, and proving an utter failure one after another: but is there not a sufficient reason for such a calamity in this systematic exclusion of the native youth from all such offices and employments under Government, as would create a demand for a superior education, and call forth the talents and energies of an ingenuous mind? [Loud and indignant expressions of assent from all quarters.] In fact there is no career open for the native youth in this their own country, under that vile system of government under which it is our calamity to live. [Continued expressions of approbation.] Unless they can get into a draper's shop or into a merchant's office as a junior clerk, which it is generally very difficult for them to do, or into a solicitor's office – in which case they will have to prowl about the Supreme Court for years together, no very safe situation for a young man of unfixed principles – they must either go as shepherds and stockmen into the interior, or open a butcher's shop, or get a publican's licence for one or other of our Colonial towns, expending their energies thenceforth in such trivial and contemptible pursuits as horse-racing, boat-racing and cricketing. And what sort of cattle are those that are sent out as heads of departments here, with the Secretary of State's brand upon them, to live at our expense and to eat the fat of the land? Why, as I told Lord Stanley once, the Treasury benches of the late Legislative Council might, with only one, or at the utmost two exceptions, have been styled with the greatest propriety, the "Refuge for the Destitute". [Great laughter and cheers of assent.] But as a Sovereign and Independent State, some native youth would in all probability rise to be one of the heads of the civilised world, instead of being the very tail of it as at present, and our country would forthwith assume one of the proudest and most influential positions on the face of the earth. [Great cheering.] Indeed there can scarcely be a limit set to the wealth and resources, the power and the grandeur of the future Australian nation. From the South Cape of Van Diemen's Land to Cape York, it will one day compromise a whole series of powerful states, and its influence will be beneficially felt over the multitude of the isles of the Western Pacific. In short, taking into account the vast galaxy of isles to the eastward and northward of Australia, in addition to the extensive coasts of this great continental island itself, I question whether even the United States of America will have a more extensive field of political power and of moral influence to expatiate over than will one day acknowledge the sovereignty of the United Provinces of Australia. [Renewed and continued cheering.]

Sons of the soil! the die is cast!
And your brothers are nailing their flag to the mast;
And their shout on the land, and their voice on the sea,
Is "The land of our birth is a land of the Free." –

[Loud cheering.]

D.H. Deniehy

SPEECH ON MR WENTWORTH'S CONSTITUTION BILL

Mr D.H. Deniehy having been called upon to second the third resolution, said:

Why he had been selected to speak to the present resolution he knew not, save that as a native of the Colony he might naturally be expected to feel something like real interest, and speak with something like real feeling on a question connected with the political institutions of the Colony. He would do his best to respond to that invitation to "speak up", and would perhaps balance deficiencies flowing from a small volume of voice by in all cases speaking plainly and calling things by their right names. He protested against the present daring and unheard-of attempt to tamper with a fundamental popular right, that of having a voice in the nomination of men who were to make, or control the making of, laws binding on the community – laws perpetually shifting and changing the nature of the whole social economy of a given state, and frequently operating in the subtlest form on the very dearest interests of the citizen, on his domestic, his moral, and perhaps his religious relations. The name of Mr Wentworth had several times been mentioned there that day, and upon one or two occasions with an unwise tenderness, a squeamish reluctant to speak plain English, and call certain shady deeds of Mr Wentworth's by their usual homely appellations, simply because they were Mr Wentworth's. Now, he for one was no wise disposed, as preceding speakers had seemed, to tap the vast shoulders of Mr

Wentworth's political recreancies – "to damn him with faint praise and mistimed eulogy". He had listened from boyhood upwards to grey tradition, to Mr Wentworth's demagogic aeropagitas – his speeches for the liberty of the unlicensed printing *régime* of Darling; and for these and divers other deeds of a time when the honourable Member for Sydney had to the full his share of the chivalrous pugnacities of five-and-twenty, he was as much inclined to give Mr Wentworth credit as any other man. But with those *fantasias*, those everlasting varieties on the "Light of other Days" perpetually ringing in his ears, he, Mr Deniehy, was fain to enquire by what rule of moral and political appraisal it was sought to throw in a scale directly opposite to that containing the flagrant and shameless political dishonesty of years, the democratic escapades, sins long since repented of, in early youth. The subsequent political conduct, or rather the systematic political principles of Mr Wentworth, had been of a character sufficiently outrageous to cancel the value of a century of service.

The British Consitution had been spoken of that afternoon in terms of unbounded laudation. That stately fabric, it is true, deserved to be spoken of in terms of respect; he, Mr Deniehy, respected it, and no doubt they all shared in that feeling. But his was a qualified respect at best, and in all presumed assimilations of the political hypothesis of our colonial constitution-makers, he warned them not to be seduced by mere words and phrases – sheer sound and fury. Relatively, the British Constitution was only an admirable example of slowly growing and gradually elaborated political experience applied and set in action, but it was also eminent and exemplary as a long history, still evolving, of political philosophy.

But, as he had said before, it was after all but relatively good for its wonderfully successful fusion of principles the most antagonistic. Circumstances entirely alter cases, and he would again warn them not to be led away by vague associations, exhaled from the use of venerable phrases that had, what few phrases nowadays seldom could boast, genuine meanings attached to them.

The patrician element existed in the British Constitution, as did the regal, for good reasons – it had stood in the way of all later legislational thought and operation as a great fact; as such it was handled, and in a deep and prudential spirit of conservatism it was allowed to stand; but as affecting the basis and foundation of the architecture of a constitution, the elective principles neutralised all detrimental influences, by conversion, practically, into a mere check upon the deliberations of the initiative section of the Legislature.

And having the right to frame, to embody, to shape it as we would, with no huge stubborn facts to work upon as in England, there was nothing but the elective principle and the inalienable right and freedom of every colonist upon which to work out the whole organisation and fabric of our political institutions. But because it was the good pleasure of Mr Wentworth, and the respectable toil of that puissant legislative body whose serpentine windings were so ridiculous, we were not permitted to form our own Constitution, but instead we were to have one and an Upper Chamber cast upon us, built upon a model to suit the taste and propriety of certain political oligarchs, who treated the people at large as if they were cattle to be bought and sold in the market, as indeed they were in American slave states, and now in the Australian colonies, where we might find bamboozled Chinese and kidnapped Coolies. And being in a figurative humour, he might endeavour to cause some of the proposed nobility to pass before the stage of our imagination as the ghost of Banquo walked in the vision of Macbeth, so that we might have a fair view of those harlequin aristocrats, those Australian magnificos. We will have them across the stage in all the pomp and circumstance of hereditary titles. First, then, stalked the hoary Wentworth. But he could not believe that to such a head the strawberry leaves would add any honour. Next comes the full-blooded native aristocrat, Mr James Macarthur, who would, he supposed, aspire to an earldom at least; he would therefore call him Earl of Camden, and he would suggest for his coat of arms a field vert, the heraldic term for green, and emblazoned on this field should be the rum keg of a New South Wales order of chivalry. There was also the much-starred Terence Aubrey Murray, with more crosses and orders – not orders of merit – than a state of mandarinhood. Another gentleman who claimed the proud distinction of a colonial title was George Robert Nichols, the hereditary Grand Chancellor of all the Australias. Behold him in the serene and moody dignity of that picture of Rodias that smiled on us in all the public-house parlours. This was the gentleman who took Mr Lowe to task for altering his opinions, this conqueror in the lists of jaw, this victor in the realms of gab. It might be well to ridicule the doings of this miserable clique, yet their doings merited burning indignation; but to speak more seriously of such a project would too much resemble the Irishman "kicking at nothing, it wrenched one horribly". But though their weakness was ridiculous, he could assure them that these pigmies might work a great deal of mischief; they would bring contempt upon a country whose best interests he felt sure they all had at heart, until the meanest man that walked the streets would fling his gibe at the aristocrats of Botany Bay. He confessed he found extreme difficulty in the effort to classify this mushroom order of nobility. They could not aspire to the miserable and effete dignity of the worn-out grandees of continental Europe. There, even in rags, they had antiquity of birth to point to; here he would defy the most skilled naturalist to assign them a place in the great human family. But perhaps after all it was only a specimen of the remarkable contrariety which existed at the

Antipodes. Here they all knew that the common water-mole was transformed into the duck-billed platypus; and in some distant emulation of this degeneracy, he supposed they were to be favoured with a bunyip aristocracy.

However, to be serious, he sincerely trusted this was only the beginning of a more extended movement, and from its commencement he argued the happiest results. A more orderly, united, and consolidated meeting he had never witnessed. He was proud of Botany Bay, even if he had to blush for some of her children. He took the name as no term of reproach when he saw such a high, true, and manly sensibility on the subject of their political rights; that the instant the liberties of their country were threatened, they could assemble, and with one voice declare their determined and undying opposition. But he would remind them that this was not a mere selfish consideration, there were far wider interests at stake.

Looking at the gradually increasing pressure of political parties at home, they must, in the not distant future, prepare to open their arms to receive the fugitives from England, Ireland, and Scotland, who would hasten to the offered security and competence that were cruelly denied them in their own land. The interests of those countless thousands were involved in their decision upon this occasion, and they looked, and were justly entitled to look, for a heritage befitting the dignity of free men.

Bring them not here with fleeting visions and delusive hopes. Let them not find a new-fangled Brummagem aristocracy swarming and darkening these fair, free shores. It is yours to offer them a land where man is bountifully rewarded for his labour, and where a just law no more recognises the supremacy of a class than it does the predominance of a creed. But, fellow citizens, there is an aristocracy worthy of our respect and of our admiration. Wherever human skill and brain are eminent, wherever glorious manhood asserts its elevation, there is an aristocracy that confers eternal honour upon the land that possesses it. That is God's aristocracy, gentlemen; that is an aristocracy that will bloom and expand under free institutions, and for ever bless the clime where it takes root. He hoped they would take into consideration the hitherto barren condition of the country they were legislating for. He himself was a native of the soil, and he was proud of his birthplace. It is true its past was not hallowed in history by the achievements of men whose names reflected a light upon the times in which they lived. They had no long line of poets or statesmen or warriors; in this country, Art had done nothing but Nature everything. It was theirs, then, alone to inaugurate the future. In no country had the attempt ever been made to successfully manufacture an aristocracy *pro re nata*. It could not be done; they might as well expect honour to be paid to the dusky nobles of King

Kamehamaka, or to the ebony earls of the Emperor Souloque of Hayti.

The stately aristocracy of England was founded on the sword. The men who came over with the conquering Norman were the masters of the Saxons, and so became the aristocracy. The followers of Oliver Cromwell were the masters of the Irish, and so became their aristocracy. But he would enquire by what process Wentworth and his satellites had conquered the people of New South Wales, except by the artful dodgery of cooking up a Franchise Bill. If we were to be blessed with an Australian aristocracy, he should prefer it to resemble, not that of William the Bastard, but of Jack the Strapper. But he trespassed too long on their time, and would in conclusion only seek to record two things – first, his indignant denunciation of any tampering with the freedom and purity of the elective principle, the only basis upon which sound government could be built; and, secondly, he wished them to regard well the future destinies of their country. Let them, with prophetic eye, behold the troops of weary pilgrims from foreign despotism which would ere long be flocking to these shores in search of a more congenial home, and let them now give their most earnest and determined assurance that the domineering clique which made up the Wentworth party were not, and should never be, regarded as the representatives of the manliness, the spirit, and the intelligence of the freemen of New South Wales. He had sincere pleasure in seconding the resolution, confident that it would meet with unanimous support and approval.

Raffaello Carboni

[EVENTS AT EUREKA]

Abyssus, Abyssum Invocat

"Joe, Joe!" No one in the world can properly understand and describe this shouting of "Joe", unless he were on this El Dorado of Ballaarat at the time.

It was a horrible day, plagued by the hot winds. A blast of the hurricane winding through gravel pits whirled towards the Eureka this shouting of "Joe". It was the howl of a wolf for the shepherds, who bolted at once towards the bush; it was the yell of bulldogs for the fossickers who floundered among the deep holes, and thus dodged the hounds: it was a scarecrow for the miners, who now scrambled down to the deep, and left a licensed mate or two at the windlass. By this time, a regiment of troopers, in full gallop, had besieged the whole Eureka, and the traps under their protection ventured among the holes. An attempt to give an idea of such disgusting and contemptible campaigns for the search of licenses is really odious to an honest man. Some of the traps were civil enough; aye, they felt the shame of their duty; but there were among them devils at heart, who enjoyed the fun, because their cupidity could not bear the sight of the zig-zag uninterrupted muster of piles of rich-looking washing stuff, and the envy which blinded their eyes prevented them from taking into account the overwhelming number of shicers close by, round about, all along. Hence they looked upon the ragged muddy blue shirt as an object of their contempt.

Are diggers dogs or savages, that they are to be hunted on the diggings, commanded, in Pellissier's African style, to come out of their holes, and summoned from their tents by these hounds of the executive? Is the garb of a digger a mark of inferiority? *"In sudore vultus lue vesceris panem"* † is then an infamy now-a-days!

Give us facts, and spare us your bosh, says my good reader. – Very well.

I, CARBONI RAFFAELLO, da Roma, and late of No. 4, Castle-court, Cornhill, City of London, had my rattling "Jenny Lind" (the cradle) at a water-hole down the Eureka Gully. Must stop my work to shew my licence. "All right." I had then to go a quarter of a mile up the hill to my hole, and fetch the washing stuff. There again – "Got your licence?" "All serene, governor." On crossing the holes, up to the knees in mullock, and loaded like a dromedary, "Got your licence?" was again the cheer-up from a third trooper or trap. Now, what answer would you have given, sir?

I assert, as a matter of fact, that I was often compelled to produce my licence twice at each and the same licence hunt. Anyone who knows me personally, will readily believe that the accursed game worried me to death.

Jam Non Estis Hospites et Advenœ

It is to the purpose to say a few words more on the licence-hunting, and have done with it. Light your pipe, good reader, you have to blow hard.

Our red tape, generally obtuse and arrogant, this once got rid of the usual conceit in all things, and had to acknowledge that the digger who remained quietly at his work, always possessed his licence. Hence the troopers were despatched like bloodhounds, in all directions, to beat the bush; and the traps who had a more confined scent, creeped and crawled among the holes, and sneaked into the sly-grog tents round about, in search of the swarming unlicensed game. In a word, it was a regular hunt. Any one who in Old England went fox-hunting, can understand pretty well, the detestable sport we had then on the goldfields of Victoria. Did any trooper succeed in catching any of the "vagabonds" in the bush, he would by the threat of his sword, confine him round a big gum-tree; and when all the successful troopers had done the same feat, they took their prisoners down the gully, where was the grand depot, because the traps were generally more successful. The commissioner would then pick up one pound, two pounds, or five pounds, in the way of bail, from any digger that could afford it, or had friends to do so, and then order the whole pack

† "In the sweat of thy brow thou shalt eat bread."

of the penniless and friendless to the lock-up in the camp.† *I am a living eye-witness, and challenge contradiction.*

This job of explaining a licence-hunt is really so disgusting to me, that I prefer to close it with the following document from my subsequently gaol-bird mate, then reporter of the *Ballaarat Times:* –

> *Police Court, Tuesday, October 24th*
>
> HUNTING THE DIGGER. – Five of these fellows were fined in the mitigated trifle of £5, for being without licences. The nicest thing imaginable is to see one of these clumsy fellows with great beards, shaggy hair, and oh! such nasty rough hands, stand before a fine gentleman on the bench with hands of shiny whiteness, and the colour of whose cambric rivals the Alpine snow. There the clumsy fellow stands, faltering out an awkward apology, "My licence is only just expired, sir – I've only been one day from town, sir – I have no money, sir, for I had to borrow half a bag of flour the other day, for my wife and children." Ahem, says his worship, the law makes no distinctions – fined £5. Now our reporter enjoys this exceedingly, for he is sometimes scarce of news; and from a strange aberration of intellect, with which, poor fellow, he is afflicted, has sometimes, no news at all for us; but he is sure of not being *dead beat* at any time, for digger-hunting is a standing case at the police office, and our reporter is growing so precocious with long practice, that he can tell the number of diggers fined every morning, without going to that sanctuary at all. – *Ballaarat Times*, Saturday, October 28, 1854.

Salvum Fac Populum Tuum Domine

The more the pity – I have not done yet with the accursed gold licence. I must prevail on myself to keep cooler and in good temper.

Two questions will certainly be put to me:

1st. Did the camp officials give out the licence to the digger at the place of his work, whenever required, without compelling him to leave off work, and renew his licence at the camp?

2nd. It was only one day in each month that there was a search for licences, was it not? Why therefore did not the diggers make it a half-holiday on the old ground, that "all work and no play, makes Jack a dull boy"?

The first question is a foolish one, from any fellow-colonist who knows our silver and gold lace; and is a wicked one, from any digger who was on Ballaarat at the time.

"Fellah" gave the proper answer through the *Ballaarat Times*,

†The Camp – administrative buildings, officials' and officers' quarters, stores, police cantonment, tents for various personnel including soldiers, gaol (including the "logs" to which prisoners were at times chained).

October 14th; – here it is:

To the Editor of the *Ballaarat Times*, October 14, 1854,
Sir,

Permit me to call your attention to the miserable accommodation provided for the miner, who may have occasion to go to the Camp to take out a licence. Surely, with the thousands of pounds that have been expended in government buildings, a little better accommodation might be afforded to the well disposed digger, who is willing to pay the odious tax demanded of him by government, and not be compelled to stand in the rain or sun, or treated as if the "distinguished government official" feared that the digger was a thing that would contaminate him by a closer proximity; so the "fellah" is kept by a wooden rail from approaching within a couple of yards of the tent. In consequence of so many persons mistaking the licence-office for the commissioner's water-closet, a placard has been placed over the door.

I am, Sir, yours &c.,
FELLAH DIGGER,

Who had to walk a few miles to pay away the money he had worked hard for, and was kept a few hours standing by a rail – not "sitting on a rail, Mary".

Now I mean to tackle in right earnest with the second question, provided I can keep in sufficiently good temper.

On the morning of Thursday, the 22nd June, in the year of Grace, One thousand eight hundred and fifty-four, His Excellency SIR CHARLES HOTHAM, Knight Commander of the Most Noble Military Order of the Bath, landed on the shores of this fair province, as its Lieutenant-Governor, the chosen and commissioned representative of Her Most Gracious Majesty, the QUEEN! "Never (writes the Melbourne historian of that day) never in the history of public ovations, was welcome more hearty; never did stranger meet with warmer welcome, on the threshold of a new home":

VICTORIA WELCOMES VICTORIA'S CHOICE,

was the Melbourne proclamation.

The following is transcribed from my diary:

Saturday, August 26th, 1854

His Excellency dashed in among us "vagabonds" on a sudden, at about five o'clock p.m., and inspected a shaft immediately behind the Ballaarat Dining Rooms, Gravel-pits. A mob soon collected round the hole; we were respectful, and there was no "joeing". On His Excellency's return to the camp, the miners busily employed themselves in laying down slabs to facilitate his progress. I was among the zealous ones who improvised this shabby foot-path. What a lack! we were all of us as cheerful as fighting-cocks. – A crab-hole being in the way, our Big Larry actually pounced on Lady Hotham, and lifting her up in his arms, eloped with her ladyship safely across, amid hearty peals of laughter, however colonial they may have been. – Now Big Larry kept the crowd from annoying the couple, by properly laying about him with a switch all along the road.

His Excellency was hailed with three-times-three, and was proclaimed on the Camp, now invaded by some five hundred blue shirts, the "Diggers' Charley".

His Excellency addressed us miners as follows: "Diggers I feel delighted with your reception – I shall not neglect your interests and welfare – again I thank you."

It was a short but smart speech we had heard elsewhere, he was not fond of "twaddle", which I suppose meant "bosh". After giving three hearty cheers, old Briton's style to "Charley", the crowd dispersed to drink a nobbler to his health and success. I do so this very moment. Eureka, under my snug tent on the hill, August 26, 1854. C.R.

Within six short months, *five thousand* citizens of Melbourne, receive the name of this applauded ruler with a loud and prolonged outburst of indignation!

Some twenty Ballaarat miners lie in the grave, weltering in their gore! double that number are bleeding from bayonet wounds; thirteen more have the rope round their necks, and two more of their leading men are priced four hundred pounds for their body or carcase.

Tout cela, n'est pas precisement comme chez nous, pas vrai?

Please, give me a dozen puffs at my black-stump, and then I will proceed to the next chapter.

Sufficit Diei Sua Vexatio

Either this chapter must be very short, or I had better give it up without starting it at all.

Up to the middle of September, 1854, the search for licences happened once a month; at most twice: perhaps once a week on the Gravel Pits, owing to the near neighbourhood of the Camp. Now, licence-hunting became the order of the day. Twice a week on every line; and the more the diggers felt annoyed at it, the more our Camp officials persisted in goading us, to render our yoke palatable by habit. I assert, as an eyewitness and a sufferer, that both in October and November, when the weather allowed it, the Camp rode out for the hunt every alternate day. True, one day they would hunt their game on Gravel-pits; another day, they pounced on the foxes of the Eureka; and a third day, on the Red-hill: but, though working on different leads, are we not all fellow diggers? Did not several of us meet again in the evening, under the same tent, belonging to the same party? It is useless to ask further questions.

Towards the latter end of October and the beginning of November we had such a set of scoundrels camped among us, in the shape of troopers and traps, that I had better shut up this chapter at once, or else whirl the whole manuscript bang down a shicer.

"Hold hard, though, take your time, old man: don't let your Roman blood hurry you off like the hurricane, and thus damage the merits of your case. Answer this question first," says my good reader.

"If it be a fair one, I will."

"Was, then, the obnoxious mode of collecting the tax the sole cause of discontent: or was the tax itself (two pounds for three months) objected to at the same time?"

"I think *the practical miner*, who had been *hard at work, night and day*, for the last four or six months, and, after all, had just bottomed a shicer, objected to the tax itself, because he could not possibly afford to pay it. And was it not atrocious to confine this man in the lousy lock-up at the Camp, because he had no luck?"

Allow me, now, in return, to put a very important question, of the old Roman stamp, *Cui bono?* that is, *Where did our licence money go to?* That's a nut which will be positively cracked by-and-bye.

* * *

Remember This Sabbath Day (December Third), To Keep It Holy

I awoke. Sunday morning. It was full dawn, not daylight. A discharge of musketry – then a round from the bugle – the command "forward" – and another discharge of musketry was sharply kept on by the red-coats (some 300 strong)† advancing on the gully west of the stockade, for a couple of minutes.

The shots whizzed by my tent. I jumped out of the stretcher and rushed to my chimney facing the stockade. The forces within could not muster above 150 diggers.

The shepherds' holes inside the lower part of the stockade had been turned into rifle-pits, and were now occupied by Californians of the I.C. Rangers' Brigade, some twenty or thirty in all, who had kept watch at the "outposts" during the night.

Ross and his division northward, Thonen and his division southward, and both in front of the gully, under cover of the slabs,

†The force used in the attack consisted of 100 mounted (including 70 mounted police) and 176 foot (including 24 police), plus the officers; a total of 288. The number of diggers under arms in the Stockade at the time of the attack probably was few more than 100.

answered with such a smart fire, that the military who were now fully within range, did unmistakably appear to me to swerve from their ground: anyhow the command "forward" from Sergeant Harris was put a stop to. Here a lad was really courageous with his bugle. He took up boldly his stand to the left of the gully and in front: the red-coats "fell in" in their ranks to the right of this lad. The wounded on the ground behind must have numbered a dozen.

Another scene was going on east of the stockade. Vern floundered across the stockade eastward, and I lost sight of him. Curtain whilst making coolly for the holes, appeared to me to give directions to shoot at Vern; but a rush was instantly made in the same direction (Vern's) and a whole pack cut for Warrenheip.†

† To chop the gaseous factory of the following electrifying blather, Toorak had offered £500 reward!! Great works.

VERN's LAST LETTER

(From *The Age*, Monday, January, 15th, 1855)

The following letter – the last written in these colonies by the now celebrated Vern – has been sent to us for publication. Our readers may rely on its authenticity.

Ship —, Sydney Heads,
Dec. 24th, 1854.

Farewell to thee, Australia! A few moments more, and then Australia, land of my adoption, adieu! adieu!

Thy rocky shores
Fade o'er the waters blue.

The ship that bears me to exile has spread her wings; but Australia, and you my late companions in arms, I cannot leave you without bidding you (it may be my last) farewell. I part from you, perhaps forever; but wherever fickle fortune may banish me to, your memory will help to beguile the dreary hours of exile; and I hope that a name once so familiar to you, now an outlaw from injustice and tyranny, may be kindly remembered by you.

Oh, that a kind fate had laid me low in the midst of you, and given me a final resting-place, Australia, in thy bosom. But no! Fate denied me a warrior's death, a patriot's grave, and decreed that I should languish in banishment. [*Fate? be d–d; the immoderate length of your legs was fatal to your not getting a "warrior's grave"*.]

There was a time when I fought for freedom's cause, under a banner made and wrought by English ladies – [*Ah, ah, I thought you would soon bring in the ladies* – where, please?]

Victoria! thy future is bright – [*sweet and smart if Vern be the operator*.] I confidently predict a Bunker's Hill, or an Alma – [*Great works!*] as the issue of your next insurrection. [*No more truck with your legs, though; let's see your signature and be off*.]

Farewell, Australians!
Yours, truly, and for ever,
C.harles H.otham's F.ootman DE LA VERN.

Hold hard, leave us the address where you got your soap last. I want to shampoo my red hair, so as to make my head worth £500. Yankee speculation I guess.

There was, however, a brave American officer, who had the command of the rifle-pit men; he fought like a tiger; was shot in his thigh at the very onset, and yet, though hopping all the while, stuck to Captain Ross like a man. Should this notice be the means to ascertain his name, it should be written down in the margin at once.

The dragoons from south, the troopers from north, were trotting in full speed towards the stockade.

Peter Lalor, was now on the top of the first logged-up hole within the stockade, and by his decided gestures pointed to the men to retire among the holes. He was shot down in his left shoulder at this identical moment: it was a chance shot, I recollect it well.

A full discharge of musketry from the military, now mowed down all who had their heads above the barricades.

Ross was shot in the groin. Another shot struck Thonen exactly in the mouth, and felled him on the spot.

Those who suffered the most were the score of pikemen, who stood their ground from the time the whole division had been posted at the top, facing the Melbourne road from Ballaarat, in double file under the slabs, to stick the cavalry with their pikes.

The old command, "Charge!" was distinctly heard, and the red-coats rushed with fixed bayonets to storm the stockade. A few cuts, kicks and pulling down, and the job was done too quickly for their wonted ardour, for they actually thrust their bayonets on the body of the dead and wounded strewed about on the ground. A wild "hurrah!" burst out and "the Southern Cross" was torn down, I should say, among their laughter, such as if it had been a prize from a Maypole.

Of the armed diggers, some made off the best way they could, others surrendered themselves prisoners, and were collected in groups and marched down the gully. The Indian dragoons, sword in hand, rifle-pistols cocked, took charge of them all, and brought them in chains to the lock-up.

Dirigat Dominus Reginam Nostram

The red-coats were now ordered to "fall in"; their bloody work was over, and were marched off, dragging with them the "Southern Cross".

Their dead, as far as I did see, were four, and a dozen wounded, including Captain Wise, the identical one, I think whom I speak of in relating the events of Tuesday evening, November 28.

Dead and wounded had been fetched up in carts, waiting on the road, and all red-things hastened to Ballaarat.

The following is for the edification of all the well-affected and well-disposed of the present and future generation:

V.R.
NOTICE

Government Camp,
Ballaarat, Dec. 3rd, 1854.

Her Majesty's forces were this morning fired upon by a large body of evil-disposed persons of various nations, who had entrenched themselves in a stockade on the Eureka, and some officers and men killed.

Several of the rioters have paid the penalty of their crime, and a large number are in custody.

All well-disposed persons are earnestly requested to *return to their ordinary occupations, and to abstain from assembling in large groups*, and every protection will be afforded to them by the authorities.

ROBT. REDE,
Resident Commissioner.

God save the Queen.

Veritatem Dico Non Mentior

Here begins a foul deed, worthy of devils, and devils they were. The accursed troopers were now within the stockade. They dismounted, and pounced on firebrands from the large fire on the middle of the stockade, and deliberately set in a blaze all the tents round about. I did see with both eyes one of those devils, a tall, thick-shouldered, long-legged, fast Vandemonian-looking trooper, purposely striking a bundle of matches, and setting fire at the corner end, north of the very store of Diamond, where we had kept the council for the defence.

The howing and yelling was horrible. The wounded are now burnt to death; those who had laid down their arms, and taken refuge within tents, were kicked like brutes, and made prisoners.

At the burning of the Eureka Hotel, I expressed it to be my opinion that a characteristic of the British race is to delight in the calamity of a fire.

The troopers, enjoying the fun within the stockade, now spread it *without*. The tent next to mine (Quinn's) was soon in a blaze. I collected in haste my most important papers, and rushed out to remonstrate against such a wanton cruelty. Sub-inspector Carter pointing with his pistol ordered me to fall in with a batch of prisoners. There were no two ways: I obeyed. In the middle of the gully, I expostulated with Captain Thomas; he asked me whether I had been made a prisoner within the stockade. "No, sir," was my answer. He noticed my frankness, my anxiety and grief. After a few words in explanation, he, giving me a gentle stroke with his sword, told me "If you really are an honest digger, I do not want you, sir; you may return to your tent."

Mr Gordon – of the store of Gordon and McCallum, on the left of the gully, near the stockade – who had been made prisoner, and was liberated in the same way, and at the same time as myself, was and is a living witness to the above.

On crossing the gully to return to my tent, an infernal trooper trotting on the road to Ballaarat, took a deliberate aim at me, and fired his Minie rifle pistol with such a tolerable precision, that the shot whizzed and actually struck the brim of my cabbage-tree hat, and blew it off my head. Mrs Davis, who was outside her tent close by, is a living witness to the above.

At this juncture I was called by name from Doctor Carr, and Father Smyth, directed me by signs to come and help the wounded within the stockade.

Quis Dabit Capiti Meo, Aquam et Oculis Meis Fontem Lacrymarum et Plorabo Die ac Nocte!

I hastened, and what a horrible sight! Old acquaintances crippled with shots, the gore protruding from the bayonet wounds, their clothes and flesh burning all the while. Poor THONEN had his mouth literally choked with bullets;† my neighbour and mate Teddy More, stretched on the ground, both his thighs shot, asked me for a drop of water. Peter Lalor, who had been concealed under a heap of slaps, was in the agony of death, a stream of blood from under the slabs, heavily forcing its way down hill.

The tears choke my eyes, I cannot write any further.

Americans! your Doctor Kenworthy was not there, as he should have been, according to Humffray's letter.

Catholics! Father Smyth was performing his sacred duty to the dying, in spite of the troopers who threatened his life, and *forced* him at last to desist.

Protestants! spare us in future with your sabbath cant. Not one of your ministers was there, helping the digger in the hour of need.

John Bull! you wilfully bend your neck to any burden for palaver and war to protect you in your universal shop-keeping, and maintain your sacred rights of property; but human life is to you as it was to Napoleon: for him, fodder for the cannon; for you, tools to make money. A dead man needs no further care, and human kind breeds fast enough everywhere after all. – *Cetera quando rursum scribam.*

†Carl Wiesenhavern has one of the bullets in his possession.

Henry Parkes

THE FEDERAL AND SEPARATE INTERESTS OF THE COLONIES

[On Saturday March 16th 1867, a number of gentlemen connected with New South Wales entertained the Hon. Henry Parkes, the Colonial Secretary, and the Hon. Joseph Docker, the Postmaster-General of New South Wales, at dinner at Scott's Hotel, Melbourne. After the usual loyal toasts had been proposed, the Chairman proposed the healths of his honourable friends, the Chief Secretary and Postmaster-General of New South Wales. The toast was received with all the honours.]

Speech Delivered at Melbourne, March 16th 1867.

MR PARKES said: I am sure I express the feelings of my colleague as well as of myself, when I say that we are deeply gratified by the kind and cordial manner in which you have drunk this toast. We were told when we were invited to this entertainment that the gentlemen inviting us were colonists of New South Wales – gentlemen having a deep interest in the prosperity of that colony. This circumstance invests the present gathering with peculiar interest, because we ought not to forget – and I admit it freely and generously – that we are assembled in the capital of another colony, which is at the same time the greatest city in Australasia. The circumstance that we, the members of the Government of New South Wales – the parent of all the colonies – are met in this room in so cordial a manner by our fellow colonists, is one that I regard with special interest. In returning thanks for the compliment you have paid us, I set a special value upon this circumstance. Our worthy friend the chairman – and I am sure you must be wise men to place this gentleman in the chair – has told us pretty distinctly the occupation in which you are all engaged. I give our worthy friend the utmost credit for ingenuity and good nature; but if he expects me to make any serious revelations regarding the land policy of the Government, I fear he will be disappointed. If in the exercise of his bounteous good nature he has any design of tying me to a buggy and carrying me on to Fort Bourke, in order that I may acquire a knowledge of Riverine interests, all I can say is, he will not catch me on the other side of the Murray. I appreciate his kindness but would rather be excused from his services. Gentlemen, considering the few opportunities that I have had of understanding the country with which you are more particularly identified, considering that I have no personal interest in common with yours, I think there are few persons who have shown more consideration for the exceptional circumstances of the Border districts, or more sincere anxiety to do all that can be fairly done to place you on a level with the people of the other portions of New South Wales. On the question of the Border duties I have always felt very strongly the impolicy of collecting those duties along the River Murray. Years ago, before they were collected in accordance with law – for nothing could be more irregular than their collection at that time – I felt that if continued for any length of time they would be fraught with such serious evils that it would be better to lose the revenue than risk the danger of their collection. I have always regarded the establishment of inland Custom-houses as a positive evil which no circumstances could to any great extent modify or decrease, and I would rather have assented to any imaginable arrangements than see a whole body of custom-house officers stationed along the narrow river dividing the territory of Victoria from New South Wales. We know that the duties entrusted to officers at a remote distance from the central authority are seldom well performed; but however well they may be carried out, they must necessarily and inevitably lead to bickerings, to bad feeling, to much of that kind of evasion of the law which, if it goes on for any length of time, settles down into the inveterate vice of smuggling; and rather than see a numerous class of petty smugglers disseminating the virus of their bad habits and disaffected feeling throughout society along the banks of a river like the Murray, I would submit to almost any conceivable law. This is and always has been and always will be my view of the question. I expressed this view to the colonists on both sides of the Murray when I had the honour of visiting those districts during last year; and I am sure my honourable colleague will say that I did not lose any opportunity of enforcing those views upon the Government on my return to Sydney. With regard to distant portions of these Australian colonies, I am one of those who believe that where self-government can be carried out it is better that it should be carried out. I am a colonist sufficiently old to remember the time when the country which is now the colony of Victoria was part of the colony of New South Wales. I took some interest in public life when the agitation was going on for the separation of this portion of the territory. I was in this city of Melbourne on the very day when the separation from New South Wales was celebrated, and all my sympathies were with my fellow-colonists in this part of the territory. I thought it was only just to them, and must necessarily be beneficial to the whole of the population, that they should be separated from the old colony and erected into a separate community. Later still I was in the Legislature of the colony when the separation of Queensland took place, and if anyone chooses to search the records of Parliament he will find that my vote was recorded for motions previously made in favour of the separation of that colony. I believe that persons considerable in numbers, considerable in property, and considerable in their industrial enterprises, who are carrying on the work of colonisation at a remote distance of 600 or 700 miles from the seat of Government, should be allowed as they attain to numerical strength sufficient for the purpose – and if other circumstances conform to such a condition of things – to form a colony of themselves. I have great sympathy for any class of my fellow-colonists who are placed under the disadvantages and difficulties which remoteness from the seat of Government will at all times carry with it. I should not like to be misunderstood or to be supposed, even by implication, to be the advocate for the creation of a new colony to be called Riverina. However earnest some gentlemen may be as Riverine patriots, I am sure they will not be displeased with me for candidly declaring my own sentiments; and I do think that the colony of New South Wales, within the boundaries fixed by the Constitution Act under which we now live, has not yet been proved to be too large. I think, before we split up any portion of this territory, we should try better than we hitherto have done – and this I confess candidly – to govern these outlying districts satisfactorily and beneficially for the whole community. I think the Government in Sydney ought to devote all its energies, without the loss of a single year, to connecting the metropolis of the colony with those districts by railway. I am bound to acknowledge that one of the finest and noblest examples of statesmanship that I know of in the Australian colonies is the conception of the Victorian railway from Melbourne to Echuca, and the vigorous action of the Government in carrying it out to completion. I don't know who were the authors of that scheme, but I think it was sagacious in conception, and that it has been carried out with true patriotism; and I give the colony of Victoria every credit for its far-sightedness in this great work. But I should like to see the Government of New South Wales do something more than copy that example. I should like to see the parent colony putting forth all her spirit of enterprise, and constructing a railway to the Murrumbidgee with even double the energy of her ardent offspring. I should go further even than this. I should be disposed to devote all the revenue derived from those outlying districts in the interior to their improvement. I believe it is a sound principle to dedicate the revenue derived from the public lands of a new country to the improvement of that country, and that the mere expenditure incurred in carrying on the civil government should be met by the ordinary means of taxation. The land once alienated can never be alienated again, and the revenue derived from that source is collected once and for all. I think, therefore, it is a correct principle that the Governments of these new countries should devote the whole of this revenue to making the land more accessible for the purposes of settlement and civilisation. I held this doctrine years ago, and I hold it still. At all times I shall be prepared to support the doctrine with reference to the outlying districts of the country. Our worthy chairman has alluded to the occasion which has brought my honourable colleague and myself to the city of Melbourne; and I am sure you possess that interest which intelligent men must feel in anything which draws the colonies into closer intercourse and into a better understanding. For my own part, I do not hesitate to say that I regard this occasion – though I am in no sense the author of it – as one full of interest, as one from which much may be expected, and from which I believe many good results will undoubtedly flow. For the first time in the history of these Australian colonies they have all assembled, including New Zealand – I may say all of them, because they are all represented, with the exception of Western Australia – with no feeling of emulation less worthy than the desire to have the largest share in effecting a common end to promote their common interests. It appears to me a very important occasion; and from my intercourse with the gentlemen who have been entrusted with this important mission I have formed so good an opinion of their judgment, of their sound understanding, and of their disinterested desire to promote the good of the entire group of colonies, to lose sight of individual interests as far as they can be lost sight of consistently with a proper feeling of patriotism; that, although I am restricted from saying anything about our proceedings, I think I may venture to say that the results will not fail to be satisfactory to the Australian people, and productive of great good to the Australian family. Apart from all personal interest I take in this occasion, I think the time has arrived when these colonies should be united by some federal bond of connexion. I think it must be manifest to all thoughtful men that there are questions projecting themselves upon our attention which cannot be satisfactorily dealt with by any one of the individual Governments. I regard this occasion, therefore, with great interest, because I believe it will inevitably lead to a more permanent federal understanding. I do not mean to say that when you leave this room tonight you will see a new constellation of six stars in the heavens; I do not startle your imagination by asking you to look for the footprints of six giants in the morning dew, when the night rolls away; but this I feel certain of, that the mother-country will regard this congress of the colonies just in the same light as a father and mother may view the conduct of their children, when they first observe those children beginning to look out for homes and connexions for themselves. I am quite sure that the report of this meeting in your city of Melbourne, little as it may be thought of here, will make a profound impression upon the minds of thoughtful statesmen in England. They will see that, for the first time, these offshoots of empire in the Southern hemisphere can unite, and that in their union they are backed by nearly two millions of souls. They will see in them in reality an infant empire, and a power which they will feel must be treated with respect, and whose claims must receive a steady and respectful attention. Gentlemen, I have again to thank you for the compliment you have paid us by inviting us to this entertainment; and I can assure you that, if it shall ever lie in my power to serve the district with which you are connected, it will afford me a real happiness to do so. It may be, if we can only obtain a distinct promise that we are not to be carried to Fort Bourke, that we shall venture to cross the Murray on leaving this city; and if we do we shall employ the occasion to make ourselves better acquainted with those important portions of our great colony. Gentlemen, I freely admit the great advantages which belong to this colony of Victoria. I give credit to its people and Government for their enterprise and for the vigour displayed in the management of their affairs; I admit in the fullest degree its ample resources. But unless I am prepared wilfully to shut my eyes, I cannot conceal from myself that we possess a colony much vaster in territory, with much more varied gifts of nature – a colony rich in coal, rich in iron, rich in gold, with pastoral lands unequalled under the sun, and with wide regions fit for nearly every kind of production. With such vast variety and richness of resources, if we don't march ahead of all the other colonies it will be our own blame. We have on our north the young colony of Queensland, which is making vigorous steps onwards, and any man with common sagacity may see that the more rapidly that colony advances the more will it give us a central position in the Australian group. With our splendid harbour, our beautifully situated city, our vast territory, all our varied and inexhaustible natural wealth, if we don't convert our colony into a great and prosperous nation, it will be a miracle of error for which we shall have to answer as for a gigantic sin. I believe in the greatness of New South

Wales, and I hope there can be no disrespect, after what I have stated, in expressing the opinion that she will eventually be the leading colony of Australia. I don't think that it is possible to be otherwise. If I were asked to account for the superior progress made hitherto by our younger sister, I should account for it simply on the ground that Victoria has a new population, all whose energies are awakened and directed to a precipitate progress; while the elder colony, having a much larger range of family life and having more stable interests, has been more conservative in all its instincts, and more disposed to question every new idea and every new project. But the time will come when by the very force of enlightenment a new order of things will arise, and the energies of our population will be directed to a wise development of those resources that must yet give us a splendid position in the family of the Australian colonies.

Ned Kelly

FROM THE JERILDERIE LETTER

It will pay Government to give those people who are suffering innocence, justice and liberty. If not I will be compelled to show some colonial strategm which will open the eyes of not only the Victoria Police and inhabitants but also the whole British army and now doubt they will acknowledge their hounds were barking at the wrong stump and that Fitzpatrick will be the cause of greater slaughter to the Union Jack than Saint Patrick was to the snakes and toads in Ireland.

The Queen of England was as guilty as Baumgarten and Kennedy Williamson and Skillion of what they were convicted for when the horses were found on the Murray River I wrote a letter to Mr Swanhill of Lake Rowan to acquaint the Auctioneer and to advertise my horses for sale I brought some of them to that place but did not sell I sold some of them in Benalla Melbourne and other places and left the colony and became a rambling gambler soon after I left there was a warrant for me and the Police searched the place and watched night and day for two or three weeks and when they could not snare me they got a warrant against my brother Dan And on the 15th of April Fitzpatrick came to the eleven mile creek to arrest him he had some conversation with a horse dealer whom he swore was William Skillion this man was not called in Beechworth besides several other witnesses, who alone could have proved Fitzpatricks falsehood after leaving this man he went to the house asked was dan in Dan came out I hear previous to this Fitzpatrick had some conversation with

Williamson on the hill. he asked Dan to come to Greta with him as he had a warrant for him for stealing Whitty's horses Dan said all right they both went inside Dan was having something to eat his mother asked Fitzpatrick what he wanted Dan for the trooper said he had a warrant for him Dan then asked him to produce it he said it was only a telegram sent from Chiltern but Sergeant Whelan ordered him to relieve Steel at Greta and call and arrest Dan and take him in to Wangaratta next morning and get him remanded Dans mother said Dan need not go without a warrant unless he liked and that the trooper had no business on her premises without some authority besides his own word.

The trooper pulled out his revolver and said he would blow her brains out if she interfered in the arrest she told him it was a good job for him Ned was not there or he would ram his revolver down his throat Dan looked out and said Ned is coming now, the trooper being off his guard looked out and when Dan got his attention drawn he dropped the knife and fork which showed he had no murderous intent and slapped Hennan's hug on him took his revolver and kept him there until Skillion and Ryan came with horses which Dan sold that night.

The trooper left and invented some scheme to say that he got shot which any man can see is false, he told Dan to clear out that Sergeant Steel and Detective Brown and Strachan would be there before morning Strachan had been over the Murray trying to get up a case against him and they would convict him if they caught him as the stock society offored an enticement for witnesses to swear anything and the germans over the Murray would swear to the wrong man as well as the right.

Next day Williamson and my mother was arrested and Skillion the day after who was not there at all at the time of the row which can be proved by 8 or 9 witnesses and the Police got great credit and praise in the papers for arresting the mother of 12 children one an infant on her breast and those two quiet hard working innocent men who would not know the difference a revolver and a saucepan handle and kept them six months awaiting trial and then convicted them on the evidence of the meanest article that ever the sun shone on it seems that the jury was well chosen by the Police as there was a discharged Sergeant amongst them which is contrary to law they thought it impossible for a Policeman to swear a lie but I can assure them it was by that means and hiring cads they get promoted I have heard from a trooper that he never knew Fitzpatrick to be one night sober and that he sold his sister to a chinaman but he looks a young strapping rather genteel more fit to be a starcher to a laundress than a policeman. For to a keen observer he has the wrong appearance for a manly heart the deceit and cowardice is too plain to be seen in the puny cabbage hearted looking face.

I heard nothing of this transaction until very close on the trial I being then over 400 miles from Greta when I heard I was outlawed and a hundred pound reward for me for shooting a trooper in Victoria and a hundred pound for any man that could prove a conviction of horsestealing against me so I came back to Victoria knew I would get no justice if I gave myself up I enquired after my brother Dan and found him digging on Bullock Creek heard how the Police used to be blowing that they would not ask me to stand they would shoot me first and then cry surrender and how they used to rush into the house upset all the milk dishes break tins of eggs empty the flour out of bags onto the ground and even the meat out of the cask and destroy all provisions and shove the girls in front of them into the rooms like dogs so as if anyone was there they would shoot the girls first but they knew well I was not there or I would have scattered their blood and brains like rain I would manure the Eleven Mile with their bloated carcasses and yet remember there is not one drop of murderous blood in my veins.

Superintendent Smith used to say to my sisters see all the men all I have out today I will have as many more tomorrow and we will blow him into pieces as small as paper that is in our guns Detective Ward and Constable Hayes took out their revolvers and threatened to shoot the girls and children in Mrs Skillions absence the greatest ruffians and murderers no matter how deprived would not be guilty of such a cowardly action, and this sort of cruelty and disgraceful and cowardly conduct to my brothers and sisters who had no protection coupled with the conviction of my mother and those men certainly made my blood boil and I don't think there is a man born could have the patience to suffer it as long as I did or ever allow his blood to get cold while such insults as these were unavenged and yet in every paper that is printed I am called the blackest and coldest blooded murderer ever on record But if I hear any more of it I will not exactly show them what cold blooded murder is but wholesale and retail slaughter something different to shooting three troopers in self defence and robbing a bank. I would have been rather hot blooded to throw down my rifle and let them shoot me and my innocent brother. They were not satisfied with frightening my sisters night and day and destroying their provisions and lagging my mother and infant and those innocent men but should follow me and my brother into the wilds where he had been quietly digging neither molesting or interfering with anyone he was making good wages as the creek is very rich within half a mile where I shot Kennedy. I was not there long and on the 25th of October I came on Police tracks between Table top and the bogs. I crossed them and returning in the evening I came on a different lot of tracks making for the shingle hut I went to our camp and told my brother and his two mates. Me and my brother went and found their camp at the shingle hut about a mile from my brothers house. We saw they carried long firearms and we knew our doom was sealed if we could not beat those before the others would come as I knew the other party of Police would soon join them and if they came on us at our camp they would shoot us down like dogs at our work as we had only two guns we thought it best to try and bail those up, take their firearms and ammunition and horses and we could stand a chance with the rest We approached the spring as close as we could get to the camp as the intervening space being clear ground and no battery we saw two men at the logs they got up and one took a double barreled fowling piece and fetched a horse down and hobbled him at the tent we thought there were more men in the tent asleep those outside being on sentry we could have shot those two men without speaking but not wishing to take their lives we waited McIntyre laid his gun against a stump and Lonigan sat on the log I advanced, my brother Dan keeping McIntyre covered which he took to be Constable Flood and had he not obeyed my orders, or attempted to reach for the gun or draw his revolver he would have been shot dead, but when I called on them to throw up their hands McIntyre obeyed and Lonigan ran some six or seven yards to a battery of logs instead of dropping behind the one he was sitting on, he had just got to the logs and put his head up to take aim when I shot him that instant or he would have shot me as I took him for Strachan the man who said he would not ask me to stand he would shoot me first like a dog. But it happened to be Lonigan the man who in company with Sergeant Whelan Fitzpatrick and King the Bootmaker and Constable O'Day that tried to put a pair of handcuffs on me in Benalla but could not and had to allow McInnis the miller to put them on, previous to Fitzpatrick swearing he was shot, I was fined two pounds for hitting Fitzpatrick and two pounds for not allowing five curs like Sergeant Whelan O'Day Fitzpatrick King and Lonigan who caught me by the privates and would have sent me to Kingdom come only I was not ready and he is the man that blowed before he left Violet Town if Ned Kelly was to be shot he was the man would shoot him and no doubt he would shoot me even if I threw up my arms and laid down as he knew four of them could not arrest me single handed not to talk of the rest of my mates, also either he or me would have to die, this he knew well therefore he had a right to keep out of my road, Fitzpatrick is the only one I hit out of the five in Benalla, this shows my feeling towards him as he said we were good friends and even swore it but he was the biggest enemy I had in the country with the exception of Lonigan and he can be thankful I was not there when he took a revolver and threatened to shoot my mother in her own house it is not true I fire three shots and missed him a yard and a half I don't think I would use a revolver to shoot a man like him when I was within a yard and a half of him or attempted to fire into a house where my mother brothers and sisters was according to Fitzpatricks statement all around him a man that is such a bad shot as to miss a man three times at a yard and a half would never attempt to fire into a house among a house full of women and children while I had a pair of arms and bunch of fives at the end of them they never failed to peg out anything they came in contact with and Fitzpatrick knew the weight of one them only too well as it run up against him once in Benalla and cost me two pound odd as he is very subject to fainting. As soon as I shot Lonigan he jumped up and staggered some distance from the logs with his hands raised and then fell he surrendered but too late I asked McIntyre who was in the tent he replied no one. I advanced and took possession of their two revolvers and fowling piece which I loaded with bullets instead of shot.

I asked McIntyre where his mates was he said they had gone down the creek and he did not expect them that night he asked me was I going to shoot him and his mates. I told him no I would shoot no man if he gave up his arms and leave the force he said the police all knew Fitzpatrick had wronged us and he intended to leave the force as he had bad health and his life was insured he told me he intended going home and that Kennedy and Scanlon were out looking for our camp and also about the other Police he told me the N.S.W. Police had shot a man for shooting Sergeant Walling I told him if they did they had shot the wrong man and I expect your gang came to do the same with me he said no they did not come to shoot me they came to apprehend me I asked him what they carried spencer rifles and breech loading fowling pieces and so much ammunition for as the Police was only supposed to carry one revolver and 6 cartridges in the revolver but they had eighteen rounds of revolver cartridges each three dozen for the fowling piece and twenty one spencer rifle cartridges and God knows how many they had away with the rifle this looked as if they meant not only to shoot me but to riddle me but I don't know either Kennedy Scanlon or him and had nothing against them, he said he would get them to give up their arms if I would not shoot them as I could not blame them, they had to do their duty I said I did not blame them for doing honest duty but I could not suffer them blowing me to pieces in my own native land and they knew Fitzpatrick wronged us and why not make it public and convict him but no they would rather riddle poor unfortunate creoles. but they will rue the day ever Fitzpatrick got among them. Our two mates came over when they heard the shot fired but went back again for fear the Police might come to our camp while we were all away and manure bullock flat with us on our arrival I stopped at the logs and Dan went back to the spring for fear the troopers would come in that way but soon I heard them coming up the creek I told McIntyre to tell them to give up their arms, he spoke to Kennedy who was some distance in front of Scanlon he reached for his revolver and jumped off, on the offside of his horse and got behind a tree when I called on them to throw up their arms and Scanlan who carried the rifle slewed his horse around to gallop away but the horse would not go and as quick as thought fired at me with the rifle without unslinging it and was in the act of firing again when I had to shoot him and he fell from his horse.

I could have shot them without speaking but their lives was no good to me. McIntyre jumped on Kennedys horse and I allowed him to go as I did not like to shoot him after he surrendered or I would have shot him as he was between me and Kennedy therefore I could not shoot Kennedy without shooting him first. Kennedy kept firing from behind the tree my brother Dan advanced and Kennedy ran I followed him he stopped behind another tree and fired again. I shot him in the armpit and he dropped his revolver and ran I fired again with the gun as he slewed around to surrender I did not know he had dropped his revolver, the bullet passed through the right side of his chest and he could not live or I would have let him go had they been my own brothers I could not help shooting them or else let them shoot me which they would have done had their bullets been directed as they intended them. But as for handcuffing Kennedy to a tree or cutting his ear off or brutally treating any of them is a falsehood if Kennedy's ear was cut off it was not done by me and none of my mates was near him after he was shot I put his cloak over him and left him as well as I could and were they my own brothers I could not have been more sorry for them this cannot be called wilful murder for I was compelled to shoot them, or lie down and let them shoot me it would not be wilful murder if they packed our remains in, shattered into a mass of animated gore to Mansfield, they would have got great praise and credit as well as promotion but I am reconed a horrid brute because I had not been cowardly enough to lie down for them under such trying circumstances and insults to my people certainly their wives and children are to be pitied but they must remember those men came into the bush with the intention of scattering pieces of me and my brother all over the bush and yet they know and acknowledge I have been wronged and my mother and four or five men lagged innocent and is my brothers and sisters and my mother not to be pitied also who has no alternative only to put up with the brutal and cowardly conduct of a parcel of big ugly fat-necked wombat headed big bellied magpie legged narrow hipped splay-footed sons of Irish Bailiffs or english landlords which is better known as offices of Justice or Victorian Police who some calls honest gentlemen but I would like to know what business an honest man would have in the Police as it is an old saying it takes a rogue to catch a rogue and a man that knows nothing about roguery would never enter the force and take an oath to arrest brother sister father or mother if required and to have a case and conviction if possible any man knows it is possible to swear a lie and if a policeman looses a conviction for the sake of swearing a lie he has broke his oath therefore he is a perjuror either ways, a Policeman is a disgrace to his country not alone to the mother that suckled him, in the first place he is a rogue in his heart but too cowardly to follow it up without having the force to disguise it. Next he is a traitor to his country ancestors and religion as they were all catholics before the Saxons and Cranmore yoke held sway since they were persecuted massacred thrown into martyrdom and tortured beyond the ideas of the present generation. What would people say if they saw a strapping big lump of an Irishman shepherding sheep for fifteen bob a week or tailing turkeys in Tallarook ranges for a smile from Julia or even begging his tucker, they would say he ought to be ashamed of himself and tar-and-feather him. But he would be a king to a policeman who for a lazy loafing cowardly bilit left the ash corner deserted the shamrock, the emblem of true wit and beauty to serve under a flag and nation that has destroyed massacreed and murdered their fore-fathers by the greatest torture as rolling them down hill in spiked barrels pulling their toe and finger nails and on the wheel and every torture imaginable more was transported to Van Diemand's Land to pine young lives away in starvation and misery among tyrants worse than the promised hell itself all of true blood bone and beauty, that was not murdered on their own soil, or had fled to America or other countries to bloom again another day were doomed to Port McQuarie Toweringabbie Norfolk island and Emu plains and in those places of tyrany and condemnation many a blooming Irishman rather than subdue to the Saxon yoke were flogged to death and bravely died in servile chains but true to the shamrock and a credit to Paddys land What would people say if I became a policeman and took an oath to arrest my brother and sisters and relations and convict them by fair or foul means after the conviction of my mother and the persecutions and insults offered to myself and people Would they say I was a decent gentleman and yet a policeman is still in worse and guilty of meaner actions than that The Queen must surely be proud of such heroic men as the Police and Irish soldiers as It takes eight or eleven of the biggest mud crushers in Melbourne to take one poor little half starved larrakin to a watchhouse. I have seen as many as eleven, big and ugly enough to lift Mount Macedon out of a crab hole more like the species of a baboon or Guerilla than a man actually come into a court house and swear they could not arrest one eight stone larrakin and them armed with battens and niddies without some civilians assistance and some of them going to the hospital from the effects of hits from the fists of the larrakin and the Magistrate would send the poor little larrakin into a dungeon for being a better man than such a parcel of armed curs. What would England do if America declared war and hoisted a green flag as it is all Irishman that has got command of her armies forts and batteries even her very life guards and beef tasters are Irish would they not slew around and fight her with their own arms for the sake of the colour they dare not wear for years and to reinstate it and rise old Erins isle once more from the pressure and tyrannism of the English yoke which has kept it in poverty and starvation and caused them to wear the enemy's coat. What else can England expect.

Is there not big fat-necked Unicorns enough paid to torment and drive me to do thing which I don't wish to do, without the public assisting them I have never interfered with any person unless they deserved it and yet there are civilians who take fire-arms against me, for what reason I do not know unless they want me to turn on them and exterminate them with out medicine. I shall be compelled to make an example of some of them if they cannot find no other employment If I had robbed and plundered ravished and murdered everything I met young and old rich and poor the public could not do any more than take firearms and assisting the police as they have done, but by the light that shines pegged on an ant-bed with their bellies opened their fat taken out rendered and poured down their throat boiling hot will be cool to what pleasure I will give some of them and any person aiding or harbouring or assisting the Police in any way whatever or employing any person whom they know to be a detective or cad or those who would be so deprived as to take blood money will be outlawed and declared unfit to be allowed human buriel their property either consumed or confiscated and them theirs and all belonging to them exterminated off the face of the earth, the enemy I cannot catch myself I shall give a payable reward for, I would like to know who put that article that reminds me of a poodle dog half clipped in the lion fashion called Brooke E. Smith Superintendent of Police he knows as much about commanding Police as Captain Standish does about mustering mosquitoes and boiling them down for their fat on the back blocks of the Lachlan for he has a head like a turnip a stiff neck as big as his shoulders narrow hipped and pointed towards the feet like a vine stake and if there is any one to be called a murderer regarding Kennedy, Scanlan and Lonigan it is that misplaced poodle he gets as much pay as a dozen good troopers if there is any *good* in them, and what does he do for it he cannot look behind him without turning his whole frame it takes three or four police to keep sentry while he sleeps in Wangaratta, for fear of body snatchers do they think he is a superior animal to the men that has to guard him if so why not send the men that gets big pay and reconed superior to the common police after me and you shall soon save the country of high salaries to men that is fit for nothing else but getting better men than himself shot and sending orphan children to the industrial school to make prostitutes and cads of them for the Detectives and other evil disposed persons send the high paid and men that received big salaries for year in a gang by themselves after me, As it makes no difference to them but it will give them a chance of showing whether they are worth more pay than a common trooper or not and I think the Public will soon find they are only in the road of good men and obtaining money under false pretences. I do not call McIntyre a coward for I reckon he is as game a man as wears the jacket as he had the presence of mind to know his position, directly as he was spoken to, and only foolishness to disobey, it was cowardice that made Lonigan and the others fight it is only foolhardiness to disobey an outlaw as any Policeman or other man who do not throw up their arms directly as I call on them knows the consequence which is a speedy dispatch to Kingdom come I wish those men who joined the stock protection society to withdraw their money and give it and as much more to the widows and orphans and poor of Greta district where I spent and will again spend many a happy day fearless free and bold as it only aids the police to procure false witnesses and go whacks with men to steal horses and lag innocent men it would suit them far better to subscribe a sum and give it to the poor of their district and there is no fear of anyone stealing their property for no man could steal their horses without the knowledge of the poor if any man was mean enough to steal their property the poor would rise out to a man and find them if they were on the face of the earth it will always pay a rich man to be liberal with the poor and make as little enemies as he can as he shall find if the poor is on his side he shall loose nothing by it. If they depend in the police they shall be drove to destruction, as they can not and will not protect them if duffing and bushranging were abolished the police would have to cadge for their living I speak from experience as I have sold horses and cattle innumerable and yet eight head of the culls is all ever was found I never was interfered with whilst I kept up this successful trade. I give fair warning to all those who has reason to fear me to sell out and give £10 out of every hundred towards the widow and orphan fund and do not attempt to reside in Victoria but as short a time as possible after reading this notice, neglect this and abide by the consequences, which shall be worse than the rust in the wheat in Victoria or the druth of a dry season to the grasshoppers in New South Wales I do not wish to give the order full force without giving timely warning, but I am a widows son outlawed and my orders *must be obeyed*.

EDWARD KELLY.

William Lane

ONE-MAN-ONE-VOTE

As a natural result of common school education the common man is beginning to have opinions and to criticise institutions. In every country where common thought is thus started its first encounter is with the customs which give one man authority over other men regardless of the consent of those others. If there is an absolute dictator men ask by what right John dictates to Tom. If there is a despotic emperor men ask who William is that Peter should be born to stand up or lie down as William directs. And if there is so-called representative government through which a quarter of the community puts a ring in the nose of the other three-quarters, the common men whose noses are ringed enquire energetically why this is thusly. Here in Queensland, as in other parts of the world, we have found out that our noses are ringed by gross electoral inequalities; here, a small minority of squatters and land-grabbers have hold of the legislative rope with which they haul us about as much as they like. One-man-one-vote means equal voice in law-making for all men, thereby giving the men of Queensland opportunity to be the rulers of Queensland and effectively snapping the ring-in-the-nose wherewith the propertied classes now control us for their own selfish purposes.

Based Upon General Principles

If we reason upon general principles, if we take into consideration accepted ideas of Freedom and Justice, particularly if we suppose that it is right to do to others as we would have others do to us, there can be no two answers about one-man-one-vote. Free states are manifestly those in which government is by the will and with the consent of the governed, in which every man stands equal before the law. And it is as manifestly unjust for one man or one set of men to make laws for others who are allowed no opportunity to take part in the making of such laws as it is manifestly necessary for men associated in a state to recognise some equitable method of arriving at a mutually authoritative decision upon disputed points. The broadest and the narrowest conceptions of Freedom, Justice, Right, Fair Dealing, both imply this: That laws shall be mutually agreed upon by those who by act of citizenship have agreed not only to keep for themselves but to maintain against attack all constitutional regulations instituted for the common well being.

A More Equitable Method of Government

One-man-one-vote is an attempt to reach a more equitable method of governance; it is a protest against the usurpation of governance which reached its climax under kingcraft and has been passed along from autocrat to aristocrat, from aristocrat to plutocrat, until it nearly confronts the democrat whom it has so long wronged. The term one-man-one-vote expresses a principle which appeals to the hearts of all who desire a better world and a higher civilisation, for it means that Man himself is to be recognised as the unit in the State, that at the ballot box Humanity alone shall be known, that as far as the law can do it every man shall enter the polling booth a simple citizen and no more.

The Truth that Man Is Equal

Blind fools may laugh at idealism all they like, but idealism, the recognition of Truths, is what moves mankind up the ladder of progress. And this has been one divine Truth, known and loved and preserved for our betterance, through ages of darkness and degradation, that in spite of all his inequalities Man is equal. We have had the world bowing enslaved before an Alexander. We have had Russian boyars puddling their feet in the gutted entrails of human foot-warmers. We have had the French lords claiming the *droit de seigneur*, taking the peasant's bride for the bridal-night. And among our own people we have seen and see still millions upon millions living like imbruted beasts. But all the time the ideal has lived, enshrined in the religions that sprung from the aching heart of the common people. At the Judgment-seat of God there was Equality, there the robes of the king and the rags of the beggar fell to the ground together and each man stood naked as he was born and as he died. This is the ideal conception of Justice, that men in themselves are equal – and we want Justice to be with us a little for it is only through Justice that good can come.

The Right of the Citizen

It is clearly Just and Right that all those who are citizens of a state should have equal voice in the making of the laws which all citizens are equally bound not only to obey but to maintain. The alien – that is the citizen of another state who enters our state as a visitor *on suffrance only* and who is not part and parcel of our community – may justly have demanded of him that while he is with us he should, without having a voice in their making, submit to our laws and conform to our regulations; his interests are not our common interests, he may be and often is more interested in weakening our social organisation than in strengthening it, like the Chinaman his only object is generally to get wealth wherewith to return again to his own people; the claims of the citizen to recognition naturally do not apply to the alien. Nor can the minors, the children, and the insane, those who are not yet grown to years of discretion or who are regarded by the laws very differently to adults, be presumed to rank as full citizens, as independent electors. But the adult members of any community, whether men or women, can in Justice demand an equal voice with any other member in the making of the laws which each and every one of them must commonly obey and maintain.

Women Should Have Justice, Too!

One-man-one-vote has this weakness, this failing, that it does not include the women. Not a single principle can be advanced in support of the rights of men which does not apply with equal force to the rights of women. Our mothers, our wives, our sisters and our daughters are as essentially citizens of the State as any man of us. They must obey all laws, they suffer from unjust laws, they benefit by good laws, equally with the rest of us. We men deserve to have Justice denied to us if we deny Justice to our women. But there is this about the one-man-one-vote agitation that it does not deny the rights of women. It simply deals with one part of an Injustice, leaving another part of the same Injustice to be dealt with in the future. And of this we may be sure and certain that the men of Queensland or of any other state, as a mass, will be far more inclined to secure for the womenfolk the same Justice which they have managed to secure for themselves than will any propertied section which wields authority in defiance of all Justice and in antagonism to all conception of free and equal government.

Class Government Is Usurpation

For this we must never lose sight of: class governance is a usurpation, a tyranny which has its root in the ages when armed robbers, military castes, ground the peaceful tillers of the soil into slavery. Our parliamentary system, of which the very opponents of one-man-one-vote profess to be so proud, is only a degenerated survival of the assembly at which in primitive times our Teutonic forefathers gathered, free and equal, to make for themselves laws for their common governance. And it is because for countless generations the race we come of governed itself thus, knowing neither king nor landlord nor rank nor wealth nor place nor privilege in its tremendous march from Central Asia to the Atlantic coast that the desire for self-governance is so instinctive in us today. It is told of these fathers of ours that, when they burst upon the rotten Empire of Rome, a band of Goths stormed and took a Roman town. Their chief, a man elected by his fellows to lead them to war, saw among the plunder a beautiful porcelain vase and set it aside for himself. "Why is that apart?" asked an old warrior. "It is the chief's," said a young one. Down came the old Goth's battleaxe, smashing the porcelain into atoms. "The Goths are equal," he cried, "next time he steals let him look to his head." So much for privilege in the old Teutonic day, but wrong begot wrong and those who began by plundering others ended by being plundered themselves. The chiefs stole and stole and there were none left to break their heads and finally it came to be that the common lands and the common cattle and the common law-making and the common liberties, the free conditions, which gave our race its brains and its vigour and its courage and its contempt for danger and its respect for women and its hatred of lying and all that is good and true and loyal and brave in us, were all stolen away from us and we are what we are. To win back our liberties is our duty. We have a right to have them back and to govern ourselves for our own good in our own way. One-man-one-vote is simply self-governance, a right lost indeed by the crimes of some and follies of others and the weakness of all, but still our right when we can get it for truths live always and Justice never dies.

The Plea of the Usurpers

The classes which have usurped government, which make pretence of representative authority while controlling the laws and domineering over the community by means of plural voting for themselves, wholesale disfranchisement of the workers, unequal electoral districts and nominee chambers, have certain specious arguments against one-man-one-vote with which they seek to lull their own consciences and to delude and bewilder us. They ask if the drunken and the sober, the industrious and the idle, the ignorant and the intelligent, and so on through a whole catalogue of opposites, are to be equal at the ballot-box. What do they really mean?

The Inequality of Intellect

This specious and pretentious argument against one-man-one-vote is used by opponents so often that it necessitates notice otherwise undeserved. "You cannot make men equal," they say. "There will always be the intellectual and the foolish and some who will exert a personal influence not only over a whole people but for all time." Just so! We cannot make men equal where they are not equal but we can maintain the equality of men where it exists, as it does exist where it is now denied. In our individuality, in our personality, in ourselves, as Men, we are all equal – and the only true inequality is in the influence which one personality wields over other personalities. For what do men like Sir George Grey, like Griffith, like McIlwraith, want more votes than the humblest when by their personal power they move hundreds and thousands, Sir George Grey hundreds of thousands, of minds? Is there a single man of superior intellect in Queensland, or in Australia, or in the world, who does not affect somewhat the individuality of all who come within his sphere, no matter what he may be? And will one-man-one-vote impede this influence of the superior intellects, will it not rather strengthen and enlarge it in every way? For as things are, power is given not to the more intellectual, through a desirable influence on others, but to pickers-up of corner allotments, grabbers of squatting land, holders of various properties, whatever their intellectuality may be. This is absurd.

Morality as a Qualification

As a matter of fact sobriety, industriousness, intelligence and general virtuousness are not intended by the usurping classes to be the tests of electoral rights. Drunkenness is too usual among the working mass but is even more frequently seen among the rich and well to do. The Queensland Assembly of today, the meeting place of legislators who do not represent the people of Queensland, is often no better than the lobby of a pot-house and witnesses scenes which would not be tolerated for an instant in any friendly society or trade union meeting. As for industriousness, it is only by the industry of the labouring people, so largely disfranchised, that wealth exists at all. While as for intelligence, that is similarly not an attribute peculiar to those who by inheritance, luck, skin-flinting, or profit-mongering shrewdness have got to possess the property which is supposed to indue them with the prerogative of ruling over their poorer fellow men. If we were to set up a standard of morality as the qualification for those who would claim full citizenship, then we should have to disfranchise a very considerable percentage of plural voters and to admit to the franchise the vast majority of those now denied any share in the governance of their country. This twaddle about sobriety, industry, intellect and so forth is worthless sophistry, used only by those who for another reason desire to withhold from the people the inborn right of self-governance.

The Real Cause of Opposition

What is this other reason, the real reason, why one-man-one-vote is opposed? It is opposed only by the propertied classes in their own selfish self-interest, by the great land monopolists, by the great mine-monopolists, by the importing and trading monopolists, by the banks, the syndicates, the employers' associations, and the hundred and one cringing dependents of these high priests of the great god Mammon. They oppose it for this reason only, that the masses are intelligent enough, sober enough, earnest enough, to see that Society as it is constructed is not sound, that the Laws as they stand are not Just, that Government as we have it is a farce which is exerted for the advantage of Capitalism regardless of the well-being of the People at large. They fear that if one-man-one-vote is secured by the common people, the labourers who toil and have nothing, the masses who are worse off amid all the luxury and glitter of our Christian civilisation than ever savages were in so-called heathen lands, that the first use made of that power will be legislative "interference" with existing industrial conditions. They are afraid of Eight Hour Bills and Factories Bills and Lien Bills, of the abolition of imprisonment for "absconding" labourers, of resumption of the squatter-lands and reform of the land laws generally, of work being found for the unemployed and of the refusal of popular parliaments to let workmen be shot down like dogs at the bidding of tyrannical Capitalism. They object to Reform: that is the only reason for this opposition to one-man-one-vote.

The Enemy of the People

The man who opposes one-man-one-vote is the enemy of the people. Whoever he is, wherever he is, no matter what he is, he would defraud his fellow men of their political rights solely in order to maintain the iniquitous laws and unbearable industrial conditions which every thoughtful man must see and which every honest man must admit to be wrong. We may not all agree as to the best way to right these wrongs, we may differ bitterly but honestly as to the unhappy inequalities which cause such world-wide misery and discontent, but we must agree, if we are honest, that peaceful remedy can only come by the untrammelled play of that self-governance which is based upon Justice and ignores class and privilege. It is not from the squatter and the land-grabber, the syndicator and the speculator that we can look for help. We must look to ourselves. And how can we look to ourselves so long as we are so disfranchised and handicapped while these gentry vote and count over and over again?

Our Duty to Ourselves

We must have one-man-one-vote. We know now that we owe no duty to a law which usurpers impose upon us, that the government which denies rights to any people is a tyranny and that our duty to ourselves and to our fellows and to our children and to all Humanity is to make such tyranny impossible. We know also that this usurpation of government by the classes over the masses is the great barrier to the changes which are absolutely necessary if Civilisation, with all that it implies, is not to go to pieces under our feet. We want to get to the ballot box, free and equal, and they are trying to prevent us. The employers' associations are organised to prevent us. Griffith quibbles when he is asked his intentions. The Government, the magistracy, the whole machinery of Capitalism, is doing everything in its power to bar the common man from the polling booth, to conserve the privileges of the favoured few. And then they rave at us about "law and order". Have we not been as tolerant of their "law and order" as ever people could be who had the faintest inkling of what Justice was and who know that the laws have been deliberately designed to oppress the people by the privileged classes who have usurped law-making and who now defend their usurpation against the one-man-one-vote?

JOHN MILLER.

Notes

FIRST IMPRESSIONS

George Worgan

Journal of a First Fleet Surgeon (Sydney: Library of Australian History, 1978), a publication of the William Dixson Foundation, is an exact transcription of the original manuscript now in the Mitchell Library. Pages 1 to 10 reproduced here are part of a coherent narrative of Worgan's first months in Australia.

Thomas Watling

Watling's letters to his aunt, Marion Kirkpatrick, who had raised him after his parents' early death, were first printed in Scotland in 1794, as *Letters from an Exile at Botany-Bay, to his Aunt in Dumfries; giving a particular account of the settlement of New South Wales, with the Customs and Manners of the Inhabitants* (Penrith: Ann Bell, n.d.). Pages 1–2 and 7–21 are reproduced here, as transcribed by George Mackaness for vol. XII of Australian Historical Monographs, 1945. The omitted pages relate to Watling's thwarted attempt to escape while at Cape Town, messages to friends in England and his proposal to execute "a Picturesque Description" of New South Wales if patronage was forthcoming.

Henry Savery

These sketches of life and characters in early Hobart originally appeared in the Hobart newspaper the *Colonial Times* between 5 June and 25 December 1829. Its editor and printer, Andrew Bent, issued them in volume form, under the same title, *The Hermit in Van Diemen's Land*, early in 1830 and was immediately charged with libel. Savery's model had been Felix McDonough's *The Hermit in London; or, Sketches of English Manners* (1821). This type of sketch remained popular throughout the nineteenth century, with Savery's

"Hermit" being succeeded by Marcus Clarke's "The Peripatetic Philosopher" and J.S. James's "The Vagabond", to mention only authors included here.

Ellen Clacy

A Lady's Visit to the Gold Diggings of Australia in 1852–53, "written on the spot" (London: Hurst and Blackett, 1853), has been reprinted (ed. Patricia Thompson, Melbourne: Lansdowne, 1963). Clacy's description of the diggings has been extracted from the end of chapter V and the middle of chapter VI.

John Mitchel

Jail Journal; or, Five Years in British Prisons (New York: *Citizen* Office) first appeared in 1854; there have been several later editions.

Ada Cambridge

The extract from *Thirty Years in Australia* (London: Methuen, 1903) consists of the second half of chapter II.

ABORIGINAL ENCOUNTERS

Watkin Tench

A Narrative of the Expedition to Botany Bay; with an account of New South Wales . . . (London: J. Debrett, 1789) could be called the first Australian bestseller since it had, in 1789 alone, three editions in London, two in Paris, and one in each of Dublin, New York, Amsterdam and Frankfurt. Chapter VIII is reproduced here, together with most of chapter III of *A Complete Account of the Settlement at Port Jackson . . .* (London: G. Nichol, 1793). These two works by Tench have been reprinted together as *Sydney's First Four Years* (ed. L.F. Fitzhardinge, Sydney: Library of Australian History, 1979).

Charles Sturt

All of the explorers' journals included in this selection are available in modern facsimile editions, as well as the journals of many others, such as those of Edward John Eyre, Ludwig Leichhardt and John McDowall Stuart. Charles Sturt's *Two Expeditions into the Interior of Southern Australia, During the years 1828, 1829, 1830, and 1831: with observations on the soil, climate and general resources of the Colony of New South Wales* (2 vols, London: Smith, Elder and Co.) first appeared in 1833. The extract comes from volume 2, the second half of chapter IV of "Expedition down the Morumbidgee and Murray Rivers in 1829, 1830 and 1831" (pp. 102–10).

Thomas Mitchell

Five years after Charles Stuart, Thomas Mitchell produced his *Three Expeditions into the Interior of Eastern Australia; with descriptions of the newly explored region of Australia Felix, and of the present colony of New South Wales* (2 vols, London: T. and W. Boone, 1838). The extract, taken from the "carefully revised" second edition of 1839, comes from the opening of chapter VI of the second expedition, "Sent to explore the course of the River Darling, in 1835" (vol. 1, pp. 245–51).

John Morgan

The extract from *The Life and Adventures of William Buckley, Thirty-Two Years a Wanderer among the Aborigines of . . . Victoria* (Hobart: Archibald Macdougall, 1852) comes from the opening of chapter II. A modern edition of this work is available (ed. C.E. Sayers, Melbourne: Heinemann, 1967).

John West

The History of Tasmania (2 vols, Launceston: Henry Dowling, 1852), a mammoth work, is available in both a South Australian Library Board facsimile edition and a reprint edited by A.G.L. Shaw (Sydney: Angus and Robertson, 1971). West divided his history into ten parts: the first six dealt with the island's European discovery and subsequent history, part 7 with its zoology, part 8 with the Aborigines, part 9 with transportation, while part 10 was the conclusion. The whole of section III of part 8 is reprinted here.

Audrey Tennyson

The passages from Audrey Tennyson's letters are reprinted from Alexandra Hasluck, ed., *Audrey Tennyson's Vice-Regal Days. The Australian letters of Audrey Lady Tennyson to her mother Zacyntha Boyle, 1899–1903* (Canberra: National Library of Australia, 1978), pp. 46–54. In editing the letters, Dame Alexandra left out family news and other material seen as unimportant; her omissions are indicated by four stops. I have made further cuts, indicated by three asterisks.

SETTLING DOWN

Elizabeth Macarthur

The letter to Miss Kingdon is taken from Sibella Macarthur-Onslow (ed.), *Some Early Records of the Macarthurs of Camden* (Sydney: Angus and Robertson, 1914), pp. 46–52.

W.C. Wentworth

The bias in Wentworth's *Statistical, Historical, and Political Description of the Colony of New South Wales, and its dependent Settlements in Van Diemen's Land: with a particular enumeration of the advantages which these colonies offer for emigration, and their superiority in many respects over those possessed by the United States of America* (2 vols, London: G. and W.B. Whittaker, 1819) is indicated by both its complete title and the title page description of Wentworth as "A Native of the Colony". Part of the opening chapter is reproduced here, showing Wentworth's habit of using long extracts from others. Elsewhere he reprints the letter from Oxley to Governor Macquarie included in "Travelling", part 4 of this anthology.

Peter Cunningham

Two Years in New South Wales; Comprising Sketches of the Actual State of Society in that Colony; of its Peculiar Advantages to Emigrants; of its Topography, Natural History etc. etc. (2 vols, London: Henry Colburn, 1827) was written as a series of letters rather than as chapters. The extract here comes from letter XXI. Modern reprints include a facsimile edition in the South Australian Library Board series and one edited by D.S. Macmillan (Sydney: Angus and Robertson, 1966).

G.T.W.B. Boyes

The extracts from Boyes's diary are taken from Peter Chapman's edition of *The Diaries and Letters of G.T.W.B. Boyes*, vol. 1, 1820–32 (Melbourne: Oxford University Press, 1984), pp. 340–41; 406; 485–89.

Eliza Brown

These letters to her father, William Bussey, have been selected from a collection edited by Peter Cowan, Eliza Brown's great-great-grandson, in *A Faithful Picture: the letters of Eliza and Thomas Brown at York in the Swan River Colony 1841–1852* (Fremantle: Fremantle Arts Centre Press, 1977), pp. 20–24; 75–79; 131–33.

George Gordon McCrae

The journal extracts are taken from Hugh McCrae (ed.), *Georgiana's Journal: Melbourne 1841–1865* (Sydney: Angus and Robertson, 1934), pp. 236–41; 245–46.

Annie Baxter

Memories of the Past: By a Lady in Australia (Melbourne: W.H. Williams, 1873) draws on the author's journals, now in the Dixson Library. The extract comes from the first half of chapter VI.

Rolf Boldrewood

Yambuck, the Baxters' Victorian station, is also the subject of the final chapter of Rolf Boldrewood's *Old Melbourne Memories* (Melbourne: George Robertson, 1884).

TRAVELLING

John Oxley

This letter to Governor Macquarie, summarising the first of the journeys of exploration recounted in *Journals of Two Expeditions into the Interior of New South Wales, Undertaken by Order of the British Government in the Years 1817–18* (London: John Murray, 1820), was printed there as appendix III, pp. 170–76.

William Dumaresq

"A Ride to Bathurst" originally appeared in the Sydney newspaper the *Australian* in March and April 1827, signed "X.Y.Z". It has been reprinted in George Mackaness, ed., *Fourteen Journeys over the Blue Mountains of New South Wales, 1813–1841* (3 vols, Sydney: the author, 1950–51).

Richard Rowe

The journalist Richard Rowe, though only in Australia for five years, chose to write under the colonial pseudonym of "Peter Possum". Some of the poems, essays and stories he contributed to the *Month, Sydney Punch* and the *Sydney Morning Herald* were collected in *Peter Possum's Portfolio* (Sydney: J.R. Clarke, 1858), source of "A Trip up the Hunter". Three moderately long passages have been omitted.

Louisa Atkinson

"Cabbage-Tree Hollow, and the Valley of the Grose" was published in the *Sydney Mail*, 12 January 1861; "A Night Adventure in the Bush" in the *Sydney Morning Herald*, 22 October 1861. The latter has been collected in *A Voice from the Country* (Canberra: Mulini Press, 1978).

Edmund Marin La Meslée

The New Australian first appeared as *L'Australie Nouvelle*, in 1883. The extract published here is taken from chapter VII of the edition translated and edited by Russel Ward (London: Heinemann, 1973), pp. 71–83, omitting some passages on colonial loans.

David Blair

The extracts from "Dottings from the Diary of a Travelling Technological Commissioner" have been transcribed from the original manuscript in the National Library of Australia, MS302.

Ernest Giles

The extract from *Australia Twice Traversed: The Romance of Exploration, Being a Narrative Compiled from the Journals of Five Exploring Expeditions into and through Central South Australia, and Western Australia, from 1872 to 1876* (2 vols, London: Sampson Low, Marston, Searle and Rivington, 1889) consists of the whole of chapter II (vol. II, pp. 106–26) of Giles's account of his third expedition.

Henry Lawson

Lawson's letters to his aunt, Emma Brooks, are reprinted from Colin Roderick, ed., *Henry Lawson Letters 1890–1922* (Sydney: Angus and Robertson, 1970), pp. 49-51; 53–54. Lawson's pair of travel sketches, "In a Dry Season" and "In a Wet Season", first appeared in the *Bulletin* on 5 November 1892 and 2 December 1893 respectively. They were collected in *While the Billy Boils* (Sydney: Angus and Robertson, 1896).

FLOODS, FLIES, FAUNA

George Grey

The extract from *Journals of Two Expeditions of Discovery in North-West and Western Australia during the years 1837, 38, and 39* (2 vols, London: T. and W. Boone, 1841), comes from the first half of chapter V of the first volume and describes Grey's visits to Hanover Bay on the first expedition (pp. 81–86).

Louisa Anne Meredith

Facsimile editions of *Notes and Sketches of New South Wales, During a*

Residence in that Colony from 1839 to 1844 (London: John Murray, 1844) have been produced by the National Trust and Penguin Books, both in 1973. The first part of chapter VI is reproduced here.

Frank Fowler

The passage reproduced from *Southern Lights and Shadows: being brief notes of three years' experience of social, literary, and political life in Australia* (London: Sampson Low, 1859) comes from pages 83–92 of the facsimile edition published by Sydney University Press in 1975.

George Bennett

The description of the platypus comes from *Gatherings of a Naturalist in Australasia: Being Observations Principally into the Animal and Vegetable Productions of New South Wales, New Zealand, and some of the Austral Islands* (London: Jan van Voorst, 1860), pp. 94–97; 105–113.

W.H.L. Ranken

The extract from *The Dominion of Australia: An Account of its Foundation* (London: Chapman and Hall, 1874) consists of the second half of chapter II and most of chapter III.

TOWN AND BUSH

William Howitt

This character sketch of a crazed shepherd comes from Howitt's *Land, Labour, and Gold; or, Two Years in Victoria: with Visits to Sydney and Van Diemen's Land* (2 vols, London: Longman, Brown, Green and Longmans, 1855). Modern reprints include a facsimile edition by Sydney University Press, 1972, and one by Lowden Publishing Co., 1972.

J.E. Neild

The account of "The Hippodrome" appeared in the *Examiner and Melbourne Weekly News*, 10 July 1858.

Marcus Clarke

"Nasturtium Villas" first appeared in Melbourne's *Weekly Times*, 14 February 1874; it has been reprinted in L.T. Hergenhan, ed., *A Colonial City: High and Low Life. Selected Journalism of Marcus Clarke* (St Lucia: University of Queensland Press, 1972).

A.J. Boyd

Boyd's character sketches of bush types first appeared in the *Queenslander* in 1875–76. They were collected as *Old Colonials* (London: Gordon and Gotch, 1882). A facsimile edition was published by Sydney University Press in 1974.

Richard Twopeny

"Dress" is one of the chapters of *Town Life in Australia* (London: Elliott Stock, 1883).

Francis Adams

"Melbourne, and Her Civilization, As they Strike an Englishman" was included in his *Australian Essays* (Melbourne: William Inglis and Co., 1886).

Edmund Finn

The two theatrical anecdotes come from Edmund Finn, *The Chronicles of Early Melbourne, 1835 to 1852. Historical, Anecdotal and Personal* (2 vols, Melbourne: Fergusson and Mitchell, 1888).

Mary Gaunt

"Riverina" first appeared in E.E. Morris, ed., *Cassell's Picturesque Australasia* (4 vols, Melbourne: Cassell and Company, 1890), vol. III, pp. 123–39.

Rosa Praed

"The Old Scenes" appeared in Lala Fisher, ed., *By Creek and Gully: Stories and Sketches . . . by Australian Writers in England* (London: Unwin, 1899).

FRIENDS, LOVERS, SEXUAL COMMERCE

Charles Harpur

These letters to Henry Parkes, now among the Harpur manuscripts in the Mitchell Library, are reprinted from Adrian Mitchell, ed., *Charles Harpur* (Melbourne: Sun Books, 1973), pp. 179–85; 191–92.

David Blair

The love letter to Annie Grant is now in the David Blair Papers, MS302, National Library of Australia, Canberra.

Cora Ann Weekes

This lecture on "Female Heroism in the Nineteenth Century" was given at the Sydney School of Arts on 30 December 1858 and printed in Weekes's journal the *Spectator* on 22 January 1859. A lengthy description of Mrs Jellyby from Charles Dickens's *Bleak House* (1852–53) has been omitted.

D.H. Deniehy

"The Social Evil" first appeared in Deniehy's Sydney newspaper the *Southern Cross* in 1859 and was reprinted in E.A. Martin, *The Life and Speeches of Daniel Henry Deniehy* (Melbourne: George Robertson, 1884).

Marcus Clarke

"Melbourne Streets at Midnight" originally appeared in the *Argus*, 28 February 1868, and is reprinted in L.T. Hergenhan, ed., *A Colonial City*.

J.E. Neild

The review of Ibsen's *A Doll's House* appeared in the *Australasian*, 21 September 1889, and has been reprinted in Harold Love, ed., *The Australian Stage. A Documentary History* (Sydney: University of New South Wales Press, 1984).

Louisa Lawson

These two editorials, "That Nonsensical Idea", on women's suffrage, and "Method", on how to improve housekeeping, appeared in Louisa Lawson's newspaper, the *Dawn*, on 5 June 1890 and 1 July 1891.

A.G. Stephens

"A Poet's Mother – Louisa Lawson" first appeared in the *Bulletin* on 24 October 1896. It was reprinted, with much other material, in Leon Cantrell, ed., *A.G. Stephens: Selected Writings* (Sydney: Angus and Robertson, 1978). Cantrell also edited Stephens's *Bulletin* diary for publication in Bruce Bennett, ed., *Cross Currents: Magazines and Newspapers in Australian Literature* (Melbourne: Longman Cheshire, 1981), pp. 35–85. Pages 43–47 are reproduced here.

RITUALS AND CELEBRATIONS

Sydney Gazette

This report of a trial for murder first appeared in a special supplement to the *Sydney Gazette*, 14 September 1811.

True Colonist

The account of the opening of the Theatre Royal at Hobart was printed in the *True Colonist*, 10 March 1837. It has been reprinted in Harold Love, ed., *The Australian Stage*.

Georgiana McCrae

Her description of the celebration of the separation of Victoria from New South Wales comes from *Georgiana's Journal* (1934).

James Smith

Lurline Stuart edited the extracts from Smith's diary, in "The Year 1863", *Meanjin*, 37 (1978), pp. 411–33. Smith's notorious put-down of the Heidelberg School first appeared in the *Argus*, 17 August 1889. It is reprinted in Bernard Smith (ed.), *Documents in Art and Taste in Australia* (Melbourne: Oxford University Press, 1975), with a reply from the artists.

J.S. James

Like Smith and Marcus Clarke, James was a regular contributor to Melbourne's *Argus* newspaper, where his "Vagabond Sketches" began appearing in April 1876. They were collected in four parts, as *The Vagabond Papers: Sketches of Melbourne Life, in Light and Shade* (Melbourne: George Robertson, 1877). "The Cup Day – 1876" comes from the second collection. A selection has been edited by Michael Cannon as *The Vagabond Papers* (Melbourne: Melbourne University Press, 1969).

Bulletin

"A Centennial Oration" appeared in the *Bulletin* for 21 January 1888.

Jane Isabella Watts

Family Life in South Australia Fifty-Three Years Ago, Dating from October, 1837 (Adelaide: W.R. Thomas, 1890) was originally issued "for private circulation only". A facsimile edition has been produced by the South Australian Libraries Board.

Nat Gould

Town and Bush; Stray Notes on Australia (London: George Routledge and Sons, 1896) has been reprinted in facsimile by Penguin Books, 1974.

Catherine Spence

This sermon is taken from *Each in His Own Tongue: Two Sermons Delivered in the Unitarian Church, Adelaide, July 17 and 24, 1904* (Adelaide: Vardon and Pritchard, 1904).

PROTEST AND REVOLUTION

J.D. Lang

The extract chosen is the concluding part of the second of the lectures printed in *The Coming Event; or, the United Provinces of Australia: two lectures delivered in the City Theatre and School of Arts, Sydney* (Sydney: D.L. Welch [1880]).

D.H. Deniehy

The speech on the constitution bill was printed in *The Life and Speeches of Daniel Henry Deniehy*, pp. 51–56.

Raffaello Carboni

The Eureka Stockade: The Consequence of Some Pirates Wanting on Quarter-Deck a Rebellion (Melbourne: the author, 1855) has been reprinted many times. Chapters IX-XII and LVI-LIX are included here.

Henry Parkes

This speech is taken from Parkes's *Speeches on Various Occasions Connected with the Public Affairs of New South Wales, 1848–1874* (Melbourne: George Robertson, 1876), pp. 252–58.

Ned Kelly

The Jerilderie letter is reprinted here from Max Brown, *Ned Kelly: Australian Son* (Sydney: Angus and Robertson, 1981), pp. 249–58.

William Lane

"One-Man-One-Vote" first appeared in the Brisbane newspaper the *Worker* on 13 June 1891.

ALTERNATIVE CONTENTS LIST

This contents list is included as a guide for readers interested in categorisation under *types* of writing.

Letters

Journals

Reminiscences, Autobiography and Biography

Historical, Descriptive and Travel Writing

Edmond Marin La Meslée *from The New Australia* 1883
Edmund Finn *from Chronicles of Early Melbourne* 1888
Mary Gaunt Riverina 1890
Nat Gould *from Town and Bush* 1896

Exploration and Science

Charles Sturt *from Two Expeditions into the Interior of Southern Australia* 1833
Thomas Mitchell *from Three Expeditions into Eastern Australia* 1839
George Grey *from Expeditions into Western Australia* 1841
George Bennett *from Gatherings of a Naturalist in Australasia* 1860
Ernest Giles *from Australia Twice Traversed 1889*

Lectures, Speeches and Sermons

J.D. Lang *from* a lecture on The Coming Event 1850
Daniel Deniehy Speech on the Constitution Bill 1854
Cora Ann Weekes Lecture on Female Heroism in the Nineteenth Century 1859
Henry Parkes The Federal and Separate Interests of the Colonies 1867
Bulletin A Centennial Oration 1888
Catherine Spence Sermon on Each in his Own Tongue 1904

Essays and Sketches

Henry Savery *from The Hermit in Van Diemen's Land* 1829
Richard Rowe *from* A Trip up the Hunter 1858
Louisa Atkinson Cabbage-Tree Hollow and the Valley of the Grose; A Night Adventure in the Bush 1861
Marcus Clarke Melbourne Streets at Midnight 1868; Nasturtium Villas 1874
A.J. Boyd The Shepherd; The Fencer; The Bush Butcher 1875–76
J.S. James The Cup Day 1876
Francis Adams Melbourne and Her Civilization 1886
Henry Lawson In a Dry Season; In a Wet Season 1893

Editorials, Reports and Reviews

Sydney Gazette Report of a Trial for Murder 1811
William Dumaresq A Ride to Bathurst 1827
True Colonist The Opening of the Theatre, Hobart 1837
James Smith The Hippodrome 1858; review of *A Doll's House* 1889
Daniel Deniehy The Social Evil 1859
James Smith An Impressionist Exhibition 1889
Louisa Lawson Editorials from the *Dawn* 1890–91
William Lane One-Man-One-Vote 1891
A.G. Stephens A Poet's Mother – Louisa Lawson 1896

Notes on the Authors

Francis Adams (1862–93) was born in Malta and came to Australia suffering from tuberculosis in 1884. He became a journalist in 1887, and wrote for the *Boomerang* and the *Brisbane Courier*, later contributing fiction and poetry to the *Bulletin*. He published a collection of poetry, *Songs of the Army of the Night*, 1881, two books of non-fiction, and four of fiction. After spending six years in Australia he returned to England, where he had been educated, and, in poor health, suicided; he was, however, an important and radical voice in Australian literature of the 1890s.

Louisa Atkinson (1834–72), the first Australian-born woman novelist, was born near Berrima, New South Wales, to Charlotte Barton, author of the earliest Australian children's book, and James Atkinson, an early writer on agriculture. Despite poor health, she became an active naturalist and botanist, contributing regular articles to newspapers and journals; her popular series, "A Voice from the Country", appeared in the *Sydney Mail* from 1860 to 1865. Louisa Atkinson's first novel, *Gertrude the Emigrant*, 1857, was published in parts in Sydney with illustrations by her; she wrote six further novels, most of which were serialised in the *Sydney Mail*.

Annie Maria Baxter (1816–1905) was born in Devon, England, and as a bride of seventeen accompanied her lieutenant husband to his regimental posting in Tasmania. *Memories of the Past*, 1873, is based upon the 35 volumes of diary and memoirs written over a period of about 30 years, 1834–65, through two unhappy marriages and over various locations in Tasmania, New South Wales and Victoria. An experienced settler and pastoralist, Annie Baxter revisited England and also travelled to Ireland, Europe and New Zealand before returning to Victoria where she died.

George Bennett (1804–93) was a traveller and naturalist who was born in Plymouth, England, and visited Australia twice before settling in Sydney in 1836 where he established a medical practice and continued his interest in natural history. He published *Wanderings in New South Wales, Batavia, Pedir Coast, Singapore and China*, 1834, and *Gatherings of a Naturalist in Australasia*, 1860.

David Blair (1820–99) was a journalist and politician who was born in Ireland and originally came to Australia in 1850 to train as a Presbyterian minister under John Dunmore Lang. He twice became a member of parliament in Victoria. As a journalist he wrote for the *Age*, the *Empire*, and the *Sydney Morning Herald*, and also published *The History of Australasia*, 1878, and *Cyclopaedia of Australasia*, 1889.

Rolf Boldrewood was the pseudonym of **Thomas Alexander Browne** (1826–1915), born in London, who arrived in Australia in 1831, where he became a whaler, land speculator, cattle-man, sheep-station owner, police magistrate and journalist. He published several novels during the 1870s but became a literary success with the appearance of the bushranging adventure classic, *Robbery Under Arms*, 1882–83. This prompted a further seventeen books published at regular intervals until 1905. As well as writing *Old Melbourne Memories*, 1884, Rolf Boldrewood had articles published in *Cornhill Magazine* and the *Town and Country Journal*; he also published two books on agriculture.

A.J. [William Alexander Jenyns] Boyd (1842–1928) was born in France and arrived in Australia in 1860. He farmed a selection in Queensland and worked as a schoolteacher before becoming editor of the *Queensland Agricultural Journal* in 1897 and also a contributor to the *Queenslander* (under the pseudonym "Old Chum"). His sketches of life and characters in rural Queensland were collected in *Old Colonials*, 1882. A.J. Boyd's other publications included *Queensland*, 1882, a guide for immigrants, and *Some Fragments of Old Sydney*, 1898.

G[eorge] T[homas] W[illiam] B[lamey] Boyes (1787–1853), diarist, was born in Hampshire, England, and appointed deputy-assistant-commissary-general in New South Wales in 1823. Later he transferred to Van Diemen's Land to become the civil auditor, and in 1840 was appointed to the Legislative Council. G.T.W.B. Boyes's diaries reveal a man of artistic aspirations who was scornful of his contemporaries and unhappy in his political and social context.

Eliza Brown (1810?–96) was born in Oxfordshire, England, and arrived in Western Australia with her husband to settle in the York district. She began writing letters home, mostly to her father, in 1840 whilst still in London waiting to board ship. The letters continued until 1852 when Eliza Brown accompanied her husband to Perth.

Ada Cambridge (1884–1926) was born in Norfolk, England, and accompanied her clergyman husband (referred to as "G" in her writing) to Melbourne in 1870. By the end of the nineteenth century she had become a successful and well-loved novelist who by the time of her death had published nearly thirty novels (some as serials in popular Australian newspapers), five collections of verse, and two autobiographical books. Ada Cambridge was also the first significant Australian woman poet, and her 1887 volume, *Unspoken Thoughts*, is of particular importance.

Raffaello Carboni (1820–75) was born in Italy and came to Australia during the gold rush. In Ballarat he played a central role in organising miners, and was charged with treason following the famous Eureka Stockade attack in December 1854. He published *The Eureka Stockade* in the following year and shortly afterwards departed for Europe, finally returning to a modest literary and musical career in Italy. In 1980 a long poem by Raffaello Carboni concerning the goldfields and Eureka was discovered in Rome.

Ellen Clacy was born in England and visited Australia during the gold rush. *A Lady's Visit to the Gold Diggings of Australia in 1852–53*, 1853, is one of the best accounts of life on the Victorian goldfields. Ellen Clacy also published a collection of fiction, *Lights and Shadows of Australian Life*, 1854.

Marcus Clarke (1846–81) was born in London and emigrated to Australia in 1863. He worked in a bank and began a career as a journalist in Melbourne, writing for various newspapers including the *Argus* and the *Australasian*. He also wrote novels, stories, theatre criticism and plays, was a founder of the men's literary Yorick Club, and a leading figure in the cultural milieu of the 1870s. An assignment he was given by his paper, the *Argus*, to research the convict history of Tasmania led to his massive and best-known work, the novel, *His Natural Life*, serialised in the *Australian Journal* in 1870–72 (later in book form as *For the Term of His Natural Life*). From the early 1870s Marcus Clarke worked as a librarian and continued to publish novels, pamphlets and freelance articles in various papers and journals until his death.

Peter Cunningham (1789–1864) was born in Scotland and as a surgeon in the Royal Navy made several voyages to New South Wales on convict ships. He also attempted farming from 1825 onwards but finally returned to England in 1830. *Two Years in New South Wales*, 1827, combined memoirs and guidance for emigrants, and was followed in 1841 by *Hints for Australian Emigrants*.

D[aniel] H[enry] Deniehy (1828–65) was born in Sydney, educated there and in Europe, and returned to Sydney to study law. During the early 1850s he became a well-known literary and political figure and in 1857–60 was a member of parliament. He also worked as an editor in Melbourne in the years 1862–64 before returning to his legal practice in Sydney in the following year, but died shortly afterwards as a consequence of a fall. D.H. Deniehy published an early novel, poetry, speeches, articles and satires in various periodicals, some of which were included in the posthumous *The Life and Speeches of Daniel Henry Deniehy*, 1884. His satire, *How I Became Attorney-General of New Barataria*, was first published in the *Southern Cross* in 1859.

William Dumaresq (1793–1868) was born in Shropshire, England, became a captain in the army and served in Canada before accompanying his brother-in-law, Governor Ralph Darling, to Sydney in about 1825. Here he held a number of unofficial public posts before retiring in 1829 under the pressure of constant charges of nepotism. He established a large estate in the Scone district but returned to live in Sydney in 1840 (where he was elected to the Legislative Council three times), finally moving to Queensland where he died.

Edmund Finn (1819–98) was born in Ireland and in 1841 came to Melbourne where he worked as a journalist and a public servant. As "An Old Colonialist" and "Garryowen" he published two books based upon his experiences in Melbourne, *The Garryowen Sketches*, 1880, and *The Chronicles of Early Melbourne, 1835 to 1852*, 1888.

Frank Fowler (1883–63) came from London to Australia in 1855 to become a journalist, contributing to the *Empire* and the *Sydney Morning Herald*; he was also editor of the *Month*, a playwright and an unsuccessful politician. He returned to London in 1858 where he continued to publish; on the way home he wrote *Southern Lights and Shadows*, 1859.

Mary Gaunt (1861–1942), novelist, travel writer and journalist, was born in Victoria where she was educated (briefly attending the University of Melbourne) and began her career as a journalist. She contributed reviews and articles to the major Melbourne papers and wrote nine chapters for *Cassell's Picturesque Australasia*. In 1894 Mary Gaunt published the first of nearly twenty novels. By 1900 she was living in London, following the death of her husband. An avid traveller, she also published books describing her journeys throughout Africa, China and the West Indies.

Ernest Giles (1835–97) was born in Bristol, England, and came to Australia during the gold rush. He explored the western regions of New South Wales and in the 1870s tried to cross the continent westwards through central Australia, eventually making the crossing from South Australia in 1875. He published three accounts of his explorations: *Geographic Travels in Central Australia from 1872 to 1874*, 1875, *The Journal of a Forgotten Expedition*, 1880, and *Australia Twice Traversed*, 1889.

Nat Gould (1857–1919), journalist and sporting novelist, was born in Manchester, England, and worked as a reporter before arriving in Australia in 1884. After contributing to newspapers in various cities, in 1891 he successfully published the first of a long series of popular novels, which were mainly on racing and sporting topics. Despite returning to England in 1895, his novels relied greatly upon his Australian experiences. Nat Gould also published three books of reminiscences, including *Town and Bush: Stray Notes on Australia*, 1896.

George Grey (1812–98) was born in Lisbon, Portugal, and entered the army before arriving in Australia, where he planned to conduct exploratory expeditions. He tried without success to found a settlement in the north-west of the continent in the late 1830s before becoming governor of South Australia from 1840 to 1845. He published *A Vocabulary of the Dialects of South Western Australia*, 1840, and *Journals of Two Expeditions of Discovery in North-West and Western Australia during the years 1837, 38, and 39*, 1841.

Charles Harpur (1813–68), the first important Australian poet, was born in Windsor, New South Wales, the son of emancipists. He worked unsuccessfully at a number of different occupations before becoming a farmer and, briefly, an assistant gold commissioner at Araluen in 1859. His first collection of verse, *Thoughts: A Series of Sonnets*, appeared in 1845. He published a further five collections (some quite short), all demonstrating his struggle to produce an authentic Australian voice. Charles Harpur also published essays and articles on a wide range of topics in papers such as the *Empire* and the *Sydney Morning Herald*.

William Howitt (1792–1879) was born in Derbyshire, England, and came to Australia during the gold rush. He spent two years in the colony before returning home where, with his wife, he published numerous literary works. *Land, Labour and Gold*, 1854, together with *A Boy's Adventures in the Wilds of Australia*, 1857, and *The History of Discovery in Australia, Tasmania and New Zealand*, 1865, resulted from William Howitt's brief but fruitful Australian visit.

J[ohn] S[tanley] James (1843–96) was born in Walsall, England, and worked in London as a journalist, then in Wales for the railways before travelling to America where he took the name "Julian Thomas". He arrived in Australia in 1875 and in the following year, as "The Vagabond", began a popular series of articles for the *Argus*, which reappeared as *The Vagabond Papers* in 1877. J.S. James also travelled in Queensland, the Pacific, Asia and Europe, and continued writing his anonymous articles for the *Argus* until his death. Eight other travel and descriptive books appeared, as well as *The "Vagabond" Annual*, 1877.

Ned Kelly (1855-80) was born in Victoria of Irish convict parents and lived with his family on a selection near Glenrowan. He achieved notoriety as a bushranger and leader of the Kelly Gang. Eventually captured during a raid at Glenrowan, he was executed on 11 November 1880 after allegedly uttering the famous last words, "Such is life". Ned Kelly attempted to have his Jerilderie letter, an apologia for his actions, published in 1879, but without success; it first appeared in print in 1956.

Edmond Marin La Meslée (1852-93) was born in France and served in the navy before leaving for Mauritius where he taught in the Jesuit College. In 1876 he arrived in Melbourne and became private secretary to the French consul-general. After touring New South Wales and Queensland and briefly revisiting France, he returned to Australia shortly before the publication of his book, *L'Australie Nouvelle*, 1883. Back in Sydney he became an important force in the establishment of the Geographical Society of Australasia.

William Lane (1861-1917) was born in England and left for America in about 1877 where he began a career in printing and journalism and developed radical, socialist ideas. He arrived in Australia in 1885, settling in Brisbane where he established the *Boomerang* in 1887 and became editor of the *Worker* in 1890. An advocate of unionism and racism (in the guise of nationalism) he attempted to establish a utopian society through the New Australia Settlement Association and its ill-fated Paraguayan settlement in 1893. As "John Miller" he published *The Workingman's Paradise*, 1892, a novel designed to raise funds for striking shearers.

John Dunmore Lang (1799-1878), minister of religion and politician, was born in Scotland and arrived in Australia in 1823 to become the first Presbyterian minister to the colony; he founded the Scots Church, Sydney. A vocal and persistent critic of convict transportation, he became a member of the Legislative Council and a campaigner for separation, republicanism and federation, lecturing and publishing on these and other contemporary issues. His books included *An Historical and Statistical Account of New South Wales Both as Penal Settlement and as a British Colony*, 1834, and *Freedom and Independence for the Golden Lands of Australia*, 1852, as well as several volumes of verse.

Henry Lawson (1867-1922) was born in Grenfell, New South Wales, the son of Louisa Lawson. He published articles and poems in various newspapers but established himself as a writer from the early 1890s with stories regularly published in the *Bulletin*. Its editor, J.F. Archibald, funded the 1892–93 trip to Bourke and Hungerford which resulted in the letters and sketches included here. He continued writing for journals, publishing, in all, seventeen collections of prose and verse. There have been numerous subsequent editions of his work. Despite his erratic literary output, and serious mental and emotional problems, Henry Lawson achieved a legendary status in his own day which has not been diminished by time.

Louisa Lawson (1848–1920), feminist, journalist, poet and editor, was born and raised in the bush, in Mudgee, New South Wales, where she lived until 1883 when with her children she moved to Sydney to become a journalist and publisher. She edited the *Republican* and founded and operated the *Dawn*, 1888–1905, Australia's first significant feminist journal. Louisa Lawson also published a book for children and a collection of poetry, *The Lonely Crossing and Other Poems*, 1905.

Elizabeth Macarthur (1769–1850) was born in England and accompanied her husband, New South Wales Corps lieutenant John Macarthur, to New South Wales in 1790. From Elizabeth Farm in Parramatta, established in 1794, and later Camden Park, she managed their now famous merino sheep empire, fostering the fine-wool industry of the colony during the prolonged absences of her husband. Some of her journal entries and letters to her family and friends in England were published in the *Elizabeth Farm Occasional Series*, 1984.

George Gordon McCrae (1833–1927) was born in Scotland, the son of Georgiana Huntly McCrae, and arrived in Australia with his mother in 1841. He became a public servant as well as a literary personality in Melbourne, publishing poetry (including some of Australia's earliest verses concerning the Aborigines) and a novel, *John Rous*, 1918. He was a founder of the Yorick Club and a close associate of many contemporary writers and artists.

Georgiana Huntly McCrae (1804–90), diarist, was born and educated in London and later studied art and worked as a portraitist before her marriage in 1830. She followed her husband to Australia in 1841 and settled in Melbourne where she became a well-known identity within the literary, political and artistic world of her day. Her grandson, poet Hugh McCrae, first published her diaries as *Georgiana's Journal* in 1934.

Louisa Anne Meredith (1812–95) was a successful published poet and artist in England before her marriage in 1839 to her cousin and their departure for his family properties in Tasmania. She published eleven descriptive volumes, some of which she also illustrated, as well as poetry, fiction, essays and song lyrics. *Notes and Sketches of*

New South Wales, 1844, like most of her work, was highly popular and went into several editions. Louisa Meredith was the only literary figure ever granted a pension by the Tasmanian government.

John Mitchel (1815–75) was born in Derry, Ireland, and became a lawyer and editor. Along with other Young Ireland nationalists he was convicted of sedition and transported to Tasmania where he arrived in 1850. In 1853 he became one of the few to escape from the Australian transportation system, making his way to America where he published *Jail Journal*, 1854, and became a journalist.

Thomas Mitchell (1792–1855) was born in Craigend, Scotland, arrived in New South Wales in 1827, and became surveyor-general in the following year. His three major expeditions, in northern New South Wales, along the Darling and to the Murray rivers, and along the Leichhardt and Murrumbidgee rivers, are described in *Three Expeditions into the Interior of Eastern Australia*, 1838. He also published *Journal of an Expedition into the Interior of Tropical Australia*, 1848.

John Morgan (1792?–1866) was born near Portsmouth, England, and published *The Emigrant's Note Book and Guide* in 1824 before coming to Western Australia as part of the first Swan River settlement in 1829. Here he was a magistrate and justice of the peace before leaving for Van Diemen's Land in 1834 where he eventually became a journalist, founding two short-lived newspapers and working on several others. *The Life and Adventures of William Buckley*, 1852, was written in collaboration with its subject.

J[ames] E[dward] Neild (1824–1906) was born in Yorkshire, England, and studied medicine before arriving in Australia in 1853 where he fossicked for gold at Castlemaine, worked as a pharmacist, and joined the *Age* newspaper in 1855. Despite practising medicine in Melbourne and teaching at the university, his chief interest was the theatre; he wrote theatre reviews for various papers including the *Argus* and *Melbourne Punch*, and served as the *Australasian*'s theatre critic from 1865 to 1880. J.E. Neild also had his own plays performed and published a novel, *A Bird in a Golden Cage*, 1867.

John Oxley (1783?–1828) was born in Yorkshire, England, and in 1820 came to Australia as a member of the Royal Navy. Appointed surveyor-general of New South Wales, he embarked upon several expeditions attempting to trace the sources of various rivers, which later led to the discovery of the Brisbane and Tweed rivers. John Oxley's *Journals of Two Expeditions into the Interior of New South Wales*, 1820, was the first publication of its kind.

Henry Parkes (1815–96), politician and poet, was born in England. Forced by poverty to leave in 1839, he worked at a number of jobs in Australia before embarking upon a political career which began with his editorship of the *Empire* in 1850 and his election to the Legislative Council in 1854. He served as premier of New South Wales six times and was a major figure in the achievement of federation. Henry Parkes also published six volumes of poetry, the historical and autobiographical *Fifty Years in the Making of Australian History*, 1892, and various other pamphlets, speeches and articles; his letters appeared in *An Emigrant's Home Letters*, 1896.

Rosa Praed (1851–1935), born and raised on stations in Queensland, was one of the first successful Australian-born novelists. Although she departed for England in 1876, and only returned for a visit about eighteen years later, she maintained strong connections with her native land. About half of her forty novels and four collections of stories are set in Australia; the best known of these is her second novel, *Policy and Passion*, 1881. Rosa Praed also published the descriptive works, *Australian Life Black and White*, 1885, and *My Australian Girlhood*, 1902.

William Logan Ranken (1839–1902) was born in British Guiana of Scottish parents and came to Australia after travelling in Europe, Asia and the Pacific. He spent some time exploring the continent before settling on a station in northern New South Wales, becoming an authority on stock. His *Dominion of Australa*, 1874, is an imaginative and interesting geography handbook.

Richard Rowe (1828–79) was born in Doncaster, England, and came to Australia in 1853 where as "Peter Possum" he became a Sydney journalist contributing to a number of newspapers including the *Sydney Morning Herald*; he was also a member of the men's literary club known as the Stenhouse Circle. In 1858 he published a collection of essays and poems, *Peter Possum's Portfolio*, and in the same year returned to England where he wrote boys' books.

Henry Savery (1791–1842), born in Somerset, England, was transported for forgery, arriving in Van Diemen's Land in 1825. Here he worked as a clerk and journalist and wrote the first novel to be published in Australia, *Quintus Servinton*, 1831. Charged and convicted of forgery for a second time, he was sent to Port Arthur, where he died. Henry Savery was also the author of *The Hermit in Van Diemen's Land*, 1830, Australia's first collection of essays, originally published in the *Colonial Times* under the pseudonym "Simon Stukeley".

James Smith (1820–1910) was born in England. He worked as a publisher and editor before migrating to Australia in 1854. He settled in Melbourne, and was a well-known journalist and editor, initially employed by the *Age* and then editing the *Leader*, *Melbourne Punch*, the *Australasian* and the *Evening Mail*. He published three books, including the *Cyclopaedia of Victoria*, 1903–5, and had a play performed in 1860. James Smith also founded two journals, *Touchstone* and the *Victorian Review*, helped to establish a number of literary societies, and was an influential force in the National Gallery of Victoria and the Public Library.

Catherine Helen Spence (1825–1910) was born in Scotland and with her family emigrated to South Australia in 1839. One of the first women to write fiction in and about Australia, she published seven novels, including *Clara Morison*, 1854 (an eighth novel, *Handfasted*, was considered too provocative for publication in her day and only appeared in 1984). Catherine Spence also gained a reputation as a social reformer, journalist and suffragist and published many articles, pamphlets and lectures on topics such as child welfare, democracy and electoral reform.

A[lfred] G[eorge] Stephens (1865–1933) was born in Toowoomba, Queensland, and went to Sydney in 1880 to become an apprentice printer. He returned to Queensland to edit the *Gympie Miner*, later to sub-edit and write for the *Boomerang*. He then became editor of the *Argus* (of which he was also part-owner) before taking up a position on the *Bulletin* in 1894, beginning an important and productive association which continued until 1906 and saw the fostering of much literary talent. Later activities included establishing and operating the *Bookfellow* and its bookshop of the same name. A.G. Stephens also published two collections of poetry, various pamphlets, a novel and plays as well as critical studies of various authors. A selection of his essays from the *Bulletin*'s "Red Page" appeared as *The Red Pagan*, 1904.

Charles Sturt (1795–1869) was born of British parents in India and came to Australia in 1827 where he became one of Australia's best-known explorers, discovering several important rivers and travelling into central Australia in 1844–46. He published *Two Expeditions into the Interior of Southern Australia*, 1833, and *Narrative of an Expedition into Central Australia*, 1849.

Watkin Tench (1758?–1833) was a Marine Corps officer who arrived at Sydney Cove with the First Fleet in 1788. Before he left New South Wales four years later he had also been a successful explorer in a number of expeditions. His publications, *A Narrative of The Expedition to Botany Bay*, 1789, and *A Complete Account of the Settlement at Port Jackson in New South Wales*, 1793, have long been regarded as two of the most important and interesting early accounts of the colony.

Audrey Tennyson (1854–1916) was born in England and accompanied her husband, Hallam Tennyson (son of the poet) to Australia when he was appointed governor of South Australia in 1899, and later governor-general. Her letters from 1899 to 1903 to her mother from Adelaide and Melbourne offer a vivid account of personal and social life in those years; they were published in *Audrey Tennyson's Vice-Regal Days*, 1978.

Richard Twopeny (1857–1915), journalist and editor, was born in England and came to Australia in 1876 to work for the *South Australian Register* but left shortly after to work on the Paris Exhibition of 1878; he also had a similar appointment managing the Melbourne Centenary Exhibition of 1888. In 1891 he became founding editor of the *Australian Pastoralists' Review*, with which he remained associated until his death. *Town Life in Australia*, 1883, was based upon his observations in Adelaide, Melbourne and Sydney.

Thomas Watling (1762–?), an artist, was born in Scotland and in 1791 transported to New South Wales as a convicted forger. He began writing to his aunt during the voyage to the colony and his letters appeared as *Letters from an Exile at Botany-Bay*, 1794. He returned to Scotland after receiving a pardon in 1797. "J.W." was the surgeon-general John White, author of *Journal of a Voyage to New South Wales* (1790), to whom Watling was assigned when he arrived in Sydney in 1792.

Jane Isabella Watts (1824–94) was born in England and with her family emigrated to South Australia, arriving in 1837. The family lived on Kangaroo Island and later in Adelaide, where Jane Watts married in 1842. *Family Life in South Australia*, 1890, a chronicle of over fifty years, was published for private circulation.

Cora Ann Weekes was the first woman to edit an Australian magazine, the *Spectator: Journal of Literature and Art*, published in Sydney from July 1858 to January 1859. An Englishwoman, she had edited newspapers in Texas and California before coming to Australia. Her lecture on "Female Heroism" was probably the first to be given in Australia by a woman.

William Charles Wentworth (1793–1872) was born on board ship from Sydney to Norfolk Island, the son of convict Catherine Crowley and surgeon D'Arcy Wentworth. He was one of the famous trio who crossed the New South Wales Blue Mountains in 1813. His *Statistical, Historical, and Political Description of the Colony of New South Wales*, 1819, advocated radical, emancipist reforms. Educated in England, he returned there twice to study and finally to live in 1862, having become both a large landholder and politically conservative as his age and wealth increased.

John West (1809–73) was an English congregational minister who arrived in Tasmania in 1838 and became a well-known anti-transportationist. In 1854 he became editor of the *Sydney Morning Herald*, remaining in that position for nearly twenty years until his death. *The History of Tasmania*, 1852, contains many of his views on the abolition of transportation.

George Worgan (1757–1838) was born in London. He trained as a naval surgeon and sailed on board the *Sirius* in the First Fleet to New South Wales. He made several expeditions in the Hawkesbury River and Broken Bay regions, spent a year on Norfolk Island, and returned to England in 1791 where he retired to a farm.

Select Bibliography

Adelaide, D., ed. *A Bright and Fiery Troop: Australian Women Writers of the Nineteenth Century*. Ringwood: Penguin, 1988.

Andrews, B.G. and W.H. Wilde. *Australian Literature to 1900: A Guide to Information Sources*. Detroit: Gale Research Library, 1980.

Baker, A.W. *Death is a Good Solution: The Convict Experience in Early Australia*. St Lucia: University of Queensland Press, 1984.

Barton, G.B. *Literature in New South Wales*. Sydney: Thomas Richards, Government Printer, 1866.

______. *The Poets and Prose Writers of New South Wales*. Sydney: Gibbs, Shallard and Co., 1866.

Bennett, B., ed. *Cross Currents: Magazines and Newspapers in Australian Literature*. Melbourne: Longman Cheshire, 1981.

Blainey, G.N. *The Tyranny of Distance*. Melbourne: Macmillan, 1982 (revised ed., first published 1968).

Burgmann, V. and J. Lee, eds. *A People's History of Australia since 1788*. 4 vols. Melbourne: McPhee Gribble/Penguin, 1988.

Cannon, M. *Australia in the Victorian Age*. 3 vols. Melbourne: Thomas Nelson, 1971, 1973, 1975.

Carter, P. *The Road to Botany Bay*. London: Faber and Faber, 1987.

Clark, C.M.H. *A History of Australia*. 6 vols. Melbourne: Melbourne University Press, 1962–87.

Crowley, F., ed. *Colonial Australia*. 3 vols. Melbourne: Thomas Nelson, 1980.

Denholm, D. *The Colonial Australians*. Ringwood: Penguin, 1979.

Dixon, R. *The Course of Empire. Neo-Classical Culture in New South Wales 1788–1860*. Melbourne: Oxford University Press, 1986.

Dixson, M. *The Real Matilda: Women and Identity in Australia 1788–1975*. Ringwood: Penguin, 1976.

Ferguson, J.A. *Bibliography of Australia*. 7 vols. Sydney: Angus and Robertson, 1941–69.

Frost, L., ed. *No Place for a Nervous Lady*. Melbourne: McPhee Gribble/Penguin, 1984.

Gilbert, A. and K.S. Inglis, eds. *Australians: A Historical Library*. 10 vols. Sydney: Fairfax, Syme and Weldon, 1987.

Green, H.M. *A History of Australian Literature, Pure and Applied*. 2 vols. Sydney: Angus and Robertson, 1984 (revised ed. by Dorothy Green, first published 1961).

Greenop, F. *History of Magazine Publishing in Australia*. Sydney: K.G. Murray, 1947.

Healy, J.J. *Literature and the Aborigine in Australia, 1770–1975*. St Lucia: University of Queensland Press, 1978.

Hergenhan, L., ed. *The Penguin New Literary History of Australia*. Ringwood: Penguin, 1988.

Hughes, R. *The Fatal Shore: A History of the Transportation of Convicts to Australia 1787–1868*. London: Collins Harvill, 1987.

Inglis, K.S. *The Australian Colonists: An Exploration of Social History 1788–1870*. Melbourne: Melbourne University Press, 1974.

Johnston, G. *Annals of Australian Literature*. Melbourne: Oxford University Press, 1970.

Jordens, A.M. *The Stenhouse Circle. Literary Life in mid-Nineteenth Century Australia*. Melbourne: Melbourne University Press, 1979.

Kramer, L., ed. *The Oxford History of Australian Literature*. Melbourne: Oxford University Press, 1981.

Lawson, S. *The Archibald Paradox*. Melbourne: Allen Lane, 1983.

Love, H., ed. *The Australian Stage: A Documentary History*. Sydney: University of New South Wales Press, 1984.

McQueen, H. *A New Britannia*. Ringwood: Penguin, 1975 (revised ed., first published 1970).

McQuilton, F.J. *The Kelly Outbreak, 1878–1880*. Melbourne: Melbourne University Press, 1979.

Matthews, B. *Louisa*. Melbourne: McPhee Gribble/Penguin, 1987.

Miller, E. Morris. *Pressmen and Governors: Australian Editors and Writers in Early Tasmania*. Sydney: Angus and Robertson, 1952.

Moyal, A. *A Bright and Savage Land: Scientists in Colonial Australia*. Sydney: Collins, 1986.

Nadel, G. *Australia's Colonial Culture*. Melbourne: Cheshire, 1957.

Palmer, V. *The Legend of the Nineties*. Melbourne: Melbourne University Press, 1954.

Pike, D., B. Nairn and G. Serle, eds. *Australian Dictionary of Biography*. 10 vols. Melbourne: Melbourne University Press, 1966–86.

Reynolds, H. *The Other Side of the Frontier*. Ringwood: Penguin, 1981.

Ryan, L. *The Aboriginal Tasmanians*. St Lucia: University of Queensland Press, 1981.

Serle, G. *From Deserts the Prophets Come: The Creative Spirit in Australia 1788–1972*. Melbourne: Heinemann, 1973.

Smith, B. *European Vision and the South Pacific*. Oxford: Oxford University Press, 1960.

Stuart, L. *Nineteenth Century Australian Periodicals: An Annotated Bibliography*. Sydney: Hale and Iremonger, 1979.

Summers, A. *Damned Whores and God's Police*. Ringwood: Penguin, 1975.

Turner, I., ed. *The Australian Dream*. Melbourne: Sun Books, 1968.

Walker, R.B. *The Newspaper Press in New South Wales 1803–1920*. Sydney: Sydney University Press, 1976.

Ward, R. *The Australian Legend*. Melbourne: Oxford University Press, 1966 (revised ed., first published 1958).

White, R. *Inventing Australia: Images and Identity 1688–1980*. Sydney: Allen and Unwin, 1981.

Wilde, W.H., J. Hooton and B. Andrews. *The Oxford Companion to Australian Literature*. Melbourne: Oxford University Press, 1985.